lonely planet

Israel
& the Palestinian
Territories

Paul Hellander
Andrew Humphreys
Neil Tilbury

LONELY PLANET PUBLICATIONS
Melbourne • Oakland • London • Paris

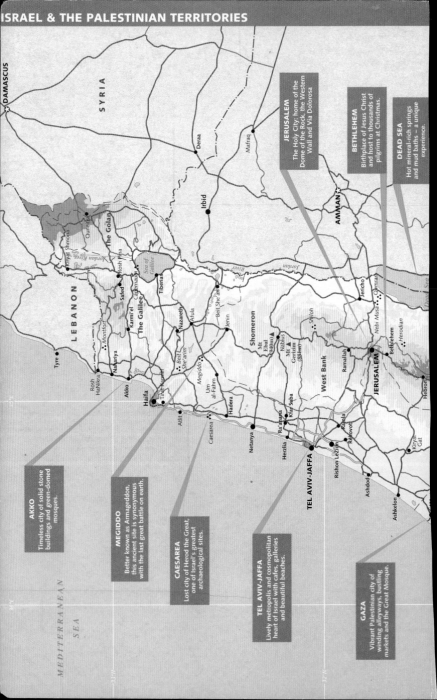

ISRAEL & THE PALESTINIAN TERRITORIES

JERUSALEM
The Holy City: home of the Dome of the Rock, the Western Wall and Via Dolorosa.

BETHLEHEM
Birthplace of Jesus Christ and host to thousands of pilgrims at Christmas.

DEAD SEA
Hot mineral-rich springs and mud baths – a unique experience.

AKKO
Timeless city of solid stone buildings and green-domed mosques.

MEGIDDO
Better known as Armageddon, this ancient site is synonymous with the last great battle on earth.

CAESAREA
Lost city of Herod the Great, one of Israel's greatest archaeological sites.

TEL AVIV-JAFFA
Lively metropolis and cosmopolitan heart of Israel with cafes, galleries and beautiful beaches.

GAZA
Vibrant Palestinian city of winding alleyways, bustling markets and the Great Mosque.

DAMASCUS

SYRIA

LEBANON

AMMAN

Deraa

Mafraq

Irbid

Tyre

Qiryat Shmona

The Golan

Rosh Pina

Sea of Galilee

Tiberias

Safed

Nahariya

Karmi'el

The Galilee

Akko

Haifa

Nazareth

Afula

Beit She'an

Jenin

Shomeron

Mt Ebal
(940m)

Mt Gerizim
(881m)

Nablus

Shiloh

West Bank

Ramallah

JERUSALEM

Bethlehem

Herodian

Nebi Musa

Qumran

Hebron

Kiryat Gat

Megiddo

Um al-Fahm

Hadera

Netanya

Caesarea

Atlit

Ra'anana

Kfar Saba

Herzlia

TEL AVIV-JAFFA

Rishon LeZiyon

Rehovot

Ramla

Ashdod

Ashkelon

Rosh HaNikra

Montfort

Beit She'arim

Tel Hazor

Jordan River

Jordan River

Jericho

MEDITERRANEAN SEA

Dead Sea

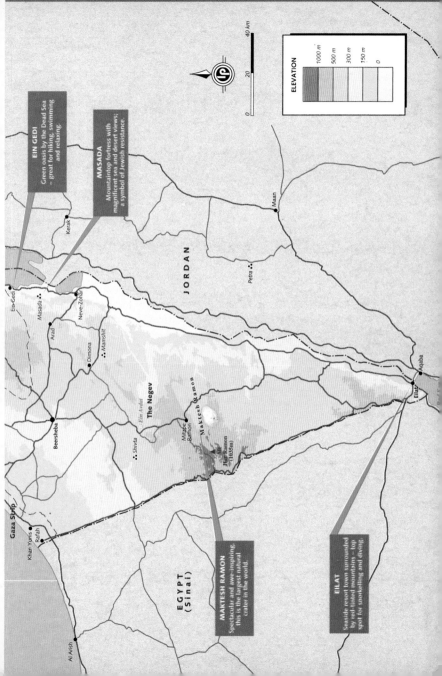

EIN GEDI
Green oasis by the Dead Sea – great for hiking, swimming and relaxing.

MASADA
Mountaintop fortress with magnificent sea and desert views; a symbol of Jewish resistance.

MAKTESH RAMON
Spectacular and awe-inspiring, this is the largest natural crater in the world.

EILAT
Seaside resort town surrounded by red-tinted mountains – top spot for snorkelling and diving.

ELEVATION

1000 m
500 m
300 m
150 m
0

0   20   40 km

JORDAN

Maan

Petra

Ein-Gedi
Masada
Neve-Zohar
Arad
Dimona
Mamshit
Kerak

Beersheba

Shivda
Ein Avdat

The Negev

Mitzpe Ramon
Maktesh Ramon
Har Ramon (1035m)

Eilat
Aqaba

Gaza Strip
Khan Yunis
Rafah
Al Arish

EGYPT
(Sinai)

Israel & the Palestinian Territories
4th edition – September 1999
First published – August 1989

Published by
Lonely Planet Publications Pty Ltd A.C.N. 005 607 983
192 Burwood Rd, Hawthorn, Victoria 3122, Australia

Lonely Planet Offices
Australia PO Box 617, Hawthorn, Victoria 3122
USA 150 Linden St, Oakland, CA 94607
UK 10a Spring Place, London NW5 3BH
France 1 rue du Dahomey, 75011 Paris

Photographs
Many of the images in this guide are available for licensing from
Lonely Planet Images.
email: lpi@lonelyplanet.com.au

Front cover photograph
Historic Ein Avdat waterhole, Negev (JL Stage)

ISBN 0 86442 691 7

text & maps © Lonely Planet 1999
photos © photographers as indicated 1999

Printed by Colorcraft Ltd, Hong Kong

Contents – Text

LANGUAGE 433

GLOSSARY 436

INDEX 442

MAP LEGEND back page

METRIC CONVERSION inside back cover

Contents – Maps

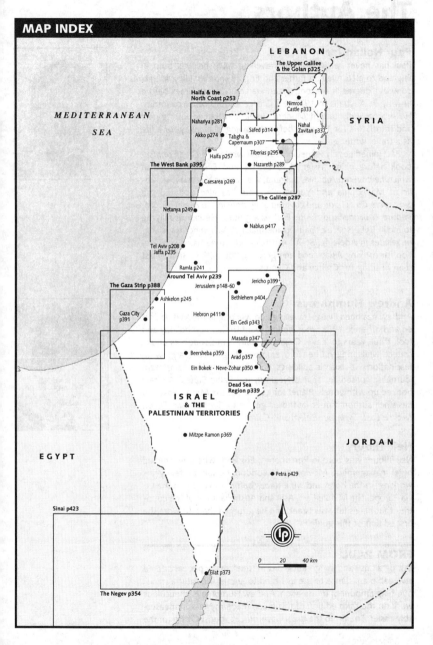

MAP INDEX

LEBANON

The Upper Galilee & the Golan p325

Haifa & the North Coast p253

Nimrod Castle p333

MEDITERRANEAN SEA

SYRIA

Nahariya p281

Safed p314

Akko p274

Nahal Zavitan p337

Tabgha & Capernaum p307

Tiberias p295

Haifa p257

The West Bank p395

Nazareth p289

Caesarea p269

The Galilee p287

Netanya p249

Nablus p417

Tel Aviv p208

Jaffa p235

Ramla p241

Around Tel Aviv p239

Jericho p399

The Gaza Strip p388

Jerusalem p148-60

Bethlehem p404

Ashkelon p245

Hebron p411

Gaza City p391

Ein Gedi p343

Masada p347

Beersheba p359

Arad p357

Ein Bokek - Neve-Zohar p350

Dead Sea Region p339

ISRAEL & THE PALESTINIAN TERRITORIES

JORDAN

EGYPT

Mitzpe Ramon p369

Petra p429

Sinai p423

0   20   40 km

The Negev p354

Eilat p373

The Authors

Paul Hellander

Paul has never really stopped travelling since he was born in England to a Norwegian father and English mother. He graduated with a degree in Ancient, Byzantine and Modern Greek before arriving in Australia in 1977, via Greece and 30 other countries. He subsequently taught Modern Greek and trained interpreters and translators for 13 years before throwing it all away for a life as a travel writer.

Paul joined Lonely Planet in 1994 and wrote LP's *Greek phrasebook* before being assigned to *Greece* and *Eastern Europe* in which he covered Albania, Bulgaria, the Former Yugoslav Republic of Macedonia and Yugoslavia. Paul has also updated the *Singapore City Guide* and covered Singapore in the *Malaysia, Singapore & Brunei* and *South-East Asia* guides. He can usually be found in Cyberspace at paul@planetmail.net. When not travelling, he resides in Adelaide, South Australia, where he has a predilection for cooking Asian food and growing hot chillies. He was last seen heading for Greece and Cyprus.

Andrew Humphreys

Andrew has been living, travelling and working in the Middle East on and off since 1988 when he first went to Cairo on holiday and took three years to leave. Originally trained in London as an architect, while in Egypt he slid over into writing through a growing fascination with Islamic buildings. Following a spell in mainstream journalism based for several years in the Baltic States, Andrew hooked up with Lonely Planet for a return to the Middle East and has since authored or co-authored guides to *Central Asia, Egypt, Middle East, Syria, Jerusalem* and *Cairo*.

Neil Tilbury

Neil Tilbury was born in Portsmouth, England, where he studied hotel management. Moving up to London, he spent a few years working in the hotel and wine trades before travelling to the US via Europe, the Middle East, Asia and Australia. One of the countries that he visited was Israel, and he returned there to write the first edition of this guide.

FROM PAUL

During a busy and invigorating stay in Israel, many people offered invaluable assistance to me as I tried to juggle and filter a mind-numbing amount of information. Andrew Humphreys' meticulous work on the third edition of this guide made my task immeasurably easier. Thanks to the Israel Government Tourist Office for the wealth of printed material and especially to David Beirman from the Sydney office. A big 'todah' to fellow-author Daniel Robinson for his selfless assistance with background data; to Ohad & Einav Sharav for their invaluable contributions to the glossary; to David Martin of the British Council in East Jerusalem for help with the West Bank; to Amichay Ne'eman of Tel Aviv for his generous hospitality; to Deborah Lipson of the Tower of David Museum for her insight into history; to Dave Cohen of Tel Aviv for his views on the travel scene; to Danny Flax and Chaim Rockman of Jerusalem for their practical help; to Vincent Simmons for last-minute information on Jerusalem; to the people of Israel for their patience and understanding of my often seemingly trivial questions and for their enduring tenacity and resilience while sometimes living 'on the edge'.

Thanks also to Verity Campbell and Michelle Glynn at Lonely Planet who gave me much-needed encouragement and support and who put this book together with a lot of TLC. Without Stella's blessing these assignments and long absences from home would not happen – efharisto! Byron and Marcus, here's another one to remember your old man by.

This Book

Neil Tilbury researched and wrote the first and second editions of this book. Andrew Humphreys extensively researched and revised the third edition. Paul Hellander updated this fourth edition.

From the Publisher

This edition of *Israel & the Palestinian Territories* was edited at Lonely Planet's Melbourne office by Elizabeth Swan, with assistance from Susan Holtham, Russell Kerr, Lyn McGaurr, Kristin Odijk, Julia Taylor and Chris Wyness. Rodney Zandbergs coordinated the cartography and design, with cartographic assistance from Katie Butterworth, Hunor Csutoros, Piotr Czajkowski, Brett Moore, Csanád Csutoros, Shahara Ahmed and Sarah Sloane. Quentin Frayne organised the language section as well as the Arabic and Hebrew scripts, Kate Nolan drew the illustrations and Maria Valianos designed the cover.

Acknowledgments

Many thanks to the travellers who used the last edition and wrote to us with helpful hints, useful advice and interesting anecdotes:

Will & Aaron, Chuck & Lee, Nick & Bob, Dr RE Alexander, Uwe Altrock, Marc David Baer, Yossi Bahalul, Frederick Bang, George Bangian, Katie Bannister, Aviva Bar-Am, Talya Bar-Lev, Javier Barrera, Paddy Barrett, Sally Barrett, Julie Bauker, Allie Beard, Roland Beibel, Tomm Ben-David, Patricia Bernard, Mathias Bischer, Arthur Blake, Caroline Blake, H Blumenthal, Theo Borst, Derek & Jennifer Bowett, Oliver Bradley, Richard Brail, Cynthia Brill, Ron Broadfoot, R Brock, Fyonna Brooman, Michael Brown, Arnout Bruins, Gal Bruttmann-Brandes, Alison Buckholtz, Rafael Builes, Tanya Burke, Howard Burrows, L Burt, Amanda Caddy, Priska Caesar, Margie Carlson, Shelden Cashdan, Lisa Catterall, Renata Cervenkova, Kit Chan, Vicky Clayton, C Cloix, Jim & Elayne Coakes, Mat Coakley, Doron Cohen, Natalie Connors, Elena Corona, Gerald Coulter, Brian Crawford, Frans Crone, MC Croucher, Rabbi Jacques Cukierkorn, Dan Dahlberg, Jonathan Danilowitz, Irene Day, Julie Delahunt, Johan Delbaere, Inge Detlefsen, Bruno Di Pietro, Chris Dixon, Robert Dorin, Emma Dornan, Br John Dougherty, Paul Doyle, Yohana & M Dragot, Dr Andrea Eggenstein, Vered Ehsani, Anthony Elgort, Shimrit Elisar, A & S Elkayam, Michael Fassbendner, Susanne Fechner, Marvin Feldman, Jurgen Felkel, Carl A Ferris, Jerome Fishkin, Uirike Flackl, Br John Francis, Elisha Freund, Royce Froehlich, Dave Fuller, Horesh Galil, Matthias Gamrath, Jeanette Gash, M Gats, Anne Gilliland, Ron Ginther, Jeremy Goldman, Simon Goldsmith, Jacquelyne Goodfellow, Titus Graf, Susan Gray, Al Green, Alasdair Green, Liz Green, Clare Greenway, Monique Gringlas, Hanna Grossman, Deborah Gyan, Avraham Hampel, Peter Hardy, Joe & Cindy Harris, UJ Hashem, Julie Hassenmiller, Abu Hasson, Meir Hatkak, Janine Heath, Renate Hermann, Alfred Heuperman, Jonathon Hibbs, Susanne Hill, Friedrich Holst, Mitch Horowitz, Petr Hruska, Yoram Ilan, Richard Ilomaki, Karin Jeck, Lasse Jeremiassen, Christian Jessen, Margit Johansen, K Johnson, Sarah Johnson, Noel Joliffe, Sharon August Jones, Paul

Jorgensen, E Joseph, Abu Kalim, Ian Kazin, Karel Klicka, Lutz Kloska, Kevin Kluetz, Reinhard Koppenleitner, Michael Kroyter, Bianca Kuttroff, Sam La Hood, Stefan Lammens, Lucy Lant, George A LeDuc & Family, P & J Leigh, Kathryn Leishman, Andy Leitner, Chris Leonard, Tamara Lesser, Eleanor Leverson, Joan Levin, Michael Levine, Tara Levy, David Lewis, Shlomi Lifshits, Eric Linder, Rob Lober, Edgar Locke, Caroline Logan, Stephanie Luckerath, Filip Lundberg, L Mackie, Morag Maclean, LJ & F Macquet, Jamie Maler, John Davis Malloy, Christopher Manley, Bella Marckmann, Andrew Martin, David Martin, Ursula & Dick Mattson, Guy Maytal, Suzanne Medeley, Hans Mey, Fizh Mike, Jack Milstein, Richard Milton, Dr Justine Minshull, Jason Moore, Philip Mordecai, Nina Morrison, Hiroshi Nakayama, Alon Nechushtan, Ben Nicholls, S Joshua Ogawa, Dvora Olinsky, Julian O'Loughlin, Pete Onni, Andrew Osborne, Vera Ovchinnikov, Brian Pancott, Robert Patterson, Allen L Pauly, Carol Pavarno, Bertrand Pawlas, Karen Pender, Margaret Pense, Babette Peperkamp, Maria Perr, Catherine Philip, Samus Phillips, Rob Plummer, Judith Polsky, Laura Pomerance, Rob Pos, Annett Prelle, Jim Proctor, Michele Puliti, Dr J Puliyel, Karen L Rae, Benjamin Rassell, David Reibscheid, Jennifer Rinconi, Alexandra Ringleb, James Rix, B & Y Robinson, Felix Rollin, Fanny Rosenblad, Armin Rosenchung, Rufus Rottenberg, John Rydzewski, Steve & Jocelyn Sacks, Richard Safra, Shalom Salaam, Markus Salfer, D Salmon, Jacqueline Schaalje, Etienne Scheeper, Gunnar Schubert, Stefan Schutt, Jeff Seinfeld, T Selby, Vicente Serra, Karl Shea, K Sherlock, Rabbi Nachum Shifren, Peggy Shoeuort, Frederick Siegmund, I Siersema, SM Silverman, Janna Silverstein, Toby Simon, Rudiger Simonides, Fletcher Simpkins, Jean Sinclair, Tanya Singer, Robert Sitomer, Jeffrey Skinner, Alex Sky, David & Lynne Smith, Mascha Snoyink, Ido Sokolovsky, Jeff Soul, Caroline Spicer, Wilma Spiers, John Spriggs, Edith Starr, George Stauer, David Stemp, David Sterasburg, Derek Stewart, L Stewart, Johanna Stiebert, Laura Stobart, Bethna Stoess, A Stojicevic, David Strasburg, Ida Strasser, Susan Subak, Wanda & Barry Syner, Angela Taft, Charity Tan, Liz Tena, Mark Tinker, Susan Tomlinson, Gabi Treidel, Lieuwe van der Veen, J & C van Kranenburg, Kees Anton van Welie, Tim Venner, Cathy & Frank von Hippel, Radim Vovesny, Larry Wade, David Wakim, Gina Wales, Antonia Walker, Kevin Wall, Dave & Lorrie Watts, Stuart Welerter, Fern Westernoff, Thomas White, Linda Whitnall, Roy Wiesner, Alun Williams, Bernard Wittmann, Darren Woodley, Alan Woodward, Kim Wroth-iu, Nerissa Wu, Samantha Yeoman, Malanie Youle, Theresa Young, Sabastian Zedlilz, Patricia Zelkowitz, Christina Zubelli.

Foreword

ABOUT LONELY PLANET GUIDEBOOKS

The story begins with a classic travel adventure: Tony and Maureen Wheeler's 1972 journey across Europe and Asia to Australia. Useful information about the overland trail did not exist at that time, so Tony and Maureen published the first Lonely Planet guidebook to meet a growing need.

From a kitchen table, then from a tiny office in Melbourne (Australia), Lonely Planet has become the largest independent travel publisher in the world, an international company with offices in Melbourne, Oakland (USA), London (UK) and Paris (France).

Today Lonely Planet guidebooks cover the globe. There is an ever-growing list of books and there's information in a variety of forms and media. Some things haven't changed. The main aim is still to help make it possible for adventurous travellers to get out there – to explore and better understand the world.

At Lonely Planet we believe travellers can make a positive contribution to the countries they visit – if they respect their host communities and spend their money wisely. Since 1986 a percentage of the income from each book has been donated to aid projects and human rights campaigns.

Updates Lonely Planet thoroughly updates each guidebook as often as possible. This usually means there are around two years between editions, although for more unusual or more stable destinations the gap can be longer. Check the imprint page (following the colour map at the beginning of the book) for publication dates.

Between editions up-to-date information is available in two free newsletters – the paper *Planet Talk* and email *Comet* (to subscribe, contact any Lonely Planet office) – and on our Web site at www.lonelyplanet.com. The *Upgrades* section of the Web site covers a number of important and volatile destinations and is regularly updated by Lonely Planet authors. *Scoop* covers news and current affairs relevant to travellers. And, lastly, the *Thorn Tree* bulletin board and *Postcards* section of the site carry unverified, but fascinating, reports from travellers.

Correspondence The process of creating new editions begins with the letters, postcards and emails received from travellers. This correspondence often includes suggestions, criticisms and comments about the current editions. Interesting excerpts are immediately passed on via newsletters and the Web site, and everything goes to our authors to be verified when they're researching on the road. We're keen to get more feedback from organisations or individuals who represent communities visited by travellers.

> Lonely Planet gathers information for everyone who's curious about the planet – and especially for those who explore it first-hand. Through guidebooks, phrasebooks, activity guides, maps, literature, newsletters, image library, TV series and Web site we act as an information exchange for a worldwide community of travellers.

Research Authors aim to gather sufficient practical information to enable travellers to make informed choices and to make the mechanics of a journey run smoothly. They also research historical and cultural background to help enrich the travel experience and allow travellers to understand and respond appropriately to cultural and environmental issues.

Authors don't stay in every hotel because that would mean spending a couple of months in each medium-sized city and, no, they don't eat at every restaurant because that would mean stretching belts beyond capacity. They do visit hotels and restaurants to check standards and prices, but feedback based on readers' direct experiences can be very helpful.

Many of our authors work undercover, others aren't so secretive. None of them accept freebies in exchange for positive write-ups. And none of our guidebooks contain any advertising.

Production Authors submit their raw manuscripts and maps to offices in Australia, USA, UK or France. Editors and cartographers – all experienced travellers themselves – then begin the process of assembling the pieces. When the book finally hits the shops, some things are already out of date, we start getting feedback from readers and the process begins again …

WARNING & REQUEST

Things change – prices go up, schedules change, good places go bad and bad places go bankrupt – nothing stays the same. So, if you find things better or worse, recently opened or long since closed, please tell us and help make the next edition even more accurate and useful. We genuinely value all the feedback we receive. Julie Young coordinates a well travelled team that reads and acknowledges every letter, postcard and email and ensures that every morsel of information finds its way to the appropriate authors, editors and cartographers for verification.

Everyone who writes to us will find their name in the next edition of the appropriate guidebook. They will also receive the latest issue of *Planet Talk*, our quarterly printed newsletter, or *Comet*, our monthly email newsletter. Subscriptions to both newsletters are free. The very best contributions will be rewarded with a free guidebook.

Excerpts from your correspondence may appear in new editions of Lonely Planet guidebooks, the Lonely Planet Web site, *Planet Talk* or *Comet*, so please let us know if you *don't* want your letter published or your name acknowledged.

Send all correspondence to the Lonely Planet office closest to you:

Australia: PO Box 617, Hawthorn, Victoria 3122
USA: 150 Linden St, Oakland, CA 94607
UK: 10A Spring Place, London NW5 3BH
France: 1 rue du Dahomey, 75011 Paris

Or email us at: talk2us@lonelyplanet.com.au

For news, views and updates see our Web site: www.lonelyplanet.com

HOW TO USE A LONELY PLANET GUIDEBOOK

The best way to use a Lonely Planet guidebook is any way you choose. At Lonely Planet we believe the most memorable travel experiences are often those that are unexpected, and the finest discoveries are those you make yourself. Guidebooks are not intended to be used as if they provide a detailed set of infallible instructions!

Contents All Lonely Planet guidebooks follow roughly the same format. The Facts about the Destination chapters or sections give background information ranging from history to weather. Facts for the Visitor gives practical information on issues like visas and health. Getting There & Away gives a brief starting point for researching travel to and from the destination. Getting Around gives an overview of the transport options when you arrive.

The peculiar demands of each destination determine how subsequent chapters are broken up, but some things remain constant. We always start with background, then proceed to sights, places to stay, places to eat, entertainment, getting there and away, and getting around information – in that order.

Heading Hierarchy Lonely Planet headings are used in a strict hierarchical structure that can be visualised as a set of Russian dolls. Each heading (and its following text) is encompassed by any preceding heading that is higher on the hierarchical ladder.

Entry Points We do not assume guidebooks will be read from beginning to end, but that people will dip into them. The traditional entry points are the list of contents and the index. In addition, however, some books have a complete list of maps and an index map illustrating map coverage.

There may also be a colour map that shows highlights. These highlights are dealt with in greater detail in the Facts for the Visitor chapter, along with planning questions and suggested itineraries. Each chapter covering a geographical region usually begins with a locator map and another list of highlights. Once you find something of interest in a list of highlights, turn to the index.

Maps Maps play a crucial role in Lonely Planet guidebooks and include a huge amount of information. A legend is printed on the back page. We seek to have complete consistency between maps and text, and to have every important place in the text captured on a map. Map key numbers usually start in the top left corner.

Although inclusion in a guidebook usually implies a recommendation we cannot list every good place. Exclusion does not necessarily imply criticism. In fact there are a number of reasons why we might exclude a place – sometimes it is simply inappropriate to encourage an influx of travellers.

Introduction

Irrespective of whether they have ever visited the place or not, it seems everyone has their own perception of just what Israel and the Palestinian Territories are about: it's a travel agency package of beaches and sun; it's the Promised Land of the Jews, the 'land of milk and honey'; it's a schismatic time bomb at the heart of the Middle East; it's the birthplace of Christ and a biblical treasure trove. To some extent, it is all of these things, but it's much more besides.

Smaller in square kilometres than Belgium or the US state of New Jersey, and less than half the size of the Australian state of Tasmania, Israel and the Palestinian Territories nevertheless contain geographical terrain of incredible contrasts, from snowcapped mountains and cedar forests, to sunbaked deserts and subtropical valleys. It's possible to be skiing on the slopes of Mt Hermon in the morning and floating in the desert-locked Dead Sea that same afternoon.

Due to its geographical position between Africa and Asia and on the edge of Europe, this small landmass has acted as a fulcrum of history. At one time or another all or part of what is now Israel and the Palestinian Territories has been a Roman province, a Crusader kingdom, a domain of Mamluk Egypt and later Ottoman Turkey, and a British protectorate. Bit-players in all of this have included Perseus and Hercules, Solomon and Sheba, Alexander the Great, Cleopatra, Richard the Lionheart, Saladin (Salad ad-Din) and Napoleon. To that list can be added Abraham, Moses, Jesus and also Mohammed, whose traditionally held presences in this particular part of the world have laden it with far more spiritual significance than is perhaps healthy.

From footprints set in stone to wispy strands of saintly hair, Israel and the Palestinian Territories is filled with physical landmarks, handmade monuments and unearthed

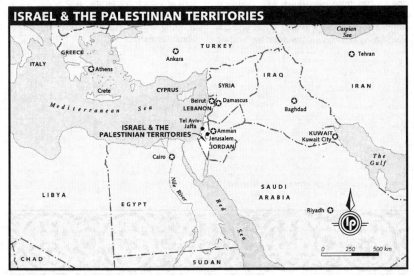

ISRAEL & THE PALESTINIAN TERRITORIES

relics linked to these and many other characters, making it a vast open-air storybook of human history. On the evidence of bones dug up and dated by archaeologists, this human history goes back over 500,000 years.

Yet despite being a cradle of humankind, as a nation Israel has only recently passed its 50th birthday. It is a country in its infancy with a lively, still fermenting society that is a cocktail of ingredients mixed from Europe, America, Africa and the Arab world. The one element that unites most of these different peoples and cultures is a shared Jewish faith. Living alongside the Jews, however, are venerable neighbours like the Samaritans, who claim an unbroken lineage dating back to the time of the Old Testament, the mysterious Druze, Armenian Christians who have maintained a constant presence in Jerusalem since 300 AD.

And, of course, there are also the Palestinian Arabs, co-claimants to the land and possessors of a strongly traditional and conservatively Islamic society, greatly at odds with that of the brash, fast-track Israelis.

With such an extraordinary diversity of peoples, past and present, and all the overlaid and overlapping of culture and faiths, it would be hopelessly optimistic to expect order and calm. So it is that Israel and the Palestinian Territories constitutes the world's longest running trouble spot. The Bible tells of some of the earliest blood letting in the wars between the tribes of Israelites and Canaanites, and you can catch the most recent instalments in the saga most nights on CNN or the BBC. As a visitor, however, be reassured that your experience of the more volatile nature of Israel and the Palestinian Territories will almost certainly be limited to newspaper headlines and TV reports.

For the independent traveller, the contradictions and contrasts of Israel and the Palestinian Territories offer the chance of a multitude of memorable experiences, embracing the spiritual, the cultural, the outdoor and the outright hedonistic. You can go from dining in Bedouin tents and watching dawn creep across the desert to diving through schools of iridescent fish in the Red Sea and partying until sun-up in the bars of Eilat, Tel Aviv or Jerusalem. You could also sign yourself up for a month of banana picking on a kibbutz or visit the refugee camps of Gaza and be humbled by Palestinian hospitality.

The most important thing is not to approach Israel and the Palestinian Territories with any preconceptions. If you do, you'll almost certainly have them confirmed, but in doing so you run the risk of missing a whole lot more.

Facts about the Country

HISTORY
Tribes, Patriarchs & Prophets

While Europe was still frozen in its Ice Age, nomads in what is now Israel had already begun to give up their wanderings. They were opting for a new settled existence, developing agriculture, domesticating animals and cultivating crops. Notable Stone Age remains have been excavated at Tel as-Sultan (Jericho) dating to 7000 BC, making it the world's oldest known town.

The settled environment resulted in the development of copper and bronze-making skills. However, evolution had progressed faster in the valleys of the Nile and Tigris. Squeezed between the two greater civilisations, the coastal strip of Canaan – which roughly corresponds to modern-day Israel – served primarily as a trade route and also occasional battlefield between Egypt and Assyria.

Into this no-man's-land between the two regional superpowers new elements were constantly arriving. The Philistines from Crete settled on the southern part of the coastal plain, while in about 1800 BC a group of nomads from Mesopotamia settled in the mountains of Canaan.

The leader of these nomads was a man named Abraham, and it's generally agreed that he and his group are the ancestors of the Israelites. Most of what we know of them comes from the Old Testament Books of Genesis, Exodus, Leviticus and Deuteronomy. The Bible relates the story of the descendants of Abraham, who entered Egypt and so terrified the Pharaoh with their rapid rate of reproduction that he had them enslaved. But as Exodus 1:12 tells it 'the more they were oppressed the more they multiplied' and a law was passed that any baby boy born to an Israelite was to be killed. It became expedient to make an exit and, as the Bible relates, God appointed Moses to lead his 'Chosen People', the Israelites, out of Egypt. After a 40 year exodus in the wilderness they returned to the land promised to Abraham (Genesis 17:8).

They set about a gradual conquest winning most of the mountain areas from the Canaanites, but they were unable to dislodge the better-armed Philistines from the coastal plain.

Rise of the Israelites

Initially the Israelites existed as numerous tribes each headed by a 'judge', but the threat of the neighbouring Philistines and Canaanites made it wise to unify under a centralised monarchy. The Israelites' first king was Saul (circa 1023-1004 BC) under whose leadership they secured a succession of military victories. His adopted son and successor was David (circa 1004-965 BC), a former shepherd boy from Bethlehem and the legendary slayer of Goliath. David is remembered today largely because it was he who captured Jerusalem from the Canaanites and proclaimed it the new capital of the Israelites. There he installed the Ark of the Covenant (2 Samuel 6), the chest believed to contain the stone tablets on which the Ten Commandments were written. It was also during the reign of David that the Israelites finally vanquished the Philistines.

Solomon (circa 965-928 BC), son of David, built on his father's successes. He extended his domain north to the Euphrates River and south to the Red Sea, made an alliance with Egypt and received a visit from the Queen of Sheba. Noted for his literary skills, he is believed to have written the Books of Proverbs, Ecclesiastes and the Song of Songs. Most importantly, as far as Judaism is concerned, he undertook the construction of a vast temple in Jerusalem in approximately 950 BC – in Jewish history this time is known as the First Temple period.

Fall of the House of David

Despite the popular perception of the First Temple period as the golden era of Israel,

Solomon's heavy taxes had fermented discontent among his people. The kingdom failed to survive his death and split in two. Ten northern tribes seceded to become the House of Israel. That left only two remaining tribes faithful to the House of David to maintain the Kingdom of Judah centred on Jerusalem.

The House of Israel was ruled from the new capital of Samaria and it flourished for a time under the kings Omri and Ahab (married to the eternally maligned Jezebel) before being conquered by the Assyrians in about 721 BC. The Israelites were exiled, scattered among distant lands, earning them the epithet of the Ten Lost Tribes. The Kingdom of Judah submitted without resistance to the Assyrians and so was allowed to remain intact. But the Assyrians were replaced by the Babylonians against whom Judah rebelled. Under the command of Nebuchadnezzar in 586 BC the Babylonian army smashed Judah, seizing Jerusalem and destroying the First Temple (2 Kings 25, 2 Chronicles 36).

Rebirth Under the Maccabees

The people of Judah were exiled to Babylonia. ('By the rivers of Babylon, where we sat down, oh oh we wept when we remembered Zion.' – Boney M fans, remember?) When the Babylonian Empire fell in to the Persians in 537 BC, the Persian king Cyrus allowed the exiles to return to Judah. Although the erstwhile kingdom was now just a small province of the Persian Empire, the Jews (as the people of Judah became known) were able to rebuild Jerusalem and the Temple (Ezra 3). In Judaic history this is commonly referred to as the Second Temple period.

The Persian Empire came to an end in 331 BC at the hands of Alexander the Great. When he died about eight years later, his short-lived empire was carved up by his generals. Of the three main dynasties that emerged, the Seleucids won control over the swathe of land from modern Israel and Lebanon through to Mesopotamia to Persia.

Since their defeat and exile, the Israelites' high priest had assumed many of the duties previously undertaken by the king. The Se-

leucids needed to control this office to ensure their dominance, but their attempts to influence and Hellenise the Jews' religion sparked off a revolt led by the Maccabee brothers in 167 BC. The fight, initially for religious freedom, became a successful bid for political independence.

After inflicting a series of defeats on the Seleucids, the Maccabees founded the Hasmonean dynasty and extended Jewish dominance to the whole of Palestine, the Golan, and the east bank of Jordan.

Romans, Nazarene & Revolts

Internal strife once again undermined the Jewish kingdom and it was easily swallowed up by the inexorably advancing Romans. As the Latinised Judea, it became a vassal state of Rome but flourished under Herod the Great, an egotistical and ambitious administrator. Following Herod's death his sons proved to be less able rulers and in 6 AD the Romans installed a direct representative in the person of the procurator (or governor). The most famous of these officials is Pontius Pilate (in office 26 to 36 AD) whose name is well known to us as the man who oversaw the crucifixion of Jesus Christ.

Jesus had very little impact on the course of history while he was alive and it wasn't until some 300 or more years after his death with the conversion of Constantine that the ministry of the Nazarene began to make any historical impact. He was one of many orators critical of the materialism and decadence of the wealthy Jerusalemites, and contemptuous of Roman authority. These were views representative of a large proportion of the Jewish population, among whom religious and political upheaval was fermenting. The insistence of the mad emperor Caligula that his image be installed in the Temple was a catalyst for extremist elements to whip up the more moderate Jews into a countrywide open revolt in 66 AD (the First Revolt). It took four years for the Romans to quell the uprising; and it was only after a prolonged siege that in 70 AD the Roman general Titus breached the walls of Jerusalem. In retaliation for this, the

Temple was completely destroyed and the Jews were sold into slavery or exiled abroad. The Dead Sea fortress of Masada held out for a further three years; its fall marked the final extinguishing of a recognised Jewish state, something that wasn't to be reborn for 1874 years.

While Jerusalem remained standing it acted as a focus for renewed Jewish nationalist aspirations, which is why the Emperor Hadrian decided to have the city completely razed to the ground. The action provoked the Second Revolt (132-35 AD), led by Simon Bar Kochba. Again, it took three years but the Romans prevailed. As a precaution against further rebellion they put to death Jewish leaders and elders, broke up communities and on the levelled ruins of Jerusalem they built their own city of Aelia Capitolina, which was made centre of the newly named province of Palestine.

Diaspora

As a result of the First and Second Revolts, the Jews were flung far and wide in a scattering known as the Diaspora – derived from the Greek word for dispersion. Jews called it the 'Golah'. Many were sent as slaves to Rome from where they spread throughout the empire; others fled south to join the large Jewish communities already established in Egypt and Babylon. The Jews suffered some oppression at the hands of the new religions of Christianity and later Islam, but generally flourished. Maimonides, a Jewish scholar and one of the 12th century's most highly regarded sages, was personal physician to Egypt's ruler, Sultan Saladin (Salah ad-Din), while Islamic Spain became an important spiritual centre for biblical study.

Matters worsened in the Middle Ages when the Christian Church began sponsoring violent anti-Jewish activities. Crusaders wanted to purge Europe of the 'killers of Christ' and travelled through Europe on their way to liberate the Holy Land. In Spain, after driving out the Muslims, the Christians turned their attention to the large Jewish community to which they gave the

choice of either conversion or death. To escape this persecution the Jews migrated further north and east into Central Europe, to territories that would later constitute Lithuania, Poland and, ominously, Germany.

Holy Land of Palestine

In 331 AD, the Byzantine emperor Constantine, legalised Christianity. As a consequence of his patronage there was a sudden rush of interest in Palestine, or as it now became, 'the Holy Land'. A first wave of biblical building got underway with churches and monasteries erected over many of the sites associated with the life of Jesus. The earliest parts of Jerusalem's Church of the Holy Sepulchre and Bethlehem's Church of the Nativity date from this time, as do remains uncovered at Avdat, Capernaum, Hammat Gader, Latrun and Mar Saba, near Bethlehem.

Challenge of Islam

After weathering a short-lived invasion by the Persians, the Byzantines were bundled out of Palestine by the sudden onslaught of Islam, in the form of the armies of Caliph Omar. Jerusalem fell in 638 AD and was designated a Holy City of Islam because of the Muslim belief that their Prophet Mohammed had ascended to heaven from within its walls. Christians were allowed access to the city under the early Muslim dynasties; however, in 1071 Jerusalem was captured by the Seljuks, who closed the gates on the stream of pilgrims. In response, Pope Urban II called for a crusade to liberate the Holy Places.

Crusading Response

Although the more hospitable Fatimids managed to kick the Seljuks out of Jerusalem in early 1099, the Crusaders were on their way, determined to rid the Holy Land of Islam. They occupied Jerusalem on 15 June of the same year and massacred indiscriminately both the city's Muslim and Jewish inhabitants.

In 1187 Saladin, ruler of Egypt, routed the Crusaders at the Horns of Hittin. There followed a series of increasingly ill-fated campaigns by the Christian knights to recoup their losses which reached a nadir with the Crusaders' sacking of Constantinople, a fellow Christian city. The end of the Crusades came with the fall of their last remaining stronghold, Akko, in 1291 to the Mamluks, the Egyptian dynasty that had superseded Saladin and the Fatimids.

Notable remains from the Crusader period can be seen at Akko, Belvoir, Caesarea, Hebron, Jerusalem (Bethany, Cathedral of St James, Holy Sepulchre, St Anne's, Virgin's Tomb), Latrun and Nimrod.

Mamluks & Ottomans

For much of their reign, the Mamluks were preoccupied with a power struggle in Egypt and a defence of Syria against Mongol attacks. This meant Palestine was relegated to backwater status. Jerusalem continued to attract pilgrims, scholars and renewed Jewish settlement. Jewish numbers in Palestine were also boosted in 1492 by mass expulsions from Spain.

The Mamluks were eventually defeated in 1517 by an Ottoman Turkish army under the command of Sultan Selim the Grim. Selim's successor was Süleyman the Magnificent (1520-66) who returned prosperity to the region. Süleyman is credited with the rebuilding of Jerusalem's city walls.

Unfortunately, these two effective administrators were followed by less able leaders, who were mostly occupied by power struggles with Egyptian pashas. Again Palestine was relegated to minor league status and left in the hands of petty officials, remarkable only for their corrupt and violent brand of administration. The local warlords and Bedouins took advantage of the lack of law and order to carve out independent domains.

Although Jews and Christians were often subjected to harsh treatment, the end of the 17th century saw an increase in Jewish immigration, as they sought to escape from even harsher persecution elsewhere in the Diaspora.

By the 19th century it was apparent that the aged Ottoman Empire was becoming frail and vulnerable and the Jews and major European powers began jockeying for a share of the inheritance. In 1838, the first regular British consulate was opened in Jerusalem, proclaiming itself a protector of the Jewish and Druze elements in Syria and Palestine. Evangelistic activities, ostensibly involving the custody of the holy shrines, often looked suspiciously like the manoeuvring of international politics.

Meanwhile, the Jews of Palestine and the Jewish Diaspora, who had retained close ties throughout the centuries, were strengthening their resolve that one day they should all be able to meet in the Holy Land – a major part of their religious observance.

In 1839, in London, the Jewish philanthropist Sir Moses Montefiore proposed the establishment of a Jewish state, an idea that garnered some support from influential Christians in Europe, thus setting the stage for the eventual founding of political Zionism and the modern State of Israel.

The Beginnings of Zionism

In Palestine, the revival of Jewish nationalism began in 1878 with the founding of Petah Tikva, the first wholly Jewish colony. The fledgling movement was strengthened just four years later by the arrival of large numbers of refugees fleeing pogroms (anti-Jewish riots and killings) in Russia, Romania and Yemen. As well as integrating into existing communities, the newcomers established their own agricultural settlements such as Rishon LeZion, Zichron Ya'acov and Rosh Pina. This late-19th century wave of immigration was later termed the First Aliyah – aliyah means literally 'ascent to the land'. Even today, Jews who move to Israel are not 'immigrating' but 'making aliyah', or achieving a more exalted state.

In 1894, Austrian journalist Theodor Herzl published The Jewish State, a book outlining his ideas that the only solution to Jewish persecution would be a Jewish state in Palestine. In 1897, the World Zionist Organisation (WZO) was founded at the First Zionist Conference, convened by Herzl in Basel, Switzerland (Zion is the traditional

Jewish synonym for Jerusalem and Israel). The aim of the WZO was to bring together international Jewry and to publicise their cause. In 1901, the Jewish National Fund (JNF) was founded to purchase land in Palestine for the Zionists.

Acting on behalf of the WZO, Herzl approached the Ottomans with a request for land in Palestine, but they refused. He turned to the British and asked for part of Cyprus or Sinai Peninsula. Their response was to offer Uganda as a possible site for a new Jewish homeland; this was rejected by the WZO.

Propelled by the WZO and the JNF, the return of the Jews to Palestine gathered momentum. In 1904, Jews escaping more pogroms in Russia and Poland made up the body of the Second Aliyah. In 1909, a group of Russian Jews established Degania, the first kibbutz, on the shore of the Sea of Galilee. The same year also saw the founding of Tel Aviv, the first modern Jewish city.

The Invisible Tenants

A popular Zionist catechism of the time was 'A land without a people for a people without a land'; however, this failed to take into account that under the suzerainty of the Ottoman Empire, Palestine was home to a significant Arab population, albeit one that lacked any national identity. This had begun to change by the end of the 19th century when heavy and seemingly indiscriminate taxation had created a groundswell of anti-Turkish sentiments. This hostility, aligned with local distrust of the increasing European presence, was laying the foundations of Palestinian Arab nationalism. This nationalism was only strengthened even more by the arrival in Palestine of the Zionists.

The Question of Recognition

At the time of WWI, Britain and her Allies sought support from both the Arabs and the Jews in their ambitions to topple the Ottoman Empire. However, in return for their support both the local Arab population and the Jews were looking to the Europeans to back their sovereign claims on Palestine. In response, British policy was at best inconsistent, at worst duplicitous and deceitful.

In 1916, a secret British-French agreement provided for the recognition of an independent Arab state, or a confederation of Arab states, but with an international administration for Palestine. At the same time the WZO, petitioning the British Government for support in the creation of a Jewish state in Palestine, were answered with the Balfour Declaration in 1917. This was a statement of policy by the British Foreign Secretary, Balfour, directed at the WZO, which said the British Government offered support for the 'establishment (in Palestine) of a national home for the Jewish people'.

The British Mandate

Following the Allied victory in WWI, the British ruled Palestine under the mandate of the League of Nations (forerunner of the United Nations), who had decreed that certain territories should be put under the 'tutelage ... of advanced nations' until those territories were deemed ready for political self-determination.

While the Allies were dividing up the spoils, ever greater numbers of Jews were arriving in Palestine. From less than 75,000 Jews in the early 1900s, the number of Jews in Palestine by 1939 was approaching 430,000 or 25% of the population. In the face of rapidly increasing Zionist colonisation and British colonial rule, the Arab response was to initiate a campaign of violence and revolt.

Hitler's declared intention of exterminating the Jewish race sent a tidal wave of refugees rolling toward Palestine. The British, however, did not want Jews flooding in and exacerbating the already tense racial situation. Their policy was to stop immigration and between 1945 and 1948 they created the ironic situation of concentration camp refugees being turned away from Palestine by the very same British army that had helped liberate them.

Unable to rely on the great powers for help, the Palestinian Jews embarked upon a program of smuggling in immigrants through the British land and sea blockade. At the same time they were determined to rid the country of British rule. The Haganah and Irgun, two Jewish resistance movements, embarked on a campaign of sabotage, bombing and kidnappings causing civilian casualties.

Partition & the British Departure

In the wake of WWII, Britain looked to wash its hands of Palestine and passed the buck to the newly formed United Nations. A UN Special Committee on Palestine (UNSCOP) was formed to take on the issue. Following much intense and lengthy debate UNSCOP fell back on an earlier British plan for partition which, in 1937, had been rejected by both the Arabs and the WZO. The Partition Resolution was approved on 29 November 1947. The document called for the creation within Palestine of an Arab state and a Jewish state with an internationalised Jerusalem.

It pleased no one. The Palestinian Arabs rejected it outright. They argued that the Jewish community at the time constituted only a third of Palestine's population, held less than 10% of the land and that the UN did not have the right to surrender Palestinian land to the Zionists. The Zionists publicly accepted the resolution, but documents later showed they actually had no intention of honouring it.

Violence in Palestine had risen while the UN debated the partition program. As a result, Britain decided to withdraw several months in advance of the date anticipated in the Resolution.

1948 War

On 14 May 1948, just one day before the last of the British forces were due to withdraw from Palestine, David Ben-Gurion proclaimed the creation of the independent Jewish State of Israel. Almost immediately, fierce fighting erupted between the Arabs and Jews. The Palestinian Arabs, primarily a peasant society, were no match for the Jewish immigrants familiar with modern weaponry and strategy.

David Ben-Gurion was the first prime minister of the independent State of Israel.

When at the end of May 1949, a UN-sponsored cease-fire came into effect, Israeli forces controlled the major part of Palestine, including the coastal plain, the Galilee region and the Negev Desert. The Gaza Strip was occupied by Egypt, and Transjordan (soon to become Jordan) held the West Bank of the Jordan River and part of Jerusalem.

What came to be known to the Israelis as the War of Independence was to the Palestinians *Al-Naqba* (The Catastrophe). Defeat meant confiscation of homes and land and hundreds of thousands of Palestinians were made refugees.

Following a failed first application, in May 1949 Israel was admitted to the UN, though with reservations expressed at the Jewish occupation of Palestinian Arab land. Israel has since been subjected to continued criticism for its lack of observation of UN resolutions and principles, most of which it has vigorously argued against. The issue of the Palestinian Arabs' rights was designated as a 'refugee problem' to be handled mainly by the UN Relief and Works Agency in Palestine (UNRWA).

Israel's Initial Development

The Zionists now set about attracting increased Jewish immigration to Israel and planning the rapid development of their new national home. The 1950 Law of Return granted citizenship to every Jewish person requesting it. By the end of the next year the Jewish population had grown by some 750,000, with more than half of the new immigrants being refugees from Muslim Arab countries.

Controversy surrounds the treatment of many of these new arrivals from the Arab countries. Many of them complained about discrimination by European Jews; that they were given the worst jobs or forcibly sent to the less appealing areas of the country.

Pioneering the generally barren and inhospitable areas became a vital priority for the new country and this saw the development of *kibbutzim* (collective farms) and *moshavim* (cooperative farms).

In a remarkably short time the Jews managed to develop the infrastructure of a nation.

Suez Crisis & Six Day War

The establishment of the State of Israel sent ripples of turbulence through the Middle East. In 1951, King Abdullah of Jordan was assassinated in Jerusalem for suspected collaboration with the Jews, and the next year Egypt's puppet monarchy (Britain held the strings) was overthrown by the Arab nationalist, Nasser. One of the new Egyptian president's first actions was to nationalise the Suez Canal, a private company in which the British and French were the majority shareholders. In 1956, this resulted in military action by the two European powers during which the Israelis extended their territories into the Gaza Strip and Sinai. Under the terms of a UN-brokered ceasefire, however, the land gains were relinquished to Egypt.

The mid-1960s saw an increase in small-scale attacks on Israel, launched from Syria

and Jordan, and in the anti-Israel rhetoric used by Arab leaders. In early summer 1967, Egypt blockaded the Tiran Straits – the Red Sea access to Eilat – and ordered the UN peacekeeping forces out of Sinai. Two battalions of the Egyptian army moved into Sinai, and in response the Israelis launched a pre-emptive strike which destroyed the Egyptian airforce on the ground.

Jordan and Syria attacked, but in six days of fighting, from June 5 to 10, Israeli forces under the command of Defence Minister Moshe Dayan, defeated the combined Arab armies. At the end of the Six Day War, Israel was in possession of the Golan Heights, the West Bank region, the Gaza Strip and Sinai Desert.

The New Middle East

The astounding success in the Six Day War redefined the popular international image of Israel from a state of wan European Jewish refugees to the military superpower of the Middle East. Victory for the Israelis gave rise to the promise that the Jewish state was here to stay. In the years immediately after the war large numbers of Jews arrived from Western Europe, North and South America and the British Commonwealth, perhaps the first major wave of immigrants to be drawn by the pull of Israel rather than propelled by the push of anti-Jewish persecution at home.

Defeat for the Arabs led to a second great Palestinian exodus as almost 500,000 left their homes rather than remain in the Israeli occupied West Bank and the Gaza Strip. The refugees often found themselves unwelcome in the neighbouring Arab states and UNRWA has been looking after most of them ever since.

Yom Kippur War

Perhaps made complacent by the ease of their victory in the Six Day War, Israel was caught completely unaware when on 6 October 1973 the Egyptians and Syrians struck on the holiest day of the Jewish calendar, Yom Kippur, the Day of Atonement. With most of the army off-duty and at prayer in the synagogues, the first three days of the war almost resulted in an Arab victory. However, the Israeli Defence Force (IDF – Israel's national army, founded in 1948 as a successor to the Haganah) was quickly mobilised and the initial Egyptian gains were reversed. The fighting was brought to a halt 18 days after it had started, by a UN call for a cease-fire.

Heavy losses and, more crucially, the loss of face caused at being caught so off-guard had a sobering effect; the Israeli's national confidence was severely shaken. The Labour Party, in power since independence, was severely criticised and the prime minister, Golda Meir, was forced to resign.

The Palestine Liberation Organisation

The aftermath of the 1967 defeat saw the emergence of a more covert Palestinian resistance in the form of terrorism. The Palestine Liberation Organisation (PLO), an organisation founded in 1964 at a summit meeting of Arab leaders and initially led by Ahmad Shukeiri and then by Yasser Arafat from 1969 onwards, carried out a campaign of bomb attacks, hijackings and murder that dominated world headlines during the early 1970s including the notorious massacre at the 1972 Munich Olympics in which 11 Israeli athletes were killed. The PLO justified the violence by quoting the UN General Assembly's affirmation of 'the legitimacy of the people's struggle for liberation from foreign domination and alien subjugation by all available means including armed struggle'.

Despite the worldwide condemnation of PLO-sponsored terrorism, the international community did recognise the Palestinian cause. At the same time, the PLO was granted observer status at the UN where it received support from several countries and also established offices in major cities, just like any leading political body.

In 1974, the Palestinian National Council (PNC), the body responsible for electing the leaders of the PLO, decided that their policy was not working, and resolved to settle for a Palestinian state in the West Bank and the Gaza Strip. This would exist alongside, and not in place of, Israel. It was also decided to achieve this goal through diplomacy, not force. Some supporters of the PLO therefore claimed to have accepted since 1974 the existence of Israel behind its pre-1967 borders, and blamed the Israelis and their supporters for suppressing news of this policy. Nevertheless a clause in the Palestinian National Covenant calling for the 'destruction of the State of Israel' was not abrogated until the Palestinian Authority (PA) was pressured to do so following the Wye River Accord of November 1998.

The Beginnings of Peace

The shock of near defeat in the Yom Kippur War instilled in Israel an urgent desire to reach some kind of peaceful compromise with its Arab neighbours. In June 1977, the new Israeli Prime Minister, Menachem ˇBegin, called for the leaders of Jordan, Syria and Egypt to meet with him to end the

Golda Meir was the prime minister of Israel from 1969 to 1974.

dispute. President Sadat of Egypt accepted Begin's challenge and after both had broadcast messages to each other's respective populations, Sadat visited Israel on 19 November 1977.

The importance of his visit cannot be overstated – a top Arab leader, who had previously denied the Jewish state's right to exist, was now flying there to negotiate peace. Begin then reciprocated with a visit to Egypt. Brokered by the US government of Jimmy Carter, the historic Egypt-Israel Camp David Peace Treaty was signed by Sadat and Begin on 26 March 1979.

Within the Arab world, Egypt's recognition of Israel was seen as traitorous, and for his collusion President Anwar Sadat was assassinated by one of his own soldiers in 1981. His successor, Hosni Mubarak, who as Sadat's vice president was against the peace agreement, has maintained the terms of the Treaty, if not the spirit, and the relationship between the two countries is best characterised as a 'cold peace'.

The Invasion of Lebanon

In June 1982, Israeli forces invaded Lebanon to force out the PLO who had been using the country as a base to attack the Golan and the Galilee regions. It's also now known that certain instigators of the invasion had a secondary, unstated agenda to install in Lebanon a pro-Israeli Christian government. The action was condemned by the international community but, more significantly, for the first time thousands of Israelis demonstrated against the military actions of their own government.

Boys, Girls & Guns

Israel is still technically at war with more than a few of its fellow Middle Eastern countries. This, in addition to being enmeshed in battling Palestinian terrorist groups and struggling to contain the sporadically violent extremist factions within its own society, means that wherever you go you'll see armed soldiers. Bus stations, in particular, are filled with soldiers in olive green uniforms either arriving home on leave or heading off back to base. Having on occasion to ask, 'Excuse me, could you move your gun so I can sit down there', is an accepted part of bus travel.

What takes more getting used to is the prepubescent appearance of some of the soldiers. Unlike most standing armies, the Israeli Defence Force (IDF) is a citizens' army made up of draftees – both men and women – plucked from civilian life at age 18, fresh from high school. With the conscripts barely out of adolescence, it's an army where fatigues are supplemented by RayBans, and M16 rifles double as crucial fashion accessories. Nor is it always necessary to wear a uniform to carry a gun. Any soldier who loses their weapon (though rarely are women assigned to the weapon-carrying infantry units) is liable to seven years imprisonment, therefore off-duty, jeans and T-shirt-clad soldiers sometimes haul their rifles around if there's no secure place to leave them. We once spotted two young men attempting to groove on a Jerusalem dance floor encumbered with machine guns slung across their backs – although we suspect this had a lot more to do with narcissism than security.

The initial spell of compulsory service in the IDF stretches for three years in the case of men and 18 months for women. Once this has been completed, every male is assigned to a reserve unit to which they are recalled for about 30 days service each year, until the age of 35. Single women are also liable to reserve service up until the age of 34, but in practice they're exempted once they're about 25 years old. Presumably, once a person hits their mid-30s they're assumed to have finally grown out of teenage things like guns.

Israel's action was further fouled by massacres that occurred at the Lebanese Palestinian refugee camps of Sabra and Shatilla – although the killing (800 dead according to the Red Cross) was carried out by Christian Phalangists, IDF forces surrounding the camps had failed to intervene. Amid the controversy, Prime Minister Begin resigned.

The Israelis withdrew from Lebanon in 1985 but retained a security zone in the south of the country as a buffer. Despite this, rocket attacks in the north of Israel have continued to occur intermittently. In recent years Hezbollah, rather than the PLO, have been the responsible party. Ostensibly in response to such attacks, during the run-up to Israel's spring 1996 elections Prime Minister Shimon Peres sought to prove his political virility by ordering the IDF into action once more against Lebanese targets. Tragically, this resulted in another massacre of Palestinian refugees when Israeli shells ripped apart a UN compound at Qana.

Shimon Peres became Israel's prime minister after the assassination of Yitzhak Rabin in Tel Aviv in November 1996.

The Intifada

After the Israeli capture of the Palestinian Arab areas of the Gaza Strip and the West Bank during the Six Day War, groups of politically motivated Jews began establishing settlements in these 'occupied territories'. The settlers argued that their right to live in the Gaza Strip and the West Bank dated to God's promise to Abraham. The issue of the settlements became one of the most contentious within Israeli politics, while the settlers themselves were involved in frequent flare-ups and clashes with Palestinians. The real explosion was sparked by a traffic incident in the Gaza Strip. In December 1987, four Palestinians were believed to have been deliberately killed by a settler driving a car. The response was a spontaneous popular uprising which became known as the *Intifada* (the 'shaking off'). Demonstrations and rallies were accompanied by boycotts of Israeli goods, the withholding of taxes, frequent strike days and of course, the volleys of rocks, bricks and Molotov cocktails hurled at Israeli armed forces.

The Intifada succeeded in bringing the Palestinian cause back to the international centre stage at a time when it had largely been forgotten. It also resulted in a great deal of unfavourable publicity for the Israelis who were responding to the sticks and stones with beatings, house demolitions and gunfire. Worldwide, TV audiences became quite familiar with the scenes of Israeli soldiers firing on running Palestinian youths armed only with stones.

With world opinion swinging behind him, Yasser Arafat announced in 1988 that the PLO was willing to forgo the use of terrorism, that it recognised Israel's right to exist, and that it accepted UN resolutions 242 and 338 – these were the conditions the US had said must be met before they would enter talks with the PLO. After a few anxious days, some incredulity and a request to rephrase the announcement, the US announced that talks with the PLO would begin – much to the dismay of the Israeli Government who had vowed never to deal with the 'terrorists' and said the US had given in. In 1990, after its leadership failed to condemn an unsuccessful Palestinian terrorist raid on a Tel Aviv beach, the US broke relations with the PLO.

Sitting Tight Through Desert Storm

In a strange twist of history, Arab-Israeli peace was furthered the following year, 1991, by Iraq's invasion of Kuwait. The US together with a coalition army made up of international and Muslim Arab contingents sought to take on Saddam Hussein and gathered together. Under the umbrella of Desert Storm, Israel found itself in the unusual position of sitting out the gathering storm and ensuing war neither able to participate in the US-led coalition forces for fear of antagonising the Arab elements in the coalition, nor able to retaliate independently for the same reasons.

In an effort to break the alliance Saddam Hussein claimed that his invasion had been carried out under the banner of anti-Imperialism and anti-Zionism, and to reinforce this notion he targeted Israel with Scud missiles. If the Israelis had retaliated it could have transformed the Gulf War into another Arab-Israeli conflict, shattering the Desert Storm coalition. As Iraqi missiles landed on Tel Aviv, at the urging of the US the Israeli airforce remained grounded.

The fact that Iraq, not even a neighbour, could inflict destruction on Israel from such a distance engendered a great sense of vulnerability. Coupled with the early defeats of the Yom Kippur War and the disastrous Lebanon campaign, the lessons of the Gulf War rekindled Israelis' appetite for peace, while realising that the threat to its national security could come not only from within its borders, but from strategic threats from further afield. In August 1991, the Israeli Government announced that it was willing to enter into talks with the Palestinians.

Oslo & the Handshake

In October that year, US Secretary of State George Baker managed to achieve a breakthrough by bringing together Israel's Prime Minister Yitzhak Shamir with representatives of Syria, Lebanon, Jordan, Egypt and, most importantly, with a Palestinian delegation for three days of face to face meetings in Madrid, Spain. In July 1992, the Labour Party was returned to power after some 15 years of Likud Party rule. With Yitzhak Rabin as leader, they won a relatively decisive victory based largely on the philosophy that it was time to approach the peace talks in a more conciliatory way than that practised by the Likud.

In September 1993, in a ceremony that took place on the White House lawn, the Israelis and Palestinians signed a declaration of principles known as the Oslo Accords, and Arafat and Rabin made their Nobel Peace Prize-winning handshake.

The State of Play Today

The Oslo Accords outlined a two stage settlement. During a period that would begin almost immediately, both sides would negotiate a final settlement that would be implemented on or before 4 May 1999. The interim section of the accords called for, among other things, an Israeli withdrawal from almost all of the Gaza Strip and parts of the West Bank, and the holding of Palestinian elections.

Accordingly, in the summer of 1994, the Gaza Strip (except for a number of Israeli settlements) and the West Bank town of Jericho were granted a limited form of self-rule. This was followed in September 1995 by the signing of and agreement known as Oslo II, a further statement of commitment between the Israelis and the PLO. This resulted in the withdrawal of the IDF from six other West Bank towns by the end of 1995, namely Bethlehem, Jenin, Jericho, Nablus, Qalqilya and Ramallah. Palestinian elections went ahead in 1996 with Arafat voted in as president and head of the Palestinian National Authority (PNA), known more commonly as the Palestinian Authority or PA for short.

Support for Arafat, however, is far from universal. Many Palestinians believe that he is selling them out, bargaining with the

Mossad – Keeping Tabs

Mossad is Israel's CIA – otherwise known as the Institute for Intelligence and Special Tasks (in Hebrew *Ha-Mossad le-Modiin ule-Tafkidim Meyuhadim*). Mossad is responsible for human intelligence collection, covert action, and counterterrorism in Israel and overseas where Israeli interests are at stake. While its main focus is on Arab nations and organisations around the world, Mossad is also responsible for the clandestine movement of Jewish refugees out of Syria, Iran, and Ethiopia. Mossad agents are active in the former communist countries, in the west, and at the UN.

The secretive organisation is based in Tel Aviv and has an estimated staff of around 1200 operatives. The identity of the director of Mossad was traditionally a state secret (or at least not widely publicised), but in March 1996 the Government announced the appointment of Major General Danny Yatom as the replacement for Shabtai Shavit, who resigned in early 1996.

Formerly known as the Central Institute for Coordination and the Central Institute for Intelligence and Security, Mossad was formed on 1 April 1951. The organisation was established by then prime minister David Ben-Gurion, who gave as Mossad's primary directive: 'For our state which since its creation has been under siege by its enemies. Intelligence constitutes the first line of defence. We must learn well how to recognise what is going on around us'.

Despite having earned themselves a respected reputation within the global intelligence community as being a fearless and often ruthless organisation, as well as being highly efficient in the carrying out of its tasks (see the boxed text 'Martyr Spy' in the Negev chapter), Mossad's bungles have been equally spectacular. On 15 November 1995, Mossad agents failed to prevent the assassination of then prime minister Yitzhak Rabin by a right-wing extremist law student Yigal Amir despite having prior knowledge of the possibility of such an assassination attempt.

On 24 September 1997, Mossad operatives attempted to assassinate Khalid Meshaal, a top political leader of the Palestinian group Hamas. The assassins entered Jordan on fake Canadian passports, and injected Meshaal with a poison. The attempt failed and the agents were caught red-handed. Only after the personal intervention of the late King Hussein of Jordan was an antidote to the poison supplied, and the agents returned in disgrace to Israel. As a further concession to the failed fiasco, the Israeli government released from jail the blind Hamas spiritual leader Sheikh Ahmad Yassin.

Israelis for his own political future. Critics claim that all that has been achieved with Oslo I and II is the creation of a number of 'cantons', geographically non-contiguous political entities without true sovereignty, surrounded by Israeli forces which far from withdrawing have simply redeployed.

The main opposition to Arafat and the PNA comes from two militant Islamic groups Hamas and Islam Jihad. They reject the peace process as a surrender to Zionism and a legitimising of the occupation of Palestine. Since self-rule began in 1994, both groups have launched suicide bombing attacks in Jerusalem, Tel Aviv and elsewhere in Israel in an attempt to derail the peace process.

Israeli society is also split over the peace process between those who believe that the only hope for the future lies in dialogue with the Palestinians, and those who are opposed to any compromise with the Palestinians that would mean relinquishing land and control over strategically or religiously significant sites. Approximately three quarters of Israel – including most of the Likud Party – support some form of territorial compromise

('Land for Peace'). Opponents of the peace process are mainly the Zionist orthodox, from whose ranks Gush Emunim was formed, and the hardline old guard. The most dramatic indication of this rift in thinking came with the assassination of Prime Minister Yitzhak Rabin at a peace rally in Tel Aviv in November 1995. The stated intention of his killer, an orthodox law student named Yigal Amir, had been to stop Rabin from handing over 'God-given Israeli lands' to the Palestinians. In 1996, in the first-ever direct election of a prime minister, the Likud candidate Binyamin Netanyahu was elected.

In October 1998, President Bill Clinton, morally encouraged by the ailing King Hussein of Jordan, rekindled the peace process by getting Yasser Arafat and Binyamin Netanyahu together in Wye River, USA. The ensuing Wye River Accord called for the Israelis to hand over a further 13% of the West Bank to the Palestinians. It also demanded that the Palestinians abrogate the clauses in the Palestinian National Charter calling for the destruction of the State of Israel and redouble their efforts against terrorism. A foiled attack on a school bus at the Israeli settlement of Gush Katif in the Gaza Strip and a failed suicide bomber attack in Jerusalem's Mahane Yehuda Market in November 1998, combined with increasing opposition from within Netanyahu's coalition government, all but completely stalled the peace process. During the General Elections of May 1999, Netanyahu was defeated by Ehud Barak, the Labour Party candidate.

The Future

At the time of writing the implementation of the Wye River Accord had almost completely halted as a result of both right-wing opposition within the Israeli government and a perceived lack of vigilance by the PA against sporadic Islamic fundamentalist terrorism emanating from its territory. Following the May elections, it is still unclear whether the situation will remain frozen. Arafat's repeated promise to declare an independent Palestinian State around the same time as the elections are in doubt and the delicate issues such as the status of Jerusalem, the fate of Israeli settlements in the Gaza Strip and the West Bank, and the future of Palestinians still living as refugees in Jordan, Lebanon and Egypt, are still to be discussed.

GEOGRAPHY

Israel, including the West Bank and the Gaza Strip, has a total land area of just 25,970 sq km and is part of the Asian continent. Its western border is the Mediterranean Sea, to the north it is bounded by Lebanon and Syria, to the east by Jordan and to the south by Egypt, with just a small seven kilometre stretch of Israeli coastline giving access to the Red Sea. Some of these borders are subject to interpretation and it's impossible to define the exact boundaries of Israel without upsetting someone.

Israel's physical geography is dominated by the 'Rift Valley', which is part of the great Syrian-African Rift and the longest valley in the world, stretching from East Africa to southern Turkey. This great trough runs the entire length of the eastern side of Israel, starting off in the south as the arid Arava Valley, then filling with the Dead Sea before becoming the Jordan Valley, swelling to contain Lake Galilee and furrowing between the mountains of the Golan Heights and the Galilee as the Hula Valley.

The valley floors and plains in the north of the country, irrigated by Israel's scant few rivers, provide the country's main swathes of agricultural land. The major watercourse is the Jordan River, the most important source of water. It flows from the mountains of the northern Galilee southward to the Dead Sea.

The Dead Sea, in the Jordan Valley where the Jordan River finally ends, is the lowest area on earth at 386m below sea level. No use as a water source because of the high salt content, the Dead Sea does provide a useful yield of minerals, including potash, bromide and magnesium.

The Judean Desert flanks the Dead Sea, a suitably barren but beautiful landscape.

Moving south it merges into the Negev, a hot, seemingly inhospitable flatland of loess, a fine deposit of windblown dust and limestone.

CLIMATE

Climatic conditions vary considerably from region to region. In general, Israel's climate is temperate, with two seasons: winter, at which time it's cold and rainy, and summer, which is hot and dry. Rainfall is concentrated from between November to March, and can vary from over 1000mm a year on Mt Hermon in the Golan to less than 100mm in Eilat on the Red Sea.

Temperature-wise, Israeli winters can be surprisingly severe, often catching travellers unaware. Even in the summer months a warm sweater is needed in many places, as the evening temperatures drop considerably from the daytime high.

The hottest areas are those below sea level: the Jordan Valley, the shores of the Sea of Galilee and the Dead Sea, and the Arava Valley. During the spring, the temperatures are pushed up by strong winds known as the *khamseen* (Arabic for '50' – not, mercifully, for the temperatures attained but for the number of days the winds are supposed to last). The widespread use of solar energy means that for much of the winter in the Jerusalem area and parts of the north, there is a distinct lack of hot water and heating in some accommodation, especially at the budget end. The lack of sun in these areas means that returning to the hostel in the early afternoon in the hope of getting a hot shower can become part of the routine.

The regional climatic variations are part of what makes Israel so fascinating. For example, in Jerusalem during the winter months it is generally cold and wet and you may even experience snow, but hop on a bus down to the Dead Sea, little more than an hour's ride away, and you can change into your shorts and T-shirts and bask in 23°C sunshine.

ECOLOGY & ENVIRONMENT

Israel generally has not the best track record when it comes to issues pertaining to ecology and the environment. A devil-may-care attitude often prevails among some Israelis, perhaps born out of the original need to develop the nation rapidly and exploit what resources were available. Litter is discarded wantonly and water courses, such as Tel Aviv's Yarkon River, are thoughtlessly polluted by industrial and agricultural effluent.

The Jordan River is a prime example of where a fundamental resource (water) has been overexploited for agriculture – the Jordanians who share the river are equally culpable. The over-use of water resources from the Jordan River basin has resulted in a considerable drop in water levels in both the Sea of Galilee and the Dead Sea, both of which are fed by the Jordan River.

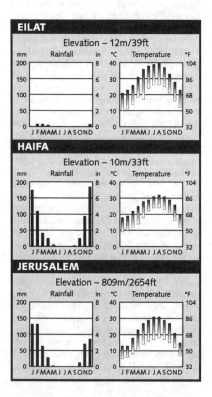

Israeli agriculture has made extensive use of drip irrigation to water large tracts of previously unusable land using the minimum amount of water needed. However, this is still greater than what the fragile Jordan River ecosystem can support.

The Society for the Preservation of Nature in Israel (SPNI – see the following Flora & Fauna section) has been in operation since 1953 and exists to support and promote development that is ecologically sustainable. The Society also runs tours for visitors and maintains a network of Field Study Centres around the country that are involved in research and the preservation of nature. See also the Responsible Tourism section in the Facts for the Visitor chapter.

FLORA & FAUNA

Due to its position at the junction of three natural zones, Israel enjoys a diverse wealth of plant and animal life. In the wet, mountainous Upper Galilee, otters dive in highland streams and golden eagles circle dense laurel forests, while away to the south in the desert landscapes of the Negev, ibex water at date palm-shaded wadis (river beds).

The climatic differences mean that parts of the Israeli countryside blossom at different times. In the north, March and April see the appearance of wild tulips, irises, lilies and hyacinths. To the south, the desert blooms as early as February, the Negev has lion's leaf, groundsels and wild tulips, and in the wadis white broom and purple irises grow.

Israel's skies are also teeming with an enormous variety of birds. Some, such as storks and swallows, rest en route to other climes. Coots and ducks spend the winter; African species, such as the turtle dove, prefer the summer. As it is for certain plants and animals, Israel is the northern limit for many southern bird species, and the southern limit for many northern ones. This makes it the world's second largest fly way (after South America) for migratory birds. See Birdwatching under Activities in the Facts for the Visitor chapter.

As far as plants and animals are concerned, the richness and abundance of species

is not entirely due to nature. The Israelis have devoted a lot of energy to reviving the land after centuries of neglect and abuse. Nearly 300 protected nature reserves have been created covering over one-fifth of the country. The Jewish National Fund has spearheaded an extensive campaign of tree planting, particularly of the fast-growing Jerusalem pine, and the result has been the re-creation of large areas of forest in the central region. There's even a tree planting festival, Tu B'Shevat, celebrated annually every February/March.

There has also been an attempt to reintroduce into Israel some of the animal species mentioned in the Bible as endemic to the Holy Land but that have long since disappeared. They include the Asiatic wild ass, brought from the Copenhagen zoo; the Mesopotamian fallow deer, brought from Iran; and the white oryx, rediscovered in the private zoo of King Faisal of Saudi Arabia. The animals are kept in reserves, known as Hai-Bar reserves after the program sponsoring their reintroduction to Israel.

Society for the Protection of Nature in Israel (SPNI)

SPNI activities encompass all aspects of nature conservation – research and surveys, educational activities, public campaigns for the protection of the environment and the preservation of historical sites. For the traveller, the SPNI provides an excellent source of information on all of these areas and at the various SPNI Field Study Centres dotted around Israel, you're likely to find enthusiastic staff quite willing to answer questions, advise on places to visit and help plan hikes.

Their bookshops, which are both large and extremely well stocked, have the best range of books and pamphlets on nature and wildlife that you're going to find in Israel (much of this is of course in Hebrew, but there is also a lot of English-language material). They also have an extensive range of large-scale maps specifically produced for hikers.

The organisation's touring department, Israel Nature Trails, operates a wide range of guided tours from afternoon hikes to week-long major camping expeditions. Even if a tight budget rules against a guided tour, it's a good idea to browse through their brochure to get an idea of some areas for independent exploration.

The SPNI's head office and bookshop is in Tel Aviv (☎ 03-638 8674, fax 688 3940) at 3 HaShefela St, Tel Aviv 66183 (see the Tel Aviv chapter for directions). The Jerusalem office and bookshop (☎ 02-624 1607) is at 13 Heleni HaMalka St, (PO Box 930), Jerusalem 91008.

The main Field Study Centres are:

Central Israel
  Har Gilo (☎ 02-676 8678, fax 993 2644) 5km west of Bethlehem
The Dead Sea
  Ein Gedi (☎ 07-658 4288, fax 658 4257) at the Ein Gedi Reserve on the Dead Sea shore
The Galilee
  Alon Tavor (☎ 06-676 6250, fax 676 6272) next to Mt Tabor just off Route 65, 10km south of Golani Junction which is 14km west of Tiberias on Route 77
  Har Meron (☎ 06-698 0024, fax 698 7723) on the road to Har-Meron, just off Route 89, 18km west of Safed
  Achziv (☎ 04-982 3762, fax 982 3015) 7km north of Nahariya on Route 4
Haifa & the North Coast
  Carmel Coast (☎ 06-639 4166, fax 639 1618) at the Nahal Taninim Nature Reserve near Kibbutz Ma'agan Michael, just north of Caesarea
The Negev
  Eilat (☎ 07-637 1127, fax 637 1771) south of the town centre, on the coastal road to the Egyptian border at Taba
  Har HaNegev (☎ 07-658 8615, fax 658 8385) at the edge of the crater at Mitzpe Ramon
  Hatzeva (☎ 07-658 1546, fax 658 1558) 50km south of the Dead Sea on Route 90
  Sde Boker (☎ 07-653 2902, fax 653 2721) on the campus of the Ben-Gurion University at Sde Boker
The Upper Galilee & the Golan
  Golan (☎ 06-696 1352, fax 696 1947) in Katzrin
  Hermon (☎ 06-694 1091, fax 695 1480) south off Route 99, near Kibbutz Snir, midway between the Tel Dan and Banias nature reserves

National Parks

The National Parks Authority maintains 34 of the country's top historical sites. If you're planning to visit a least five sites, you should save some money and purchase a 'Green Card'. Valid for 14 days from the date of the first visit and nontransferable, it costs about 60NIS (US$15) per person and allows the holder to visit every site. With an entrance fee of about 17NIS (US$4) per site, this is a very good buy.

The card can only be purchased from the National Parks Authority head office (☎ 03-576 6888, fax 751 1858), Twin Tower, 35 Jabotinsky St, Ramat Gan 52511, or from the following sites: Masada, Tel Jericho, Tel Hazor, Herodion, Caesarea and Megiddo.

GOVERNMENT & POLITICS

Israel is a secular, parliamentary and democratic republic, headed by a president. While not a theocracy in any sense politically, religious groups particularly from the ultraorthodox Jews have a large say in matters of state. The president, whose powers are basically formal, is responsible to the parliament. At the time of writing, the president is Ezer Weizmann.

The government, headed by the prime minister, is the main policy-making body. The Knesset is Israel's parliament, a single-chamber house of 120 members (MKs). All MKs are protected by the Act of Immunity from prosecution or arrest for anything they say or do in the course of their parliamentary duties. Proceedings in the Knesset can get rather high-spirited, with MKs constantly losing their tempers and shouting at each other.

Israel's political parties predate the founding of the state, having been formed during the time of the British Mandate. Despite the quadrupling of the population between 1948 and 1970, the scene was still dominated by the Labour Party, which held power for 29 years until being bumped into opposition in 1977 by the Likud Party, always a close second runner. The two rival parties were joined in a coalition government toward the end of the 1980s until a 1992 election put Labour back in the driving seat. Labour is generally characterised as being left of centre and moderate on issues pertaining to the future of the West Bank and Gaza. It was led by Yitzhak Rabin until his assassination in 1995, at which point Shimon Peres took over as prime minister. Peres was ousted from office little more than six months later when he lost in elections to the Likud candidate, Binyamin Netanyahu. Likud follows an essentially centrist line in a party that is predominantly right-wing and advocates tougher policies on the Palestinian issue. The General Election that took place in May 1999 saw the return of the Labour Party under the leadership of the former Chief of Staff, Ehud Baruk.

The 120 seats of the Knesset are held by members of about a dozen different parties, drawn from across the political spectrum. Some smaller parties representing religious, ideological and special interest groups have loyal, if limited sectoral support among voters. Y'Israel Ba'Aliyah, headed by former Soviet dissident Natan (Anatoly) Sharansky, has concentrated on trying to capture the Russian immigrant vote.

Y'Israel Ba'Aliyah and the parties representing the orthodox and ultraorthodox communities received an increased number of parliamentary seats in the 1996 election, obliging Prime Minister Netanyahu to include them in his coalition government.

ECONOMY

In the years immediately following independence, the economy of Israel was a triumph of skill and initiative over lack of natural resources. The rapid growth of the population and constant cash injections from overseas in the form of aid and investment stimulated steady expansion and development. Roads were built, vast tracts of desert were made cultivable, swamps were drained and a modern well-equipped and well-trained army was put together from scratch. However, the burden of that military spending along with antiquated state restrictions on private enterprise began to show in chronic inflation which by 1985 was running at around 500%.

The currency was changed from lirot to shekels to new shekels in the struggle to control its devaluation. After a series of severe cuts in the government budget and food subsidies, followed by a freeze on prices, wages and taxes, the Israeli government eventually managed to reduce the inflation rate to around 20%. It now stands at around 4 to 4.5% annually.

In the past two decades Israel has switched from an agricultural to a post-industrial economy concentrating on the production of chemicals, plastics, electronic equipment, military technology (get the T-shirt: 'Uzis Do It Better') and computers. The country is now a world leader in various fields, such as computerised printing techniques and the genetic crossbreeding of plants and livestock, and it's also a world-class centre for diamond cutting.

A crippling 60% of the national budget is still eaten up by defence spending and foreign debt – the annual trade deficit in 1995 hit an all-time high of US$9.2 billion – but as long as the peace process stays on course prospects are good. A lasting peace with the Palestinians may lead to a lifting of the Arab boycott on all foreign companies that do business with Israel and result in increased investment from abroad. Additionally, since the signing of the Oslo Accords, tourism to Israel has risen from 1.5 million in the late 1980s to over 2.5 million in 1998. Predictions are that it could hit a figure of five million by the year 2000.

POPULATION & PEOPLE

Israel, including the West Bank and the Gaza Strip, has a population of 6.03 million people. Of this number 4.78 million (or 79.2%) are Jews, 901,000 (15%) are Muslims, 129,000 (1.7%) are Christians and 99,000 are Druze (1.3%). The population of Arabs in the West Bank and the Gaza Strip – including areas under both Israeli and Palestinian authority control – is about 2.9 million.

Jews

Despite the international image of Israeli Jews as a homogenous people, the truth is that they are a deeply divided nation, split by a bewildering array of schisms. 'Two Jews equals three opinions' is more than just an amusing aphorism. Divisions exist along the lines of secular vs nonsecular, hawks vs doves, oriental Jews vs European, those who use creamer vs those who don't – everything is an issue here to be debated and argued in cafes and newspaper columns, on TV talk shows and over the dining room table. As one Israeli Jew interviewed by *National Geographic* put it, 'If we ever get peace around here we'll have a civil war that'll make us wish we had the Arabs back as enemies'.

Ashkenazi In classic Hebrew, Ashkenaz means 'Germany', and these Jews originate from Central and Eastern Europe, particularly Germany. They are also descendants of Ashkenazim who emigrated to North and South America, South Africa and Australia. Some of them still use Yiddish (a combination of Hebrew and medieval German) as their common language, written in Hebrew characters.

The early Zionist pioneers were Ashkenazim, Polish and Russian socialists, and they administered the setting up of the Jewish state and later organised the mass immigration of the Sephardim.

Sephardi Sephard is the Hebrew for 'Spain' and these Jews are descendants of those expelled from Spain and Portugal in the 15th century. Most of the Jews in Palestine until the 19th century were Sephardim. The Spanish Jews spoke Ladino, a mixture of Hebrew and Spanish, written in Hebrew characters. It's still spoken today by some older Sephardim.

Less educated and, generally speaking, less wealthy than the Ashkenazim, the Sephardim claim that they have been treated as second-class citizens. The prevalence of Ashkenazim in politics and other positions of power is often cited as proof of this.

Oriental Also referred to as Sephardi, these Jews originate from various Muslim and Arabic-speaking countries. The most

high profile – if only because of their restaurants – are the Yemenite Jews (or Teymanim after the Hebrew name for Yemen). They arrived in Israel soon after its independence, when a massive airlift called 'Operation Magic Carpet' brought virtually the whole community to Israel. The Iraqi Jews arrived at around the same time, fleeing the persecution brought on by Israel's defeat of the Iraqi army in 1948. There are also Afghan, Bukharan (from Central Asia), Cochin (from Cochin in India) and Iranian Jewish communities in Israel.

Ethiopians Airlifted to Israel from their famine-struck country in two massive operations in 1985 and 1991, many Jews, especially Ashkenazim, have found it hard to accept that these black people really share their faith. Questioning their Jewishness, some argued that the Ethiopians should go through a religious conversion ceremony, including a 'ritual' bath. The discovery in early 1996 that the Israeli authorities had been routinely throwing out blood donated by Ethiopians because of alleged AIDS fears is indicative that the Africans have still not been accepted by Israeli society.

Palestinian Arabs

Since 1948, the Arab population is concentrated mainly in the Gaza Strip and the West Bank. Over 80% of Arabs in Israel are Sunni Muslims, the remainder are Christians or Druze.

Considerable controversy exists over the origins of the Palestinians and this subject along with land tenure and ownership issues is at the very heart of the Palestine 'problem'. The Israelis commonly contend that the Palestinians are descended from the Arab Muslims who invaded Palestine in the 7th century or even that most of them are descendants of immigrants from neighbouring countries who came to Palestine at the turn of the 19th century. Palestinians, on the other hand, claim that their ancestry goes back beyond that and that their ancestors appeared along the south-east Mediterranean coast more than five millennia ago and settled down to a life of fishing, farming and herding. They endured war with the Israelites, domination from Assyrians, Persians and Romans and 400 years of rule by the Ottoman Turks.

Nearly 10% of the Arabs are Bedouins. These are tribes of traditionally nomadic people and they are Muslims. They are still mainly concentrated in the Negev, continuing to live in tents and breeding sheep, goats and camels. The Israeli Government has encouraged them to settle permanently and many have, mainly in the region near Beersheba.

Christians

Most Christians in Israel are Arabs. The remainder consist mainly of Armenians, foreign clergymen, monks, nuns and those working for Christian organisations. See Religion later in this chapter.

Druze

Nearly 10% of the non-Jewish population belong to this mysterious religious sect. The Druze have no homeland or language of their own and their nation, such as it is, is defined by their religion, an offshoot of Islam. Like Muslims, the Druze believe in Allah and his prophets but they believe that Mohammed was succeeded by a further divine messenger. The Druze also hold the non-Islamic belief of reincarnation and for this reason headstones on their graves carry no name.

Within Druze society there is a select inner core made up of men and women who have passed severe tests and are considered to have led exemplary lifestyles of honesty and modesty. The men are identifiable by their white turbans, and only these *'uqqal* ('the wise') are permitted to read the Druze holy books and take place in the Thursday night religious ceremonies. The rest of the community, *juhhal* ('the ignorant'), have to hope that they might qualify in their next incarnation.

Most of the Druze nation lives in Lebanon and Syria; in Israel they inhabit a few villages in the Galilee, on Mt Carmel, and in the Golan. Having never had a state of their own the Druze tend to hold allegiance to whatever country they live in. Most of the Druze are Israeli citizens and, like any other citizen perform military service. However, the situation is a little different in the Golan where up until 1967 the Druze towns and villages were part of Syria. These Syrian Druze resent Israel's annexation and have remained fiercely supportive of Syrian claims to the area. From either side of the political fence, the Druze will be among the friendliest people travellers will meet in Israel.

Samaritans

One of the world's smallest minorities, numbering only 584 people the Samaritans claim to be both Palestinians and Israelites – they speak Arabic but pray in ancient Hebrew.

According to their history they are descendants of the tribes of Joseph, and until the 17th century they possessed a high priesthood descending directly from Aaron through Eleazar and Phinehas.

The Samaritans' faith is based solely on the first five books of the Bible, so the only prophets they recognise are Moses and Joshua. As in Judaism they observe Shabbat, but the Samaritans' interpretation of biblical laws is stricter than that of the most ultra-orthodox Jews. During their menstrual period, women are obliged to remain separated from their families for seven days and after giving birth, a woman is considered to be unclean; if the child is a son, the impure state lasts for 40 days, twice that if it's a girl.

For the Samaritans, Jerusalem's Temple Mount is replaced in importance by Mt Gerazim, near Nablus. It was here they say, not Mt Moriah, that Abraham brought his son to sacrifice, an event celebrated on the mount every year at Pesah.

Over the years, the Samaritans have been greatly affected by the political turmoil in the region. From a one-time powerful community, their numbers were reduced by conquest and forced conversion, first by the Byzantines then by Arabs. During the time of the British Mandate the Samaritan community, then numbering less than 150, separated, with about half of them moving away from Nablus to Holon, now a suburb of Tel Aviv. After 1948 the communities became split between Israel and Jordan, reunited only by the Jewish successes in the Six Day War. As a consequence, these days the Samaritans of Nablus are recognised as Palestinians while those in Holon are seen as Israelis and relations between the two communities are fraught with difficulties.

Black Hebrews

The Black Hebrews have attracted controversy ever since the first arrivals in 1969. They claim to be the most authentic descendants of the Jews exiled from Israel 4000 years ago, but this is treated with deep scepticism by the authorities and they have been refused Israeli citizenship.

The community was founded in Chicago by Ben Carter (now known as Ben-Ami Carter), a steel worker who claims he had a vision through which he learnt that African-Americans were descended from the early Israelites and the time had come to return to the Promised Land. Rather than travel directly to Israel, the Hebrews, led by Carter, first tried to settle in Liberia from were they were ultimately expelled.

In Liberia the community developed their principles of a vegetarian diet, and abstinence from smoking, alcohol (except their own wine) and pharmaceutical drugs, and complete isolation from the corrupting influences of the world. They took up wearing colourful African clothing and made efforts to teach themselves Hebrew. Men were surnamed Ben Israel (Son of Israel) and the women called Bat Israel (Daughter of Israel).

The first Black Hebrews entered the country posing as tourists before making claims for citizenship under the Law of Return which states that any Jew is entitled to become an Israeli. They were refused but the Israelis feared to deport them and be accused of racism. Ben Ami attacked the authorities declaring that the 'White' Jews had stolen the language, history and culture of the original Jews, the Black Hebrews.

They never got their citizenship, but the Israeli Government eventually compromised and granted the Black Hebrews temporary residency on the condition that they brought no more members into the country. Their insular community is located in Dimona, on the edge of the Negev Desert, and now numbers 1200; the Black Hebrews welcome visitors.

As a further sign of their grudging acceptance into Israeli society the band Eden – chosen to represent Israel in the 1999 Eurovision Song Contest – had Black Hebrews as two of its members.

Circassians

An independent group in the Muslim community, the Circassians number some 4000. They originated in the Caucasian Mountains of Russia, immigrating to Palestine in the 1890s. Mostly loyal to the State of Israel, the community is concentrated in two villages in the Galilee.

ARTS

Israelis have a great enthusiasm for the arts in all forms – the country sustains several world-class orchestras, the cities and towns are crowded with art galleries, theatre performances are well attended, and bookshops are plentiful and well stocked. By no means is it all great art, but that's to miss the point – the arts in Israel serve to stimulate and provoke discussion, and on that level they succeed completely.

Music

Classical Israel has long been associated with excellence in classical music. This started in the 1930s when Jewish musicians, including the best of Europe's composers, performers and teachers, fled to Palestine to escape Nazism. The Israeli musical pedigree was further boosted by the waves of Soviet Jews who arrived in the country during the 1980s – the joke went that if a Soviet Jew was not carrying a violin case upon arrival at Ben-Gurion airport, then they must be a pianist.

The violinist Yitzhak Perlman and the Israel Philharmonic Orchestra are world-renowned, and there are numerous other musicians and groups worthy of note. The major orchestras and groups perform regularly, mainly by subscription, from October to July – visitors will not always find it easy to get tickets to these concerts. The most important venues are the Mann Auditorium in Tel Aviv and Jerusalem's Binyanei Ha'-Umah. Cultural centres elsewhere regularly host classical concerts, and the historic settings of Caesarea's Roman amphitheatre and Akko's Crusader castle are often used.

In 1986, the Nuyha/Al-Hakawati Theatre in East Jerusalem produced the first-known Arabic operetta. Their music department teaches the use of traditional Arab instruments and incorporates a recording studio.

Klezmer Klezmer is traditional Yiddish dance music, born in the Ashkenazi Jewish communities of Eastern and Central Europe – think *Fiddler on the Roof*. Centred on violins, the sound can range from weeping melancholy through to wild thigh-slapping, high-kicking exuberance. In the past 20 years, klezmer has experienced something of a revival and it's no longer confined to wizened old men turning out hoary old standards at wedding parties. Bands such as the New York-based Klezmatics have extended the boundaries with new compositions and eclectic fusions which draw large audiences

Traditional Arab instruments such as the *rabab* (above) and the *oud* are still popular.

wherever they perform. Renowned classical violinist, Yitzhak Perlman, recently recorded a klezmer album which was extremely well received (*In The Fiddler's House* released on EMI). If you happen to be around at the time there is an annual Klezmer Festival held in Safed each August which is reputedly well worth attending.

Popular To listen to Israeli pop is to be transported to a world of permed blonde hair, white pressed trousers, held hands and wistful smiles. How bad is it? Well, gaining a Eurovision song contest nomination is still considered a mark of success. It's little wonder that the last (and, as far as we can remember, only) impact that Israeli pop had on the international scene was back in the late 1980s when Ofra Haza made it big with her much-sampled *Im Nin' Alu* (from her album *Yemenite Songs*). Connoisseurs of kitsch might want to look out for *Umpatampa* by Dana International, a lollipop sucking, transsexual disco queen – she won the 1998 Eurovision song contest with a song called *Diva*, that can be found on the album of the same name. See the boxed text 'Dana International' in the Tel Aviv chapter.

More discerning listeners might look out for Noa (Achinoam Nini) a sprite-like Yemenite Israeli singer sporting a wistful, soaring voice who sings in both Hebrew and English. Her 1994 album *Noa* is considered by many to be her best. Israeli jazz is best represented by the silky voice and smooth piano playing of Nurit Galron who sings laid-back jazz numbers in Hebrew. Check out her self-titled album *Nurit Galron* for a sample of some of her best work.

Literature

Israeli The Zionist movement was founded by writers whose main contribution lay initially in the writing of political pamphlets and newspaper articles as opposed to *belles lettres*. The efforts of Israel's literary community have remained intensive ever since with a considerable proportion of Israel's better literary figures coming from the left of the political spectrum.

That support comes not just from within Israel (where half of the adult population reads at least one book a month), but also internationally, with Israeli literature garnering far more attention and recognition than might be expected for a country with such a small population. In fact, Israel has been honoured with a winner of the Nobel Prize for Literature in SY Agnon.

Pioneers of the early age of modern Hebrew literature include Hayim Nahman Bialik, Shaul Tchernikowsky and Yosef Hayim Brenner. However, the best-known novelist of that generation of writers prior to 1948 is Moshe Shamia.

The most well-represented Israeli author in translation these days is Amos Oz whose books appear in 22 languages. Although much of the charm and colour in his novels is drawn from the Israeli characters and settings, the themes are universal. Almost anything he's written including *In the Land of Israel* is worth reading.

Almost rivalling Oz in his collection of international accolades, is David Grossman. whose novels *See Under Love* and *The Yellow Wind* have drawn comparisons with Günter Grass and Gabriel García Márquez.

Worth particular mention is the superb lyrical description of Jerusalem by Amos Elon in *Jerusalem: City of Mirrors* – first published in 1991, but re-released in 1996 with additions. It is a gripping description of a fascinating city and a must for any would-be visitor to the country's spiritual heart.

Belonging to a generation older than Oz and Elon, AB Yehoshua, a native of Haifa, is still producing highly regarded work. One of his most recent works in English translation is *Mr Mani*, a six-generational, sweeping epic of a wandering Jewish family.

In the field of poetry, *The Great Tranquility: Questions & Answers* by Yehuda Amichai was published in 1997 prompting Mark Rudman, an amazon.com online reviewer to write: 'Yehuda Amichai is by now one of the half-dozen leading poets in the world. He has found a voice that speaks across cultural boundaries and a vision so sure that he can make the conflicts of the

citizen soldier in modern Israel stand for those of humankind. His wit is considerable: he can say virtually anything and give his words enough sting to defuse both sentimentality and hyperbole'.

After the First Rain: Israeli Poems on War and Peace – published in June 1998 – is a collection of poems in English translation by contemporary Israeli poets, and edited by poet Moshe Dor. It provides insight into Israeli feelings on a painful topic that they find hard to avoid in their daily life.

For adventure lovers, Abraham Rabinovich's *The Boats of Cherbourg* is a modern-day thriller in the Tom Clancy style. Published in 1997, it is based on the planned use of clandestine missile boats by the Israelis during the Yom Kippur War against the navies of Egypt and Syria. It is an excellent read for fans of modern warfare stories.

Palestinian Palestinian literature was born of adversity and has been fostered by the nation's political misfortunes. One of its best-known exponents, Emile Habibi, a long-time representative in the Israeli Knesset for the Communist Party, only took up the pen after a leading Israeli politician said in 1967 that the Palestinians did not exist; if they did they would have produced their own literature. Habibi's response was to embark on a series of short stories and novels, one of which, *The Pesoptimist*, was translated into 16 languages, including Hebrew. A lifelong resident of Haifa, he died in May 1996.

Another of the Palestinian's most esteemed writers is Mahmoud Darwish, born in the Galilee. For Palestinians, as in the Arab world as a whole, verse has always been more highly regarded than prose and Darwish is primarily a poet. Highly political, Darwish was a member of the PLO in the 1970s, and during the Intifada years (which saw a flourishing of poems and literature, much of it of a bland nationalist flavour) he composed the Declaration of Independence for Palestine.

Another Palestinian Israeli renowned for his writing is the poet Tawfiq Zayad who was also a member of the Knesset for the Communist Party before being killed in a motor accident in 1997.

Israeli control over Jerusalem led to Beirut becoming the centre of Palestinian literary life and later to Tunis when the PLO were forced out of Lebanon. Liana Badr fled there, via Jordan, after the Israelis captured her hometown of Jericho in 1967. Her first-hand experience of upheaval informs *The Eye of the Mirror*, the story of a Palestinian girl caught up in the Lebanese civil war.

Hassan al-Kanafani also wrote about Palestinian refugees in Lebanon, Kuwait and Iraq in *Man In The Sun* which was published by AUC Press, Egypt (email auc@aucacs.eun.eg). In al-Kanafani's case, the Palestinian relationship between literature and politics proved fatal; he was assassinated in Beirut in 1972.

Architecture

Israeli For a new land, a new architecture was desired. For the Zionists, Palestine was a clean sheet and for the society they were creating they wanted an architecture that reflected their vision. They brought with them the latest and most progressive ideas from the drawing boards of Europe and used them as a blueprint. The mantra of the time was 'form over function' and the style it gave rise to is known as 'International Style'. While architects in Europe struggled for the opportunity to put the ideas into practice, the sands of the Promised Land were fertile ground where cast concrete was concerned. A couple of the best examples of this would-be utopian style of architecture are the Weizmann House in Rehovot (1936) and the Shocken Library (1936) in Jerusalem.

Some of the first people to flee Germany after Hitler's rise to power in 1933 were the artists and architects, and a great many of them found refuge in Palestine. As a result, the influential Bauhaus school of architecture, widely admired in Europe but less frequently built, found a foster home among the Zionists. For sheer quantity of Bauhaus buildings, Tel Aviv probably rivals Berlin, but framed by spindly palms and lit by a Mediterranean sun they look much better here.

Israel's independence brought huge waves of immigrants, and much more housing was required. The centralisation of construction work under a single authority resulted in identical housing projects throughout the country. The architecture looked bureaucratic, with the emphasis on low cost and speed of construction rather than any more aesthetic concerns. With a decreased rate of immigration and increased prosperity, the need to economise on building costs is no longer such a major consideration. Since the 1950s and 1960s standards of architecture have improved in Israel, but there has yet to emerge a distinctive home-grown style. Instead, the cues come from America and the resulting buildings are no worse, or better, than the majority of modern-day architecture the world over.

Islamic When the Zionists arrived in Palestine the area did, of course, have its own architectural traditions, but these were hardly likely to appeal, belonging as they did to the Islamic world. The majority of the architecture in Israel that predates this century is Arabic or Turkish in origin. During the 400-year reign of the Ottoman Turks, Palestine was a backwater so little building of much significance went on. The exception perhaps is Akko which was largely rebuilt in the 18th century and has a beautiful, typically Turkish mosque and some fine caravanserai.

In common with Egypt and Syria, much of the country's finest Islamic-era architecture dates from the Mamluk period (1250-1517). Unfortunately, their buildings are confined almost solely to the Jerusalem's Old City (see that chapter for more information), with just a few other isolated examples dotted around, such as the Ibrahimi Mosque in Hebron and a couple of structures in the Gaza Strip.

Film

Israeli cinema has enjoyed limited international critical acclaim with films like *Othello* and *Runaway Train*, as well as commercial success with lower quality productions that have kept ex-Israeli Hollywood producers Golan and Globus in a job.

Film-making in what is now Israel can be traced back to the beginning of the century, when Edison camera operators came to Jerusalem to shoot footage of the local inhabitants. The first locally produced movies were Zionist fundraising films. The characters in these early movies were portrayed as idealised 'new Hebrew men' that socialist Zionism sought to create as the antithesis of the stereotypically weak, cowering Diaspora Jew. Postindependence, a couple of small film studios were established and one or two features made, but these were overshadowed by a series of British and Hollywood productions filmed in Israel in the 1950s and early 1960s, such as Otto Preminger's *Exodus*.

A 1964 production, *Salah Shabati*, is said to have signalled the emergence of Israel's own film industry. Since that time, the staple diet of Israeli cinema has been the *bourekas* film. The name derives from a pastry, and is used to indicate a low-budget comedy of a stereotyped emotional, lazy and vulgar Sephardi, competing with a snobbish, humourless and dull Ashkenazi. However, this tacky movie genre has seen little activity since the 1970s.

In recent times there has been a swathe of popular and well-produced Israeli films including *Rabbi Fishke Goes to War*, an outrageous comedy that broke all box office records in Israel and in the US. Starring Paul Smith (*Midnight Express*), the film is about a soldier – who's really a rabbi – that joins the top-secret department of the Israeli army to take practical and moral care of a friend who joined the unit.

Six Days to Eternity is the untold story of the Six Day War, which includes the first release of documentary clips shot by the Arab army. The film brings to life the War from the hours before the conflict to the actual battles and the ultimate victory of Israel's airforce.

There is currently no domestic Palestinian film industry, but there are some Pales-tinian film makers working outside Israel. In particular, Michel Kleifi's *Wedding In Galilee* and *Fertile Memory* enjoyed critical acclaim both at home and abroad.

Theatre

In a fantasy that Broadway couldn't ever conceive of, it is claimed that more than half of all adult Israelis visit the theatre at least once a year. And, what's more, those attendances are achieved without the faintest stirrings of an Andrew Lloyd Webber tune. Instead, Israeli theatre companies fill the house with a mix of American and European classics such as Brecht, Chekhov and Shakespeare, alternated in repertory with home-grown farces and social satire. It's the local fare that's the best received, with playwrights, actors and audiences all sharing a love of parody and slapstick. The subject matter of the native plays also often better satisfies the Israeli propensity for navel gazing.

The Israeli theatre tradition has its origins in immigrants from Eastern and Central Europe, like Moscow's Habimah company who settled in then-Palestine during the 1920s. The Habimah today is the country's official national theatre, but it shares the applause with at least five other major companies including Tel Aviv's Cameri Theatre, the Khan Theatre in Jerusalem and municipal theatres in Haifa and Beersheba.

SOCIETY & CONDUCT
Israeli Society

If America with its rich mix of peoples and creeds can be described as a melting pot, Israeli society is more of a chaotic and far from cohesive mosaic as visualised by Jackson Pollock.

The nation-founding, pioneering spirit is still very much in evidence, and Israel remains an outdoor society with a strong emphasis on healthy living and hard work – it sometimes feels like the country is one big scout jamboree. However, the pre-eminence of the kibbutz ethos, which is the complete embodiment of all of the above, is on the wane; only about three percent of the population actually live on a kibbutz.

Instead, the last 20 years have seen the emergence of an Israeli nouveau riche with a serious addiction to consumerism. While hedonism may be an exaggeration, the prevailing credo is 'live now pay later'. As put by one resident of Tel Aviv with little faith in the peace process, 'Why worry about bills when you may never get to pay them'.

Adam's Rib: Women in Israel

An ultraorthodox man wakes up in the morning and one of the first things he does is mutter a prayer that thanks God for not making him a woman. This little tradition has been a thorn in the side of Jewish feminists for decades. In traditional synagogues in Israel, women are still separated from men by a latticed divider and are deemed 'impure' during and for seven days after their menstrual cycle. But despite the fact that orthodox Judaism relegates women to a secondary role, Israeli women generally enjoy a status on par with many of their western counterparts.

Working women and collective childcare were realities in Israel 40 years before western feminists adopted their practice. Turn-of-the-century pioneer women worked in the swamps and fields alongside men and fought combat in the 1948 War of Independence. Israel was also one of the first countries to elect a female Prime Minister, Golda Meir.

Look around. The majority of Israeli women are not orthodox. They are, however, self-confident and single-minded. They are lawyers, politicians, doctors, and journalists. Some are even rabbis. While they tend to marry young – by their mid-20s – most continue to work afterward.

That said, there are still problems with discrimination and abuse, and as such Israel is entangled in certain steadfast cultural traditions that belie its western appearance. Women lag behind men in many careers, and while laws exist to support equal pay, women still earn less. One problem is the military. The army is a major trainer of skilled, technical labour and serves as a jump-start to many civilian careers. A man's value in society is often related to his job in the army. But women soldiers only serve an administrative or educational role, which carries little prestige and rarely translates into a post-army profession.

The biggest discrepancy, however, exists in divorce court, which is governed by orthodox Jews. A man holds the divorce decree in his hands and can legally refuse to grant his wife her freedom and prevent her from remarrying. While the husband is free to then have relationships with other women (even father children legally), any child his estranged wife has with another man is considered illegitimate, and cannot later get married by a rabbi in Israel. It's a law that feminists have been trying to change for years, but for political reasons, the orthodox have been given free reign over marriage and divorce laws, and have no interest in amending them.

Domestic violence is also increasing. Women's organisations and psychologists have long claimed that Israel's violent occupation of the Palestinian Territories has spilled over to the domestic front. It's a problem that has only recently been addressed, since for many years no one wanted to acknowledge that abuse could happen in Jewish homes.

All of these, combined with the periodic influx of immigrants from countries less versed in feminism – the Ukraine, Ethiopia, Iraq – make the fight for women's rights a difficult task. The biggest obstacle, however, is probably national security. Many social problems in Israel are ignored or swept under the carpet due to more pressing concerns. Domestic violence and the religious regard for women are simply not high priorities and probably won't be for a long time.

Kim Zetter

Sorry For What?

Two recent immigrants, one from Russia and one from America, and a native Israeli are at the supermarket where they come across a sign reading 'We're sorry, but due to shortages we have no meat'. The Russian turns to the other two and says, 'What is meat?'. The American shrugs, 'What do they mean by shortages?'. The Israeli shakes his head and looks perplexed, 'What do they mean by this sorry?'.

The Israelis tell this joke about themselves, and any visitor who's been in the country for more than five minutes will nod despairingly at the punch line. The Israelis, as they'll readily agree, are not hot on the niceties of social intercourse. No official or sales assistant will acknowledge your presence until addressed directly. Dining out, staff will frisbee a menu at the table, then indicate they're ready to take the order with a disinterested, 'Yeah?'. Likely looking places to ask for directions or timetables ward off all potential enquiries with prominently displayed 'No Information' notices.

For those who perceive the difference, it's not, explains writer Stephen Brook, that the Israelis are bad mannered, but rather that they have no manners at all. Faced with a waiter who shrugs aside your complaints of cold food with 'People don't like it if it's too hot', anyone might feel that such subtleties are irrelevant; but one thing to remember is never lose your temper and start shouting, because there's nothing Israelis love more than a good row.

Even though most regard themselves as secular, they still maintain such traditions as circumcision and bar mitzvah – the spiritual roots of the country lie firmly in Judaism. Because of this, the country's outspoken religious minority wields a disproportionate influence in the life of all Israeli Jews. The religious courts have exclusive jurisdiction of several areas including marriage and education. This is no doddering bunch of old men issuing unread and ignored edicts either; the religious community frequently goes head-to-head against slacking politicians and community leaders, and occasionally engages in a bit of hand-to-hand in street confrontations. In recent years orthodox Jews have burnt down bus stops for carrying lewd advertising, invaded football pitches hosting Shabbat fixtures, and punched out a mayor of Jerusalem for his backing of a mixed-sex swimming pool.

Palestinian Society

The traditional Palestinian lifestyle revolves strongly around the extended family. Despite the adversities of the past 50 years, outside the big cities and towns the Palestinians are extremely friendly and helpful to strangers and have no qualms about opening up their homes. Weddings are big events and tend to involve whole villages.

In general, the Palestinians are quite accepting of foreigners' ways, but when visiting the Gaza Strip or the West Bank towns it is essential that you dress modestly – both men and women should cover their legs, and women should not expose their shoulders or upper arms.

RELIGION

As far as two out of the three monotheistic faiths are concerned, Israel is where it all started and no other country in the world has so much religious significance to so many. Jews have lived here, in varying numbers, since the time of the Old Testament; Christianity began here 2000 years ago; and Muslims revere Jerusalem as their third holiest site. In addition, Israel is also the world centre of the Baha'i faith.

Judaism

Judaism is the dominant faith of Israel. An orthodox minority of the country's Jews spend most of their lives studying their faith, so don't expect to find all your questions answered in this book.

According to Jewish doctrine, Jews are in the world to be witnesses to the claim that there is one God with whom humans can have contact: God has chosen them to act as messengers whose task it is to pass on these details to the rest of the world. What God has said is written in the Torah (the first five books of the Old Testament). The Torah contains God's will as revealed to the Jews through their leader, Moses, over 3000 years ago. It contains 613 commandments, interpretations of which cover fundamental issues such as avoiding idolatry, murder and sexual transgression, and apparent trivialities such as never eating cheeseburgers and not driving a car or making toast on Satur-

Shabbat

The most important meal of the week in most Jewish homes is the Friday night dinner at the start of Shabbat (the Jewish holy day). In Judaism, the 'day' begins when the sun sets. Before Shabbat starts, the house is cleaned and the dinner table is set with the best crockery and table linen. Traditionally, religious fathers and sons go to the synagogue while the women prepare the meal. On his return the father blesses the children and recites from the Old Testament. To religious Jews, Shabbat is a joyful day and a time to appreciate what they have been too busy to notice during the week.

No work of any kind may be carried out on Shabbat, unless it is necessary to save life. The orthodox maintain a particularly meticulous code which forbids writing, handling of money, and the operation of machinery of any kind.

Jewish communities tend to be concentrated because religious Jews need to be within walking distance of the synagogue, as driving, using public transport and even walking too far are forbidden on Shabbat.

day. Judaism is an extremely complex faith, and the Torah is only the foundation of Jewish sacred literature. There are also the prophetic, historical and 'poetical' books that constitute the rest of the Old Testament. The prophetic books rank second only to the Torah in Judaism, with Isaiah being one of the most important.

Another major written part of the Jewish faith is the Talmud, which includes the Mishnah (a Hebrew commentary on the laws of the Torah assembled in the land of Israel around the year 200 AD) and the Gemara (a collection of legal and philosophical debates and homiletic stories, mainly in Aramaic). There are in fact two Talmuds – the Jerusalem (or Palestinian) Talmud edited in Tiberias around the year 400 AD; and the Babylonian Talmud, a much more extensive work that was edited in Babylonia (modern-day Iraq) almost a century later.

This great collection of writings was completed during the early centuries of the Christian Era. About 2000 authors contributed towards the 63 books of the Talmud, covering rabbinical interpretations of the scriptures and commentaries. Virtually every aspect of life is touched upon and it is this work that many spend a lifetime studying. In days gone by, some scholars in Eastern Europe were said to know it all by heart.

Dress The most religious, or ultraorthodox Jews are known as Hasidim (or Haredim). The men are easily identifiable by their black hats (on Shabbat often replaced by grand fur hats known in Israel as *streimels*), long black coats, tieless white shirts, beards and cropped hair with *peyot* (side curls). Some groups do have more modern permutations of this clothing code, but it is always in black. Women's clothing is not as distinctive, but they do wear long coats and skirts to ensure that as little flesh as possible is visible. After marriage they are usually obliged to wear a hat, a scarf or a snood (hair net). Some women wear a wig, and although it is usually made of real hair, is considered as 'covering' the original hair, and as such conforms to the letter of Jewish law.

When saying their morning prayers many orthodox males don the *tallit* (prayer shawl) and in the reform and conservative movements, a growing number of women don the tallit also. On each of the four corners of the tallit are *tzitzit* – symbolic tassles as directed by the Torah. While the regular tallit is specifically for prayer, the Torah's instruction is to wear a garment with tzitzit all day; therefore, traditional Jews wear the *tallit katan* (small prayer shawl) all day, and the larger tallit just for prayers.

The Hasidic clothes are worn, year-round and are based on outfits worn by Christian noblemen in the 15th century. The outfits were designed to distinguish the wearer from other Jews and from non-Jews. Many modern orthodox groups follow all the commandments but wear basically the same clothes as other members of their societies

The most common sign of a religious Jew is the *kippa* (skullcap) known in Yiddish and outside Israel as *yarmulke*. There is no universally recognised size for kippa and you'll see various styles, colours and materials used.

Wearing a kippa is essentially a tradition, not a *mitzvah* (commandment) though many Jews are unaware of this. The kippa is a symbol of one's orthodoxy; secular Jews do not wear one because they do not identify with the orthodox worldview. See also the boxed text 'Jews & Kippa' in the Galilee chapter.

Childhood By Jewish law, a boy is circumcised on the eighth day after birth. The more traditional, though not necessarily religious, Jews treat it as an important ceremony with family and friends gathered to witness the occasion.

When he reaches the age of 13, a Jewish boy becomes 'bar mitzvah', meaning that he is now subject to Jewish law and therefore, for religious purposes, an adult. On the Shabbat after his 13th birthday he reads from the Torah in the synagogue for the first time. This involves about a year's preparation and it's often an emotional and noisy occasion with older relatives making their

presence felt. Witnessing a bar mitzvah at the Western Wall can be one of the highlights of a visit to Jerusalem. Nowadays there is also a 'bat mitzvah' ceremony for Jewish girls, but only in the reform and conservative movements does the girl read from the Torah.

Synagogues, Rabbis & Prayers Unlike, say, Christian churches, the synagogue's function isn't limited to that of a prayer hall. The Diaspora synagogues usually function as community centres whereas in Israel, where Jewish culture is reflected throughout the society, most synagogues are almost exclusively places to pray, though some are used for studying. In medieval Europe, some synagogues would have had an attached bakery to prepare *matzah* (special unleavened bread) that's baked once a year for Pesah (Passover), and maybe a *mikveh* (bathhouse) for ritual washing.

Synagogue architecture is so unprepossessing because originally neither Christian rulers in Europe nor Muslim overlords allowed Jews the ostentatiousness that their own churches and mosques were allowed. There are no domes or minarets, flying buttresses or spires; in fact from the outside it's very often quite difficult to identify a synagogue. You have to look for small indicators such as *menorahs* (the seven-branched candelabra), or the Star of David.

The menorah is a symbol of Judaism.

Gay Orthodoxy – Oxymoron or Reality?

It is almost inconceivable for outside observers to reconcile the black-suited, white button-down shirt image of Hasidic Jewry with the world of homosexuality. Yet the few Hasidim who have spoken out on this always controversial topic confirm that gays and lesbians do exist, if not exactly flourish, in a closeted religious community.

The research of sociologist Alfred Kinsey in the 1940s and 50s suggested that at least 10% of humanity has homosexual preferences. While this figure is disputed, it is evident that an increasing number of ultraorthodox Jews are confessing to having sexual preferences for their own gender. In an interview given in 1998 to the *Jerusalem Post* a young Hasidic man complained that the ultraorthodox rabbis pretend that 'homosexual orthodox' is an oxymoron and that gays can only be secular.

Previously, most declared orthodox gays and lesbians either abandoned their orthodoxy altogether or left Israel to seek freedom in gay-tolerant Jewish communities in the US or Europe. Progressive Jewish congregations such as the Reform or Conservative movements accept openly gay members and many orthodox gays and lesbians simply swapped allegiance to these more tolerant groups.

The revulsion felt by the Hasidim against homosexuality is legendary. First and foremost it is considered a biblical sin – and the lives of the ultraorthodox are ruled by down to the last minutiae by the Torah. Shlomo Benziri, deputy health minister and member of the Sephardic Shas party claims that homosexuality is an illness, an abomination, and not a legitimate lifestyle.

Relief for Israel's orthodox gay and lesbian population could be at hand with the creation of several new Web sites. The OrthoDykes and OrthoGays home pages can be reached via the inclusive www.gayjews.org site.

The focal point of the interior of a synagogue, normally located in the eastern wall, is a cupboard containing one or more copies of the Torah. These are written in Hebrew on parchment, by a scribe with a quill pen, and kept as a scroll on two rollers. The cupboard is known as the *Aron Hakodesh* (Holy Ark) and is covered by a *parochet* (curtain). A light is kept burning continually in front of the Ark, in remembrance of the continual light in the Temple and as a mark of respect to the holiness of the Scrolls.

In the centre of the synagogue (or in more modern structures, at the front) is the reading desk, normally on a *bimah* (raised platform). On Shabbat and festivals, readings from the Torah are made from here; the Torah is also read in the morning on Monday and Thursday.

As in the Temple, the sexes are seated separately, often with a gallery for the women who, according to orthodox Jewish law, must be strictly segregated from the men. However, in reform and conservative synagogues mixed seating is allowed.

Jews should pray three times a day, in the morning, afternoon and evening, with certain additional prayers to be said on Shabbat and holidays.

Heads must be covered at all times in a synagogue, but otherwise the apparent lack of decorum during services often surprises first-time visitors. People talk to each other and wander in and out of the synagogue, and children play.

Tefillin You may notice at the Western Wall, and perhaps in some of the bus stations, Jewish men wrapping a leather strap around their arm and wearing a small box strapped to their head. These are phylacteries or *tefillin* – *tefillin shel yad* is the strap wrapped around the arm and hand and *tefillin shel rosh* is placed around the head. Both parts include a box, enclosed in which is a parchment enscribed with a stipulated portion of the Torah. The shel yad binds the arm, therefore the body; the shel rosh binds the mind. The purpose is to remind Jews that the mind, heart and body are to be used for good and not evil. Tefillin are traditionally worn by men during the morning service except on Shabbat and holidays.

Death & the Afterlife Jewish teaching says that at death the body returns to God, and funerals take place within 24 hours as a token of respect for the dead. It's also considered a humiliation to leave the dead unburied for any longer than necessary. According to Jewish law the body belongs to God throughout one's life and for that reason tattoos are forbidden.

There is no cremation in traditional Judaism, because Jews believe in a physical resurrection on the Day of Judgment. Many Jews are bitterly opposed to autopsies for this reason.

It is a Jewish gesture of mourning that a man rips his clothes. This puts the mark of his broken heart on his clothing and can also provide an outlet for the anguish and emotion that a mourner feels. Today this is usually expressed by a symbolic tearing of a lapel. There is no prayer for the dead, as such, but *kaddish*, a prayer that praises God, is recited on their behalf, preferably by a son of the deceased.

Visitors to Jewish grave sites place stones rather than flowers on the grave because this is considered a more permanent way of showing that a visit has been made; it also involves the mourner in the act of burying the deceased, therefore helping to return them to God.

Non-Jews & Conversion Most Jews believe that the future of their people can only be ensured by the continuity of Jewish families. Therefore the idea of one of their own marrying a non-Jew strikes them with horror – it means the end of a family line. Even if the non-Jew is willing to convert, the orthodox view is that wanting to marry a Jew is not sufficient reason for wanting to enter Judaism. Conversion is not supposed to be undertaken for reasons other than a genuine spiritual desire to join the Jewish people and share its fate. In fact, Jews are not at all keen on the idea of outsiders joining into their faith, and as a deterrent conversion to Judaism is usually a rigorous and slow process.

The good news is that according to a rabbinical teaching, non-Jews can earn themselves a place in the world to come by following the 'Seven Laws to the Sons of Noah' that God has prescribed as being universal. Idolatry, blasphemy, murder, theft and incest are no-goes, as is eating meat that has been cut from a living animal. 'Acting justly' is a little trickier as it is wide open to interpretation.

Other Jewish Sects
For a discussion about the Black Hebrews and Samaritans, see Population & People earlier in this chapter.

Karaites A Jewish sect of about 15,000 members, founded in Babylonia in the 8th Century, the Karaites reject the rabbinical traditions and rulings, recognising the Scriptures as the only source of religious law. They have a strange status in that they are Jews yet not quite Jews. They are recognised under the Law of Return and they serve in the IDF, but both Karaite and Jewish law forbid intermarriage between Jews and Karaites.

They are settled mainly in Ashdod, Beersheba and Ramla, but there are also communities in Istanbul, the Crimea and the San Francisco Bay area.

Islam
The Arabic word Islam means voluntary surrender to the will of Allah (God) and

obedience to his commands. A Muslim is a person who accepts and practices the Islamic way of life.

Muslims recognise the existence of Judaism and Christianity, but within Islam Moses and Jesus are only two in a line of prophets that also includes Adam, Noah, Abraham, Ishmael, Isaac, Lot, Jacob and Joseph. The last of the prophets was Mohammed, born in Mecca in 571 AD, who began receiving revelations from Allah when he was aged 40. He began to preach in his home town attracting a few followers and a lot of persecution, before moving to Medina in 622 (year zero in the Muslim calendar) where he established the first Islamic state.

Through the Angel Gabriel (Jibrail), Mohammed received the word of Allah enshrined in the Quran (or Koran), the sacred book of the Muslims. It consists of 114 *suras* (chapters) and 6236 verses providing teachings and guidance on all areas of life and the afterlife.

To a Muslim, Christians and Jews share the same religion, but they haven't subscribed to the update.

The Muslim Way of Life Simplicity and modesty are encouraged. Muslims are required to cover their bodies properly and decently. Men must be covered from navel to knees, and must not wear pure silk or gold. Women must cover the whole body except the face and hands. A woman's outfit must not arouse a man's base feelings, so skin-tight, transparent or revealing styles are out.

The Five Pillars of Islam

The life of a good Muslim is theoretically guided by what are known as the five pillars.

The first and most fundamental of the five is *Ash-Shahadah* or the declaration of faith; *'La ilaha lah Muhammadur rasalul lah'* ('There is no God except Allah, and Mohammed is Allah's messenger').

Second in importance is *Salah* or prayer, offered five times a day, either individually or as part of a congregation. Prayers are supposed to be said at dawn, around noon, late afternoon, after sunset and late in the evening (times shift slightly because they're set by the cycle of the moon). In practice, few Muslims do pray five times daily; many consider once a day sufficient with a weekly Friday visit to the mosque.

Contemporary Muslims are also equally flexible in their observance of *Zakah*, the third pillar, the act of donating a part of their earnings to those less fortunate. Not a tax or a charity payment, the follower of Islam is expected to voluntarily give away approximately 2.5% of any money earned. In practice this only happens during the holy month of Ramadan. Fasting during Ramadan, or *Sawm*, constitutes the fourth tenet. From dawn to sunset every day during the ninth month of the Islamic calendar, Muslims should refrain from eating, drinking, smoking and having sex. This is supposed to be an exercise in self control, designed to raise a person's moral and spiritual standards above selfishness, laxity and other vices and to remind everyone of those less fortunate who often have to go hungry. In reality, what happens is that many Muslims adjust their day so that they get up late and don't have too long to wait before the sun goes down and the call to prayer announces *iftar*, or breakfast time.

During every Muslim's lifetime it is expected that he (it's optional for 'she') will make a pilgrimage to the Kabaa at Mecca, the birthplace of the prophet Mohammed. This is known as the *Haj* and it's the fifth pillar of Islam. Muslims who have made the Haj often paint the outside walls of their house with crude representations of the Kabaa or of airplanes to represent their journey.

Non-Muslims should be aware of these dress codes and, out of respect, should adhere to them when in predominantly Muslim areas.

Islam strictly forbids the free mixing of the sexes after puberty, a rule that applies to all types of socialising, not just premarital sex (hence the often unwelcome interest that many Muslim males show towards western women – their own women are out of bounds). Marriages are generally arranged by parents with the couple's consent. According to Muslims, there is no sexual discrimination in Islam. Muslims believe that the husband and wife are equal partners in the family, playing their role in respective fields. Divorce is permitted but is regarded as the most abominable of legal acts. Although extramarital sex is strictly forbidden, Islam permits polygamy – it's illegal under Israeli law, but this doesn't apply to Muslims in the Palestinian Territories, although most of them are monogamous anyway.

Islam is not as complex as Judaism when it comes to food and drink, but Muslims are only allowed to eat animals that are slaughtered in the Quranically prescribed manner, and never pigs nor carnivorous animals. Alcohol is also prohibited.

Mosques The word 'mosque' comes from the Arabic word *mesjid*, meaning a place of adoration. Most mosques have domes and minarets, making them easy to recognise. Inside, facing the holy city of Mecca, is the *mihrab* (prayer niche), normally an arched alcove about 1.5m high. The *minbar*, a free-standing pulpit, is usually nearby and it's from here that the *imam* (preacher) gives the Friday sermon. Also at the front of the mosque is the *khatib*, a low, railed wooden platform where the reader, sits to recite the Quran to the worshippers.

There are no professional 'priests' attached to a mosque. The imam who gives the weekly sermon normally has a regular full-time job. At one time every mosque would have had a *muezzin* to cry the call to prayer five times a day from atop the minaret; these days he's largely been replaced by taped recordings.

Not all mosques welcome non-Muslims. Sometimes a sign saying 'For Prayers Only' is posted prominently by the entrance. If unsure then ask. You must always remove your shoes before entering any mosque.

Christianity

The relative standing of Christian denominations elsewhere in the world counts for little in Israel. While in an international sense the Vatican-based Roman Catholic Church may be the richest and most high-profile branch of Christianity, being relative newcomers to the Holy Land (established only during the Crusades) they get to administer only 17% of Jerusalem's holy sites. The Protestants have even less.

In fact, in the Holy Land the balance of power lies with the Greek Orthodox Church, who have jurisdiction over more than half of Jerusalem's Church of the Holy Sepulchre and a bigger portion of Bethlehem's Church of the Nativity than anybody else. The Greek Orthodox patriarchate has seniority in the Christian hierarchy of Israel, despite the fact that this church constitutes only a fraction of the world's Christian population and is geographically confined mainly to Greece and the Slavic countries. Similarly, by dint of being one of the first into Palestine, the Armenian Church, with a world congregation of only six million, owns a third of Jerusalem's holy sites. Obscure in the church councils of the world, the Copts and Assyrians are also highly visible in Israel.

There are, of course, age old disputes over who owns what. In an attempt to settle the issue in 1757 the Turkish authorities drew up the rights of possession for nine of the most important shrines. This ruling is known as the 'Status Quo' and is still applicable today. However, it has done nothing to put an end to the intense rivalry in the Holy Land between the various factions in the Christian world, which occasionally erupts in fisticuffs in the aisles of the sacred sites.

Greek Orthodox Church The Greek Orthodox Church is the oldest ecclesiastical body in Israel and is probably the closest successor to the original Judaeo-Christian community of St James. A Greek-speaking Christian community emerged in Jerusalem in the mid-2nd century, gaining importance during the rule of Constantine when most of the holy sites were discovered.

The Greek Orthodox Church community of today is predominantly Arabic-speaking, but led by an almost exclusively Greek-speaking hierarchy. The Orthodox patriarchate of Jerusalem is the only autonomous church in the country, with all the others being dependent to various degrees on a head office abroad.

Israel is also home to two Russian Orthodox missions. Both in Jerusalem, one represents the Moscow patriarchate, the other the Russian Church Abroad; each claims to be the legitimate successor of a 19th century Russian Government mission. The Moscow mission is in possession of the green-domed cathedral in Jerusalem's Russian Compound and other churches in Jaffa, Nazareth, Tiberias and Haifa; the Church Abroad is in charge of the photogenic, onion-domed Church of St Mary of Magdalene in Gethsemane, on the Mount of Olives. Being out of communion with the patriarch of Moscow, the Church Abroad is not recognised by the Orthodox patriarch of Jerusalem.

The Romanian Orthodox patriarch is also represented by a church and small community in Jerusalem.

Armenian A small country and formerly a province of the ex-Soviet Union, Armenia is represented by one of the Holy Land's more powerful Christian communities. Much of Mt Zion in Jerusalem is the property of the Armenian Church, and has been since the 10th century. During the Mandate, the Armenians formed a prosperous community of some 5000 with their own churches, schools and culture, but due to emigration they number only about 2500 today.

The Armenian patriarchate, also based in Jerusalem, shares the churches of the Holy Sepulchre and the Nativity with the Orthodox and Latin patriarchates.

Syrian Orthodox & Copts The Syrians have had a bishop in Jerusalem since 1140, the Copts since 1236. Also called the Jacobites, the Syrian Orthodox are headed by an archbishop whose residence is the monastery of St Mark in Jerusalem. The Copts, from Egypt, have a monastery upstairs at the back of the Church of the Holy Sepulchre. Both these groups celebrate Christmas at the Armenian altars in the Church of the Nativity, but otherwise they use their own small chapels in the Church of the Holy Sepulchre.

Ethiopian From the Middle Ages until the 16th century, the Ethiopians owned chapels and altars in various holy places. Today they are confined to a ramshackle monastery on the roof of the Church of the Holy Sepulchre in Jerusalem, where they also have the chapel of St Helena, as well as a lovely church and monastery in West Jerusalem and a chapel near the Jordan River.

Catholic The Latin patriarchate of Jerusalem was established by the Crusaders in 1099, ceased to exist in 1291, and was re-established in 1847-48. Most Catholic religious groups were established here over the past 130 years except the Franciscans, who for more than 500 years were the sole body in charge of Catholic interests in Palestine and the Middle East. It was the Franciscans who regained and maintained the rights of worship and possession in the major holy places, established programs for their restoration, catered for the huge numbers of pilgrims and ministered to the small Catholic communities that sprang up around their monasteries and convents.

The Latin community includes over 45 religious orders and congregations. There are around 30 female communities and several hundred houses.

Uniate These are the Oriental churches in communion with Rome, and they are all represented in Israel by some relatively small communities. The largest comprises the Melkites, who are mostly in Akko and The Galilee. The next in size are the Maronites, mostly near the Lebanese border. The Chaldeans and the Syrian and Armenian Catholics are far fewer in number. The Uniate churches do not have any rights in the principal Holy Places.

Protestant The Anglican and Prussian Lutherans first arrived in Palestine 160 years ago. Their main objective was missionary work among Jews and Muslims, but the Greek Orthodox Church proved the source of most of the converts. Today, the Evangelical Episcopal Church is primarily Arab-speaking, and the Anglican Archbishop in Jerusalem presides over a synod made up of Egyptian, Libyan, Sudanese, Iranian and Jordanian bishops.

The Anglicans have no rights in the Church of the Holy Sepulchre, but an arrangement with the Greek Orthodox Church allows them to occasionally celebrate mass in the nearby Chapel of St Abraham. The Anglican cathedral in Israel is St George's in East Jerusalem.

The German Lutherans established several schools, hospices and hospitals in Palestine, including the Hospice of the Order of St John in Jerusalem and the Augusta Victoria Hospice (now a hospital) on Mt Scopus. There are some non-German Lutheran institutions in Israel including the Swedish Theological Institute and the Finnish Missionary School in Jerusalem, the Swedish school and hospital in Bethlehem, and the Scandinavian Seamen's churches in Haifa and Ashdod. There are also several minor Protestant groups representing reformed Christianity such as Presbyterians, Baptists, Pentecostalists, Quakers and Adventists.

Christian Zionism & the International Christian Embassy In 1980, when the Israeli Government insisted on claiming Jerusalem as the capital of the Jewish state, 13 countries closed their embassies in the city in protest and transferred them to Tel Aviv. Reacting to what they saw as the unfair treatment of the Israelis, a group of Christians already living in Israel established the International Christian Embassy in Jerusalem (ICEJ).

The ICEJ does not claim to represent all Christians, rather it represents a nation of Christian Zionists who interpret the Bible (eg Romans II) as supporting the Jewish people and the modern State of Israel. In fact, one suspects that the pro-Jewish stand of the ICEJ has its foundations in a fear of Islam. For instance, the ICEJ believe that the borders of Israel should include the area which is now Jordan. Christian Zionists also consider Islam's claim of Jerusalem as its third holiest site to be highly questionable.

The Druze
The name is derived from Al-Darazi, one of the founders of the sect, but beyond that the Druze are a very difficult people to understand. The Druze religion has its roots in Ismailism, a religious-political movement that has its origins in 11th century AD. Their faith, which they call Din al-Tawhid, hinges on a belief in one supreme God who operates through a complex system of cosmic principles and periodically manifests himself in human form. The prophets (eg Moses, Jesus and Mohammed) were the bearers of esoteric truth only. See also the Druze section in Population & People.

Baha'ism
A world religion which has established its centre in Haifa, Baha'ism is named after its founder Baha'u'llah (The Splendour of God). It's a development of a Muslim mystical movement founded in Persia in 1844 and teaches that religious truth is progressive, not final. Like Islam, Baha'ism believes that the human race is educated by God through a series of prophets who reiterate the same fundamental teachings which are adapted to suit the requirements of the age in which they appear. But whereas Islam stopped at Mohammed, Baha'ism adds Baha'u'llah to the list.

Since its founding Baha'ism has developed a worldwide following. One of the largest communities is in Iran, but membership of the faith is expanding rapidly in India (now with the largest Baha'i community), Africa, South-East Asia, the Pacific region and among the South American Indians.

Messianic Movement

This small group with its origins in Judaism differs from the majority of Jews in that they accept Jesus Christ as the Son of God and all that he has said, as written in the New Testament. They have formed their own denomination within the Christian Church, as they still have major differences with some interpretations of Jesus' teachings in relation to their understanding of the Old Testament and the status of the Jewish people. Jews consider them to be Christians not Jews.

LANGUAGE

The national language of Israel is Hebrew (see the boxed text 'Ben Yehuda & the Revival of Hebrew' in the Tel Aviv chapter). It is the most spoken language, followed by Arabic. English is also widely spoken and you will almost always be able to find someone who understands it. Most of the important road and street signs are in all three languages. With Jews arriving in Israel from around the world, many other languages are commonly understood too – French, German and Yiddish are the main ones, but also Spanish and Russian.

For the meanings of common terms used throughout this book, refer to the Glossary provided at the back of this book. For a basic guide to Hebrew and Arabic and a list of useful words and phrases, see the Language Guide chapter, also at the back of this book.

Facts for the Visitor

SUGGESTED ITINERARIES
One Week

Base yourself in **Jerusalem** and spend two or three days exploring the **Old City**, including visits to the Citadel Museum, the Dome of the Rock, the Western Wall (at least once) and the Church of the Holy Sepulchre. Make an early-morning visit to the Mount of Olives to catch the ascending sun rousing the city.

A day trip to the **Dead Sea** is a must – Ein Gedi is the most convenient spot – as is a visit to **Masada**; the two can be combined in one of the excellent 12 hour tours you'll see advertised in many of the city's hostels.

Head up to **Tiberias** on the shores of the Galilee and aim to spend a full day there, perhaps cycling around the lake to the biblical sites of **Tabgha** and **Capernaum**. There's plenty of good accommodation in Tiberias. Next morning take a bus for **Safed** to wander around the old quarters of town, then in the afternoon travel on to **Akko** for a waterfront evening meal. Again, there are a couple of reasonable places to stay in Akko.

Depending on how much time you have left, you might want to visit **Caesarea** on your way back down the coast and then spend a last day in **Tel Aviv** topping up your tan on the beaches.

Two Weeks

Plan on four to six nights in **Jerusalem** doing everything mentioned in the one week itinerary, but also exploring the newer parts of town such as the orthodox Jewish Mea She'arim district and the Mahane Yehuda Market. Pay a visit to the Yad Vashem Holocaust Museum. As well as visits to the **Dead Sea** and **Masada**, reserve a day for **Bethlehem** and, if you feel up to it, the half-day hike through **Wadi Qelt** is worth doing.

Spend a couple of nights in **Tiberias** using it as a base to visit **Nazareth** (half a day here is more than enough), **Tabgha** and **Capernaum** on the lake, and **Safed** – allow for a full day in Safed though the lack of good ac-

commodation here means it may be preferable to return to Tiberias for the evening or move directly on to Akko. From Tiberias you could also visit **Beit She'an** (a few hours) and make a one day excursion up into the **Golan**.

Spend a day and a night in **Akko** and, as you have to change buses here anyway, you may care to take a look around **Haifa**, though there really isn't much of interest here. En route back down the coast stop by **Caesarea** for a few hours.

Underrated by many, **Tel Aviv** is nonetheless worth two or three days of anyone's time; for one thing, the beaches here are far better than those in Eilat. Other sights worth visiting include **Jaffa** and the Carmel Market/Nahalat Binyamin area, and the superb Diaspora Museum and Museum of Modern Art, both of which can take up three or four hours of your time.

More than Two Weeks

With more than two weeks at your disposal you can cover pretty much the whole of Israel. Make sure that you visit all of the places listed above, perhaps staying an extra day in Akko to make the excursion up to **Rosh HaNikra** on the Lebanese border. You would also have the luxury of being able to eschew a packaged trip to the **Golan** and exploring it independently over a couple of days; **Nimrod Castle** and **Banias** are the places not to miss.

From Jerusalem we would really recommend that anyone who has time pay a day's visit (generally speaking there are no hotels available for overnight stays) to a busy Palestinian town – **Nablus** probably being the prime choice. And if you are in Israel any length of time, you may feel it appropriate to balance the experience with a trip to **Gaza** – not necessarily a comfortable place to visit but certainly an enriching experience.

We also recommend that you head down to **Eilat** – stopping off en route at **Mitzpe Ramon** for a few hours – but don't hang around, hop on a No 15 bus to the **Taba** border and spend a couple of days sunning and diving off Egypt's Sinai coast. It's also worth remembering that from Eilat, Petra is only a couple of hours away and Jordanian visas, though pricey, can be obtained at the border.

PLANNING
When to Go

Each season has both advantages and disadvantages (see the table on page 52), but other than perhaps cost and availability of air tickets, few of the factors given are going to drastically affect the enjoyment of your visit. Israel's climate is not so extreme that there's any specific time to make a point of avoiding, and while the Jewish religious holidays do cause the country to fill up with pilgrims, accommodation prices to double and public transport to grind to a halt, they are usually mercifully brief.

See also Climate in the Facts about the Country chapter and Public Holidays & Special Events section later in this chapter.

What Kind of Trip?

Israel's relatively small size is a major boon, one which allows for leisurely exploration as opposed to the usual frenetic new town, new hostel dash. Visitors can find somewhere comfortable in Tel Aviv or, more often, Jerusalem, and use it as a luggage dump and base from which to cover the country in a series of two or three day sorties. With easy border crossings, Israel can also serve as a convenient launching point for short excursions into neighbouring Egypt and Jordan; so, time permitting, a holiday in Israel can quite easily incorporate two of the Middle East's most spectacular sites: the Pyramids and the rose-coloured stone city of Petra (see the Getting There & Away chapter).

It's also a very unintimidating country which, while maintaining much of the exoticism of the Middle East, presents far less of the hassle for solo travellers, and women in particular. Many people do choose to come as part of an organised tour but most places are accessible to the individual by public transport. Local operators are fairly well attuned to the needs of independent travellers, and there are a variety of budget tours to places that might otherwise be a little awkward to get to.

Alternatively, for the less culturally inquisitive the country competes strongly with other Mediterranean destinations as a good sea and sand holiday spot; it has the climate, the beaches, some beautiful landscapes and the added attractions of unique phenomena, such as the Dead Sea. There are also plenty of accompanying leisure facilities, including horse riding, rafting, diving and other water sports.

WHEN TO GO

Month	Advantages	Disadvantages
January	Hotel accommodation is at its cheapest and you have the place to youself. The Dead Sea and Eilat are still hot enough to pick up a tan.	Jerusalem is very cold and even Tel Aviv is overcast and deep in hibernation.
February	Hotel prices are still low and there's a chance of seeing Jerusalem under snow. You can go skiing in the Golan.	Except for the Dead Sea and the Negev Desert, it is still raining and overcast.
March	Street cafes are back in business and most places are showing signs of life.	Jerusalem and Bethlehem are booked solidly towards the end of the month with Easter pilgrims.
April	Temperatures are just about right, not too hot but warm enough to hit the beach. For hikers the Golan is blooming, streams are swollen and waterfalls are at their most dramatic.	Orthodox Easter means Jerusalem is colourful and crowded early in the month but accommodation is scarce. Prebooking is recommended. In the last week of the month the country closes down for Pesah and hotel prices soar.
May	Temperatures are perfect for the mainly outdoor annual Israel Festival held in Jerusalem.	Disadvantages? There don't seem to be any.
June	The serious sun worshipping begins and the Israel Festival continues.	There are no major disadvantages to visiting during this month.
July	If you really like it hot, this is for you. Temperatures consistently creep over 30°C in Haifa and rusalem, and close to 40°C in Eilat.	The heat is really turned up making sightseeing an endurance test. Kibbutzim are oversubscribed so have something arranged in advance.
August	Klezmer Festival in Safed.	The heat is extremely uncomfortable and the kibbutzim are still oversubscribed.
September	The weather is cooling off to a nice medium heat – still plenty of action on the beach but no need to change your shirt three times daily.	This is another good month to visit. We couldn't think of any disadvantages.
October	Almost everyone's gone home so it's back to hassle-free sightseeing. The Fringe Theatre Festival in Akko is worth attending if only for the venues.	The country is closed most of the month for Rosh HaShanah, Yom Kippur and Sukkot; transport is an on/off thing, restaurants and cafes are shut for days at a time and hotel prices go out of control.
November	A good time for photography and you now stand a chance of getting a spot on the bikini-friendly beach at Eilat.	Tel Aviv and most places north of the Negev are packing up and battening down.
December	Christmas in Jerusalem; romantic or what?	Few in Israel celebrate Christmas except for the masses of pilgrims block-booking the hotels. Due to demand at this time of year, book your flight well in advance.

Maps

Lonely Planet has a highly detailed, slimline 1:250,000 *Israel & the Palestinian Territories travel atlas*, to complement this guide. Otherwise, the best of the internationally available sheet maps is Hallwag's 1:500,000 *Israel Road Map* which clearly marks the hierarchy of roads, denotes the territory of the West Bank (many maps don't), includes within its bounds Beirut, Damascus and Amman, and also has inset street plans of the major Israeli cities. Hildebrand's 1:360,000 *Travel Map of Israel* isn't bad either, although despite the larger scale it's not as clear as the Hallwag map.

If you intend travelling beyond the borders of Israel then Kümmerly & Frey's *Israel & Adjoining Countries* (1:750,000) could be a good choice – it covers the whole of Sinai plus the greater part of Jordan. Avoid Bartholomew's *Israel & Jordan* – it is extremely crude and looks like it was produced in the days of quill pens.

For a wider choice or something more specialised, wait until you reach Israel. There are numerous local cartographic companies producing some high quality work. The most prolific is Carta. *Carta's Map of Israel* (1:525,000) isn't actually that good, but their large-scale city plans (currently they do Jerusalem, Tel Aviv and Haifa) are excellent. Another company called Map does a superb 1:100,000 road atlas, a bit bulky and also perhaps extravagant for backpackers, but invaluable for drivers. It also produces a not so good Jerusalem pocket atlas. Hikers should check out the range of special topographical sheet maps with marked trails produced by the Society for the Protection of Nature in Israel (SPNI) – see Flora & Fauna in the Facts about the Country chapter.

Most of these maps are sold at bookshops throughout Israel, particularly at branches of Steimatzky and at the SPNI shops in Jerusalem and Tel Aviv. Free country and city maps of varying quality are also handed out at the better tourist information offices.

What to Bring

The usual traveller's rule applies: bring as little as possible but enough so that you don't have to buy too many things. Although most consumer items and medications you might want are easily available in Israel, they tend to be expensive, particularly clothing and toiletries.

Bring a sun hat and sunglasses, some kind of sunscreen and comfortable walking shoes (worn in but not worn out) but, most importantly, choose your clothes carefully. You need to pack something which is both suitable for the hot climate and is also acceptable for visiting religious sites. Most religious sites are not open to anyone dressed immodestly, which means that both men and women must have their legs, shoulders and necklines covered. Heads need to be covered too in synagogues but there is usually something provided.

One thing many travellers fail to realise is how chilly Israel can be in the winter; anyone visiting from October to March and not intending to spend all their time in Eilat should bring a sweater.

RESPONSIBLE TOURISM

Israel is a small country and receives a large number of visitors each year – over two million in 1997 alone. That's an extra third of the total population of Israel moving around the country visiting sites, using resources and placing increasing pressure on the infrastructure. Let us not forget that Israelis also love to travel around their own country.

The great majority of visitors move around the country in buses, coaches and cars adding considerably to the carbon monoxide (and other pollutants) soup that exhaust emissions create. It's a heavy burden for a geographically small nation.

Individual travellers will find it hard to avoid motorised transport, but might consider hiking or cycling tours of the country which are becoming more and more popular. The SPNI (see entry under Flora & Fauna in the Facts about the Country chapter) runs a wide range of ecologically sound tours catering for all tastes and budgets. A company in Jerusalem called Walk Ways (see Jerusalem chapter for details) organises cycling tours of the Galilee, the Jordan Valley and the Negev and Sinai deserts. This is an excellent way to visit the country while minimising the impact on the environment.

Desert safaris in an off-road vehicle while exciting and fun, ultimately damage fragile ecosystems and could perhaps be avoided in favour of camel safaris such as those provided by a company called Shacharut in the Negev Desert (see that chapter for details).

Low-impact, low-polluting travel should be the aim of all responsible tourists. Choose your transport with forethought and take out of the environment whatever you take in. That way Israel will continue to cater for its visitors long into the future.

TOURIST OFFICES
Local Tourist Offices
Most Israeli towns have at least one tourist office. The performance of these offices can vary a lot; some are friendly, but others suffer from the Israeli bureaucratic disease, and seem very disinclined to offer anything that might be categorised as information. The addresses of local tourist information offices are given in the individual city sections.

Tourist Offices Abroad
Australia
   (☎ 02-9326 1700, fax 9326 1676, email aicc@mpx.com.au) 395 New South Head Rd, Double Bay, NSW 2028
Canada
   (☎ 416-964 3784, fax 964 2420, email igto@indirect.com) 180 Bloor St West, Suit 700, Toronto, Ontario M5S-2V6
Denmark
   (☎ 033-119 711, fax 914 801) Vesterbrogade 6D, DK-1620 Copenhagen
France
   (☎ 01-42 61 01 97, fax 49 27 09 46, email infos@otisrael.com) 22 Rue des Capucines, F-75002 Paris
Germany
   (☎ 030-203 9970, fax 2039 9730) Friedrichstr 95, D-10117 Berlin
   (☎ 069-7561 1920, fax 7561 9222) Bettinastr 62, D-60325 Frankfurt-am-Main
   (☎ 089-212 3860, fax 2123 8630) Stollbergstr 6, D-80539 Munich

Italy
   (☎ 02-7602 1051, fax 7601 2477) Corso Europa 12, I-20122 Milano
Japan
   (☎ 3-3238 9081, fax 3238 9077, email listman@clal-ns.or.jp) 22 Ichibancho, Chiyoda-ku, Tokyo 102
Netherlands
   (☎ 020-612 8850, fax 689 4288, email igto.adam@wxs.nl) Stadhouderskade 2, 1054 ES Amsterdam
South Africa
   (☎ 011-788 1703, fax 447 3104, email igto@icon.co.za) 5th floor, Nedbank Gardens, 33 Bath Avenue, Rosebank 2196
UK
   (☎ 020-7299 1111, fax 7299 1112, email igto-uk@dircon.co.uk) 180 Oxford St, London W1N 9DJ
USA
   (☎ 213-658 7462, fax 658 6543) 6380 Wilshire Blvd 1718, Los Angeles, California 90048
   (☎ 312-782 4306, fax 782 1243, email igtochicago@aol.com) 5 South Wabash Ave, Chicago, Illinois 60603-3073
   (☎ 212-499 5660, fax 499 5665, email info@goisrael.com) 800 Second Ave, New York, NY 10017
   (☎ 972-991 9097, fax 392 3521, email igtotx@onramp.net) 5151 Belt Line Rd, Suite 1280, Dallas, Texas 75240

See also the Israel Government Tourist Office's Web site: www.infotour.co.il.

VISAS & DOCUMENTS
Visas
With all but a few exceptions, a tourist visa is not required to visit Israel; all you need is a passport, valid for at least six months from your date of entry. The exceptions include holders of passports from most African and Central American countries, India, Singapore and some of the ex-Soviet republics.

As a tourist you are normally allowed a three month visit, although visitors entering through the land borders with Egypt and Jordan are often initially only granted a month's stay. On arrival, Israeli immigration officials will give you a duplicate entry permit to fill in. The second copy will be returned to you and you need to keep this until you leave the country. Do not lose this small, and very losable, piece of paper or you'll face a long delay in the already lengthy departure procedure.

If you look 'undesirable', or are suspected of looking for illegal employment, immigration officials may question the purpose of your visit and ask to see evidence of a return flight/ferry ticket and financial support. Travellers singled out and then found to have insufficient money to cover their proposed stay have, in the past, been prevented from entering the country and put on the next flight home. More commonly, if unimpressed, immigration may only allow you a shorter stay, say one month.

Visa Extensions If you want to extend your stay beyond the initial three months, you need to apply for a visa. You can do this at any of the Ministry of the Interior offices located in most major towns and cities. Most travellers use one of the following:

Eilat
    (☎ 07-376 332) Ministry of the Interior (Visa Renewal) on HaTemarim Blvd
Jerusalem
    (☎ 02-622 8211, 629 0231) 1 Shlomzion St, in the central area of the New City
Tel Aviv
    (☎ 03-651 941, 657 758) Shalom Tower, just west of Allenby St

Along with trying to prise information from the Egged bus staff (who don't like people who ask questions), dealing with bureaucracy is about the most unpleasant side of Israel. Applying for a visa extension involves an early start to beat the long queues. Most offices open at 8 am and by that time the queue is usually depressingly long. Once you've gained an audience, convincing the civil servants that you should be allowed to stay can be hard; one crucial requirement is that you must have proof that you can support yourself without needing to work illegally. If the petition is accepted your stay will be extended for typically three months, although sometimes it can be for one month only and sometimes for six. The process costs 120NIS, and one passport-sized photo

How Safe Is It?

Stability has never been a strong point in this part of the world. In his book *Return to the Desert*, author David Praill estimates that over the last 4000 years the parcel of land now known as Israel 'has suffered an invasion or undesired incursion on average once every 40 years'. However, with both Egypt and Jordan committed to peace and ongoing talks with Syria, the present situation is as favourable to tourism as it has been almost any time this century.

Israel is not nearly as dangerous as the accumulated impact of suicide bombing and assassination headlines might suggest. The violence, which indisputably does afflict the country, has almost exclusively involved the local population, and popular tourist areas have never been targeted. The Palestinians are in no way hostile to foreign visitors (although they may be a little cool towards anybody blatantly Jewish) and, especially outside of Jerusalem, you'll find them courteous and welcoming.

is required. There's no fee for citizens of Belgium, Luxembourg or the Netherlands.

The offices are normally open from 8 am to noon and are closed on Friday and Saturday. On Sunday and Wednesday they often reopen for a late afternoon shift (in Tel Aviv, for instance, from 4 to 7 pm).

The maximum period a foreigner can stay in Israel varies according to which official you ask. It can be one month if they don't like the look of you or several years if they do. Usually, one year is the most you can stay without pulling strings.

Expired Visas The 55 shekel question is, what happens if you try to leave Israel after overstaying the initial three months without having obtained an extension? Well, at Ovda airport and the Taba and Arava land borders, you'll almost certainly be turned away and told to return to the Ministry of the Interior in Eilat – pretty inconvenient if you had a flight to catch. At Ben-Gurion airport, if the overstay is less than a month you may be let off but then again you may be charged the cost of the visa renewal (110NIS) *and* have a fine slapped on top; if the overstay is more than a month then you're definitely going to have to dig deep into your pockets. It has also happened that people wildly over the mark have had their passports stamped to bar them from returning to Israel for a period of five years.

It is, however, OK to apply for your extension some days after your initial three months are up, so don't worry about rushing back to town if you're out wandering in the wilderness.

Egyptian Visa If you are travelling to Egypt from Israel you will need a visa, unless you are only visiting the east coast of Sinai in which case you'll receive a 14 day pass at the border.

The Israeli Stamp Stigma

Israel is, of course, the venue for that popular Middle Eastern game, the Passport Shuffle, which involves getting in and out of the country, but avoiding being stamped with any incriminating evidence to tell that you were ever there. This game was devised because those countries which refuse to recognise Israel (including Lebanon, Syria and the Gulf States) refuse to allow anyone across their borders whose passport is marred by evidence of a visit to the Jewish state. Israeli immigration officials will, if asked, stamp only your entry permit and not your passport. This is fine if you are flying both into and out of Israel, but if crossing by land into either Egypt or Jordan, the Arab immigration officers are generally not so obliging and their entry stamps will be a dead giveaway – although some wily travellers have reported getting away with stamps on a separate piece of paper, especially at the Allenby Bridge crossing into Jordan.

At the Egyptian embassy (☎ 03-546 4151), 54 Basel St, just off Ibn Gvirol St in Tel Aviv, visas are processed the same day (hand in applications, passports and photo in the morning, then pick up that afternoon), except for Israelis, who have to wait 15 days.

At the time of writing, single-entry tourist visas with one-month validity, cost 80NIS (US$20). Nationals of the Commonwealth countries, Germany, Cyprus, Finland, Sweden, Norway, and the USA only pay 50NIS (US$12.50). One photo is required. The embassy is open Sunday to Thursday from 9 to 11 am for visa applications, closed Friday and Saturday. Return between 2 and 3 pm the same day for collection. The office closes at 11 am regardless of any queue, so arrive as early as possible.

Visas can also be issued at the Egyptian consulate (☎ 07-637 6882) at 68 HaAfroni St in Eilat; the procedure and cost are exactly the same as in Tel Aviv. The consulate is open Sunday to Thursday from 9 am to 11 am; it's closed Friday and Saturday. Return between 1 and 2 pm the same day to collect your visa.

Jordanian Visa The Jordanian embassy (☎ 03-751 7722), inconveniently located at 14 Abba Hillel St, in the Tel Aviv suburb of Ramat Gan, issues visas Sunday to Thursday from 9 am to 1 pm. They can also be obtained at the Arava and Jordan River crossing points (not at the Allenby/King Hussein Bridge). The cost of the visa varies by nationality; for UK citizens it's JD26, for US citizens JD33, for Australians and New Zealanders JD16, for Canadians JD38 and down to just JD6 for French, Belgians and the Irish. South Africans and Japanese get their visas free. (JD1 = US$1.50/UK£1, approximately). See the section on Petra in the Excursions from Israel chapter.

Travel Insurance

However you're travelling, it's worth taking out travel insurance. Work out what you need. You may not want to insure that grotty old army surplus backpack, but everyone should be covered for the worst possible case scenario: an accident, for example, that will require hospital treatment and a flight home. It's a good idea to make a copy of your policy, in case the original is lost. If you are planning to travel for a long time, the insurance may seem very expensive but if you can't afford it, then you certainly won't be able to afford any medical emergency in Israel.

Hostel & Student Cards
The only officially required document for travellers in Israel is a valid passport but, if you have them, bring along your Hostelling International (HI) card and International Student Identity Card (ISIC) as they can be very useful.

HI membership will save you money at their affiliated hostels – although they still tend to be way more expensive than the privately owned competition – while an ISIC card entitles the holder to a 10% discount on Egged bus fares over 10NIS, 20% off fares on Israel State Railways and substantial discounts at most museums and archaeological sites. Even if signs don't mention student discounts produce your card and ask anyway. Student cards issued by your individual university or college are often not recognised.

Photocopies
It's a good idea to make photocopies of all vital documents – such as the data pages of your passport, your birth certificate, credit cards, airline tickets, serial numbers of your travellers cheques and other travel documents – and keep them separate from your real documents. Add to this an emergency stash of about US$50. Also leave copies of all these things with someone at home.

EMBASSIES & CONSULATES
Your Own Embassy
It's important to realise what your own embassy – the embassy of the country of which you are a citizen – can and can't do to help you if you get into trouble.

Generally speaking, it won't be much help in emergencies if the trouble you're in

is remotely your own fault. Remember that you are bound by the laws of the country you are in. Your embassy will not be sympathetic if you end up in jail after committing a crime locally, even if such actions are legal in your own country.

In genuine emergencies you might get some assistance, but only if other channels have been exhausted. For example, if you need to get home urgently, a free ticket is highly unlikely – the embassy would expect you to have insurance. If you have all your money and documents stolen, it might assist with getting a new passport, but a loan for onward travel is out of the question.

Some embassies used to keep letters for travellers or have a small reading room with home newspapers, but these days the mail holding service has usually been stopped and even newspapers tend to be out of date.

Israeli Embassies & Consulates
These are some of the Israeli embassies abroad. Some consulates are also listed:

Australia
   Embassy: (☎ 02-6273 1309/1300, fax 6273 4273, email IsrEmb.Canberra@u030.aone.net.au) 6 Turrana Ave, Yarralumla, Canberra, ACT 2600
   Consulate: (☎ 02-9264 7933, fax 9290 2259, email isconsyd@infinet.net.au) 37 York St, Sydney, NSW 2000
Canada
   Embassy: (☎ 613-567 6450, fax 237 8865, email embisrott@cyberus.ca) 50 O'Conner St, Suite 1005, Ottawa, Ontario K1P 6L2
   Consulate: (☎ 514-393 9372, fax 393 8795 email cgisrmtl@videotron.net) 1155 Blvd Rene Levesque Ouest, Suite 2620, Montreal, Quebec H3B 4S5
France
   Embassy: (☎ 01-40 76 55 00, fax 40 76 55 55) 3 rue Rabelais, F-75008 Paris
   Consulate: (☎ 04 91 53 39 90/87, fax 91 53 39 94, email isconsulat@aol.com) 146 rue Paradis, Marseille F-13006
Germany
   Embassy: (☎ 0228-934 6500, fax 934 6555, email Botschaft@israel.de) Simrockallee 2, Bonn D-53173
   Consulate: (☎ 030-893 2203, fax 892 8908, email israel@berlin.snafu.de) Schinkelstrasse 10, Berlin D-14193

Ireland
    Embassy: (☎ 01-668 0303, fax 668 0418,
    email embisrae@iol.ie) Carrisbrook House,
    122 Pembroke Road, Ballsbridge, Dublin 4
Netherlands
    Embassy: (☎ 070-376 0500, fax 376 0555,
    email ambassade@israel.nl) 47 Buitenhoff,
    The Hague 2513 AH
New Zealand
    Embassy: (☎ 04-472 2362/8, fax 499 0632,
    email israel@central.co.nz) DB Tower, 111
    The Terrace, PO Box 2171, Wellington
UK
    Embassy: (☎ 020-7957 9500, fax 7957 9555,
    email isr-info@dircon.co.uk) 2 Palace Green,
    London W8 4QB
USA
    Embassy: (☎ 202-364 5500, fax 364 5607,
    email ask@israelemb.org) 3514 International
    Drive NW, Washington DC 20008
    Consulate: (☎ 212-499 5400, fax 499 5555,
    email nycon@interport.net) 800 Second Ave,
    New York NY 10017

There are nine Israeli consulates in the USA;
phone one of the above two for other contact
details.

Embassies & Consulates in Israel

Although the Israelis lay claim to Jerusalem
as their capital, this is not recognised by
most of the international community. Instead, most foreign embassies are in Tel
Aviv, though some countries also maintain
consulates in Jerusalem.

Unless otherwise stated, the following
embassies and consulates are closed on Saturday and Sunday. Several of them maintain separate offices for passport and/or visa
inquiries.

Australia
    Embassy: (☎ 03-695 0451) 37 Shaul Ha
    Melekh Ave, Tel Aviv
Canada
    Embassy: (☎ 03-636 3300) 3 Nirim St, Tel
    Aviv
Denmark
    Embassy: (☎ 03-544 2144) 23 B'nei Moshe St,
    Tel Aviv
    Consulate: (☎ 02-625 8083) 5 B'nei Brit St,
    West Jerusalem
Egypt
    Embassy: (☎ 03-546 4151) 54 Basel St, off Ibn
    Gvirol, Tel Aviv

Consulate: (☎ 07-637 6882) 68 HaAfroni St,
    Eilat
France
    Embassy: (☎ 03-524 5371, fax 527 0062) 112
    Herbert Samuel Esplanade, Tel Aviv
    Consulate: (☎ 02-625 9481, fax 625 9178,
    email consulate@p-d.com) 6 Emile Botta St,
    West Jerusalem
    Consulate: (☎ 02-628 2387) Sheikh Jarrah,
    East Jerusalem
    Consulate: (☎ 07-360 111) 8 Kikar Nemerim,
    Eilat
    Consulate: (☎ 04-851 3111, fax 851 3931) 37
    HaGefen St, Haifa
Germany
    Embassy: (☎ 03-693 1313) 3 Daniel Frisch St,
    Tel Aviv
Ireland
    Embassy: (☎ 03-950 9055) 266 HaYarkon St,
    Tel Aviv
Jordan
    Embassy: (☎ 03-751 7722) 14 Abba Hillel Sil-
    ver St, Ramat Gan, Tel Aviv
Netherlands
    Embassy: (☎ 03-695 7377) Asia House, 4
    Weizmann St, Tel Aviv
    Consulate: (☎ 04-824 3298) 24A Vitkin, Haifa
South Africa
    Embassy: (☎ 03-525 2566) 16th Floor, 50
    Dizengoff St, Tel Aviv
UK
    Embassy: (☎ 03-524 9171, 510 0497) 192 Ha-
    Yarkon St, Tel Aviv
    Consulate: (☎ 02-582 8281, fax 532 2368,
    email britain@palnet.com) 19 Nashashibi St,
    Sheikh Jarrah, East Jerusalem
    Consulate: (☎ 07-372 344) 14 Tsofit Villas,
    Eilat
USA
    Embassy: (☎ 03-519 7575, fax 516 0315,
    email acs.amcit-telaviv@dos.us-state.gov) 71
    HaYarkon St, Tel Aviv
    Consulate: (☎ 02-625 3288, fax 627 2233) 18
    Agron St, West Jerusalem
    Consulate: (☎ 02-622 7200, fax 628 5455) 27
    Nablus Rd, East Jerusalem
    Consulate: (☎ 04-853 1470) 12 Yerushalayim
    St, Haifa

CUSTOMS

You can bring duty free into Israel up to one
litre of spirits and two litres of wine for
every person over 17 years of age, as well
as up to 250g of tobacco or 250 cigarettes.
Animals, plants, firearms and fresh meat

may not be brought into the country. Additionally, video equipment, personal computers and diving apparatus must be declared at customs and a deposit paid to be collected on departure (to prevent travellers bringing any of this stuff in and flogging it while here).

MONEY
Currency
The national currency is the new Israeli shekel (NIS). The correct plural in Hebrew is *shekelim* but even Israelis when speaking English tend to anglicise the word and use 'shekels'. Expats tend to call them 'sheks'. The 'old shekel' was dropped in 1985 as part of a rescue plan to help reduce inflation. The new shekel is divided into 100 *agorot*. There are coins of 10 and 50 agorot and 1 and 5NIS, and notes of 5, 10, 20, 50, 100 and 200NIS.

Exchange Rates

country	unit		shekel
Australia	A$1	=	2.7NIS
Canada	C$1	=	2.8NIS
Egypt	E£1	=	1.2NIS
euro	€1	=	4.3NIS
France	10FF	=	6.6NIS
Germany	DM1	=	2.4NIS
Japan	Y100	=	3.3NIS
Jordan	JD1	=	5.8NIS
New Zealand	NZ$1	=	2.2NIS
UK	UK£1	=	6.6NIS
US	US$1	=	4.1NIS

Exchanging Money
In the major towns and cities there is no shortage of places to change money – not only are there countless banks and specialist exchange bureaus, but many Arab shopkeepers double as moneychangers and the reception at your hostel or hotel is probably quite likely to indulge in a little banknote barter too.

Generally speaking there is little variation in the rates of exchange on offer, but you ought to check on the commission charged by the banks because sometimes

this can be extremely voracious. The best deals are offered by the Arab moneychangers in Jerusalem and the specialist exchange bureaus in Jerusalem and Tel Aviv, none of which charge any commission at all.

Some bank branches also have currency exchange ATMs which accept several of the major international currencies and offer the convenience of 24 hour accessibility, seven days a week; the drawback is a whopping transaction charge.

At the end of your stay you can convert your shekels at the airport or at the port in Haifa. You are allowed to freely reconvert up to US$500 but for anything over that you must produce a bank receipt as proof of the original exchange.

Cash Most Israelis talk in terms of US dollars, not shekels, a habit acquired in the days when the national currency was constantly being devalued. Upmarket hotels still quote their prices in dollars as do the HI hostels, most car hire companies and many airlines. At such places, payment in dollars is accepted and, for the customer, it's preferable because payments made in foreign currency are free of the 17% value-added tax (VAT).

After the dollar, one foreign currency is as good as any other and moneychangers and banks will take whatever you've got, though exchange rates on the Egyptian pound are very poor.

Travellers Cheques Travellers cheques are also widely accepted and you will have no trouble getting them cashed – bearers of Eurocheques can even exchange them at branches of the post office. Beware though, commission charges can be as high as 130NIS *per cheque* regardless of the amount, so shop around. The best bet is to go to one of the currency exchange bureaus or to one of the American Express or Thomas Cook offices or agents that don't charge a commission– see the individual city chapters for addresses. These offices can also refund or replace lost or stolen cheques.

ATMs Many bank foyers are equipped with cash dispensing ATMs accepting all of the major international credit cards. If you don't have your PIN number but are carrying a Visa card, Bank Leumi will give you a cash advance (subject to a credit status check). In case of loss of your plastic, call: American Express (☎ 03-524 2211); Diners Club (☎ 03-572 3572); Visa (☎ 03-572 3572); and Eurocard (☎ 03-576 4444).

Credit Cards Israelis live on credit and owe their free-wheeling lifestyles to Visa, American Express, Diners Club and the like. Nearly every establishment takes credit cards because if it didn't it wouldn't have any business. We've witnessed breakfasting Israelis cover the cost of their cappuccino and croissant with a piece of plastic.

International Transfers For anyone unfortunate enough to run out of money, the Israeli post operates a Western Union international money transfer service. For details, go to any post office or call ☎ 177-022 2131, toll-free.

Black Market There is no black market in Israel and no one will hassle you on the street to change your money.

Security

Keeping your cash, plastic and travellers cheques in body pouches is of course a secure method of protecting your money, but if you retrieve it in public to pay for transactions you'll be showing would-be thieves exactly where you keep it. It's better to keep some cash handy in a secure inside pocket and dip into your security pouch only in the safety of your hostel or hotel room.

'Fanny packs' or 'bumbags', while enormously popular and convenient, do scream 'tourist' and can easily be slashed or removed by accomplished thieves. It is probably better to avoid them. Keep your money in more than one location on your person (keep a spare US$50 in your shoe!) and never keep two or more credit cards together in the same place. They may all be stolen.

Israel is generally safe from active pickpocketing or even mugging, but market places and popular crowded tourist haunts like Jerusalem's Old City have their fair share of bag snatchers and thieves.

Costs

You can bring an unlimited amount of foreign and local currency into Israel – and you're going to need it by the barrowload. Compared to other countries in the region like Egypt, Jordan, Greece or Turkey, there are no two ways about it, Israel is expensive. Compare prices with Australia, New Zealand, the UK or USA, however, and there's little to complain about. And in Israel you generally do get what you pay for, which is more than can be said for many other places.

Accommodation can be quite cheap. Most budget travellers opt for a bed in a hostel dormitory; pick the right place and that's not an unpleasant option. Most establishments offer clean sheets, hot showers and possibly air-con for somewhere between 20 and 30NIS (US$7 to US$10) per night. Moving a little upmarket, decent private double rooms with en suite bathroom start at around 150NIS (US$50).

Dining could well be the area that busts your budget apart. The food in Israel can be excellent, but it's not a place for cheap eating. It is possible to survive on a couple of *felafel* sandwiches a day – and many travellers we met were doing just that – at a cost of around 20NIS (US$5.25), but that's like watching TV through the shop window. A more realistic figure would be 30 to 50NIS (US$8 to US$13) per day, which allows for a little indulgence bolstered with a lot of street food.

Museum and gallery admission prices are quite expensive, often in the region of 20NIS (US$5.25), but this is offset by the relatively cheap cost of transport; the hour-long bus ride between Tel Aviv and Jerusalem, for instance, is about 20NIS (US$5.25).

On an individual budget of 100 to 150NIS per day (about US$26 to US$40), it should be possible to get dormitory accommodation, eat a couple of budget meals and travel around. Of course, you can spend a great deal more (your beer tab can sometimes match your daily budget) visiting galleries and museums, hiring bicycles, joining tours and so on, and we recommend that you do a lot of these things. Conversely, it's also possible to scrape by on as little as 50 to 80NIS a day but then what are you going to Israel for?

Tipping & Bargaining

Not so long ago, apparently, no one tipped in Israel. Now your bill arrives appended with a large handwritten 'Service is not included' and delivered by a waiter or waitress with a steely smile that reads, '15%. No less'. You may frequently feel the money is undeserved, but that's not the point – serving staff salaries in Israel are customarily low and the system relies on tips from the customers to even the balance. Although we know it goes against the grain with many budget travellers, tipping is something you have to get used to in Israel and when pricing a menu always allow for that extra percentage on top.

Note that taxi drivers in Israel do not expect to be tipped; they're usually content just to overcharge.

Bargaining is not always the fun it is made out to be. Mostly limited to Arab markets, it can be time-consuming, frustrating and, in general, an unwelcome hassle. The golden rules are: don't start bargaining with a shopkeeper unless you are really interested in buying; have a good idea of the item's value both locally and back home; and don't be intimidated. Easier said than done. Do not use large notes or travellers cheques, as getting change can be a problem.

Basically, the bargaining game is played like this: the shopkeeper usually attracts your attention and gives you a price three to 10 times above the realistic going rate. If you are genuinely interested you pull a face showing disgust or amusement at this quote and state your offer in a 'take it or leave it' manner. This should, of course, be substantially below the amount you are actually willing to pay. Whatever, stick to your guns

and do not be bullied or cajoled into paying too much. Turning away from a bargaining session can often cut a price in half. A good idea is to observe the shopkeepers at work. Note how they may flirt with young women, or else bully them and the older tourists. They can also act respectfully towards potential customers.

Traditionally, Arab shopkeepers sell something cheaper early in the day, as a quick first sale means good business later. However, this line is often used to persuade customers to pay more, thinking that they are getting a bargain.

Taxes & Refunds

Israel slaps a value-added tax (VAT) on a wide range of goods, but tourists in Israel are entitled to a refund on most items purchased with foreign currency in shops that are registered with the Ministry of Tourism (there'll be a sign in the window or at the till). Few like to part with money – the Israeli Government included – and the procedure for claiming your 17% seems to have been designed with the specific aim of deterring the faint-hearted.

The net figure on one invoice must be at least US$50, with the exception of electrical appliances, cameras, films, photographic accessories and computers. Be sure to get a discount of at least 5% on the displayed price and a copy of the invoice showing the VAT amount paid in both Israeli shekels and US dollars. The purchases need to be wrapped in a sealed plastic bag, of which at least one side must be transparent with the original invoice displayed inside so that it can be read without opening the bag. The bag needs to remain sealed for the duration of your time in Israel.

If leaving from Ben-Gurion airport or Haifa port, go to the Bank Leumi counter in the departure lounge and present your sealed bag. The bank will stamp the invoice, identify the goods and refund in US dollars the VAT paid (less a commission). At other departure points, customs officials do the honours, but the refund will be mailed to your home address.

POST & COMMUNICATIONS
Post
Letters posted in Israel take seven to 10 days to reach North America and Australia, and a little less to Europe. Incoming mail is reasonably quick, taking about three or four days from Europe and around a week from places further afield. At the time of writing, a normal airmail letter to Europe cost 1.80NIS, to the USA 2.20NIS and to Australia 2.70NIS.

Poste restante seems to work quite well; for post restante addresses see the individual city chapters. Remember that American Express offices (in Jerusalem and Tel Aviv) will receive mail for card holders.

Telephone
Israel has a state-of-the-art, card-operated public telephone system and international calls can be made from any street call box. Telecards are bought from lottery kiosks, newsagents, bookshops, vending machines or 24-hour kiosks, and come in denominations of 20 units (11NIS), 50 units (24NIS) and 120 units (52NIS). The international access code is 012, 013 or 001 – depending on which company you use (see table on opposite page) – followed by the country code, city code and the number you wish to connect with.

Standard rates apply between 8 am and 10 pm; from 10 pm to 1 am and all day Saturday and Sunday calls are 25% cheaper, while all week between 1 am and 8 am calls are 50% cheaper.

You can also make discount international calls from the offices of Solan Telecom which are located in most towns and cities throughout Israel and open 24 hours, although in practice the savings are nothing substantial.

There is a wide range of local and international phonecards available. The Lonely Planet eKno Communication Card (see the insert at the back of this book) is aimed specifically at travellers and provides cheap international calls, a range of messaging services as well as free email – for local calls, you're usually better off with a local phonecard. You can join online at www.ekno.lonelyplanet.com; or to join by phone from Israel, dial 1-800-945-9176. Once you have joined, to use eKno from Israel, dial 1-800-945-9177. To join from another country and for further information, check out the eKno Web site at www.ekno.lonelyplanet.com.

The international country code for Israel is 972. Other useful numbers are:

fire service	☎ 102
first aid/ambulance	☎ 101 or ☎ 911
information	☎ 144
police	☎ 100

Telephone Codes Israel has now standardised all its area access codes to a few easily remembered local area codes. Mobile phones use the 052 prefix.

☎ 02	Jerusalem and the West Bank
☎ 03	Tel Aviv and surrounds
☎ 04	Haifa and the North Coast
☎ 06	The North including the Galilee, the Upper Galilee and the Golan
☎ 07	The Negev, down to Eilat, the Gaza Strip and the Dead Sea region
☎ 08	The coastal plain (south of Tel Aviv)
☎ 09	Sharon district (north of Tel Aviv)

Mobile Phones Most mobile phone users with GSM-equipped mobile phones will not be able to use their phones in Israel on international roaming. The system currently in use is specific to Israel only, though some of the more recent mobile handsets on sale in your country may be equipped to handle both carrier systems. However, a new mobile phone service called Orange has entered the market and can apparently handle GSM-equipped mobile phones from overseas. Check with your own mobile phone service provider before heading for Israel.

Fax
To send a fax, call by a post office. Faxes are charged at 20NIS for the first sheet and 10NIS for any subsequent ones. Faxes can also be sent from Solan offices for 15NIS

Calling Overseas

Costs for calling overseas vary depending on which company you use and also on the time of day or night that you make your call. Off-peak is usually between midnight and 7 am. The three companies offering overseas connections compete quite rigorously and their prices, while on the whole quite low, can differ quite considerably. Compare the sample charges in the table below, but be aware that these may have changed by the time you read this. Use the appropriate ISD prefix to select the company you wish to use, then dial the country code, city code and your phone number. Charges are listed in shekels and per unit used.

Country called	Barak 013 prefix	Golden Lines 012 prefix	Bezeq 001 prefix
Australia	0.81	1.85	1.84
Canada	0.73	0.84	1.77
Egypt	2.09	1.85	4.62
France	0.98	1.04	0.98
Germany	0.62	1.04	1.19
Greece	0.76	1.04	1.19
Ireland	0.73	0.76	0.71
Italy	1.42	1.04	1.32
Jordan	1.13	1.28	3.23
Netherlands	1.31	1.04	0.98
South Africa	1.15	1.85	1.84
Sweden	1.22	1.04	0.98
UK	0.62	1.04	1.19
USA	0.73	0.84	0.71

per sheet, irrespective of the destination, and they'll receive your faxes for a small fee.

Email & Internet Access

Israel is a remarkably well-connected Internet society with many businesses now sporting email addresses and Web sites. This perhaps accounts for the seeming dearth of public Internet access points like cafes and public libraries (presumably Israelis netsurf at home).

Internet cafes do come and go and Jerusalem currently leads the pack with about four places where you can access your email and surf the Net. Strudel (☎ 02-623 2101, fax 622 1445; email strudel@ inter.net.il), is the longest-standing NetCafe in Jerusalem (see that chapter). Customers can open an account here and send and receive mail.

In Tel Aviv the monopoly on Internet access is essentially held by the In Bar (☎ 03-528 2228, fax 528 2225, email barak@ isralink.co.il). See also their Web site: www .isralink.co.il. However, the British Council Library provides access for members, and Momos Hostel offers access for guests and probably nonguests too (see Tel Aviv chapter for all details).

Palnet@K5M (☎ 02-995 6813), the first Palestinian Internet cafe and Internet Service Provider, is in Ramallah on the West Bank. See their Web site (www.palnet.com) for full details.

Check the Israel Internet cafe Web site (www.internet.cafe.il) to see what's new. Alternatively, you could easily take out a temporary Internet account if you are travelling with a laptop PC equipped with a modem card. There are a number of service providers, but we used Netvision (☎ 04-856 0660, fax 04-855 0345, email admin@netvision.net.il) with considerable success and lack of fuss. Visit their Web site (new.netvision.net.il) for full details. They are based in Haifa, but have local access numbers all over the country. Connection speed is nominally up to 56K, but is commonly hampered by poor local phone connections resulting in maximum speeds of 24K or even as low as 12.2K from Eilat.

Internet Resources

Israel is very much a computer-literate society and one that has been quick to seize upon the possibilities offered by the Internet. Point and click surfers can drop by Tel Aviv's In Bar, book domestic air tickets or even 'ask the rabbi'. There is also heaps of practical information on the Net and World Wide Web that may be of use to anyone planning a visit to Israel, and the following are just a few suggestions of places to start:

www.lonelyplanet.com
This is the Lonely Planet site home page – follow the links to the Travellers' Reports for the latest postings on Israel.

www.iguide.co.il
Bills itself as the Complete Guide (almost) to the World Wide Web in Israel and boasts over 950 links broken down into categories such as arts, reference etc.

www.city.net/countries/israel
More links specifically geared to the visitor, including categories such as travel & tourism, maps, museums and galleries and lodgings.

www.infotour.co.il
The Israel Government Tourist Office's Web site. Good for checking out what the IGTO want you to know and has other useful links on the country.

www.israel.org
The home page of the Israeli Foreign Ministry, this includes biographies of ministers, a guide to the peace process, a weekly survey of the Israeli press and links to the Web sites of Israeli embassies worldwide.

www.birzeit.edu/index.html
The Web site of Birzeit University, 20km north of Jerusalem. A one-stop shop for all you could want to know about the Palestinian Territories, including a link to all the useful Palestinian Web sites.

www.visit-palestine.com
The official tourism Web site of the Palestinian Ministry of Tourism & Antiquities. Comprehensive data on the seven main Palestinian towns.

www.jpost.co.il
The Internet version of the English-language newspaper the *Jerusalem Post*, which includes daily news, columns, features and reviews – and there's no subscription fee.

www1.huji.ac.il/jeru/jerusalem.html
A virtual tour through the Old City of Jerusalem with links to information on other parts of the country.

www.israelhotels.org.il
The home page of the Israel Hotel Association. Good for getting an overview of hotels in Israel. Only members of the IHA are listed.

www.bnb.co.il
Provides good information on B&B accommodation options in Jerusalem.

BOOKS

Annually, thousands of books are published on the subjects of Israel, Palestine, Judaism, the Middle East conflict and other related topics. A search on any online or library bibliography will turn up scores of them. A search on amazon.com on the Internet will give you an idea of what books are available for sale. All of these books should be available in paperback from most good English-language bookshops; though bear in mind that in most countries, books are published in different editions by different publishers.

The majority of these books are also available in bookshops in Tel Aviv and Jerusalem. Check out the stores belonging to the Steimatzky chain which, alongside shelves of Hebrew publications, have sizeable English-language sections carrying everything from Kerouac to Calvin and Hobbes and biographies of Arafat to volumes of Talmudic teachings. They often also have smaller selections of French and German-language titles.

For literature by Israeli and Palestinian authors, see Arts in the Facts about the Country chapter.

Lonely Planet

There was just too much good material to limit Jerusalem to a chapter in this book, so we've expanded the coverage, added more colour photos, maps and diagrams and packaged the lot up as the comprehensive, newly revised *Jerusalem city guide*. Lonely Planet also publish guides to Israel's neighbouring countries in the form of *Egypt* and *Jordan & Syria*. There's also *Middle East* which distils the above books down to a hyperdensity of basic information for cheap travel, and adds in chapters on Iran, Iraq, Lebanon, Libya, Turkey, Yemen and the Arab Gulf States.

Guidebooks

Not a book to lug around but one for the shelf is Insight Guides' *Israel* which, in addition to superb photography, contains some good essays on contemporary Israeli society. Anyone whose visit to Israel is primarily motivated by the country's biblical and ancient history should take a look at *The Holy Land from the Air* by Amos Elon. This book uses spectacular aerial photography to illustrate the many legendary and religious sites in the region. Narrowing the scope somewhat, the *Blue Guide to Jerusalem* is the ultimate reference guide to the art, culture and history of the Holy City.

There are also many locally produced guides on sale in Israel: tightly focused titles which cover a town or region. You'll find most of them at branches of Steimatzky.

Travel

Considering that it's written by a former Anglican minister and it concerns his spiritual pilgrimage through Jesus country, *Return to the Desert* by David Praill is surprisingly unself-absorbed and entertaining. It's basically an account of the author's sponsored 40 day walk from Mt Hermon on the Syrian-Israeli border to Mt Sinai in Egypt, and it's particularly good reading for anyone sharing Praill's fascination with silent and solitary landscapes.

Howard Jacobson's particular thing in *Roots Schmoots* is his Jewishness – or rather, lack of. A secular English intellectual and author, he visited Israel in 1992 in order to investigate what it meant to others to be a Jew. He doesn't seem to have liked what he found there and the result is, on occasion, acerbicly funny, though all too often Jacobson resorts to supercilious put-downs of the people and places he encountered.

In *To Jerusalem and Back – a Personal Account,* Saul Bellow, the prolific essayist and novelist, describes the trip he made to Israel in 1975, the year before he won the Nobel Prize for Literature.

First published in 1969, *Jerusalem* by Colin Thubron is one of the earliest books by the now feted travel writer. It's as oblique and ethereal as a Lennon lyric from the Sgt Pepper era but, sadly, it's far less enjoyable, made leaden with pomposity. Far, far more illuminating and entertaining is *Jerusalem: City of Mirrors* by Amos Elon, an internationally respected Israeli writer who has spent most of his life in the city of which he writes. He has a good store of humorous quotes and anecdotes supplied by the many distinguished visitors to the city. For example, according to Elon, George Bernard Shaw when visiting in 1930 advised the Zionists to set up notices at every holy site saying 'do not trouble to stop here: it isn't genuine'.

Not to forget *The Innocents Abroad* by Mark Twain, written in 1871 – it's still one of the best books dealing with the tourist experience in the Holy Land.

History & Politics

Books on Israeli/Arab-Israeli politics and history are plentiful, but the same can't always be said for objectivity. Browsing the bookshelves, it's a case of choosing a title to cater to your prejudices. The fast pace of events in the region also means that books are quickly dated so only titles published within the last few years are mentioned here.

For the uninitiated a good place to start is with Amos Oz, long viewed in the west as Israel's voice of conscience. Although he's primarily a novelist, Oz is also one of the leaders of the Peace Now movement, a left-wing political group, and he has three collected works of nonfiction *(In the Land of Israel, The Slopes of Lebanon* and *Israel, Palestine and Peace)* which eloquently and passionately outline his beliefs. Along the way they shed a great deal of illumination on modern-day Israeli society.

From Beirut to Jerusalem by Pulitzer Prize-winning journalist Thomas Friedman is the recent history of the Middle Eastern conflicts as witnessed by an outsider. It's excellent for anyone seeking a fuller understanding of the causes and effects of the constant strife that afflicts the region.

There are a number of books written specifically from a Palestinian point of view. Edward Said is a respected American-Palestinian academic whose views roughly coincide with those of Oz. If Oz speaks to the west for Israel, then it is Edward Said who speaks for the Palestinians. Said is a staple in literary and intellectual magazines in the USA, Europe and in the Middle East. His most recent book *Peace and its Discontents* (1995) is a collected series of essays arguing the poor dividends of the peace process where the Palestinians are concerned.

Gaza: Legacy of Occupation by Dick Doughty & Mohammed El-Aydi focuses on the arduousness of Palestinian life in the Gaza Strip. The writing is extremely matter of fact, but the tragedies of daily life don't need any dressing up; reported straight as they are, they make for very sobering reading. In *Against the Stranger* Janine di Giovanni, a feature writer on the *Sunday Times*, aims for something similar, but her book is undermined by a tendency towards journalistic exhibitionism.

The BBC's *The Fifty Year's War – Israel & the Arabs* was published in 1998 to accompany the television series of the same name. It is a concise, seemingly unbiased account of the conflict co-written by both a Jew (Ahron Bregman) and an Arab (Jihan El-Tahri) and contains some previously unpublished secret interviews with key players on both sides.

Published also in 1998 is *Israel – A History* by Martin Gilbert, an authoritative, somewhat dry, but very readable account of the history of Israel over the last 100 years. *Soldier of Peace* by Dan Kurzman (also published in 1998), is a detailed and gripping account of the life of former prime Minister Yitzhak Rabin who was assassinated in Tel Aviv in 1995.

General

To be enjoyed rather than believed at face value, *The Source* by James A Michener and *Exodus* by Leon Uris are two of the all-time most popular novels with an Israeli theme. Muriel Spark, the distinguished part-Jewish British writer, also employs divided Jerusalem as a backdrop in her mannered novel of uptight expatriates, *The Mandelbaum Gate*.

As a cataclysmic event which still very much haunts and shapes modern Israeli society, you might want to read up on the Holocaust. One of the most respected works on the subject is *Holocaust* by Martin Gilbert, but as a more personal testimony we would also strongly recommend *If This Is A Man* by Primo Levi, a powerful and harrowing account of survival in Auschwitz.

CD ROM

There's an international-release CD ROM entitled *Jerusalem*, produced by Tyrell Multimedia and published by Simon & Schuster Interactive. It's a visual exploration of 3000 years of the city's history through animation, film clips and fancy graphics. There's also a similar Israeli-produced disk, *Jerusalem 3000*, which, from the packaging, purports to do the same thing. It's unlikely you'll find this title outside of Israel, however.

All issues of the *Jerusalem Post*, from January 1990 onward, are available on CD ROMs, kept current with six-monthly updates. As of early 1999 the cost was US$199 for a subscription to four CDs – the initial disk with news items from January 1990 to August 1998, and a further three CDs as they become available. Address inquiries and orders to Jerusalem Post on CD ROM, PO Box 81, Jerusalem 91000 or call ☎ 02-531 5603, fax 531 5622; email jpost@elronet.co.il.

NEWSPAPERS & MAGAZINES

Israelis as a nation are news addicts. Over 90% of the nonorthodox population regularly read the papers – hardly surprising considering the volatile and unpredictable state in which they live. To not keep up with the news is to miss the latest episode in a tense drama in which all Israelis are part of the supporting cast.

The largest circulation papers are *Yedioth Ahronoth* and *Ma'ariv*, both of which are slightly right of centre. The left-leaning Tel Aviv-based daily *Ha'aretz* is available in both English and Hebrew editions and enjoys the reputation of being the country's most intellectual paper. The internet editions are available at www.haaretzdaily.com, but the site has been very unstable of late. The biggest Arabic-language daily is the Jerusalem-based *Al-Quds*. However, unless you read Hebrew or Arabic, your appreciation of Israel's extensive press will be limited.

The *Jerusalem Post* is the country's only English-language daily (there's no Saturday edition). Though indispensable for its coverage of Israeli life, its pronounced right-wing leanings are a turn-off to many. Buy it on Friday, however, for the extensive 'what's on' supplement. The *Post* also has a weekly international edition available abroad.

The alternative to the *Post* is no alternative at all; the poorly funded, weekly *Jerusalem Times*, published in East Jerusalem, carries little news but lots of pro-Palestinian polemics. Choose your poison. You'll normally only find the *Times* sold in East Jerusalem and the Old City. See the Useful Organisations section in this chapter for information about other periodicals covering local political issues.

Look out in the hostels and bars for the freebie *Traveller*, an occasional features-based newspaper aimed squarely at the backpacking fraternity. It carries some useful pieces like a round-up of the Jerusalem and Tel Aviv bar scenes, and hints on budget eating. However, as of January 1999 this excellent publication seemed to have ceased circulation, so it may no longer be around when you read this.

Despite being perceived as largely hostile to Israel, western newspapers are easily found and they're usually only a day old – try Steimatzky. And if the contents of your wallet are equal to your craving, Steimatzky is also the place to pick up your copy of the *Economist*, *Paris-Match* or *Wired*.

RADIO & TV

National Radio 1 (576AM in Tel Aviv and the central region; 1458AM in Jerusalem and Eilat) has English-language news bulletins at 7 am, and 1 and 8 pm, as well as a current affairs magazine at 5 pm daily.

The BBC World Service can be picked up on 639 and 1323kHz and 227MW, while Voice of America is on 1260kHz.

If you're looking for something more relaxing than news, you might try Kol HaMuzika, whose playlist consists almost exclusively of western classical music. For pop – Israeli, 'Mediterranean' (mainly Greek and Turkish) and international – good bets include Reshet Gimel (Radio 3), the IDF-run Galei Tzahal; and Galgalatz, whose music mix and traffic reports are intended to calm edgy drivers.

Very popular with travellers as well as Israelis is the Voice of Peace (100FM, 1540 AM). Broadcasting 24 hours from a ship anchored off the coast of Tel Aviv, often in English, this station plays a great selection of popular music virtually nonstop. Its founder, Abie J Nathan, is a well-known peace campaigner and has led many colourful campaigns to further the cause. Voice of Peace broadcasts do not reach beyond Haifa to the north and Beersheba to the south.

Israel has two state television stations, both of which carry masses of English-language programs – English news on Channel 1 is at 6.15 pm during the week, 4.30 pm Friday and 5 pm Saturday. Palestinian TV broadcasts news in English daily at 10.30 pm, in French on Sunday, Tuesday and Thursday at 5.30 pm, and in Hebrew on Saturday, Monday and Wednesday at 5.30 pm. Jordan TV's Channel 2 has English news from 10 to 10.30 pm, and French news from 7 to 7.30 pm. The majority of the nonorthodox Israeli population also has cable which brings access to an additional 32 channels including CNN, Sky, BBC World, Discovery and MTV.

For TV and radio listings pick up the Friday editions of the *International Herald Tribune* (in the HaAretz supplement) and the *Jerusalem Post* which carries a seven day entertainment supplement.

PHOTOGRAPHY & VIDEO

Whatever you run out of or whatever needs replacing, you'll be able to find it in Israel, but there's little doubt that it would have been way cheaper back home.

Photography in Israel presents no special problems, although if you take it seriously then you might want to bring along a polarising filter to counter sun glare. Other than military installations there's little that can't be photographed – even IDF soldiers are happy to preen and pose for a visitor's camera. The exceptions are the Hasidic Jews who extremely dislike having their photograph taken. Arab women often react angrily too if they're snapped unawares, so ask first.

For good photography, the best time of the year to visit Israel is between November and April, when the sky is clear of high-temperature haze and the afternoon sun warms rather than bleaches.

TIME

Israel is two hours ahead of GMT/UTC, eight hours behind Australian Eastern Standard Time and seven hours ahead of American Eastern Standard Time – when it's noon in Tel Aviv it's 5 am in New York, 10 am in London and Paris, and 8 pm in Melbourne.

ELECTRICITY

Israel uses 220V, 50 cycles, alternating current. Wall plugs are the round, two prong type. Bring an adaptor if required, it's cheaper than buying one in Israel.

WEIGHTS & MEASURES

Israel uses the metric system. See the conversion table at the back of this guide.

LAUNDRY

Many of the better hostels have a laundry room, otherwise coin-operated laundromats are common. One machine load costs about 8NIS and dryers are about 4NIS for a 10 minute cycle. Laundromats are open on Sunday, Monday, Wednesday and Thursday from 8 am to 7 pm, Tuesday and Friday from 8 am to 1 pm, and they're closed Saturday.

HEALTH

Travel health depends on your predeparture preparations, your daily health care while travelling and how you handle any medical problem that does develop. While the potential dangers can seem quite frightening, in reality few travellers experience anything more than an upset stomach.

Israel presents no major health hazards for the visitor and no vaccinations are legally required. Vaccinations you may wish to consider are listed below. However, probably the biggest health worries you can expect are overexposure to the sun and possibly an upset stomach caused by the change in diet.

In the case of emergencies anywhere in Israel, dial ☎ 101 (Hebrew speaking) or ☎ 911 (English speaking), or contact the local branch of the Magen David Adom (Red Star of David), the Israeli equivalent of the Red Cross – details are given under Information in each town or city. There is also a medical helpline for tourists on ☎ 177-022 9110. Every day the *Jerusalem Post* carries a list of the late-opening pharmacies.

Doctors and hospitals in Israel generally expect immediate cash payment for health services.

Pre-departure planning

Immunisations Plan ahead for getting your vaccinations: some of them require more than one injection, while some vaccinations should not be given together. Note that some vaccinations should not be given during pregnancy or in people with allergies – discuss with your doctor.

It is recommended you seek medical advice at least six weeks before travel. Be aware that there is often a greater risk of disease with children and during pregnancy.

Discuss your requirements with your doctor, but vaccinations you should consider for this trip include the following (for more details about the diseases themselves, see the individual disease entries later in this section). Carry proof of your vaccinations, especially yellow fever, as this is sometimes needed to enter some countries.

Diphtheria & Tetanus Vaccinations for these two diseases are usually combined and are recommended for everyone. After an initial course of three injections (usually given in childhood), boosters are necessary every 10 years.

Hepatitis A Hepatitis A vaccine (eg Avaxim, Havrix 1440 or VAQTA) gives long-term immunity (possibly more than 10 years) after an initial injection and a booster at six to 12 months. Alternatively, an injection of gamma globulin can provide short-term protection against hepatitis A – two to six months, depending on the dose given. It is not a vaccine, but is ready-made antibody collected from blood donations. It is reasonably effective and, unlike the vaccine, it is protective immediately, but because it is a blood product, there are current concerns about its long-term safety. Hepatitis A vaccine is also available in a combined form, Twinrix, with hepatitis B vaccine. Three injections over a six-month period are required, the first two providing substantial protection against hepatitis A.

Hepatitis B Travellers who should consider a vaccination against hepatitis B include those on a long trip, as well as those visiting countries where there are high levels of hepatitis B infection, where blood transfusions may not be adequately screened or where sexual contact or needle sharing is a possibility. Vaccination involves three injections, with a booster at 12 months. More rapid courses are available if necessary.

Polio Everyone should keep up to date with this vaccination, which is normally given in childhood. A booster every 10 years will maintain immunity.

Rabies Vaccination should be considered by those who will spend a month or longer in a country where rabies is common, especially if they are cycling, handling animals, caving or travelling to remote areas, and for children (who may not report a bite). Pretravel rabies vaccination involves having three injections

Medical Kit Check List

Following is a list of items you should consider including in your medical kit – consult your pharmacist for brands available in your country.

☐ **Aspirin** or **paracetamol** (acetaminophen in the USA) – for pain or fever

☐ **Antihistamine** – for allergies, eg hay fever; to ease the itch from insect bites or stings; and to prevent motion sickness

☐ **Antibiotics** – consider including these if you're travelling well off the beaten track; see your doctor, as they must be prescribed, and carry the prescription with you

☐ **Loperamide** or **diphenoxylate** –'blockers' for diarrhoea; **prochlorperazine** or **metaclopramide** for nausea and vomiting

☐ **Rehydration mixture** – to prevent dehydration, eg due to severe diarrhoea; particularly important when travelling with children

☐ **Insect repellent, sunscreen, lip balm** and **eye drops**

☐ **Calamine lotion, sting relief spray** or **aloe vera** – to ease irritation from sunburn and insect bites or stings

☐ **Antifungal cream** or **powder** – for fungal skin infections and thrush

☐ **Antiseptic** (such as povidone-iodine) – for cuts and grazes

☐ **Bandages, Band-Aids (plasters)** and other wound dressings

☐ **Water purification tablets** or **iodine**

☐ **Scissors, tweezers** and a **thermometer** (note that mercury thermometers are prohibited by airlines)

☐ **Syringes** and **needles** – in case you need injections in a country with medical hygiene problems. Ask your doctor for a note explaining why you have them.

☐ **Cold** and **flu tablets, throat lozenges** and **nasal decongestant**

☐ **Multivitamins** – consider for long trips, when dietary vitamin intake may be inadequate

over 21 to 28 days. If someone who has been vaccinated is bitten or scratched by an animal, they will require two booster injections of vaccine; those not vaccinated require more.

Typhoid Vaccination against typhoid may be required if you are travelling for more than a couple of weeks in many parts of the world, including Israel. It is now available either as an injection or as capsules to be taken orally.

Health Insurance Make sure that you have adequate health insurance. See Travel Insurance under Visas & Documents in the Facts for the Visitor chapter for details. Health care in Israel is very expensive so do not skimp on taking out insurance.

Travel Health Guides If you are planning to be away or travelling in remote areas for a long period of time, you may like to consider taking a more detailed health guide.

CDC's Complete Guide to Healthy Travel, Open Road Publishing, 1997. The US Centers for Disease Control & Prevention recommendations for international travel.
Travellers' Health, Dr Richard Dawood, Oxford University Press, 1995. Comprehensive, easy to read, authoritative and highly recommended, although it's rather large to lug around.
Travel with Children, Maureen Wheeler, Lonely Planet Publications, 1995. Includes advice on travel health for younger children.

There are also some excellent travel health sites available on the Internet. The Lonely Planet home page (www.lonelyplanet.com /weblinks/wlprep.htm#heal) has links to the World Health Organization and the US Centers for Disease Control & Prevention.

Other Preparations

Make sure you're healthy before you start travelling. For long trips, make sure your teeth are OK. If you wear glasses take a spare pair and your prescription.

If you require a particular medication take an adequate supply, as it may not be available locally. Take part of the packaging showing the generic name rather than the brand, which will make getting replacements easier. It's a good idea to have a legible prescription or letter from your doctor to show that you legally use the medication to avoid any problems.

Basic Rules

Food There is an old colonial adage which says: 'If you can cook it, boil it or peel it you can eat it ... otherwise forget it'. Vegetables and fruit should be washed with purified water or peeled where possible. Beware of ice cream which is sold in the street or anywhere it might have been melted and refrozen; if there's any doubt (eg a power cut in the last day or two), steer well clear. Shellfish such as mussels, oysters and clams should be avoided as well as undercooked meat, particularly in the form of mince. Steaming does not make shellfish safe for eating.

If a place looks clean and well run and the vendor looks clean and healthy, then the food is probably safe. In general, places that are packed with travellers or locals will be fine, while empty restaurants are questionable. The food in busy restaurants is cooked and eaten quite quickly with little standing around and is probably not reheated.

Overall street food in Israel is generally hygienically prepared and the only problems travellers are likely to face are stomach upsets or diarrhoea caused by unfamiliar food.

Water Tap water in Israel is safe to drink anywhere. However, for those who prefer to drink bottled water, there are some reputable brands of bottled water and soft drinks of the highest quality, but expensive.

Water Purification If you have any concerns about the water or are trekking in remote areas such as the Golan, you might want to consider purifying the water. The simplest way of purifying water is to boil it thoroughly. Vigorous boiling should be satisfactory; however, at high altitude water boils at a lower temperature, so germs are less likely to be killed. Boil it for longer in these environments.

Consider purchasing a water filter for a long trip. There are two main kinds of filter. Total filters take out all parasites, bacteria and viruses and make water safe to drink. They are often expensive, but they can be more cost effective than buying bottled water. Simple filters (which can even be a nylon mesh bag) take out dirt and larger foreign bodies from the water so that chemical solutions work much more effectively; if water is dirty, chemical solutions may not work at all.

It's very important when buying a filter to read the specifications, so that you know exactly what it removes from the water and what it doesn't. Simple filtering will not remove all dangerous organisms, so if you cannot boil water it should be treated chemically. Chlorine tablets will kill many pathogens, but not some parasite cysts like giardia and amoeba. Iodine is more effective in purifying water and is available in tablet form. Follow directions carefully and note that too much iodine can be harmful.

Medical Problems & Treatment

Self-diagnosis and treatment can be risky, so you should always seek medical help. An embassy, consulate or five-star hotel can usually recommend a local doctor or clinic. Although we do give drug dosages in this section, they are for emergency use only. Correct diagnosis is vital. In this section we have used the generic names for medications – check with a pharmacist for brands available locally.

Note that antibiotics should ideally be administered only under medical supervision. Take only the recommended dose at the prescribed intervals and use the whole course, even if the illness seems to be cured earlier. Stop immediately if there are any serious reactions and don't use the antibiotic at all if you are unsure that you have the correct one. Some people are allergic to commonly prescribed antibiotics such as penicillin; carry this information (eg on a bracelet) when travelling.

Environmental Hazards

Heat Exhaustion Heat exhaustion in Israel is most likely to be incurred in the Dead Sea

***

Everyday Health

Normal body temperature is up to 37°C (98.6°F); more than 2°C (4°F) higher indicates a high fever. The normal adult pulse rate is 60 to 100 per minute (children 80 to 100, babies 100 to 140). As a general rule the pulse increases about 20 beats per minute for each 1°C (2°F) rise in fever.

Respiration (breathing) rate is also an indicator of illness. Count the number of breaths per minute: between 12 and 20 is normal for adults and older children (up to 30 for younger children, 40 for babies). People with a high fever or serious respiratory illness breathe more quickly than normal. More than 40 shallow breaths a minute may indicate pneumonia.

***

and the Negev Desert region. The climate in Tel Aviv in midsummer is extremely humid and likely to cause discomfort to travellers not used to humidity.

Dehydration and salt deficiency can cause heat exhaustion. Take time to acclimatise to high temperatures, drink sufficient liquids and do not do anything too physically demanding.

Salt deficiency is characterised by fatigue, lethargy, headaches, giddiness and muscle cramps; salt tablets may help, but adding extra salt to your food is better.

Anhidrotic heat exhaustion is a rare form of heat exhaustion that is caused by an inability to sweat. It tends to affect people who have been in a hot climate for some time, rather than newcomers. It can progress to heatstroke. Treatment involves removal to a cooler climate.

Heatstroke This serious, occasionally fatal, condition can occur if the body's heat-regulating mechanism breaks down and the body temperature rises to dangerous levels. Long, continuous periods of exposure to high temperatures and insufficient fluids can leave you vulnerable to heatstroke.

The symptoms are feeling unwell, not sweating very much (or at all) and a high body temperature (39°C to 41°C or 102°F to 106°F). Where sweating has ceased, the skin becomes flushed and red. Severe, throbbing headaches and lack of coordination will also occur, and the sufferer may be confused or aggressive. Eventually the victim will become delirious or convulse. Hospitalisation is essential, but in the interim get victims out of the sun, remove their clothing, cover them with a wet sheet or towel and then fan continually. Give fluids if they are conscious.

If planning to trek in Israel's desert regions make sure you start very early and finish by lunchtime if at all possible.

Hypothermia Too much cold can be just as dangerous as too much heat. In Israel the only time you are likely to encounter extremely cold weather is while skiing or trekking on Mt Hermon in the Golan during winter.

Hypothermia occurs when the body loses heat faster than it can produce it and the core temperature of the body falls. It is surprisingly easy to progress from very cold to dangerously cold due to a combination of wind, wet clothing, fatigue and hunger, even if the air temperature is above freezing. It is best to dress in layers; silk, wool and some of the new artificial fibres are all good insulating materials. A hat is important, as a lot of heat is lost through the head. A strong, waterproof outer layer (and a 'space' blanket for emergencies) is essential. Carry basic supplies, including food containing simple sugars to generate heat quickly and fluid to drink.

Symptoms of hypothermia are exhaustion, numb skin (particularly toes and fingers), shivering, slurred speech, irrational or violent behaviour, lethargy, stumbling, dizzy spells, muscle cramps and violent bursts of energy. Irrationality may take the form of sufferers claiming they are warm and trying to take off their clothes.

To treat mild hypothermia, first get the person out of the wind and/or rain, remove their clothing if it's wet, and replace it with dry, warm clothing. Give them hot liquids –

not alcohol – and some high-kilojoule, easily digestible food. Do not rub victims: instead, allow them to slowly warm themselves. This should be enough to treat the early stages of hypothermia. The early recognition and treatment of mild hypothermia is the only way to prevent severe hypothermia, which is a critical condition.

Jet Lag Jet lag is experienced when a person travels by air across more than three time zones (each time zone usually represents a one-hour time difference). It occurs because many of the functions of the human body (such as temperature, pulse rate and emptying of the bladder and bowels) are regulated by internal 24-hour cycles. When we travel long distances rapidly, our bodies take time to adjust to the 'new time' of our destination, and we may experience fatigue, disorientation, insomnia, anxiety, impaired concentration and loss of appetite. These effects will usually be gone within three days of arrival, but to minimise the impact of jet lag:

- Rest for a couple of days prior to departure.
- Try to select flight schedules that minimise sleep deprivation; arriving late in the day means you can go to sleep soon after you arrive. For very long flights, try to organise a stopover.
- Avoid excessive eating (which bloats the stomach) and alcohol (which causes dehydration) during the flight. Instead, drink plenty of non-carbonated, nonalcoholic drinks such as fruit juice or water.
- Avoid smoking.
- Make yourself comfortable by wearing loose-fitting clothes and perhaps bringing an eye mask and ear plugs to help you sleep.
- Try to sleep at the appropriate time for the time zone you are travelling to.

Motion Sickness Eating lightly before and during a trip will reduce the chances of motion sickness. If you are prone to motion sickness try to find a place that minimises movement – near the wing on aircraft, close to midships on boats and near the centre on buses. Fresh air usually helps; reading and cigarette smoke don't. Commercial motion-sickness preparations, which can cause drowsiness, have to be taken before the trip commences. Ginger (available in capsules) and peppermint (including mint-flavoured sweets) are natural preventatives.

Prickly Heat Prickly heat is an itchy rash caused by excessive perspiration trapped under the skin. It usually strikes people who have just arrived in a hot climate. Keeping cool, bathing often, drying the skin and using a mild talcum or prickly heat powder or resorting to air-conditioning may help.

Sunburn In the tropics, the desert or at high altitude you can get sunburnt surprisingly quickly, even through cloud. Use a sunscreen, a hat, and a barrier cream for your nose and lips. Calamine lotion or a commercial after-sun preparation are good for mild sunburn. Protect your eyes with good quality sunglasses, particularly if you will be near water, sand or snow. The glare in the Negev Desert can be especially strong.

Infectious Diseases

Diarrhoea Simple things like a change of water, food or climate can all cause a mild bout of diarrhoea, but a few rushed toilet trips with no other symptoms is not indicative of a major problem.

Dehydration is the main danger with any diarrhoea, particularly in children or the elderly; and can occur quite quickly. Under all circumstances *fluid replacement* (at least equal to the volume being lost) is the most important thing to remember. Weak black tea with a little sugar, soda water, or soft drinks allowed to go flat and diluted 50% with clean water are all good. However, with severe diarrhoea a rehydrating solution is preferable to replace minerals and salts lost.

Commercially available oral rehydration salts (ORS) are very useful; add them to boiled or bottled water. In an emergency you can make up a solution of six teaspoons of sugar and a half teaspoon of salt to a litre of boiled or bottled water. You need to drink at least the same volume of fluid that you are losing in bowel movements and vomit-

ing. Urine is the best guide to the adequacy of replacement – if you have small amounts of concentrated urine, you need to drink more. Keep drinking small amounts often. Stick to a bland diet as you recover.

Gut-paralysing drugs such as loperamide or diphenoxylate can be used to bring relief from the symptoms, although they do not actually cure the problem. Only use these drugs if you do not have access to toilets, eg if you *must* travel. Note that these drugs are not recommended for children under 12 years.

In certain situations antibiotics may be required: diarrhoea with blood or mucus (dysentery), any diarrhoea with fever, profuse watery diarrhoea, persistent diarrhoea not improving after 48 hours and severe diarrhoea. These suggest a more serious cause of diarrhoea and in these situations gut-paralysing drugs should be avoided.

In these situations, a stool test may be necessary to diagnose what bug is causing your diarrhoea, so you should seek medical help urgently. Where this is not possible the recommended drugs for bacterial diarrhoea (the most likely cause of severe diarrhoea in travellers) are norfloxacin 400mg twice daily for three days or ciprofloxacin 500mg twice daily for five days although these are not recommended for children or pregnant women. The drug of choice for children would be co-trimoxazole with the dosage dependent on weight. A five day course is given. Ampicillin or amoxycillin may be given during pregnancy, but medical care is necessary.

Two causes of persistent diarrhoea in travellers are giardiasis and amoebic dysentery. Giardiasis is caused by a common parasite, *Giardia lamblia*. Symptoms include stomach cramps, nausea, a bloated stomach, watery, foul-smelling diarrhoea and frequent gas. Giardiasis can appear several weeks after you have been exposed to the parasite. The symptoms may disappear for a few days and then return; this can go on for several weeks.

Amoebic dysentery is caused by the protozoan *Entamoeba histolytica* and is characterised by a gradual onset of low-grade diarrhoea, often with blood and mucus. Cramping abdominal pain and vomiting are less likely than in other types of diarrhoea, and fever may not be present. It will persist until treated and can recur and cause other health problems.

You should seek medical advice if you think you have giardiasis or amoebic dysentery, but where this is not possible, tinidazole or metronidazole are the recommended drugs. Treatment is a 2g single dose of tinidazole or 250mg of metronidazole three times daily for five to 10 days.

Fungal Infections Fungal infections are more common in hot weather and are usually found on the scalp, between the toes (athlete's foot) or fingers, in the groin and on the body (ringworm). You get ringworm (which is a fungal infection, not a worm) from infected animals or other people. Moisture encourages these infections.

To prevent fungal infections wear loose, comfortable clothes, avoid artificial fibres, wash frequently and dry yourself carefully. If you do get an infection, wash the infected area at least daily with a disinfectant or medicated soap and water, rinse and dry well. Apply an antifungal cream or powder like tolnaftate. Expose the infected area to air or sunlight as much as possible and wash all towels and underwear in hot water, change them often and let them dry in the sun.

Hepatitis Hepatitis is a general term for inflammation of the liver. It is a common disease worldwide. There are several different viruses that cause hepatitis, and they differ in the way that they are transmitted. The symptoms are similar in all forms of the illness, and include fever, chills, headache, fatigue, feelings of weakness and aches and pains, followed by loss of appetite, nausea, vomiting, abdominal pain, dark urine, light-coloured faeces, jaundiced (yellow) skin and yellowing of the whites of the eyes. People who have had hepatitis should avoid alcohol for some time after the illness, as the liver needs time to recover.

Hepatitus A is transmitted by contaminated food and drinking water. You should seek medical advice, but there is not much you can do apart from resting, drinking lots of fluids, eating lightly and avoiding fatty foods. Hepatitis E is transmitted in the same way as hepatitis A; it can be particularly serious in pregnant women.

There are almost 300 million chronic carriers of hepatitis B in the world. It is spread through contact with infected blood, blood products or body fluids, for example through sexual contact, unsterilised needles and blood transfusions, or contact with blood via small breaks in the skin. Other risk situations include having a shave, tattoo or body piercing with contaminated equipment. The symptoms of hepatitis B may be more severe than type A and the disease can lead to long-term problems such as chronic liver damage, liver cancer or a long term carrier state. Hepatitis C and D are spread in the same way as hepatitis B and both can also lead to long term complications.

There are vaccines against hepatitis A and B, but there are currently no vaccines against the other types of hepatitis. Following the basic rules about food and water (hepatitis A and E) and avoiding risk situations (hepatitis B, C and D) are important preventative measures.

HIV & AIDS Infection with the human immunodeficiency virus (HIV) may lead to acquired immune deficiency syndrome (AIDS), which is a fatal disease. Any exposure to blood, blood products or body fluids may put the individual at risk. The disease is often transmitted through sexual contact or dirty needles – vaccinations, acupuncture, tattooing and body piercing can be potentially as dangerous as intravenous drug use. HIV/AIDS can also be spread through infected blood transfusions; some developing countries cannot afford to screen blood used for transfusions. Israel is fortunately equipped with a high level of medical services so this should not be a problem.

If you do need an injection, ask to see the syringe unwrapped in front of you, or take a needle and syringe pack with you. A fear of HIV infection should never preclude treatment for serious medical conditions.

Sexually Transmitted Diseases HIV/AIDS and hepatitis B can be transmitted through sexual contact – see the relevant sections earlier for more details. Other STDs include gonorrhoea, herpes and syphilis; sores, blisters or rashes around the genitals and discharges or pain when urinating are common symptoms. In some STDs, such as wart virus or chlamydia, symptoms may be less marked or not observed at all, especially in women. Chlamydia infection can cause infertility in men and women before any symptoms have been noticed. The symptoms of syphilis eventually disappear completely, but the disease continues and can cause severe problems in later years. While abstinence from sexual contact is the only 100% effective prevention, using condoms is also effective. The treatment of gonorrhoea and syphilis is with antibiotics. The different sexually transmitted diseases each require specific antibiotics.

Typhoid Typhoid fever is a dangerous gut infection caused by contaminated water and food. Medical help must be sought.

In its early stages sufferers may feel they have a bad cold or flu on the way, as early symptoms are a headache, body aches and a fever which rises a little each day until it is around 40°C (104°F) or more. The victim's pulse is often slow relative to the degree of fever present – unlike a normal fever where the pulse increases. There may also be vomiting, abdominal pain, diarrhoea or constipation.

In the second week the high fever and slow pulse continue and a few pink spots may appear on the body; trembling, delirium, weakness, weight loss and dehydration may occur. Complications such as pneumonia, perforated bowel or meningitis may occur.

Cuts, Bites & Stings
See Immunisations for details of rabies, which is passed through animal bites.

Cuts & Scratches Wash well and treat any cut with an antiseptic such as povidone-iodine. Where possible avoid bandages and Band-Aids, which can keep wounds wet. Coral cuts are notoriously slow to heal and if they are not adequately cleaned, small pieces of coral can become embedded in the wound.

Bedbugs & Lice Bedbugs live in various places, but particularly in dirty mattresses and bedding, evidenced by blood spots on bedclothes or on the wall. Bedbugs leave itchy bites in neat rows. Calamine lotion or a sting relief spray may help.

When in Israel do check the sleeping quarters at some of the cheaper hostels, as readers have advised us of bedbug problems in some places. If in doubt move on.

All lice cause itching and discomfort. They make themselves at home in your hair (head lice), your clothing (body lice) or in your pubic hair (crabs). You catch lice through direct contact with infected people or by sharing combs, clothing and the like. Powder or shampoo treatment will kill the lice and infected clothing should then be washed in very hot, soapy water and left in the sun to dry.

Bites & Stings Bee and wasp stings are usually painful rather than dangerous. However, in people who are allergic to them severe breathing difficulties may occur and require urgent medical care. Calamine lotion or a sting relief spray will give relief and ice packs will reduce the pain and swelling. There are some spiders with dangerous bites, but antivenins are generally available.

Jellyfish Avoid contact with these sea creatures, which have stinging tentacles – seek local advice. Dousing in vinegar will deactivate any stingers which have not 'fired'. Calamine lotion, antihistamines and analgesics may reduce the reaction and relieve the pain.

Snakes & Scorpions To minimise your chances of being bitten always wear boots, socks and long trousers when walking through undergrowth where snakes may be present. Don't put your hands into holes and crevices, and be careful when collecting firewood. You are more likely to come across scorpions in the desert in Israel, so be alert, if camping rough, for scorpions that may take refuge in your shoes or even your sleeping bag.

Snake bites do not cause instantaneous death and antivenins are usually available. Immediately wrap the bitten limb tightly, as you would for a sprained ankle, and then attach a splint to immobilise it. Keep the victim still and seek medical help, if possible with the dead snake for identification. Don't attempt to catch the snake if there is a possibility of being bitten again. Tourniquets and sucking out the poison are now comprehensively discredited.

Less Common Diseases

The following diseases pose a small risk to travellers, and so are only mentioned in passing. Seek medical advice if you think you may have any of these diseases.

Cholera This is the worst of the watery diarrhoeas and medical help should be sought. Outbreaks of cholera are generally widely reported, so you can avoid such problem areas. *Fluid replacement is the most vital treatment* – the risk of dehydration is severe as you may lose up to 20L a day. If there is a delay in getting to hospital, then begin taking tetracycline. The adult dose is 250mg four times daily. It is not recommended for children under nine years nor for pregnant women. Tetracycline may help shorten the illness, but adequate fluids are required to save lives.

Rabies This fatal viral infection is found in many countries. Many animals can be infected (such as dogs, cats, bats and monkeys) and it is their saliva which is infectious. Any bite, scratch or even lick from an animal should be cleaned immediately and thoroughly. Scrub with soap and running water, and then apply alcohol or iodine solution.

Medical help should be sought promptly to receive a course of injections to prevent the onset of symptoms and death.

Tetanus This disease is caused by a germ which lives in soil and in the faeces of horses and other animals. It enters the body via breaks in the skin. The first symptom may be discomfort in swallowing, or stiffening of the jaw and neck; this is followed by painful convulsions of the jaw and whole body. The disease can be fatal. It can be prevented by vaccination.

Tuberculosis (TB) TB is a bacterial infection usually transmitted from person to person by coughing but can also be transmitted through consumption of unpasteurised milk. Milk that has been boiled is safe to drink, and the souring of milk to make yoghurt or cheese also kills the bacilli. Travellers are usually not at great risk as close household contact with the infected person is usually required before the disease is passed on. You may need to have a TB test before you travel as this can help diagnose the disease later if you become ill.

Typhus This disease is spread by ticks, mites or lice. It begins with fever, chills, headache and muscle pains followed a few days later by a body rash. There is often a large painful sore at the site of the bite and nearby lymph nodes are swollen and painful. Typhus can be treated under medical supervision. Seek local advice on areas where ticks pose a danger and always check your skin carefully for ticks after walking in a danger area such as a tropical forest. An insect repellent can help, and walkers in tick-infested areas should consider having their boots and trousers impregnated with benzyl benzoate and dibutylphthalate.

Women's Health
Gynaecological Problems Antibiotic use, synthetic underwear, sweating and contraceptive pills can lead to fungal vaginal infections, especially when travelling in hot climates. Fungal infections are charac-

terised by a rash, itch and discharge and can be treated with a vinegar or lemon-juice douche, or with yoghurt. Nystatin, miconazole or clotrimazole pessaries or vaginal cream are the usual treatment. Maintaining good personal hygiene and wearing loose-fitting clothes and cotton underwear may help prevent these infections.

Sexually transmitted diseases are a major cause of vaginal problems. Symptoms include a smelly discharge, painful intercourse and sometimes a burning sensation when urinating. Medical attention should be sought and male sexual partners must also be treated. For more details see the section on Sexually Transmitted Diseases earlier. Besides abstinence, the best thing is to practise safer sex using condoms.

Pregnancy It is not advisable to travel to some places while pregnant as some vaccinations normally used to prevent serious diseases are not advisable during pregnancy (eg yellow fever). In addition, some diseases are much more serious for the mother (and may increase the risk of a stillborn child) in pregnancy (eg malaria).

The majority of miscarriages occur during the first three months of pregnancy. Miscarriage is not uncommon and can occasionally lead to severe bleeding. The last three months should also be spent within reasonable distance of good medical care. A baby born as early as 24 weeks stands a chance of survival, but only in a good modern hospital.

Pregnant women should avoid all unnecessary medication, although vaccinations and malarial prophylactics should still be taken where needed. Additional care should be taken to prevent illness and particular attention should be paid to diet and nutrition.

WOMEN TRAVELLERS

In Israel, harassment can be a big problem for women travellers, especially in Arab neighborhoods and towns where the male-dominated culture is not particularly conducive to female tourists travelling without an escort. Even on the more liberal streets and beaches of Tel Aviv, Israeli men can also act in an overly forward and familiar manner. The harassment is rarely physical, but even persistent staring and verbal taunts can be very irritating and threaten the enjoyment of your visit. There are one or two guidelines you can observe to help minimise unwanted attention.

In most places, the best advice is not to walk alone. Never hitch, either with other female friends or alone, and avoid deserted areas. The Mount of Olives, in particular, has a bad reputation, and Lonely Planet has also received letters from women who've had unpleasant encounters on the ramparts of the Old City walls of Jerusalem.

In places like East Jerusalem and the Old City, and particularly in Arab towns in the West Bank, it's vital that you dress modestly. While a headscarf isn't necessary, a long skirt and blouse that covers your elbows, or even baggy T-shirts are better than shorts or tight jeans. How you conduct yourself will also determine the attention you draw. Western women are often viewed as promiscuous, so a little flirtation or even simple friendliness can quickly be misconstrued as an invitation for sex. It's best to remain businesslike and respectful in your conduct, and remember that accepting the minimum of attention will usually invite more.

How you deal with harassment once it starts is a matter of choice. In late 1995, the *Jerusalem Post* reported on three women tourists who had responded to the unwanted physical advances of their escorts with a little black-belt karate; their attackers required medical treatment. Of course, not everyone has this level of retaliation at her disposal. Before any attention gets out of hand, politely but firmly turn down whispered invitations and completely ignore come-ons. If this doesn't work and the attention does get out of hand, seek out a person of authority, or a local woman if possible, to intervene on your behalf. Usually the spectre of communal shame is enough to put someone back in line.

GAY & LESBIAN TRAVELLERS

Homosexuality is not illegal in Israel, but it's anathema to the country's large religious population and as a result the gay and lesbian community are obliged to keep a low profile.

The Society for the Protection of Personal Rights (SPPR), which represents gays and lesbians in Israel, has successfully lobbied in recent years for legislative changes, and in April 1998, the Knesset passed a law banning anti-gay actions and sexual harassment, particularly in the workplace.

The biggest scene – and the annual gay-pride parade – is in largely secular, free-wheeling Tel Aviv, with Sheinkin St, near the Carmel Market popular for its cafes and shops. Cafe Nordau (see Places to Eat) is the most venerable of Tel Aviv's gay venues and is a good place to pick up information on what else is going on; see also Bars and Organised Tours in the Tel Aviv chapter. In the Jerusalem chapter see Bars & Clubs, and in Haifa see Entertainment.

For further information about what is going on, call the gay switchboard (☎ 03-629 2797) Sunday, Tuesday, Wednesday and Thursday from 7.30 to 11.30 pm, and Monday 7 to 11 pm. The Society for the Protection of Personal Rights (SPPR) (☎ 03-620 4327, fax 525 2341, email sppr@netvision.net.il), PO Box 37604, Tel Aviv 61375, also operates a gay hotline (☎ 03-629 3681) and publishes an English-language newsletter titled *Israel Update* – send them a self-addressed envelope. In Haifa, the gay information and counselling line operates on Mondays from 7 to 11 pm; call ☎ 04-852 5532.

Useful Web sites include The Other 10% – Gay & Lesbian Student Union of the Hebrew University (www.ma.huji.ac.il/~dafid/asiron.html); and A Gay Guide to Tel Aviv (www.agmonet.co.il/list/li04059.htm).

We also recommend that you take a look at the *Spartacus International Gay Guide*, which has a brief section on Israel. It's published annually by Bruno Gmünder and should be available from better bookshops.

DISABLED TRAVELLERS

Many hotels and most public institutions in Israel provide ramps, specially equipped toilets and other conveniences for the disabled. Several of the HI-affiliated hostels in particular, including the one in Tel Aviv and the lovely Beit Shmuel in Jerusalem, have rooms specially adapted for wheelchair access. Anyone with any particular concerns might try contacting in advance Milbat – The Advisory Centre for the Disabled (☎ 03-530 3739) at the Sheba Medical Centre in Tel Aviv for information and advice.

The Yad Sarah Organisation (☎ 02-624 4242) at 43 HaNevi'im St in Jerusalem loans out wheelchairs at no charge, crutches and other aids, though a deposit is required. It's open Sunday to Thursday from 9 am to 7 pm, Friday from 9 am to noon.

USEFUL ORGANISATIONS
Alternative Information Centre

Located at 6 Koresh St, PO Box 31417, Jerusalem, this centre (☎ 02-624 1159, fax 625 3131) is a joint Israeli-Palestinian project that provides information on developments in Palestinian society and the Israeli response. Specifically geared to assisting visiting journalists, the AIC will also help individual travellers interested in learning more about local politics. They publish two periodicals, the weekly *The Other Front* and the monthly *News From Within*.

Christian Information Centre

The Christian Information Centre (☎ 02-627 2692, fax 628 6417), PO Box 14308, is near Jaffa Gate in Jerusalem's Old City. This is the best source of information in Israel regarding the Christian community, holy sites etc. For further details see Information in the Jerusalem chapter.

Volunteer Tourist Service

In operation for over 20 years, the VTS has assisted hundreds of thousands of tourists during their visits to Israel. Completely voluntary, the organisation aims to provide assistance to visitors with problems, answer queries, and trace lost relatives and friends.

They can also arrange a visit to an Israeli home, matching up the visitor's profession or hobby with that of the host. They are at Ben-Gurion airport between noon and 8 pm or in the lobbies of major hotels from 6 to 8.30 pm except Friday and Jewish holidays.

DANGERS & ANNOYANCES

While security and safety in a large sense are not matters which should concern the aver-age visitor (see the boxed texts at the begin-ning of this and the Gaza Strip & the West Bank chapters), theft is just as much of a problem in Israel as it is anywhere else. The standard precautionary measures should be taken. Always keep valuables with you or locked in a safe – never leave them in your room or in a car or bus (unhappily there are more than a few fellow travellers who make their money go a little bit further by helping

---

Security in Israel – a Travel Survival Kit

Israel has admittedly had a bad international profile when it comes to danger from within the country. Stories of bombings and shootings, demonstrations and uprisings are common enough through the images of the electronic media. As a result many would-be visitors keep away from Israel. The reality, as in the case of most media manufactured perceptions, is some-what different.

The main exponents of domestic terrorism are Hamas (in Arabic an acronym for 'Harakat Al-Muqawama Al-Islamiya' or Islamic Resistance Movement). Since 1989 Hamas has taken part in the kidnapping and murdering of soldiers, shooting attacks, bombings in crowded places, car bombings and suicide bombings.

Israel is nevertheless a very security-conscious and essentially safe country to travel in and you have more chance of being hit by a bus than being blown up in one. Either way the prospect is not attractive for an unsuspecting traveller. There is not a lot you can do to avoid random acts of terrorism, but you can stack the odds in your favour by keeping a few point-ers in mind.

Urban buses, bus stations and markets are popular spots for intended bombing missions. Keep your time spent in or around them as short as possible. Walk in preference to taking an urban bus. Security is generally good at interurban bus stations, but it is next to impossible to monitor markets and city bus stops. Some urban stops in Jerusalem are patrolled, however, by volunteer security brigades. Be alert for suspicious people around you and avoid congested places. Jerusalem's Mahane Yehuda Market is a magnet for shoppers and lovers of markets, but it was bombed once in 1997 killing 16 and injuring 170 people, and a suicide bombing attempt made in November 1998 injured 20 bystanders.

Keep away from developing hotspots and move on quickly out of harm's way if you acci-dentally come across a demonstration. Incidents of this nature are more likely to happen in West Bank towns such as Hebron or Ramallah. Tourists are not deliberately targeted, but you may get caught up in any ensuing crossfire if things get nasty.

In order to avoid the scrupulous attention of the IDF, do not do silly things like wearing Palestinian *keffiyahs* in obviously Jewish areas. Never leave luggage or bags unattended any-where: it is likely to be declared a *hefetz hashud* (suspicious object) and blown up by secu-rity personnel. Conversely, do not wear a *kippa* or other Jewish items of clothing in the West Bank and try for once to look like a tourist. This is one scenario where wearing a bum-bag/fanny pack and funny hat might save your bacon. Keep your wits about you, sprinkle them with a healthy dose of common sense and enjoy your stay – safely!

themselves to other people's). Use a money belt, a pouch under your clothes, a leather wallet attached to your belt, or extra internal pockets in your clothing. Keep a record of your passport, credit card and travellers cheque numbers.

Travelling on intercity buses, you generally stow large bags in the luggage hold. This is a virtually trouble-free system, but keep valuables with you just in case. Crowded tourist spots and markets are an obvious hunting ground for pickpockets, so take extra care.

LEGAL MATTERS

Although more widely available than ever before, the possession of drugs in Israel is still a serious offence, often punished by a spell in prison and deportation. Purchasing drugs here is a risky business, as suppliers and police informers can be one and the same. Eilat is particularly hot on anti-drug enforcement and, periodically, the police sweep-search the hostels up behind the bus station. This also happens in Tel Aviv with the hostels at the southern end of Ben Yehuda St, but far less frequently. Bringing drugs in and out of the country yourself is plain dumb – the thoroughness of Israeli security searches is legendary.

BUSINESS HOURS

The most important thing to know is that on Shabbat, the Jewish Sabbath, all Israeli shops, offices and places of entertainment close down. Shabbat begins at sundown Friday and ends at sundown Saturday. During this time you will find it difficult to get anything to eat, you can't easily change money and your movements are restricted because most buses aren't running. You need to plan for Shabbat in advance and work out where you'll be and what you can do to avoid being overtaken by the countrywide inactivity. Israel kicks back into action on Saturday evening when all the cafes, bars and restaurants always experience a great post-Shabbat rush.

Predominantly Muslim areas like East Jerusalem, the Gaza Strip and the West Bank towns remain open on Saturday, but are closed all day Friday. And, of course, Christian-owned businesses (concentrated in Jerusalem's Old City and in Nazareth) close on Sunday.

Standard Israeli shopping hours are Monday to Thursday from 8 am to 1 pm and 4 to 7 pm or later, and Friday from 8 am to 2 pm, with some places opening after sundown on Saturday, too.

Although banking hours vary, generally they are Sunday to Tuesday and Thursday from 8.30 am to 12.30 pm and 4 to 5 or 5.30 pm, and Wednesday, Friday and eves of holy days from 8.30 am to noon. In Nazareth, banks are open Friday and Saturday morning, but are closed on Sunday.

PUBLIC HOLIDAYS & SPECIAL EVENTS

One patient researcher some years ago sat down to compile a list and discovered that between the various religions and their different denominations the people of Israel celebrate more festivals each year than there are days. Our list below describes just some of the more notable holidays in the annual calender.

Jewish

Be well prepared for any Jewish religious holidays that are celebrated during your visit. The Jewish holidays are effectively like long bouts of Shabbat, and if you're caught off-guard you can be rendered immobile for a couple of days at a time, maybe without food, maybe without money. The main ones to beware of are Rosh HaShanah, Yom Kippur, Sukkot and Pesah.

Rosh HaShanah This is one of the two days of the Jewish calendar known as Days of Judgement or Days of Awe (the other is Yom Kippur). It is a time for contemplation and meditation for every Jew and is accompanied by soul-searching and the seeking of atonement for past wrongdoings. As with all Jewish holidays, prayer services begin the eve of the holiday – in this case continuing for two days and are heralded by the ritual

For the young and old of Jewish, Muslim and Christian faiths, the Holy Land – especially Jerusalem – has an overwhelming religious significance.

People – A Multicultural Cross Section

Didi Ben Arosh Didi Ben Arosh, young chef/owner of the French restaurant Cavalier in Jerusalem, is part of a new wave of foodies working to change the perception of Israel as a gastronomic desert. A prime example of Israeli chutzpah, this self-taught son of Moroccan immigrants opened his celebrated restaurant six years ago with no professional training. Working from 6 am until 2 am, he did everything in the beginning from buying the groceries to washing the windows. Today he receives invitations to cook with renowned chefs in Paris and frequently hosts Israeli and French officials in his dining room.

Halina Birenbaum Halina Birenbaum was 15 when she 'graduated' from the concentration camps of WWII. Born in Poland, she lost all her family in the Holocaust except for one brother. A survivor of four camps, including Auschwitz, she wrote a remarkable memoir called *Hope Is the Last to Die*, and speaks regularly to school children. In 1946 she immigrated to Israel where she lives in Herzliya with her husband, Haim. One of her two sons, songwriter Yaakov Gilad, recorded a popular album of Holocaust songs (Ashes and Dust) with singer/songwriter Yehuda Poliker, which includes one of Birenbaum's poems set to music.

Nadim Khoury Nadim Khoury, the 'Samuel Adams of the Middle East', owns the Taybeh Brewing Company, the Arab world's first microbrewery, a concept that might seem a hard sell since Islam forbids alcohol consumption. But Khoury, one of the West Bank's 5% Christian-Arab minority, says his only obstacles to selling suds to Christians, Muslims, and Jews are the occasional military roadblocks that prevent deliveries into Israel. The father of four spent 18 years in the US studying business and brewing techniques before returning to Taybeh following the Oslo Accords. His sister heads the business department at Birzeit University near Ramallah.

Einat Ramon For many Israelis, 'female rabbi' is an oxymoron. Indeed, Rabbi Ramon, member of Judaism's more liberal Conservative movement and Israel's first native-born female rabbi, has been a pioneer since her ordination in 1989. She teaches Judaic studies and performs unrecognised weddings (only weddings performed by an orthodox rabbi, and civil ceremonies performed outside of Israel, are officially recognised). Born in Jerusalem to ardent Zionists and married to a Reform rabbi, Einat descends from the 'Mayflower' generation of immigrants who came to Palestine from Russia in the 1920s to establish a socialist Jewish utopia.

People – A Multicultural Cross Section

Martin Pielstocker 'I feel good here', says German-born archaeologist Martin Pielstocker, who works with the Israel Antiquities Authority and plays volleyball in his spare time. 'If they fired me tomorrow I'd still stay. I'd probably open a pub.' Living in Israel since 1989 and married to an Israeli woman, Martin has blended seamlessly into his adopted society and finds Israelis friendly and welcoming. If they question his presence in Israel at all, it's only to wonder why a non-Jew would leave economically strong Europe for the less stable Middle East. 'The economy here is difficult', Martin says, 'but Israelis are more connected to family and country'.

Ernest 'Jackie' Moeketsi Jackie is one of a new breed of Israelis – neither Jewish nor an Israeli citizen, he represents a growing number of new residents building another branch of Middle Eastern multiculturalism. Jackie, a devout Christian, came to Israel from Lesotho in 1994 as a kibbutz volunteer. He married Dessie Saba, an Ethiopian Jew, and in November 1998 they had a son, Shmul Moeketsi. With the assistance of the Israeli government, they secured a mortgage and bought their first apartment. Jackie summarised his feelings for Israel when, beaming a happy smile, he declared, 'Israel is a place to live and feel free like home. God bless Israel'.

Sharon Sasson-Brunsher & Limor Yizhaki-Amslalem Tel Aviv sets the trends that the rest of Israel follows. Cafes and restaurants open and close at a dizzying pace, and whatever's hot (achla) and not (alhapanim) changes as swiftly as the slang that describes them. In that mode, Limor, half Iraqi/half Finnish, and Sharon, also of Iraqi origin, represent the youthful energy and ethnic mix that feed 'The City That Never Sleeps'. Friends since design school, they co-own 'Charlotte', a stylish boutique in Neve Tzedek, Tel Aviv's oldest neighborhood, which has become a hip area for young bohemians attempting to inject the area's dusty streets with new life.

Golda Yamburg In 1953, conditions in Israel were so austere that before 20-year-old Golda could immigrate from Argentina to help found Kibbutz Revadim, she had to prove that she possessed a blanket, underwear and shoes. Home during those years was an unfurnished shack, breakfast was often half an egg, and the border settlement was subject to periodic attacks from Jordanian marauders – a far cry from Buenos Aires, where Golda's grandfather had been a respected rabbi. 'We never suffered', Golda says. 'We didn't enjoy either, but we didn't suffer'. She still resides on Revadim with husband, Arieh, an artist, and their three children.

Text: Kim Zetter, Photos: Eddie Gerald (Except E Moeketsi text & photo by Paul Hellander)

Whether you have a sweet tooth or a craving for savouries, you'll be delighted by the abundance of delicious foods available in the stalls and markets all over the country.

blowing of the *shofar* (ram's horn) which serves to remind Jews to follow God's commandments and to follow their heritage.

Characteristic foods eaten on Rosh Ha-Shanah include pomegranates, apples dipped in honey or other honeyed foods to augur a sweet year, and tongue or fish heads to mark the 'head of the year', a direct translation of 'Rosh HaShanah'. People greet each other with the phrase 'Shanah Tovah' (Happy New Year) during this period.

Yom Kippur Known as the Day of Atonement, Yom Kippur ends the 10 days of penitence which begin on New Year's Day. For the observant, Yom Kippur means 25 hours of complete abstinence from food, drink, sex, cosmetics (including soap and toothpaste) and animal products. The time is spent in prayer and contemplation and all sins are confessed. As the only Jewish holiday equivalent to Shabbat in sanctity, Yom Kippur is the quietest day of the year in most of Israel.

Sukkot The Festival of Sukkot is the third of the Jewish Pilgrimage Festivals. On this day the majority of Jews, religious or not, erect homemade *sukkot* (shelters) in commemoration of the 40 years which the ancient Israelites spent in the wilderness following the Exodus. The sukkot, which is hammered together from plyboard, but with a roof only of loose branches of palm leaves through which the stars can be seen, sit out on the balconies of apartments, in gardens and even in hotels and restaurants. For the seven day duration of the festival, all meals are taken in the sukkot and the ultraorthodox even go as far as sleeping in these makeshift huts.

Hanukkah Also known as the Festival of Lights, Hanukkah celebrates the triumphant Maccabean Revolt against the king of the Syrian Greeks, Antiochus IV. Its symbol is the *hanukiah* (eight-branched candelabra), and one of its candles is lit for each night of the holiday. The significance of the number eight dates back to the time when the Jews,

after reclaiming their temple in Jerusalem in 165 BC, entered the temple and discovered only one flask of holy oil, sufficient for one day. According to tradition the oil lasted eight days, which was just long enough to prepare a new supply of oil.

A special Hanukkah lamp should also be displayed by each house, usually hung in the window – in Mea She'arim these are often hung outside the building, making it an enchanting district to wander through during the time of the festival.

Tu B'Shevat The Mishnah names this day as the New Year for Trees and it is customary to eat fruit and nuts, especially the carob fruit. Since independence, Tu B'Shevat has been observed as a time for tree-planting.

Purim Purim, the Feast of Lots, is a remembrance of the hatred born of the Jews' refusal to assimilate and their unwillingness to compromise religious principle by bowing before the secular authority. Despite such a serious, if highly relevant, theme, the holiday has a carnival atmosphere with fancy dress as the order of the day. The streets are filled with proud parents and their Batmen, Madonnas and Power Rangers. In the evening it's the turn of the dames, fairies and gangsters.

For a nation of nondrinkers, Purim is an annual opportunity for the Israelis to atone: according to tradition they are supposed to get so drunk that they can't distinguish between the words 'Bless Mordechai' and 'Curse Haman'. One of the most popular foods eaten during Purim are *Oznei Haman* (Haman's Ears), fried, three-cornered pastries filled with apricots or other fruits and covered in poppy seeds.

Pesah Pesah, the Feast of Passover, celebrates the exodus of the Jews from Egypt led by Moses. The festival lasts a full week during which time most Jewish stores (including foodstores and markets) are closed (or open for limited hours only). The production of everyday bread is substituted for *matza*, a flat tasteless variety which is made in discs of up to a metre in diameter. There's no public transport on either the first or last day of the festival.

The Samaritans celebrate their version of Pesah on Mt Gerizim near Nablus. To them this is the authentic Mt Sinai as well as the site of Abraham's sacrifice of his son, Isaac. Here they sacrifice a lamb, watched by a crowd of onlookers, as they have done for over 2500 years.

Yom HaSho'ah (Holocaust Day) Periodically throughout the day, sirens wail to signal two minutes of silence in remembrance of the six million victims of the Holocaust. It's an incredibly moving and eerie experience as everyone on the streets stops and puts their bags down; all traffic comes to a halt, engines are extinguished and nothing moves.

Mimouna This festival takes place the day after the last day of Pesah, and has been celebrated by the North African Jewish communities for generations. Mimouna's exact origins are unknown – one theory is that it's an Arabisation of the Hebrew word *emunah*, meaning faith or belief in the coming of the Messiah and the redemption of the Jews. Certainly the theme of Mimouna is confidence in God and patience in awaiting the Messiah. It's a good chance to experience Israeli hospitality, which traditionally excels itself on this occasion. North African Jews organise street parties and open-house celebrations and foreigners (Jews and non-Jews alike) are warmly invited to join in. Check a government tourist information office for the local arrangements.

Yom Ha'Atzmaut (Independence Day) On 14 May 1948 Israel became an independent state and since then the day has been celebrated by Jews worldwide (note that the date changes with the lunar calendar). In Israel, expect parades, concerts, picnics, aerial flypasts and fireworks all over the country.

Lag B'Omer Ending 33 days of mourning, Lag B'Omer is interpreted as a rite of spring

or as the day when a plague was lifted in Jewish history. The modern-day celebrations include such festivities as parades, parties and bonfires.

It's worth being around Meiron on this day, up near Safed in the Galilee. This small village is the focus of a torchlit parade, accompanied by much singing and dancing. On arrival at Meiron, the celebrants place their candles on the tomb of Rabbi Shamon and light a giant bonfire. Some of the Hasidim throw their clothes onto the fire and the festivities go on all night. In the morning, three-year-old boys are given their first haircuts and the hair is thrown onto the still-blazing fire.

Shavuot This is the Jewish celebration of Pentecost, the Feast of Weeks. A happy harvest event, Shavuot is celebrated most avidly on kibbutzim and moshavim where the children are adorned with wreaths.

Muslim

Muslim holidays are not as disruptive as the Jewish ones unless you happen to be travelling in the West Bank or the Gaza Strip at the time. Ramadan is the important one to be aware of because the ban on eating and drinking during the day will mean that no cafes, restaurants or street-food stalls will be open – you could of course carry your own supplies, but it's a little inconsiderate to openly consume food when everyone else around you is fasting.

Birth of the Prophet Mohammed's birthday, celebrated with heavy consumption of sticky, sickly sweets and confectionery.

Lailatul Miraj This holiday remembers the night Mohammed ascended to heaven from the Temple Mount in Jerusalem.

Ramadan For non-Muslim visitors, the major effect of this month-long dawn-to-sunset fast is that the less commercial Muslim Arab areas are extremely quiet, with numerous businesses open for only limited hours.

Eid al-Fitr This is the great feast to mark the end of Ramadan. Muslims express their joy at the end of their fast by offering a congregational prayer, preferably in an open field. They express their gratitude to Allah for enabling them to observe the fast, thus preparing them for life as a Muslim. Special dishes are prepared and it is customary to visit relatives and friends, to go out for a day trip and to give presents to children. Everyone eats a great deal.

Eid al-Adha The most important feast of the Muslim calendar, Eid al-Adha commemorates the occasion when Allah asked Abraham to sacrifice his son, Ishmael. A lamb was sacrificed instead of the boy after Abraham had shown his readiness to obey Allah. Today Muslims offer congregational prayer on the day and follow it with a sacrifice mainly of sheep, but also goats or cows. The meat of the sacrificed animal is given to needy people and to older relatives; clothes and money are sometimes given, too.

Christian

Many visitors with a Christian background will find the festivals are celebrated very differently from the way they are used to. This is largely due to the domination of the Greek Orthodox Church, and also to the fact that Christianity is very much in third place in the religious stakes here. Christmas Day, for example (ignoring the fact that it is celebrated on three separate occasions by the various denominations), is just another day for most people. Even in Jerusalem there are no highly visible signs of the great event, such as decorated trees or street lights. Simply being here is the key for most of the pilgrims.

Christmas Day Apart from 25 December, Christmas is celebrated on 7 January by the Greek Orthodox and on 19 January by the Armenians. The event to attend is the midnight mass on Christmas Eve (24 December) which is held at Bethlehem's Church of the Nativity. During the day a procession

departs from Jerusalem for the church; however, due to the huge popularity of the service not everyone gets in. Pew space inside the church is reserved for ticket-holding observant Catholics only. The tickets, which are free, must be applied for in advance at the Terra Sancta office in the Christian Information Centre at Jaffa Gate in Jerusalem. The rest of the crowd, along with an international mass choir, congregates outside the church in Manger Square where a large video screen relays the service being conducted inside. It can be an extremely cold night, so wrap up well if you're going. Buses back to Jerusalem run irregularly all night.

Easter Celebrated first by the Protestants and the Roman Catholics, and then about two weeks later by the Orthodox Church, Easter means absolute chaos in Jerusalem's Old City. The Via Dolorosa and the narrow streets surrounding the Church of the Holy Sepulchre become clogged with pilgrims staking out their spots for the numerous services and processions. Take note that at this time of the year, pilgrims fill many of the cheap hotels and hostels in Jerusalem's Old City and completely block-book everything in Bethlehem.

Celebration of the Baptism of Jesus Christ The traditional site where John the Baptist baptised Jesus Christ is on the west bank of the Jordan River, a few kilometres from Jericho. The area has long been off-limits for security reasons and a baptism site further up the river was provided near the Sea of Galilee at Kibbutz Degania. However, the Roman Catholics have recently been able to organise a special celebration at the revered site in October. Contact the Christian Information Centre in Jerusalem for details, including transport arrangements.

Armenian Holocaust Day Every year on 24 April, the Armenians commemorate their overlooked tragedy with a parade and service in Jerusalem's Old City.

Public Holidays 2000

Jewish holidays follow a lunar calendar and so fall on a different date each year according to the western Gregorian calendar. For instance, in 1999 Rosh HaShanah, which marks the beginning of the Jewish new year, fell on 11 September, while in 2000, it is on 30 September. However, it will always fall around this time, unlike the Muslim holidays which, following the Islamic calendar, move back a number of days each year. Therefore, Ramadan, which starts on or around 9 December in 1999, will begin again around 28 November in 2000.

January
   Orthodox Christmas (5-6)
   Armenian Christmas (19)
   Tu B'Shevat (22)
March
   Eid al-Adha (16)
   Purim (21)
   Shushan Purim (22)
April
   Good Friday (2)
   Easter Sunday (4)
   Ras as-Sana (Muslim New Year) (6)
   Pesah (Passover) (20-26)
   Armenian Holocaust Day (24)
   Mimouna (27)
   Orthodox and Armenian Easter Sunday (30)
May
   Yom HaSho'ah (Holocaust Day) (2)
   Yom Ha'Atzmaut (Independence Day) (10)
   Lag B'Omer (23)
June
   Jerusalem Day (2)
   Shavuot (Pentecost) (9)
   Moulid an-Nabi (Prophet's Birthday) (15)
August
   Tish'a be-Av (10)
September
   Rosh HaShanah (30)
October
   Yom Kippur (9)
   Sukkot (14-20)
November
   Ramadan (28)
December
   Hanukkah (22-28)
   Western Christmas (25)
   Eid al-Fitr (28)

Special Events

February
   Jerusalem Musical Encounters (Jerusalem)
March
   International Festival of Poets (Jerusalem)
   International Judaica Fair (Jerusalem)
April
   Ein Gev Music Festival (Ein Gev, The Galilee)
   Music & Nature Days (Misgav)
May, June
   Israel Festival (Jerusalem)
June
   Blues Festival (Haifa)
July
   Hebrew Song Festival (Arad)
   Israel Folkdance Festival (Karmiel)
   International Film Festival (Jerusalem)
August
   International Puppet Theatre Festival
      (Jerusalem)
   Klezmer Festival (Safed)
   Red Sea Jazz Festival (Eilat)
September
   Early Music Workshop (Jerusalem)
October
   Fringe Theatre Festival (Akko)
   Film Festival (Haifa)
   Jerusalem Marathon (Jerusalem)
December
   International Christmas Choir Assembly
      (Nazareth)

For further details on the above holidays and special events, you should contact an Israeli Government tourist information office in your own country or any of the local tourist information offices within Israel. You could also consult an Israeli tourist information office for details of the public holidays in 2001.

ACTIVITIES

Israelis are very much outdoor types, belonging to a youthful nation still imbued with a pioneering spirit. They're encouraged in this by dint of living in such a geographically and geologically very diverse, yet at the same time compact, country. Two hours driving from Tel Aviv can have you skiing on the slopes of Mt Hermon or rafting on the Jordan River; alternatively, head off in another direction and you're into the desert, riding dune buggies or camel trekking. The majority of these activities have been developed for the benefit of the locals; however, they are also a great way for visitors to further experience the natural beauty of the country.

Hiking

With its changing landscapes, Israel offers a wealth of superb hiking opportunities, both leisurely and more strenuous. The regional chapters feature some of the more rewarding routes. In particular, look at exploring the Maktesh Ramon (see Mitzpe Ramon in the Negev chapter), the world's largest crater, and Ein Avdat (also in the Negev), which involves some canyon climbing to reach an ice-cold spring. Other excellent hikes include the route through Wadi Qelt (see Jerusalem to Jericho in The Gaza Strip & the West Bank chapter) and various trails up in the Golan region – see the introduction to that particular chapter.

We really can't stress enough that anyone interested in hiking should visit the SPNI shops in Jerusalem and Tel Aviv (see Information in the individual chapters for details etc), which carry an enormous range of specialist hiking maps – mainly in Hebrew, unfortunately, but the staff are willing to talk you through the routes and share their own experiences.

Cycling

Tours can be arranged with the Israel Cyclists' Touring Club, an affiliate of the International Bicycle Touring Society. Each tour is accompanied by a certified guide and an escort to handle any technical problems. You might also contact the Jerusalem Cycle Club (☎ 02-561 9416). See also Bicycle in the Getting Around chapter.

Horse Riding

Horse riding is widely available in the Galilee and the Golan regions (see Activities in that chapter) and at many places along the coast north of Tel Aviv, including: Kibbutz Nahsholim (☎ 06-639 9533, fax 639 7614) at Dor Bay on the coast north of Netanya; the Farm (☎ 09-866 3525) at HaVatzelet HaSharon, near Netanya; the Cactus Ranch

(☎ 09-865 1239), in Netanya; Herod's Stables (☎ 06-836 1181) at Caesarea; the Mekhora Stables (☎ 04-984 2735) at Kerem Maharal, 5km north of Zichron Ya'acov; and the Riders' Ranch (☎ 04-830 7242) at Beit Oren, 10km south of Haifa.

Elsewhere, try Moshav Neve Ilan (☎ 02-534 8111), 15km from Jerusalem, the Municipal Farm (☎ 07-672 6608) at Migdal in Ashkelon and the Texas Ranch in Eilat (see the Negev chapter).

Rafting & Kayaking

See the activities section in the Upper Galilee & the Golan chapter.

Beaches & Watersports

Although it's a bit of a distance from Tel Aviv, one of Israel's most attractive stretches of sand is at Dor, on the northern coast 29km south of Haifa. Otherwise, the beaches at Bat Yam (a suburb of Tel Aviv), Tel Aviv itself, Netanya and Dor are all excellent. As you start getting up towards Haifa, the water becomes polluted and jellyfish start to be a problem. The beaches at Eilat are almost certainly crowded and aren't all that enticing.

With the Red and Mediterranean seas and the Sea of Galilee, there are ample opportunities to enjoy the pleasures of swimming, windsurfing and sailing. Eilat is the watersports capital offering everything from parasailing to water-skiing. It's also a major scuba diving centre – although the sites along the Sinai coast are far superior. An interesting option is to dive at Caesarea where you can explore the underwater ruins of Herod's city. Contact the diving club at Caesarea (☎ 06-636 1787).

Skiing

Israel has just the one ski centre, at Mt Hermon in the extreme north of the country. The season begins in late December/January and lasts until mid-April. There are long and short-distance chair lifts, a ski school and equipment for hire. It's not cheap, however. See the Mt Hermon Ski Centre section in the Upper Galilee & the Golan chapter.

Birdwatching

Israel is the world's second-largest bird migratory fly way after South America. Eilat's International Birdwatching Centre (see Eilat in the Negev chapter) is the best site to appreciate this and to find out about other locations. The other major place for birdwatching is up in the Golan and there are special birdwatching centres at Beit Ussishkin, Kibbutz Dan and at the Hula and Gamla nature reserves.

For raptors and migratory route information call ☎ 02-932 383/4. There's also an ornithological centre in Tel Aviv (☎ 03-682 6802) at 155 Herzl St, south of the Shalom Tower.

COURSES

Some of the Israeli universities run overseas student programs in various subjects, including Hebrew, Arabic and Middle Eastern studies. It is not always necessary to speak Hebrew to enrol, although you will often need to study the language as part of the curriculum. Contact the nearest Israeli Government tourist information office in your home country for information.

Language

After a few weeks in Israel, it's not uncommon for travellers to find that they want to learn Hebrew or Arabic. Unfortunately, finding a place to learn Hebrew in Israel is neither cheap nor easy, and to learn Arabic can be even harder.

The *ulpanim* (language schools) network caters for new Jewish immigrants and is generally not welcoming of non-Jews; however, you might try contacting the Ulpan Office, Division of Adult Education (☎ 02-625 4156), 11 Beit Ha'am, Bezalel St, Jerusalem 94591.

The Ulpan Akiva Netanya (☎ 09-835 2312/3, fax 865 2919, Web site www.virtual.co.il/education/u_akiva/), PO Box 6086, Netanya 42160, is an international school for Jews and non-Jews and has various programs for learning Hebrew and Arabic. Fees for the 24 day program are US$1875, including tuition, cultural activities, accommodation and meals. Courses of eight, 12 and 16 to 20 weeks are also available for varying fees.

Kibbutz Ulpan is a 4½ or six month program for those who want to learn Hebrew and experience life on a kibbutz. Students spend half the day at work and the other half studying, six days a week. For more information you can contact your nearest kibbutz office or the Kibbutz Aliyah Desk (☎ 212-318 6130, fax 318 6134) at 110E 59th St, 4th Floor, New York, NY 10022, USA.

Birzeit University, north of Jerusalem on the West Bank, offers numerous courses in Arabic language and literature to beginners and more experienced students. For full details check out the Birzeit University Web site (see Internet Resources earlier in this chapter).

Bible Studies

St George's College (☎ 02-589 4704/5, fax 589 4703) PO Box 19018, 20 Nablus Rd, Jerusalem, describes itself as a centre for fieldwork, study and reflection in the Holy Land, allowing you to study the Bible in its appropriate geographical setting. The college has courses that include Bible study, field trips throughout the Holy Land as well as to Sinai, lasting from 16 days (US$1500) to three (US$1720), four (US$2250) or 10 weeks (US$5100). Course headings include The Bible and the Holy Land Today, The Palestine of Jesus, and The Bible and its Setting. Food and board are included.

Diving

For details of scuba diving courses, see the Eilat section in the Negev chapter.

WORK

Many people automatically associate a visit to Israel with a spell as a kibbutz or moshav volunteer and every year thousands of young people descend on the Holy Land for the experience. However, the reality of life on a kibbutz or moshav is often clouded by inaccurate images presented by recruitment organisations, many of which (especially those dealing with moshavim) seem to be motivated more by making a fast buck than developing the flow of milk and honey.

Many volunteers are actually extremely disappointed with what they find. The hostels of Tel Aviv are packed with ex-kibbutzers who couldn't wait to get out. Before committing yourself to a volunteer program you should study carefully what it actually involves.

When it comes down to discussing which kibbutzim or moshavim are the 'best', it's difficult to recommend individual sites. Location and the type of work carried out are often less important than the more random factors like who you work with, the kibbutzniks you work for and your relationships with both parties. What might be a fantastic place for one volunteer may well be a living hell for another.

Kibbutz Volunteers

To be accepted as a kibbutz volunteer you need to be 18 to 32 and in good physical and mental health. You will be expected to work hard at whatever job is assigned to you, eight hours a day, six days a week for a minimum of two months.

Agriculture has always been the mainstay of every kibbutz, but as most now have some form of light industry as well, volunteers can as easily find themselves working on production lines in factories as out in the fields picking fruit. Another possibility is that you will be assigned as a service worker, attached to the dining room, kitchen or laundry. Working with kibbutz children is uncommon because of the language barrier.

Volunteers are accommodated in separate quarters from the kibbutzniks, usually two or four to a room. The conditions in these quarters vary; some are extremely pleasant, but most, however, are old and/or have been poorly treated over the years by a succession of bored, frustrated and drunk volunteers.

In effect, volunteers work for their keep. The kibbutz generally provides the basic needs and also pays a small personal allowance (about US$50 per month). The facilities of the kibbutz are usually available

for volunteers to enjoy and these can include a swimming pool, sports facilities, a library and a cinema. Kibbutz-organised trips are also part of the deal and volunteers are taken on excursions to interesting sites around the country, often including places that most visitors would not get to see.

There is sometimes friction between volunteers and kibbutzniks. To earn any respect, a volunteer usually has to prove their efficiency at work over months rather than days or weeks. Even then, with volunteers arriving and leaving constantly, there's little motivation for the kibbutzniks to open up.

For their part, the volunteers are often aggrieved that their 'working holiday' is plenty of the former and little of the latter; too many days spent labouring under the Levantine sun rather than lying in it. However, the biggest cause of discontent is often not the work but the boredom.

Another preconceived idea about kibbutz volunteering is that it enables you to see the sights of Israel. It doesn't. With only one day off a week plus three more per month, it takes several months of snatched short trips to visit a significant amount of the country. Neither do kibbutzim make ideal tour bases, sited as they often are, well off the beaten track.

Despite all, most volunteers really enjoy their time on kibbutzim, even if it often does turn out to be very different to what they had expected. See the boxed text 'My Kibbutz Experience' in the Negev chapter.

Joining a Kibbutz There are basically four ways to go about becoming a volunteer. The first two involve contacting a kibbutz representative office in your own country, and either joining a group of about 15 people or travelling as an individual.

Groups fly out to Israel together, are met at Ben-Gurion airport and taken directly to the kibbutz. They normally stay on the kibbutz for three months and will have had an opportunity to meet one another and hear about their kibbutz before flying out.

If you travel as an individual you don't have to arrive on a preset date like the group, but within a month of your allocation. You are then given instructions on how to reach the kibbutz office and a letter of introduction guaranteeing you a place. As an individual you are not met at the airport in Israel and you will not necessarily get a place on a kibbutz immediately; you may have to wait a day or two in Tel Aviv, the expense of which is your own responsibility. Try not to arrive in Israel on a Friday, Saturday or just before a Jewish festival when the kibbutz office will be closed.

The kibbutz representatives charge a basic registration fee (about US$50) and arrange your flight – which generally costs more than you'd pay if you shopped around yourself. If you choose to join a group, you have no option but to fly with them, but as an individual you can register and then make your own travel arrangements. To find out more, contact your nearest kibbutz representative's office:

Australia
  Kibbutz Programme Centre (☎ 02-9360 6300) 104 Darlinghurst Rd, Darlinghurst NSW 2010
  Kibbutz Programme Desk (☎ 03-9272 5331, fax 9272 5640) 306 Hawthorn Rd, South Caulfield, Victoria 3162
Belgium
  Bureau de Volontaires (☎ 02-538 1050) 68 Ave Ducpetiaux, 1060 Bruxelles
Canada
  Israel Aliya Centre (☎ 604-257 5141) 950 W 41st Ave, Vancouver, BC V5Z 2N7
  Israel Programme Centre (☎ 613-789 5010) 151 Chapel St, Ottawa, ON K1N 7Y2
France
  Dror-Habonim, 32 rue Estelle, Marseille 13001
  Dror-Habonim, 9 rue Clement-Roassal, Nice 06000
  Dror-Habonim, 8 rue Idrac, Toulouse 31000
  Hachomer Hatsair, 12 rue Mulet, Lyon 69000
  Objectif Kibbutz, 15 rue Beranger, 75003 Paris
Germany
  Kibbutz Bewegung (☎ 69 740 14) Savignystr 49, 6600 Frankfurt 17
Netherlands
  Volunteers Desk, Jon Veermeerstr 24, Amsterdam 1071
New Zealand
  Kibbutz Programme Desk (☎ 04-384 4229) Jewish Community Centre Building, Kensington St, PO Box 27-156, Wellington

UK
  Kibbutz Representatives (☎ 020-8458 9235) 1A Accommodation Rd, London NW11
  Kibbutz Representatives (☎ 0151-722 5671) Harold House, Dunbabin Rd, Liverpool
  Kibbutz Representatives (☎ 0161-795 9447) 11 Upper Park Rd, Salford, Manchester M7 OHY
  Kibbutz Representatives (☎ 0141-620 2194) 222 Fenwick Rd, Glasgow
  Project 67 (☎ 020-7831 7626, fax 404 5588) 10 Hatton Garden, London EC1
USA
  Israel Aliyah Centre (Kibbutz), 6505 Wiltshire Blvd, Room 807, Los Angeles, California 90048
  Israel Aliyah Centre (Kibbutz), 4200 Biscayne Blvd, Miami, Florida 33137
  Israel Aliyah Centre (Kibbutz), Suite 1020, Statler Office Building, 20 Providence St, Boston, Massachusetts 02116
  Israel Aliyah Centre (Kibbutz), 10103 Fondern Rd (354), Houston, Texas 77096
  Kibbutz Aliyah Desk, 870 Market St (1083), San Francisco, California 94102
  Kibbutz Aliyah Desk, 2320 W Peterson, Suite 503, Chicago, Illinois 60659
  Kibbutz Aliyah Desk, 6600 West Maple Rd, West Bloomfield, Michigan 48033
  Kibbutz Aliyah Desk (☎ 212-318 6130, Web site www.kibbutz.qpg.com) 110 East 59th St, New York

Alternatively, would-be volunteers can make their own way to the kibbutz offices in Tel Aviv to apply there in person for a place. The movement discourages this path, but as only a few 'mavericks' adopt this approach there's a good chance that your application will be successful. Men stand a better chance of being placed as there are only two male applications for every eight female ones. The worst time to turn up is during July and August. Your success at being accepted is dependent not only on there being a suitable vacancy, but on you being able to convince the kibbutz officials that you are not a drug-crazed, beer-guzzling, youngster-perverting layabout.

The four offices in Tel Aviv are:

Kibbutz HaDati
  (☎ 03-525 7231) 7 Dubnov St. Only Jews are accepted here, with some religious observance

required. Office hours are limited so phone in advance.

Kibbutz Programme Centre
(☎ 03-527 8874) 18 Frishman St, corner of Ben Yehuda St; open Sunday to Thursday from 8 am to 2 pm

Meira's
(☎ 03-523 7369, fax 524 3811) 73 Ben Yehuda St, entrance behind the restaurant; open Sunday to Thursday from 9.30 am to 3 pm

Project 67
(☎ 03-523 0140, fax 524 7474) 94 Ben Yehuda St

The final way to become a volunteer is to apply directly to a kibbutz. This is not normally possible but can be done, for example if there is a desperate need for volunteers due to a crop harvest. It helps if you have a friend who is a volunteer already and can pull a few strings with the volunteer leader.

For further details, check out the Web site www.kibbutz.co.il or get hold of the excellent *Kibbutz Volunteer* by John Bedford (published in the UK by Vacation Work), which includes a breakdown of each kibbutz describing the work available, accommodation, entertainment and other facilities.

Moshav Volunteers

Moshav volunteers need to be aged 18 to 35 and have to commit themselves to a minimum five week stay. A moshav volunteer is normally assigned to an individual farmer although he or she will be bunked with other volunteers in shared accommodation. Most volunteers provide their own meals. Pay is US$260 per month for an eight hour day, six day working week. If food is provided, expect half of that. Overtime is often available although complaints about farmers not paying up are not uncommon.

The major differences between being a volunteer on a moshav as opposed to on a kibbutz are that the work is generally much harder (though often more varied and occasionally more interesting), and that the money is slightly better. However, relations between volunteers and moshavniks are just as strained as those on kibbutzim, and the isolation of the farming communities and the lack of social activities again contribute

to the pressure on volunteers to spend the small amount of money earned on drink.

Joining a Moshav Although there are moshav representatives in some countries, prospective volunteers can save themselves around US$100 by making their own way to Tel Aviv. The official moshav main office (☎ 03-695 8473) is downstairs at 19 Leonardo de Vinci St. From the central bus station in Tel Aviv, take bus No 70 on the opposite side of Petah Tikva St. It's open Sunday to Thursday from 9 am to noon.

You can also try Project 67 or Meira's (see earlier for addresses). Each volunteer has to take out a health insurance policy which includes coverage for hospitalisation. Volunteers are often in short supply, so as long as you present yourself as hard-working, punctual and well-behaved, you should have no problems and probably find work in a day or two.

Other Volunteer Projects

Palestinian Work Camps While these work camps are less well known than the kibbutz and moshav, their purpose is to promote solidarity with the Palestinian community, provide an opportunity for foreigners to meet Palestinians and also to assist them in community projects like road maintenance, rubbish collecting, painting, decorating and other odd jobs.

The work camps are mostly held during July/August and December. Volunteers pay their own travel expenses, a US$20 registration fee and provide their own spending money. Accommodation and some meals are provided, either with a family or in a school or tented camp. The work can be mundane, but for the politically motivated it's a very popular way to do something constructive and rewarding. If you want to participate, it's best to write both directly to the work camps and to the following UK/USA organisations as early as possible for the current schedules.

Israel
Al Hadaf (☎ 06-631 2040, fax 631 2915) PO Box 169, Um al-Fahm 30010

Al-Nahdah Centre (☎ 02-993 3035, fax 993 3018) PO Box 92, Taybeh 40400
Arab Association for Human Rights (☎ 06-656 1923, fax 656 4934) PO Box 215, 34/604 Mary's Well St, Nazareth 16100

UK

Friends of Beir Zeit University (FOBZU) (☎ 020-7373 8414) 21 Collingham Rd, London SW5 ONU
Witness for Palestine (☎ 020-7263 7187) 20 Dartmouth Park Hill, London NW5 1HL
Medical Aid for Palestine (☎ 020-7226 4114, Web site www.map-uk.demon.co.uk) 33A Islington Park St, London N1 1QB
Universities Fund for Palestinian Refugees (☎ 01223-211 864) 63 Holbrook Rd, Cambridge CB1 4SX

USA

Volunteers for Peace (☎ 802-259 2759, Web site www.vfp.org) 43 Tiffany Rd, Belmont, VT 05730

Medical & Social Work The organisations listed under work camps can also help with inquiries regarding other volunteer and salaried projects such as teaching, nursing and counselling.

Christian hospitals in Jerusalem and Nazareth, in particular, use volunteer nurses. These can be trained and qualified people or those willing to assist in feeding patients. In Jerusalem inquire at St Louis' French Hospital, next door to Notre Dame outside the Old City's New Gate; and in Nazareth, ask at the EMS, French and Italian hospitals. In Gaza, the Ahli Arab Hospital often requires experienced volunteer nurses. Inquire in person or write in advance to The Director, Ahli Arab Hospital, PO Box 72, Palestine Square, Gaza.

Volunteers for Israel During the dark days of Operation Peace for Galilee, when Israel invaded Lebanon (1982), this program was launched to place volunteers in noncombat support jobs in the IDF. The idea is to give more reserve soldiers time off to attend to family and business matters.

The 23 day program involves very menial duties in kitchens, stores – even some boot polishing. Volunteers are issued with military fatigues (you have to give them back at the end) and housed on a base, but are not armed.

Your air ticket to/from Israel is partially subsidised by the program if you stick it out, and you are allowed free time to travel (after all your work is done) before flying home. Contact the Israeli Government tourist information office in your own country or write to Volunteers for Israel (☎ 212-643 4848), 330 West 42nd St 1818, New York 10036.

Archaeological Digs Definitely not for gold-diggers, most archaeological digs require that you pay to work. In January of each year the Israeli Antiquities Authority (IAA), part of the Ministry of Education & Culture, publishes a list of the archaeological excavations open to volunteers for the coming year. To get yourself a copy, contact the IAA at the Rockefeller Museum (☎ 02-629 2627, fax 629 2628), PO Box 586, Jerusalem 91004. The requirements are that you be over 18 years old, fit and come fully insured.

The busy archaeological season is between May and September when universities are not in session and the weather is hot and dry. No previous excavating experience is usually necessary (it's not Indiana Jones they're wanting but his mule), but volunteers should be prepared to participate for a minimum of one or two weeks, depending on the individual dig. A fee for food and accommodation (varying from sleeping bags in a field to three star-type hotels) is required. Some expeditions do provide volunteers with an allowance for food, accommodation and/or travel expenses within Israel. The Institute of Archaeology at the Hebrew University of Jerusalem (☎ 02-588 2403/4, fax 582 5548), Mt Scopus, Jerusalem 91905, takes on board volunteers for week-long digs at a cost of around US$180, including room and meals, lectures and field trips.

For those interested in trying archaeology one day at a time, there's a tourist-oriented 'Dig for a Day' program operating during July and August and involving a three hour excavation, seminars and a tour. It costs about US$55. Contact Archaeological Seminars (☎ 02-627 3515, fax 627 2660, email office@archesem.com), PO Box 14002, 34 Habad St, Jerusalem 91140.

For further leads on what digs may be accepting volunteers, try contacting the Department of Antiquities & Museums in Jerusalem (☎ 02-629 2607, fax 629 2628, email harriet@israntique.org.il).

ACCOMMODATION

Israel has a wide range of accommodation with plenty of scope for both the big spenders and the budget travellers. Before you convert all your currency into shekels, remember that by paying in US dollars – where the option exists – you avoid the 17% VAT; in such cases we give the rates in US dollars rather than shekels.

Camping

While there are numerous country-wide camping areas, usually equipped with all necessary amenities, they aren't always the expected cheap alternative, and it's often better value to check into a hostel. Still, there are plenty of opportunities to pitch your tent for free. Camping seems to be tolerated on most public beaches, though notable exceptions include the Dead Sea shore, the Mediterranean coast north of Nahariya and in the Gaza Strip. Be careful – theft is very common on beaches, especially in Eilat, Tel Aviv and Haifa. For site locations and advance bookings contact the Israeli Camping Organisation (☎ 04-925 392), PO Box 53, Nahariya 22100.

Hostels

Israel has, at last count, 32 Hostelling International HI hostels. In the Dead Sea region and Mitzpe Ramon they are the sole budget accommodation choice, but elsewhere, privately owned hostels usually offer better value and service. Also, most HI hostels insist that you take breakfast rather than allowing you to provide your own at a fraction of the cost. Nonmembers can stay at HI hostels for usually only a couple more shekels than card holders so it isn't worth buying a card especially.

For a list of HI hostels and further information, contact the Israel Youth Hostels Association (☎ 02-655 84006, fax 655 8432, email iyha@netvision.net.il), International Convention Centre (6th Floor), PO Box 6001, Jerusalem 91060. The International Convention Centre is west of the city centre, about 500m south of the new bus station and the office is open Sunday to Thursday from 8.30 am to 3 pm and Friday from 9 am to noon. Visit their Web site (www.youth-hostels.org.il) for further details.

Kibbutz Guesthouses

The kibbutzim have had to search for alternatives to agriculture for their income, and in recent years they have been developing the concept of running guesthouses. Originally designed for fellow Israelis as a rustic escape from city life, they are now more upmarket and attract overseas visitors as well. They mainly fit into the mid-range price and have good facilities such as swimming pools or beaches, renowned restaurants and special activities for guests. Mostly located in the countryside, they can be inconvenient for travellers relying heavily on public transport. However, for those with a car they can be a great alternative to hotels, especially in the Dead Sea area, the Galilee and the Golan.

The Kibbutz Hotels Reservations Centre (☎ 03-524 6161, fax 527 8088, email info@kibbutz.co.il) at 90 Ben Yehuda St, PO Box 3194, Tel Aviv 61031, publishes a booklet listing all their hotels, restaurants and campsites with prices, amenities and a map (also available at government tourist information offices). They will make all bookings for you and do not charge any commission, but they will accept only faxed reservations.

Christian Hospices

Various Christian denominations have accommodation in the vicinity of their religious sites. They are often the best value in the low to moderate price range, with cleanliness seemingly the top priority. You do not need to be a Christian to stay in most of these hospices, but you must be prepared to abide by the rules, which usually involve a strict curfew, an early check-out time and no double rooms for unmarried couples. Some hospices, however, are extremely informal and are more like regular guesthouses or hotels.

Hotels

In comparison to the number of lower and mid-range priced beds available, Israel has a disproportionately high percentage of luxury accommodation –, but then this is a country in which the Minister of Tourism once told an international travel trade conference that Israel 'does not want budget travellers'. In fact, the Israeli state goes as far as to sponsor and subsidise the construction of new upmarket hotels. Except during the high season (see the boxed text 'When To Go' at the beginning of this chapter), prices at these hotels compare favourably with those in other parts of the world and, attuned as they are to a predominantly North American clientele, the facilities and level of service are top class.

However, some of these hotels also have some very iniquitous 'service charges'; for instance, at the Tel Aviv Ramada, on top of the usual outrageous prices for bar fridge items, a little green plastic tab stuck on the fridge door reads 'Daily charge for rental of fridge – US$3'. The tab has to be torn to open the fridge so, if you buy a Coke from a shop and want to keep it cool in your room, management are going to know and you'll be charged for use of fridge space.

Many of the luxury hotels in Israel are, of course, equipped to cater for the needs of the observant Jew which means kosher kitchens, in-hotel synagogues and Shabbat clocks and elevators (on the Sabbath observant Jews must refrain from operating machinery, which extends even to pushing buttons. To get around that Shabbat lifts automatically stop on every floor).

Note that the Israeli Ministry of Tourism no longer operates a star system (apparently it was too much of a headache dealing with slighted four-star managers), so in this book we use terms like five star-type and three star-type purely in a descriptive sense.

The Israel Hotel Association (☎ 03-517 0131, fax 510 0197, email info@israelhotels .org.il) has a Web site listing all its hotels (www.israelhotels.org.il) and publishes a useful booklet listing all member hotels and kibbutz hotels. The head office is at 29 Ha-Mered St, Tel Aviv (PO Box 50066).

B&Bs

In many popular tourist areas you will find B&B accommodation in private homes. In some places they form the bulk of moderately priced rooms. They can be found by inquiring at the local tourist information office, looking for signs posted in the street or, in some places, by simply hanging out at the bus station with your bags.

Jerusalem is particularly well served by B&B establishments. The Home Accommodation Association of Jerusalem (HAAJ) maintains a growing list of over 30 establishments. These range from self-contained apartment studios to simple rooms with private facilities. In many cases, breakfast is offered as part of the deal. Prices range from US$25 to US$70 and, in at least 13 cases, bookings can be made effortlessly via email.

Check the HAAJ's Web site (www.bnb .co.il) for further details.

FOOD

Despite the loud and constant claims that Israel offers an incredible variety of international cuisine, you may find that outside of cosmopolitan Tel Aviv, the majority of the food is disappointing and almost definitely expensive.

Budget travellers will find that eating out on a regular basis will ruin them financially. Fortunately most of the hostels have a communal kitchen for guests, so you can go shopping in the street markets, grocery stores and supermarkets and then cook your own meals.

Other than that, the travellers' staple in Israel is *felafel*, ground chickpeas blended with herbs and spices, shaped into a ball and then deep-fried in oil. They are not particu-

Big Mac Attack

According to Judaism, every meal is a religious rite and so has to be *kosher*, which roughly translated means 'ritually acceptable'. Defining what is and is not kosher, however, is not so simple.

Genesis 1:29 permits all fruit and vegetables, and 'clean' animals (7:2). 'Clean' is taken to mean animals that chew the cud and have wholly cloven hooves (Leviticus 11; Deuteronomy 14). 'Clean' birds, according to the Mishnah, must have a crop, a gizzard and an extra talon – for example chicken and turkey – while only fish that have at least one fin and easily removable scales are acceptable.

There are other rules that specify exactly how an animal must be slaughtered and which parts may be eaten. But of all the rules of *kashrut* (the noun from kosher), the most intriguing is that forbidding the mixing of meat and dairy products. Exodus 23:19 states that 'you shall not seethe a kid in its mother's milk', which is interpreted by orthodox Jews to mean that they cannot cook or eat meat and milk (including all dairy products) together. So, no chicken in cream sauce, no fish in batter, no tea with milk in a meat restaurant. American-style fast food chains have failed in the past in Israel because they cannot put cheese or mayonnaise on top of hamburgers.

Despite the largely secular nature of modern Israeli society, a 1995 survey revealed that 90% of Jewish Israelis observe at least some of the requirements of the dietary laws. It makes sense then for local restaurants to be kosher. To gain official recognition as such they have to submit to regular check-ups carried out by rabbinical inspectors. Kosher criteria doesn't stop at the kitchen, either; in recent years one Jerusalem restaurant found itself threatened with the removal of its kosher licence for having a Christmas tree on the pavement outside.

That said, on Shamai St in central Jerusalem, there is a large cheeseburger-selling McDonald's and it is always crowded. A spokesperson for the restaurant has said that its meat is kosher and anybody is free not to eat cheese with their burger. This has failed to placate the orthodox community, which has responded by fly-posting denunciations of the company and exhorting Jews to stay off the Big Macs. In light of the considerable ultraorthodox gains in the elections to the Knesset, don't count on having burger, fries and a shake as part of your Jerusalem diet.

larly tasty, but covered in *tahina* (a thin paste made from sesame seeds) and served with an assortment of salads in a pitta bread, they are palatable, fairly substantial and, more importantly, cheap at anywhere from 6 to 12NIS (US$1.50 to US$3).

The most popular way to eat meat is as *shwarma*, also known elsewhere as doner kebab. This is lamb, or sometimes turkey or chicken, sliced from a revolving vertical spit and stuffed, along with salad, into a pitta or rolled in a plate-sized piece of *laffa* bread. Shwarma typically costs 14 to 18NIS (US$3.50 to US$4.50).

The other good deal on offer is fruit, of which Israel (with its varied climate) produces a wide range, including oranges, apples, mangoes, guava, melons, persimmons, pomegranates, lemons, figs, dates and avocadoes. Visit the street markets late in the afternoon for the best bargains, especially on a Friday. Look out, in particular, for the *sabra*, a cactus fruit that looks like a hand grenade which was imported to Palestine from Mexico a few centuries ago. Israeli-born Jews are nicknamed 'sabra' after the fruit; tough and prickly on the outside, soft and sweet on the inside. Sabra is sold on the streets everywhere when in season, but it's an acquired taste. The seeds give the locals another chance to use their unsurpassed spitting skills.

Vegetarian Food

The kosher laws of Judaism ensure that Israel is a dream for vegetarians, with numerous dairy-only restaurants.

One place in particular worth visiting is Taste of Life (60 Ben Yehuda St) in Tel Aviv run by Black Hebrews. This place uses no animal products whatsoever, meat or dairy, and they're inexpensive. They make and serve their own tofu dishes, with convincing versions of such meat dishes as shwarma and hot dogs, and dairy foods like cheese, yoghurt, ice cream and shakes. There's a sister establishment in Tiberias.

Oriental Jewish

Oriental food was brought to Israel by Jews immigrating from the Arab countries, most notably, in terms of cuisine, from Yemen. In addition to salads, felafel and shwarma, oriental restaurants specialise in flame-grilled meats, either *shashlik*, which is chunks, or *kebab*, which is minced. Lamb, beef and chicken are the most popular meats cooked this way, but oriental kitchens are especially renowned for offal dishes. Turkey testicles, cow's udder, spleen and heart all taste a lot better than they sound and they also tend to be relatively inexpensive.

One of the tastiest aspects of oriental Jewish cooking is the art of stuffing vegetables and meat with rice, nuts, meat and spices. Most Yemenite restaurants have a varied selection of stuffed vegetables as starters, but one or two on their own make for an ample meal.

Eastern European Jewish

Eastern European food is characterised by the familiar Viennese schnitzel, Hungarian goulash, and *gefilte* fish. Most Israelis we met completely denied enjoying the latter, which consists of ball-shaped pieces of fish heads and tails served chilled. Much more appetising are *blintzes*, a type of heavy pancake typically filled with something savoury such as mushrooms or cheese – though never meat because of kosher laws. Romanian restaurants are also among some of Israel's best, particularly good for steaks and liver.

On Shabbat, most secular Jews join the religious and follow the traditional rule of no cooking. For many, this will mean eating *cholent*, a heavy stew prepared before sunset on Friday.

Palestinian

Felafel originates from the Arab world, as does tahina and its close cousin, *humous* (a thick paste made from chickpeas, tahina and seasonings). These three, with accompanying vinegary salads and bread, form the backbone of most menus at the cheap sit-down Arab restaurants, along with *fuul* (pronounced 'fool'), mashed up fava beans often flavoured with garlic.

More upmarket places will also serve grilled chicken, shwarma and shashlik and, if you're lucky, *mansaf*, a Palestinian dish of rice with small pieces of lamb, nuts, lemon juice and herbs.

Mansaf is a speciality of Hebron and Jericho, while specific to the Jerusalem region is *maklubi*, an upside-down dish of rice, lamb, eggplant and other vegetables. From Nablus and the north comes *musakan*, chicken cooked on the fire with olive oil, onions and *sumak*, a red-coloured lemony spice, served on pitta bread.

Other Palestinian dishes include *melok*, a soup made from greens, and *kubbe*, minced spiced lamb or beef mixed with *burghul* (cracked wheat) and deep fried. Kubbe is also available in oriental Jewish and Armenian establishments.

If in a restaurant you are offered *mezze*, this is a selection of starters which typically includes humous, stuffed vine leaves, brain salad, eggplant puree, olives and pickles.

Arab Sweets & Pastries

Usually soaked in honey and full of sugar, these edible highlights of Arab cuisine can't be good for you, but who cares? *Baklava* is like toasted shredded wheat, stuffed with pistachios or hazelnuts and drowned in honey, while *katayeef* and *kunafeh* are concoctions of cheese, wheat, sugar and honey. For the best kunafeh, visit Nablus where you can also get the Arab version of Turkish Delight.

Breads

Israel has a delicious selection of breads, both Jewish and Arabic. Many travellers make the mistake of assuming that the cheapest is *pitta*, the small, flat, round loaves produced by the Arabs and oriental Jews. Not true. If you are counting every agorot, then buying the subsidised Jewish standard white loaves from grocery stores and supermarkets will cost you around half the price. *Hallah*, a softer style of bread, is baked for Shabbat. Jewish bakeries produce sweet breads, too. Glazed with sugar syrup, filled with currants or chocolate, they vary in quality, but can be great. *Matza* is the unleavened bread eaten by Jews during Passover.

Oriental Jewish bakeries produce similar breads to the Arabs. Iraqi pitta is very thin and resembles a large pancake. Arabs mainly bake pitta, and it can be thickly covered with sesame seeds or sprinkled with *za'atar* or *dogga*, a mixture of herbs (mainly oregano) and spices – it's served separately with pitta and bagels, which you dip into the mixture after dipping them in olive oil.

Bagels are very popular; originally from Eastern Europe, Israeli bagels are different from most others, being crisper and drier. In Tel Aviv, a softer style – sprinkled with sesame seeds – is produced. A traditional way to end a night out is to visit the bagel factory and pick up a hot bagel or two. Arab bagels are similar, but larger. In East Jerusalem and the Old City they are sold from carts everywhere. A variation of the Arab bagel is *ka'ak*, a ring of bread covered with sesame seeds and eaten with za'atar, hard boiled eggs, cheese or felafel.

DRINKS
Nonalcoholic Drinks

Tea and coffee are Israel's most popular beverages. The Arabs usually serve tea in a glass, black, very sweet (if you don't want sugar say so when you order) and often with *na'ana* (mint), which is extremely refreshing even on a hot day. Jews serve tea black, with lemon, milk or nondairy creamer to satisfy the kosher laws.

Coffee here is generally strong, black coffee; if what you want is something like a Nescafé then ask for 'milk coffee' or 'nes'. Beware the cappuccino which often resembles something closer to a knickerbocker glory minus the fruit. Arabs and oriental Jews often serve bitter Turkish-style coffee flavoured with *hehl* (cardamom).

Soft drinks in Israel are expensive. Save a small fortune by buying family sized bottles at supermarkets and grocery shops. For example, a small bottle of Coke from a street vendor can be 7 or 8NIS, while a 1.5 litre bottle of the same from a grocery shop may be only a few shekels more. Freshly squeezed fruit juices are widely available.

Tamar hindi (tamarind juice), *asir tamar* (date juice) and *asir loz* (almond juice) are traditional Palestinian drinks. Very sweet, they're sold in the Damascus Gate area of East Jerusalem, dispensed from a big silver 'coffee pot' worn on the seller's back. At Arab cafes you may also see a yellowish-green hot drink called *yansoon*, which is an aniseed herbal tea; it may taste a little too medicinal for your liking. *Sahlab*, served hot in winter, cold in summer, is made from a tapioca-like powder mixed with milk, coconut, sugar, raisins and chopped nuts.

Alcoholic Drinks

Beer The National Brewery Ltd controls 98% of the beer market. At the bottom of the range is the little-seen Nesher (3.8% alcohol), which is not served by most bars or cafes but, when found, is the cheapest beer on the market. Goldstar (4.7%) is the most popular beer with travellers, both bottled and draught, while Maccabee (4.9%) is the Israeli favourite, considered upmarket and the only beer that Israel exports.

A relative newcomer is Taybeh, the product of a small, private Palestinian-run brewery in the West Bank town of the same name. It's available in most supermarkets and you will probably find it on tap in places like Ramallah in the West Bank.

Of the imported beers, Carlsberg and Heineken predominate and cost between 8 and 20NIS for a half-litre glass. Boutique beer lovers will appreciate Tel Aviv's only brewery-pub where you can sample some pretty decent if expensive locally brewed ales.

Wine & Spirits Although you will see several shelves in supermarkets and grocery shops lined with bottles of wine and spirits, Israelis don't drink much. There has been an increase in consumption among younger Israelis, but for most Jews wine is only drunk on holy days such as Shabbat and during Passover and Purim. Spirits are hardly touched at all. The Arab Muslim population also, of course, abstains.

However, vines and wines have existed in the Holy Land since 3000 BC, making it one of the world's oldest wine-producing areas. The pre-eminent producer today is the Carmel cooperative which produces some internationally competitive wines, although to date the best efforts have come from the the Golan's Yarden and Gamla vineyards.

The quality of Israeli wines is often exaggerated, but some fierce competition has at least kept prices low and you'll always find the best buys in supermarkets where a decent Chardonnay goes for about 14NIS a bottle.

Arak and brandy are the best-selling Israeli spirits. *Arak* is an Arabic word and covers many different spirits. It is distilled from various fermented bases such as vine, rice, palm sap, yams and dates. Ramallah is reputedly the best arak in Israel; normally only available in Jaffa, its label is written in Arabic and it comes in a square-shaped bottle. Good Israeli brandies are Stock, Carmel's 777 and Carmei-Zion's Grand 41.

Vermouths and fortified wines, mainly sherry and port, are also produced locally. Other than the Stock range, their dusty state on shop shelves is more than justified. More successful are some of the Israeli liqueurs, especially Carmei-Zion's Hallelujah, a sort of Jewish Grand Marnier.

ENTERTAINMENT

With a much more liberal society than its Middle East neighbours, Israel has a variety of entertainment sources, much of it similar to what you find in the west. Under a general heading of 'nightlife', you can find an increasing number of bars in most towns, along with different versions of discos and live music venues. Classical music concerts, usually of an excellent standard, are frequently staged throughout the country.

Cinema is very popular with Israelis and most cities and larger towns have at least one multiscreen movie house. Standard Hollywood fare prevails, although there are a couple of specialist art house-type places in Tel Aviv, and the Cinematheque chain screens a lot of European as well as non-mainstream stuff. Films are nearly always left in their original language and subtitled into Hebrew. Tickets cost about 27NIS.

Israel has an active theatre and dance scene but, as in many places, it faces an increasing struggle for funds and an audience. Most performances are in Hebrew, although if you look in the Jerusalem and Tel Aviv chapters you will find some concessions to the English-language speakers.

For sports fans, Israel's small population and political isolation reduces the choice of spectator sports to soccer, basketball, the occasional tennis tournament and the Maccabiah Games.

Arab entertainment sources are limited to music of neighbouring Arab nations, mainly Egypt, and a small theatre in East Jerusalem (see the Entertainment section in the Jerusalem chapter). An invitation to a wedding is the best way of seeing a performance of some wonderful music, song and dance.

SHOPPING

Israel is full of shops stocked with tacky souvenirs for gullible tourists. To find bargains and quality items you'll need to shop around and haggle (see Tipping & Bargaining under Money earlier in this chapter).

Products made out of minerals and mud from the Dead Sea are popular and presumably healthy souvenirs, but they tend to be very expensive if bought at the Dead Sea tourist shops. Consider buying directly from, say, the Ahava store in Jerusalem or even the airport duty free shop, if you are keen.

Not all your shopping needs to be done in markets. Some of Israel's best buys are luxury items from regular shops and galleries. It's worth remembering that some shops give a special discount if you pay in foreign currency. Check prices elsewhere all the same, even without a discount, they may be cheaper. Don't forget you can always pick up duty free gifts at the airport where there is a wide range of products available.

Sandals

Most travellers seem to feel that they have to buy a pair of sandals, with Jerusalem's Old City being the obvious place. If you are passing through Greece at some point on this trip, buy your sandals there – the Old City Arabs do. Jewish shoe shops offer better quality, but they are more expensive.

Ceramics

Some good quality ceramics in modern and traditional styles are available. Tiles and plates are very popular – the Armenians are recognised as the leading makers of these. The best selection is in Jerusalem's Old City – take a look at Jerusalem Pottery on the Via Dolorosa near the 6th Station, at the two places on Armenian Patriarchate Rd and at the Palestinian pottery workshop across from the US consulate in East Jerusalem.

Copper & Brassware

Oriental coffee pots and trays, *nargilas* (hubble-bubble pipes), and other ornaments are ubiquitous. Shop around and check Jaffa's flea market, Jerusalem's Old City and Mea She'arim, Nazareth and Akko in particular.

Antiquities

Israel is alone among the Mediterranean seaboard nations in allowing the free sale and export of its antiquities. What could earn you a stiff jail sentence in Greece or Egypt, can provide you with an unusual and often inexpensive memento from biblical times for your mantelpiece or your collection of travel artefacts. For about US$10 you can pick up the odd Roman coin or two, or for a hefty US$50,000 you can have a very ancient, though admittedly a rather scabby-looking sword from the time of Abraham. However, an Abraham-era arrowhead will only set you back a mere US$250. Jerusalem's Old City is the best place to find antiquities to buy.

Woodwork

Olive wood is very popular and there are souvenirs for all budgets. The most common items are crucifixes, camels, worry beads and carvings of biblical characters. Olive woodcarvings are available everywhere.

Glassware

Loud claims are made about this industry in Israel, but we saw little to inspire. Hebron is the recognised leader in the field and buying there should save money.

Canework & Basketware

Gaza produces the best canework and it's sold all over the country – furniture, baskets, decorative pieces and trays. Basketware materials include rushes and raffia and are coloured with different interwoven shades.

Jewellery

Israel is one of the world's diamond centres, but if you're reading this book then it's a safe bet you are not a 24 carat shopper. Anyway, where's the originality in a diamond? For uniqueness take a look at the jewellery handmade by the Black Hebrews – Jerusalem's Ben Yehuda St and Tel Aviv's Dizengoff St are the busiest street-selling zones. Yemenite jewellery is characterised by a delicate style of intricately joined metals and is really quite beautiful. We saw some attractive examples in Jaffa, and they weren't too expensive. Bedouin work is heavier and more roughly executed – it goes well with pit boots and attitude. Worth visiting is the Thursday morning market in Beersheba to see some of this work (see that section in the Negev chapter).

Getting There & Away

Air is the most common means of getting to Israel. Ben-Gurion airport, situated midway between Jerusalem and Tel Aviv, is the country's busy international air gateway. There is also the option of sailing from Cyprus or Greece or coming in overland via Jordan or, more likely, Egypt (the borders with Syria and Lebanon are closed).

AIR

Airfares to Israel vary considerably according to season. July to September, and Jewish holidays in particular, mean much higher prices (see the boxed text 'When to Go' at the beginning of the Facts for the Visitor chapter). When checking out fares also look into flights to Ovda, a small military airport 60km north of Eilat which is commonly used by cheap charters from Manchester, London and Amsterdam from December to March. Also, with daily bus connections to both Tel Aviv and Jerusalem from Egypt (see under Egypt in the Land section later in this chapter), flying in to Cairo, or Sharm el-Sheikh in Sinai, may be an option worth considering.

Airports

The country's main international air terminal is Ben-Gurion airport at Lod, 18km east of Tel Aviv and 50km from Jerusalem. There are regular buses to both cities, as well as to Haifa and Beersheba.

On arrival at Ben-Gurion airport, passage through the arrivals terminal is usually fairly swift. Outside to the right are the taxi stands and to the left are the *sheruts* (minibuses/service taxis) to Jerusalem and buses for destinations including Jerusalem, Tel Aviv, Beersheba and Haifa.

Israel's other international airport is Ovda, located in the desert about 60km north of Eilat, which is used mainly by charter flights. Two regular buses shuttle between the airport and Eilat from where bus connections can be made for the rest of the country.

There's also Eilat airport, used mainly for domestic services (flown by Arkia), although a few international El Al flights land here too. Bizarrely, Eilat airport is located smack in the centre of town, which at least puts it within walking distance of almost all the hotels and hostels. Plans are afoot to scrap Eilat airport because of the rising value of the real estate it occupies. Eilat airport and Ovda will eventually be replaced by a new major international airport somewhere on the outskirts of town, built in cooperation with the Jordanians. This is unlikely to be completed during the lifetime of this book.

From Ben-Gurion Airport to Tel Aviv

For Tel Aviv, take Tourbus bus No 222, which departs hourly and makes several stops along HaYarkon St in the city's central hotel and hostel district. The trip takes 35 minutes and costs 15NIS. Alternatively, Egged buses take you to the city's central bus station (45 minutes) where you take a city bus to get to your ultimate destination (see Getting Around in the Tel Aviv chapter).

The buses run between 4 am and midnight except on Friday when the last bus departs at 6.45 pm and on Saturday when the first bus is at noon. Don't rely on getting to the airport on the last (midnight) scheduled bus. Reliable sources suggest it never arrives. At other hours you may be lucky and find a sherut heading to the city centre (ask at the Jerusalem sherut stand) otherwise you'll have to resort to a taxi.

From Ben-Gurion Airport to Jerusalem

The only cheap way into Jerusalem is by the regular Egged buses No 947 or 945 which depart every half-hour to Jerusalem's central bus station (35-40 minutes, 17NIS), then take an Egged city bus to wherever you want to go (see Getting Around in the Jerusalem chapter).

The most convenient but more expensive way to get to the Old City or East Jerusalem is to take a sherut from just outside the arrivals building. The sheruts run all night, departing whenever they're full, and the fare is US$10 (40NIS). 'Special' (ie nonshared) taxis are available for all destinations but are much more expensive. To protect arrivals from rip-off tactics, authorities have posted most fares on a massive sign. Check this carefully before you're hustled into a cab.

There are two rates: daytime rates apply from 5.30 am to 9 pm; night-time rates from 9 pm to 5.30 am. Sample daytime fares are Tel Aviv 60NIS (US$20), Haifa 220NIS (US$72), Netanya 90NIS (US$30) and Jerusalem 95NIS (US$32); night-time fares are approximately 30% higher.

Buying Tickets

The plane ticket will probably be the single most expensive item in your budget, and buying it can be an intimidating business. There is likely to be a multitude of airlines and travel agents hoping to separate you from your money, and it is always worth putting aside a few hours to research the current state of the market. Start early: some of the cheapest tickets have to be bought months in advance, and some popular flights sell out early. Talk to other recent travellers – they may be able to stop you making some of the same old mistakes. Look at the ads in newspapers and magazines and watch out for special offers. Then phone around different travel agents for bargains. (Airlines can supply information on routes and timetables; however, except at times of interairline war, they do not supply the cheapest tickets.) Find out the fare, the route, the duration of the journey and any restrictions on the ticket (see Restrictions in the Air Travel Glossary), then sit back and decide which is the best option for you.

You may discover that those impossibly cheap flights are 'fully booked, but we have another one that's a bit more ... '. Or the flight is on an airline notorious for its poor safety standards and then leaves you in the world's least favourite airport in mid-journey for 14 hours. Or they claim only to have the last two seats available for that country for the whole of July, which they will hold for you for a maximum of two hours. Don't panic – keep ringing around.

Use the fares quoted in this book as a guide only. They are approximate and based on the rates advertised by travel agents at the time of going to press. Quoted airfares do not necessarily constitute a recommendation for the carrier.

If you are travelling from the UK or the USA, you will probably find that the cheapest flights are being advertised by obscure bucket shops whose names haven't yet reached the telephone directory. Many such firms are honest and solvent, but there are a few rogues who will take your money and disappear, to reopen elsewhere a month or two later under a new name. If you feel suspicious about a firm, don't give them all the money at once – leave a deposit of 20% or

WARNING

The information in this chapter is particularly vulnerable to change: prices for international travel are volatile, special deals come and go, routes are introduced and cancelled, schedules change, and rules and visa requirements are amended. Airlines and governments seem to take a perverse pleasure in making price structures and regulations as complicated as possible. You should check directly with the airline or a travel agent to make sure you understand how a fare (and ticket you may buy) works. In addition, the travel industry is highly competitive and there are many lurks and perks.

The upshot of this is that you should get opinions, quotes and advice from as many airlines and travel agents as possible before you part with your hard-earned cash. All the details given in this chapter should be regarded as pointers and are not a substitute for your own careful, up-to-date research.

Air Travel Glossary

Baggage Allowance This will be written on your ticket and usually includes one 20kg item to be stored in the hold, plus one item of hand luggage.

Bucket Shops These are unbonded travel agencies specialising in discounted airline tickets.

Bumped Just because you have a confirmed seat doesn't mean you're going to get on the plane (see Overbooking).

Cancellation Penalties If you have to cancel or change a discounted ticket, there are often heavy penalties involved; insurance can sometimes be taken out against these penalties. Some airlines impose penalties on regular tickets as well, particularly against 'no-show' passengers.

Check-In Airlines ask you to check in a certain time ahead of the flight departure (usually one to two hours on international flights). If you fail to check in on time and the flight is overbooked, the airline can cancel your booking and give your seat to somebody else.

Confirmation Having a ticket written out with the flight and date you want doesn't mean you have a seat until the agent has checked with the airline that your status is 'OK' or confirmed. Meanwhile you could just be 'on request'.

Courier Fares Businesses often need to send urgent documents or freight securely and quickly. Courier companies hire people to accompany the package through customs and, in return, offer a discount ticket which is sometimes a phenomenal bargain. In effect, what the companies do is ship their freight as your luggage on regular commercial flights. This is a legitimate operation, but there are two shortcomings – the short turnaround time of the ticket (usually not longer than a month) and the limitation on your luggage allowance. You may have to surrender all your allowance and take only carry-on luggage.

Full Fares Airlines traditionally offer 1st class (coded F), business class (coded J) and economy class (coded Y) tickets. These days there are so many promotional and discounted fares available that few passengers pay full economy fare.

ITX An ITX, or 'independent inclusive tour excursion', is often available on tickets to popular holiday destinations. Officially it's a package deal combined with hotel accommodation, but many agents will sell you one of these for the flight only and give you phoney hotel vouchers in the unlikely event that you're challenged at the airport.

Lost Tickets If you lose your airline ticket an airline will usually treat it like a travellers cheque and, after inquiries, issue you with another one. Legally, however, an airline is entitled to treat it like cash and if you lose it then it's gone forever. Take good care of your tickets.

MCO An MCO, or 'miscellaneous charge order', is a voucher that looks like an airline ticket but carries no destination or date. It can be exchanged through any International Association of Travel Agents (IATA) airline for a ticket on a specific flight. It's a useful alternative to an onward ticket in those countries that demand one, and is more flexible than an ordinary ticket if you're unsure of your route.

No-Shows No-shows are passengers who fail to show up for their flight. Full-fare passengers who fail to turn up are sometimes entitled to travel on a later flight. The rest are penalised (see Cancellation Penalties).

Air Travel Glossary

On Request This is an unconfirmed booking for a flight.

Onward Tickets An entry requirement for many countries is that you have a ticket out of the country. If you're unsure of your next move, the easiest solution is to buy the cheapest onward ticket to a neighbouring country or a ticket from a reliable airline which can later be refunded if you do not use it.

Open Jaw Tickets These are return tickets where you fly out to one place but return from another. If available, this can save you backtracking to your arrival point.

Overbooking Airlines hate to fly empty seats and since every flight has some passengers who fail to show up, airlines often book more passengers than they have seats. Usually excess passengers make up for the no-shows, but occasionally somebody gets 'bumped' onto the next available flight. Guess who it is most likely to be? The passengers who check in late.

Point-to-Point Tickets These are discount tickets that can be bought on some routes in return for passengers waiving their rights to a stopover.

Promotional Fares These are officially discounted fares, available from travel agencies or direct from the airline.

Reconfirmation If you don't reconfirm your flight at least 72 hours prior to departure, the airline may delete your name from the passenger list. Ring to find out if your airline requires reconfirmation.

Restrictions Discounted tickets often have various restrictions on them – such as needing to be paid for in advance and incurring a penalty to be altered. Others are restrictions on the minimum and maximum period you must be away, such as a minimum of 14 days or a maximum of one year.

Round-the-World Tickets RTW tickets give you a limited period (usually a year) in which to circumnavigate the globe. You can go anywhere the carrying airlines go, as long as you don't backtrack. The number of stopovers or total number of separate flights is decided before you set off and they usually cost a bit more than a basic return flight.

Stand-by This is a discounted ticket where you only fly if there is a seat free at the last moment. Stand-by fares are usually available only on domestic routes.

Transferred Tickets Airline tickets cannot be transferred from one person to another. Travellers sometimes try to sell the return half of their ticket, but officials can ask you to prove that you are the person named on the ticket. This is less likely to happen on domestic flights, but on an international flight tickets are compared with passports.

Travel Agencies Travel agencies vary widely and you should choose one that suits your needs. Some simply handle tours, while full-service agencies handle everything from tours and tickets to car rental and hotel bookings. If all you want is a ticket at the lowest possible price, then go to an agency specialising in discounted fares.

Travel Periods Ticket prices vary with the time of year. There is a low (off-peak) season and a high (peak) season, and often a low-shoulder season and a high-shoulder season as well. Usually the fare depends on your outward flight – if you depart in the high season and return in the low season, you pay the high-season fare.

so and pay the balance when you get the ticket. If they insist on cash in advance, go somewhere else. And once you have the ticket, ring the airline to confirm that you are actually booked on the flight.

Once you have your ticket, write its number down, together with the flight number and other details, and keep the information separate. If the ticket is lost or stolen, this will help you get a replacement.

Web surfers might like to try their luck on www.travel.com where you can check your own itinerary, get a price quote and book your ticket online.

Cheap Tickets in Israel Despite the long queues, the Israel Student Travel Association (ISSTA) offices do not always offer very competitive fares. (For their office locations see Travel Agencies under Information in the individual city entries.) In Tel Aviv, Mona Tours (see the Tel Aviv chapter for details) is *the* place to go for cheap tickets and the Lametayel Adventure Store in Tel Aviv (see also Tel Aviv chapter) might be another good place to look.

It's worth checking around the hostels and travellers' bars as many of these advertise cut-price flights, though the East Jerusalem hostels tend to be between US$10 and US$20 more expensive than elsewhere. In Tel Aviv, for example, ask at the No 1 or Gordon hostels and look at the notice board in the Buzz Stop; in Jerusalem ask at the Al-Arab, Palm or Tabasco hostels; and in Eilat try at Max & Merran's. The average cheap-

Painful Departures

The advice to air travellers departing Israel is to turn up at the airport a good three hours before the scheduled flight time. The reason for this is that everyone boarding a plane out of one of Israel's airports (and that includes domestic flights) is subject to a rigorous cross-examination as part of security procedures. Middle-aged American couples with names like Weintraub can waltz through this in minutes and can probably turn up at the departure hall only 1½ hours before the flight. Everyone else, especially the independent traveller with a backpack, ought to bring a long engrossing novel.

The questioning, carried out before check-in, is to establish whether you pose a security threat – ie is there any likelihood that in among your three weeks worth of unwashed smalls there is something of an even more explosive nature. Factors that will arouse the suspicions of your inquisitors are things like whether you have visited the Gaza Strip or the West Bank and whether you've made any Palestinian acquaintances. If this is the case, chances are that your baggage will receive a thorough and time-consuming search.

On one occasion I went to the airport to see my wife off; she had been helping me out for three weeks but had to go home to work in Australia. It was a scenario that guaranteed a grilling for both of us! The interrogation – both together and separately – conducted by a pretty young thing just out of the army, was apparently to determine the relationship I had with my wife (were we really married?) and to ascertain whether there was the slightest possibility that I had seeded her luggage with Semtex.

Apparently in a similar interrogation conducted at a UK airport and prior to an El Al flight to Israel, a young and pregnant English woman was escorted to the airport by her Palestinian boyfriend who was taking her home to meet his parents. He was to follow a few days later. The scenario raised the suspicions of the Israeli security guard who ordered a search of the young woman's luggage and found enough explosives to send the aircraft and its passenger into oblivion. Do not fret over security checks: they are for your own safety.

est single ticket prices that we dug up were US$113 to Athens, US$130 to London and US$350 to New York.

Travellers with Special Needs

If you have special needs of any sort – you've broken a leg, you're vegetarian, travelling in a wheelchair, taking the baby, terrified of flying – you should let the airline know as soon as possible so that they can make arrangements accordingly. You should also remind them when you reconfirm your booking (at least 72 hours before departure). It may be worth ringing around the airlines before you make your booking to find out how they can handle your particular needs.

Airports and airlines can be surprisingly helpful, but they do need advance warning. Most international airports will provide escorts from the check-in desk to the plane where needed, and there should be ramps, lifts, accessible toilets and reachable phones. Aircraft toilets, on the other hand, are likely to present a problem; travellers should discuss this with the airline at an early stage and, if necessary, with their doctor.

Guide dogs for the blind will often have to travel in a specially pressurised baggage compartment with other animals, away from their owner, though smaller guide dogs may be admitted to the cabin. All guide dogs will be subject to the same quarantine laws (six months in isolation etc) as any other animal when entering or returning to countries currently free of rabies such as the UK or Australia.

Deaf travellers can ask for airport and inflight announcements to be written down for them.

Children under two travel for 10% of the standard fare (or free, on some airlines), as long as they don't occupy a seat. They don't get a baggage allowance either. 'Skycots' should be provided by the airline if requested in advance; these will take a child weighing up to about 10kg. Children between two and 12 can usually occupy a seat for half to two-thirds of the full fare, and do get a baggage allowance. Pushchairs/strollers can often be taken as hand luggage.

Departure Tax

The tax for foreigners flying out of Ben-Gurion airport is around 41NIS (US$13), but this is included in the cost of your ticket.

The USA & Canada

New York offers the widest choice of carriers, but you can also fly from Los Angeles, Chicago, Miami, Atlanta and Toronto. Many North American travellers prefer to fly with El Al nonstop for security reasons. El Al also flies via London, Manchester or Paris. Tower Air and TWA both fly nonstop and via Paris. Return flights from New York on El Al and Tower Air cost US$1287. All of these airlines have discounted fares from time to time. The Belgian carrier Sabena, includes an overnight stay in Brussels; fares cost around US$1100-1500 return and $900 one way to Ben-Gurion airport from New York. If you are a student (under 26) check for special discount fares. For example, Lufthansa (via Frankfurt) is currently offering $862 and Air France (via Paris) $844.

The *New York Times*, the *LA Times*, the *Chicago Tribune* and the *San Francisco Examiner* produce weekly travel sections in which you'll find any number of ads. Council Travel (☎ 800-226-8624, Web site www .counciltravel.com) and STA Travel (☎ 800-777-011222, Web site www.sta-travel.com) have offices in major cities nationwide. The magazine *Travel Unlimited* (PO Box 1058, Allston, MA 02134) publishes details of the cheapest air fares and courier possibilities for destinations all over the world.

In Canada, Travel CUTS (☎ 888-838-2887, Web site www.travelcuts.com) has offices in all major cities. The *Toronto Globe & Mail* and the *Vancouver Sun* carry travel agents' ads.

Australia & New Zealand

From Australia there are several airlines that fly into Israel, most via Europe. One-way tickets range from about A$1350 to A$1950 in the low season, while high season return tickets range from A$2125 to A$2459.

Some of the cheaper airlines flying to Israel are Alitalia via Rome, Olympic via

Athens, and Singapore Airlines. Other airlines which offer slightly more expensive flights include Lauda Airlines via Vienna and KLM via Amsterdam. At the top end of the price range are flights with Qantas and El Al via Bangkok and EgyptAir via Cairo. Another option is to buy a round-the-world ticket (RTW) with Qantas or British Airways, or a cheaper one with Alitalia and United Airlines. RTW fares range from A$1800 in the low season to $A2500 in the high season.

Two well-known travel agents for cheap fares are STA Travel and Flight Centre. STA (☎ 03-9349 2411, Web site www.statravel.com.au), has its main office at 224 Faraday St, Carlton, 3053 and offices in all major cities and on many university campuses. Call ☎ 131 776 Australia-wide for the location of your nearest branch. Flight Centre (☎ 131 600 Australia-wide, Web site www.flightcentre.com.au) has a central office at 82 Elizabeth St, Sydney and there are dozens of offices throughout Australia.

Flights between New Zealand and Israel fly either via Los Angeles or London; flights via London are usually the cheaper option. One-way fares to Israel from Auckland start at NZ$1824. In New Zealand, Flight Centre (☎ 09-309 6171) has a large central office in Auckland at National Bank Towers, on the corner of Queen & Darby Sts, and numerous branches throughout the country. STA Travel (☎ 09-309 0458, Web site www.sta travel.com.au) has its main office at 10 High St, Auckland and has other offices in Auckland as well as Hamilton, Palmerston North, Wellington, Dunedin and Christchurch.

The UK

Discount air travel is big business in London. Check out the travel sections in the weekend newspapers – such as the *Independent* on Saturday and the *Sunday Times* – and the travel classified sections in London's weekly *Time Out* and *TNT* magazines. Whether looking around for cheap fares or just some advice, the Israel Travel Service (☎ 0161-839 1111) in Manchester is a private and extremely helpful outfit with extensive experience.

Of the two international airports in Israel, Ovda tends to be used for organised tours in the south and Ben-Gurion for all other flights. British Airways (☎ 0345-222111) and El Al (☎ 020-7957 4100) both fly direct to Tel Aviv once or twice a day. In the high season, British Airways fares are around UK£300 – slightly less than El Al with fares of around UK£320. It is often cheaper to fly via a destination in Europe. Lufthansa Airlines (☎ 0845-603 0747) flies via Munich or Frankfurt for around UK£250. At the time of writing, Olympic Airways (☎ 020-7409 2477) had the cheapest flight for UK£208 via Athens.

The lowest fares are not usually through the airlines direct; discount agencies such as Trailfinders (☎ 020-7938 3939) and City Bond Travel (☎ 020-7408 1535) are reliable sources of cheap flights.

For travellers under 26-years-old or students, fares may be even lower. The two leading agencies in the UK are USIT Campus (☎ 020-7730 3402, Web site www.usit campus.co.uk) and STA Travel (☎ 020-7361 6262, Web site www.statravel.co.uk), both of which have branches across the UK and sell tickets to all travellers but cater especially to young people and students.

Charter flights can work out as a much cheaper alternative to the scheduled flights available, especially if you do not qualify for the under-26 and student fare discounts. At the time of writing, WST (☎ 020-7224 0504), specialists in flights bound for Israel, were offering fully flexible fares for UK£259.

Elsewhere in Europe

Most European countries offer frequent flights to Israel. Air France, Austrian Airlines, Sabena and Swissair all fly regularly from the major European cities via their home countries. Sample fares to Tel Aviv start at 74,000dr from Athens, f550 from Amsterdam, L800,000 from Rome, DM660 from Berlin and 2250FF from Paris.

In Europe many travel agencies have ties with STA Travel, where cheap tickets can be purchased and STA-issued tickets can be altered (usually for a US$25 fee). Outlets in major cities include:

France
Voyages Wasteels (☎ 08-03 88 70 04, fax 01-43 25 46 25; this phone number can only be dialled from within France) 11 rue Dupuytren 756006, Paris
Germany
STA Travel (☎ 030-311 0950, fax 313 0948) Goethestrasse 73, 10625 Berlin
Greece
ISYTS (☎ 01-322 1267, fax 323 3767) 11 Nikis St, Upper Floor, Syntagma Square, Athens
Italy
Passaggi (☎ 06-474 0923, fax 482 7436) Stazione Termini FS, Gelleria Di Tesla, Rome

In continental Europe, Athens and Amsterdam have a reputation as good sources of cheap fares. In Athens, check the many travel agencies in the backstreets between Syntagma and Omonia squares. For student and nonconcessionary fares, try Magic Bus (☎ 01-323 7471, fax 322 0219). In Amsterdam, try NBBS Travelshop (☎ 020-624 0989), Rokin 38 or Flyworld/Grand Travel (☎ 020-657 0000, fax 648 0477).

Egypt
There are El Al flights available between Ben-Gurion airport and Egypt (Cairo and the Red Sea port of Hurghada), which will save you having an Egypt-Israel border stamp in your passport. The flights cost about US$150 one way and US$328 return.

Asia
Although most Asian countries are now offering fairly competitive air fare deals, Bangkok, Singapore and Hong Kong are still the best places to shop around for discount tickets. Hong Kong's travel market can be quite unpredictable, but some excellent bargains are available if you are lucky.

In Bangkok, the budget traveller's headquarters is on Khao San Rd. There are several good travel agents but there are also some suspect ones; ask the advice of other travellers before handing over your cash. STA Travel (☎ 02-236 0262) at 33 Surawong Road is a good, reliable place to start.

Singapore, like Bangkok, has hundreds of travel agents so you can check and compare prices on flights. STA Travel (☎ 65-737 7188) in the Orchard Parade Hotel, 1 Tanglin Road offers competitive discount fares for Asian destinations and beyond. Chinatown Point shopping centre on New Bridge Road also has a good selection of travel agents.

Hong Kong has a number of excellent, reliable travel agencies (and some not so reliable ones). A good way to check on a travel agent is to look it up in the phone book: fly-by-night operators don't usually stay around long enough to get listed. Many travellers use the Hong Kong Student Travel Bureau (☎ 2730 3269) 8th floor, Star House, Tsim Sha Tsui. You could also try Phoenix Services (☎ 2722 7378) 7th floor, Milton Mansion, 96 Nathan Rd, Tsim Sha Tsui.

LAND
Egypt and Jordan have open land borders with Israel; Lebanon and Syria do not. If you are planning to visit either of the latter two then do so before going to Israel, as evidence of a visit to the Jewish state will, without exception, bar you from entry.

Private cars are permitted to cross the borders but not taxis or hire cars. Drivers and riders of motorbikes will need the vehicle's registration papers and liability insurance. For Israel, an international drivers permit is not necessary – your domestic licence will do.

Egypt
Forbidden until the signing of the 1979 peace accord, travel between Israel and Egypt is now a thriving part of the tourist scene, although it's mainly confined to international travellers. Israelis tend to limit their trips south across the border to the beaches of Sinai, while for most Egyptians

a visit to Israel is unthinkable for fear of attracting the unwanted attention of their own national security service.

There are two border crossings – Rafah (or Rafiah) and Taba. Which one you use depends on where you are in Israel and whether it's Sinai or Cairo you're heading for.

If your visit to Egypt is confined to just Sinai (crossing at Taba only) then no Egyptian visa is necessary – you'll be issued a 14 day pass at the border. See the boxed text 'Israeli Stamp Stigma' and Egyptian Visa, under Visas & Documents, both in the Facts for the Visitor chapter.

From Tel Aviv & Jerusalem There is currently one tour operator providing coach services from Tel Aviv and Jerusalem. The buses travel nonstop to Cairo via the border at Rafah (where there is a change of bus) in the Gaza Strip. The journey takes roughly 10 hours and a ticket from Tel Aviv or Jerusalem is about 115NIS (US$38) one way or 171NIS (US$57) return. To that has to be added an Israeli departure tax of 90NIS (US$30) (payable usually to the bus company) and an Egyptian entry tax of E£7 (US$2.50). You can change money at the border.

There is currently one main operator:

Mazada Tours
  (☎ 03-544 4454) 141 Ibn Gvirol St, Tel Aviv; daily buses departing at 9 am, arriving Cairo at 7 pm. Also Tuesday, Thursday and Sunday overnight buses departing at 8.30 pm, arriving at 7 am next morning.
  (☎ 02-623 5777) 9 Koresh St, Jerusalem; buses depart Monday to Friday at 7.30 am. There are also overnight services on Tuesday and Thursday, departing at 7 pm.

Alternatively, you can do it yourself from Tel Aviv. An Egged bus departs for Rafah at 9 am each day from the central bus station. The journey takes about two hours and costs 35NIS. After passing through the Israeli immigration, catch the shuttle bus (about US$2.50) to the Egyptian hall. Once through procedures there, you can catch a local Egyptian bus or service taxi for Cairo

which takes about five hours. As all the buses from here go to the city, do not go to Rafah if you want to go directly to Sinai.

On the return leg, the bus departs from the Cairo Sheraton at 5.30 am on Sunday, Monday, Wednesday and Thursday only. Tickets are bought at the hotel from Masr Travel; the fare is US$50 one way.

From Eilat Taba, just 4km south of central Eilat, was for a long time the subject of a territorial diplomatic tug of war which the Egyptians eventually won. The border with Egypt is now that little bit closer. This is the most convenient place to cross if you are planning a visit to Sinai. While there are no organised buses from Eilat into Egypt, a solo crossing is simple enough and once over the border it's possible to pick up local Egyptian transport both for Sinai destinations and for Cairo (see the Sinai section in the Excursions from Israel chapter).

The border is open 24 hours, but this is subject to occasional change and you will want to time your crossing to be able to find transport on the other side. Unlike Rafah, where you can be held up for three or four hours, it's normally possible to stroll through the formalities at Taba in around 30 minutes. There is a 61NIS (US$14.50) Israeli departure tax to be paid at Taba as well as a E£17 (US$5) Egyptian entry tax. Visitors to Taba only are exempt from these costs as payment is made some way past the Taba Hilton compound at a small roadside booth. When leaving Egypt there is a E£2 exit tax, so make sure you retain some small change.

Once on the Egyptian side you can change money at the Taba Hilton, or in a small exchange booth in the customs and passport control building. It's then a further 1km walk to the small tourist village and the bus stop. Alternatively, shared minibuses to Nuweiba (E£30) await arrivals just past the customs area.

Jordan

Unlike Egypt, which maintains a 'you keep to your side of the fence and I'll keep to mine' peace with Israel, Jordan and Israel have become best buddies, exchanging coach loads of visitors on a daily basis. The Allenby/King Hussein Bridge, which until very recently served as the only meeting point of the two neighbours, has been supplemented by two other crossings – Jordan River and Arava. Travellers now no longer have to collude in the pretence that they suddenly materialised on the King Hussein Bridge without ever stepping foot in anywhere called Israel. There is absolutely no problem entering Jordan with an Israeli visa in your passport. See Jordanian Visa under Visa & Documents in the Facts for the Visitor chapter.

Allenby/King Hussein Bridge This crossing is only 30km from Jerusalem on one side and 40km from Amman on the other. You can get here easily by taking a 30NIS service taxi from opposite Damascus Gate in Jerusalem – ask for 'Jisr Al-Malek Hussein', not Allenby Bridge which is the Israeli name and may not be understood. The journey takes about 45 minutes. Remember, anyone turning up here without a valid visa will be sent back. However, the flip side is that the Jordanian officials here can be asked not to stamp visa holders' passports – this is the only crossing at which travellers looking to move on to Syria or Lebanon can avoid incriminating evidence of a trip to Israel.

Note that if you are entering Jordan this way and intend to return to Israel, you must keep the entrance form given to you by the Jordanians – they could well insist on you prolonging your stay in Jordan if you cannot present it on departure.

Crossing at this border can take anything up to three hours depending on the traffic – try to avoid being there between 11 am and 3 pm which is the busiest time. The Israeli exit tax is a steep 140NIS, which is considerably higher than the other land border crossings. The rationale for this high fee is that you are supposedly paying for the privilege of exiting both Palestinian *and* Israeli territory. Once through all the immigration procedures and out the other side, look for

the white service taxis which charge JD2 per person to Amman; the yellow cars are 'special' taxis which charge JD10 to 12 for the same ride.

The bridge is open Sunday to Thursday from 8 am to midnight. These times are subject to frequent change and it's advisable to check with the tourist information office in Jerusalem.

Jordan River The least used of the three border crossings, Jordan River is 6km east of Beit She'an in the Galilee region. It is not a particularly convenient border crossing, but it's modern, well used and has good facilities. If you don't already have your Jordanian visa, they are issued here and it is considerably closer to Jerusalem than the Arava crossing at Eilat. You can take a Tiberias bus and change at Beit She'an for one of four daily buses to the border (6.60NIS). They leave Beit She'an at 8.40 and 9.20 am and 3 and 6 pm returning from the border back to Beit She'an some 15-20 minutes after the above departure times. Once across the border, however, you're in the middle of nowhere. The options are to take a minibus to Irbid or take a taxi to the main road some 3km distant, from where you can try and hitch to somewhere more life-supporting.

The border is open Sunday to Thursday from 8 am to 8 pm, and Friday and Saturday from 8 am to 5 pm. The Israeli exit tax here is 57NIS.

The Jordanians refer to this border crossing as Jisr Sheikh Hussein (Sheikh Hussein Bridge).

Arava Opened in August 1994, this crossing (known as Wadi Araba to the Jordanians) is just 4km from central Eilat. Once over the border, the carved stone city of Petra, arguably the Middle East's second greatest attraction after the pyramids, is less than two hours drive away. We do not, however, recommend that you try making a day trip of it – there's simply too much to see. Also, the huge volume of coach traffic at this crossing often means lengthy delays, sometimes up to three hours. Border opening times are Sunday to Thursday from 6.30 am to 10 pm, and Friday and Saturday from 8 am to 8 pm. We strongly advise getting here before opening time to be ahead of the buses which start rolling up soon after.

A direct and much-needed bus service between Eilat and Aqaba has been on the cards ever since the border reopened, but at the time of research nothing was happening. Inquire at Eilat central bus station or tourist information office for the latest information or monitor feedback on LP's Thorn Tree Web site for any changes.

There's an Israeli exit tax of 61NIS and anyone without a Jordanian visa can get one here. Jordanian visas can be expensive, ranging from JD6 for French passport holders to an outrageous JD38 for Canadian passport holders. Australians, New Zealanders, British, Irish and Americans all pay something between these two extremes. South Africans and Japanese get their visas free.

Both sides of the border have money-changing facilities, but the Jordanians offer far more favourable rates. Once across the border you will have to take a taxi to the Aqaba bus station (JD5), from where buses can be caught to Petra (JD3), departing at 8.30 and 10 am and noon, 2 and 3.30 pm. If there are enough of you it may be worth sharing a taxi direct from Aqaba to Petra and back at a cost of JD40 with two hours waiting time thrown in or for JD50 with five hours waiting time. Rates are fixed.

SEA
Routes & Fares
Israel is connected to mainland Europe by a regular ferry service between Haifa and Piraeus, near Athens in Greece. The Piraeus-Haifa run usually involves a stop in Rhodes, or sometimes in Crete instead, with all ferries stopping additionally at Limassol (Lemesos) in Cyprus. Departures from Haifa at the time of writing were on Thursday and Sunday evenings, but these times are open to frequent seasonal change and you should check with a ticket agent in good time before making concrete travel plans. Depar-

tures from Piraeus are currently on Mondays and Thursdays.

The cheapest tickets to Piraeus are US$96 for deck, US$106 for a Pullman seat and from US$125 per person in a four-berth cabin. Students and those under 26 get a discount of about 20%. These prices are for one-way voyages in the low season; in the high season, prices go up by between 11 and 15%. It varies slightly between the different shipping companies, but the high season is roughly from mid-June to mid-September. A disembarkation fee of US$22 is charged for each stopover en route; US$44 per vehicle. For return voyages, 20% reductions are made on the tickets (although not from the student and under-26 prices). Travellers with campervans can sleep in the van on deck and avoid expensive cabin costs when travelling on Poseidon Line's *FB Sea Symphony*.

The Piraeus-Haifa run takes about 58 hours, so take plenty of food and drink (or money) for the voyage.

Alternatively, it's possible to travel by ferry only as far as Rhodes and change there for Marmaris in Turkey. Low season fares to Rhodes from Haifa are US$91 for deck class, US$101 for Pullman and US$120 for a cabin berth. Passengers from Rhodes to Haifa are charged a hefty disembarkation fee of US$44. From Rhodes the fare to Marmaris is 12,000GRD one-way (19,000GRD return). Low season fares departing Haifa for Limassol (Lemesos) only are deck class US$58, Pullman seat US$68 and a cabin berth US$87.

Buying Tickets
There are two major ferry companies, Poseidon Lines and Salamis Lines. The former is Greek-owned and run and the latter is Cypriot-owned and run. Travellers' tales about the comfort level of both lines vary, so keep your ear to the ground for current opinions.

Tickets can be purchased at all ports of call as well as directly from the ferryline offices. Here are the contact details for both lines:

Poseidon Lines

Cyprus:

(☎ 05-745 666, fax 745 666) Poseidon Lines (Cyprus) Ltd, 124 Franklin Roosevelt St, Limassol

Greece:

(☎ 01-965 8300, fax 965 8310, email poseidon .lines@ath.forthnet.gr) Poseidon Lines Shipping Co., Alkyonidon 32, 166 73 Voula, Athens

Israel:

(☎ 04-867 4444, fax 866 1958) Caspi Travel, 76 Ha'Atzmaut St, Haifa

UK:

(☎ 020-7431 4560, fax 7431 5456, email ferries@viamare.com) Viamare Travel Ltd, 2 Sumatra Rd, London NW6 1PU

Salamis Lines

Cyprus:

(☎ 05-355 555, fax 364 4100) Salamis Tours, PO Box 351, Limassol

Greece:

(☎ 01-429 4325, fax 429 4557) Salamis Lines (Hellas), Fillelinon 9, 185 36 Piraeus

Israel:

(☎ 04-861 3670, fax 861 3613) A Rosenfeld Shipping Ltd, 104 Ha'Atzmaut St, Haifa

UK:

(☎ 020-7431 4560, fax 7431 5456, email ferries@viamare.com) Viamare Travel Ltd, 2 Sumatra Rd, London NW6 1PU

Sailing details and ticket prices for both companies can be viewed on the following Web sites: www.greekislands.gr/greece.htm (Poseidon Lines) and www.viamare.com/salamis/salprc.htm (Salamis Lines).

Take note that for sailings scheduled for Friday, or on the eve of a Jewish public holiday, the port closes at 1 pm and access to the port and ferry is not possible – even though the ferry usually leaves at 8 pm. Check-in in this instance must take place before 1 pm. No departures are currently scheduled for Fridays, but this may situation may change depending on the sailing season.

Getting Around

AIR

Arkia, Israel's domestic airline (which now has charters to and from abroad), operates scheduled flights variously connecting Jerusalem, Tel Aviv, Haifa, Rosh Pina, Kiryat Shmona and Eilat. Not surprisingly, prices don't come close to being competitive with bus fares. As nowhere in Israel is more than eight hours drive from anywhere else (and usually far less), it does make you wonder how Arkia stays aloft. Sample fares are Tel Aviv to Eilat US$80, Tel Aviv to the Galilee US$46 and Haifa to Eilat US$94.

These Arkia offices take bookings:

Ashdod
(☎ 08-852 1212, fax 856 8838)
Kanyon Ashdod, Nordau St
Bat Yam
(☎ 03-507 3366, fax 507 6657)
35 Rothschild Blvd
Beersheba
(☎ 07-628 7444, fax 628 7450)
183 Keren Kayemet St
Eilat
(☎ 07-638 4888, fax 637 3370)
Red Canyon Centre
Haifa
(☎ 04-861 1606, fax 867 1661)
80 Ha'Atzmaut St
Jerusalem
(☎ 02-625 5888, fax 623 5758)
Klal Centre, 97 Jaffa Rd
Kiryat Shmona
(☎ 06-695 9901, fax 695 9904)
Pal Building
Netanya
(☎ 09-884 3143, fax 882 5904)
110 Shtamper St
Rosh Pina
(☎ 06-693 5302)
Airport
Tel Aviv
(☎ 03-524 0220, fax 524 0229)
11 Frishman St

See Arkia's Web site (www .arkia.co.il) for the latest timetables and prices.

BUS

The relatively small size of Israel, combined with an excellent road system, make travel by bus *the* way to get around.

Egged buses

Israel's bus network is dominated by Egged, the second largest bus company in the world after Greyhound. Egged is a cooperative with about 6000 members and 3500 employees. They operate about 4000 buses on over 3000 scheduled routes, as well as numerous special trips. Other than in the Golan and Dead Sea regions, where getting around can be a problem, the service provided by Egged is very good. The buses are frequent, fast and well looked after.

Egged also operate almost all urban services. Within city limits there's one flat fare which stays the same whether you ride just one stop or 10. At the time of writing, this fare is 4.30NIS and it applies in every town from Akko down to Eilat. You buy your ticket from the bus driver. Despite the frequency of most services they do fill up, especially in the rush hours which occur roughly every Monday to Thursday between 7 and 8 am and 4 and 6 pm, and most of Saturday evening. It varies with the route but most buses operate from about 5.30 am to about 10.30 pm.

Remember, beware of Shabbat: on Friday, and the eve of Jewish holidays, all buses, urban and intercity, only operate until 3 or 4 pm and on Saturday services don't resume until sunset.

For Egged bus information call ☎ 1770 225 555 (it is not necessary to dial an area code for connection).

Arab Buses

In Nazareth, East Jerusalem and the West Bank, there are around 30 small Arab companies providing services to the area. While Jewish buses tend to be air-conditioned, clean, fast and modern, the Arab buses are virtual antiques, and not well kept ones at that. If you have the choice you are better off using a *sherut* (service taxi) instead – they are only slightly more expensive but are much faster.

Costs

Israel's bus system is not the absolute bargain it used to be (what is?), but it's still reasonably cheap.

The most lengthy journey that the average visitor is likely to make is the run between Eilat and Jerusalem (four hours) or Tel Aviv (five hours) which costs around 54NIS and 58NIS respectively, or roughly around US$0.04 per km. That certainly takes some beating.

On routes between towns and cities, buying a return ticket can sometimes save you money especially as they have no time limits; for example, you could buy a Tel Aviv-Beersheba return ticket and from Beersheba wander around the Negev region before, some days later, using the return portion of the ticket to get from Beersheba back to Tel Aviv.

ISIC holders are entitled to a discount of 10% on interurban fares costing more than 10NIS.

Bus Passes

There are several discount bus passes which may be worth frequent travellers looking into.

Israbus Pass Like most unlimited travel passes available, the value of this bus pass is totally dependent on the amount of travelling done. An Israbus Pass is valid for all Egged services, which means more or less all buses, long-distance and urban. It does not, however, cover the Arab network. You can be pretty certain of saving money if you get the 21 day Israbus Pass and then use it extensively for three weeks, but it's unlikely many people will get the full worth of a seven day pass; that would roughly mean making a two hour or more journey (for example, Tel Aviv to Haifa or Jerusalem to Beersheba) every day for a week.

Israbus Passes can be bought at most major bus stations or Egged Tours offices. The rates are:

days	cost in NIS	NIS per day
7	270	38.5
14	430	30.7
21	540	25.7

Multifare Discount Passes This is a card valid for a calendar month (it's sold from the 27th of the preceding month until the 5th of the month in question) which permits a set number of single rides at a 25% discount. These passes are not valid for interurban rides, only for routes within a specified city or town, so unless you are going to be making two or three bus journeys a day in one particular place for a whole month, you're not going to see any benefit from this pass.

TRAIN

The small passenger network of the Israel State Railways (ISR) is slightly cheaper than the buses, but this is offset by its extremely limited scope and the generally inconvenient location of most of the railway stations, away from city and town centres. However, the rolling stock is modern and well maintained and if you are a rail lover, taking the train is an ideal way to see the countryside in a relaxed manner away from the often frenetic and stressful driving habits of Egged's bus drivers. The once popular and scenic route from Tel Aviv to Jerusalem has closed down indefinitely pending much-needed repairs to the track. It is anyone's guess, however, when and if the line will reopen. ISIC holders get a 20% discount on all rail fares.

The main line is Haifa-Tel Aviv Central (North Tel Aviv), and is used as much by commuters as travellers seeking alternative transport. If you are heading to Akko or Nahariya from Tel Aviv, taking the train is probably a better option since it doesn't involve the change of transport that you would have to make if you were travelling by bus. Rehovot and Ashdod (south of Tel Aviv) are served by primarily commuter links.

Distances Between Major Cities & Towns (km)

	Beersheba	Eilat	Haifa	Jerusalem	Tel Aviv	Tiberias
Akko	223	464	22	174	108	63
Ashdod	84	325	125	66	40	164
Ashkelon	66	307	134	71	53	180
Beersheba	-	241	200	81	115	246
Ben-Gurion airport	110	351	115	44	15	137
Bethlehem	76	319	168	10	73	169
Eilat	241	-	427	307	356	473
Ein Gedi	106	232	210	78	153	179
Gaza	44	288	172	128	77	212
Haifa	200	427	-	131	85	57
Hebron	52	291	195	37	100	186
Jericho	115	287	147	38	99	114
Jerusalem	81	307	131	-	59	176
Masada	64	216	261	109	169	183
Netanya	144	385	58	92	29	100
Ramallah	98	341	140	15	75	150
Tel Aviv	115	356	85	59	-	131
Tiberias	246	473	57	176	131	-

TAXI
Sherut (Service Taxi)
Sheruts, or service taxis, are usually stretch-Mercedes, seating up to seven passengers, or 13-person minivans, which operate on a fixed route for a fixed price just like a bus. If you are uncertain about the fare, just ask your fellow passengers. Regular rates are normally about 20% more than the bus, but are sometimes on a par.

Most sheruts travel between towns and cities from recognised taxi ranks, leaving when they're full. This can sometimes mean waiting for six other people but you'll be surprised how popular the system is. Long delays are rare. Also, the locals tend not to sit inside and wait but stand outside instead, so what often appears to be an empty vehicle will rapidly fill up when you climb in.

With a sherut you can get out anywhere along the way, but you pay the same fare regardless. After dropping off a passenger, the sherut then picks up replacement passengers wherever possible.

Most notably in Tel Aviv, but also in Jerusalem, some sheruts operate as bus stand-ins on Shabbat, providing the only transport on certain major intercity routes while Egged is off the road.

In the West Bank, where the Egged service is limited to Jewish settlements, the service taxis (in Arabic, drop the 'taxi' bit and just say, 'servees') are a better, faster alternative to the local Arab buses.

'Special' Taxis
Throughout Israel, drivers of 'special' (that is, nonshared) taxis have a terrible reputation with tourists and locals alike for overcharging and being generally unhelpful and impolite. The usual 'my meter doesn't work' or 'for you, friend, special price' (more likely to be double than a discount) tricks are popular. Be sure that the meter is used or risk paying too much.

These highwaymen of the Middle East are so notorious at ripping off passengers that even the luxury King David Hotel in

Jerusalem has official fares posted up in its lobby to protect guests. Tourist information offices can also advise how much to pay.

Just insist as soon as you enter the taxi that you want the meter *on*. Point at the meter and the driver will get the drift. If he refuses to switch it on, get out of the cab – assuming it is not moving – and look for another taxi.

All complaints about taxi rip-offs or other complaints should be addressed to the Controller of Road Transport at the following regional authorities:

Haifa
(☎ 04-852 6107, fax 851 1621)
121 Jaffa Rd, 31200
Jerusalem
(☎ 02-622 8456, fax 622 8452)
97 Jaffa Rd, 91008
Tel Aviv
(☎ 03-565 7272, fax 565 7216)
8 HaMelakha St, 67150

CAR

Good roads, beautiful scenery and short distances make Israel a great place to hire a car. Also, in places like the Golan and the Negev, the buses serve only a limited area and having your own vehicle can be a real boon. Even if you're on a tight budget, a few people sharing a car can be an economically viable way to see specific areas, if not the whole country.

Except for Tel Aviv and Jerusalem and the main coastal highways between Haifa and

---

Road Orthodoxy

When death and disablement prove insufficient incentives to get drivers to slow down, the ultraorthodox road safety campaigners play on even greater fears. Signs in Jerusalem's Mea She'arim district display the macabre message, 'Drive Carefully the Pathologist Awaits' – a reference to autopsies that they claim have been carried out indiscriminately in Israel's hospitals in violation of Jewish religious law.

Tel Aviv, traffic is pretty light. Be wary of roads that look and feel like freeways (a prime example is Route 4) but which are punctuated by frequent junctions and traffic lights.

If you are driving a hire car you may safely travel Route 90 from Tiberias to Eilat through the Jordan Valley and the West Bank, though you should desist from detouring off the road into Palestinian territory proper.

Israelis do seem to exhibit near suicidal tendencies once behind the wheel and over 18,500 people have been killed in road accidents since 1948 – more than the total killed in all the wars with their Arab neighbours. Don't let this put you off but do be extra cautious.

Road Rules

In Israel you drive on the right-hand side of the road. Seat belts should be worn at all times by front seat occupants. The speed limit is 50 km/h (31 mph) in built up areas and 90 km/h (56 mph) elsewhere unless stated, but this is typically ignored. There seems to be a lack of regulatory road signs, but virtually all major cities, towns and places of interest are signposted in English.

Parking With a rapid increase in private car ownership, parking is a major problem in urban centres. In most places, but especially in Tel Aviv, street parking is strictly regulated. To avoid a ticket or having your car towed, be sure to follow the rules.

Generally, there is no free street parking in most city or town centres; parking cards need to be purchased from the post office or newspaper kiosks. Each parking card has five hours worth of street parking, and costs about 35NIS.

With a parking card affixed to the car's front window, you can park where the kerb is marked by blue and white stripes. You cannot legally park anywhere else. Between 7 am and 5 pm, you can only park for one hour. Between 5 and 10 pm you can park for longer, but you must display parking cards to indicate the number of hours parked.

Driving in the West Bank

Although the air is considerably less stone-filled than it was in the days of the *Intifada*, it is still not entirely advisable to drive a car with yellow Israeli licence plates in the West Bank (Palestinian licence plates are green on white). You can check your itinerary with the car rental company.

No cars in any case may be taken into Gaza. All Israeli *and* Jordanian-registered vehicles must be left at the large car park north of the Erez crossing into Gaza. Foreign-registered vehicles may be taken into Gaza, but are subject to a rigorous inspection by the Israelis at Erez.

However, it is still perfectly OK to travel by car – hire or otherwise – along Route 90 from Tiberias to Eilat or vice versa. This route which effectively runs along the eastern flank of the West Bank along the Jordan River Valley and the Dead Sea is the shortest way from the Galilee to the Negev and is used extensively by drivers with Israeli-licenced cars.

When approaching Jericho, be sure to take the Route 90 bypass so as to avoid driving through the centre of Jericho. This road runs east of Jericho and swings wide of the Palestinian-controlled town. When coming from Jerusalem follow the signs for the Dead Sea, but keep left at the Dead Sea turn-off. When approaching from the north, keep left at the turn-off for the Jericho town centre and follow the bypass around to Almog junction just south of Jericho. (See the map Around Jericho in The Gaza Strip & the West Bank chapter.)

Overnight parking on the blue and white stripes is unregulated. If you need to park for a longer period during the day, it's better to use a public car park.

Rental

Local car hire firms generally offer lower rates than the international companies like Avis, Budget and Hertz. Eldan, in particular, stands out with good rates and offices nationwide. If you are planning to drive throughout the country, it can be a good idea to use a company that has a few offices just in case you need a replacement car. Note that you are not allowed to take hired vehicles into Sinai or over the border into Jordan.

Prices do vary dramatically and shopping around is recommended. Based on three days rental, look at around US$55 to US$75 per day for a Fiat Uno or similar, with aircon, insurance and unlimited mileage. July and August rates are substantially higher than the rest of the year. Be wary of initial quotes – check if insurance and unlimited mileage are included, and if there is a minimum rental period.

Most car hire companies require drivers to be over 21-years-old with a clean, valid drivers licence (an International Driving Permit isn't needed for most nationalities).

An often overlooked alternative to the Jewish-owned companies are the Palestinian operations. In addition to any political reasons for giving them your business, their cars are considered 'protected' in East Jerusalem and other Arab areas, including the West Bank, and should be spared the hostility and stones that can be targeted towards Jewish cars with yellow plates.

Note that these vehicles can theoretically be driven throughout Israel, although you will undoubtedly attract some unfriendly stares from Israelis as you cruise around the country, not to mention the zealous attention of the IDF. Realistically you are better off sticking to the West Bank. Rates can be competitive, especially for a week or more and if you bargain.

The Palestinian companies include:

Holy City
   (☎ 02-582 0223, fax 582 4329) East Jerusalem, behind the American consulate

Orabi
  (☎ 02-995 3521 [24 hours], 995 5601, fax 995 3521) Jerusalem St, Al-Bireh, near Ramallah. Branches are also in Bethlehem, Jericho and Nablus; credit cards accepted.
Petra
  (☎ 02-582 0716, fax 582 2668) Main St, East Jerusalem. Their cars have yellow plates, but with the Arabic company insignia they should be safer than Jewish-owned vehicles.

BICYCLE

Cycling is a cheap, convenient, healthy, environmentally sound and above all fun way of getting around Israel. The same reasons that make the country great for driving also make it appealing for cycling; namely good roads with light traffic, some beautiful scenery and relatively short distances between major towns and sights. Most major roads also have a hard shoulder, so cyclists can stay well clear of the traffic. Interurban buses can usually accommodate bikes in their underslung luggage bays without any disassembly required; you'll probably be charged an additional 50% of the fare.

The main drawback to cycling in Israel is, of course, the heat. Always set off as early as possible, carry plenty of water (preferably chilled and in an insulator pack) and aim to finish for the day around early afternoon.

Choose your route carefully; while the coastal plain is flat enough, the Upper Galilee, the Golan and the Dead Sea region have innumerable steep hills and the Negev Desert can be unmercifully hot.

You will have to bring your own bike with you. Although a few places in Jerusalem, Eilat, Jericho and Tiberias hire by the day, their machines are unsuitable for long-distance riding. Walk Ways in Jerusalem (see Cycling Tours in that chapter for details) does sell decent second-hand mountain bikes that might suit you for a cycling trip in Israel.

Bicycles can travel by air – you can take them to pieces and put them in a bike bag or box, but it's much easier to wheel your bike to the check-in desk, where it should be treated as a piece of baggage. You may have to remove the pedals and turn the handlebars sideways so that it takes up less space in the aircraft's hold. Check all this with the airline well in advance, preferably before you pay for your ticket. Before you leave home, go over your bike carefully and fill your repair kit with every imaginable spare because 10-to-one you won't be able to buy that crucial part you need to get you back on the road.

HITCHING

Hitching is never entirely safe in any country in the world, and Israel is no different. There have been incidents in which hitchers in Israel have been abducted and killed and not all, it's thought, for political reasons. Travellers who decide to hitch should understand that they are taking a small but potentially serious risk. At least hitch in pairs and let someone know where you are planning to go. And, above all, women should never hitch without male company.

You will notice a large number of soldiers soliciting lifts by the roadside. This is because it's traditional, and actively encouraged, for Israelis to give lifts to soldiers – so bear in mind that if you are hitching you will be last in line for a lift if there are any IDF uniforms to be seen. Note that even female soldiers are forbidden to hitch because of the potential danger. Also, take note that sticking out your thumb is not the locally accepted way to hitch a lift. In Israel it means something more basic and impolite, although most locals recognise the foreigner's intentions. The local way to hitch is to point down at the road with your index finger.

ORGANISED TOURS

Maintaining the centuries-old tradition of pilgrimage to the Holy Land, organised tours are big business in Israel. Egged Tours is the largest tourist carrier and they have offices in most towns (see individual city chapters and town sections); numerous smaller companies compete for the remainder of the market. For details of available tours contact any tourist information office or travel agent.

The Ministry of Tourism regulates tours and sets prices and, by law, all guides must be licensed by them. This is not a welcome ruling and in the manner of the slyly hissed 'hashshish, hashshish' which accompanies strolls in the bazaars of Morocco, cagey looking men may sidle up to you in Jerusalem's Old City and – avoiding your eyes – nervously whisper 'tour guide, tour guide'.

Major exceptions to this rule are the various Christian clergymen who lead hundreds of thousands of pilgrims around Israel. The churches maintain that their own guides are the best for their needs and that banning them would reduce the number of pilgrims. Rather than lose the good business that the Christians provide, the authorities upset other guides by allowing the priests, vicars and monks to continue.

Remember, although Israeli guides often display an impressive breadth of knowledge, not all of what you hear can be taken at face value – the guides are an important part of Israel's unofficial public relations department and they are quite often far from free of bias.

More and more private hostels are getting in on the tour business, with inexpensive trips geared to the traveller. It often makes sense to take these tours as they show you places that can involve more time and money getting there independently. In Jerusalem, for example, walking tours of the Old City and day trips to Jericho and the Wadi Qelt, the Dead Sea region and refugee camps are widely available.

Another development in the tour business are the 'soft adventure' tours to the Dead Sea region and the Judean and Negev deserts. Various operators offer trips that generally include a variation of 4WD excursions, hikes, abseiling and, in the Negev, camel safaris and a Bedouin cultural experience (a traditional meal and/or a night in a Bedouin tent). Specific information is given in the relevant chapters.

Also, don't forget the organised tours with the Society for the Protection of Nature in Israel (SPNI) (☎ 03-638 8674 in Tel Aviv, email tourism@spni.org.il) which specialise in taking you to otherwise inaccessible places. The SPNI tours are generally well planned and run the gamut from easygoing to challenging, from one-day jaunts to 15-day full-on nature experiences. Their tours tend to be viewed as rather expensive, but you probably get more than your money's worth if you can afford the investment. Tour costs run from US$59 for a four hour Moonlight Tour of the Judean Desert to US$2125 for accommodation in a deluxe hotel on a 15 day Complete Active Tour of Israel. See their Web site (www.spni.org) for further details.

Pop: 622,100   ☎ **Area Code: 02**

Jerusalem is Israel's spiritual heart and the centre of its frenetic political and cultural life. It is a city that weighs heavy on the soul of its visitors; a city of contrasts and reflections. No visitor can fail to be moved by its startling yellow-white stone and overwhelming sense of history and purpose. It is surely the holiest city of all – so many people have attached so much importance to Jerusalem, for so many different and conflicting reasons, and for so many years.

Jerusalem is a religious hearth for Jews, Christians and Muslims alike. Within its walls you will find the holiest Jewish site, the Western Wall; the third holiest Muslim site – the Haram ash-Sharif/Temple Mount, from where Mohammed rose to heaven; and the holy Christian sites of Jesus' trial, crucifixion, burial and resurrection.

Jerusalem is a contentious city that has been divided and reunited; it's claimed as the capital by both Israelis and Palestinians. Jews inhabit the sprawling suburbs of West Jerusalem and the New City while Palestinians live mainly in East Jerusalem. Muslims, Jews and Christians share tenure of the teeming Old City in a truce in which tension is never far from the surface.

No visit to Israel can be complete without a visit to Jerusalem, and the few days that most visitors devote to a visit can barely do justice to the enormity of its historical and religious legacy.

HISTORY
First Temple

The first settlement on the site of Jerusalem was on the Ophel Ridge, immediately to the south-east of the present-day Jewish Quarter. This was a small Jebusite city, mentioned in Egyptian texts of the 20th century BC, which was conquered in 997 BC by the Israelites. They were led by their king, David who brought the Ark of the Covenant to Jerusalem and made the city his capital.

HIGHLIGHTS

- **The Old City** – so much to see, never enough time; historical sites, bazaars and its animated residents

- **The Haram ash-Sharif and the Dome of the Rock** – magnificent Islamic architecture

- **The Western Wall** – where Jews come to lament the loss of the Second Temple but which comes to life when colourful *bar mitzvahs* take place

- **The Israel Museum** – guardian of the nation's historical wealth and the Dead Sea Scrolls

- **The 'City of Mirrors'** – a city of pilgrimage for the world's three most important monotheistic religions; being here is an experience in itself

- **The Church of the Holy Sepulchre** – where Jesus was crucified; Christianity's most important site

THE WEST BANK

Also in Jerusalem:
Haram ash-Sharif p129
Via Dolorosa p138
Church of the
 Holy Sepulchre p139
The Israel Museum p175
Yad Vashem p181

TEL AVIV

Jerusalem p148-60 ●

Around Jerusalem
p203

THE NEGEV

Under Solomon, the son of David, the boundaries of the city were extended north to enclose the spur of land that is now the Haram ash-Sharif/Temple Mount. The construction of the First Temple began in 950 BC. After Solomon's death, some 17 years later, the city became the capital of Judah as the 12 tribes of Israel divided. In 586 BC Jerusalem fell to Nebuchadnezzar, the King of Babylon, and the city and the Temple were destroyed. The people of Jerusalem were exiled to Babylonia until three years later, when the King of Persia, Cyrus, allowed them to return.

Second Temple

The Second Temple was constructed around 520 BC, and around 445 BC the city walls were rebuilt under the leadership of Nehemiah, Governor of Judah.

The next notable stage in the history of Jerusalem came with Alexander the Great's conquest of the city in 331 BC. On his death in 323, the Seleucids eventually took over until the Maccabaean Revolt 30 years later. This launched the Hasmonean dynasty who re-sanctified the Temple in 164 BC after it had been desecrated by the Seleucids.

Romans

Under the leadership of General Pompey, Jerusalem was conquered by the Romans around 63 BC. Some 25 years later they installed Herod the Great to rule what they called the Kingdom of Judea. Upon the death of Herod, the Romans resumed direct control, installing a procurator to administer the city. Pontius Pilate, best known for ordering the crucifixion of Jesus around 30 AD, was the fifth procurator.

Another 36 years later came the First Revolt by the Jews against the Romans, but after four years of conflict, the Roman general Titus triumphed. With the Second Temple destroyed and Jerusalem burnt, many Jews became slaves and more fled into exile marking the start of the Diaspora. Jerusalem continued as the capital but Emperor Hadrian decided to destroy it completely in 132 AD due to the threat of renewed Jewish national

aspirations. This provoked the unsuccessful Second Revolt led by Simon Bar Kochba, after which Jews were forbidden to enter Aelia Capitolina, the new city built on the ruins of Jerusalem. Aelia Capitolina is the foundation of today's Old City.

Holy City

In 331 AD Christianity was legalised by Emperor Constantine, founder of the Eastern Roman Empire, and his mother visited the Holy Land searching for Christian holy places. This sparked off the building of basilicas and churches, and the city quickly grew to the size it had been under Herod the Great.

The Byzantine Empire was defeated by the Persians, who conquered Jerusalem in 614. Their rule lasted just 15 years before the Byzantines succeeded in retaking the city. That victory, however, was short-lived, for within another 10 years an Arab army, led by Caliph Omar under the banner of Islam, swept through Palestine. Omar's entry into Jerusalem was to instigate almost 1300 years of Muslim supremacy in what had been first a Jewish city, then a Christian city and now a city of Islam. In 688 the Dome of the Rock was constructed on the site of the destroyed Temple. Under the early Islamic leaders, Jerusalem was a protected centre of pilgrimage for Jews and Christians as well as Muslims, but this came to an end in the 10th century. Under Caliph Hakim, non-Muslims were cruelly persecuted and churches and synagogues were destroyed, finally provoking the Crusades 90 years later.

Crusaders & Mamluks

The Crusaders took Jerusalem in 1099 from the Fatimids who had only just regained control from the Seljuks. After almost 90 years the Latin Kingdom was defeated by Saladin (Salah ad-Din) in 1187. This was to be the most effective administration so far. Under Saladin, Muslims and Jews were allowed to resettle in the city. From the 13th to the 16th centuries, the Mamluks constructed a number of outstanding buildings dedicated to religious study.

Ottomans

Although a Muslim academic centre, Jerusalem became a relative backwater. In 1517 the Ottoman Turks defeated the Mamluks, adding Palestine to their large empire. Yet although they, too, are remembered for their lack of efficiency in local administration, their initial impact on the city is still much admired today. The impressive Old City walls that you see now were built by their second sultan, Suleyman the Magnificent. After Suleyman, Jerusalem's rulers allowed the city, like the rest of the country, to decline. Buildings and streets were not maintained, and corruption among the authorities was rife.

Jewish Revival

As a result of the Turkish sultan's 1856 Edict of Toleration for all religions, Jews and Christians were again able to settle in the city. In the 1860s, inspired and largely financed by an English Jew, Sir Moses Montefiore, Jewish settlement outside the city walls began. As Jewish immigration rapidly increased, these settlements developed into what is now the New City.

British Mandate

After WWI Jerusalem, which had been captured by General Allenby's forces from the Turks, became the administrative capital of the British Mandate. In these times of fervent Arab and Jewish nationalism, the city became a hotbed of political tensions. Jerusalem was always the most sought-after area of the country for both the Arabs and the Jews, and the city was the stage for much terrorism and more open warfare.

Divided City

After the British withdrew from Palestine, the UN became responsible for supervising the situation. Its subsequent partition plan was accepted by the Jews, but it was rejected by the Arabs. Jerusalem was to be internationalised, surrounded by independent Arab and Jewish states. In the 1948 War the Jordanians took the Old City and East Jerusalem, while the Jews held the New

City. Patches of no-man's-land separated them and the new State of Israel declared its part of Jerusalem as its capital.

For 19 years Jerusalem was a divided city, and Mandelbaum Gate became the official crossing point between East Jerusalem and the New City for the few who were permitted to move between them. The Six Day War in 1967 saw the reunification of the whole of Jerusalem, and the Israelis began a massive program of restoration, refurbishment and landscaping.

Controversial Capital

Controversy continues to surround the status of Jerusalem, and most countries maintain their embassies in Tel Aviv. According to Palestinians and other opponents of Israel, the Jewish State has no right to declare the city its capital, and you would be unwise to underestimate the strength of this sentiment. There is a sincere resentment among local Arabs of what Israel has done and continues to do, regardless of the numerous cosmetic changes made. The Israelis, meanwhile, are determined to keep all of Jerusalem as their capital regardless of any such opposition.

ORIENTATION

As cities go, Jerusalem is actually quite small, but it's made a little confusing by its fragmentation and hide-and-seek topography. The most important aid to navigation is an understanding that the city is broken into three distinct areas: the Old City, East Jerusalem and the New City (also referred to as West Jerusalem).

The Old City

For many visitors this is Jerusalem. Encircled by fortified walls, the Old City is one tightly bound square kilometre of 20,000 people and 3000 years of history. The Western Wall is here, as is the Dome of the Rock and the Church of the Holy Sepulchre, built over the site of biblical Golgotha. There is also an entrancing bazaar and here you'll find the doorways leading up to some of Jerusalem's best cheap hostels. Navigation is difficult, as the narrow, gully-like alleys twist, turn and buck to leave the uninitiated visitor without any sense of direction.

Of the seven gates that provide entrance to the Old City, the most important are likely to be Jaffa Gate, which is the main access from the New City, and Damascus Gate, which faces East Jerusalem.

The New City

This is the predominantly Jewish, commercial and administrative district, embracing a diversity of lifestyles from the 19th century orthodoxy of the Mea She'arim neighbourhood to the Baywatch-type babes around the pool at the Hilton International. The New City is roughly centred on the triangle of Jaffa Rd, King George V St and pedestrianised Ben Yehuda St. Zion Square is at the bottom of Ben Yehuda St and connects it with Jaffa Rd. Although it is fairly cramped and not much of a public plaza, it is a popular gathering point for demonstrators. Most of the mid-range and top-end hotels and eating places are around here, along with the most popular cafes and bars. Mahane Yehuda, the New City's cheap market, is just to the west of the central area, while further out are the Knesset building, the Israel Museum, the Holocaust memorial of Yad Vashem, and the Hadassah Medical Centre with the Chagall windows.

Home also to the central bus station, the New City is most travellers' initial contact with Jerusalem. Many of these travellers then hop on a local bus down Jaffa Rd to the Old City, into which they disappear not to emerge until it's time to move on, which is a shame because the New City has a lot to offer.

East Jerusalem

This is the Palestinian part of Jerusalem, lying to the east of HaShalom Rd. It is a district of small businesses, shops, travel agencies, moneychangers, hotels and restaurants mainly based on the two main streets of Nablus Rd and Salah ad-Din St. These form a triangle with congested Sultan Suleyman St, which runs alongside the Old City walls. Despite the fumes and the noise, East Jerusalem's cheap hostels are a popular alternative to those in the Old City, and what they lack in the picturesque department they make up for in value for money.

Also in East Jerusalem are the archaeological Rockefeller Museum, the Garden Tomb, considered to be a possible site of Jesus' crucifixion, burial and resurrection, and the temporarily closed Tourjeman Post Museum.

Maps

The Jaffa Rd tourist information office hands out a very poor city plan which is not going to get you anywhere but lost; far better and a very worthwhile investment is Carta's Map of Jerusalem (24NIS). Alternatively, a company called Map produces a pocket-sized 50 page Jerusalem Street Atlas (60NIS), which is far more comprehensive than the Carta map but, for those new to the city, doesn't really give a good impression of how it all fits together. There's also an excellent 1:2500 map Jerusalem – The Old City done by the Survey of Israel (15NIS).

More a memento than an on-the-hoof aid, Steimatzky does an attractive panoramic 3D map of the Old City (9NIS). All these maps are locally produced and should be available from any branch of Steimatzky or from the Society for the Protection of Nature in Israel (SPNI) shop on Heleni HaMalka St.

INFORMATION
Tourist Offices

The main city tourist information office (Map 3, ☎ 625 8844) is in the City Hall Complex on Safra Square, at the eastern end of Jaffa Rd. It goes by the grand name of the Jerusalem Information & Tourism Centre and is open Sunday to Thursday from 8.30 am to 4.30 pm, and Friday from 8.30 am to noon, closed Saturday.

Located on Omar ibn al-Khattab Square, opposite the entrance to the Citadel, the Christian Information Centre (Map 6, ☎ 627 2692, fax 628 6417) is very good on everything pertaining to the city's Christian sites and also has a good selection of books on Jerusalem. Practising Catholics apply here for tickets to the Christmas Eve Midnight Mass in Bethlehem. The Centre is open Monday to Saturday from 8.30 am to 1 pm; closed Sunday.

At 24 King George V St (Map 3), is the Ministry of Tourism, but it's not much use for day-to-day tourist inquiries. There is a (currently nonfunctional) computerised information stand which used to be accessible 24 hours a day when it was working.

The Jewish Student Information Centre (☎ 628 2643, fax 628 8338, email jseidel@ jer1.co.il) is at 5 Beit El St in the Jewish Quarter of the Old City (adjacent to the Hurva and Rambam synagogues). It has a lounge with refreshments, a library and evening activities, and it provides assistance with accommodation, Shabbat dinners and free tours, as well as general information for the Jewish visitor.

Currently there's a city tourist information office (Map 6, ☎ 625 8844) at 17 Jaffa Rd, just north of the Old City walls. It's very small and the staff there are not always particularly helpful. It is open Sunday to Thursday from 8.30 am to 4.30 pm, and Friday from 8.30 am to noon, closed Saturday. There's also a second, now privately run tourist information office at Jaffa Gate in the Old City, open the same hours.

SPNI

The Jerusalem office of the SPNI (Map 3, ☎ 624 1607) is at 13 Heleni HaMalka St, housed in what was originally a pilgrims' hospice built by the Russian Church in the 19th century. In addition to an information and tour booking office, there is also the country's best shop for Maps and hiking-related books and pamphlets. Some of the staff are experienced trekkers and are happy to give advice. The office is open Sunday to Wednesday from 9 am to 4.45 pm, Thursday from 9 am to 5.45 pm and Friday from 9 am to 12.30 pm.

Money

If you want the best deal when changing money, go to the legal moneychangers in the Old City and East Jerusalem. The two just inside Damascus Gate seem to give a

better price than those anywhere else. The moneychanger in the Petra Hostel near Jaffa Gate seems to be open when the others are closed. Other moneychangers can be found on David St – the Old City's main bazaar street going east from Jaffa Gate – and on Salah ad-Din St in East Jerusalem.

In the New City (Map 3) go to Change Point at 33 Jaffa Rd or 2 Ben Yehuda St and neither of which charge any commission. The Jaffa Rd branch is open daily from 9 am to 9 pm, but closed on Saturday. The one on Ben Yehuda St is open from 9.30 am to 7.45 pm, except on Friday, when it closes at 2 pm, and on Saturday, when it is closed all day. Most banks are on Jaffa Rd around Zion Square, and most are open Sunday to Tuesday and Thursday from 8.30 am to 12.30 pm and 4 to 5.30 pm, and Wednesday and Friday from 8.30 am to 12.30 pm; they're closed Saturday.

The American Express Travel service office (Map 3, ☎ 624 0830, fax 624 0950) is at 19 Hillel St. It will replace lost/stolen travellers cheques, receive mail etc. It is open Sunday to Thursday from 9 am to 5 pm, but closed on Friday and Saturday. The local agent for Thomas Cook is Aweidah Tours (Map 5, ☎ 628 2365, fax 628 2366) located at 23 Salah ad-Din St in East Jerusalem.

Post & Communications

The main post office (Map 3, ☎ 624 4745) and poste restante is at 23 Jaffa Rd. The main section is open Sunday to Thursday from 7 am to 7 pm, and Friday from 7 am to noon, closed Saturday. After hours you can send letters, telegrams and telexes from the information desk here. During the night you'll need patience to wake up somebody, and chances are they will not speak English.

There are several post office branches, including one in Omar ibn al-Khattab Square inside Jaffa Gate in the Old City (Map 6), which is open Sunday to Thursday from 7.30 am to 2.30 pm, and Friday from 8 am to noon. There's another in the Jewish Quarter (Map 9), just off the Cardo by the Broad Wall which is open Sunday, Monday, Wednesday and Thursday from 8 am to

12.30 pm and 4 to 6 pm, Tuesday from 8 am to 1.30 pm, and Friday from 8 am to 12.30 pm, closed Saturday.

East Jerusalem's main post office (Map 5) is on the corner of Salah ad-Din and Sultan Suleyman Sts. It's open Sunday and Thursday from 8.30 am to 2.30 pm and 4 to 6.30 pm, Monday, Wednesday and Friday from 8.30 am to 12.30 pm, and Tuesday from 8.30 am to 2.30 pm; it's closed Saturday.

For discount international telephone calls go to Solan Telecom (Map 3), which is at 2 Luntz St, a small pedestrianised street running between Jaffa Rd and Ben Yehuda St. It's open 24 hours a day, seven days a week.

Email & Internet Access Customers can send and receive email at the Strudel Internet cafe/wine bar (Map 3, ☎ 623 2101, fax 622 1445, email strudel@inter.net.il) at 11 Monbaz St, near the Russian Compound. It has four computer stations linked through Netscape to the Web and computer time is charged at 6NIS for 15 minutes. Printouts cost 1NIS per sheet for black & white and 2NIS for colour.

Nearby, at 9 Heleni HaMalka St, is the Netcafe (Map 3, ☎ 624 6327, email info@netcafe.co.il) where you can surf and email for 14NIS for 30 minutes or 25NIS for one hour. It's open from about 10 am until late on weekdays, 10 am to 3 pm on Friday and 9 pm until late on Saturday. There are also snacks and drinks available if Net surfing whets your appetite. Smoking is banned.

Tmol Shilshom (Map 3, ☎ 623 2758, email info@tmol-shilshom.co.il) at 5 Solomon St is a little cafe-cum-bookshop that currently has the cheapest Internet access charges in town: 9NIS for 30 minutes. There are only two terminals, so phone reservations are suggested. However, Internet access is limited to 10 am to 3 pm.

If you are in Jerusalem or Israel for any length of time and you have your own computer with you, you might want to take out your own Internet account. There are a number of providers, but Lonely Planet has used Netvision (☎ 04-856 0660, fax 855 0345, email admin@netvision.net.il) with considerable success and lack of fuss. Visit their Web site (www.netvision.net.il) for full details. They are based in Haifa but have local analogue and ISDN access numbers in each telephone region.

Travel Agencies

The student travel agency ISSTA (Map 3, ☎ 625 7257), at 31 HaNevi'im St, is open Sunday to Tuesday and Thursday from 9 am to 6 pm, and Wednesday and Friday from 9 am to 1 pm, closed Saturday. Egged Tours are at 44A Jaffa Rd (Map 2, ☎ 625 3454) and 224 Jaffa Rd (Map 2, ☎ 530 4422), while Mazada Tours (Map 3, ☎ 623 5777), which operates a bus service to Cairo and tours to Jordan, is at 9 Koresh St, a couple of blocks south of Jaffa Rd.

Bookshops

Steimatzky has three branches in Jerusalem's New City (Map 3). They're at 39 Jaffa Rd, just east of Zion Square, at 7 Ben Yehuda St and at 9 King George V St. If it's magazines you're after, take a look in Tower Records, on Hillel St, behind McDonald's; it has a large range of UK and US-style music and arts publications.

Probably Jerusalem's most endearing bookshop is Sefer VeSefel (Map 3), a creaky little place with floor to ceiling new and second-hand titles, fiction and nonfiction. It's particularly good on Middle Eastern history and politics and Judaism, and has a good assortment of used Israel travel guides. It also has a small balcony cafe. Sefer VeSefel is upstairs at 2 Ya'Avetz St, a little alley off Jaffa Rd, one block east of King George V St. It's open Sunday to Thursday from 8 am to 8 pm, Friday from 8 am to 2.30 pm, and Saturday from the end of Shabbat to 11.30 pm.

In the Old City (Map 9), The Bookshelf located at the southern end of Jewish Quarter Rd has piles of dog-eared thrillers, while the Moriah Bookstore on nearby Misgav Ladakh is the best place for English-language material on Judaism. In East Jerusalem (Map 5), Educational Bookshop at 22 Salah ad-Din St has a good assortment of Palestinian-oriented publications. In the same street is Sharbain's Bookshop, good for language and children's books.

French readers will find a limited selection of books in the Steimatzky stores but are much better catered for at Alliance Française Bookshop on Jaffa Rd, across from the main post office (Map 3).

Libraries

Books on Jerusalem as well as other nonfiction and fiction titles and English-language newspapers and magazines are available to the public at two British Council libraries: 4 Abu Obeida St (Map 5, ☎ 628 2545, fax 628 3021) in East Jerusalem (turn right just past the Tombs of the Kings) and at 3 Shimshon St (Map 4, ☎ 673 6733), in the south of the New City. Both these libraries are open Monday to Thursday from 11 am to 4 pm, and Friday from 9.30 am to 1.30 pm, closed Saturday and Sunday. There is also a good library at the Hebrew Union College located at 13 HaMelekh David St in the New City (Map 3). It is open Sunday to Thursday from 8 am to 5 pm.

Cultural Centres

In addition to the two British Councils (see the Libraries section above) there is also an American Cultural Center (Map 4, ☎ 625 5755) at 19 Keren HaYesod, an Alliance Française (Map 3) on Agron St, opposite the Supersol supermarket, and a French Cultural Centre (Map 5, ☎ 628 2451) at 21 Salah ad-Din St in East Jerusalem.

Laundry

With only two machines available but plenty of charm, coffee and good home cooking while you wait, Tzipor Hanefesh (Map 3, ☎ 624 9890) is a friendly three storey cafe/laundromat. One machine load costs 7NIS and a 45 minute drying cycle costs the same. You'll find it at 10 Rivlin St, in the trendy central area of Nahalat Shiv'a. There's another good laundromat close by at 12 Shamai St, one block south of Ben Yehuda St. It's open Saturday to Thursday from 9 am to 10.30 pm, and Friday from 8.30 am to 3.30 pm.

Medical Services

In emergencies call ☎ 101 or contact the Magen David Adom (☎ 652 3133). In the Old City, the Orthodox Society (Map 6, ☎ 627 1958), on Greek Orthodox Patriarchate Rd in the Christian Quarter, operates a low-cost clinic that, we're told, welcomes travellers. It also does dental surgery. The clinic is open Monday to Saturday from 8 am to 3 pm, closed Sunday.

A more expensive alternative is the Jerusalem Medical Centre (Map 2, ☎ 561 0297) on Diskin St in the Kiryat Wolfson district of the New City.

Emergency

In emergencies dial ☎ 100. Arab police seem to be responsible for basic duties in East Jerusalem and the Old City and their station is on Omar ibn al-Khattab Square, beside the Citadel. However, they are most likely to refer you to the central police station in the Russian Compound in the New City. The city's lost and found office is also here. It's open Sunday, Tuesday and Thursday from 7.30 am to 4 pm, Monday and Wednesday from 7.30 am to 2 pm, and Friday from 9.30 am to 12.30 pm, closed Saturday.

The city's rape crisis centre can be contacted on ☎ 651 4455.

THE OLD CITY (MAPS 6–9)

A bazaar of living history, the Old City is a densely packed labyrinth of more than 100 streets, 1000 shops and stalls, and 3000 years of human experience. As you walk along Via Dolorosa you're treading on the same paving stones that were there at the time of Christ – they were uncovered while new sewers were being dug in the 1970s. Rather than store them in a museum, the municipality had them re-laid. It is this perpetuation of the ancient in the 20th century that creates the appeal of the Old City.

The Old City is administered by the Israelis but is predominantly Arab in make-up and appearance. The two do not as a rule mix (although in the past there were times when they cohabited quite peacefully) and instead the Old City is divided into four hazily defined quarters. At the same time, it's focused on three definite centres of gravity. The Christian and Armenian quarters have developed in homage to the Church of the Holy Sepulchre, the site traditionally considered to be that of Jesus' crucifixion. The Muslim Quarter huddles in the shadow of the Haram ash-Sharif/Temple Mount, site of the Dome of the Rock, while the Jewish Quarter is orientated towards the Western Wall, the last vestige of the Second Temple.

Walls & Gates

The walls as they exist today are the legacy of Suleyman the Magnificent, who oversaw their construction between 1537 and 1542. The northern wall, including Damascus Gate, was built first and then extended south, at which point it was delayed by a dispute over whether or not Mt Zion and the Franciscans' monastery should stand inside or outside the wall. To save time and expense the builders decided against looping the wall around the monastery, leaving the Franciscans out in the cold. Popular legend has it that when news reached Suleyman of the miserly cost-cutting exercise, he was furious and had the architects beheaded.

There were seven gates in his walls and, in the late 19th century, an eighth was added. All but the Golden Gate on the southern side of the Haram ash-Sharif/Temple Mount are accessible and, time permitting, you should try to make a point of entering/leaving the Old City by each of them.

Note that each of the gates has at least three names; one by which it's known to the Arabs, one by which it's known to the Jews and a more internationally recognised Anglicised name. While almost everybody recognises the names Damascus Gate and Jaffa Gate, if you wanted an Arab taxi driver to take you, for example, to Herod's Gate, you would have to ask for Bab as-Zahra.

The following description of the gates begins with the Damascus Gate and continues clockwise around the wall.

Damascus Gate One of the most impressive structures of Islamic architecture in Jerusalem, Damascus Gate is also the busiest and most photogenic of the Old City gates. The amphitheatre-like plaza out the front has become a makeshift marketplace and it's a great place to sit and observe.

The gate itself dates in its present form from the time of Suleyman the Magnificent, although there had been a gate here long before the arrival of the Turks. This was the main entrance to the city as early as the time of Agrippas, who ruled in the 1st century BC. The gate was considerably enlarged during the reign of the Roman emperor Hadrian. The foundations of Hadrian's 'Great Gate' were uncovered during renovations in 1967 and are now open to visitors. Facing the outside of the gate, take the steps to your right which lead down to a small plaza; go through the door under the walkway and the old Roman gate is on your right at the foot of the wall. It's actually only one of two small entrances which flanked a much larger central gate (clearly illustrated on an adjacent copper wall plaque).

Inside, some of the old Roman gatehouse has been excavated and the cavernous rooms are used to house a collection illustrating the development of the gate area. It's worth a visit. One of the entrances to the ramparts above is also through here. The **Roman Square excavations**, as they're known, are open Saturday to Thursday from 9 am to 5 pm, and Friday from 9 am to 2 pm. Admission is 3.50NIS.

To the Arabs, this gate is known as Bab al-Amud (Gate of the Column), after a column erected by the Roman emperor Hadrian, which once stood in the square behind the gate. This column is shown on the Madaba map, a Byzantine-era mosaic discovered in Jordan, a copy of which is on display in the Roman Square excavations. In Hebrew it's Sha'ar Shechem (Nablus Gate).

Herod's Gate It was just 100m east of this gate that the Crusaders breached the city walls on 15 July 1099. The name was derived from a mistaken belief held by 16th and 17th century pilgrims that a nearby building was at one time the palace of Herod Antipas.

In Hebrew the gate is Sha'ar HaPerahim and in Arabic, Bab as-Zahra (Flower Gate).

St Stephen's Gate This is the gate that gives access to the Mount of Olives and Gethsemane, and from their positions on that biblically famed hillside, Israeli paratroopers fought their way in through this gate on 7 June 1967 to capture the Old City.

Although Suleyman called it Bab al-Ghor (the Jordan Gate), the name never stuck and it became known as St Stephen's Gate after the first Christian martyr, who was stoned to death at a spot nearby. The Hebrew name, Sha'ar Ha'Arayot (Lions Gate) is a reference to the two pairs of heraldic lions carved either side of the archway.

Golden Gate Uncertainty surrounds this sealed entrance to the Haram ash-Sharif/ Temple Mount. The Jewish Mishnah mentions the Temple's eastern gate and there are Herodian elements in the present structure. Some believe it to be where the Messiah will enter the city (Ezekiel 44:1-3). The gate was probably sealed by the Muslims in the 7th century to deny access to the Haram ash-Sharif/Temple Mount to non-Muslims. A popular alternative theory is that the Muslims sealed it to prevent the Jewish Messiah from entering the Haram. The Golden Gate is known as Sha'ar ha-Rahamim (Gate of Mercy) in Hebrew and either Bab al-Rahma or Bab al-Dahriyya (Eternal Gate) in Arabic.

Dung Gate In Hebrew it's Sha'ar HaAshpot. The popular theory as to how these two unflattering appellations came about is that at one time the area around the gate was the local rubbish dump. Its Arabic name is Bab al-Maghariba (Gate of the Moors) because North African immigrants lived nearby in the 16th century.

Presently the smallest of the city's gates, at one time it was even more diminutive. The Jordanians widened it during their tenure in the city in order to allow cars through.

You can still make out traces of the original, narrower Ottoman arch.

Zion Gate This gate had to be punched through to give access to the Franciscan monastery left outside the walls by Suleyman's architects. During the 1948 War, Israeli soldiers holding Mt Zion also tried to burst through here in a desperate attempt to relieve the besieged Jewish Quarter. First they tried to dynamite the wall at a spot 100m east of the gate (it still bears the scar) and when that failed they launched an all-out assault which ended disastrously. A memorial plaque to the fallen is inset within the gate while the bullet-eaten facade gives some indication of how ferocious the fighting must have been.

To the Jews, the gate is Sha'ar Ziyyon, while in Arabic it's Bab Haret al-Yahud (Gate of the Jewish Quarter).

Jaffa Gate The actual gate is the small block through which the doglegged pedestrian tunnel passes (the dogleg was to slow down any charging enemy forces – you'll find the same thing at Damascus and Zion gates); the breach in the wall through which the road now passes was only made in 1898 in order to permit the visiting Kaiser Wilhelm II and his party to ride with full pomp into the city.

Just inside the gate, on the left as you enter, are two graves said to be those of Suleyman's architects, beheaded for leaving the Mt Zion monastery outside the walls.

The Arabic name for the gate is Bab al-Khalil (Gate of the Friend), which refers to the holy city of Hebron (Al-Khalil in Arabic). In Hebrew it is Sha'ar Yafo because this was the start of the old road to the historical port of Jaffa.

New Gate This is the most modern of all the gates, opened in 1887 by Sultan Abdul Hamid to allow direct access from the newly built pilgrim hospices to the holy sites of the Old City's Christian Quarter. In Hebrew it's ha-Sha'ar He-Chadash, and in Arabic, al-Bab al-Jadid.

Ramparts Walk

One of the best ways to see the Old City and its surroundings is to walk around the top of the walls. The walls are surprisingly high in parts, and the views across the Old City rooftops are a treat. Such a walk will also enable you to make some kind of sense of the layout of the place.

It's not a good idea to make the walk after rain, or especially after snow, as despite new paving and guardrails, the stone can be slippery underfoot. In addition, women should not walk unaccompanied here at any time, as to do so would be to risk sexual assault and mugging.

It isn't possible to do a complete circuit of the wall because the Haram ash-Sharif/Temple Mount stretch is closed for security reasons. Instead, the walk is in two sections: Jaffa Gate north to St Stephen's Gate (via New, Damascus and Herod's gates) and Jaffa Gate south to Dung Gate (via Zion Gate).

While you can descend at any of the gates, getting up onto the walls is only possible at two of them. At Jaffa Gate the stairs for the Damascus Gate walk are on the left as you enter the Old City, through an arch in the facade of the Golden Gate jewellery shop; the stairs for the Dung Gate stretch are outside the walls, 100m south of Jaffa Gate. At Damascus Gate the ramparts are reached by going through the Roman Square excavations (see the Damascus Gate section of Walls & Gates earlier in this chapter).

The walls are open Saturday to Thursday from 9 am to 4 pm, and Friday and holiday eves from 9 am to 2 pm. The section from the Citadel to Zion Gate is open Sunday to Thursday until 9.30 pm. Tickets cost 10NIS and are valid for four admissions over two days (three at the weekend), allowing you to do the combined 3.5km walk gradually. Note that tickets cannot be purchased on Saturday.

Rooftop Promenade

For a different perspective on the Old City, climb the metal stairway on the corner of Habad St and St Mark's Rd or the steep stone stairs in the south-western corner of the Khan as-Sultan, both of which lead onto the rooftops around the David St and Al-Wad markets. Come up during the day for a peek through the ventilation ducts at the bustle below but also make a night-time visit to appreciate the Old City in its moonlit silhouette.

The Citadel (Tower of David)

This is one of the country's most impressive restoration projects and a major museum complex, so it's worth paying a visit to the Citadel early in your stay for an excellent grounding in Jerusalem history.

The Citadel started life as the 1st century palace of Herod the Great. A megalomaniacal builder, Herod furnished his palace with three enormous towers, the largest of which was reputedly modelled on the Pharos of Alexandria, one of the seven wonders of the ancient world. The chiselled-block remains of one of the lesser towers still serve as the base of the Citadel's main keep. Following Herod's death the palace was used by the Roman procurators as their Jerusalem residence until it was largely destroyed by Jewish rebels in 66 AD. The Byzantines, who came along some 250 years later, mistook the mound of ruins for Mt Zion and presumed that this was David's palace – hence the name Tower of David. They constructed a new fortress on the site.

As Jerusalem changed hands, so did possession of the Citadel, passing to the Muslim armies and then to the Crusaders, who added the moat. It took on much of its present form in 1310 under the Mamluk sultan Malik an-Nasir, with Suleyman the Magnificent making further additions between 1531 and 1538. Suleyman is responsible for the gate by which the Citadel is now entered, and it was on the steps here that General Allenby accepted the surrender of the city on 9 December 1917, ending 400 years of rule by the Ottoman Turks.

For a site that acts as a micro-cosm of the city through the ages, the Citadel today fittingly serves as the **Tower of David Museum of the History of Jerusalem** (☎ 627 4111, fax 628 3418, email tower@netvision.net.il). Its

The Jerusalem Syndrome

The Red Sea sun can blister unprotected skin and a splash of Dead Sea in the eye is agonising, but Jerusalem can send a person mad. It happens to about 200 foreign visitors a year. Overwhelmed by the impact of the Holy City's historical and religious heritage people believe themselves to be characters from the Bible; like the Canadian Jew who, claiming to be Samson, decided to prove his ID by smashing through the wall of his room to escape. Or there was the elderly American Christian woman who believed she was the Virgin Mary and went to Bethlehem to look for the baby Jesus, inviting anyone who would listen to His birthday party. This sort of deluded behaviour has become a recognised phenomenon known as the Jerusalem Syndrome. Although many of these individuals have arrived at Ben-Gurion airport with a recorded history of mental aberration, about a quarter of those cases on file have had no previous psychiatric record.

In perhaps the most serious case so far, in 1969 an Australian Christian fanatic set fire to Al-Aqsa Mosque, causing considerable damage. He believed that he had to clear the Haram ash-Sharif/Temple Mount of non-Christian buildings to prepare for the Messiah. More recently, in spring 1992 a US Christian went into a violent rage in the Church of the Holy Sepulchre and before the security guards were able to subdue him, he had smashed lamps and icons and torn down the cross marking the traditional site of the crucifixion of Jesus.

The Jerusalem Syndrome is nothing new. In the 1930s, an English Christian woman was certain that Christ's Second Coming was imminent and would regularly climb Mt Scopus to welcome Him back to earth with a cup of tea.

Christian sufferers of the syndrome tend to break down at such traditional sites as the Mount of Olives, the Via Dolorosa or the Garden Tomb, and identify with such characters as Jesus or the Virgin Mary, although John the Baptist is apparently the most popular choice. In addition to Samson, 'incarnations' of Jewish sufferers have included Moses and King David.

As with everything else in Israel, opinions vary on what causes the Syndrome. It's been suggested that these are people who have arrived in Israel hoping to find peace and calm, possibly looking for an escape from some kind of turmoil back home, and when instead they encounter the conflict and tension that underlies life in Jerusalem, their minds snap. Although the ages and backgrounds vary, a significant proportion of those afflicted with the syndrome are unmarried 20 to 30 year old Christians or Jews from North America and Western Europe who grew up in religious homes. Men seem to outnumber women two to one.

Most of the syndrome sufferers wind up at the state psychiatric hospital, Kfar Shaul, on the outskirts of West Jerusalem. Treatment tends to take the form of observation until the patient is deemed well enough to be flown home. In most cases, this takes a week or so. Doctors at Kfar Shaul have found it virtually pointless to try to persuade the deluded that they are not who they claim to be. The hospital cites the example of two patients, both claiming to be the Messiah. Put together, each accused the other of being the impostor.

many rooms contain some impressive dioramas and artefacts, holograms and videos which tell a version of the city's story. Visitors can follow one of four or five special signposted routes through the museum, including one for the disabled. One of the highlights is a detailed large-scale model of Jerusalem, made in the late 19th century and discovered almost 100 years later, forgotten in a Geneva warehouse. It's displayed in an underground chamber reached from the central courtyard garden.

The entrance to the Citadel is just inside Jaffa Gate. From April to October it's open Sunday to Thursday from 9 am to 5 pm, and Friday, Saturday and holiday eves from 9 am to 2 pm. From November to March the museum opens at 10 am and closes at 4 pm (2 pm Saturday). At 11 am daily there's a free guided tour in English.

Every important historical site in Israel seems to feel the need to put on a sound and light show and the Citadel joins the club with a production of questionable quality. The show is presented in English each Monday and Wednesday at 9.30 pm and on Saturday at 9 pm. There are performances in French, German and Hebrew on other days of the week at differing times. Wrap up well if you're attending because evenings in Jerusalem are often surprisingly chilly, even in summer.

Entry to the above attractions is 24NIS (students 17NIS), or you can buy a combined ticket for 40NIS (students 28NIS).

Finally, as if this is not enough, there is a 'Mystery in the Citadel' event in which you become detective, judge and jury in a light-hearted historical murder case. Four suspects lead the audience around part of the museum in search of the murderer of Aristobulus III, the high priest, and brother-in-law of Herod the Great. For this pleasure, expect to fork out 28NIS (students 24NIS) or buy another combined ticket with the museum for 38NIS (students 32NIS).

Haram ash-Sharif/Temple Mount

Dominating not just the Old City but in some ways the whole country, this vast esplanade has become a spiritual keystone to the Jewish and Muslim faiths and something of an obstacle to peace between the two peoples.

All three monotheistic faiths agree on the most holy nature of this place (ancient Mt Moriah where Abraham was called to sacrifice his son in a test of his faith – Genesis 22:2-19), but in no way does a shared sense of sanctity translate into any form of kinship. Instead, the Mount (the closest spot on earth to paradise in Muslim lore) is surrounded by barbed wire and sharpshooters and carefully patrolled by watchful flak-jacketed soldiers.

Religious Jews still bristle at the presence of the Muslims on the site of Solomon's Temple (I Kings 5-8), destroyed by Nebuchadnezzar (II Kings 25) and replaced by the Second Temple which stood until its destruction by the Romans in 70 AD. Muslims, who have worshipped at their mosque here for 1300 years, rebuff all Jewish demands for access seeing in them a further erosion of Palestinian rights in the face of Zionism. Periodically there are clashes at the gates, tear gas mists the air and more blood is spilt. The angel may have stayed the hand of Abraham but he's done far less well since.

For the uninvolved visitor, the Haram ash-Sharif (Noble Sanctuary in Arabic; the Jewish term is Har HaBayit, or Temple Mount) is a relaxing contrast to the noise and congestion of the surrounding narrow streets. It's a flat paved area the size of a couple of adjacent football fields, fringed with some attractive Mamluk buildings and with the Dome of the Rock positioned roughly in the centre. There are nine gates connecting the enclosure to the surrounding narrow streets, but although you can leave the compound by any of them, non-Muslims are only allowed to enter through two: Bab al-Maghariba (Gate of the Moors), reached from the Western Wall plaza, and Bab as-Silsila (Chain Gate), at the eastern end of Bab as-Silsila St.

Entrance to the Haram itself is free, but to visit the two mosques (highly recommended) and the museum, a ticket must be purchased for 30NIS (students 22NIS). Get the ticket from the ticket kiosk just inside the Bab al-Maghariba.

Visiting hours are slightly confusing as they are based around Muslim prayer schedules, which follow the lunar calendar. Basically, the Haram is open Saturday to Thursday (closed Friday) from 8 am to 3 pm, although those inside by then are allowed to stay until 4 pm. During prayers (approximately from 11.30 am to 12.30 pm in winter and 12.30 to 1.30 pm in summer) the museum shuts and entry to the mosques

LEE FOSTER

LEE FOSTER

CHRISTINE OSBORNE

The Dome of the Rock (top & bottom left) with gold dome and fine tilework is a spectacular structure reputedly built to compete with the highly sacred Church of the Holy Sepulchre (bottom right).

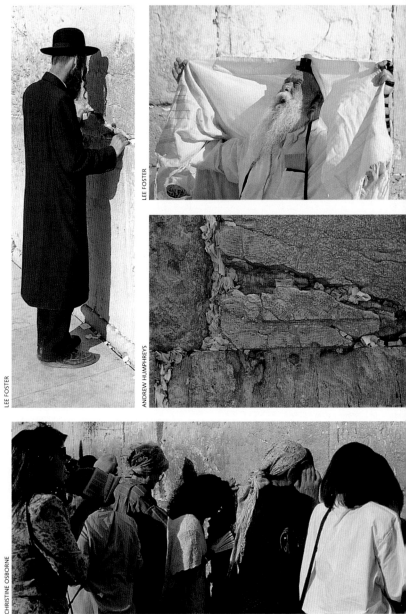

LEE FOSTER

LEE FOSTER

ANDREW HUMPHREYS

CHRISTINE OSBORNE

As the holiest of all Jewish sites, Jerusalem's Western Wall – also known as the Wailing Wall – acts as an open-air synagogue and attracts pilgrims from around the world.

HARAM ASH-SHARIF / TEMPLE MOUNT

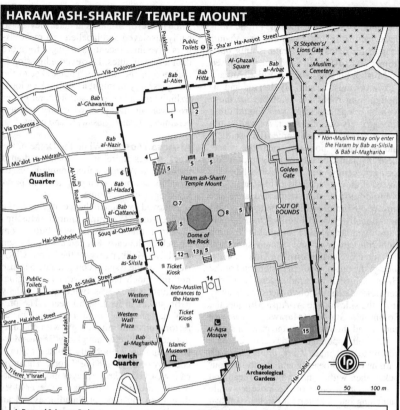

* Non-Muslims may only enter the Haram by Bab as-Silsila & Bab al-Maghariba

1 **Dome of Suleyman Pasha**
2 **Sabil – Public Fountain**
3 **Solomon's Throne**
4 **Sabil of Sheikh Budir**
5 **The Stairs of Scales of Souls**
   Muslims believe that scales will be hung from the
   column-supported arches at the top of these stairs
   on Judgment Day to weigh the souls of the dead.
6 **Small Wall**
   A little visited northern extension of the Western Wall.
7 **Dome of the Ascension**
   According to Muslim tradition Mohammed prayed
   here before his ascent.
8 **Dome of the Chain**
   This is the smaller version of the Dome of the Rock,
   in the exact centre of the Haram. Mystery surrounds
   the reason for its construction. A popular theory is
   that it was a trial-run for the real thing; another is
   that it was the Haram's treasury. Its name comes from
   the legend that Solomon hung a chain from the dome
   and those who swore falsely whilst holding it were
   struck by lightning.
9 **Gate of the Cotton Merchants**
   This is the most imposing of the Haram's gates. Make a
   point of departing through here into the Mamluk-era
   arcaded market of the Cotton Merchants (Souq al-Qattanin).

10 **Sabil of Qaitbay**
   Though overshadowed by its more illustrious neighbours,
   this is one of Jerusalem's most beautiful structures.
   It was built by Egyptians in 1482 as a charitable act to
   please Allah, and it features the only carved stone dome
   outside Cairo.
11 **Mamluk Arcade**
12 **Dome of Learning**
   Along with parts of the facade of the Al-Aqsa Mosque,
   this is one of the very few remaining Ayyubid
   (1187-1250) structures in Jerusalem. Note the very unusual
   entwined columns flanking the door.
13 **Summer Pulpit**
   Built by the Mamluks in the 14th century and renovated
   by the Ottomans, this was used to deliver outdoor
   sermons.
14 **Al-Kas Fountain**
   One of many ablutions fountains on the Haram for the ritual
   washing before prayers.
15 **Solomon's Stables**
   A cavernous vaulted hall under the Haram,
   constructed by the Crusaders to accommodate their horses.
   Unfortunately it's closed except by arrangement.
   This area is out of bounds.

is for Muslims only. Note also that during the month of Ramadan (see the Public Holidays section in the Facts for the Visitor chapter for dates) the Haram is only open from 7.30 to 10 am. It is completely closed on Muslim holidays such as Eid al-Adha.

Visitors must be suitably dressed and although long robes are available for those with bare legs and arms, you should dress appropriately out of respect. As well as patrols of Israeli Defence Force (IDF) soldiers and Palestinian police to keep the peace, there are plain-clothed Muslim guards monitoring decency, and couples will be accosted if they so much as hold hands.

In addition, certain unmarked areas are strictly off-limits and if you stray, even unintentionally, you will be lectured and perhaps even arrested. Presumably Islamic authorities are coy about casual visitors getting too close to the sensitive Golden Gate, though the out-of-bounds eastern end of the Haram ash-Sharif is a rather scruffy and dry concrete plateau of olive trees. Stay away from the sides of the Al-Aqsa Mosque, the Solomon's Stables (Marawani Moswue) corner and the garden on the eastern side.

The self-appointed guides can also be a complete nuisance. They often approach with an official bearing and ask to see your ticket, then with it in hand they'll lead you over to one or other of the mosques while launching into a historical spiel; if you had not planned on taking a guide then stop them fast. Their other trick is to fluster people by saying, 'Quick, quick the mosque is closing, you have to hurry to see it'; of course they attach themselves to explain everything 'quick, quick'. Simply don't hand over your ticket to anyone but the guy at the door, who is also the person to ask about closing times. Note that in addition to removing your footwear to enter the mosques, all bags and cameras must be left outside, too – leave someone on watch, as Lonely Planet has received letters telling us of thefts.

For best effect, visit the uninspiring Islamic Museum and understated Al-Aqsa Mosque before you visit the spectacular Dome of the Rock.

Islamic Museum Although there are some interesting objects in here, they are so badly displayed and labelled that most visitors have little incentive to linger for more than a few minutes. However, admission is included in the price of your ticket to the mosques, so you might as well take a look. Exhibits include ornate architectural pieces from various mosques, weaponry, textiles, ceramics, Qurans, glassware and coins.

Al-Aqsa Mosque While the Dome of the Rock serves more as a masthead than a mosque, Al-Aqsa is a functioning house of worship, accommodating up to 5000 praying supplicants at a time.

Believed by some to be a conversion of a 6th century Byzantine church, Muslims maintain that Al-Aqsa was built from scratch in the early 8th century by the son of Abd al-Malik, patron of the Dome. Clarification of the issue is complicated because nothing much remains from the original structure, which was twice destroyed by earthquakes in its first 60 years. The present-day mosque is a compendium of restorations and rebuildings, with columns donated, strangely enough, by Benito Mussolini and the elaborately painted ceilings courtesy of Egypt's King Farouk. The intricately carved *mihrab* (prayer niche indicating the direction of Mecca), however, does date from the time of Saladin, as did an equally magnificent carved wood pulpit which was lost in a 1969 fire started by a deranged Australian Christian.

Dome of the Rock Enclosing the sacred rock upon which Abraham prepared to sacrifice his son and from which, according to Islamic tradition, the Prophet Mohammed launched himself heavenward to take his place alongside Allah, the Dome of the Rock was constructed between 688 and 691 AD under the patronage of the Umayyad caliph Abd al-Malik. His motives were shrewd as well as pious – the caliph was concerned that the imposing Christian Church of the Holy Sepulchre was seducing Arab minds.

In asserting the supremacy of Islam, Abd al-Malik had his Byzantine architects take as their model the rotunda of the Holy Sepulchre. But not for the Muslims the dark, gloomy interiors of the Christian structures or the austere stone facades; instead their mosque was covered, both inside and out, with a bright confection of mosaics and scrolled verses from the Quran, while the crowning dome was covered in solid gold that shone as a beacon for Islam.

A plaque was laid inside honouring al-Malik and giving the date of construction. Two hundred years later the Abbasid caliph al-Mamun altered it to claim credit for himself, neglecting to amend the original date.

During the reign of Suleyman the Magnificent what remained of the original interior mosaics were removed and replaced, while the external mosaics were renewed in 1963. Essentially, however, what you see today is the building as conceived by Abd al-Malik. The gold dome also disappeared long ago, melted down to pay off some caliph's debts. The present convincing anodised aluminium dome has been financed by Gulf State Arab countries.

Inside, lying central under the 20m high dome and ringed by a wooden fence, is the rock from which Mohammed began his Night Journey (his footprint is supposedly visible in one corner). Tradition also has it that this marks the centre of the world.

Steps below the rock lead to a cave known as the 'Well of Souls' where the dead are said to meet twice a month to pray. If you descend into the cave you'll probably find Muslim women praying and you may be ushered out by an anxious guard after a few seconds.

Orthodox Jews may not enter the mosque because they might inadvertently trespass on the site of the Holy of Holies, the innermost sanctum of the Temple which only the High Priest was permitted to enter (and even then only on Yom Kippur). However, do not be surprised to see young Israeli army recruits – minus boots and weapons – being given a cultural tour of the mosque by an equally young female officer.

Mamluk Buildings Make a point of strolling around the northern section of the Haram to admire the facades on the northern and western sides. Mainly religious schools, these buildings feature some delightfully ornate stonework. See Mamluk Buildings in the Muslim Quarter section of this chapter for more information.

Western Wall

In stark contrast to the gaudy magnificence of the Dome of the Rock, the Western Wall (in Hebrew, HaKotel Hama'aravi or HaKotel) is nothing more than a stone wall but still manages to be one of the most captivating places in Jerusalem, and indeed Israel.

It is part of the retaining wall built by Herod the Great in 20 BC to contain the landfill on which the Second Temple compound stood. The Romans destroyed the Temple in 70 AD but since, according to rabbinical texts, the *shechina* (divine presence) never deserted the wall it's regarded as the most holy of all Jewish sites. The Wall grew as a place of pilgrimage during the Ottoman period where Jews would come to mourn and lament their ancient loss – hence the term the Wailing Wall. At this time, houses were pressed right up to the Wall leaving just a narrow alley for prayer.

God's Fax Line

Courtesy of Israel's national phone company, Bezek, the pious can now fax the Almighty. Messages received on fax 02-561 2222 are collected and once a day (Shabbat excepted), taken by telephone company employees down to the Western Wall to be wedged in between the stones. Bezek says that over 100 messages a day are received – more during Jewish holidays. There is no fee charged for the service. Failing that, you can make a virtual visit to the Wall at its own Web site www.kotelkam .com replete with WebCam so that you can observe the comings and goings of the faithful and post an email message.

In 1948 the Jews lost access when the whole of the Old City was taken by the Jordanians. Nineteen years later when Israeli paratroopers stormed in during the Six Day War they fought their way directly to the Wall and the first action on securing the Old City was to bulldoze the neighbouring Arab quarter to create the plaza that exists today.

The area immediately in front of the Wall now operates as a great open-air synagogue. It's divided into two areas, a small southern section for women and a more active, larger northern section for men. Here, the black-garbed Hasidim rock backwards and forwards on their heels, bobbing their heads in prayer, occasionally breaking off to press themselves against the Wall and kiss the stones. To celebrate the arrival of Shabbat there is always a large crowd at sunset on Friday and students from the nearby Yeshiva HaKotel head down there to dance and sing. The Wall is also a popular site for bar mitzvahs, held on the Shabbat or on Monday and Thursday mornings.

The fascination extends beyond the Jewish world. Madonna visited, as did Michael Jackson one Saturday in 1993. His visit in particular raised the ire of the orthodox because of the accompanying entourage of camera-clicking press corps (photography is forbidden on the Shabbat). Nevertheless, non-Jewish visitors who dress modestly and, in the case of men, don the complimentary kippa are permitted to approach the Wall.

Notice the different styles of stonework. The huge lower layers are the Herodian stones, identifiable by their carved edges, while the strata above that, which are chiselled slightly differently, date from the time of the construction of the Al-Aqsa Mosque. Also visible at close quarters are the wads of paper, from Post-It notes to half-exercise books, stuffed into the cracks in the stone wall: it's a belief that prayers inserted into the Wall have a better than average chance of being answered.

The Western Wall is accessible 24 hours a day, and admission is free. We highly recommend that you experience the plaza bathed in moonlight.

Wilson's Arch Situated to the north of the men's prayer section, this arch carries Bab as-Silsila St to the Temple across the Tyropoeon (Cheesemaker's) Valley. It was once used by priests on their way to the Temple. Look down the two illuminated shafts to get an idea of the wall's original height. Possibly Hasmonean (150 to 40 BC) but at least Herodian, the room's function is unknown. Women are not permitted into the room and the site is often closed, full stop. Theoretically, the arch room is open Sunday, Tuesday and Wednesday from 8.30 am to 3 pm, Monday and Thursday from 12.30 to 3 pm, and Friday from 8.30 am to noon, closed Saturday.

The Jewish Quarter (Map 9)

Roughly defined as the area south of Bab as-Silsila St and east of Habad St, the Jewish Quarter is an area you'll recognise immediately by its scrubbed stone, the neat, precise edges, and the air of no one being home.

Flattened during the fighting in 1948, the Jewish Quarter has been almost entirely reconstructed since it was recaptured by the Israelis in 1967. Though modern, the architecture of the quarter is traditional in style, designed to maintain the character of the Old City, though lacking a little in spirit.

There are few historic monuments above ground level but the digging that went on during construction unearthed a number of interesting archaeological finds, some of which date back to the time of the First Temple (around 1000 to 586 BC). Everything is well signposted, and while there's nothing unmissable, the area around the Quarter Cafe is very pleasant and there are great views of the Haram ash-Sharif/Temple Mount and Western Wall from the stairs beside the Church of St Maria of the Germans.

The Cardo Cutting a broad north-south swathe, this is the reconstructed main street of Roman and Byzantine Jerusalem, the Cardo Maximus. At one time it would have run the whole breadth of the city, up to what's now Damascus Gate, but in its present form it starts just south of David St, the tourist souq, serving as the main entry into the Jewish Quarter from the Muslim and Christian areas.

As depicted on the 6th century Madaba map of the Old City, a copy of which is displayed here, the Cardo would have been a wide colonnaded avenue flanked by roofed arcades. A part of it to the south has been restored to something like its original appearance while the rest has been reconstructed as an arcade of expensive gift shops and galleries of Judaica. There are wells to allow visitors to see down to the levels beneath the street where there are strata of wall from the days of the First Temple and the Second Temple.

Upstairs, above one of the Cardo galleries, is a permanent exhibition which goes under the title of *One Last Day*. This is a set of photographs taken by John Phillips, on assignment for *Life* magazine, on the day the Jewish Quarter fell to the Jordanians in 1948. They can be viewed from Sunday to Thursday from 9 am to 5 pm, and Friday from 9 am to 1 pm, closed Saturday. Admission is 4NIS.

Broad Wall Just east of the Cardo and north of Hurva Square, looking like a derelict lot between blank-faced apartment blocks, is a stretch of crumbling masonry known as the Broad Wall. This is actually an exposed portion of the remains of a fortified stone wall dating from the time of King Hezekiah (circa 701 BC).

The Israelite Tower & Rachel Ben-Zvi Centre Buried beneath a modern apartment block on Shone HaLakhot St and reached by a short flight of steps, the Israelite Tower is a gate tower from the time of the Babylonian siege and destruction of the First Temple (roughly 580 BC). The site is open Sunday to Thursday from 9 am to 5 pm, and Friday from 9 am to 1 pm. Admission is 4NIS, which also covers entry to the Burnt House and the Wohl Archaeological Museum.

Across from the Israelite Tower, the Rachel Ben-Zvi Centre (☎ 628 6288), also on Shone HaLakhot St, exhibits a scale model of Jerusalem in the First Temple period, which shows archaeological findings from the period of King David and his followers. The centre's other exhibits include an audiovisual history of the city from 1000 to 586 BC.

The centre is open to visitors Sunday to Thursday from 9 am to 4 pm, and on Friday from 9 am to 1pm. Admission is 11NIS (students 9NIS).

Hurva Square & Synagogues Hurva Square is the tree-shaded social centre of the Jewish Quarter. It's easily identifiable by its graceful landmark of a lone single-brick arch, almost all that remains of the **Hurva Synagogue**. The synagogue was originally dedicated by the Ashkenazi community in 1864 but was destroyed by the Jordanians in 1948. On regaining control of the Old City in 1967, the Jews decided to rebuild their place of worship but despite a succession of plans being submitted by various renowned architects, no agreement on how to proceed could be reached. The re-creation of one of the arches that supported the synagogue dome was as far as the matter got.

Adjoining the Hurva Synagogue is the **Ramban Synagogue**, its name is an acronym for Rabbi Moshe Ben Nahman. The synagogue was established on this site in the year 1400 in a stable bought from an Arab landlord, but problems were later caused by the building of a neighbouring mosque (the minaret of which still stands). The upshot was that in 1588 the Jews were banned from worship and the synagogue was converted into a workshop. It was reinstated as a house of worship only in 1967, some 380 years later.

South of Hurva Square, on HaTupim St, are four **Sephardic synagogues**, two of which date back as far as the 16th century. In accordance with a law of the time stating that synagogues could not be taller than neighbouring buildings, this grouping was sunk deep into the ground – a measure which certainly saved the buildings from destruction during the bombardment of the quarter in 1948. Instead, the synagogues were looted by the Jordanians and then used as sheep pens. They have been restored using the remains of Italian synagogues damaged during WWII and are back in use for morning and evening services. The synagogues are open Sunday to Thursday from 9.30 am to 4 pm, and Friday from 9.30 am to noon. There is a small admission fee.

Batei Mahseh Square & the Shelter Houses Batei Mahseh was at one time the quarter's largest square, presided over by the **Rothschild building**, a grand old thing built in 1871 with funds provided by Baron Wolf Rothschild of Frankfurt. The Shelter Houses facing the Old City walls on Batei Mahseh St were originally intended to provide housing for the poor, but during the last fortnight of the battle for the quarter in May 1948, hundreds of resident Jews also found shelter in their basements.

Museums Perhaps the most impressive complex in the Jewish Quarter is the **Wohl Archaeological Museum** (☎ 628 3448), which details the lavish lifestyle enjoyed in the Jewish neighbourhood of Herod's city. Exhibits include frescoes, stucco reliefs, mosaic floors, ornaments, furniture and household objects. It's open Sunday to Thurs-day from 9 am to 5 pm, and Friday from 9 am to 1 pm, closed Saturday. Admission is 10NIS, which also covers entry to the Israelite Tower and the Burnt House.

The **Burnt House** (☎ 628 7211), next to the Quarter Cafe, is the reconstruction of a luxurious house in what was the Upper City of the Second Temple era. There's also an audiovisual show presented in a number of different languages, including English. The Burnt House has the same opening hours as the Wohl Archaeological Museum.

The same idea but jumping way forward in time, is the **Old Yishuv Court Museum** (☎ 628 4636) at 6 Or HaChaim St (west of the Cardo) a reconstructed house in which each room illustrates an aspect of Jewish life in the quarter before the destruction of the 1948 War. This museum is open Sunday

to Thursday from 9 am to 2 pm. Admission is 12NIS (students 10NIS).

Probably of much more limited interest is the **Siebenberg House** (☎ 628 2341), a private residence with excavations in the basement. Finds include a Hasmonean cistern and parts of what may have been an aqueduct that carried water from Solomon's Pools to the Temple. The Siebenberg House is at 35 Misgav Ladakh St (on the corner of HaGittit St) and is open by appointment only.

St Maria of the Germans Located on the northern side of the steps leading to the Western Wall, this is a Crusader complex comprising a church, a hospital and a hospice. When archaeologists first unearthed these remains there were demands from the ultraorthodox Jewish community to have them destroyed because they strongly objected to the existence of a church on a major route to the Western Wall.

The Muslim Quarter (Map 7)

This is the most bustling and densely populated area of the Old City and depending on your tastes it's either claustrophobic and a hassle or completely exhilarating. Enter the melee at permanently congested Damascus Gate, squeezing by a tractor and dodging the young Arab boys riding their vendors' carts down the slope. About 100m in, the street forks, and there is a busy *felafel* stall wedged between the two prongs. Bearing to the left is Al-Wad Rd, lined with vast showrooms of brass items such as coffee pots and trays, in among sweet shops, vegetable stalls and an egg stall. This route leads directly to the Western Wall, along the way crossing the Via Dolorosa.

The section of the Via Dolorosa heading uphill to the west (right) is crowded with Christian pilgrims, tour groups and shoppers battling for the right of way. Souvenir shops line the route, with ceramics the speciality.

Bearing to the right at the fork is Souq Khan as-Zeit St, which is even busier than Al-Wad Rd. It's lined with shops selling fruit, vegetables, sweets, hardware and oriental spices and nuts.

There Goes the Neighbourhood

On Al-Wad Rd, a little south of the fork with Souq Khan as-Zeit St in the heart of the Muslim Quarter, a broad arch bridges the street and from one of its windows hangs a bed-sheet-size Israeli flag. This is the controversial home of the hawkish Israeli politician and war hero Ariel Sharon. He purchased this property as a statement of his belief that Jews should be able to live anywhere within Israel. His lead has been followed by a small band of other Jews, who have set up homes and even *yeshivot* (religious schools) in among the Muslims.

The majority of less extremist Jews, it should be noted, do regard this settlement as needlessly aggressive and it does not have widespread support. Nevertheless, Palestinians have little choice but to live with it, and a round-the-clock detachment of IDF soldiers lounges around the doorway of Beit Sharon to see that they do so quietly. Ironically, Sharon doesn't actually live here.

It's also illuminating to note that prior to Sharon's occupation, the Israeli government had forbidden an Arab family to move into the Jewish Quarter of the Old City to reclaim an ancestral plot, citing as a reason that their presence would disturb the homogeneity of the neighbourhood.

St Anne's Church Constructed in a Romanesque style, St Anne's is generally agreed to be the finest example of Crusader architecture in Jerusalem. Its popularity with pilgrims, however, has more to do with the traditional beliefs that the building's crypt enshrines the site of the home of Joachim and Anne, the parents of the Virgin Mary, while next to the church are the impressive ruins surrounding the biblical Pool of Bethesda.

The Crusaders built the church in 1140, at the same time constructing a small adjacent chapel with a stairway leading down to the pool where Jesus is supposed to have healed

a sick man (John 5:1-18). When Jerusalem fell to the armies of Saladin, St Anne's became a Muslim theological school – an inscription still to be seen above the church's entrance testifies to this. Successive rulers allowed the church to fall into decay so that by the 18th century it was roof-deep in refuse. In 1856 the Ottoman Turks presented the church to France in gratitude for its support in the Crimean War against Russia, and it was reclaimed from the garbage heap.

Apart from its architectural beauty, the church is noted for its acoustics, and a prominent sign requests that only hymns be used for sound checks.

St Anne's Church is open Monday to Saturday from 8 to 11.45 am and 2 to 6 pm (winter 2 to 5 pm), closed Sunday. Admission is 6NIS (4NIS students). The entrance is marked 'St Anne – Peres Blanc'; do not use the other door marked 'Religious Birthplace of Mary'.

Ecce Homo Arch & the Convent of the Sisters of Zion East of Al-Wad Rd an arch punctured by two windows spans the Via Dolorosa. This is the 19th century echo of an arch that was the eastern gate of the city during Roman times. The lower portion of the original Roman arch is preserved in the church belonging to the adjacent Convent of the Sisters of Zion. It's thought that the structure would have been a triumphal arch with a high portal in the middle flanked by two smaller gateways; the remains in the church are of one of the smaller arches (the bit spanning the street outside was designed to imitate the arc of the main central arch). The arch is traditionally, if improbably, the place where Pilate took Jesus out and proclaimed, 'Ecce homo' ('This is the man') – it's improbable, because the arch wasn't constructed until the time of Hadrian, some 100 years after the Crucifixion.

The convent church is open Monday to Saturday from 8.30 am to noon and 2 to 5 pm, closed Sunday. Admission is free.

Next door, and the property of the Greek Orthodox Church, is a basement chapel that's known as the **Prison of Christ**, which is supposedly the site of the hewn-rock cellars where Jesus and other criminals of the day were held.

Mamluk Buildings Overshadowed by the splendours of the Haram ash-Sharif/Temple Mount, and clustered outside its northern and western walls, are some excellent examples from the golden age of Islamic architecture. This area was developed during the era of the Mamluks (1250 to 1517), a military dynasty of former slaves ruling out of Egypt. They drove the Crusaders out of Palestine and Syria and followed this up with an equally impressive campaign of construction, consolidating Islam's presence in the Levant with masses of mosques, *madrasas* (theological schools), hostels, monasteries and mausoleums. Their buildings are typically characterised by the banding of red and white stone (a technique known as *ablaq*) and by the elaborate carvings and patterning around windows and in the recessed portals.

All of these features are exhibited in the **Palace of the Lady Tunshuq**, built in 1388 and found halfway down Aqabat at-Takiya – 150m east of the Tabasco Hostel & Tearooms. The facade is badly eroded; however, the uppermost of the three large doorways still has some beautiful inlaid marblework, while a recessed window is decorated with another Mamluk trademark, the stone 'stalactites' known as *muqarnas*. The palace complex now serves as workshops and an orphanage. Opposite the palace is the **Tomb of the Lady Tunshuq** (1398).

Continue downhill to the junction with Al-Wad Rd, passing on your right, just before the corner, the last notable piece of Mamluk architecture built in Jerusalem, the **Ribat Bayram Jawish** (1540), a one-time pilgrims' hospice. Compare this with the buildings on Tariq Bab an-Nazir St, straight across Al-Wad, which are Jerusalem's earliest Mamluk structures, built in the 1260s before the common use of ablaq. This street is named after the gate at the end which leads through into the Haram ash-Sharif/Temple Mount, but non-Muslims may not enter here.

Some 100m south on Al-Wad Rd, opposite the Old City Restaurant, is **Tariq Bab al-Hadad St**; it looks uninviting but wander down, through the archway, and enter a street entirely composed of majestic Mamluk structures. Three of the four facades belong to madrasas, dating variously from 1358 to 1440, while the single-storey building is a *ribat*, or hospice, dating from 1293. The last archway on the left gives access to the Small Wall (see that section later), while the green gate at the end of the street leads into the Haram, but again, non-Muslims may not enter here.

Back on Al-Wad Rd, continuing south the road passes the Souq al-Qattanin (see the following section) and then, on the left, a *sabil* or drinking fountain dating from Ottoman times, Sabil Suleyman. It terminates in a police checkpoint at the mouth of the tunnel down to the Western Wall plaza. However, the stairs to the left lead up to the busy Bab as-Silsila St and the Bab as-Silsila Gate, one of the two ways into the Haram for non-Muslims. Just before the gate is the tiny kiosk-like **Tomb of Turkan Khatun** (1352) with a facade adorned with uncommonly asymmetrical carved geometric designs. Earlier this century the tomb served as a stall for a lemonade seller.

Look out also for the restored **Khan as-Sultan**, which is a 14th century *caravanserai* (travellers' inn and stables) at the top end of Bab as-Silsila St. A discreet entrance just up from the large 'Gali' sign leads into a courtyard surrounded by workshops, and from a staircase tucked in the left-hand corner as you enter you can climb up to the Old City rooftops.

Souq al-Qattanin Founded on the remains of a Crusader market the Mamluks built this tunnel-like arcade in the mid-14th century. Almost 100m long, it has 50 shops on the ground floor with residential quarters above. The name means 'market of the cotton merchants'. Sadly, little trade goes on here now and most of the former stores and workshops are just used for warehousing. The complex also included two *ham-*

mams (public baths), one of which is undergoing restoration and may at some future point be open to visitors.

Small Wall This site, also known as the Hidden Wall, is at the end of the last narrow passageway off Tariq Bab al-Hadad St. It is marked by a small sign, visible from Al-Wad Rd where Tariq Bab al-Hadad St begins. This section of wall, now part of a Muslim house, is the same Western Wall that thousands of Jews flock to a few hundred metres to the south. The Arabs living here don't seem to mind the traffic of visitors and have provided an outside light on their 1st floor to enable Jews to read their prayers.

Zalatimo's A sweet shop famed for its pancakes and sticky confectionery, this place is also well known because its back room opens onto the remains of the original entrance to the Church of the Holy Sepulchre.

The Christian Quarter (Map 6)
All subject to the pull of the Holy Sepulchre, this quarter houses churches, monasteries and other religious institutions belonging to more than 20 different Christian sects.

As you enter from Jaffa Gate, the first two streets to the left – Latin Patriarchate Rd and Greek Catholic Patriarchate Rd – indicate the tone of the neighbourhood, named as they are after the offices there. The roads lead to St Francis St and in this quiet area around New Gate the local Christian hierarchy resides in comfort.

Elsewhere in the quarter, comfort and quiet give way to the chaos and crush of the tourist bazaars. Descending from Omar ibn al-Khattab Square into the heart of the Old City, **David St** is completely devoted to filling the mantelpieces and wall units of the world with multi-denominational kitsch from glitter-dusted prints of the Dome of the Rock and glow-in-the-dark crucifixes to 'Shalom Y'All' plaques. Branching north off David St, **Christian Quarter Rd** deals in a better class of souvenir with an emphasis on religious icons. South-east of the Church of the Holy Sepulchre the **Muristan Market**

is usually less crowded than the other markets and specialises in leather goods, clothes and carpets.

Towards the bottom end, David St switches over to food – a row of cavernous vaults on the left with fruit and vegetable stalls inside date from the Second Crusade. David St ends by crashing into a trio of narrow streets which, if followed to the left, converge into Souq Khan as-Zeit St, one of the main thoroughfares of the Muslim Quarter, while to the right they become the Cardo and lead into the Jewish Quarter. The squeamish should avoid the first of these narrow alleys leading to the Muslim Quarter, Souq al-Lahamin, the **Butchers' Market**.

Church of the Holy Sepulchre Despite being the central shrine of Christianity, this church is much less distinctive than something like the Dome of the Rock or the Western Wall, and it happens that many people wander in and out without any idea of what they've just visited. Then again, many who do arrive in full knowledge of what the church represents often leave sorely disappointed. Hemmed in by a bunch of other buildings, from outside the Church has no visual impact while inside it is dark, cramped and noisy. In his book *Winner Takes All* author Stephen Brook described the interior as looking like 'a cross between a building site and a used furniture depot'.

If the church is lacking a little in the appearance of exaltedness, at least its claim to stand on the true site of the crucifixion, burial and resurrection is fairly well respected. At the start of the 1st century, this was a disused quarry outside the city walls. According to John 19:17 and 41-2, Jesus' crucifixion occurred at a place reminiscent of a skull, outside the city walls and with a grave nearby. Archaeologists discovered tombs dating from the correct period, so the site is at least compatible with the story in the gospels.

Until at least 66 AD there had been a tradition for the Jerusalem community to hold celebrations of public worship at the tomb, in accordance with the Jewish practice then of

Via Dolorosa

Winding up through first the Muslim Quarter and then the Christian Quarter, the Via Dolorosa, or Way of Sorrows, is the route that Jesus took as he carried his cross to Calvary. The sanctity of the modern-day pilgrims' route, however, is based purely on faith, not fact.

The history of the Via Dolorosa can be traced back to the days when Byzantine pilgrims, on the night of Holy Thursday, would go in procession from Gethsemane to Calvary along roughly the same route as today's Via Dolorosa, although there were no official devotional stops en route. By the 8th century, some stops had become customary but the route had changed considerably and now went from Gethsemane around the outside of the city walls to Caiaphas' house on Mt Zion, then to the Praetorium of Pilate at St Sophia near the Temple and eventually to the Holy Sepulchre.

In the Middle Ages, with Latin Christianity divided into two camps, the Via Dolorosa was twinned – each of the two claimed routes primarily visiting chapels belonging to either one or the other faction. In the 14th century, the Franciscans devised a walk of devotion that included some of the present-day stations but had as its starting point the Holy Sepulchre. This became the standard route for nearly two centuries but it was eventually modified by the desire of European pilgrims to follow the order of events of the gospels, finishing at the site of the Crucifixion rather than beginning there.

Historians, however, point to one devastating flaw in the routing of the Via Dolorosa, which is that it's more likely that Jesus was condemned to death by Pilate on the other side of the city at the Citadel, next to Jaffa Gate. This was Herod's palace and Pilate's place of residence when in Jerusalem. Various Bible references to the trial taking place on a platform (Matthew 27:19) and in the open (Luke 23:4, John 18:28) support this theory, as the palace is known to have had such a structure. Hence, a more probable route for Jesus to have taken would be east along David St, north through the Butchers' Market of today, and then west to Golgotha.

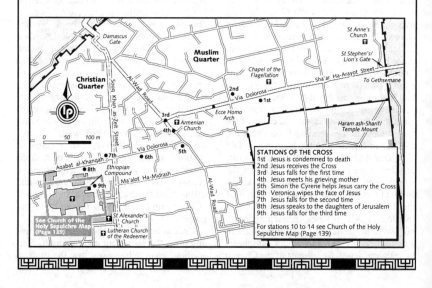

STATIONS OF THE CROSS
1st Jesus is condemned to death
2nd Jesus receives the Cross
3rd Jesus falls for the first time
4th Jesus meets his grieving mother
5th Simon the Cyrene helps Jesus carry the Cross
6th Veronica wipes the face of Jesus
7th Jesus falls for the second time
8th Jesus speaks to the daughters of Jerusalem
9th Jesus falls for the third time

For stations 10 to 14 see Church of the Holy Sepulchre Map (Page 139)

CHURCH OF THE HOLY SEPULCHRE

1 Franciscan Convent
2 Church of the Apparition
3 Franciscan Sacristy
4 Mary Magdalene Chapel
5 Seven Arches of the Virgin
6 Byzantine Arcade
7 Crusader Arcade
8 Prison of Christ
9 St Longinus Chapel
10 Division of the Rainment Chapel
11 St Dimas Altar
12 Chapel of the Discovery of the Cross

13 Church of St Helena
14 Chapel of the Mocking
15 Greek Choir
16 St Nicodemus Chapel of the Syrians
17 Three Maries Altar
18 Tombs of Crusader Kings Baldwin I & Godfrey de Bouillon
19 Armenian Chapel
20 40 Martyrs' Chapel
21 St John's Chapel
22 St James' Chapel
23 Chapel of the Franks

24 Chapel of St Michael & All Saints
25 St John's Chapel (Armenian)
26 St Abraham's Monastery
27 Cisterns of St Helena
28 Golgotha
29 Greek Chapel
30 Chapel of Calvary
31 Medici Altar
32 Franciscan Chapel

STATIONS OF THE CROSS
10th Jesus is stripped of his garments
11th Jesus is nailed to the cross
12th Jesus dies on the cross
13th The body of Jesus is taken from the cross
14th Jesus is laid in the Holy Sepulchre

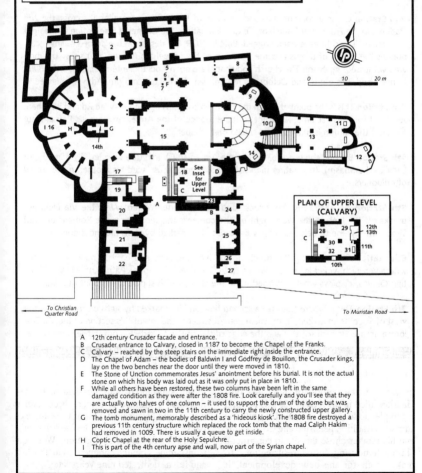

To Christian Quarter Road

To Muristan Road

A 12th century Crusader facade and entrance.
B Crusader entrance to Calvary, closed in 1187 to become the Chapel of the Franks.
C Calvary – reached by the steep stairs on the immediate right inside the entrance.
D The Chapel of Adam – the bodies of Baldwin I and Godfrey de Bouillon, the Crusader kings, lay on the two benches near the door until they were moved in 1810.
E The Stone of Unction commemorates Jesus' anointment before his burial. It is not the actual stone on which his body was laid out as it was only put in place in 1810.
F While all others have been restored, these two columns have been left in the same damaged condition as they were after the 1808 fire. Look carefully and you'll see that they are actually two halves of one column – it used to support the drum of the dome but was removed and sawn in two in the 11th century to carry the newly constructed upper gallery.
G The tomb monument, memorably described as a 'hideous kiosk'. The 1808 fire destroyed a previous 11th century structure which replaced the rock tomb that the mad Caliph Hakim had removed in 1009. There is usually a queue to get inside.
H Coptic Chapel at the rear of the Holy Sepulchre.
I This is part of the 4th century apse and wall, now part of the Syrian chapel.

Stations of the Cross

Every Friday at 3 pm, the Franciscan Fathers lead a cross-bearing procession which attracts many pilgrims, tourists and souvenir hawkers.

1st Station Supposedly the spot where Jesus was tried, the 1st station is actually inside the working Islamic Al-Omariyeh College, whose entrance is the door at the top of the ramp on the southern side of the Via Dolorosa, east of the Ecce Homo Arch. Entry is not always permitted so don't be surprised if you are asked to leave. There is nothing of official Christian value to see anyway, although there is a great view of the Haram ash-Sharif/Temple Mount through the barred windows on the upper level.

2nd Station Commemorating the condemnation of Jesus and his receiving the cross, the 2nd station is in the Franciscan Church of the Condemnation. The Chapel of Flagellation to the right is where he is said to have been flogged. Built in 1929, the design on the domed ceiling incorporates the crown of thorns and the windows of the chapel around the altar show the mob who witnessed the event. The church and chapel are open April to September, daily from 8 am to noon and 2 to 6 pm; and October to March, daily from 8 am to 5 pm. Admission is free.

3rd Station This is the point at which the Via Dolorosa joins up with Al-Wad Rd and it's where Jesus fell for the first time. Adjacent to the entrance of the Armenian Catholic Patriarchate Hospice, the station is marked by a small Polish chapel.

4th Station Beyond the hospice, next to the Armenian Church (the wonderfully named Our Lady of the Spasm), this station marks the spot where Jesus faced his mother in the crowd of onlookers.

5th Station As Al-Wad Rd continues south towards the Western Wall, the Via Dolorosa breaks off to climb to the west; right on the corner is the spot where the Romans ordered Simon the Cyrene to help Jesus carry the cross. It is marked by signs around a door.

6th Station Further along the street, on the left-hand side and easy to miss, is the place where Veronica wiped Jesus' face with a cloth. The Greek Orthodox Patriarchate in the Christian Quarter displays what is claimed to be the cloth, which shows the imprint of a face.

7th Station This is where Jesus fell a second time and it's marked by signs on the wall on the west of Souq Khan as-Zeit St, the main market street at the top of this section of the Via Dolorosa. In the 1st century, this was the edge of the city and a gate led out to the countryside,

praying at the tombs of holy persons. Hadrian filled in the area in 135 AD to build a temple dedicated to Aphrodite, but the Christian tradition persisted and Constantine and his mother chose the site to construct a church honouring Jesus' resurrection. To make room for the new development, it meant substantial buildings had to be demolished – a move of a mere 100m either way would have saved a lot of time and expense, but the community insisted that this had to be the church's location. Work on Constantine's church commenced in 326 AD and it was dedicated nine years later.

Stations of the Cross

a fact which supports the claim that the Church of the Holy Sepulchre is the genuine location of Jesus' crucifixion, burial and resurrection.

8th Station This is another station easy to miss. Cut straight across Souk Khan as-Zeit St from the Via Dolorosa and ascend Aqabat al-Khanqah. Just past the Greek Orthodox Convent on the left is the stone and Latin cross marking where Jesus told some women to cry for themselves and their children, not for him.

9th Station Come back down to where the Via Dolorosa and Aqabat al-Khanqah meet and turn right (south, away from Damascus Gate) along Souq Khan as-Zeit St. Head up the stairway on your right and follow the path round to the Coptic Church. The remains of a column in its door mark the spot where Jesus fell the third time.

Retrace your steps to the main street and head for the Church of the Holy Sepulchre; the remaining five stations are inside – see the Church of the Holy Sepulchre map.

10th Station As you enter the church, head up the steep stairway immediately to your right. The chapel at the top is divided into two naves. The right one belongs to the Franciscans, the left to the Greek Orthodox. At the entrance to the Franciscan Chapel is the 10th station where Jesus was stripped of his clothes.

11th Station Still in the chapel, this is where Jesus was nailed to the cross.

12th Station The Greek Orthodox Chapel is the site of Jesus' crucifixion.

13th Station Between the 11th and 12th stations is where the body of Jesus was taken down and handed to Mary.

14th Station This is the Holy Sepulchre, the Tomb of Jesus. Walk down the narrow stairs beyond the Greek Orthodox Chapel to the ground floor and you will see that the Holy Sepulchre is to be found in the centre of the rotunda, which would be on your left if you were entering from outside. The actual tomb is inside the Sepulchre. Candles lit by pilgrims who make a donation dominate the small tomb, with the raised marble slab covering the rock on which Jesus' body was laid. Around the back of the Holy Sepulchre is the tiny Coptic Chapel where pilgrims kiss the wall of the tomb, encouraged by a priest who expects a donation. See the Christian Quarter section in this chapter for more information about the Church of the Holy Sepulchre.

When his armies took the city in 638 AD, Caliph Omar was invited to pray in the church but he refused, generously noting that if he did his fellow Muslims would have turned it into a mosque. Instead, in 1009 the church was destroyed by the mad Caliph Hakim – which no doubt wouldn't have happened if Omar had prayed there all those years before. Unable to afford the major repairs necessary, the Jerusalem community had to wait until 1042 when the Byzantine Imperial Treasury provided a subsidy. It wasn't enough to pay for a complete reconstruction of the original church so a large part of the building was abandoned but an upper gallery was introduced into the rotunda and an apse added to its eastern side as a sort of compensation. This was the church that the Crusaders entered on 15 July 1099 as the new rulers of the city. They made significant alterations and so the church as it exists today is more or less a Crusader structure of Byzantine origins.

A fire in 1808 and an earthquake in 1927 did cause extensive damage; however, due to the rivalry between the different Christian factions who share ownership it took until 1959 for a major repair programme to be agreed upon. (See the boxed text 'Battle of Bethlehem' in the Gaza Strip & West Bank chapter for more on Christian noncooperation.) For this reason the keys to the church have been in the possession of a local Muslim family since the Ottoman period and it's their job to unlock the doors each morning and secure them again at night.

The Church of the Holy Sepulchre is open daily to anyone suitably dressed – the guards are very strict and refuse entry to those with bare legs, shoulders or backs. It's open daily from 4.30 am to 8 pm (7 pm in winter). The main entrance is in the courtyard to the south and can be reached by two points: via Christian Quarter Rd or Dabbaga Rd, running from Souq Khan as-Zeit St past Muristan Rd. Another two possible entry points are via the roof (see the Ethiopian Monastery section).

Christ Church Located just across from the Citadel in the Jaffa Gate area, this was the Holy Land's first Protestant church, consecrated in 1849. It was built by the London Society for Promoting Christianity Among the Jews (known today as CMJ: the Church's Ministry Among the Jews). The society's founders were inspired by the belief that the Jews would be restored to what was then Turkish Palestine, and that many would acknowledge Jesus Christ as the Messiah before He returned.

In order to present Christianity as something not totally alien to Judaism, Christ Church was built in the Protestant style with several similarities to a synagogue. Jewish symbols, such as Hebrew script and the Star of David, figure prominently at the altar and in the stained glass windows.

Greek Orthodox Patriarchate Museum On Greek Orthodox Patriarchate Rd this museum (☎ 628 4006) presents some of the treasures of the patriarchate, and goes a little way towards presenting the history of this locally dominant church.

It's open Tuesday to Friday from 9 am to 1 pm and 3 to 5 pm, and Saturday from 9 am to 1 pm, closed Sunday and Monday. Admission is 5NIS. Follow Greek Catholic Patriarchate Rd north from Jaffa Gate turning right into Greek Orthodox Patriarchate Rd and it's on the left.

St Alexander's Church On a corner just east of the Holy Sepulchre, this is the home of the Russian mission in exile. The attraction for visitors is a much-altered triumphal arch that once stood in Hadrian's forum, built here in 135 AD. Through the arch and to the left at the top of the steps you can see a section of the pavement which was once part of the platform of Hadrian's temple to Aphrodite.

St Alexander's Church is only open at 7 am on Thursday when prayers are said for Tsar Alexander III. The excavations are open from Monday to Thursday from 9 am to 1 pm and 3 to 5 pm; ring the bell. There's a small admission fee.

Ethiopian Monastery Follow the route to the 9th Station of the Cross: up the steps off Souq Khan as-Zeit St, at the point at which the street to the Church of the Holy Sepulchre turns to the right, there is a small grey door directly ahead that opens onto a roof of that church. The cluster of huts here has been the Ethiopian Monastery since the Copts forced them out of their former building in one of the many disputes between the various Christian groups.

The monks live among the ruins of a medi-eval cloister erected by the Crusaders where Constantine's basilica had been previously. The cupola in the middle of this roof section admits light to St Helena's crypt below. Access to the Church of the Holy Sepulchre is possible via two nearby points. One is through the Ethiopian Chapel (most of these monks do not speak much English but are very friendly, so ask for directions) and the other way is to go left out of the Ethiopian monastery and through the Copts' entrance.

Lutheran Church of the Redeemer
Dominating the Old City skyline with its tall white tower, the present church was built in 1898 on the site of the 11th century church of St Mary la Latine. The closed northern entrance porch is medieval and decorated with the signs of the zodiac and the symbols of the months. The tower is popular for its excellent views over the Old City. It's open Monday to Saturday from 9 am to 1 pm and 1.30 to 5 pm, closed Sunday. Admission is 2NIS.

Church of St John the Baptist
Jerusalem's oldest church, it stands in a hidden section of the Muristan area and is usually overlooked, having been buried by the gradual raising of surrounding street levels. However, the entrance from Christian Quarter Rd is clearly signposted. This leads you into the courtyard of a more recent Greek Orthodox monastery where a monk will usually be present to open the church for you. Originally built in the mid-5th century, it was restored after the Persians destroyed it in 614 AD. In the 11th century the merchants of Amalfi built a new church, which became the cradle of the Knights Hospitallers, using the walls of the earlier building. The present facade with the two small bell towers is a more recent addition, along with a few other alterations made to ensure the building's stability.

The Armenian Quarter (Map 8)
Though numbering only a few million in total worldwide, the Armenians have their own quarter within the Old City. Theirs was the first nation to officially embrace Chris-

tianity when their king converted in 303 AD and they established themselves in Jerusalem sometime in the following century. The Kingdom of Armenia disappeared at the end of the 4th century and Jerusalem was adopted as their spiritual capital. They have had an uninterrupted presence here ever since.

The core of the quarter is actually one big monastic compound. The Armenian presence in Jerusalem was traditionally purely religious but a large secular element arrived earlier this century following Turkish persecution. That persecution escalated in 1915 to an attempted genocide in which over 1.5 million Armenians were killed.

The community today, which numbers about 1500, is still very insular, having its own schools, library, seminary and residential quarters discreetly tucked away behind high walls. The gates to this city within a city are closed early each evening.

There's little to see for the casual visitor but if you can make it during the limited hours that its doors are open then it is well worth taking a look inside St James' Cathedral. Armenian ceramics are also famous and there are a couple of good showrooms off Armenian Orthodoxy Patriarchate Rd.

Armenian Compound
About 1200 Armenians now live in what used to be a large pilgrims' hospice. It became a residential area after 1915 when refugees from the Turkish massacres settled here. The empty, wide courtyards are a rare sight in the Old City. It is basically closed to visitors but you can call (☎ 628 2331) or ask at the entrance to St James' Cathedral to make an appointment for a visit.

St James' (Jacques') Cathedral
Attending mass here could seriously shake the nonfaith of an atheist. With the air loaded with incense, diffusely glowing golden lamps hung from the ceilings and the floors covered in dark, richly patterned carpets, this place has a palpable aura of ritual and mystery lacking in every other Christian site in this most holy of cities.

It was the Georgians in the 11th century who first constructed a church here in honour of St James, on the site where he was beheaded and became the first martyred disciple. The Armenians, in favour with the ruling Crusaders, took possession of the church in the 12th century and the two parties shared restoration duties. The tiles date from much later, from the 18th century, and they were imported from Turkey.

The church is on Armenian Orthodoxy Patriarchate Rd and is only open for services, which are held Monday to Friday from 6.30 to 7.15 am and 2.45 to 3.30 pm, and Saturday and Sunday from 2.30 to 3 pm. The Sunday service really is an impressive affair with no less than nine hooded Armenian priests taking part. There is quite a bit of to-ing and fro-ing around the altar area from the numerous helpers and there is impressive choral chanting from a 20-person choir – all in Armenian. Most of the participants are foreign tourists. There is no charge to participate.

Armenian Museum Originally a theological seminary (1843), with an attractive courtyard enclosed by arched colonnades on two levels, the building that houses this museum (☎ 628 2331) is a lot more fascinating than most of the exhibits it presents. It's reasonably well stocked and the displays are in English. There is a detailed display of the Armenian genocide which took place in 1915. Look out for the large Armenian globe dating from 1852 in the Paul Bedoukian hall. It's open Monday to Saturday from 9 am to 4.30 pm, closed Sunday. Admission is 5NIS (students 3NIS).

St Mark's Chapel This is the home of the Syrian Orthodox community in Jerusalem, whose members here number about 200. (There are only about three million worldwide, of whom two million are in Malahar in central India.) The Syrian Orthodox believe the chapel, on Ararat St, occupies the site of the home of St Mark's mother, Mary, where Peter went after he was released from prison by an angel (Acts 12:12). The Virgin Mary is claimed to have been baptised here, and according to their tradition this, not the Cenacle on Mt Zion, is where the Last Supper was eaten. One thing to look out for is the painting on leather of the Virgin and Child attributed to St Luke and, according to the caretaker, painted from life.

The chapel is open Monday to Saturday from 7 am to noon and 2 to 5 pm, closed Sunday. Admission is free but donations are welcome.

Alex de Rothschild Craft Centre This is a small gallery (☎ 628 6076) at 4 Or HaChaim St displaying ceramics, glass, enamel and textiles by Jewish artists and craftspeople. It's open Sunday to Thursday from 10 am to 4 pm and admission is free.

MT ZION (MAP 2)

הר ציון   جبل صهيون

Now meaning the part of the stern hill south of the Old City beyond Zion Gate, in the Old Testament period Mt Zion referred to a hill east of what is now known as the City of David. The name change came in the 4th century, based on new interpretations of religious texts. This compact area contains some of the most important sites in Jerusalem, including the possible site of the biblical Last Supper and a less probable tomb of King David. Also here is the **grave of Oskar Schindler**, the man with the list; from Zion Gate walk directly ahead, downhill, bearing left at the fork to go past the Chamber of the Holocaust, around the bend and cross the road to the entrance of the Christian cemetery in which he's buried. Once inside the cemetery head downwards toward the stairs that lead you to the lower section. Schindler's grave is not well marked, but it is about four rows from the end of the cemetery more or less in the middle and to your right. Ask the guard for directions if you really get lost.

The hustlers who offer themselves to you as guides on Mt Zion are a particularly unpleasant lot, persistent and occasionally quite nasty when their services are declined. They also have a scam going outside King

David's Tomb in which they ask for a donation in exchange for a cardboard kippa; men do need to cover their heads to visit but kippas are handed out gratis inside the tomb and no donations are requested.

King David's Tomb

A Crusader structure erected two millennia after his death, the Tomb of King David provides little spectacle. What's more, the authenticity of the site is highly disputable – the likelihood is that David is buried under the hill of the original Mt Zion, east of the City of David. However, this is one of the most revered of the Jewish holy places, and from 1948 to 1967, when the Western Wall was off-limits to Jews in Jordanian-held territory, the tomb was the stand-in main centre of pilgrimage. It still serves as a prayer hall.

To get to the tomb head south from Zion Gate, bear right at the fork and then left. It's open Saturday to Thursday from 8 am to 6 pm, and Friday from 8 am to 2 pm. Admission is free.

The Coenaculum

Popularly thought to be the site of the Last Supper *(coenaculum* is Latin for dining hall), this is the only Christian site in Israel administered by the local government. Part of the King David's Tomb complex, the Coenaculum (also referred to as the Cenacle) was a site of Christian veneration during the Byzantine period. In the Middle Ages the Franciscans acquired it but were later expelled by the Turks. Under the Turks the Coenaculum became a mosque, and Christians were barred from entering, just as Jews were kept from King David's Tomb.

Like the Tomb, the Coenaculum hall dates from the time of the Crusaders and to the right of the entrance there is a pair of faded Crusader coats of arms. The southern wall still bears the niche hollowed by the Muslims as a mihrab when they converted the chapel into a mosque.

The Coenaculum is above King David's Tomb, reached via a discrete stairway behind a door to the left that leads up from the courtyard. Many visitors mistake the first large room for the real thing but you need to walk across the hall to enter the much smaller chamber beyond which is where Jesus supposedly shared the Last Supper (Matthew 26:26-35; Mark 14:15-25; Luke 22:14-38; John 13, 14, 15, 17; I Corinthians 11:23-25; Acts 1:12-26 and Acts 2:1-4).

The Coenaculum chapel is open daily from 8 am to noon and 3 to 6 pm, but the Last Supper room closes at 4 pm; admission to both is free. Special services are occasionally held; contact the Christian Information Centre (see under Tourist Offices earlier in this chapter) for details.

Museum of King David

This museum next to King David's Tomb is associated with the Diaspora Yeshiva, the adjacent Jewish school for religious study. The main exhibit is some rather bizarre modern art. The only reason for the museum's existence seems to be to raise money for the yeshiva – entry is 5NIS (3NIS students). Opening times are variable depending on who is available as all members of the museum staff are volunteers.

Church & Monastery of the Dormition

This beautiful church is one of the area's most popular landmarks and is the traditional site where the Virgin Mary died, or fell into 'eternal sleep'; its Latin name is Dormitio Sanctae Mariae (Sleep of Holy Mary). The current church and monastery, owned by the German Benedictine order, was consecrated in 1906. It suffered damage during the battles for the city in 1948 and 1967 when its tower overlooking Jordanian army positions on the Old City ramparts below was manned by Israeli soldiers.

The church's interior is a bright contrast to many of its older, duller peers nearby. A golden mosaic of Mary with the baby Jesus is set in the upper part of the apse; below are the Prophets of Israel. The chapels around the hall are each dedicated to saints: St Willibald, an English Benedictine who visited the Holy Land in 724; the Three Wise Men; St Joseph, whose chapel is covered with medallions which feature kings of Judah as Jesus' forefathers; and St John the Baptist. The floor is decorated with names of saints and prophets and zodiac symbols.

The crypt features a stone effigy of Mary asleep on her deathbed with Jesus calling his Mother to heaven. The chapels around this statue were donated by various countries. In the apse is the Chapel of the Holy Spirit, with the Holy Spirit shown coming down to the Apostles.

The church is open daily from 8 am to noon and 2 to 6 pm. Admission is free. The complex also has a pleasant cafe where cakes and drinks (including beer) are served.

Church of St Peter in Gallicantu

Almost hidden by the trees and the slope of the hill, the Church of St Peter 'at the Crowing of the Cock' is the traditional site of the denial of Jesus by his disciple Peter (Mark 14:66-72) – 'before the cock crow thou shalt deny me thrice'.

Built on the foundations of previous Byzantine and Crusader churches the modern structure is also believed to stand on the site of the house of the high priest Caiaphas, where Jesus was taken after his arrest (Mark 14:53). A cave beneath the church is said to be where Christ was incarcerated. Whatever your beliefs, the view from the balcony of the church across to the City of David, the Arab village of Silwan and the three valleys that shape Jerusalem is reason enough to justify a visit.

The church is open Monday to Saturday from 8 to 11.45 am and 2 to 5 pm (May to September from 2 to 5.30 pm), closed Sunday. Admission is free. The church is reached by turning east (left) as you descend the road leading from Mt Zion down and around to Sultan's Pool. Roman steps lead down from the church garden to the Gihon Spring in the Kidron Valley.

KIDRON VALLEY (MAP 2)

עמק קידרון   وادي لخضر

Apart from the wonderful views, the points of interest here are tombs. These can be reached by following the road north from the entrance to Hezekiah's Tunnel or by heading south from Jericho Rd. The Arab village that clings to the eastern slope of the valley is Silwan.

Valley of Jehoshaphat

The most northern part of the Kidron Valley, this is the area between the Haram ash-Sharif/Temple Mount and the Mount of Olives. The word Jehoshaphat in Hebrew means 'God shall judge', and this narrow furrow of land is where the events of the Day of Judgement are to take place. All of humanity will be assembled together on the Mount of Olives, with the Judgement Seat on the Haram opposite. Two bridges will appear, spanning the valley, one made of iron and the other made of paper. According to God's judgement each person will be directed to cross one or the other. But there's no suspense. We know the ending – the Bible gives it away: the iron bridge will collapse and those sent across it die, while the paper bridge holds up with the promise of eternal life.

At the southern end of the Valley of Jehoshaphat are a series of tombs. From north to south the most prominent are:

Tomb of Jehoshaphat This 1st century burial cave is notable for the impressive frieze above its entrance.

Absalom's Pillar Also dating from the 1st century, the legendary tomb of David's son (II Samuel 18:17) is just in front of the Tomb of Jehoshaphat.

Grotto of St James or B'nei Hezir Just beyond Absalom's Pillar, this is where St James is believed to have hidden when Jesus was arrested nearby. It is probably the burial place of the B'nei Hezir's, a family of Jewish priests.

Tomb of Zechariah Carved out of the rock next to the grotto with a pyramid-like top, this tomb is where Jewish tradition believes the prophet Zechariah is buried (II Chronicles 24:25).

City of David

The oldest part of Jerusalem, dating from beyond the 20th century BC, this is the site of the city captured and developed by King David. The excavations are the result of work, still ongoing, that started in 1850.

Of interest to archaeologists is a signposted path which leads around the excavations. These include the Canaanite citadel of the Jebusite town that David conquered, a fortress built by David, and Jerusalem's Upper City where the wealthy resided and buildings destroyed in the Babylonian conquest of 586 BC once stood.

The site is open daily from 9 am to 4 pm and admission is free. From the Dung Gate, head east (downhill), take the road to the right (just past the parking lot), then take a left along the path with the sign (just past the grocery store) and follow it down to the bottom of the hill where you turn right. If you don't see a sign, ask for directions as the slopes are too steep to want to get lost on. Continue downhill to reach Warren's Shaft.

Warren's Shaft

Built by the Jebusites to ensure their water supply during a siege, it's just inside their city's defence wall and is possibly where Joab entered the City of David (II Samuel 5:8; I Chronicles 11:17). About 100m down from the entrance to the City of David excavations, a small museum features photos of the excavation work with explanations of the water supply situation as it used to be. A spiral staircase leads to a tunnel extending into the shaft, so bring a flashlight.

The shaft (☎ 628 8141) is open Sunday to Thursday from 9 am to 5 pm, and Friday from 9 am to 1 pm, closed Saturday. Admission is 5NIS (students 4NIS).

From Warren's Shaft, you can then proceed down to Hezekiah's Tunnel at the bottom of the hill.

Gihon Spring, Pool of Shiloah & Hezekiah's Tunnel

The Gihon Spring was the main reason why the Jebusites settled on the low Ophel Ridge rather than choose the adjacent higher ground. *Gihon* means 'gushing', quite suitable as the spring acts like a siphon, pouring out a large quantity of water for some 30 minutes before almost drying up for between four and 10 hours. There is believed to be enough water to support a population of about 2500 people. The tunnel was constructed in about 700 BC by King Hezekiah to bring the water of the Gihon into the city and store it in the pool of Shiloah, or Siloam. Its purpose was to prevent invaders, in particular the Assyrians, from locating the city's water supply and cutting it off (II Chronicles 32:3). The tunnel's length is 533m (335m as the crow flies).

Although narrow and low in parts, you can wade through it; the water is normally about half a metre to a metre deep. Due to the siphon effect it does occasionally rise, but only by about 15 to 20 cm.

The entrance steps leading down to the water are medieval, built due to the ground level having risen over the years. After about 20m the tunnel turns sharply to the left, where a chest-high wall blocks another channel which leads to Warren's Shaft (this can be visited near the City of David excavations). Towards the tunnel's end the roof rises. This is because the tunnellers worked from either end and one team slightly misjudged the other's level. They had to lower the floor so that the water would flow. A Hebrew inscription was found in the tunnel, and a copy can be seen in the Israel Museum. Carved by Hezekiah's engineers, it tells of the tunnel's construction.

You enter the tunnel at the Gihon Spring source on HaShiloah Rd down in the Kidron Valley and just south of the resthouse. Turn left as you get to the foot of the hill from Warren's Shaft.

It's open Sunday to Thursday from 9 am to 4 pm, and Friday from 9 am to 2 pm, closed Saturday. Admission is 10NIS (student 5NIS). The wade takes about 30 minutes; wear shorts and suitable footwear. A flashlight is also required – although candles are sold at the entrance they won't stay lit in the tunnel because of the drafts.

continued on page 161

MAP 1 – Greater Jerusalem

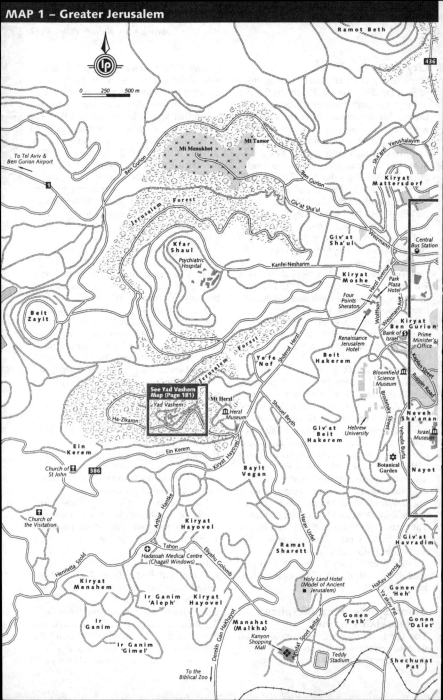

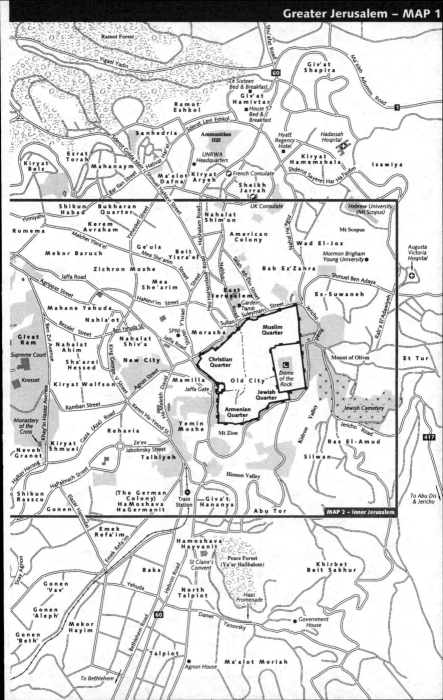

Ramot Forest

Yigael Yadin

Giv'at
Shapira

Ma'aleh Adumim Road

Le Sixteen
Bed & Breakfast

Giv'at
Hamivtar

House 57
Bed & //
Breakfast

Ramot
Eshkol

Sderot Levi Eshkol

Hyatt Regency
Hotel

Hadassah
Hospital

Sanhedria

Ammunition
Hill

Kiryat
Hamemshala

Isawiya

Ezrat
Torah

UNRWA
Headquarters

Shderot Sayeret Har HaTsofim

Kiryat
Belz

Mahanaym

Ma'alot
Dafna/

Kiryat
Aryeh

French Consulate

Sheikh
Jarrah

Shikun
Habad

Bukharan
Quarter

Nahalat
Shim'on

UK Consulate

Hebrew University
(Mt Scopus)

Augusta
Victoria
Hospital

Kerem
Avraham

American
Colony

Mt Scopus

Romema

Yirmiyahu

Malchei Yisra'el

Wad El-Joz

Mekor Baruch

Ge'ula

Mea She'arim

Jaffa Road

Beit
Yisra'el

Bab Ez'Zahra

Mormon Brigham
Young University

Zichron Moshe

Mea
She'arim

Es-Suwaneh

Shmuel Ben Adaya

Agrippas Street

Mahane Yehuda

HaNevi'im Street

East
Jerusalem

Garden
Tomb

Suleyman Street

Nahla'ot

Ben Yehuda St

Jaffa Road

Morasha

Muslim
Quarter

Mount of Olives

Et Tur

Givat
Ram

Nahalat
Ahim

Nahalat
Shiv'a

Sultan

Christian
Quarter

Dome of
the Rock

Supreme Court

Sha'arei
Hessed

New City

Old City

Knesset

Kiryat Wolfson

Mamilla

Jaffa Gate

Jewish
Quarter

Jewish Cemetery

Ramban Street

Agron Street

Armenian
Quarter

Jericho Road

Monastery
of the
Cross

Rehavia

Yemin
Moshe

Mt Zion

Ras El-Amud

Neveh
Granot

Kiryat
Shmuel

Ze'ev
Jabotinsky Street

Silwan

Talbiyeh

HaPalmach Street

Hinnon Valley

Shikun
Rassco

(The German
Colony)
HaMoshava
HaGermanit

Train
Station

Giv'at
Hananya

To Abu Dis
& Jericho

Gonen

Abu Tor

MAP 2 – Inner Jerusalem

Emek
Refa'im

Hamoshava
Hayvanit

St Claire's
Convent

Peace Forest
(Ya'ar HaShalom)

Khirbet
Beit Sakhur

Baka

Yehuda

North
Talpiot

Haas
Promenade

Gonen
'Vav'

Daniel

Yanovsky

Government
House

Gonen
'Aleph'

Mekor
Hayim

Talpiot

Agnon House

Ma'alot Moriah

To Bethlehem

MAP 2 – Inner Jerusalem

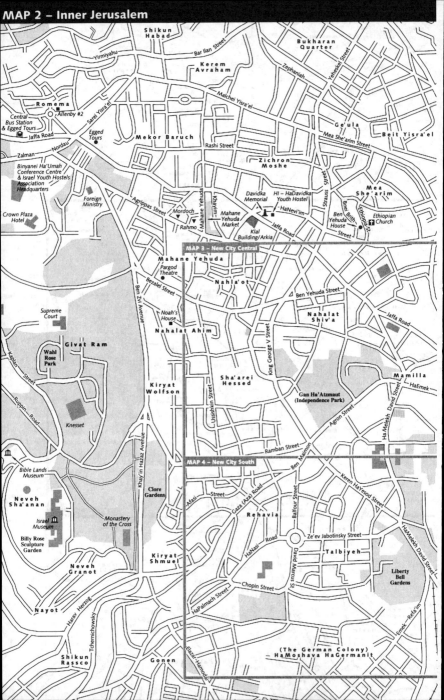

Shikun Habad

Bukharan Quarter

Yekhezkel Street

Yirmiyahu

Bar Ilan Street

Kerem Avraham

Zephaniah

Romema

Allenby #2

Sarel Yisra'el

Malchei Yisra'el

G e u l a

Mea She'arim Street

Beit Yisra'el

Central Bus Station & Egged Tours

Jaffa Road

Egged Tours

Mekor Baruch

Rashi Street

Nordau

Zalman

Z i c h r o n M o s h e

Strauss Street

M e a S h e ' a r i m

Binyanei Ha'Umah Conference Centre & Israel Youth Hostels Association Headquarters

Foreign Ministry

Agrippas Street

Mahane Yehuda

Mordoch

Khayim

Davidka Memorial

HI – HaDavidka Youth Hostel

HaNevi'im

Bnei Brith Street

Ethiopian Church

Crown Plaza Hotel

Rahmo

Mahane Yehuda Market

Klal Building/Arkia

Jaffa Road

Ben Brith Yehuda House

Ethiopian St

MAP 3 – New City Central

Mahane Yehuda

Pargod Theatre

Bezalel Street

Nahla'ot

Ben Yehuda Street

Jaffa Road

Supreme Court

Noah's House

Nahalat Ahim

Nahalat Shiv'a

Mamilla

Ben Zvi Avenue

King George V Street

HaEmek

Givat Ram

Wahl Rose Park

Kiryat Wolfson

Sha'arei Hessed

Gan Ha'Atzmaut (Independence Park)

Agron Street

Ha Melekh David Street

Kaplan Street

Ussishkin Street

Ruppin Road

Knesset

Ramban Street

Ben Maimon

MAP 4 – New City South

Khay'in Hazaz Avenue

Clore Gardens

Afasi Street

Gaza (Aza) Road

Balfour Street

Keren HaYesod Street

Bible Lands Museum

Neveh Sha'anan

Rehavia

Ze'ev Jabotinsky Street

HaMelekh David Street

Israel Museum

HaNasi Road

Talbiyeh

Billy Rose Sculpture Garden

Monastery of the Cross

David Marcus St

Neveh Granot

Kiryat Shmuel

Liberty Bell Gardens

Nayot

Chopin Street

HaPalmach Street

Emek Refa'im

Harav Herzog

Tchernichowsky

Elazar HaModa'i

Shikun Rassco

Gonen

(The German Colony) HaMoshava HaGermanit

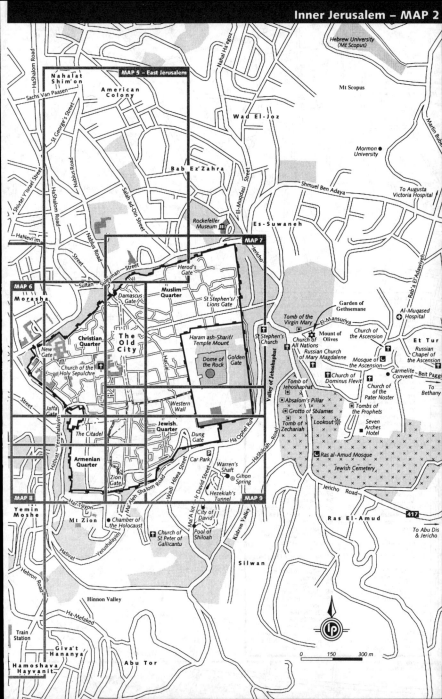

Hebrew University
(Mt Scopus)

Mt Scopus

**Nahalat
Shim'on**

MAP 5 – East Jerusalem

Sachs Van Paasen

**American
Colony**

St George's Street

HaShalom Road

Nablus Road

HaShalom Road

HaNevi'im

Wad El-Joz

Bab Ez'Zahra

El-Muqadasi Street

Salah ad-Din Street

Shmuel Ben Adaya

Mormon ●
University

To Augusta
Victoria Hospital

Es-Suwaneh

Rockefeller
Museum 🏛

MAP 7

Jericho

Martin Buber

Sultan

Suleyman Street

Damascus
Gate

Herod's
Gate

**MAP 6
Morasha**

HaShalom Road

**Muslim
Quarter**

St Stephen's/
Lions Gate

El-Mansuriya

Rab'a El-Adawiyeh

Garden of
Gethsemane

Al-Muqased 🏥
Hospital

**Christian
Quarter**

**The
Old City**

New
Gate

HaGai

Tomb of the
Virgin Mary

St Stephen's
Church

Church of
All Nations

Mount of
Olives

Church of
the Ascension

Et Tur

Russian
Chapel of
the Ascension

Church of the
Holy Sepulchre

**Haram ash-Sharif/
Temple Mount**

Dome of
the Rock

Golden
Gate

Russian Church
of Mary Magdalene

Mosque of
the Ascension

Carmelite
Convent

Beit Paggi

To
Bethany

Jaffa
Gate

Valley of Jehoshaphat

Church of
Dominus Flevit

Church of
the Pater Noster

The Citadel

**Jewish
Quarter**

Western
Wall

Tomb of
Jehoshaphat

Absalom's Pillar

Grotto of St James

Tombs of
the Prophets

Dung
Gate

Ha-Ophel Road

Tomb of
Zechariah

Lookout

Seven
Arches
Hotel

**Armenian
Quarter**

Zion
Gate

Car Park

Warren's
Shaft

HaShiloah Road

Ras al-Amud Mosque

Jewish Cemetery

MAP 8

Gihon
Spring

Ha-Tsiyon

Wadi Hilwa Street

Ma'Alot

City of
David

Pool of
Shiloah

Gihon Spring

Hezekiah's
Tunnel

MAP 9

Kidron Valley

Jericho Road

Ras El-Amud

417

To Abu Dis
& Jericho

**Yemin
Moshe**

Hativat Yerushalayim

Ma'Alei Shalom Road

Mt Zion

Chamber of
the Holocaust

Church of
St Peter of
Gallicantu

Silwan

Hebron Road

Hativat Yerushalayim

Hinnon Valley

Ha-Mefaked

Train
Station

**Giva't
Hananya**

**Hamoshava
Hayvanit**

Abu Tor

LP

0   150   300 m

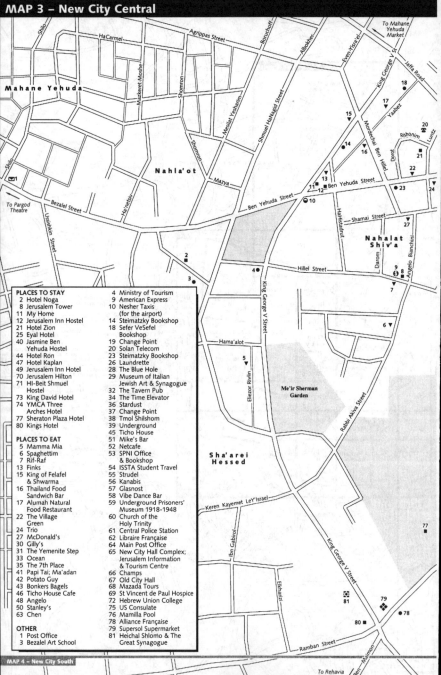

MAP 3 – New City Central

PLACES TO STAY
2 Hotel Noga
8 Jerusalem Tower
11 My Home
12 Jerusalem Inn Hostel
21 Hotel Zion
25 Eyal Hotel
40 Jasmine Ben
   Yehuda Hostel
44 Hotel Ron
47 Hotel Kaplan
49 Jerusalem Inn Hotel
70 Jerusalem Hilton
71 HI-Beit Shmuel
   Hostel
73 King David Hotel
74 YMCA Three
   Arches Hotel
77 Sheraton Plaza Hotel
80 Kings Hotel

PLACES TO EAT
5 Mamma Mia
6 Spaghettim
7 Rif-Raf
13 Finks
15 King of Felafel
   & Shwarma
16 Thailand Food
   Sandwich Bar
17 Alumah Natural
   Food Restaurant
22 The Village
   Green
24 Trio
27 McDonald's
30 Gilly's
31 The Yemenite Step
33 Ocean
35 The 7th Place
41 Papi Tai; Ma'adan
42 Potato Guy
43 Bonkers Bagels
46 Ticho House Cafe
48 Angelo
50 Stanley's
63 Chen

OTHER
1 Post Office
3 Bezalel Art School

4 Ministry of Tourism
9 American Express
10 Nesher Taxis
   (for the airport)
14 Steimatzky Bookshop
18 Sefer VeSefel
   Bookshop
19 Change Point
20 Solan Telecom
23 Steimatzky Bookshop
26 Laundrette
28 The Blue Hole
29 Museum of Italian
   Jewish Art & Synagogue
32 The Tavern Pub
34 The Time Elevator
36 Stardust
37 Change Point
38 Tmol Shilshom
39 Underground
45 Ticho House
51 Mike's Bar
52 Netcafe
53 SPNI Office
   & Bookshop
54 ISSTA Student Travel
55 Strudel
56 Kanabis
57 Glasnost
58 Vibe Dance Bar
59 Underground Prisoners'
   Museum 1918-1948
60 Church of the
   Holy Trinity
61 Central Police Station
62 Librairie Française
64 Main Post Office
65 New City Hall Complex;
   Jerusalem Information
   & Tourism Centre
66 Champs
67 Old City Hall
68 Mazada Tours
69 St Vincent de Paul Hospice
72 Hebrew Union College
75 US Consulate
76 Mamilla Pool
78 Alliance Française
79 Supersol Supermarket
81 Heichal Shlomo & The
   Great Synagogue

MAP 4 – New City South

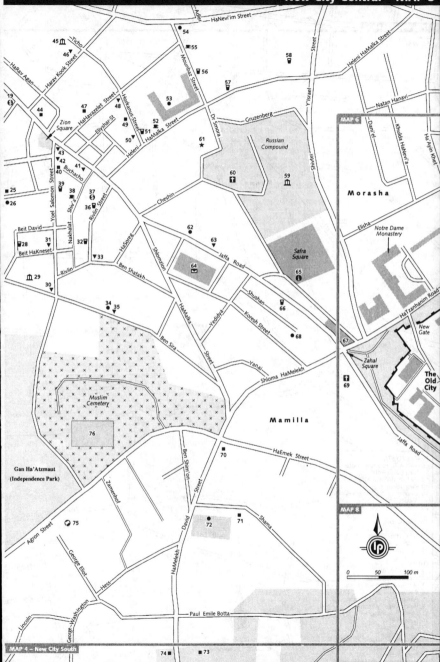

HaNevi'im Street

54
55
HaMashbir Street
56
58

45 🏛 Ticho
46
HaRav Agan
HaRav Kook Street
Mounbaz Street
57

Natan Hanavi

19 ℹ️
44 ■
47
48
HaHavazelet Street
Hachnasis Street
53
Dr Smora
Gruzenberg

Zion Square
Elyshar St
49
50
51
52
HaMalka Street
Heleni
61 ★
Russian Compound

MAP 6
Dani el
Khulda HaNevi'a
Helen HaMalka Street
Y'israel
Shivtei

43
42
41
40 Buchacho
Chcshin
60 🗒️
59 🏛️

Morasha

Yoel Salomon Street
39
38 Shiv'a
37 ℹ️
36 Rivlin Street

25
26
Beit David
28 ■
Beit HaKneset
31
29 🏛️
30
Nakhalat
32
33
HaSoreg
62 ●
Shlomzion
63 ▼
64 🗒️
Jaffa Road
Safra Square
65 ℹ️

Elisha
Notre Dame Monastery

Rivlin
Ben Shatakh

34 ●
35
Ben Sira
HaMalka Street
Yeddiya
Shushan
Koresh Street
66 🍴
68 ●
67 🚶
69 🚶

HaTzanhanim Road

New Gate
Zahal Square
The Old City

Muslim Cemetery
76

Yanai
Shloma HaMelekh
Mamilla

Jaffa Road

Gan Ha'Atzmaut
(Independence Park)
Zamenhof

70 ■
HaEmek Street
Shama

MAP 8

Agron Street
75 🅿️
George Eliot
Hess
David HaMelekh
Ben Shimon Street
72 ●
71 ■

🧭 LP
0   50   100 m

Lincoln
George Washington
Paul Emile Botta

MAP 4 – New City South
74 ■
73 ■

MAP 4 – New City South

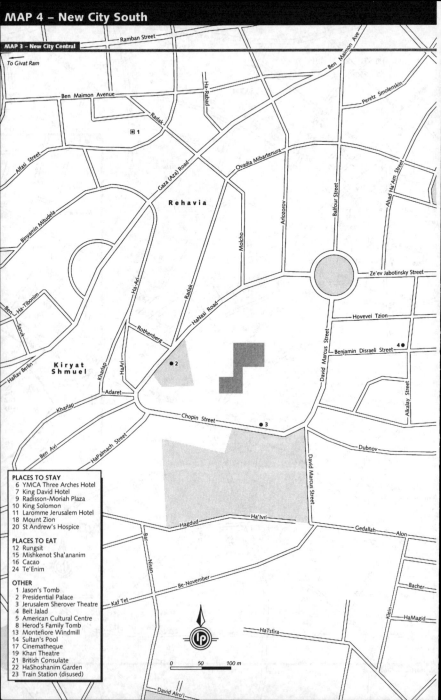

MAP 3 – New City Central

To Givat Ram

Ramban Street

Ben Maimon Ave

Ben Maimon Avenue

Peretz Smolenskin

Ha-Rabad

Radak

☒ 1

Alfasi Street

Caza (Aza) Road

Ovadia Mibartenura

Ahad Ha'Am Street

Balfour Street

Rehavia

Binyamin Mitudela

Molcho

Arlozorov

Ha-Ari

Ze'ev Jabotinsky Street

Ben Ha-Tibonim

Saruk

Radak

HaNasi Road

Rothenberg

Hovevei Tzion

David Marcus Street

Benjamin Disraeli Street 4 ●

HaKav Berlin

Kharlap

HaAri

Adaret

● 2

Kiryat Shmuel

Alkalay Street

Kharlap

Chopin Street

● 3

Ben Avi

HaPalmach Street

Dubnov

David Marcus Street

Ha'Ivri

PLACES TO STAY
  6 YMCA Three Arches Hotel
  7 King David Hotel
  9 Radisson-Moriah Plaza
 10 King Solomon
 11 Laromme Jerusalem Hotel
 18 Mount Zion
 20 St Andrew's Hospice

PLACES TO EAT
 12 Rungsit
 15 Mishkenot Sha'ananim
 16 Cacao
 24 Te'Enim

OTHER
  1 Jason's Tomb
  2 Presidential Palace
  3 Jerusalem Sherover Theatre
  4 Beit Jalad
  5 American Cultural Centre
  8 Herod's Family Tomb
 13 Montefiore Windmill
 14 Sultan's Pool
 17 Cinematheque
 19 Khan Theatre
 21 British Consulate
 22 HaShoshanim Garden
 23 Train Station (disused)

Hagdud

Gedallah

Alon

Bar

Nisan

Be-November

Bacher

Kaf Tet

Klein

HaMagid

HaTsfira

David Alro'i

0   50   100 m

LP

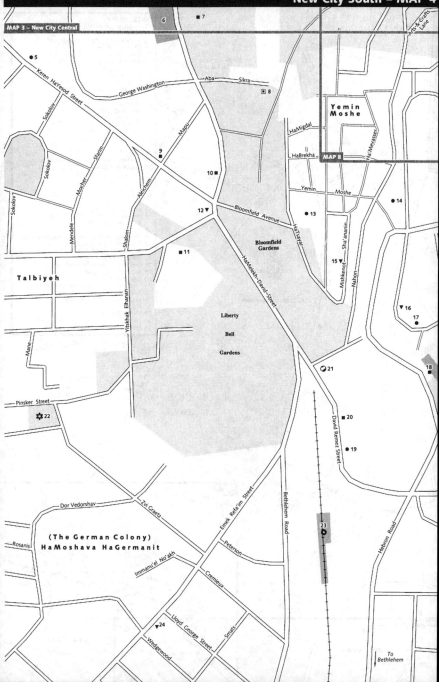

MAP 3 – New City Central

6

■ 7

● 5

Keren HaYesod Street

George Washington

Aba — Sikra

■ 8

Sokolov

Sokolov

Sfarim

Mocher

Mendele

Sholom

Sokolov

Aleichem

Mapu

Yemin
Moshe

HaMigdal

HaBrekha

MAP 8

Ha Mevasser

Arts & Crafts
Lane

9
■

10 ■

12 ▼

Bloomfield Avenue

Yemin

Moshe

● 13

● 14

HaTsayar

Mishkenot

Sha'ananin

Nahon

Bloomfield
Gardens

■ 11

Talbiyeh

Yitskhak Elhanan

15 ▼

HaMelekh David Street

Liberty

Bell

Gardens

Mane

▼ 16

17 ●

18
■

Ⓒ 21

Pinsker Street

✿ 22

● 20

David Remez Street

● 19

Dor Vedorshav

Zvi Graetz

(The German Colony)
HaMoshava HaGermanit

Rosanis

Emek Refa'im Street

Bethlehem Road

Hebron Road

Immanu'el No'akh

Peterson

Cremieux

23

To
Bethlehem

▼ 24

Lloyd George Street

Wedgewood

Smats

MAP 5 – East Jerusalem

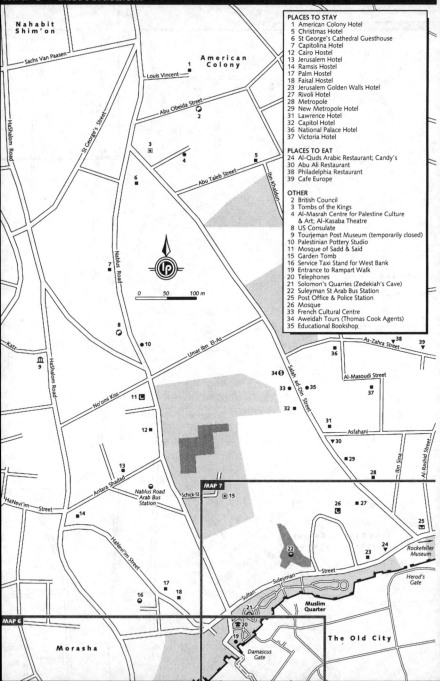

PLACES TO STAY
1 American Colony Hotel
5 Christmas Hotel
6 St George's Cathedral Guesthouse
7 Capitolina Hotel
12 Cairo Hostel
13 Jerusalem Hotel
14 Ramsis Hostel
17 Palm Hostel
18 Faisal Hostel
23 Jerusalem Golden Walls Hotel
27 Rivoli Hotel
28 Metropole
29 New Metropole Hotel
31 Lawrence Hotel
32 Capitol Hotel
36 National Palace Hotel
37 Victoria Hotel

PLACES TO EAT
24 Al-Quds Arabic Restaurant; Candy's
30 Abu Ali Restaurant
38 Philadelphia Restaurant
39 Cafe Europe

OTHER
2 British Council
3 Tombs of the Kings
4 Al-Masrah Centre for Palestine Culture
   & Art; Al-Kasaba Theatre
8 US Consulate
9 Tourjeman Post Museum (temporarily closed)
10 Palestinian Pottery Studio
11 Mosque of Sadd & Said
15 Garden Tomb
16 Service Taxi Stand for West Bank
19 Entrance to Rampart Walk
20 Telephones
21 Solomon's Quarries (Zedekiah's Cave)
22 Suleyman St Arab Bus Station
25 Post Office & Police Station
26 Mosque
33 French Cultural Centre
34 Aweidah Tours (Thomas Cook Agents)
35 Educational Bookshop

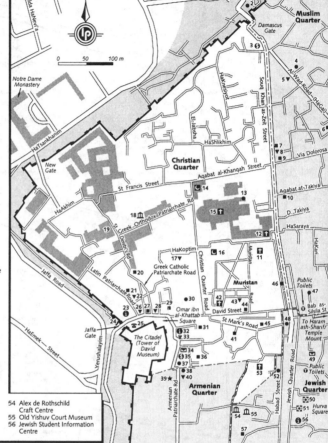

PLACES TO STAY
- 6 Al Ahram Youth Hostel
- 7 Al-Arab Hostel
- 9 New Hashimi Hostel
- 10 Tabasco Hostel & Tearooms
- 19 Casa Nova Pilgrims' Hospice
- 20 Greek Catholic
  Patriarchate Hospice
- 21 Gloria Hotel
- 27 New Imperial Hotel
- 29 Petra Hostel
- 31 Jaffa Gate Youth Hostel
- 36 Christ Church Hospice
- 41 Citadel Youth Hostel
- 44 New Swedish Hostel
- 45 Lutheran Hospice
- 57 El-Malak Youth Hostel

PLACES TO EAT
- 5 Jerusalem Star
- 8 El-A'Elat Restaurant
- 17 Kostas' Restaurant
- 22 Abu Shanab
- 26 City Restaurant
- 28 Cafeteria St Michel
- 33 Coffee Shop
- 40 Armenian Tavern
- 43 Backpackers Tearooms

OTHER
- 1 Telephones
- 2 Entrance to Ramparts Walk
- 3 Money Changer
- 4 Ariel Sharon's House
- 11 Lutheran Church
  of the Redeemer
- 12 St Alexander's Church
- 13 Ethiopian Monastery
- 14 Khanqah Salahiyya Mosque
- 15 Church of the Holy Sepulchre
- 16 Omar Mosque
- 18 Greek Orthodox
  Patriarchate Museum
- 23 Tourist Information Office
- 24 Entrance & Tickets for
  Ramparts Walk
- 25 Telephones
- 30 Pool of Hezekiah
- 32 Christian Information Centre
- 34 Branch Post Office
- 35 Bank Leumi
- 37 Zion Walking Tours
- 38 Armenian Ceramic Shop
- 39 Police Station
- 42 Church of St John the Baptist
- 46 Butchers' Market
- 48 Stairs to Rooftop Promenade
- 49 Branch Post Office
- 50 Hurva Synagogue
- 51 Ramban Synagogue
- 52 Archaeological Seminars
- 53 St Mark's Church

- 54 Alex de Rothschild
  Craft Centre
- 55 Old Yishuv Court Museum
- 56 Jewish Student Information
  Centre

Backpackers taking a break at the Damascus Gate.

CHRISTINE OSBORNE

MAP 7 – The Old City, Muslim Quarter

Rockefeller Museum

Din Street

Herod's Gate

Damascus Gate

Christian Quarter

Muslim Quarter

Sa'adiya

El-Mawlawiya

El-Bustami

Shadad

Ma'alot Sheikh Hasan

St Stephen's/ Lions Gate

Muslim Cemetery

See Haram ash-Sharif / Temple Mount Map (Page 129)

Public Toilets

Sha'ar HaArayot Street

Al-Ghazali Square

Via Dolorosa

Aqabat at-Takiya

D. Takiya

HaSaraya

Muristan

To Jaffa Gate

David Street

St Mark's

Tariq Bab-an-Nazir St

Al-Wad Road

Tariq Bab al-Hadad St

Souq al-Qattanin

HaShalshelet

Bab as-Silsila Street

Jewish Quarter

HaLakhot Street

Golden Gate

Haram ash-Sharif/ Temple Mount

Dome of the Rock

Ticket Kiosk

Non-Muslim entrances to the Haram

Wailing Wall

Western Wall Plaza

Ticket Kiosk

Al-Aqsa Mosque

Warren's Shaft

Gihon Spring

PLACES TO STAY
3 Rivoli Hotel
4 Metropole
7 Jerusalem Golden Walls Hotel
20 Convent of the Sisters of Zion
22 Austrian Hospice
23 Al-Ahram Youth Hostel
25 Armenian Hospice
31 New Hashimi Hostel
33 Al-Arab Hostel
37 Tabasco Hostel & Tearooms
40 New Swedish Hostel
42 Citadel Youth Hostel
43 Lutheran Hospice

PLACES TO EAT
6 Al-Quds Arabic Restaurant; Candy's
13 Jerusalem Star
26 Abu Shukri
32 El-A'Elat Restaurant
41 Backpackers Tearooms

OTHER
1 Garden Tomb
2 Mosque
5 Post Office & Police Station
8 Suleyman St Arab Bus Station
9 Entrance to Solomon's Quarries
10 Telephones
11 Entrance to Ramparts Walk
12 Money Changer
14 Ariel Sharon's House
15 Mosque of the Red Dome
16 Pool of Bethesda
17 St Anne's Church
18 Exit from Western Wall Tunnel
19 Chapel of the Flagellation
21 Ecce Homo Arch
24 Armenian Church

27 Ottoman-era Sabil
28 Ribat Bayram Jawish
29 Tomb of the Lady Tunshuq
33 Palace of the Lady Tunshuq
34 Ethiopian Monastery
35 Church of the Holy Sepulchre
36 St Alexander's Church
38 Lutheran Church of the Redeemer
39 Butchers' Market
44 Stairs to Rooftop Promenade
45 Stairs to Rooftop Promenade
46 Sabil Suleyman
47 Tomb of Turkan Khatun
48 Tickets & Entrance to Western Wall Tunnel
49 Viewpoint
50 Israelite Tower
51 Rachel Ben-Zvi Centre

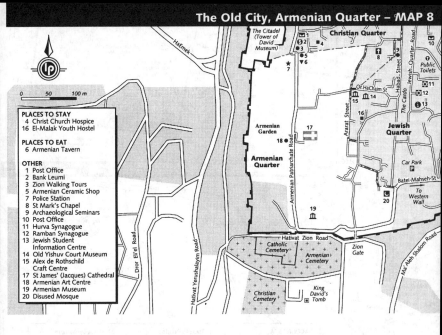

PLACES TO STAY
4 Christ Church Hospice
16 El-Malak Youth Hostel

PLACES TO EAT
6 Armenian Tavern

OTHER
1 Post Office
2 Bank Leumi
3 Zion Walking Tours
5 Armenian Ceramic Shop
7 Police Station
8 St Mark's Chapel
9 Archaeological Seminars
10 Post Office
11 Hurva Synagogue
12 Ramban Synagogue
13 Jewish Student
   Information Centre
14 Old Yishuv Court Museum
15 Alex de Rothschild
   Craft Centre
17 St James' (Jacques) Cathedral
18 Armenian Art Centre
19 Armenian Museum
20 Disused Mosque

The Old City walls and Citadel.

CHRISTINE OSBORNE

MAP 9 – The Old City, Jewish Quarter

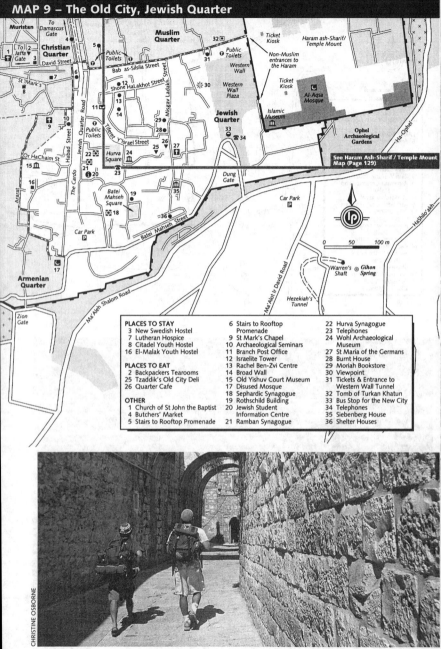

PLACES TO STAY
3 New Swedish Hostel
7 Lutheran Hospice
8 Citadel Youth Hostel
16 El-Malak Youth Hostel

PLACES TO EAT
2 Backpackers Tearooms
25 Tzaddik's Old City Deli
26 Quarter Cafe

OTHER
1 Church of St John the Baptist
4 Butchers' Market
5 Stairs to Rooftop Promenade

6 Stairs to Rooftop
  Promenade
9 St Mark's Chapel
10 Archaeological Seminars
11 Branch Post Office
12 Israelite Tower
13 Rachel Ben-Zvi Centre
14 Broad Wall
15 Old Yishuv Court Museum
17 Disused Mosque
18 Sephardic Synagogue
19 Rothschild Building
20 Jewish Student
   Information Centre
21 Ramban Synagogue

22 Hurva Synagogue
23 Telephones
24 Wohl Archaeological
   Museum
27 St Maria of the Germans
28 Burnt House
29 Moriah Bookstore
30 Viewpoint
31 Tickets & Entrance to
   Western Wall Tunnel
32 Tomb of Turkan Khatun
33 Bus Stop for the New City
34 Telephones
35 Siebenberg House
36 Shelter Houses

Jewish students exploring the Jewish Quarter's winding alleys.

The Mount of Olives, east of the Old City, is dotted with numerous churches and white-stone graves dating back to biblical times; it also has wonderful panoramic views of Jerusalem.

The facade of Jerusalem's Church of All Nations (top) is adorned with glittering images of Christian deities, which can also be seen in other churches throughout the Holy City (bottom left & right).

continued from page 147

MOUNT OF OLIVES (MAP 2)

הר הזיתים ‏ جبل الزيتون

To the east of the Old City, the Mount of Olives is dominated by the world's oldest and largest **Jewish cemetery** and the many churches commemorating the events that led to Jesus' arrest and his ascension to heaven.

The cemetery dates from biblical times. Its importance is based on the belief that this will be the site of the Resurrection of the Dead on the Day of Judgement when the Messiah comes (Zechariah 14:1-11). Waiting here to meet Him and no doubt snap up the rights to the event is Robert Maxwell, interned in one of the hillside tombs.

Most of the Mount's churches and gardens are open in the morning, closing for at least two hours towards noon and reopening again in the mid-afternoon. However, the real draw and what makes a visit to the Mount of Olives a must is the panoramic view it affords of the Old City.

Up at the top, in front of the **Seven Arches Hotel** (the cause of much controversy as it was built by the Jordanians over part of the ancient Jewish cemetery) is a promenade which triggers compulsive camera clicking in all who visit. Sunset isn't necessarily the best time to visit as usually the Old City is thrown into silhouette then; instead, come first thing in the morning, when the light is best.

You can walk from East Jerusalem or from St Stephen's Gate in the Old City, or otherwise take the bus to avoid what most find to be quite a strenuous walk; Arab bus No 75 runs from the station on Sultan Suleyman St.

Church of the Ascension

The 45m high tower has great views across to the Old City and the Judean Desert while the church itself features some notable mosaics, paintings and masonry work. A cafeteria serves refreshments. It's open Monday to Saturday from 8 am to 5.30 pm. Admission to the church is free, but it costs 2NIS to go up the tower (6NIS if you use the elevator). The church is next to Augusta Victoria Hospital, and Arab bus No 75 stops outside.

Warning

In a report in the *Jerusalem Post*, a priest who brings visitors to the Mount of Olives noted that during one week alone several people had had their pockets picked, a guide had been beaten up, and a woman had been sexually assaulted. Lonely Planet has also received letters from women readers who suffered unpleasant experiences while walking around here. Our advice is that females definitely should not visit the Mount of Olives alone.

Russian Chapel of the Ascension

Marked by a needle-point steeple – the tallest structure on the Mount of Olives – this church and monastery is built over the spot from which the Russian Orthodox church claims Jesus made his ascent to heaven. It is a bit hard to find, so look for a narrow alleyway leading off from the main street, in among the shops and cafes. It is open on Tuesday and Thursday from 9 am to noon. Entry is free.

Mosque of the Ascension

Confusingly also sometimes referred to as the Church of the Ascension, this Muslim-administered building is an odd little octagonal Crusader reconstruction of an earlier Byzantine structure. Saladin authorised two of his followers to acquire the site in 1198 and it has remained in Muslim possession since. Islam recognises Jesus as a prophet.

The stone floor bears an imprint said to be the footstep of Jesus. Perhaps the reason for its unconvincing appearance today is that pilgrims in the Byzantine period were permitted to take bits of it away.

Opening hours vary but the cost of admission is 2NIS.

Church of the Pater Noster

Beside the cave in which Jesus spoke to his disciples, Queen Helena, the mother of Emperor Constantine of Rome, had this church constructed (also known as the Church of the Eleona – a bastardisation of the Greek word *elaionas* meaning 'olive grove'). Destroyed by the Persians in 614, the site later became known as the place where Jesus had taught the Lord's Prayer, a belief which inspired the Crusaders to construct an oratory among the ruins in 1106.

The most interesting things here are the attractive tiled panels on which are inscribed the Lord's Prayer in over 60 languages.

As you enter the gate, turn left and then right. The tomb is that of Princess de la Tour d'Auvergne, who purchased the property in 1886 and built the neighbouring Carmelite convent. The actual cave can be reached by going around the cloister to the left, down some stairs and through the first door on the right.

The site is open Monday to Saturday from 8.30 to 11.45 am and 3 to 4.45 pm, closed Sunday. Admission is free.

Tombs of the Prophets

Slightly to the north and below the viewing promenade are a set of ancient tombs in which are buried the three prophets Haggai, Zachariah and Malachi, who lived in the 5th century BC.

It's open Sunday to Friday from 8 am to 3 pm, closed Saturday. Admission is free.

Church of Dominus Flevit

The original church on this site was built by medieval pilgrims who claimed to have found the rock on the Mount of Olives where Jesus had wept for Jerusalem (Luke 19:41) – hence, Dominus Flevit, meaning 'the Lord wept'.

When the present day, tear-shaped church was being built in 1954 and 1955, excavations unearthed a 5th century monastery, the mosaic floor of which is on display. Also uncovered was a large cemetery dating back to about 1500 BC. The cemetery has since been recovered but some of the tombs are still visible. The view of the Dome of the Rock from the window of the altar is particularly attractive.

The church is open daily from 8 to 1.45 am and 2.30 to 5 pm. Admission is free.

(Russian) Church of Mary Magdalene

Although badly tarnished by the weather, the golden onion domes of this White Russian church are still one of Jerusalem's most attractive and surprising landmarks. Built by Alexander III in memory of his mother, the church is now a convent and has one of the city's best choirs. A section of the Garden of Gethsemane is claimed to be within the church's grounds.

It's only open on Tuesday and Thursday from 10 to 11.30 am. Admission is free.

Church of All Nations & Garden of Gethsemane

Designed by the same architect responsible for Dominus Flevit up the hill, the classically styled Church of All Nations is notable for the glistening golden mosaic that adorns its facade (the mosaic depicts Jesus assuming the suffering of the world, hence the church's alternative name of the Basilica of the Agony). Built in 1924 it was financed by a consortium drawn from 12 nations. It's the successor to two earlier churches, the first was erected in the 4th century but destroyed by an earthquake in the 740s, and the second was an oratory built

The onion-domed Church of Mary Magdalene

over the ruins by the Crusaders but abandoned in 1345 for reasons unknown.

Around the church is the popularly accepted site of Gethsemane, the garden where Jesus was arrested (Mark 14:32-50). The garden has some of the world's oldest olive trees (in Hebrew *gat shmanim* means 'oil press'), three of which have been scientifically dated as being over 2000 years old, making them witnesses to whatever biblical events may have occurred here.

The garden is open daily from 8.30 to 11.30 am and 2.30 to 4 pm. Admission is free. The entrance is not from the main road but from the narrow, steeply inclined alleyway which you'll find leading up behind the church.

St Stephen's Church

This Greek Orthodox church is on the southern side of the main Jericho road as it curves away from the Old City walls towards the Mount of Olives. Largely ignored by guides and visitors alike, it was completed in 1968 as a 'modern Byzantine' church. It's near the site where Stephen, the first Christian martyr, was stoned to death. The two pleasant ladies who look after the church are happy to guide visitors around. There are also remains of the Roman Road which led from the Golden Gate down to the Kidron Valley and an anonymous tomb cut into the rock. Ring the church bell to see if anyone is in – there are no set hours. Admission is free.

Tomb of the Virgin Mary

On her death, sometime in the middle of the 1st century, Mary was supposedly interned here by the disciples. A monument was first constructed in the 5th century but was repeatedly destroyed. Almost hidden in the valley, the present monument is a Crusader edifice from the 12th century, built on Byzantine foundations. It is now owned by the Greek Orthodox Church, while the Armenians, Syrians and Copts have shares in the altar.

The tomb is open Monday to Saturday from 6 to 11.45 am and 2.30 to 5 pm, closed Sunday. Admission is free.

On the main road beside the stairs down to the tomb, the small cupola supported by columns is a memorial to Mujir ad-Din, a 15th century Muslim judge and historian.

MT SCOPUS (MAP 2)

הר הצופים   جبل سكوبس

From the top of Scopus (from the Greek *skopeo*, meaning 'to look over') there are marvellous views of the city and the Judean Desert towards Jordan.

Its strategic location has played a decisive role in the many battles for Jerusalem over the centuries. In 70 AD the Roman legions of Titus camped here, as did the Crusaders in 1099 and the British in 1917. During the 1948 War, Arab forces attacked from here. One of the more intriguing aspects of the 1949 cease-fire was that Mt Scopus became an Israeli-held enclave in Jordanian territory.

In addition to the Hebrew University campus and the military cemetery, other places of note here include Hadassah Hospital, renowned as one of the world's top medical centres, and the Mormon Brigham Young University, which opened against strong opposition from religious Jews. Take Arab bus No 75 to the Augusta Victoria Hospital and walk 20 minutes, or take Egged bus No 4, 4A, 9, 23 or 28 from Jaffa Rd in the New City to the university.

Hebrew University

Founded in 1925 and featuring some distinctive modern architecture, the Mt Scopus campus of the Hebrew University was the world's first secular Hebrew institute of higher learning. Between 1948 and 1967, when Mt Scopus was a Jewish enclave isolated in Jordanian-held territory, the university was moved to Givat Ram, and is now split between the two sites. There are free guided tours in English, from Sunday to Thursday at 11 am, lasting from 60 to 90 minutes. These leave from the Bronfman visitors centre in the Sherman administration building. The modern **Hecht Synagogue** stands out as the major attraction for visitors, but the best views are from the **amphitheatre**. Call ☎ 588 2819 for full details.

EAST JERUSALEM (MAP 5)
ירושלים המזרחית שرق لقدس
Solomon's Quarries

Midway between the Damascus and Herod's gates is this vast cave beneath the northern wall of the Old City. Part of a quarry, the large quantities of stone chiselled from here was, in all likelihood, used by Herod in his numerous construction projects, and maybe even by Solomon in the construction of the First Temple. Far more recently the builders of the YMCA (1933) in the New City received special dispensation to use stone from the quarry in the building of the communion room in the building's tower.

In Jewish tradition the cave is known as Me'arat Zidkiyahu (Zedekiah's Cave) because legend has it that the last king of Judah, Zedekiah, used it as an escape route to flee the armies of Nebuchadnezzar. The cave extends for over 200m beneath the Old City, and while there is little to see it does offer cool refuge on a hot day and it's actually great fun exploring all the little pathways and nooks and crannies.

The cave is open Sunday to Thursday from 9 am to 5 pm, Friday from 9 am to 2 pm, and Saturday from 9 am to 4 pm. Admission is 7NIS (students 3.50NIS).

Rockefeller Museum

Set up with a gift of US$2 million donated by the Rockefeller family in 1927, what was originally the Palestine Archaeological Museum was at one time the leading museum of antiquities in the region. However, the museum has received little attention in recent times and while some of the exhibits are impressive, particularly the carved beams from Al-Aqsa Mosque and the stone ornamentation recovered from Hisham's Palace (see the Jericho chapter), the presentation is off-puttingly dour and musty compared to other more modern Israeli museums.

The museum (☎ 628 2251, fax 620 4624) is open Sunday to Thursday from 10 am to 5 pm, Friday and Saturday from 10 am to 2 pm. Admission is 22NIS (students 14NIS).

Garden Tomb

This site is considered as an alternative to the Church of the Holy Sepulchre for the crucifixion and resurrection of Jesus. While enjoying little support for its claims, it is appreciated by many for its tranquillity and charm. As one Catholic priest is reported to have said, 'If the Garden Tomb is not the true site of the Lord's death and resurrection it should have been'.

Biblical significance was first attached to this location by General Charles Gordon (of Khartoum fame) in 1883. Gordon refused to believe that the Church of the Holy Sepulchre could occupy the site of Golgotha and on identifying a skull-shaped hill just north of Damascus Gate he began excavations. The suitably ancient tombs he discovered under the mound confirmed him in his convictions that this was the true site of the crucifixion and burial of Jesus.

Archaeologists have since scotched the theory by dating the tombs as coming from the 5th century BC. Several cynics suggest that the continued championing of the Garden Tomb has more to do with the fact that it's the only holy site in Jerusalem that the Protestants, its owners, have any stake in.

It's open Monday to Saturday from 8.30 am to noon and 2 to 5.30 pm, closed Sunday. Admission is free. On Sunday at 9 am an interdenominational service with singing is held, which lasts about 50 minutes. To get there from Sultan Suleyman St head north along Nablus Rd and turn right at Schick St.

St George's Cathedral

Named after the patron saint of England, who is traditionally believed to have been martyred in Palestine early in the 4th century (see Lod in the Tel Aviv chapter), this is the cathedral church of the Anglican Episcopal Diocese of Jerusalem and the Middle East. Consecrated in 1910, the Turks closed the church and then used the bishop's house as their army head quarters during WWI. After the British took Jerusalem in 1917, the truce was signed here in the bishop's study. The cathedral has two congregations, Arabic and English speaking, and the complex includes a popular guesthouse (see Places to Stay later in this chapter) and school.

The church compound is a piece of the Mandate frozen in time. The church features many symbols of the British presence in Jerusalem: a font given by Queen Victoria, memorials to British servicemen, a royal coat of arms, an English oak screen and the tower built in memory of King Edward VII. The cathedral is just south of the junction of Salah ad-Din St and Nablus Rd. It has no set hours for visiting and no admission fee is charged.

Tombs of the Kings

The first archaeologist to excavate here decided that this complex must be the tombs belonging to the kings of Judah because of the majesty of the facade. While the name has stuck, it has since been proved that this is the 1st century tomb of Queen Helena of Adiabene, Mesopotamia. It has been described by one scholar as one of the country's 'most interesting ancient burial places' but only archaeology buffs are likely to agree.

The tomb is north, beyond St George's Cathedral, and it's open to visitors Monday to Saturday from 8 am to 12.30 pm and 2 to 5 pm, closed Sunday. Admission is 5NIS (students 3NIS).

Tourjeman Post Museum

Overlooking the former Mandelbaum Gate area – which wasn't a gate at all but the UN-supervised access point between the Jewish New City and Jordanian-occupied Jerusalem between 1948 and 1967 – this museum is housed in an old Turkish house used by the Israelis as a frontier position. With the touchy theme of 'a divided city reunited', it presents a distinctly Zionist picture of the period when the city was physically divided by concrete barriers and barbed wire.

A little tricky to find, the museum (☎ 628 1278) is on HaShalom Rd. From the Damascus Gate area walk north up HaNevi'im St, turn right after the Ramsis Hostel onto HaShalom Rd, and it's on your left after a few minutes walk.

The museum was closed for repairs during research, though its closure may be for longer than anticipated. Check with the tourist offices for possible opening details.

THE NEW CITY (MAPS 2, 3 & 4)
Notre Dame & City Hall

Who knows what the Roman Catholic Assumpionist Fathers had in mind when they set about building the Notre Dame de France hospice in 1884. Whether it's the predominant use of stone or the result of a paranoiac defensiveness that comes from having so many various creeds and sects vying for influence in one place, much of the city's religious architecture has a distinct bastion-like appearance. This reaches an apotheosis in the Notre Dame, a hostelry for French pilgrims that takes the form of a vast, imposing fortress that even manages to dominate the Old City walls. Reinforcing the muscular imagery, up on the roofline stands a five metre high statue of Mary flanked by two crenellated turrets. It's fitting that between 1948 and 1967, when Jerusalem was divided, the south wing of the Notre Dame was used as an IDF bunker and frontier post.

As a result the building suffered heavy battle damage but it underwent major renovation in the 1970s and now Notre Dame operates as a busy international pilgrim centre with a highly rated guesthouse (see Places to Stay section later in this chapter) and restaurant (see Places to Eat section later in this chapter). It also has an arts centre promoting traditional local Christian art.

Just to the west of Notre Dame, on Zahal Square, the building with the rounded facade is Jerusalem's former City Hall. This was another front line bunker on the border between Jewish West Jerusalem and the Arab-held East Jerusalem and Old City, as evidenced by the bullet-pocked stonework. Currently this building is no longer in use, having been replaced by the new City Hall complex and plaza immediately behind. This was completed in 1993 and the municipality is quite proud of it – the Department of Information (☎ 624 1379) based here gives guided tours every Monday at 9.30 am; meet in Safra Square near the date palms, opposite the main post office.

Russian Compound

Between Jaffa Rd and HaNevi'im St and dominated by the green domes of the Church of the Holy Trinity, this area was acquired by the Russian Orthodox Church in 1860. In addition to the cathedral, facilities were constructed here for the many pilgrims from Russia who visited the Holy Land until WWI. The cathedral (closed to the public) occupies the site where the Assyrians camped in about 700 BC, and in 70 AD Roman legions assembled here during the Jewish Revolt. In front of the cathedral, the 12m high Herod's Pillar is believed to have been intended for the Second Temple; however, it cracked during chiselling and was abandoned here.

Nicknamed 'Bevingrad' by the Jews during the Mandate, after the reviled British foreign secretary Ernest Bevin, the compound is home today to the central police station and law courts.

The building behind the church to the right was the headquarters of the British in Palestine and as such a target for attacks from the Jewish underground; now, as the **Underground Prisoners' Museum 1918-1948** (☎ 623 3166), it is devoted to those same resistance organisations. It is open Sunday to Thursday from 8 am to 4 pm, closed on Friday and Saturday. Admission is 6NIS (adult) or 3NIS (youth, student, senior citizen).

Mea She'arim

Possibly the world's most reluctant tourist attraction, this ultraorthodox Jewish district is the only remaining example of *shtetl* (ghetto) which existed before the Holocaust in Eastern European Jewish communities.

The residents mostly dress in 18th century Eastern European styles. They are mainly devoted to religious study and are frequently financed by fellow ultraorthodox communities abroad. Because of the intensity of the religious aspect, this is the best place in the world for buying items of Ju-

daica. There are also many bakeries producing traditional products.

Another result of the dominant interpretation of Jewish Law here is the attitude of residents towards strangers. Signs proclaim 'Daughters of Israel! The Torah requires you to dress modestly', and give details of what this all means. When you visit Mea She'arim you should conform to the residents' standards in your dress and behaviour. This means that women should not wear shorts or even long trousers, but a loose-fitting skirt and long sleeves. Men should wear long trousers. Do not walk arm in arm or even hand in hand with anyone, and kissing is definitely taboo. Most ultraorthodox Jews dislike being photographed – in fact, their interpretation of Jewish Law forbids it.

The more extreme characters have been known to stone those – Jewish and non-Jewish – who break the codes of conduct, however unwittingly; signalled or verbal objections are more common though. Needless to say, thousands of photographs are taken each week; just be discreet and aware of what the possible rsponse to your activities may be. Abiding by the request to dress discreetly is not too difficult, though.

Mea She'arim is a few minutes walk from both Damascus Gate and the Jaffa Rd/King George V St junction.

Ethiopia St

Tucked away on narrow, leafy Ethiopia St, the impressive domed **Ethiopian Church** would be a major feature in most cities, but in Jerusalem it is often overlooked. Built between 1896 and 1904, the church's entrance gate features the carved Lion of Judah, an emblem believed to have been presented to the Queen of Sheba, Ethiopia's queen, by Solomon when the queen visited Jerusalem.

This church is open March to September daily from 7 am to 6 pm (slightly shorter hours in winter) and admission is free.

Opposite the church is the **Ben Yehuda house** where the great linguist lived and did much of his work on the revival of the Hebrew language. A plaque marking the house was stolen by ultraorthodox Jews, who strongly disapprove of the language's everyday use.

On your left as you leave Ethiopia St and descend HaNevi'im St towards the Old City is the **Ethiopian consulate**, with its mosaic-decorated facade.

Bukharan Quarter

Established towards the end of the 19th century by Jews from the Central Asian cities of Samarkand and Bukhara, this was one of Jerusalem's most wealthy and exclusive districts. Unlike neighbouring Mea She'arim, which consciously styled itself along humble lines, the Bukharan Quarter comprised numerous regal and elegant family mansions, many of which were used only as summer residences. Most impressive of all is **Beit Yehudayoff** at 19 Ezra St, a great birthday cake of a building designed by an Italian architect for a particularly well-off Bukharan family. Known locally as the Palace, it once served as the headquarters of the Ottomans in Jerusalem and now houses two girls' schools.

In the aftermath of the Russian Revolution, Central Asia's Jews were stripped of their wealth and prevented from travelling. Their quarter in Jerusalem began a slide into decline and the orthodox of Mea She'arim moved in to fill the vacuum. Though neglected and decaying, the Bukharan Quarter is still worth a visit; from HaNevi'im St follow Strauss St north onto Yeheskel St then turn left onto Ezra St.

Mahane Yehuda Market

About 1km west of Zion Square between Jaffa Rd and Agrippas St, this fabulous market is a spectacle in its own right even if you don't want to do any shopping. You'll never see bigger, redder strawberries than here, and an unflinching nature is required to buy the fish which have to be brained into submission before they can be wrapped. Other stalls laden with all manner of fruit, vegetables, pickles, olives and cheeses stand among cheap butcheries, bakeries and wholesale *mahkolets* (grocery shops).

On Agrippas St there are several great places for spicy *meorav Yerushalmi* (barbecued meats), and these are open from the early evening until early morning.

The market is at its most gloriously bustling best on Thursday and Friday during the pre-Shabbat scramble.

The Time Elevator

If you like virtual 'rides' you might enjoy this whizz-bang potted presentation of the history of the city. Opened in September 1998, the Time Elevator (☎ 625 2227, fax 625 2228) is a high-tech experience combining gut-wrenching virtual roller-coaster effects through time and space with light-hearted historical documentary. It starts with the establishment of the City of David and ends with a spectacular aerial panorama of Jerusalem today all projected onto a large split screen. It is actually a very enjoyable experience though a little pricey at 37NIS for the half-hour show. It is in the Beit Agron building at 37 Hillel St. Rides take place every half hour and it is open daily from 10 am to 9 pm, closed Saturday.

Ticho House (Beit Ticho)

The former home of Dr Abraham Ticho and his artist wife, Anna, this combination of museum, art gallery, shop, library and cafe is now administered by the Israel Museum.

Dr Ticho, a Jew, was a leader in the field of ophthalmology and during the British Mandate was responsible for saving hundreds of Palestinian Arabs from blindness. Included in the exhibits is Dr Ticho's study and some documents and letters of interest, in particular those dealing with his work for the Arabs, as well as his collection of Hanukkah (Festival of Lights) lamps and some of Anna Ticho's art.

However, the appeal of the museum is secondary to the popularity of its charming ground floor cafe, the tables from which spill out onto a terrace overlooking a large, tranquil garden.

Ticho House (☎ 624 5068), just off Harav Kook St, is open Sunday, Monday, Wednesday and Thursday from 10 am to 5 pm,

Tuesday from 10 am to 10 pm, and Friday from 10 am to 2 pm, closed Saturday. There is no admission charge.

The cafe at Ticho House is open Sunday to Thursday from 10 am to midnight, Friday from 10 am to 3 pm, and Saturday from sundown to midnight.

Museum of Italian Jewish Art & Synagogue

In 1952, with no Jews left in Conegliano Veneto near Venice, the interior of the town's 18th century synagogue was dismantled and reassembled here. It now serves the needs of Italian Jews in Jerusalem and is the only synagogue outside Italy where the ancient Italian liturgy is performed.

The architecture and art are also there for public appreciation east of King George V St at 27 Hillel St, on the next street parallel to and south of Ben Yehuda St. The synagogue/museum (☎ 624 1610) is open to visitors Sunday to Tuesday and Thursday from 10 am to 1 pm, and Wednesday from 4 to 7 pm. Admission is 10NIS. Shabbat services are held here.

Heichal Shlomo & the Great Synagogue

Facing the Sheraton Plaza Hotel and Gan Ha'Atzmaut (Independence Park) at 58 King George V St, this 1960s complex is styled along the lines of Solomon's Temple – Heichal Shlomo literally means 'Solomon's Mansion' – and is the seat of the Chief Rabbinate of Israel and the Supreme Religious Centre. The emblem of the scales of justice is on both sides of the entrance.

The **Wolfson Museum** (☎ 624 7112) housed inside the massive building features presentations of religious and traditional Jewish life. It's open Sunday to Thursday from 9 am to 1 pm, closed Friday and Saturday. Admission is 5NIS.

Next door to Heichal Shlomo, and part of the same complex, is the Great Synagogue. The building has been condemned by many as an extravagant waste of money, but attendance at a Shabbat service here is, nevertheless, recommended.

REHAVIA & TALBIYEH (MAP 4)

רחביה טלביה

Built in the earlier part of this century by wealthy Christian Arabs (Talbiyeh) and Jewish intellectuals (Rehavia), these are among the city's more fashionable neighbourhoods – although the increase in the number of ultraorthodox Jewish residents is said to be changing that. The official residences of the prime minister and president are here and many of the impressive properties display nameplates of medical and legal professionals.

Talbiyeh, also known as Kommemiyut, has some particularly wonderfully self-indulgent architecture; take a look at 17 Alkalay St, a house called **Beit Jalad**, built by an Arab contractor with a fondness for the imagery of *The Thousand and One Nights*.

These neighbourhoods lie south of Ramban St and west of Keren HaYesod St.

Jason's Tomb

It's not worth the long walk to get here because there really is nothing to see but a cave barred by a rusting iron gate in a leafy suburban street. However, for the archaeologist, this was one of the city's most interesting tombs because it provided a wealth of historical information. Built in the early 1st century BC by someone called Jason, it contains two or three generations of his family. Archaeologists learned from this tomb of that era's expressions of belief in the afterlife – cooking pots, complete with food, and lighting were provided in the individual graves, and even some dice were found (gambling in heaven?) The porch's charcoal drawings of a warship in pursuit of two other vessels indicate that Jason or a son was a naval officer.

If you're in the neighbourhood you may want to visit the tomb, which is on Alfasi St; look through the iron grille to see the burial chamber. Eight shaft graves can be seen through the small opening on the left.

MAMILLA (MAPS 3 & 4)   ממילה

Bordering the Old City walls from Jaffa Gate up to Zahal Square and rolling across the valley to busy HaMelekh David St, Mamilla links old and new Jerusalem. At the beginning of this century it was a busy commercial district shared between Arabs and Jews but the fighting in 1948 resulted in the border being drawn through Mamilla, and for 19 years the place existed as a sniper-targeted no-man's-land.

Such prime real estate wasn't going to lie fallow for too long and many new developments are either under way or have already been completed. The most high profile of these is David's Village, a clustering of prestige residential blocks across the valley from Jaffa Gate. The sales pitch for these apartments is appropriately enough 'for those who can afford to live like a king' – except the village is not named, as you might assume, for the biblical King David but for the developer behind the project, David Taic. Adjacent to the village is the luxury Jerusalem Hilton hotel; there's also a shopping centre, parks and new highways to come.

HaMelekh David St, which runs south from the New City centre down to the railway station, escaped the fighting relatively unscathed and has several important landmarks, including the architecturally noteworthy Hebrew Union College building, the King David Hotel and the YMCA. The road leads to Herod's Family Tomb, the attractive Yemin Moshe neighbourhood and Liberty Bell Gardens.

St Vincent de Paul Hospice

On Mamilla Rd down from Jaffa Gate, this large convent is another of those wonderful Jerusalem buildings that gets lost in the crowd. It's an orphanage built in the late 19th century by the Sisters of Charity, a Paris-based order of nuns.

The house at 33 Mamilla Rd bears a plaque recording that Dr Theodor Herzl, the founder of political Zionism, stayed here during his visit to Palestine in 1898.

The YMCA & the King David Hotel

Designed by the architect of New York's Empire State Building and completed in 1933, Jerusalem's YMCA building on Ha-Melekh David St is an appealing mix of Romanesque and Orientalism. The vaulted lobby is especially attractive and we recommend poking your nose inside. Although for a time closed to the public after being used for an attempted suicide, the building's distinctive tower is open again, Monday to Saturday from 9 am to 2 pm, closed Sunday. Admission is 3NIS. (See also the Places to Stay – Mid-range section of this chapter.)

The stadium behind the main building used to be home to Jerusalem's football team but it's now moved to a new, modern ground beside the Malkha shopping centre.

Opposite the YMCA, and obscuring its view of the Old City, is the ungainly bulk of the King David Hotel. What the Savoy is to London and Raffles to Singapore, so is the King David to Jerusalem. It was designed in 1930 by a Swiss architect, Emil Vogt, for an Egyptian Jewish family, and the hotel has since been host to Winston Churchill, Anwar Sadat, the last five US presidents, Elizabeth Taylor and Kirk Douglas, to name but a few. During the Mandate it was home to the British military high command and then in 1946 the hotel's southern wing was blown up by the Irgun, the underground militia led by Menachem Begin, who later became Israel's prime minister.

Herod's Family Tomb

The tomb is on Aba Sikra St just off Ha Melekh David St, south of the King David Hotel. When archaeologists discovered it, little was found inside as the tomb robbers had been there first. Herod himself is not buried here but at Herodian, near Bethlehem.

Yemin Moshe & the Montefiore Windmill

The small Yemin Moshe neighbourhood can be identified immediately by its windmill, actually one of the first Jerusalem structures to be built outside the secure confines of the Old City.

It was part of a scheme developed by Sir Moses Montefiore, who was an English Jewish philanthropist who wanted to ease the overcrowding within the city walls. He built a block of 24 apartments, a development known as **Mishkenot Sha'ananim** (Tranquil Dwellings) and the windmill was to have provided the basis for a flour industry. The scheme failed and the windmill is now an eccentric landmark serving as a museum dedicated to the life and work of Montefiore. It's open Sunday to Thursday from 9 am to 4 pm, and Friday from 9 am to 1 pm, closed Saturday.

The Mishkenot Sha'ananim complex is now a guesthouse for 'creative' visitors to Jerusalem, and past tenants have included Simone de Beauvoir, Isaiah Berlin, Marc Chagall, Milan Kundera and VS Naipaul.

Arts & Crafts Lane

Originally a small settlement of Sephardic Jews, Khutsot HaYotser was rebuilt in the 1920s as an Arab market and workshop complex. From 1948 on, it sat abandoned in the middle of no-man's-land, and it was only when the barbed wire was removed in 1967 that reconstruction could begin. Today, it's a curious arcade (curious in that the arcade leads from nowhere to nowhere) of art galleries, craft workshops and a couple of cafes. It's not really worth a special trip but you might conceivably pass this way walking from the Old City to the Cinematheque or Yemin Moshe.

Liberty Bell Gardens

Just across from the Montefiore Windmill an exact replica of the Liberty Bell in Philadelphia is the central point of this three hectare park, often a venue for public events and popular with picnickers.

St Andrew's Church

Also known as the Scottish Church, it was built in 1927 to commemorate the capture of the city and the Holy Land by the British in WWI. It's owned by the Church of Scotland and the floor features an inscription to the memory of Robert the Bruce, who requested that his heart be buried in Jerusalem when he died. Sir James Douglas made an attempt at fulfilling Bruce's wish but en route he was killed in Spain, fighting the Moors. The heart was recovered and returned to Scotland where it's now buried at Melrose.

Jerusalem Film Centre & Cinematheque

Perched on the valleyside below Hebron Rd, with great views across to Mt Zion and the Old City, this complex (☎ 671 5398) houses several cinema screens, a small museum, a library and archives relating to the film industry. It's open Sunday and Monday from 10 am to 3 pm, Tuesday and Thursday from 10 am to 7 pm, and Friday from 10 am to 1 pm. Also part of the complex is the Cinematheque (see the Entertainment section of this chapter) and a popular restaurant.

Sultan's Pool

Now a unique open-air amphitheatre used for a variety of concerts, this was originally a city reservoir created by the Mamluk sultan Barquq in the 14th century. Its location, nestled below the walls of the city, makes it a spectacularly atmospheric venue: we recommend you check the listings in the *Jerusalem Post* or ask at the tourist information office on Jaffa Rd and if anybody is performing here, get a ticket.

Sultan's Pool is between Yemin Moshe and Hebron Rd, and beside the road above it is a beautiful 16th century *sabil* (public drinking fountain) built during the reign of Suleyman the Magnificent.

TALPIOT (MAP 1)   תלפיות

To get here take bus No 8 from Jaffa Rd and get off at the Kiryat Moriah stop.

Haas Promenade

Providing another spectacular view of Jerusalem, this promenade is a popular place for Jerusalemites to visit at night. There are a couple of cafes and a restaurant here, too. In Hebrew it's known as the Tayelet.

Hill of Evil Council

To the east and below the Haas Promenade is what's known as the Hill of Evil Counsel. Now the UN headquarters site, it was the residency of the British high commissioner for Palestine during the Mandate. Going further back, it's an alternative possibility for the site of the house of Caiaphas, the high priest who paid Judas to betray Jesus.

GIVAT RAM & MUSEUM ROW (MAPS 1 & 2)

גבעת רם   שדירת המוזיאונים

West of central Jerusalem and south of the central bus station is Givat Ram, which in the last 30 years or so has developed as the institutional heart of the city. It's home to the Knesset (the seat of the Israeli parliament) and several museums, and is also the site of the prime minister's office (usually easily identified by the placard wielding protesters outside). Across the road is the Bank of Israel headquarters and the Supreme Court building. You can get here from Jaffa Rd on bus No 9, 24 or 28 (to the university).

Israel Museum
See the Israel Museum section between pages 171 and 180.

Bible Lands Museum
One of the latest additions to the New City's cultural scene, this museum is billed as 'a nondenominational centre for the appreciation of the history of the Bible'. Dating from 6000 BC to 600 AD and presented chronologically, the exhibits include some 2000 artefacts ranging from mosaics and other art pieces, seals and bronzes to household items from all over Asia, Europe and Africa.

The Bible Lands Museum (☎ 561 1066) is on Granot St, adjacent to the Israel Museum. It's open Sunday, Monday, Tuesday and Thursday from 9.30 am to 5.30 pm, Wednesday from 9.30 am to 9.30 pm, Friday from 9.30 am to 2 pm, and Saturday from 11 am to 3 pm. Admission is 18NIS.

Knesset
A few minutes walk from the Israel Museum is HaKirya (The City), the government centre, dominated by the Knesset, Israel's parliament building. Belonging to the multistorey car park school of architec-

ture, the building was inaugurated in 1966 – previously the parliament had met in what is now the Ministry of Tourism on King George V St. The present-day Knesset is at least a lot more attractive inside than out and it has a foyer decorated with three tapestries and a mosaic by Marc Chagall.

The building is open to the public on Sunday and Thursday from 8.30 am to 2.30 pm, when free guided tours are given. Bring your passport. You can also see the Knesset in session on Monday or Tuesday from 4 to 7 pm, and Sunday and Thursday from 11 am to 7 pm. The proceedings are conducted mainly in Hebrew and occasionally in Arabic. Call ☎ 675 3333 for further details.

Next to the bus stops opposite the Knesset is a bronze menorah, a gift from British supporters of the State of Israel. It's decorated with panels representing important figures and events in Jewish history.

Hebrew University
The Givat Ram campus on Brodetsky Rd, west of the Israel Museum, features a strikingly designed synagogue recognisable by its white egg-shaped cupola. Other features of interest include the Academy of the Hebrew Language, which displays the library and furniture of Ben Yehuda, who was responsible for the Hebrew language revival. Free daily guided tours of the campus start at 9 and 11 am at the old Sherman building.

The Bloomfield Science Museum
Go away on holiday, come back and impress the hell out of everybody with lucid explanations of how a fax machine works or why domes don't buckle. Part of the Hebrew University, this museum is devoted to aiding the understanding of the natural and technological worlds through a series of hands-on exhibits. It's designed primarily with the young in mind and it's a great place to take kids. The museum (☎ 561 8128) is open Monday, Wednesday and Thursday from 10 am to 6 pm, Tuesday from 10 am to 8 pm, Friday from 10 am to 1 pm and Saturday from 10 am to 3 pm. Admission is 12NIS.

continued on page 180

THE ISRAEL MUSEUM

No visit to Jerusalem or Israel could be considered complete without a visit to the country's leading showcase of its cultural and historical heritage – the Israel Museum. The coach loads of daily visitors are testament to its endurance as a major cultural attraction, and like many major museums in the world, a single day can hardly do justice to the treasures on display.

The Israel Museum is a purpose-built grouping of several buildings on a specially created, landscaped site. It includes the excellent **Arts Wing**, which brings together works that range from Islamic calligraphy to Francis Bacon and is, as would be expected, strong on Jewish artists, including Chagall and Soutine. The **Archaeological Wing** houses finds made in the Holy Land from prehistoric artefacts through to Roman and Byzantine remains. There's also a wing devoted to **Judaica & Jewish Ethnography**.

Indisputably the museum's biggest drawcard is the **Shrine of the Book**, the distinctive pot lid-shaped building at he northern end of the site. Displayed in a dimly lit subterranean chamber are five of the 2000-year-old Dead Sea Scrolls found in caves at Qumran, near the Dead Sea.

There's also an **Art Garden** with work by Henry Moore, Picasso and Rodin, among others, as well as a **Youth Wing** for children where there are always several exhibitions at any one time, as well as programs of concerts, lectures and films.

Bottom: *Vertebrae* by Henry Moore – a black-bronze sculpture in the Art Garden (see page 179)

© THE ISRAEL MUSEUM JERUSALEM/BY ADAM BARTOS

Right: Hadrian, bronze bust from Beit She'an, 2nd century AD (© The Israel Museum Jerusalem)

Beginnings

The founding of the museum had its roots in a memorable speech given by then prime minister David Ben-Gurion in the Knesset, Israel's parliament. The speech was delivered on 30 May 1960 during a debate on the budget allocation for the establishment of the National Museum of Israel. Ben-Gurion announced that Israel should have an 'impressive cultural centre' to reflect the revival of the country's 'independence in its ancient land' and the enduring spirit of the people.

The main initiator behind this move to establish a home for Israel's cultural treasures was Teddy Kollek, then director of the prime minister's office (later to serve as the mayor of Jerusalem for 28 years). It was he and a group of like-minded pioneers who had the dream to create a national museum in the new homeland of Israel, and Ben-Gurion's support was crucial in securing the funds for the building of the nascent museum.

After funding was secured, a grand debate ensued over the placement of the new museum. The present site Neveh Sha'anan (Hill of Tranquillity), west of the Old City, was decided upon mainly because of its accessibility to visitors. It wasn't until 11 May 1965 that the dream was finally realised and the museum opened its doors to the public.

Now over 30 years old, the museum has grown in stature and size and serves as a focus and repository for the nation's cultural and archaeological wealth. It attracts over 700,000 visitors each year and hosts many fascinating exhibitions. The museum itself consists of a series of low, interconnected buildings blending almost imperceptibly into Jerusalem's landscape. If you are planning to explore archaeological sites around Israel, you should make sure you begin or end your visit in the Israel Museum.

Practicalities

Get to the museum by 10 am if at all possible to avoid the long queues that form when the tour buses start arriving. The main entrance building contains the ticket office, information stand and the well-stocked museum shop. Maps showing the layout of the museum are on prominent display.

It is a good 30-40 minute hike to the museum from the Old or New City. If you're on foot the best route is to follow Agron St west from where it begins near the Jerusalem Hilton, until you come out by the big intersection with Ben Tsvi Boulevard. Cross the intersection (via the underpass) and follow Rupin St to the museum entrance which is prominently signposted.

The museum is open Sunday, Monday, Wednesday and Thursday from 10 am to 5 pm, Tuesday from 4 to 10 pm, Friday from 10 am to 2 pm, and Saturday from 10 am to 4 pm. Admission is 20NIS (students 15NIS). For recorded information, call ☎ 02-670 8811 or check the tourist information office and the *Jerusalem Post* for details of special exhibitions and events.

Guided tours in English are included in the admission price. They start from the main entrance and deal with specific areas rather than the whole complex. There's a good museum highlights tour daily (except Saturday and Tuesday) at 11 am and also at 3 pm on Sunday, Monday, Wednesday and Thursday.

If you can't get to the Israel Museum in Jerusalem, check out their Web site at www.imj.org.il.

Highlights

If you have time on your hands, you can conveniently get around most of the major exhibits in one (albeit exhausting) day. Allow two days if time and funds allow. The following section deals with the highlights of the museum.

Shrine of the Book This discrete building houses the remarkable Dead Sea Scrolls which were found by a shepherd boy at Qumran near the Dead Sea in 1947. The scrolls, totalling 800 in all, were found in

Bottom: An exterior view of the Shrine of the Book, which houses the Dead Sea Scrolls.

© THE ISRAEL MUSEUM JERUSALEM/BY ANN LEVIN

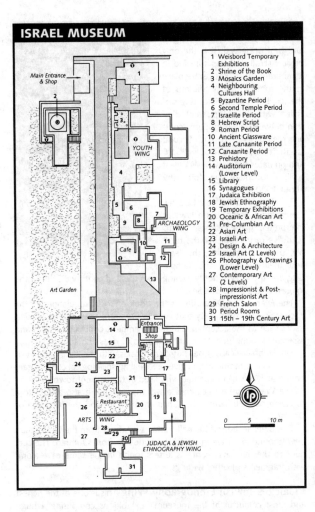

ISRAEL MUSEUM

Main Entrance & Shop

YOUTH WING

ARCHAEOLOGY WING

Cafe

Art Garden

Entrance
Shop

Restaurant

ARTS WING

JUDAICA & JEWISH ETHNOGRAPHY WING

1 Weisbord Temporary Exhibitions
2 Shrine of the Book
3 Mosaics Garden
4 Neighbouring Cultures Hall
5 Byzantine Period
6 Second Temple Period
7 Israelite Period
8 Hebrew Script
9 Roman Period
10 Ancient Glassware
11 Late Canaanite Period
12 Canaanite Period
13 Prehistory
14 Auditorium (Lower Level)
15 Library
16 Synagogues
17 Judaica Exhibition
18 Jewish Ethnography
19 Temporary Exhibitions
20 Oceanic & African Art
21 Pre-Columbian Art
22 Asian Art
23 Israeli Art
24 Design & Architecture
25 Israeli Art (2 Levels)
26 Photography & Drawings (Lower Level)
27 Contemporary Art (2 Levels)
28 Impressionist & Post-impressionist Art
29 French Salon
30 Period Rooms
31 15th – 19th Century Art

0   5   10 m

clay pots and date back to the time of the Bar Kochba Revolt (132-35 AD). Made mainly of leather, they deal with both secular and religious issues and were thought to have been written by an ascetic group of Jews called the Essenes who inhabited the area for about 300 years.

An enormous amount of often controversial and contradictory material has been written about the Dead Sea Scrolls; the bottom line is that no one really knows what they signified, or who the Essenes really were, despite several biblical references to their existence.

The most important scroll is the **Great Isaiah Scroll**, the largest and best preserved. It is the only biblical scroll that has survived in its entirety, and takes centre place in the room. The 54 columns of the scroll contain all 66 chapters of Isaiah without an apparent division between what modern scholars regard as First and Second Isaiah. It dates from about 100 BC and predates the previously oldest biblical document ever found by about 1000 years.

The **Temple Scroll** is a halachic composition dealing with laws as interpreted by the Essenes. It deals with five major subjects: the temple, the king's statutes, the feast and their sacrifices, the Temple City, and the laws of purity. Dating from the 2nd century BC, this is the longest of the Dead Sea Scrolls.

Left: Torah finials, San'a, Yemen, 20th century (© The Israel Museum Jerusalem)

The **Manual of Discipline** is the book of social regulations of the ancient Jewish community that lived in Qumran. The scroll deals with issues such as the acceptance of new members, conduct at meals and assemblies, punishment for infringements of rules and so on.

The **Habbakuk Commentary Scroll** deals with the life and times of the Qumran community and gives a revealing sociological commentary on the activities of the people who lived in this ancient town.

The **War Scroll** is in essence a war manual, but it also alludes to a so-called battle between the 'Children of Light' and the 'Children of Darkness'.

The lower section of the hall contains artefacts from the Bar Kochba Revolt found in a cave in Nahal Hever not far from Qumran. The corridor to the main hall contains letters found in the same cave along with fragments of other writings.

Judaica & Jewish Ethnography Wing

This is one of the richest and most colourful of the museum's exhibitions comprising a huge range of artefacts both large and small detailing all facets of Jewish life. The Jewish world has had a long-held interest in its own people and religion – the oldest religion still practised today. This exhibition is a repository for the spiritual and cultural wealth of the Israeli nation.

The exhibition is in two parts; the Judaica section is comprised of objects made of metal – primarily silver – and centres around five major themes: the Shabbat, the synagogue, the Torah, illuminated manuscripts, and Jewish holidays. The most outstanding features are the three complete synagogues brought from various locations and reconstructed. Of the three, the **Vittorio Veneto Synagogue** is the most impressive. It dates from 1700 and was transported from Vittorio Veneto in Italy in 1965. It was used by the Ashkenazi (European Jewish) community in Italy for more than 200 years, but fell into disuse after WWI.

Look out for the excellent examples of lavishly designed *parochets* (Torah Ark curtains), Torah mantles and scroll cases. There are also spice boxes, alms boxes, Torah ornaments, *haggadot* (illuminated manuscripts) and superb manuscripts of marriage contracts.

The second part of this exhibition focuses on Jewish ethnography; the variety of folk costumes on display is most impressive. Foremost among the exhibits are a Jewish bride's outfit from San'a in Yemen which dates back to the turn of the 19th and 20th centuries, a Druze woman's apparel from Galilee dating back to the late 19th century, and richly embroidered Palestinian costumes from Bethlehem of the 1930s. Look out also for costumes from Jewish communities in Ethiopia and Kurdistan.

The **Ortenau Room** is a replica of a middle-class Jewish home featuring domestic trappings from the early 19th century to around 1938. The room belonged to the Ortenau family of Bad Reichenhall near Munich in Germany and was preserved in its entirety through the duration of WWII before being donated to the Israel Museum. As such it is testimony not only to Jewish life in Europe before WWII, but also stands as a memorial to the victims of that same war.

Archaeology Wing If it's pots, shards, coins and bones that you like, the **Archaeology Wing** will keep you engrossed for hours. Constituting a long serpentine segment of the museum complex, the exhibition starts chronologically from the ground floor level of the main entrance building and should ideally be tackled from this starting point. It is the most comprehensive archaeological collection in the whole country and features finds made in Israel since 1948.

Right: Seated male figure, Mexico, late classic period, 600-900 AD (© The Israel Museum Jerusalem)

There is a varied display of **prehistory** material in the first gallery including hand axes, picks, chopper tools and spheroids. All of these items have been found at sites in Israel and paint a rich tableau of the country's first inhabitants. An impressive collection of Judean Treasure artefacts from the **Chalcolithic period** are worth looking out for. The collection of heads, maces, standards and sceptres are made of arsenic and antimony copper and were moulded using the *cire perdue* (lost wax) process; they were found in a Judean desert cave in 1961.

The **Canaanite period** gallerys feature anthropoid sarcophagi, gold jewellery and various clay figurines and jugs. The **Israelite period** gallery houses the *'House of David' Victory Stele* – a fragmentary monumental inscription from the First Temple period and the only extra-biblical reference to the Davidic dynasty to have come to light so far. Other notable artefacts from this period include a curious ivory pomegranate and an unusual pottery stand decorated with clay musicians, from the late 11th to early 10th century BC.

The **Roman period** is well represented by Jewish sarcophagi, ossuaries and some impressive statues including a bronze bust of Hadrian from the 2nd century AD (see the photo on page 173). Found at Beit She'an, it is considered to be one of the finest portraits of Hadrian ever discovered.

Right: Ivory pomegranate from King Solomon's Temple, 8th century BC (© The Israel Museum Jerusalem/ by Nachum Slapak)

The exhibits in the **neighbouring cultures** hall include rock reliefs from Simurrum in north-eastern Iraq, stelae from the Zagros Mountains in western Iran, an Egyptian board game called *senet* and an ingenuously entitled *Votive Statue of the Singer Imeni* from Cusae in Middle Egypt.

Arts Wing The **Arts Wing** takes up a considerable portion of the museum complex, occupying two floors of the southern wing as well as an annexe at Beit Ticho in the New City. There is a lot to see – art for every taste, from curious plastic nude statues to traditional European impressionist paintings. There are galleries for prints, drawings, paintings, sculpture and photography as well as Israeli art since 1906. There are also sections on the arts of Oceania, Asia, Africa and the Americas.

The **modern art and sculpture** collections, including the Art Garden outside the museum's main building (see on the opposite page for more details) are prominent features of the museum complex. Inside the museum proper are galleries of **impressionist** and **postimpressionist art** – admire works by Renoir, Pissaro, Gauguin, Matisse and Van Gogh. One of the most arresting displays is a complete **French Salon** from the 18th century (viewed from two entrances leading off from the postimpressionist art gallery).

Israeli art is well represented in the **Israeli Art** pavilion with striking paintings by Reuven Rubin and Yosef Zaritsky, and less conventional work by Igael Tumarkin (see his odd exhibit made of wood, textiles, iron, a stretcher and paint entitled *Mita Meshunah* – Unnatural Death). The upper floor of this pavilion has a series of changing exhibitions while the lower floor houses the permanent exhibit of modern Israeli art.

There is an extensive photography collection showing impressive works by Man Ray and Manuel Alvarez Bravo as well as Israeli photographers Mendel Diness and Yaakov Ben Dov. One of the most curious exhibits is an erotic-inspired photo-painting by Salvador Dali and Horst P. Horst – *Costume Design for the Dream of Venus* – in which Dali has painted over a photograph of a naked woman.

Art Garden The art theme extends to the **Art Garden** on the eastern side of the complex and is reached by a paved pathway from the Shrine of the Book. The hard-to-miss, black bronze sculpture called *Vertebrae* by British artist Henry Moore is a semiabstract creation reminding one of both the shape of a woman through its suggestive curvature, and the internal structure of the human body with pieces resembling the vertebrae of the spine. Also look out for the striking sculpture *Mother and Child* by Jacques Lipchitz.

The Art Garden provides visitors with a welcome respite from the heady collections of the Israel Museum. Before wandering inside, enjoy the splendid views over the western side of Jerusalem's New City.

Youth Wing The Youth Wing serves as the education department of the museum. Children can enjoy hands-on educational activities such as playing with model houses conveniently positioned at children's eyelevel. Groups of school children are given guided tours and art classes are offered to interested parties.

Left: Intricately carved Japanese *netsuke* were part of the kimono ensemble and had both functional and aesthetic purposes (© The Israel Museum Jerusalem).

JERUSALEM

continued from page 171

Monastery of the Cross

This great, walled compound is similar in appearance to a desert monastery such as that of Mar Saba or St Catherine's in Sinai, and it looks completely out of place in the middle of the large urban sprawl of the New City. Founded by King Bagrat of Georgia, it was built to commemorate the tradition that the tree from which Jesus' cross was made grew here. The monastery is basically 11th century, although various additions have been made since then. The Greek Orthodox Church purchased the complex in 1685.

It's worth a visit just to appreciate the incongruity, which is even greater once inside, but there are also some interesting 17th century frescoes, a bit of 5th century mosaic floor in the chapel and a small museum. The monastery is open Monday to Friday from 9 am to 4 pm, closed Saturday and Sunday. Admission is 5NIS. It can be reached by walking through Rehavia along Ramban St, crossing Hanasi Ben Zvi and following the path down the hillside. From the city centre take bus No 31 or 32; from Jaffa Gate, bus No 19. Get off at the first stop on Harav Herzog St and follow the path down.

WEST OF THE NEW CITY (MAP 1)
Model of Ancient Jerusalem

About 2.5km south-west of Givat Ram in the grounds of the Holy Land Hotel (☎ 643 7777) is a huge 1:50 scale model of Jerusalem as it was in 66 AD, at the end of the Second Temple era. While the model is fantastic and the attention to detail incredible, it's a long way out of town and only those with a keen interest in Jewish history or archaeology are going to find the trip worthwhile.

The model is open for viewing Sunday to Thursday from 8 am to 10 pm; admission is 20NIS (students 15NIS). Take bus No 21 or 21A.

Yad Vashem

Anyone who spends alot of time in the country will soon become aware of just how much the spectre of the Holocaust continues to haunt Israeli society. The modern Jewish state was born out of the tragic experiences of persecution, flight and the death camps, and the desire to ensure that such horrors would never be repeated. As a columnist in the *Jerusalem Report* put it, in effect the Holocaust is the civil religion of Israel and, if that is so, than Yad Vashem is its greatest shrine. It's telling that while the Western Wall doesn't necessarily make it on to the program, nearly all visiting heads of state are taken on an official visit to Yad Vashem.

While admittedly it's not going to make for the cheeriest day of your vacation, there's good reason to come here. The history and tragedy documented in the museum speak of far more than the Nazis and the nation of Israel.

Among the many commemorations is a striking 21m high memorial to honour the resistance fighters, with the path leading to it bordered by inscriptions carved into stones recording their various acts of bravery.

Yad Vashem (taken from Isaiah 56:5, meaning 'A Memorial and a Name') (☎ 675 1611) is open Sunday to Thursday from 9 am to 4.45 pm, and Friday from 9 am to 1 pm, closed Saturday; admission is free. There are free guided tours on Sunday and Wednesday at 10 am. Take bus No 13, 18, 20, 23 or 27.

Mt Herzl

In November 1995, world leaders from over 86 nations assembled here to pay their respects to the assassinated prime minister Yitzhak Rabin. He was laid to rest beside the graves of other former holders of the office, including Levi Eshkol, Golda Meir and Menachem Begin. Also buried here is the founder of political Zionism, Theodor Herzl, the man after whom this pleasant parkland area is named.

The Herzl Museum (☎ 511 108) includes a replica of Herzl's Vienna study, library and furniture. It's open Sunday to Thursday from 9 am to 5 pm, and Friday from 9 am to 1 pm, closed Saturday. Admission is free. Take bus No 13, 18, 20, 23 or 27.

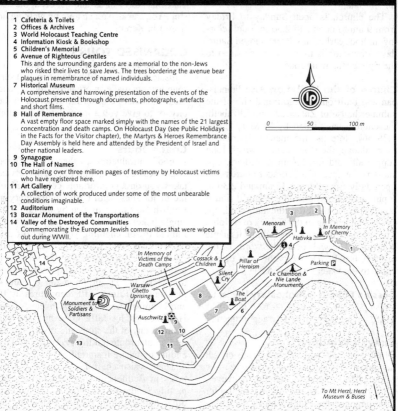

YAD VASHEM

1 **Cafeteria & Toilets**
2 **Offices & Archives**
3 **World Holocaust Teaching Centre**
4 **Information Kiosk & Bookshop**
5 **Children's Memorial**
6 **Avenue of Righteous Gentiles**
   This and the surrounding gardens are a memorial to the non-Jews
   who risked their lives to save Jews. The trees bordering the avenue bear
   plaques in remembrance of named individuals.
7 **Historical Museum**
   A comprehensive and harrowing presentation of the events of the
   Holocaust presented through documents, photographs, artefacts
   and short films.
8 **Hall of Remembrance**
   A vast empty floor space marked simply with the names of the 21 largest
   concentration and death camps. On Holocaust Day (see Public Holidays
   in the Facts for the Visitor chapter), the Martyrs & Heroes Remembrance
   Day Assembly is held here and attended by the President of Israel and
   other national leaders.
9 **Synagogue**
10 **The Hall of Names**
   Containing over three million pages of testimony by Holocaust victims
   who have registered here.
11 **Art Gallery**
   A collection of work produced under some of the most unbearable
   conditions imaginable.
12 **Auditorium**
13 **Boxcar Monument of the Transportations**
14 **Valley of the Destroyed Communities**
   Commemorating the European Jewish communities that were wiped
   out during WWII.

Ein Kerem

Now enveloped by the expanding New City
whose ugly apartment blocks threaten to
blight the terraced valley slopes, this picturesque village contains several attractive
churches commemorating the traditional
birthplace of John the Baptist.

It's a very pleasant walking area, and although bus No 17 from Jaffa Rd travels directly to the village, you might instead take
No 5, 6, 18 or 21 to reach Ein Kerem via the
Jerusalem Forest. Get off at the Sonol petrol

station on Herzl Blvd, continue walking in
the same direction and take the first right
onto Ye'fe Nof and the second left, Pirhe
Chen, to enter the forest. Head for the youth
centre in the middle of the forest and from
there the village is visible.

Church of St John This church is owned
by the Franciscan order and constructed
over the grotto where St John is believed to
have been born (Luke 1:5-25, 57-80). Steps
lead down to the grotto, with its remains of

ancient structures as well as a fine Byzantine mosaic.

The church is open Sunday to Friday from 9 am to noon and 2.30 to 5 pm (closing an hour earlier in winter), closed Saturday. Admission is free. It's on the street to the right of the main road.

Church of the Visitation Also Franciscan and built on the traditional site of the summer house of Zachariah and Elizabeth, the church was visited by St Mary (Luke 1:39-56). Note also the ancient cistern and, in an alcove, the stone behind which John supposedly hid from Roman soldiers. Upstairs is the apse of a Crusader church. It's open daily from 8 to 11.45 am and 2.30 to 6 pm, and admission is free. You'll find it on the street to the left of the main road, opposite that leading to the Church of St John. The spring which gives the village its name is nearby. The wall bears the words of the prophet Isaiah, 'Ho everyone who thirsts, come to the waters' (Isaiah 55:1).

Russian Church & Monastery Higher up the slope, this monastery (☎ 622 2565, 565 4128) can only be visited by appointment.

Chagall Windows
Often confused with its namesake on Mt Scopus, the Hadassah Medical Centre is the Middle East's largest hospital. However, it's far more well known internationally for its synagogue featuring stained-glass windows by Jewish artist Marc Chagall. His 12 colourful abstract panels each depict one of the tribes of Israel, based on Genesis 49 and Deuteronomy 33. Four of the windows were shattered during the 1967 War and had to be repaired by the artist who, as a testimony to the event, left a single symbolic bullet hole in the lower part of the green window.

The windows and tourist centre (☎ 641 6333, 644 6271) are open for viewing Sunday to Thursday from 8 am to 3.45 pm, and Friday from 8.30 am to 12.30 pm, closed Saturday. Admission is 9NIS (students 4.50NIS), which includes a guided tour (held

every hour on the half-hour until 12.30 pm). Take bus No 19 or 27 and get off at the last stop. You can also reach here by walking up from Ein Kerem.

ORGANISED TOURS
The huge number of places of interest in Jerusalem and the wealth of history that surrounds them make an organised tour a good idea. This can be as an introduction to the city, or to give you a more detailed awareness of certain areas.

Coach Tours
A good introduction to the city is Egged Tours' Route 99, Circular Line. This service takes you on a comfortable coach to 36 of the major sites, with basic commentary in English (sort of) provided by the driver. A single ticket is 20NIS valid for a day's unlimited travel, enabling you to get off and back on wherever you wish; bear in mind, however, the infrequency of the service: it operates Sunday to Thursday with departures at 10 and 11 am, noon and 1, 2 and 4 pm, and on Friday with departures at 10 and 11 am and noon. The coach leaves from Ha'Emek St by Jaffa Gate but you can board at any of the stops and it's a continuous circular route (taking 1½ hours in total), ending up where it started.

There is also a half-day tour (US$24) that takes in Bethlehem and Yad Vashem departing Sunday to Thursday at 9.30 am. Another half-day tour (US$32) takes in the Mount of Olives and the Hezekiah's Tunnel leaving at 10 am on Tuesday and Thursday from 1 April to 30 October.

Their one day tours take in Jerusalem, Bethlehem, Yad Vashem and the Old City (daily at 9.30 am, US$46) and Jerusalem New City (Monday and Wednesday at 9.30 am, US$56). This last tour includes the Chagall windows, Mount Herzl, the Israel Museum, the Knesset and the suburb of Ein Kerem.

For further information visit the Egged Tours Web site www.eggedtlalim.co.il or their offices – see the Travel Agencies section earlier in this chapter.

Walking Tours

Up-to-date details of the following and other walking tours are available at the tourist information office.

Zion Walking Tours Enjoying one of the best reputations for Old and New City tours, Zion (Map 6, ☎ 628 7866, fax 629 0774) has its office on Omar ibn al-Khattab Square, opposite the entrance to the Citadel. Particularly good value is a three-hour 'Four Quarters' tour of the Old City departing Sunday to Friday at 9 and 11 am and 2 pm and costing US$10 (students US$9) per person. A number of readers have recommended guide Stanley Ziring who takes the walking tours on Monday, Tuesday and Thursday at 11 am. Other tours include the Pre-Temple Period route, the Underground City of Jerusalem and Mea She'arim and they also offer a tour of the Judean Desert and Jericho costing US$45. Bookings are essential for this last tour.

SPNI The SPNI organises hikes and treks in the surrounding countryside but each Thursday beginning at 8 am it runs a full-day tour of the Old City. It's limited, however, only to the Jewish parts. The cost per person is 132NIS. For booking details see the Information section earlier in this chapter.

Free Walking Tours The Jaffa Rd tourist information office organises a free Saturday morning walking tour around a different part of the city each week. Meet at 10 am by the entrance to the Russian Compound at 32 Jaffa Rd. Unfortunately such a free tour inevitably attracts a large crowd so although the guides are well informed you'll often struggle to hear them.

Sheraton Plaza Hotel (Map 3, ☎ 625 9111), on the corner of King George V St and Agron St, offers free walking tours most days of the week, and they are open to non-residents. Meet in the hotel lobby at 9 am.

The Jewish Student Information Centre (see the Information section earlier in this chapter), which is committed to giving young Jews a fresh awareness of being Jewish, organises free walking tours of Jewish sites in the Old City's Jewish and Muslim quarters. Visit the centre or call ☎ 628 2643 for current schedules.

Cycling Tours

The Jerusalem Cycle Club (Map 4, ☎ 561 9416) based at 16 Rachael Imenu St, in the German Colony, organises Saturday morning cycle rides around the environs of Jerusalem. The excursions start at 7 am and usually last about four hours and the club can rent out bicycles. Call for details.

For do-it-yourself pedal power, check out Walk Ways (☎ 533 2402, fax 534 4452, email rockman@netvision.net.il). Owner Chaim Rockman rents out bikes at a reasonable rate and although his outfit is located out in Mevesseret Zion on the Tel Aviv road, he'll deliver and pick up bikes to your hotel or hostel. Walk Ways also organises adventurous cycling and camping tours through Israel, Jordan and Egypt's Sinai region.

Air Tours

Jerusalem Wings (☎ 583 1444, fax 583 1880, email lljrwing@inter.net.il) is an air tour company offering 30 minutes in a small plane over Jerusalem and its environs for US$50 per person, or a 60 minute whirl down to Masada and back for US$90 per person. Make sure you make your reservations a few days in advance.

Arkia Airlines (☎ 625 5888, fax 625 5758) runs a so-called 'Hallelujah Flight'. For US$89 per person and with a minimum of 40 people on board you can fly over the biblical sights of Israel taking in Jerusalem, Bethlehem, Nazareth and the Sea of Galilee.

Archaeological Digs

For those interested in trying archaeology one day at a time, there's a tourist-oriented 'Dig for a Day' program operating during July and August involving a three-hour excavation, seminars and a tour. It costs about US$55. Contact Archaeological Seminars (Map 6, ☎ 627 3515, fax 627 2660, email office@archesem.com), PO Box 14002, 34 Habad St, Jerusalem 91140.

SPECIAL EVENTS

Throughout the year, Jerusalem is a major venue for special events, in particular national celebrations of Jewish festivals (see Public Holidays & Special Events in the Facts for the Visitor chapter) and the annual Israel Festival. Usually held sometime during May or June, this is a three week programme of cultural events featuring music, theatre and dance which makes good use of some of the city's unique venues such as the Citadel, Sultan's Pool and the Mt Scopus amphitheatre.

PLACES TO STAY

The best location to stay in really depends on your requirements. The Old City and East Jerusalem tend to have the cheapest places and the best atmosphere, and, of course, they're the most convenient for the major sites nearby. However, some hostels and hospices have strict curfews, and being at least a good 20 minute walk from the nightlife of the city centre, they aren't so great for those who want to stay out late (the Old City and East Jerusalem completely close down at dusk). On the other hand, accommodation in the New City tends to be considerably more expensive.

B&B accommodation is becoming more and more popular and is a good mid-range option. If you plan to stay a week or more, ask about reduced rates.

PLACES TO STAY – BUDGET

In general, hostel prices in Jerusalem are the cheapest in all Israel, and it's possible to get a bed for as little as 15NIS – half of what you might expect to pay in Tel Aviv. Nevertheless, anyone intending to spend two months or more in Jerusalem might want to consider renting a room or an apartment. If you look around you should be able to pay less rent than you would in a hostel (the going rate for a room in a flatshare is around 750NIS or US$250 per calendar month), and you will have privacy and independence.

To find a cheap room or studio, or someone who needs an extra person to share an apartment, scan the 'In Jerusalem' section

The Colony

The *American Colony Hotel* (Map 5, ☎ 627 9777, fax 628 3357, email reserv@amcol.co.il) is the East Jerusalem counterpart to the King David Hotel. Both places have served as unofficial no-man's-lands where in recent Middle Eastern history the key players and observers have gathered. But while the King David has been host to statesmen and women, the Colony has been the favoured haunt of journalists, writers, diplomats and spies. Past residents have included TE Lawrence, John Le Carre, Graham Greene, Lord Allenby and, intriguingly, Lauren Bacall.

Once the home of a Turkish pasha, it is the city's only top-class Arab hotel (albeit English-owned and Swiss-managed), although the Israelis used to disparagingly refer to it as the PLO hotel because of alleged links between staff and the Palestinian movement. It has beautiful Oriental architecture, a lovely swimming pool, a popular garden terrace and serves non-kosher food, including a renowned lunchtime buffet on Saturday.

Singles cost from US$207 to US$219 while doubles range from US$253 to US$276. The American Colony is at 1 Louis Vincent St, off Nablus Rd.

of Friday's *Jerusalem Post*, or better still, get someone who reads Hebrew to take a look with you at the classifieds in *Kol Ha'ir*, a local weekly. The notice boards at the two campuses of the Hebrew University, at the Israel Centre on the corner of Strauss and HaNevi'im Sts, and at the Sefer VeSefel and Tmol Shilshom bookshops can also be good places to look. (See both Email & Internet Access and Bookshops earlier in this chapter.)

She'al (☎ 622 6991), at 21 King George V St, is a property agency that keeps lists in English, although it charges a small fortune to let you look at them. It is open Sunday to Thursday from 8.30 am to 1 pm and

4 to 7 pm, and Friday from 8.30 am to 1 pm, closed Saturday.

Old City

Most of the Old City's budget accommodation is found near Jaffa and Damascus gates, which is convenient because they're the main access points and well served by buses. From outside the Jaffa Rd central bus station (Map 2) take bus No 6, 13 or 20 for Jaffa Gate and bus No 23 or 27 for Damascus Gate (4.30NIS).

The main contender in the popularity stakes is *Tabasco Hostel (Maps 6 & 7, ☎ 628 3461, fax 628 3461)* on Aqabat at-Takiya St (you can see the sign from Souq Khan as-Zeit St). This place is very lively and clean, though often crowded. It has a busy notice board and no curfew, though you'll have to identify yourself to get in after 1 am. Downstairs is the Old City's most partyin' venue. Plus it's cheap – dorm beds are 18NIS, a mattress on the roof is 15NIS, while a rather small private room is a hefty 75NIS.

In the vicinity of Damascus Gate, *Al-Arab Hostel (Maps 6 & 7, ☎ 628 3537)* on Souq Khan as-Zeit St is another backpackers' hangout. Its reputation has waxed and waned over the years as has the attitude of staff to guests. As well as large airy, cat-prowled dorms (beds 15NIS), there are beds on the roof (12NIS) and a couple of private double rooms at 50NIS. Showers and toilets are shared by all and are perhaps too few and not well maintained, but it has a tiny kitchen with free tea, a table tennis room, and each night videos are shown in the cushion-strewn common room. Curfew is 1.30 am. Take note, though: don't get involved in political discussions here. Sensitivities are rather high and a misplaced opinion may lead to a misunderstanding.

Far cleaner, far quieter and a much better option altogether is the fairly austere *New Hashimi Hostel (Maps 6 & 7, ☎ 628 4410, fax 628 4667)*. The dorms have only eight beds (20NIS), and each room has its own shower and toilet, as do the very attractive private doubles at 90NIS. There's a large common area with plenty of tables and chairs and a well-equipped kitchen. Reception is open 24 hours a day. Note that this is primarily a Muslim hostel which means no alcohol and no open association of the sexes, or you'll be out on the street. The New Hashimi is just two doors along from Al-Arab on Souq Khan as-Zeit St.

Right next to the mosque on Al-Wad Rd is *Al-Ahram Youth Hostel (Maps 6 & 7, ☎ 628 0926, fax 992 1027)*, another fairly quiet and reasonably clean place that seems to attract an older crowd. Dorm beds are 20NIS and between 24NIS and 30NIS for a comfortable mattress up on the roof terrace. There is an enforced midnight curfew. Across from the Al-Ahram, on the corner of the Via Dolorosa, is *Austrian Hospice (Map 7, ☎ 627 1466)*. Secluded behind high walls, this place is almost monastic in its asceticism and sobriety. However, you may find it redeemed by the wonderful garden terraces which overlook the streets below. Dorm beds are US$26 for the first night and US$13 for each subsequent night. Double rooms (married couples only) cost US$72 including breakfast. There's a midnight curfew but a US$20 deposit gets you a night key. The hospice is open from 7 am to 10 pm.

In the Jaffa Gate area is *Petra Hostel (Map 6, ☎ 628 6618)* which has a superb location on Omar ibn al-Khattab Square, so see if you can get into a dorm with a balcony overlooking the action. It's an airy place, with lots of room to move and breathe. Located in what was once a grand hotel in the old Jerusalem, it's now a popular backpackers' home. Dorm beds are 23NIS or a spot on the roof with a great view of the Dome of the Rock – if you ignore the abandoned wasteland of Hezekiah's Pool below – is 15NIS.

New Swedish Hostel (Maps 6, 7 & 9, ☎ 626 4124, fax 628 7884, 29 David St), is about 100m down into the bazaar. While it's clean and draws a regular backpacker crowd, many from Sweden, it is somewhat cramped and pokey. Dorm beds cost 15NIS and tiny private rooms cost between 50NIS and 75NIS. There's a 3 am curfew.

Jaffa Gate Youth Hostel (Map 6, ☎ 627 6402), is behind the Christian Information

Centre and is a popular, often crowded place with a kitchen and cosy TV lounge. Dorm beds (women only) are 25NIS; a double room is 90NIS. There's a midnight curfew.

For a couple of better hostels, head into the bazaar along David St from Omar ibn al-Khattab Square, take the first right and then turn left immediately onto St Mark's Rd. *Citadel Youth Hostel (Maps 6, 7 & 9, ☎ 627 4375, email citadelhostel@netscape .net)* is 50m down here on the right. The reception and the small double rooms (60 to 100NIS) on the ground floor look like they've been burrowed into stone. A tight, narrow stairway leads up to some clean and comfortable dorms (beds are 20NIS), a small lounge, a kitchen, and access to the roof with views over the Old City.

Just beyond the Citadel Youth Hostel, on the opposite side of the street, is *Lutheran Hospice (Maps 6, 7 & 9, ☎ 628 2120, fax 628 5107, email luthhosp@netvision.net.il)*, the closest thing to a 'five star' hostel. It is beautiful. There are shady cloisters, a huge spotless kitchen and a palm garden with a fountain and views of the Dome of the Rock. The dorms are single sex and beds are 25NIS. Private single rooms are priced in deutschmarks and go for between DM66 and DM78 and doubles from DM59 and DM65. The hospice is closed from 9 am to noon and has a strict 10.30 pm curfew, though you may stay out later if you tell the front desk when you'll be back.

Finally, tucked away on quiet El-Malak St is the only private accommodation option in the Jewish Quarter. This is *El-Malak Youth Hostel (Map 9, ☎ 628 5362)*, a cool, cosy oasis in the basement of an old house not far from the Western Wall. Dorm beds go for 20NIS and small private rooms, some of which are in a separate part of the house, go for between and 75 and 100NIS. Ask for Isaac, the custodian of the hostel.

East Jerusalem

'Hostel Row' is the stretch of HaNevi'im St across from Damascus Gate, beside the service taxi rank. There are four possibilities here, the best of which are the two nearest

the Old City walls. *Faisal Hostel (Map 5, ☎ 627 2492, 4 HaNevi'im St)* is the closest and has a good terrace on which guests can laze around and watch the activity around the gate. There's a kitchen with free tea and coffee and a common room. The hostel's occupants, however, seem to be a semi-permanent migrant crowd rather than backpackers. Dorm beds (a bit cramped) are 20NIS and there are a few doubles at 50NIS. There's a flexible 1 am curfew.

Palm Hostel (Map 5, ☎ 627 3189, 6 HaNevi'im St), next door to the Faisal, has a great common room with plants and a glass roof. There's also a kitchen with a fridge, and videos are shown most nights. There is no curfew. Beds in large, spacious dorms are 20NIS, and there are a few private rooms at 80 and 100NIS.

Just north of the Nablus Rd Arab bus station is *Cairo Hostel (Map 5, ☎ 627 7216, 21 Nablus Rd)*. It's a bit soulless and not particularly friendly, but there's a large lounge with satellite TV, and free coffee and tea in the kitchen. Dorm beds are 15NIS, and there are also some private rooms for 60NIS that take three or maybe four people.

New City

Although it is way more expensive than the Old City and East Jerusalem hostels, *Jerusalem Inn Hostel (Map 3, ☎ 625 1294, 6 HaHistradrut St)* just off pedestrianised Ben Yehuda St right in the centre of the New City, is recommended. It's a converted apartment building with dorms on three floors, all kept immaculately clean. It further endears itself to some by having a strictly enforced no smoking policy (and you don't want to mess with Olga, the manageress). There's no kitchen, but at the reception/bar area you can get breakfast, snacks, tea, coffee and beer. The place has a midnight curfew but a popular will get you a front door key. Dorm beds are 42NIS and singles are 96NIS, while doubles start at 120NIS.

Another good option on the hostel scene is *My Home (Map 3, ☎ 623 2235, fax 623 2236, email myhome@netvision.net.il, 15 King George St)*, close to Ben Yehuda St.

It's clean enough, though the floors are a bit grungy and could do with a scrub, and dorm beds are certainly not as cheap (US$14 to US$17) as in the Old City or even nearby. Double rooms are a better buy from US$20 to US$24 and breakfast is included. Nevertheless, it is handy for city nightlife and most amenities.

Another possible option is *Jasmine Ben Yehuda Hostel (Map 3, ☎ 624 8021, fax 625 3032, 1 Solomon St)* more or less above the Underground disco. This place is reasonably clean and well run but the management are a bit diffident and timeworn as is the feel of the hostel generally. There is a small kitchen area as well as tea, coffee and breakfast if you want them. There's no curfew. Dorm beds are 30NIS.

Hotel Noga (Map 3, ☎ 625 4590 mornings only, or 566 1888, 4 Bezalel St) is something different altogether – a clean family owned apartment in a quiet part of town alongside the Bezalel Art School. The comfortably furnished rooms share a well-equipped kitchen and bathroom. Singles/doubles are 75/90NIS, and there's also a triple for 120NIS and a quad for 144NIS. There's no curfew, as guests get their own front door key. Reservations must be made in advance.

There are six HI-affiliated hostels in and around Jerusalem, two of which are central. The better of the two is *HI-Beit Shmuel Hostel (Map 3, ☎ 620 3491, fax 620 3467, 6 Shama St)* next to the Hebrew Union College near the junction of HaMelekh David and Agron Sts. This place is highly recommended. It's a beautiful building, more like a hotel than a hostel, and it's only a few minutes walk from both the Old City and the central area of the New City.

HaDavidka Youth Hostel (Map 2, ☎ 538 4555, fax 538 8790, 67 HaNevi'im St) is at the junction of HaNevi'im St and Jaffa Rd. It's just a few minutes walk from the city centre and a bus ride (Nos 23 and 27 stop outside on their way to Damascus Gate) from the Old City. The HaDavidka has good facilities and are well maintained, but is not particularly friendly and it's often busy with

Israeli school groups. In both the HI hostels, dorm beds cost between US$13 and US$19 and there are usually private singles for around US$42, with breakfast included in all cases.

PLACES TO STAY – MID-RANGE
Old City

The majority of the mid-range accommodation in the Old City is offered by the Christian hospices in the Jaffa Gate area. They all have strict curfews and tend to be quiet, sober places from which unmarried couples are most likely to be turned away. *Christ Church Hospice (Map 6, ☎ 627 7727, fax 627 7730, email christch@netvision.net.il)* at Omar ibn al-Khattab Square, across from the Citadel entrance, has pleasant staff and is very clean and quiet with a pretty courtyard and comfortable public rooms (see Christ Church earlier in this chapter for more information). Singles cost from US$41 to US$50, and doubles from US$72 to US$90. As well as its cheap dorm beds, the very popular *Lutheran Hospice* (see Places to Stay – Budget earlier for directions) has an attached guesthouse in which singles go for between DM66 and DM78 and doubles from DM59 and DM65, with breakfast provided.

Casa Nova Pilgrims' Hospice (Map 6, ☎ 628 2791, fax 626 4370, 10 Casa Nova St) is run by the Franciscans with the help of some officious Arab staff. It is clean and has vaulted ceilings and massive marble pillars in the dining room. The food is great and the rooms, mainly twins with bathrooms and central heating, are pleasant. The hospice is often full with European pilgrims. Singles/doubles are US$32/42. From Jaffa Gate take the second left, Greek Catholic Patriarchate Rd, and follow it until it becomes Casa Nova St. The hospice is on your left after you enter a narrow alley and climb a set of stairs.

Greek Catholic Patriarchate Hospice (Map 6, ☎ 628 2023, fax 628 6652) is a bit unfriendly, but the basic singles/doubles at US$36/52 are comfortable and breakfast is included. It's on St Dimitri's Rd; from Jaffa

Gate take the second left (Greek Catholic Patriarchate Rd which becomes St Dimitri's Rd) and the hospice is on the right.

Although the building is owned by the Greek Orthodox Church, *New Imperial Hotel* (*Map 6*, ☎ *628 2261*), on your left as you enter Jaffa Gate, has few religious trappings. It was built in the late 19th century, and Kaiser Wilhelm stayed here when he visited in 1898. The hotel retains an air of dusty, faded grandeur, although the rooms have all been cleaned up and are reasonably comfortable. Heating might be a problem in winter, though renovations of the heating system are on the planning board. Singles/doubles are a bargain, starting at US$30/33.

Behind the New Imperial on Latin Patriarchate Rd, *Gloria Hotel* (*Map 6*, ☎ *628 2431, fax 628 2401*) is very modern inside and has large, quiet rooms, with pleasant views across the Citadel from the dining room. Singles/doubles cost from US$50/75 with breakfast, and there's no curfew.

Deep in the Muslim Quarter on the Via Dolorosa, 50m west of the junction with Al-Wad Rd, is perhaps the most comfortable of the Christian-run establishments; *Armenian Hospice* (*Map 7*, ☎ *626 0880, fax 626 1208*) has been renovated and now offers immaculate double rooms with en suite bathroom and TV for $US60. Around 100m further east along the Via Dolorosa, on the left, is the *Convent of the Sisters of Zion* (*Map 7*, ☎ *627 7292, fax 628 2224, eccehomo@inter.net.il*), run by the Sisters of Zion. It's very clean, with a study area and kitchen. Singles/doubles are US$40/66 with breakfast. The hospice reception is open from 7 am to 12.30 pm and from 5.30 to 8.00 pm. There is an 11 pm curfew.

East Jerusalem

This was where all the pilgrims to the Old City would stay when Jerusalem was a divided city, so most of these hotels are found mainly on or around Salah ad-Din St and date from the 1950s and 1960s – and the majority are still firmly stuck there. The facilities are generally not as good as those in the New City hotels of comparable prices, but the East Jerusalem places tend to be friendlier.

One of the best accommodation deals in the city, *St George's Cathedral Guesthouse* (*Map 5*, ☎ *628 3302, fax 628 2253, email sghotel@netvision.net.il, 20 Nablus Rd*) is part of the St George's Cathedral compound, just 10 minutes walk from the Old City. It's a delightful cloistered building with an attractive garden and the atmosphere is very relaxed and friendly, with no curfew. The comfortable rooms, most with private bathroom, cost in high season US$50/78 for singles/doubles with breakfast.

On the same street but a little closer to Damascus Gate is *Capitolina Hotel* (*Map 5*, ☎ *628 6888, fax 627 6301, 29 Nablus Rd*) next door to the US consulate and once the Jerusalem YMCA. The decor is dowdy but there are good facilities, including a swimming pool and squash and tennis courts; singles/doubles are US$55/75.

Of the more conventional hotels, *Jerusalem Golden Walls Hotel* (*Maps 5 & 7*, ☎ *627 2135, fax 589 4658, email admin@pilgrimpal.com*) definitely has the prime location, on Sultan Suleyman St facing the Old City walls, but it's also next to the bus station so rooms on that side suffer from chronic noise pollution. It's one of East Jerusalem's best-appointed hotels, though; singles cost US$105, doubles US$140.

Not much further from the Old City (just a few minutes walk from Damascus Gate), *Jerusalem Hotel* (*Map 5*, ☎/fax *628 3282*), just off Nablus Rd facing the Nablus Rd Arab bus station, is not a bad option. It's a beautiful building with an attractive courtyard and has a cool, welcoming stone-clad interior; singles are US$59, doubles US$85.

Many of the other hotels in East Jerusalem suffered badly from a lack of trade in the Intifada years and are now seriously in need of some money being spent on them. A case in point is *Rivoli Hotel* (*Maps 5 & 7*, ☎ *628 4871, fax 627 4879, 3 Salah ad-Din St*) on the corner of Sultan Suleyman St. It has rooms that are adequate if a little dingy, and what was once quite a decent lounge. Singles/doubles here are US$50/70.

Over the road and 50m along is *Metropole (Maps 5 & 7, ☎ 628 2507, fax 628 5134, 6 Salah ad-Din St)* another downmarket down-at-heel place where singles cost US$40 and doubles US$60. Do not confuse it with the adjacent *New Metropole Hotel (Map 5, ☎ 628 3846, fax 627 7485, 8 Salah ad-Din St)* which is a much better place. It has a roof garden with views of Mt Scopus, the Mount of Olives and the Rockefeller Museum. Comfortable air-con singles/doubles with good facilities cost US$45/70.

Continuing north up the same street is the aged *Lawrence Hotel (Map 5, ☎ 626 4208, fax 627 1285, email karine@actom .co.il 18 Salah ad-Din St)*, which has basic singles/doubles from US$40/60, while over the road is the more modern *Capitol Hotel (Map 5, ☎ 628 2501, fax 626 4352, email hotcap@p-ol.com)*, with a bar and well-equipped air-con rooms with balconies facing the Mount of Olives. The hotel is very popular with tours from Europe. Singles/doubles start from US$65/85.

From the Capitol Hotel, continue north up Salah ad-Din St and turn right into As-Zahra St, where you'll find *National Palace Hotel (Map 5, ☎ 627 3273, fax 628 2139, email ranzi@trendline.co.il)*, which is rather characterless but does well from the pilgrim trade, packing them into singles/doubles at US$70/96. Equally unexceptional though smaller and more private are the *Victoria Hotel (Map 5, ☎ 627 3858, fax 627 4171, 8 Al-Masoudi St)* around the corner to the right of the National Palace, which has singles/doubles at US$45/65, and the *Christmas Hotel (Map 5, ☎ 628 2588, fax 626 4417, email garo@netvision.net.il)*, off Salah ad-Din St opposite St George's Cathedral, which has clean and comfortable singles from US$75 and doubles at around US$95.

New City

A wonderful location outside one of the Old City gates (and just 10 minutes walk from the city centre) help make the guesthouse at the *Notre Dame of Jerusalem Centre (Map 6, ☎ 627 9111, fax 627 1995)* one of the city's better mid-range accommodation op-

tions. The rooms have three-star-style facilities, while the majestic surroundings and views are just excellent. Singles cost US$79 and doubles US$98, breakfast included.

The *YMCA – Three Arches Hotel (Maps 3 & 4, ☎ 569 2692, fax 623 5192, email y3arches@netvision.net.il, 26 HaMelekh David St)*, is most probably the best-looking YMCA in the world. Guests have free use of the pool, gym and squash and tennis courts. Singles/doubles are US$104/127. The YMCA can be reached on bus No 7, 8, 21 or 30 from Jaffa Rd. If you are walking, it will take you about 10 minutes to reach Jaffa Gate, while the city centre area is some 15 minutes away.

Another place of great character is *St Andrew's Hospice (Map 4, ☎ 673 2401, fax 673 1711,)* which, belonging to the church of the same name, has a friendly Scottish country house atmosphere – very comfortable and peaceful. Singles/doubles are US$50/75 with breakfast included. However, despite its appealing location near Bloomfield Gardens, overlooking Mt Zion and the Old City, the hospice is a little far away from the action. It's a 15 to 20 minute steep walk to Jaffa Gate and more than that to the New City centre. During the day take bus No 4, 7, 14, 15, 21 or 30; later at night you may find yourself having to resort to pricey taxis.

If you value being in the middle of it all then there are several extremely central options, the best of which is possibly *Jerusalem Inn Hotel (Map 3, ☎ 625 2757, fax 625 1297, 7 Horkenos St)*, which has an almost Scandinavian looking interior with masses of open space, a large lounge and a bar/restaurant. Singles range in price from US$52 to US$72 and doubles from US$58 to US$78. It's not far from Zion Square. Head north up Eliyshar St (look for MacDavid's on the corner), up the steps at the end and it's on the left.

Right across from Zion Square is *Hotel Ron (Map 3, ☎ 622 3122, fax 625 0707, email ronhotel@inter.net.il, 44 Jaffa Rd)*. It's from one of this building's balconies that Menachem Begin, former underground leader and future prime minister, made his first major public speech. The rooms are large and reasonably pleasant, although those facing the front may be a little noisy; singles/doubles are US$89/94. Around the corner from the Ron is the less appealing **Hotel Kaplan** (Map 3, ☎ 625 4591, fax 623 6245, 4 HaHavazelet St) which has rooms without toilets at US$28/38 or with shower and toilet at US$40/60.

Eyal Hotel (Map 3, ☎ 623 4161, fax 623 4167, 21 Shamai St), one block south of Zion Square has a good central location but prices now have crept up to US$86 per person. The Eyal also has a sister hotel in **Hotel Zion** (Map 3, ☎ 623 2367, fax 625 7585), which is as central as it gets, lying between Jaffa Rd and Ben Yehuda St on Luntz St, one of the small cafe-filled pedestrian alleys. It's reasonably attractive inside, but the staff's attitude is a bit gruff. It is surrounded on all sides by some of Jerusalem's liveliest all-night streets. Some people might have problems with the noise. Singles are from US$53 to US$72, and doubles from US$76 to US$80.

B&Bs

Within this category fall the majority of B&B establishments (see earlier in this chapter). A very convenient and excellent option for arrivals by bus is **Allenby #2** (Map 2, ☎ 052-578 493, fax 534 4113, email nmr@netvision.net.il) an old, homey Jerusalem house on Allenby Square and a five minute walk east of the central bus station. Here you will find several single and double rooms and a roomy self-contained apartment that can accommodate up to five people. Danny Flax, the irrepressible owner, is a fountain of knowledge on Jerusalem and a most delightful host. Prices range from US$45 to US$70.

Over in the Giv'at Hamivtar neighbourhood, some 3km north of the Old City are a couple of places that merit serious consideration. **House 57** (Map 1, ☎ 581 9944, fax 532 2929, email house57@netvision.net.il, 57 Midbar Sinai) was the first of the now popular B&B options. Built on the side of a

hill, the location offers comfortable rooms with a view and easy bus access to the Old and New Cities. Single/double accommodation goes for US$45/65.

Further along the same street is **Le Sixteen** (Map 1, ☎ 532 8008, fax 581 9159, email le16@virtual.co.il, 16 Midbar Sinai) run by French and English-speaking Ari. This beautifully designed house has five small studio apartments, all opening out onto a green lawn – a rarity in Jerusalem – and views over the valley to the north. Rooms have air-con and cable TV and range in price from US$35 to US$70 for singles/doubles.

Down in the German Colony, 3km south of the New City, are three places worth looking at. Just off the main drag, Emek Refa'im is **B-Green Guest House** (☎ 566 4220, fax 563 8505, email b-green@virtual.co.il, 4 Rachel Imenu) a friendly place with a relaxing garden. Owner Boaz Green has well-appointed single/double rooms averaging US$50.

Not far away and next to the Smadar Cinema is **A Little House In The Colony** (☎ 563 7641, fax 563 7645, email melonit@netvision.net.il, 4/a Lloyd George St) – an obvious play on the TV series of a similar name. The location is good but the rooms are quite small and range in price from US$49 to US$59 for singles and from US$59 to US$71 for doubles. Breakfast is included.

Finally, in sight of the Knesset in the Nahalat Ahim district just west of the New City is **Noah's House** (Map 2, ☎ 625 0842, fax 625 0849, email katsir@hum.huji.ac.il, 33 Narkiss St), so named in reference to its passing similarity to the Ark of the same name. These are more like apartments than B&B rooms and are great for longer term stays or for families with children. Rates range from US$40 to US$90 for singles in low season to US$55 to US$110 for doubles in high season. Lower rates apply for long-term stays.

For further details on the above and on other B&B accommodation see the Home Accommodation Association of Jerusalem's Web site www.bnb.co.il.

PLACES TO STAY – TOP END

Jerusalem is top-heavy with luxury hotels. Most are in the New City, with just one or two in East Jerusalem and none in the Old City. During 1997 the Hilton chain opened *Jerusalem Hilton (Map 3, ☎ 621 1111, fax 621 1000, email jrshiew@netvision.net.il, 7 King David St)* the city's brashest and most glitzy hotel located in Mamilla, a champagne cork's arc away from the Old City walls. Singles run from US$236 to US$333, while doubles rev up at US$282 to US$380.

The country's top hotel is probably still *King David Hotel (Maps 3 & 4, ☎ 620 8888, fax 620 8882, email danhtls@dan hotels.co.il, 23 HaMelekh St)* and has been given the seal of approval by a stream of visiting kings and queens, presidents and prime ministers. While the place does have the benefits of a distinguished history, a superb high-class restaurant and excellent, uninterrupted views of the Old City from its eastern side, it's difficult not to suspect that the major attraction of the King David is its pure, traditional snob appeal. Singles cost from US$283 to US$506, while doubles go from US$306 to US$529.

Not far behind the King David in the luxury stakes is *Laromme Jerusalem Hotel (Map 4, ☎ 675 6666, fax 675 6777, email managmnt@laromme-hotel.co.il, 3 Ze'ev Jabotinsky St)* beside the Liberty Bell Gardens and overlooking the Old City. Owned by El Al, this place has excellent standards of service and is again an occasional host to heads of state. Singles cost from US$151 to US$348 while doubles range from US$170 to US$368.

Next in ranking is *Sheraton Plaza Hotel (Map 3, ☎ 629 8666, fax 623 1667, 47 King George V St)* overlooking Ha'Atzmaut Park, although the upper floors of this 18 storey slab enjoy views across the whole city. The Plaza is very convenient for the New City and about 15 minutes walk from the Old City. Singles cost from US$173 to US$303 and doubles from US$193 to US$322.

The other two five-star-style hotels that are within an easy walk of the Old City are

King Solomon (Map 4, ☎ 569 5555, fax 624 1774, email solhotel@netvision.net.il, 32 HaMelekh David St) just south of the King David Hotel, and *Radisson-Moriah Plaza (Map 4, ☎ 569 5695, fax 623 2411, 39 Keren HaYesod St)*. The Solomon was originally built for the Sheraton chain and it maintains their high standards. Rooms here are US$136 to US$230 for singles and US$135 to US$245 for doubles. The prices at Radisson-Moriah Plaza are US$170 to US$242 and US$212 to US$327.

Jerusalem's other top rank hotels suffer badly from unfavourable locations. The village-size *Hyatt Regency (Map 1, ☎ 533 1234, fax 581 5947, email hyattjrs@trendline .co.il, 32 Lehi St)* has excellent facilities, and the Hyatt reputation ensures the hotel's popularity with US visitors. However, the hotel is stuck out over towards Mt Scopus, miles from anywhere of interest and impossible to get to by public transport; singles range from around US$154 to US$236 and doubles from US$169 to US$251.

Similarly isolated up on the Mount of Olives is *Seven Arches (Map 2, ☎ 627 7555, fax 627 1319, email svnarch@trendline .co.il)* It has a classic view over the Old City but once that's savoured and the nearby churches have been explored there's a long way to go to get anywhere else. Business has not been great here and singles/doubles are a low US$100/130.

For good value and a central location we recommend *Kings Hotel (Map 3, ☎ 620 1201, fax 620 1211, 60 King George V St)*, close to Sheraton Plaza – it's just over the road from a late night Supersol supermarket. Singles are from US$105, doubles from US$130. Even more central but with inferior facilities to the Kings, *Jerusalem Tower (Map 3, ☎ 620 9209, fax 625 2167, 23 Hillel St)* is a three or four-star-style hotel. It's very popular with package tour operators. Singles are in the US$121 to US$138 range while doubles are priced between US$145 and US$182.

One final good place, located just south of the Cinemathèque, is the modest *Mount Zion (Map 4, ☎ 568 9555, fax 673 1425, 17*

Hebron Rd). It has an unusual design in that it's built into the side of the valley and the street level reception area is actually on the top floor. Most rooms have good views of the Old City; singles range from US$132 to US$184, doubles from US$145 to US$196.

There are also several hotels west of the New City centre in the Givat Ram area, quite a bus or cab ride from the Old City. *Crown Plaza (Map 2, ☎ 658 8888, fax 651 4555)* was originally a Hilton and has five-star specifications, but because of the awful location (behind the conference centre, which is the great glass block facing the central bus station) prices are as for a four star-style establishment; singles/doubles are priced from US$198/218.

Even further afield are *Park Plaza (Map 1, ☎ 658 2222, fax 658 2211, 2 Vilnai St),* *Four Points Sheraton (Map 1, ☎ 655 8888, fax 623 1667, 4 Vilnai St)* and *Renaissance Jerusalem Hotel (Map 1, ☎ 659 9999, fax 651 1824, email renjhot@netvision.net.il, Ruppin Bridge at Herzl Blvd),* all good top-class hotels with, in the case of the latter, pools, health clubs, restaurants and all the trimmings. They are hindered, however, by being located to the west of Givat Ram virtually on the outskirts of the city but seem to do well servicing a steady flow of foreign tour groups. As a result room rates are reasonable for the quality of hotel – in the region of US$100 to US$175 for singles and US$110 to US$198 for doubles.

PLACES TO EAT

With all the exotic and varied international ingredients that go into making up Jerusalem's society, much of the food on offer in the city's restaurants and cafes is, not surprisingly, diverse and representative of the city's ethnic mix. It is unfortunately often overpriced and eating out can be a strain on a modest budget. You can find anything from Jewish home cooking to Argentinian steaks, from Chinese banquets to Persian grills. Finding a good restaurant at a reasonable price can take some searching, however.

Mahane Yehuda Market (Map 2), is Jerusalem's cheapest food source, cheaper even than the Old City. To save even more, go along just as the market closes (Sunday to Thursday between about 7.30 and 8.30 pm, and Friday between about 3 and 4 pm) when prices are at their lowest. It's closed on Saturday.

Elsewhere in the New City, the basement *supermarket* in the Hamashbir department store on the corner of King George V and Ben Yehuda Sts has a good selection of bread and dairy products at regular prices. Better still is the large *Supersol supermarket (Map 3)* on Agron St near the junction with King George V St – it's open until late, 24 hours some days. Also in the New City is *Bonkers Bagels*, a 24 hour bakery almost on Zion Square.

Nearer the Old City, *Nasser Eddin Bros* on Sultan Suleyman St, across from Damascus Gate, stocks a wide range of dry goods for self-caterers. It's closed Sunday.

Vegetarian & Health Food

Established for over 30 years, *The Village Green (Map 3, ☎ 625 2007, 10 Ben Yehuda St)* restaurants (also at 1 Bezalel), both in the New City centre, are reliable places for good-value vegetarian food and refreshment. Also worth a visit is the attractive stone and foliage-filled *Alumah Natural Food Restaurant, (Map 3, ☎ 625 5014)* close to the first Village Green at 8 Yaabez St. Service is pretty laid-back and slow and main dishes are 30 to 40NIS, but they do cheaper takeaways. It's open Sunday to Thursday from 10 am to 11 pm, Friday until 2 pm only, closed Saturday.

Next to the Underground disco is the *Potato Guy (Map 3).* Simple, unassuming, tasty and quick. Choose your own fillings and get your calories and carbohydrates in an easy-to-eat package. A basic spud costs 10NIS and fillings are 2.9NIS each.

The 7th Place (Map 3, ☎ 625 4495, 37 Hillel St) is a Southern Indian-style restaurant with a dairy and vegetarian-only menu. Prices are very reasonable, with most of the menu going for 25 to 35NIS. Try the popular *thali* dish at 34NIS. The restaurant's in the Beit Agron building just east of the

St James' Cathedral door, Armenian Quarter

The Church of the Holy Sepulchre, Old City

An Ethiopian priest contemplates his Bible at an entrance of the Church of the Holy Sepulchre.

GADI FARFOUR

PAUL HELLANDER

EDDIE GERALD

Jerusalem has more to offer than just famous religious sites – you can pass through the Damascus Gate (top left), shop in the David St Bazaar (top right) or stop for a drink in Ben Yehuda St (bottom).

junction with Yoel Salomon St. It is open Sunday to Thursday from 8 am to 1 am, Friday from 8 am to 3 pm, and Saturday from sunset until 1 am.

Te'Enim (Map 4, ☎ 563 0048, 21 Emek Refaim St) at the eastern end of the restaurant strip in the German Colony is a vegetarian's delight. This place will even appeal to hard-core carnivores. The menu is varied and imaginative: mouth-watering dishes such as skewered mushrooms with tofu, and vegetables in red wine with olives and herbs go for 32NIS, imaginative salads for around 30NIS and sandwiches for 25 to 30NIS.

Felafel, Shwarma & Humous

Old City There are surprisingly few felafel places in the Old City, and none of their felafel is particularly good. The most convenient is a stall at the bottom of the slope as you enter from Damascus Gate, in the narrow frontage between the two forking roads. For good humous head down Al-Wad Rd, and by the 5th Station of the Cross, where the Via Dolorosa turns west (right), is *Abu Shukri (Map 7)*. A good humous platter will cost about 13NIS, but stay off the *fuul* and felafel, which are not as good as elsewhere.

Most *shwarma* and grilled-meat shops are along Souq Khan as-Zeit St, but sadly, they're not very good either, and they overcharge, possibly as a result of the large numbers of tourists around.

East Jerusalem For better food overall, head out of Damascus Gate and try the places on Sultan Suleyman St. Down towards the junction with Salah ad-Din St, *Al-Quds Arabic Restaurant* and neighbouring *Candy's (Maps 5 & 7)* both do superb shwarma and *shashlik* (chunks of meat grilled on a spit). For those with skip-size appetites, they sell roasted chicken, whole or half, hot off the skewer.

Something of a cult among humous freaks is *Abu Ali Restaurant (Map 5)*, although it may be greeted with something less than enthusiasm by the hygiene conscious. It's hidden away off Salah ad-Din St; head north from Herod's Gate and turn right

along an alley at the sign for 'Geneve Exhibition' it's downstairs on your left. Abu Ali is open daily from 6 am to about 2 pm.

New City Most New City felafel is sold on King George V St between Jaffa Rd and Ben Yehuda St – just follow the trail of *tahina* and squashed felafel balls on the pavement. Many of the places selling felafel also have shwarma. None of them stand above the others in price or quality, but one of the most popular with locals is *King of Felafel & Shwarma (Map 3)* on the corner of King George V and Agrippas Sts. If you want to sit while eating go to the curiously named *Thailand Food Sandwich Bar (Map 3, 6 Ben Hillel St)*, the pedestrianised street running between Ben Yehuda and King George V Sts, and get yourself a similar deal for between 7NIS for felafel and 12NIS for shwarma.

Humous is available in most Oriental restaurants and is reputably very good at *Ta'ami (Map 3, 3 Shamai St)* (no English sign), parallel with and to the south of Ben Yehuda St, and at the long-established *Rahmo (Map 2)* just off the Mahane Yehuda Market, on the corner of Ha'Armonium and HaEshkol Sts.

Cafes & Snacks

Old City For breakfast, *Cafeteria St Michel (Map 6, Omar ibn al-Khattab Square)* at Jaffa Gate does a decent spread of omelette, bread and jam, and tea or coffee. Two doors away to the left, *City Restaurant* also serves up good breakfasts and has various Middle Eastern snacks including grilled cheese and felafel or humous platters. It's open daily except Sunday from 8 am to 8 pm. Across the square, *Coffee Shop*, next to the Christian Information Centre, is a lovely place – clean, and decorated with Christian-theme Jerusalem tiles on the tables and walls. It features a modestly priced all-you-can-eat salad bar with soup and bread. It's open daily except Sunday from 10 am to 6 pm.

A popular meeting point for travellers and proud of it, *Backpacker Tearooms (Maps 6,*

7 & 9, 100 Aftimus St), in the Christian Quarter's Muristan area, offers all-day cheap food and beer as well as nightly videos. In the sanitised New York-accented Jewish Quarter, *Tzaddik's Old City Deli (Map 9)* fuels hungry diners with heavily loaded submarine rolls, plus things like chilli dogs and draught beer. It's open Sunday to Thursday until 8 pm, and Friday until mid-afternoon.

East Jerusalem Decorated with pink lacy curtains and embroidered 'God Bless Our Home' pennants, and with a waiter who switches effortlessly between Arabic and half a dozen different European languages, *Cafe Europe (Map 5, 9 As-Zahra St)* seems way out of place in the heart of blaring, wailing Arab East Jerusalem. The menu is similarly quirky but the food is superb and offers some of the best-value quality eating in the whole of the city, East, New and Old. The platters are particularly recommended, and the ice cream cocktails are excellent too, although a little pricey. It's open daily from 10 am to 10.30 pm, but is closed on Sunday. Try their famous chicken sandwiches or hamburgers, the meat for which has been marinated in a 15-year-old recipe.

New City Cafes literally line the streets of the city centre, especially Ben Yehuda, Luntz and those in the Nahalat Shiv'a area. Take your pick; there's little difference between most of them. The majority offer basic hot dishes and salads as well as cakes, ice cream and beverages. Service may be anything from indifferent to downright lousy, and even basic items such as coffee are often prepared badly. There are, of course, some happy exceptions.

Tmol Shilshom (Map 3, ☎ 623 2758, 5 Yoel Salomon St) is a crowded little restaurant sandwiched between Salomon and Shiv'a Sts. It doubles as a bookshop and meeting place for frequent literary readings in Hebrew and sometimes English, and its walls are lined with shelves of second-hand and some new titles. You can also check your email here (see Internet Resources). The place is packed at lunchtimes but it's

quieter early on and there's a good breakfast spread, including waffles with homemade jam. Try their delicious salmon steak, cooked in a fig and wine sauce with secret spices.

Another good place to sit and read (bring your own book) is the tranquil *Ticho House Cafe (Map 3, ☎ 624 4186, 9 Harav Kook St)*. The house provides cool and pleasant surroundings, or you can sit out in the tree-shaded garden. Ticho House is open Sunday to Thursday from 10 am to midnight, Friday from 10 am to 3 pm, and Saturday from sunset to midnight. On Thursday from 8.30 pm onwards they have live jazz plus wine and cheese evenings. Phone for bookings.

Despite the name, *Strudel (Map 3, ☎ 623 2102, 11 Monbaz St)* is a pastry-free zone – the name comes from the Hebrew term for the '@' common to all email addresses. It's an Internet cafe/wine bar, with tables for dining, a sofa area and four computer stations in alcoves. It has a menu of homemade soups, salads and sandwiches and an impressive array of beers and wines, including a mean draft Guinness. Strudel is in the Russian Compound area. It is open from noon until late, and from 3 pm onwards on Saturday.

Back down in the centre of the New City is a popular cafe/restaurant called *Trio (Map 3, ☎ 623 4888, 5 Luntz St)*. It is open 24 hours a day, offers a dance party every Friday at noon and live jazz music on Tuesday and Saturday from 7 pm onwards. They serve a hearty Israeli breakfast for between 22 and 26NIS and pasta dishes in the 30 to 38NIS range.

Rif-Raf (Map 3, Hillel St) is a 24-hour cafe very popular with the student community. It's a great place to get a snack or just to hang out and watch or be watched. It's opposite American Express on the corner of Rabbi Akiva St.

Away from the city centre, *Cacao (Map 4, ☎ 671 0632, 1 Hebron Rd)* the vegetarian cafe at the Cinematheque, has great views from its terrace of the Old City, Mt Zion and the Judean Desert. It's open seven days a week from 10 am until after midnight.

Restaurants – Budget

Old City There are very, very few sit down places to eat in the Old City and even fewer that we could recommend. About the best place to eat in the Old City is *Abu Shanab (Map 6, 35 Latin Patriarchate Rd)* near Jaffa Gate. It specialises in excellent pizza, made on the premises, which comes in three sizes: filling (10NIS), very filling (20NIS) and 'do you want half of this?' (35NIS). Abu Shanab also does hot sandwiches, salads, lasagne and spaghetti, all about 15NIS. It's open daily from 9 am until midnight.

A favourite backpacker hangout is *Tabasco Tearoom (Maps 6 & 7)* downstairs from Tabasco Hostel. Food is mainly western, though they throw in the odd curry or two. Travellers mainly come here for the cheap beer and the company. A feed and a beer should not cost much more than 20NIS.

Close to Damascus Gate, the *Jerusalem Star (Map 7)*, serves basic grilled meat dishes; half a grilled chicken with potatoes and salad costs 15NIS. There are often special offers – check the door. It's open daily until 9.30 pm.

In the Jewish Quarter of the Old City, just up from the Western Wall is the self-service *Quarter Cafe (Map 9, ☎ 628 7770, 11 Tiferet Y'Israel St)* (upstairs). It has decent, reasonably priced kosher food (20 to 35NIS) in pleasant surroundings, with a great view across to the Dome of the Rock and the Mount of Olives from the upper level. It's open Sunday to Thursday from 8.30 am to 6.30 pm, and Friday from 8.30 am to 4 pm, closed Saturday.

El-A'Elat Restaurant (Map 7, ☎ 628 3435, 77 Khan as-Zeit St) open since 1950 is worth giving a look-in for its good shwarma (25NIS). This place also hosted King Hussein of Jordan's wedding party when he married his first wife Dina.

Another little place worth seeking out is *Kostas' Restaurant (Map 6, HaKoptim St)* tucked away in a corner of the Christian Quarter of the Old City. The menu is limited and nominally Greek but the food is tasty and reasonably cheap and is popular with local Arabs who tend to patronise the es-

tablishment. Chicken fillet goes for 33NIS. Open only from lunchtime to early evening.

Near Jaffa Gate is the *Armenian Tavern (Map 8, ☎ 627 3854, 79 Armenian Patriarchate Rd)*, which has a beautiful tiled interior with a fountain gently splashing in one corner. The strongly flavoured meat dishes (30 to 40NIS) are – without exception – excellent and it's recommended you try the *khaghoghi derev*, a spiced mince meat mixture bundled in vine leaves, served in a light, yoghurt-based sauce.

East Jerusalem At the cheaper end of the range, *Al-Quds Arabic Restaurant* (see Felafel, Shwarma & Humous earlier in this chapter) specialises in grilled chicken; walk through to the back to be seated and served with half a bird, fries, salad and bread for 15NIS. It closes around midnight. *Cafe Europe* (see the Cafes & Snacks earlier in this chapter) also has a good selection of European-style entrees in the 25 to 35NIS range.

New City Nonvegetarians should not miss trying the city's speciality, *meorav Yerushalmi* – literally 'Jerusalem meats'. This is a mix of chopped livers, kidneys, hearts and beef with onions and spices sizzled on a great hot plate and scooped into pockets of bread. The best place to try it is on Agrippas St, in the vicinity of Mahane Yehuda, where there are dozens of restaurants frying from early evening through until early morning.

Halfway along this street is *Mordoch (Map 2, ☎ 624 5169, 70 Agrippas St)* a popular lunchtime stop for students and local workers alike, with not a tourist in sight. It's only a small joint but very popular so get here before 1 pm. The *kubeh* soup is their speciality, thought their *musaka* and stuffed courgettes are pretty tasty too. Prices are between 14 and 20NIS for any of the above dishes.

A cheap Asian fast-food joint is *Papi Tai (Map 3, 35 Jaffa Rd)*. It's nothing flash but it's cheap (around 17NIS for stir-fry) and convenient and they do takeaway. Jerusalem has a huge *McDonald's (Map 3, 4 Shamai*

St) one block south of Ben Yehuda St with all the usual McFavourites. You can even get decidedly nonkosher cheeseburgers here.

Grilled meats as well as other oriental favourites like salads, soups and stuffed vegetables are served up at *Chen (Map 3, ☎ 625 7317, 30 Jaffa Rd)*, a busy lunchtime stop-off point in the New City where you can eat well for under 25NIS. Israel's President Chaim Herzog is said to have favoured this place. It's across from the main post office (no English sign) and sandwiched between a pastry shop and a gift shop. It is open Sunday to Thursday from 8 am to 6 pm and Friday from 8 am to 3 pm, closed Saturday. *Ma'adan (Map 3, 35 Jaffa Rd)* is a similar sort of place, where a full meal including soup or salad starts at around 25NIS. The menu is wider than that at Chen, and it's open until late.

There are several good pasta places in the city centre, the best of which is probably *Spaghettim (Map 3, ☎ 623 5547, 8 Rabbi Akiva St)*, off Hillel St. Occupying the ground floor of a villa, Spaghettim has a spacious, cool, bare stone interior, which is refreshingly uncluttered, compared to most Jerusalem restaurants. The menu is spaghetti only, but it's served in over 50 different ways, from the predictable bolognaise through to ostrich in hunter sauce. Prices are 20 to 40NIS and it's open from noon to midnight.

Mamma Mia (Map 3, ☎ 624 8080, 38 King George V St) is also very good. The pastas here, all homemade, cost between 36 and 40NIS. It's at the back of the car park, 100m south of the junction with Hillel St, and is open Sunday to Thursday from noon to midnight, Friday from noon to 4 pm, and Saturday from sunset to midnight.

Another neat Italian place is *Angelo (Map 3, ☎ 623 6095, 9 Horkanus St)* near the Russian Colony. It is a 'no meat' kosher establishment which will obviously appeal to vegetarians. It offers cosy streetside dining in a quiet corner of the New City. Main pasta dishes range in price from 33 to 35NIS. It is open from noon to 11 pm, Sunday to Thursday and from half an hour after sunset on Saturday.

The Yemenite Step (Map 3, ☎ 624 0477, 10 Yoel Salomon St), open from 10 am to midnight is an oriental Jewish establishment. The mainstay of the menu is *malawach*, a thin, flaky-pastry bread stuffed with meat, mushrooms or other savouries. It's extremely filling, though a little monotonous eaten on its own. It costs 15NIS.

Romanian restaurants are particularly good for steaks and liver, and one of the best is *Gilly's (Map 3, ☎ 625 5955, 33 Hillel St)* on the corner of Yoel Salomon St. It is quite pricey though, with main dishes in the 60 to 110NIS price range.

One of Jerusalem's better known secrets is that one of the city's great kitchens is at the *Notre Dame (Map 6)* opposite New Gate. The Vatican-owned complex features a terrace coffee shop, open all day, and a restaurant with excellent food served in grand surroundings. The restaurant is open daily to nonresidents for lunch and dinner; expect to pay about 40NIS per person.

Restaurants – Mid-Range

The *Philadelphia Restaurant (Map 5, ☎ 628 9770, 9 As-Zahra St)*, off Salah ad-Din St in East Jerusalem, is one of the city's best Arab restaurants. Named after Amman as it was known in ancient times, the restaurant specialises in *mazzas* (traditional appetisers) as well as grilled lamb dishes and seafood. It's open seven days a week from noon to 10 pm.

Stanleys (Map 3, ☎ 625 9459, 3 Horkanus St) gets raves reviews from the local press. The emphasis is on South African meat dishes, from sirloin to *Boerwoers*, a kind of farmer's sausage and, if you're lucky, some of Stanley's homemade *biltong* which is sliced dried beef (similar to jerky) served with salad. The lunchtime specials costing 24 to 35NIS are a good deal and the restaurant is open seven days a week from midday to midnight.

The kind of people to whom the romantically tinged Colony appeals (see the boxed text 'The Colony' in this chapter) also tend to be enthusiastic fans of *Fink's (Map 3, ☎ 623 4523, King George V St)*, 50m north of Ben Yehuda St in the New City. It's the bar that was rated as one of the best in the world in a 1994 *Newsweek*; as well as the vast array of fine wines and spirits, Finks serves a menu of consistently excellent Austro-Bavarian food. A speciality is the goulash soup, described as a 'Jewish ploughman's lunch'. With less than a dozen stools at the bar and only six tables, reservations are advisable. Finks is open Saturday to Thursday from 6 pm until midnight, closed on Friday.

Mishkenot Sha'ananim (Map 4, ☎ 625 4424) below the Montefiore Windmill, serves award-winning French cuisine combined with a few Moroccan appetisers. It also claims to possess one of the largest and best restaurant wine cellars in the world. Whether or not its cellar is that good (this writer is sadly unqualified to comment), the views of the floodlit Old City walls are undeniably terrific. Some of their more imaginative advertised dishes include mixed Kissinger hors d'oeuvres, terrine de foie gras and goose liver with strawberry. It's open seven days a week from 11 am to 1 am. Business lunches are offered at US$28 per person.

Not far from Mishkenot Sha'ananim is *Rungsit (Map 4, ☎ 561 1757, 2 Jabotinsky St)* which offers superior Thai/Japanese food in opulent Oriental (Far Eastern as opposed to Middle Eastern) surroundings. It's a sister restaurant to the Rungsits in New York and Bangkok. In Jerusalem it's diagonally opposite Laromme Hotel in Talbiyeh and is open Sunday to Thursday from noon to midnight, Friday from 12.30 pm to one hour before Shabbat, and Saturday from one hour after Shabbat to midnight.

For superior seafood, head for *Ocean (Map 3, ☎ 624 7501, 7 Rivlin St)*, a restaurant described by the Jerusalem correspondent of the London *Times* as 'unhappily pretentious', but also as having fresh fish on a par with anything served in any European capital. The Ocean is open daily from 1 to 4 pm and 7 to 11 pm. It's probably the most expensive restaurant in Jerusalem.

ENTERTAINMENT

Pick up the *Jerusalem Post*, in particular the Friday edition, for an up-to-date and comprehensive list of events and also stop by the Jaffa Rd tourist information office for their current 'Events in Jerusalem' brochure. The *Traveller* newspaper, available free in bars and hostels, also has a good entertainment guide. At last count, however, the *Traveller* was struggling to survive so it may be gone or suspended by the time you read this.

Bars & Clubs

While East Jerusalem and the Old City close up completely at sunset, with just *Abu Shanab*, *Tabasco Tearooms* and *Backpacker Tearooms* providing any alternative to beer and a book back at the hostel, *New City (Map 3)* stays buzzing 'til sunup. Yoel Salomon and Rivlin Sts, the two parallel main streets in Nahalat Shiv'a are lined with enough late night bars and cafes to defeat even the most alcohol-absorbent of pub-crawlers.

Down at the bottom of Rivlin St, *The Tavern Pub* was the original Jerusalem pub and it attracts a mainly ex-pat, bar-propping, beer drinking crowd. It's nothing special, but it's at the centre of the action and the tables outside make a good vantage point for people watching.

The Blue Hole, down a little side alley about midway along Yoel Salomon St, is a similar sort of place to The Tavern, but considerably more dingy and away from the real action. Like most of the bars, it has a popular happy hour – only in the case of The Blue Hole it's a whole 3½ hours long.

Possibly Jerusalem's most popular nightspot is the *Underground (Yoel Salomon St)*, near Zion Square. It has a very crowded pub on the ground floor, a disco downstairs and is not ideal for those who enjoy breathing. This place doesn't get going until around 10 or 11 pm and stays open until everyone's way past caring what time it is. It's had some negative travellers' reports about its rowdiness and it really is for the under-25s so, if you are past your 'use by' date, go prepared.

What to do on Shabbat in Jerusalem

'Shabbat Shalom' for the unobservant and the non-Jew in Jerusalem, need not be a password to boredom. As a large part of Jerusalem belongs to the Arabs, Shabbat is just another day and nothing is closed in most of the Old City, Mt Zion, the Mount of Olives and East Jerusalem. The exception in the Old City is, of course, the Jewish Quarter, which completely shuts down for the day, but you can wander over to the Western Wall to see the crowds, the singing and the dancing that welcomes the Shabbat on Friday at sunset.

While the Egged buses are off the road, the Arab bus network and service taxis are still operating from the Damascus Gate area, and Shabbat is as good a time as any to head for Bethlehem, Jericho, Hebron, Ramallah or Nablus.

You might also try beating Shabbat by taking a bus down to the Dead Sea on Friday before the shutdown and staying somewhere overnight like Ein Gedi or Masada – the parks and reserves are all open seven days a week. You can return later in the day when the buses start running again. Even better, sign up for the all-inclusive trip to Masada-Ein Gedi-Qumran-Jericho offered by many of the Old City hostels. This departs every morning, Shabbat included, at 3 am and would get you back into Jerusalem at about 3 pm – time then for a quick snooze before sundown when the city comes back to life for its busiest night of the week.

You could always elect for a day trip to Tel Aviv where there's the beach and usually a fair number of eating places and watering holes open to satisfy the cravings of the nonobservant. Sheruts still run on Shabbat and they depart from near Zion Square.

If you do elect to stay in town on Friday night then you'll find that, much to the annoyance of observant Jews, most of the bars on and around Yoel Salomon and Rivlin Sts and the Russian Compound defy Shabbat and open as usual.

Stardust (6 Rivlin St) is a small, cosy bar with different musical offerings. Monday is club night considered by the local beat press a true standout on the sometimes stagnant music scene. The *Vibe Dance Bar (15 Heleni HaMalka)* is sometimes sporadic in its operation, but usually kicks in between Wednesday and Saturday. It the alternative for ravers who want to dance, but don't like the Jerusalem club scene.

The other main concentration of bars is in the Russian Compound area, crowded around the upper part of Heleni HaMalka. These places are less congested with travellers and visitors and tend to be where the local Israelis hang out. Best of the lot are the suitably laid-back *Kanabis* on Monbaz St and the ever-popular *Glasnost*, which features live music four nights a week – see the following Live Music section. Also worth dropping by is *Strudel (11 Monbaz St)*, the Internet cafe/wine bar.

Decent Guinness (18NIS, but 9NIS during happy hour) is served at *Champs (19 Jaffa Rd)* a lone English-style pub midway between the New City centre and the Old City walls, opposite the new City Hall complex. It's open from 1 pm to 5 am. Happy 'hour' is from 4 to 7 pm and again from 10 to 11 pm when drinks listed in red on the menu are all half price.

Do check out the free *Traveller* newspaper for what's hot and what's not. It's available in most bars and traveller hangouts.

Live Music

Live music has been having a hard time of late, with the Jerusalem municipality making it hard for live music to keep off the ground. Be prepared for changes to the following listings, since venues may change on a whim.

To find the best place for live music nightly between 10 pm and midnight – rock, folk and blues – squeeze in at *Mike's Place (Map 3)* on Horkanus St, a tiny bar which, aside from the guy with the guitar and the bartender, has room for only about a dozen customers. It's off Heleni HaMalka St in the Russian Compound area.

Up the hill, *Glasnost (Map 3, 15 Heleni HaMalka St)* has live music, varying from rock to reggae to jazz funk and samba, depending on what night of the week it is. At the time of research, Monday, Tuesday and Friday were music nights. There's a cover charge of 15NIS.

A newcomer on the scene is *NetCafe* (see Email & Internet Access earlier this chapter) near the Russian Compound which usually has live music a couple of nights a week, from acoustic folk to hippiejamrock, starting at 9.30 pm.

For jazz, ethnic and Arabic music, and the odd buzzsaw guitar band, check the schedule at *Pargod Theatre (Map 2, ☎ 625 8819, 94 Bezalel St)*. Friday afternoons feature free jazz jamming sessions from 1.30 to 4.30 pm.

Elsewhere, *The Yellow Submarine (Map 1, ☎ 678 1387)* on HaRakavim St way down in Talpiot usually has sessions of Israeli rock and Israeli alternative.

Cinemas

See the *Jerusalem Post* for listings of what's showing. The city's centrally located cinemas are listed below:

Cinemathèque
(Map 4, ☎ 672 4131) on Hebron Rd; shows a variety of classics, avante-garde, new wave and off-beat films, and presents a festival each July. It's a membership cinema but usually a sufficient number of tickets are available just before the performance. The complex of the cinema, cafe, archives and museum is tucked below Hebron Rd, down from St Andrew's Church

Gil 1-10
(☎ 678 8448) out at the Malkha shopping mall; take bus No 19 or 24 from Jaffa Rd

Lev
(☎ 624 7507) at 37 Hillel St, just two blocks south of Ben Yehuda St

Orion
(☎ 625 2914) on Shamai St, just one block south of Ben Yehuda St

Rav-Chen 1-7
(☎ 679 2799) at 19 Ha'Oman St in the Rav Mecher building, way down in Talpiot near the Haas Promenade

Ron
(☎ 623 4176) at 18 Hillel St, near the Jerusalem Tower

Semadar
(☎ 561 8168) at 4 Lloyd George St, in the German Colony, just south of the Liberty Bell Gardens

Films are also shown at the *Jerusalem Sherover Theatre* in Talbiyeh (see later) and at the Israel Museum, while French films are screened regularly (in fact, nightly we were told) at the Alliance Française on Agron St.

Theatre

Most theatre is performed in Hebrew, although there are the occasional foreign-language productions.

Al-Masrah Centre for Palestine Culture & Art and Al-Kasaba Theatre
(Map 5, ☎ 628 0957) on Abu Obeida St off Salah ad-Din St, behind the Tombs of the Kings in East Jerusalem. Plays, musicals, operettas and folk dancing are performed here in Arabic, often with an English synopsis.

Jerusalem Sherover Theatre
(Map 4, ☎ 561 7167) at 20 David Marcus St in Talbiyeh. This modern complex features the classics and modern works. Simultaneous English-language translation headsets are available for certain performances.

Khan Theatre
(Map 4, ☎ 671 8281) on David Remez St across from the railway station entrance. In a converted and refurbished Ottoman-era caravanserai, this complex features mainly Hebrew plays in its theatre. It also has a nightclub. Take bus No 6, 7, 8 or 30 to get here.

Train Theatre
(Map 4, ☎ 561 8514) in the Liberty Bell Gardens. This is a converted railway carriage that now serves as a puppet theatre.

Music & Folk Dancing

Classical music lovers are well catered for in Jerusalem. The Jerusalem Sherover Theatre is home to the Jerusalem Symphony Orchestra while *Binyanei Ha'Umah Conference Centre (Map 2, ☎ 622 2481)*, opposite the central bus station and adjacent to the Crown Plaza Hotel, is the national residence of the Israel Philharmonic Orchestra.

Free classical performances are held on occasion at a number of venues like the **YMCA auditorium** (Maps 3 & 4) on Ha-Melekh David St, the **Music Centre of Mishkenot Sha'ananim** (alternate Fridays) and **Beit Shmuel** (Map 3), part of Hebrew Union College on King George V St (Saturday morning). Immigrant musicians also perform at Ticho House every Friday morning.

At the **International Cultural Centre for Youth** (ICCY, Map 4, ☎ 566 4144/6, 563 0900, 566 9838) at 12A Emek Refaim St in the German Colony, south of Talbiyeh, the Pa'amez Teyman Folklore Ensemble regularly perform from a repertoire that includes Israeli folk dances and Yemenite, Hasidic and Arabic traditional dances, Israeli folk singing and Khalifa Arabic drummers. Tickets are sold at the door and at many hotels.

For jazz, try the **Pargod Theatre** (Map 2, ☎ 623 1765) at 94 Bezalel St. Friday afternoon used to be jam sessions from 1.30 to 5.30 pm; maybe they still are – call and find out.

GETTING THERE & AWAY
Air
Arkia flights depart from the airport at Atarot, north of the city directly with Eilat and Rosh Pina, with further connections to Haifa and Tel Aviv. There are no flights on Saturday. Arkia's office in the city centre (Map 2, ☎ 625 5888) is in room 121 in the Klal building at 97 Jaffa Rd, beside the junction with HaNevi'im St.

Other airline offices, all in the New City unless otherwise stated, are:

Air France
   (☎ 625 2495) 3 Shlomzion HaMalka
   (☎ 628 2535) As-Zahra St, East Jerusalem
Alitalia
   (☎ 625 8653) 23 Hillel St
British Airways
   (☎ 625 6111) 33 Jaffa Rd
El Al
   (☎ 625 6934) 236 Jaffa Rd
KLM
   (☎ 625 1361) 33 Jaffa Rd

Lufthansa
   (☎ 624 4941) 16A King George V St
Olympic Airways
   (☎ 623 4538) 33 Jaffa Rd
Sabena
   (☎ 623 4971) 23 HaMelekh David St
SAS
   (☎ 628 3235) 14 El Zahara St, East Jerusalem
Swissair
   (☎ 623 1373) 31 HaNevi'im St
Tower Air
   (☎ 625 5137) 14 Hillel St
TWA
   (☎ 624 1576) 34 Ben Yehuda St

For airport information call ☎ 03-971 0000; for recorded English-language flight information call ☎ 03-973 1122.

Bus
Egged Buses The central bus station on Jaffa Rd is where most people first arrive. Buses here connect with all the major areas in the country. Always busy, the interurban buses arrive in and depart from the main concourse, with the city buses operating from stops outside on Jaffa Rd and Zaiman St, reached by an underpass.

Although the interurban buses are always busy, those heading for the Dead Sea and in particular Eilat are the only ones for which you need reserve seats in advance. Buses for the Dead Sea are always busy and seem to run independently of official timetables. The simple rule is to make as early a start as possible.

Unless otherwise stated buses run daily between about 5.30 am and 11 pm, with the last buses on Friday being at around 3 pm and the first buses on Saturday leaving at about 6 pm. Call ☎ 530 4555 for intercity bus information.

The left-luggage office is at 195 Jaffa Rd, out of the station and directly opposite. It's open Sunday to Thursday from 7 am to 7 pm, and Friday from 7 am to 1 pm, closed Saturday. The charge is 5NIS per item per day.

Beersheba – 27.5NIS, 90 minutes; departing every 30 minutes until 8.30 pm

Eilat – 58NIS, 4½ hours; departing 7 and 10 am, 2 and 5 pm; book a day in advance

Ein Gedi – 18NIS, 90 minutes; departing 8.40 am
and 4, 7.45 and 9.40 pm (you can also take the
Eilat or Masada buses)

Haifa – 38NIS, two hours; departing every 45
minutes, last bus 7.15 pm

Masada via Ein Gedi – 35.50NIS, 1¾ hours; departing Sunday to Thursday 8.45, 9.40 and 11
am, noon and 1 pm, Friday 8.45 and 9.50 am
and 1 pm (you can also take one of the Eilat
buses)

Safed – 40NIS, three hours, only one or two a
day; take a Tiberias bus and change

Tel Aviv – 17NIS, one hour; departing every 10
to 15 minutes; bus No 405 goes to the central
bus station, bus No 480 goes to the Arlosoroff
terminal

Tiberias – 39NIS, 2½ hours; departing every hour
until 7 pm

Arab Buses The Arab buses run from two
stations in East Jerusalem. Their schedules
are not to be relied upon but the last Arab
buses usually leaves from the station by
6.30 pm. The main station is on Sultan Suleyman St, between Nablus Rd and Salah
ad-Din St, while the other station is on
Nablus Rd, just up from Damascus Gate, on
the left-hand side; some Egged city buses
also run from this station, most notably Nos
23 and 27.

From the Sultan Suleyman St Station

Bethany	No 36
Bethlehem	No 22
Hebron	No 23
Mount of Olives	No 75

From Nablus Rd

Nablus	No 23
Ramallah	No 18

Train

The scenic rail route that runs between
Jerusalem and Tel Aviv has been closed indefinitely and there are no indications when
and if it will reopen. The track is in need of
extensive repairs and upgrading, and there
neither seems to be the money nor the will to
get it up to scratch. Whether it will reopen
during the life of this book is anyone's guess.
The forlorn and now locked train station is in
David Remez St, at the southern end of
HaMelekh David St.

Car Rental Most of these places are along
King David St, north of the YMCA.

Avis	☎ 624 9001
Budget	☎ 624 8991
Eldan	☎ 625 2151
Europcar	☎ 623 5467
Hertz	☎ 623 1351
Reliable	☎ 624 8204
Sa-Gal	☎ 624 8003
Splendid	☎ 624 2488
Thrifty	☎ 625 0833
Traffic	☎ 624 1410

For a listing of Palestinian car rental companies, see under Rental in the Car section
of the Getting Around chapter.

Sheruts (Service Taxis) Sheruts make an
affordable alternative to the buses, and on
Shabbat they are the only way of getting
around all but the Palestinian areas. In the
New City regular services include the following main destinations:

Tel Aviv
HaBirah (☎ 623 2320) 1 Harav Kook St, opposite Zion Square
Kesher-Aviv (☎ 625 7366) 12 Shamai St,
south of and parallel to Ben Yehuda St Cost:
11NIS per person, Friday and Saturday 20NIS.
Ben-Gurion Airport
Nesher (Map 3, ☎ 623 1231, 257 227, fax 624
1114) 21 King George V St, on the corner of
Ben Yehuda St. Cost: 34NIS to be picked up
from your hostel/hotel; it's a seven day a week,
24 hour a day service but reserve one day
ahead, especially on Saturday.
Haifa & Eilat
Yael Daroma (☎ 622 6985) Shamai St, next
door to Kesher-Aviv; reservations a day in advance are normally necessary.

In East Jerusalem the sherut rank is across
from Damascus Gate and all vehicles to
West Bank and Gaza destinations depart
from here. The taxis are much faster than
the buses, leave more frequently and cost
only a few shekels more – see individual
place entries in The Gaza Strip & the West
Bank chapter for exact fares. They operate
daily and regularly from about 5 am until
about 5 pm, after which time the service

becomes less dependable, with less passengers to fill the vehicles.

GETTING AROUND
Airport
The only cheap way into Jerusalem from Ben-Gurion airport is by the Egged bus No 947 or 945 which leaves every half-hour from just outside the arrivals terminal at the airport (17NIS, 30-35 minutes,). From Jerusalem's central bus station, buses leave with similar frequency for Ben-Gurion. Egged bus services are not very convenient for the Old City or East Jerusalem, especially if you are re carrying heavy luggage and need to look for a place to stay.

The most convenient but more expensive way to get to the Old City or East Jerusalem is to take a sherut from outside the arrivals building. The sheruts run all night, leaving whenever they're full; the fare is US$10 (40NIS). 'Special' (ie nonshared) taxis are available for all destinations, but are much more expensive. To protect arrivals from rip-off tactics, the authorities have posted most fares on a massive sign. Check it carefully before you're hustled into a cab.

To get to the airport call Nesher Taxis (see Sheruts earlier in this chapter) on the corner of Ben Yehuda St.

If you want to get a 'special' taxi (a nonshared one), it will cost you around 95NIS from the airport to the city centre. This fare goes up about 30% between 9 pm and 5.30 am. The prices are displayed on a board at the airport, so you shouldn't have to haggle with the drivers.

Bus
Currently, these are the major routes:

Bus No 1 goes from platform D of the central bus station to Mea She'arim, Jaffa Gate, Mt Zion and then to the Old City's Jewish Quarter.
Bus No 27 goes from Hadassah Medical Centre to Mt Herzl and Yad Vashem, central bus station, down Jaffa Rd, left along HaNevi'im and via Strauss and Yezehekel Sts to the Nablus Rd bus station near Damascus Gate.

For city bus information call ☎ 530 4555.

Taxi
Although all Jerusalem taxis comply with the law that requires them to stick to charging by the meter, they are still an extremely expensive way of getting around the city.

AROUND JERUSALEM
Kibbutz Ramat Rachel
Its location between Jerusalem and Bethlehem made this kibbutz a scene of bloody fighting during the 1948 War. Today, that same location has helped the kibbutz develop itself as a full-scale tourist attraction. Its name means 'the Heights of Rachel', referring to Jacob's wife whose tomb is in Bethlehem. It offers visitors a glimpse of life on the collective farm with tours, a guesthouse, a restaurant and a bar. There's also a museum with exhibits on the 1948 War, open daily from 8 am to noon. Call ☎ 670 2555 for details about guided tour schedules. To get there take bus No 7

Kennedy Memorial
South of the Hadassah Medical Centre and about 11km from the city centre, this fine memorial to John F Kennedy sits atop Mt Orah. Unfortunately, you may need a car to get here as the nearest buses (Nos 20 and 50) still stop a good 30 minutes walk away.

Sorek/Avshalom Stalagmite & Stalactite Cave
The stunning Sorek, which is also known as Avshalom (Absalom's), cave is some 20km west of Jerusalem along the road from Ein Kerem. The predominance of limestone in the region has caused these geological formations, which are floodlit for effect. The pleasant scenery en route from Jerusalem is almost worth an excursion itself. No regular bus goes directly to the cave, but Egged Tours offers two half-day guided tours, each for around US$20.

Shoresh Junction
West of this junction on the Jerusalem-Tel Aviv highway, the road descends into a gorge. On both sides you can see the rusted remains of vehicles that were part of the

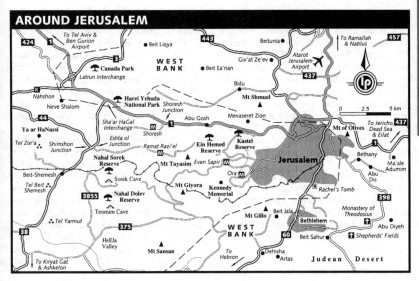

AROUND JERUSALEM

Jewish supply convoys attacked by the Arabs during the 1948 siege of Jerusalem. Some have been daubed with red paint and inscriptions, and they form a memorial to the Jews who were killed here.

Abu Gosh

This peaceful and picturesque Arab village (13km from Jerusalem and off the main highway to Tel Aviv) is significant because it is the site of biblical Kiriath-Jearim (Town of Forests) where the Ark of the Covenant was located for 20 years until David moved it to Jerusalem (I Chronicles 13:5-8). The village is known from the time Joshua conquered it. Sheikh Abu Gosh once charged a toll on the caravans of pilgrims passing through on the way to Jerusalem. Before the new highway bypassed the village it was a popular beauty spot for Israelis but now it sees fewer visitors.

There are two interesting churches here. **Notre Dame de l'Arche** (Our Lady of the Ark of the Covenant) was built in 1924 and is a local landmark, with its statue of St Mary carrying the baby Jesus. It belongs to the French Sisters of St Joseph of the Apparition, and they believe that it stands on the site of Abinadab's house where the Ark was kept (I Samuel 7:1). Ring the bell at the door of the adjacent building if no one is about and the church is closed. The church is built on the same site as a larger Byzantine church, and you can see its mosaic floor inside and out. Reach the church from the top of the hill overlooking the village and facing Jerusalem. Turn right coming out of the Caravan Restaurant and head up the hill. It's open daily from 8 to 11.30 am and 3.30 to 6 pm. Admission is free.

The **Crusader Church and Monastery** is one of the country's best-preserved and most attractive Crusader remains. It was built about 1142 and destroyed in 1187. Used for many centuries as an animal shelter, it was acquired in 1859 by the French government, who placed it under the guardianship of the French Benedictine Fathers. Since 1956 it has belonged to the Lazarist Fathers. In the subterranean section of the building is a small spring. It is believed that the monastery stands on the remains of a Roman castle. A stone from it is displayed in the church and bears an inscription of the 10th Legion, a renowned Roman unit stationed in Jerusalem in the 1st century. The complex is next door to the mosque, so look for the minaret in the valley. The sign outside reads, 'Eglise de Croisse – Crusaders' Church'. Ring the bell to enter. The monastery is open Monday to Wednesday, Friday and Saturday from 8.30 to 11 am and 2.30 to 5.30 pm, closed Sunday and Thursday. Admission is free, but donations are requested.

Places to Eat *Caravan Restaurant* is halfway between the two churches and next to a bus stop. You can eat reasonably well and cheaply on humous or stuffed vine leaves or spend more on meat and dessert while enjoying the view across the village towards Jerusalem.

Getting There & Away Abu Gosh is most conveniently reached from Jerusalem on bus No 185 or 186, both of which depart frequently between 6 am and 11 pm from the central bus station.

Bethany

On the western slopes of the Mount of Olives, Bethany is renowned as the site of the resurrection of Lazarus (John 11:1-44). A Franciscan church commemorates the traditional site of the miracle performed by Jesus. Bethany is also named as the place where Jesus was anointed, much to the disapproval of his disciples (Matthew 26:6-13; Mark 14:3-9; John 12:1-8). The church features some impressive mosaics, one of which illustrates the resurrection. Built in 1954, this is the fourth church to occupy the area. The first was constructed in the mid-1st century, the second in the Byzantine period and the third by the Crusaders.

A Greek Orthodox church stands by the Tomb of Lazarus. In the 16th century, Muslims built a mosque here and Christians later dug their own entrance to enable them to worship. Local guides are often on hand and do a decent job of telling their interesting version of the local history. If you listen,

you should tip a couple of shekels. The tomb is open daily from 8 am to noon and 2 to 6 pm. Admission is 2NIS.

The church itself is only open to the public on the Feast of Lazarus, usually in early April. The Greek Orthodox convent, a 10 minute walk away from Jerusalem, boasts the rock upon which Jesus sat while waiting for Martha to arrive from Jericho. Ring the bell to enter.

To reach Bethany you can take either of two Arab buses – the Bethany service, No 36 (there are two No 36 services, so ask for El-Azariya (Lazarus) before boarding), or No 28 to Jericho – and get off on the way through. Another option is to walk. If it's not too hot (or too wet), you can walk up and over the Mount of Olives and around the side to Bethany, or choose other routes. You can't really get lost, and you're never far from a busy road on which to hitch or hail a sherut.

Latrun

About halfway between Jerusalem and Tel Aviv lies Latrun. Its popular wine-producing monastery enjoys views of many biblical sites: Emmaus, Ayalon, Bethoron, Gezer, Modin, Lydda and Sorec. Also nearby is Canada Park, a result of the tree-planting programme initiated by the Jewish National Fund. Latrun means 'Home of the Good Thief'; it is believed to have been the home of one of the thieves crucified with Jesus.

A modern highway cuts through the area, and to the west (the left-hand side heading towards Tel Aviv) is the attractive Latrun Monastery, while to the east (the right-hand side) is Canada Park and the ruins of the Emmaus Church.

In the 1948 War, the Arabs closed the road here, thus cutting off supplies to Jerusalem. It was not until the Six Day War that the Israelis took Latrun. Going further back in time, the area has seen its fair share of conflict. Greeks, Romans, Arabs, Crusaders, the British and the Ottoman Turks have all passed through en route to Jerusalem.

Latrun Monastery Founded in 1890 by the French Trappist Order of monks as a contemplative monastery, Latrun Monastery is now widely renowned for its wine, and its lovely location, architecture and gardens.

The wine making started in around 1899. The monks reclaimed and cultivated the land and planted olive groves, grain and vegetables as well as vineyards. In the rocky areas pine trees and cypresses were chosen. In WWI the monks were expelled by the Turks, but they were able to return, and in 1926 the present monastery was constructed.

Visitors are welcome to enjoy the gardens and the architecture and to buy the wine, spirits, vermouths and the olive oil produced here. The shop by the gate is open Monday to Saturday from 8.30 to 11.30 am and 2.30 to 4.30 pm, closed Sunday.

Emmaus Church Above the ruins rises the monastery formerly belonging to the Beit-Haram Brothers, but now functioning as the French Prehistorical Research Centre. The church commemorates Christian tradition that this is where Jesus appeared to two of his disciples after his resurrection (Mark 16:12-13; Luke 24:13-31).

Canada Park This park is one of the country's many beautifully forested areas, and you can wander around and picnic here. You can find a well-preserved Roman bath near the church, dating from around 640. Various water holes, conduits and the remains of an amphitheatre are also to be found in the park.

Getting There & Away Latrun can be reached most easily by bus from Jerusalem, with a service every 30 minutes. From Tel Aviv only one bus (in the morning) passes through, although you can change at Ramla where there are frequent connections. Remind the driver that you want to go to Latrun before he flies past.

Tel Aviv

תל-אביב   تل أبيب

Pop: 349,200 ☎ Area Code: 03

Tel Aviv is the yin to Jerusalem's yang. Barely a century old, the modern metropolis thumbs its nose at the 3000 year history of the Holy City with its shackles of tradition, confrontational religions and its petty politicking. Forsaking synagogues for stock exchanges and tradition for faddism, the concerns of secular Tel Aviv are finance, business and fun. While the pious scurry to the Western Wall for their sundown prayers, the beautiful people of Tel Aviv pose furiously as they check out the evening's competition at the city's many promenade cafes and bars.

The initial impression of many visitors is that Tel Aviv is brash and soulless – a rare point on which ultraorthodox Jews and fundamentalist Muslims would agree. Few trav-ellers stay longer than a day or two, believing that the city offers little to see or do. This is a shame because, in fact, Tel Aviv is a greatly underrated Mediterranean city.

The city possesses an absorbing array of distinctive neighbourhoods, a result of the diverse backgrounds of its inhabitants. A short walk can encompass the spicy orientalism of the Yemenite Quarter, the seedy vodka cafes of Russianised lower Allenby St and the Miami chic of pastel pink and blue glass beachfront condominiums.

The key to enjoying Tel Aviv is to treat it as a resort (a role it plays far better than Eilat); cruise the cafes, hang out at the bars and make good use of the city's superb beaches. But also make some time for a few explorations around town – take a wander in areas like Jaffa and the Yemenite Quarter and don't miss the excellent Diaspora Museum and Tel Aviv Museum of Art.

Tel Aviv is also an extremely comfortable base from which to make day trips to some surrounding places of interest like Ramla, Caesarea, or other haunts, which are great for beach-bums, such as Netanya or Ashkelon. However, its midsummer wea-

HIGHLIGHTS

- **Nightlife** – the best restaurants, bars, cafes and nightclubs in Israel
- **Old Jaffa** – former Arab port and point of arrival for many Jews making *aliyah* (immigrating to the Holy Land)
- **Diaspora Museum** – the best introduction to the history of the Jewish Diaspora with the largest photo-documentation centre of Jewish life in the world
- **Beaches** – Tel Aviv's glorious fee-free beaches and beautiful boardwalk
- **Tel Aviv's Neve Tzedek district** – a trip back in time
- **Carmel Market** – a maelstrom of tastes, smells, people and products

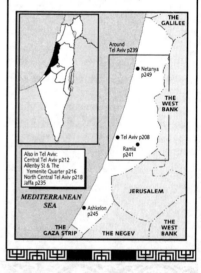

ther is usually very hot and humid making a stay in Tel Aviv then a potentially trying experience.

206

History
Dune Staking While the history of Jerusalem is a grand biblical epic, the making of Tel Aviv is a modern short story centred on drive and ambition coupled with town planning blunders.

Tel Aviv was begun by small groups of Jews who wished to migrate from the cramped and unsanitary confines of long-established, predominantly Arab Jaffa. Initially they settled in two small communities, Neve Tzedek (1886) and Neve Shalom (1890), among the dunes on the sandy coastal plane just north of the Arab town. Before long they were joined by another 60 families who were led by Meir Dizengoff, an ambitious figure who had plans to create a major Jewish town.

Taking as a model the English garden city, several town planners were invited to submit schemes for the new town. The plan adopted was that of Professor Boris Schatz, founder of the Bezalel Art School in Jerusalem. It centred around what is now Herzl St and the new town was given the name Tel Aviv (Hill of Spring), from a reference in Ezekiel 3:15.

Best-Laid Plans Progress on the new town was briefly halted when the Turks broke up the settlement and expelled the Jews from the area, but with the British victory in WWI development was permitted to continue. Arab riots in Jaffa in 1921 sent many Jews fleeing for Tel Aviv, swelling the numbers from a founding 550 people in 65 homes to an outsized 40,000 inhabitants.

The town grew quickly to accommodate the newcomers, but the development was on occasion a little eccentric. Allenby St, for instance, planned as the new main thoroughfare, was meant to run north-south parallel to the seafront but it was diverted in order to reach a coffeehouse on the beach. The Neve Shanan district in the south was planned in the shape of the seven-branched menorah merely because of the associated Jewish symbolism. And the immigrants kept coming. The 1930s saw waves of arrivals from overseas, many fleeing the threat of Nazi Germany.

When war did break out in 1939, Tel Aviv played host to about two million Allied troops. It also became a centre of the Zionist resistance against Britain's anti-immigration policies. In 1948, as the British pulled out, Jewish forces attacked Jaffa and after bloody fighting most of the Arab population fled, leaving the old town in Israeli hands.

All this was a far cry from the English garden city envisaged just 40 years earlier.

Moving Up Tel Aviv struggled through the early years of Israel's independence, contending with further immigration and urban expansion which placed crippling demands on far from bottomless municipal coffers. It wasn't until the 1970s and the growth of the private sector that the city experienced any kind of economic upturn.

Private investment has since transformed the face of the city with outgrowths of voluminous commercial and office buildings, skyscraping apartment towers and multilevel shopping complexes. Tel Aviv has basically stopped expanding outwards in favour of building upwards. The playful mirrored glass and sculpted concrete structures that have sprung up in recent years are the most visible sign of the city's wealth, with the twin Azrieli Towers of the Shalom Centre east of the city centre a bold statement of Tel Aviv's confidence and self-assurance.

Orientation
Tel Aviv is a large conglomeration of connecting suburbs sprawling across a coastal plain. Most of your time will be spent in the city's well-defined central district which occupies about 6km of seafront estate and is focused on four main streets running north-south, more or less parallel to the beachline. Closest to the sand is hotel-lined HaYarkon St, while a block inland is the central backpacker accommodation area, Ben Yehuda St. Further back is the trendy shopping zone, Dizengoff, and then more or less marking the easternmost limit of Central Tel Aviv is Ibn Gvirol St. These all run virtually the entire length of the central city area, from the northern tip bordered by the Yarkon River,

down as far as Allenby St and the Yemenite Quarter, the original 1930s centre of town.

Allenby St, almost a continuation of Ben Yehuda St, is a fifth major street which runs south from the city centre towards the central bus station.

For the purposes of this book we have broken down the central city area into three zones: North Central, Central Tel Aviv and Allenby St & the Yemenite Quarter. This has been done to better organise the information and help with orientation – North Central and Central Tel Aviv are not necessarily labels that Tel Avivians would recognise.

Information

Tourist Offices The city tourist information office (☎ 639 5660, fax 639 5659) is on the 6th floor of the central bus station, opposite stand 630. While the staff is not always particularly friendly the office has masses of hand-outs, not only on Tel Aviv but on most other places in Israel. It's open Sunday to Thursday from 9 am to 6 pm, Friday from 9 am to 1.30 pm, closed Saturday.

There is also another office in the Municipal Building (☎ 521 8500) on Rabin Square with similar opening hours.

SPNI The Society for the Protection of Nature in Israel (SPNI) offices (☎ 638 8674, 638 8688 (after 5 pm), fax 688 3940, email tourism@spni.org.il) occupy three floors and a basement at 3 HaShefela St, not far from the central bus station. SPNI tours are booked on the 1st floor but if it's just general information you are after then go downstairs to the shop where staff are happy to dole out advice.

To get to the SPNI from the city centre take bus No 5 from Dizengoff St and get off on Petah Tikva Rd by the Electricity Company; cross over and head north, the way you've come, and HaShefela St is the first on the right.

From the central bus station, take bus No 4 or 5 and get off at the first stop; walk on in the direction the bus is heading and take the first right, HaSharon St, which intersects with HaShefela St after 200m. The

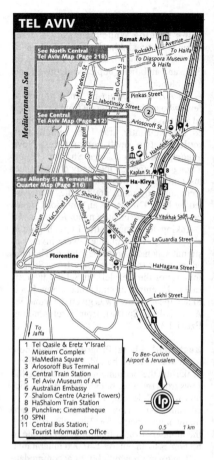

TEL AVIV

1 Tel Qasile & Eretz Y'Israel
  Museum Complex
2 HaMedina Square
3 Arlosoroff Bus Terminal
4 Central Train Station
5 Tel Aviv Museum of Art
6 Australian Embassy
7 Shalom Centre (Azrieli Towers)
8 HaShalom Train Station
9 Punchline; Cinematheque
10 SPNI
11 Central Bus Station;
   Tourist Information Office

To Ben-Gurion
Airport & Jerusalem

0   0.5   1 km

SPNI is open Sunday to Thursday from 8 am to 5 pm, Friday from 8 to 11.30 am.

Money The best currency exchange deals are given at the private bureaus around town, which don't charge commission. Try Sinai Exchange at 68 Ben Yehuda St, Change Point at 94 HaYarkon St, Change Spot at 140 Dizengoff St and Change at 37 Ben Yehuda St. These offices are generally open for business Sunday to Thursday from 9 am to 8 or 9 pm, Friday from 9 am to 2 pm and are closed Saturday. The Sinai Exchange reopens after sundown on Shabbat from 7 to 11 pm.

Banks are most easily found on Ben Yehuda and Dizengoff Sts. Banking hours are normally Sunday, Tuesday and Thursday from 8.30 am to 12.30 pm and 4 to 5.30 pm, Monday from 8.30 am to 1.30 pm, and Wednesday and Friday from 8.30 am to noon; they're all closed on Saturday.

A number of banks with ATMs that dispense cash off a credit card also have foreign currency exchange ATMs. These are accessible 24 hours a day and accept most of the major currencies. The ATMs are located, among other places, at 29 Ben Yehuda St, at 104 HaYarkon St and at the junction of Dizengoff and HaMelekh George Sts. Use these, however, only as a last resort as they offer very unfavourable rates.

Tel Aviv's American Express Travel Service Office (☎ 524 2211, fax 523 1030) is at 120 Ben Yehuda St (PO Box 3292). It's open Sunday to Thursday from 9 am to 5 pm, closed Friday and Saturday. Thomas Cook is represented by Unitours (☎ 520 9999) at 90a HaYarkon St, which is open Sunday to Thursday from 9 am to 5 pm, and Friday from 8 am to 1 pm.

Post & Communications The main post office is at 132 Allenby St, on the corner of Yehuda HaLevi St. It's open Sunday to Thursday from 7 am to 6 pm, and Friday from 7 am to noon. It's closed Saturday. The poste restante is two blocks east at 7 Mikve Y'Israel St – cross Allenby St to Yehuda HaLevi St and then bear right at the fork. This is also the international telephone office which is open Sunday to Thursday from 8 am to 6 pm, Friday from 8 am to 2 pm, closed Saturday.

There are convenient Central Tel Aviv post office branches on the corner of HaYarkon and Trumpeldor Sts and at 1 Zamenhoff St, just off Dizengoff Square. Branch post offices are generally open from 8 am to 6 pm, Sunday to Thursday.

The Internet may be accessed at the In Bar (☎ 528 2227, fax 528 2225, email barak@isralink.co.il) at 2 Shlomo Hamelech on the corner of HaMelekh George St. Since this place has the virtual monopoly on private Internet access they charge an exorbitant 40NIS an hour or 30NIS per half-hour. Students with student card pay 30NIS and 20NIS respectively.

The British Council Library (see Libraries) offers free Internet access to its members, and Momo's Hostel (see Places to Stay) offers Internet access for 15NIS per half-hour and 10NIS for each subsequent half-hour.

For discount international phone calls, faxes and telegrams go to Solan Telecom (☎ 522 9424, fax 522 9449) at 13 Frishman St, between HaYarkon and Ben Yehuda Sts. It's open 24 hours a day, seven days a week. Change Spot, a currency exchange bureau at 140 Dizengoff St, also offers cut-price international phone and fax rates.

Travel Agencies The Israel Student Travel Association (ISSTA, ☎ 517 0111) is at 109 Ben Yehuda St, on the corner of Ben-Gurion Ave. It's open Sunday to Thursday from 8.30 am to 1 pm and 3 to 6 pm, Friday from 8.30 am to 1 pm and closed Saturday. Possibly the best place to get discounted one-way tickets out of Israel is at Mona Tours (☎ 621 1433, fax 528 3125, email miridave@netvision.net.il) at 25 Bograshov St. A one-way ticket to London at the time of research was selling for US$120.

Another place to look for cheap flights is the Travel Centre (☎/fax 528 0955) upstairs at 15 Bograshov. It's also worth checking the notice boards at the No 1 Hostel and Gordon Hostel, though they may simply refer you back to Mona Tours.

For excursions around Israel, try Egged Tours (☎ 527 1212, fax 527 1229) 59 Ben Yehuda St or simply walk along that street between Allenby and Frishman Sts and check the posters in the windows.

Bookshops Steimatzky, the largest bookshop chain in Israel, has branches at 71 and 103 Allenby St, in the central bus station, in the Dizengoff and Opera Tower shopping centres, on the corner of Dizengoff and Frishman Sts and just a few doors along at 109 Dizengoff St. Of these, the branch on Dizengoff St and that at 103 Allenby St carry the best selections of English-language (and French) books, newspapers and magazines.

Lametayel (☎ 528 6894), in the Dizengoff Centre (see also Camping Gear) has an excellent range of travel guides including the most popular Lonely Planet titles – including copies of this book which may be difficult to find at other stockists. Here you can browse books at your leisure and the store even provides cushions and bean bags for your comfort.

With masses of alphabetically ordered fiction, easily the best second-hand bookshop is Book Boutique at 190 Dizengoff St. Other possible places to browse are Pollack's at 36 HaMelekh George St, White Raven at 1 Yona HaNevi St and an unnamed shop with plenty of magazines and old comics at 152 Dizengoff St, tucked away down a little alley.

Libraries At 140 HaYarkon St is the British Council Library (☎ 522 2194, email bc .telaviv@britcoun.org.il). It has a reading room with a fairly large selection of both fiction and nonfiction. English newspapers and magazines can be read at the Shakespeare Cafe downstairs. The library is open to all nationalities, Monday to Thursday from 10 am to 1 pm and 4 to 7 pm, Friday from 10 am to 1 pm; it's closed Saturday and Sunday. See their Web site www.britcoun.org.il for details.

The Australian embassy (☎ 695 0451) also has a library which includes books on Israel and Australian newspapers and magazines. It is open Monday to Thursday from 8 am to 4 pm, closed Friday to Sunday. The embassy is at 37 Shaul HaMelekh Blvd. HaNevi'im St becomes Shaul HaMelekh Blvd and the embassy is just past the Tel Aviv Museum of Art.

Cultural Centres If you're British, American or French you'll find magazines and books from home, as well as details of events being organised, at your country's

cultural centre. Aside from the British Council mentioned above there's an American Cultural Center (☎ 510 6935) on the 8th floor at 1 Ben Yehuda St but it only provides information on the USA and by appointment only. For the Gallics, there's a French Institute (☎ 510 3848) at 38 Ge'ula St, which runs between Allenby and HaYarkon Sts, north of Carmel market.

Laundry Tel Aviv is well endowed with laundromats, which cater to a large group of transient workers. Each neighbourhood will normally have at least one laundromat. The Uni Wash laundromat at 9 Mendele St, Central Tel Aviv, is particularly good as there's a friendly cafe next door. For visitors based in the Dizengoff Square area there is the very convenient Kikar Dizengoff Laundry Laundrette right next to Dizengoff Apartments on Dizengoff Square. It's open 24 hours a day. Otherwise try the junction of Idelson and Pinsker Sts, Nikita at 98 or 191 Ben Yehuda St, 45 Bograshov St, or opposite the Gordon Hostel on Gordon St. Rates for all laundromats are in the region of 10NIS for a 7kg load plus 1NIS for five minutes of drying.

Camping Gear Lametayel (☎ 528 6894), in the Dizengoff Centre, has a great array of travellers' supplies from groundsheets and hiking boots to a near complete range of Lonely Planet guides. It's open Sunday to Thursday from 9.30 am to 7 pm, Friday from 9.30 am to 1 pm and closed Saturday. Look for it up on the top floor, near McDonald's.

Emergency The city's central police station (☎ 564 4444) and the lost and found office are just off Yehuda HaLevi St, east of the junction with Allenby St; in emergencies call ☎ 100. For emergency medical aid call ☎ 101 or contact the Magen David Adom (☎ 546 0111).

If you need to contact the rape crisis centre, the number in Tel Aviv is ☎ 523 4819.

Dangers & Annoyances We have received numerous letters of complaint from

Ben Yehuda & the Revival of Hebrew

Perhaps one of the most remarkable achievements in the foundation and development of the Jewish nation is the almost single-handed revival and dissemination of the biblical language of the Jews, Hebrew. This language had long ceased to function as a lingua franca for the Jews of the world and was limited at the time of the rise of Zionism to the holy Jewish texts that were read in the synagogues in the Jewish Diaspora.

The man responsible for this remarkable achievement was Eliezer Ben Yehuda, a Lithuanian Jew born on 7 January 1858. Like most children of his age he was introduced to classical Hebrew through a thoroughly religious upbringing and came to the nascent State of Israel in 1881 imbued with the idea of making the previously biblical language a secular tool which would enable Jews of Palestine and the Diaspora to communicate in one unified tongue.

While the Hebrew language was essentially intact it had remained static from biblical times and was not spoken as a 'living' language. Consequently it did not have words for such modernities as 'electricity' and 'car' and new terms had to be coined from scratch. It is believed that Ben Yehuda spoke Hebrew for the first time at a cafe in Montmartre in Paris prior to departing for Palestine. Upon arrival he took it upon himself to speak only Hebrew to anyone he met and his firstborn son was the first all Hebrew-speaking child in modern history.

His persistence and proselytising paid off and his teachings took hold among an equally enthusiastic corpus of would-be Hebrew speakers. Ben Yehuda also contributed to the revival of the Hebrew language by establishing the 17 volume *Complete Dictionary of Ancient and Modern Hebrew*, and it is now the first language of choice for just under six million people in Israel.

women who have been harassed and hassled on Tel Aviv's beaches by over-amorous males. These Jewish Romeos, while ultimately harmless, can be very annoying for a woman or even a couple of women on their own. Other than bringing your own male along for company, there is little you can do other than try to ignore their overtures or attempt to send them packing by some carefully chosen words of dismissal; such as 'Azov oti' (a-ZOV o-TI, 'Leave me alone').

Central Tel Aviv

For the backpacker, the heart of Tel Aviv is **Ben Yehuda St** where the few remaining hostels are clustered. Named after the man

credited with the revival of the Hebrew language, this street was originally populated mainly by German Jews who, ironically, were among the most stubborn opponents of Ben Yehuda's ideas. Many of the children of these people now run the local shops while the older generation can be seen sitting over espresso reminiscing about the times when nearby **HaYarkon St** was just a camel path. These days HaYarkon St, just one block back from the beach, is the upmarket hotel zone with more than a dozen international standard establishments lining its 3km length.

Though it is modern, the sun-bleached, whitewashed architecture along HaYarkon St is not offensive, apart from the hideous

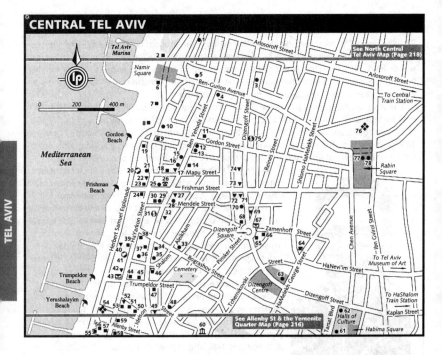

CENTRAL TEL AVIV

lapse of **Namir Square**, or Atarim Square. A dismal concrete complex of shops, restaurants, cafes and bars, Namir Square is squalid, gloomy and stinks of urine. Situated just over 100m north-west, however, at **181 HaYarkon St**, is an architectural delight – an apartment block with a bizarre sculpted and lushly foliated facade, like a vertical rockery. Be sure to look at both the front and back of the building.

Dizengoff St, named after the city's first mayor (1910-37), is Tel Aviv's prime street for window-shopping and people-watching. It gets classier the further north you go but the most vibrant bit is around Dizengoff Square with its ludicrous performing **Fire and Water Fountain**, designed by Ya'acov Agam, a leading Israeli artist whose most prominent local work prior to this was the paint job on the Dan Hotel. The colourful drum of the fountain spins round spurting

jets of water and occasionally shooting skywards jets of flame, all accompanied by a musical soundtrack. You can witness this phenomenon at 11 am, and 1, 7 and 9 pm every day.

A little south-east of the square and fountain is the **Dizengoff Centre**, a multilevel shopping mall that crosses the street, both above and below ground level. One of Israel's prime retailing areas, it houses plenty of cafes, fast-food joints, banks and a couple of cinemas. Fully air-conditioned, it's a great place to duck into to escape the afternoon heat.

Tel Aviv Museum of Art Part of an attractive modern development that includes law courts and the municipal central library, the Tel Aviv Museum of Art (☎ 696 1297, fax 695 8099), at 27 Shaul Ha Melekh Blvd, is home to a superb collection, particularly

CENTRAL TEL AVIV

PLACES TO STAY		PLACES TO EAT		21	Unitours
2	Carlton Hotel	17	Chicken 'n' Chips		(Thomas Cook Agents)
6	Radisson-Moriah Plaza	22	International Bar	25	Arkia Booking Office
7	Crowne Plaza	27	Espresso Mersand		(Domestic Flights)
8	Ramada Continental	32	Taste of Life	26	Solan Telecom
9	Gordon Hostel	40	Planet Hollywood;	28	Uni Wash Laundromat
11	Gordon Inn Guest House		Buzz Stop	29	Egged Tours
14	No 1 Hostel	42	The Chicago	31	American Express
18	City Hotel	49	Brazilian Sandwich Bar &	33	Mona Tours
19	Tel Aviv Sheraton		Bakery	35	El Al Offices
23	Astor Hotel	52	Mongolian Bar & Grill	36	Orange (Tapuz) Walking
24	Dan Tel Aviv; Regatta Cafe	69	Derby Bar Restaurant		Routes start
30	Hotel Adiv	71	Chin Chin Restaurant;	41	US Embassy
34	Noah Hostel		Frishman Felafel;	43	Branch Post Office;
37	Top Hotel		Cameri Theatre;		Soweto Club
38	Aviv Hotel		Steimatzky Bookshop	46	Camelot Bar
39	Yamit Park Plaza	72	Basta La Pasta	48	First Town Hall
44	Hotel Imperial	73	Acapulco	54	Opera Tower
45	Hotel Metropolitan	74	Kassit Restaurant	60	Bailik House
47	Seaside Hostel			61	Habima Theatre
50	Hotel Nes Ziona	OTHER		62	Helena Rubenstein
51	Hotel Moss	1	181 HaYarkon St		Pavilion
53	Hotel Eilat;	3	Book Boutique	63	Lametayel Adventure Store
	Down South Pub	4	ISSTA Student Travel		& Bookshop
55	Ambassador	5	Ben-Gurion's House	64	In Bar Internet Café
56	Tayelet Hotel	10	British Council;	67	Branch Post Office
57	Miami Hotel		Shakespeare Cafe	70	Steimatzky Bookshop
58	Hotel Bell	12	Project 67	75	Change Spot
59	Hayarkon 48 Hostel	13	Kibbutz Hotels		(Currency Exchange,
65	Kikar Dizengoff Apartments;		Reservation Office		Phones & Fax)
	24 Hour Laundromat	15	Supersol Supermarket	76	Gan Ha'Ir
66	Center Hotel	16	Meira's Kibbutz &		Shopping Centre
68	Dizengoff Square Hostel;		Moshav Office	77	City Hall
	Subway	20	French Embassy	78	Rabin Memorial

strong on late 19th and early 20th century works. Alongside the ubiquitous Monets, Pisarros and sundry other impressionists, some Jewish post-Impres sionists such as Chagall and Soutine are well represented and there are pleasant surprises in little seen works by Dali, Klimt and Magritte.

The museum often screens films and holds special exhibitions – check the *Jerusalem Post* on Friday or ask at the tourist information office for the Tel Aviv-Jaffa tourist booklet which usually lists current exhibitions. The museum is open Sunday, Monday, Wednesday and Thursday from 10 am to 10 pm, Friday and Saturday from 10 am to 2 pm. Admission is 27NIS (students 20NIS), which includes entrance to the Helena Rubenstein Pavilion.

To get to the museum take bus No 7a, 9, 18, 28 or 70 from HaMelekh George St, Dizengoff St or Rothschild Ave. Or it's not far to walk from Dizengoff Square.

The impressive building with the fountain in front, just west of the museum, is the new Centre of Arts (Mishkan Ha'Omanuyut), home to the Israeli Opera company.

Helena Rubenstein Pavilion Named for the cosmetics woman, the Helena Rubenstein Pavilion of Contemporary Art (☎ 528 7196) at 6 Tarsat Blvd is part of the Tel Aviv Museum of Art and is used for temporary exhibits by guest artists, both Israeli and foreign. Admission is sometimes free depending on the exhibit, but a Tel Aviv Museum of Art ticket is valid for here, too.

It is open Sunday to Thursday from 10 am to 4 pm (until 10 pm on Tuesday), Saturday from 10 am to 2 pm, closed Friday.

The Pavilion is part of the large Heychal Ha'Tarbut (Halls of Culture) complex which includes the Mann Auditorium and Habima Theatre.

Jabotinsky Institute This is an historical research organisation with a museum on the 1st floor presenting the history and activities of the national resistance movement, founded and led by Ze'ev Jabotinsky. The several departments show his political, literary and journalistic activities, and also document the creation of the Jewish Legion in WWI (a paramilitary force set up to aid illegal immigration during the time of the British Mandate).

The museum (☎ 528 7320) is at 38 HaMelekh George St – no signs in English. It's open Sunday to Thursday from 8 am to 4 pm, and is closed Friday and Saturday. Admission is free.

Ben-Gurion's House At 17 Ben-Gurion Ave close to Namir Square is the former house (☎ 522 1010) of Israel's first prime minister, David Ben-Gurion. Maintained more or less as it was left at the time of his death, the small rooms are simply furnished and contain part of the revered politician's library of some 20,000 books as well as his correspondence with various world leaders. The house is open Sunday to Thursday from 8 am to 3 pm (Monday until 5 pm), Friday from 8 am to 1 pm; it's closed Saturday. Admission is free.

Allenby St & the Yemenite Quarter

The bright lights and fancy shops that formerly lined Allenby St, once making it Tel Aviv's main fashionable artery, have moved elsewhere. Today the trade is in bargain basement clothing, secondhand books and the tawdry sex of ten shekel peep shows and 'Amsterdam-style' video stores. Reminders of the street's more stately past are few, though the old stock exchange building still

functions and, on the corner of Ahad Ha'am and Allenby Sts, the **Great Synagogue**, built in 1926, stands as one of the city's rare monuments to spirituality.

Allenby St may be past its prime, but there are still plenty of places worth exploring, from the youthful hipness of **Sheinkin St** to the stately elegance of Rothschild Ave and Bialik St, and the bustle and burlesque of Carmel Market. Several of these areas come together at **Magen David Circle**, so named because here six streets intersect in a manner not unlike the Israeli six-pointed Star of David (*magen* means 'star of').

Bialik St A short street lined with attractive buildings, Bialik St is a repository of Tel Avivian history. At No 14 is **Reuven Rubin House** (☎ 525 5961), the former residence of the artist of the same name. On display is a selection of his work and part of the artist's private collection of photographs and furnishings. It's open Sunday, Monday and Wednesday from 10 am to 1 pm, Tuesday from 10 am to 1 pm and 4 to 8 pm, Saturday from 11 am to 2 pm, and closed Friday.

A few doors along at No 22 is **Bialik House** (☎ 525 4530), former home of Chaim Nachman Bialik, Israel's national poet. It contains memorabilia connected with his life and work, though most of the labelling is in Hebrew only. It's open Sunday to Thursday from 9 am to 5 pm, Saturday from 10 am to 2 pm, closed Friday; admission is free.

The Yemenite Quarter A maze of narrow dusty streets lined with crumbling buildings, the Yemenite Quarter (Kerem Hateimanim) is imbued with an oriental flavour at odds with the clean-cut modernism of the rest of the city. It's one of the few places in the city that reminds the visitor of Tel Aviv's Middle Eastern location. For a long time the quarter suffered badly from neglect – although it could be argued that this, in fact, has added greatly to its charm – but in recent years speculators have begun to reinvest and the place is booming.

The biggest success story has been that of **Nahalat Binyamin St**. Formerly a run-down province of the textile and haberdashery trade, private investment has seen it rejuvenated as a busy pedestrianised precinct full of fashionable cafes and arty shops. On Tuesday afternoon and Friday the street is also host to a craft market and filled with buskers, mime artists and dancers. Divert your eyes upwards, too, where there are the vestiges of some very elegant architecture. Take note in particular of No 16 (Rosenberg House), No 8 (Degel House), and No 13 (Levy House), with its beautiful tiled panels depicting caravans of camels.

Carmel Market Tel Aviv's crowded and lively market meets Allenby St at Magen David Circle, from where it incises itself through the Yemenite Quarter. The main market street is HaCarmel St, and you need to push your way past the first few metres of clothing and footwear to reach the more aromatic and enticing stalls of fruits and vegetables, hot breads and spices. When in form, the stallholders have an amusing sales patter, singing songs to promote their goods and often joining in with one another.

Each of the narrow sidestreets specialises in produce ranging from poultry or fish to dried fruit and nuts or spices, sold from sacks. The best prices are to be had as the market closes, especially around 3 or 4 pm on Friday when everyone wants to sell up before the Shabbat.

Shalom Tower One block west of Nahalat Binyamin St is the imposing bulk of Tel Aviv's major landmark, the Shalom Tower (☎ 517 7304). Built on the site of the city's very first building, the Gymnasia Herzlia (1909), the tower was at the time Israel's tallest building (a status it has since ceded to the twin Azrieli Towers on the eastern side of the city centre).

The lower floors of the tower are a shopping mall while higher up are the offices of the Ministry of the Interior (this is where you go to renew your visa). For desperate tourists there is a terrible **Wax Museum** (admission 13NIS, students 11NIS) which attempts to present events and characters

from the history of Israel but fails dismally – the only convincing piece in the whole place is Moshe Dayan's eye patch.

More worthwhile is a visit to the top (34th) floor **observation deck** for great views of the city and beyond. Admission is 10NIS or you can content yourself with a free ride up to the 29th floor and the partial views from the windows at the end of the corridor.

The tower is open Sunday to Thursday from 10 am to 6.30 pm, Friday from 10 am to 2 pm, and Saturday 11 am to 4 pm.

Rothschild Ave This pleasant leafy boulevard was named after the Jewish family of financiers. At one time Rothschild Ave was *the* address to have. It's no longer so exalted but former glories are invoked at No 16, **Independence Hall** (☎ 517 3942), where on 14 May 1948, Ben-Gurion declared the establishment of the State of Israel. Previous to that the building had been the home of Meir Dizengoff, one of the founders of Tel Aviv. It's now open to the public Sunday to Thursday from 9 am to 2 pm and Friday 9 am to 1 pm, closed Saturday. Admission is 12NIS (adults) and 7NIS (students).

West of the junction with Allenby St, at 23 Rothschild Ave, the **Haganah Museum** (☎ 560 8642) chronicles the formation and activities of the Haganah, the military organisation that was the forerunner of today's Israeli Defence Force. The museum is open Sunday to Thursday from 9 am to 4 pm, closed Friday and Saturday. Admission is 10NIS or 7NIS with a student card.

Neve Tzedek One of the first quarters to be built in the new city in 1887, this area south-west of the Shalom Tower is a delightful maze of narrow streets squeezed between high, sun-bleached walls. It fell into decay before being adopted by the textile industry, which filled its northernmost streets with workshops and fashion showrooms with the result that in the past few years it has become a trendy enclave of artistic types. The quarter is well worth a casual wander; look out for **36 Rokach St**, with its gilded copper dome and courtyard

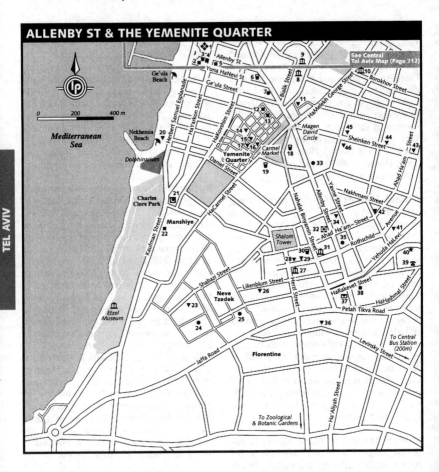

ALLENBY ST & THE YEMENITE QUARTER

full of bizarre sculptures, and for **2 Lilien-blum St**, home of the first cinema in Israel. The district is also home to the **Suzanne Dellal Centre** (☎ 510 5656), a theatre, music and dance complex with sublimely tranquil gardens that are a great place to linger over a coffee (see Theatre, Music & Dance later in this chapter).

Manshiye Located at the southern, sea-front end of Carmel Market, Manshiye was at one time an Arab district but it was largely destroyed during the 1948 War and its inhabitants fled. The sole evidence of the neighbourhood's Arab heritage is the **Hassan Beq Mosque**, currently being reno-vated under the auspices of the Ministry of Religious Affairs. The project has received criticism from some sections of the Jewish community because the mosque's minaret was used by Arab snipers during the war.

That particular episode is recorded in the **Etzel Museum** (☎ 517 2044), an attractive smoked-glass structure built within the re-

ALLENBY ST & THE YEMENITE QUARTER

PLACES TO STAY			
2	Ambassador	26	Chaim's
3	Tayelet Hotel	28	Tel Aviv Brewhouse
4	Miami Hotel	29	Kashmir
5	Hotel Bell	34	Spaghettim
12	Home Hostel	36	Poondak Chem;
13	Hotel HaGalil		bakery
22	Dan Panorama	41	Ying Yang
38	Central Hostel	43	Slice Pizza
		44	Orne Ve'Ela
		45	KaCafe Kazze
PLACES TO EAT		46	Souss Etz
11	Bezalel (Felafel) Market		
14	Shaul's Inn	OTHER	
15	Big Mama	1	Opera Tower
16	Maganda	6	Joey's Bar
17	Restaurant Zion	7	White Raven Bookshop
20	Banana Beach	8	Reuven Rubin House
23	Suzana	9	Bialik House

10	Jabotinsky Institute
18	The Balcony
19	Logos/He-She
21	Hassan Beq Mosque
24	Suzanne Dellal Centre
25	36 Rokach St
27	Independence Hall
30	Swing
31	Haganah Museum
32	Great Synagogue
33	Steimatzky Bookshop
35	Steimatzky Bookshop
37	Main Post Office
39	International Telephone Office; Poste Restante
40	Police Station; Lost & Found
42	Cafe Noir

TEL AVIV

mains of an old Arab house on South Herbert Samuel Esplanade. The museum presents a mainly photographic history of the Jewish victory against the Arabs in Jaffa in April 1948. It's open Sunday to Thursday from 8.30 am to 4 pm, and closed Friday and Saturday; admission is 8NIS (students 4NIS).

North Central

North of Central Tel Aviv private residences begin to heavily outnumber the commercial properties and the streets become more sedate. They're also very elegant, with an appealing mix of clean-cut Bauhaus-inspired architecture and lanky curving palm trees. Anyone who appreciates fine architecture must take a look at **219 Dizengoff St**, on the corner of Jabotinsky St.

The upper ends of HaYarkon, Ben Yehuda and Dizengoff Sts knot together in an area known as **Little Tel Aviv**, a distinctly upmarket gathering of shops, cafes and restaurants. Some years ago this was the trendiest area of Tel Aviv and, though the smart set has moved on, it's still quite lively most evenings. On Shabbat and Jewish festivals, especially Purim, this junction of streets is closed to traffic and used as a children's playground and extra seating area for the local cafes.

Some of the activity from Little Tel Aviv has migrated south a little to **Basel St**, where a small pedestrianised area is saturated with cafes in which the important thing is to be seen, not served.

Port Area Originally opened in 1936 to give newly established Tel Aviv sea-trafficking independence of Jaffa, the port fairly soon went into decline with the construction of a better, deeper harbour at Ashdod. The municipality has plans to redevelop the port area, but to date it is a gloomy shadow of the trendy upmarket dash of its sister port down in Jaffa. Other than a few scattered restaurants the area is still blighted by uninspiring abandoned warehouses and is favoured mainly by fishermen and wave watchers.

Ramat Aviv Sitting just north of the Yarkon River, the wealthy suburb of Ramat Aviv is home to the nation's elite (both the president and prime minister have apartments here) as well as, in the form of Tel Aviv University, the nation's future elite. The university campus features some striking modern architecture and its departments cover the widest spectrum of all the country's universities. However, for the visitor, there is a couple of good museums here, one of which, the Diaspora Museum, should not be missed.

A less obvious attraction is **HaYarkon Park**, a green wooded expanse beside the

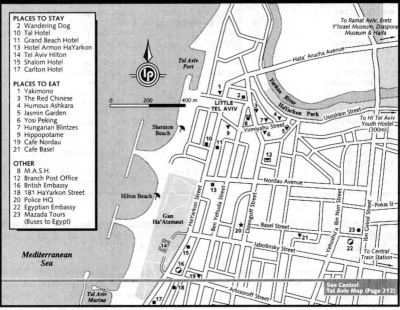

NORTH CENTRAL TEL AVIV

PLACES TO STAY
2   Wandering Dog
10 Tal Hotel
11 Grand Beach Hotel
13 Hotel Armon HaYarkon
14 Tel Aviv Hilton
15 Shalom Hotel
17 Carlton Hotel

PLACES TO EAT
1   Yakimono
3   The Red Chinese
4   Humous Ashkara
5   Jasmin Garden
6   Yosi Peking
7   Hungarian Blintzes
9   Hippopotame
19 Cafe Nordau
21 Cafe Basel

OTHER
8   M.A.S.H.
12 Branch Post Office
16 British Embassy
18 181 HaYarkon Street
20 Police HQ
22 Egyptian Embassy
23 Mazada Tours
    (Buses to Egypt)

river which offers some respite to the traffic and noise. The river is a little dirty and the surroundings are marred by some prominent electricity pylons but it doesn't stop students from the nearby campus flocking down here to take advantage of the rowing boats for hire.

Diaspora Museum The museum, also known as Beit Hatefutsoth (☎ 646 2020, fax 646 2134, email bhwebmaster@bh.org.il), doesn't actually display any artefacts from the past. Rather, this is a good collection of models, dioramas, films and presentations chronicling the diversity of Jewish life and culture in exile. The main role of the Beth Hatefutsoth is to relate the unique story of the continuity of the Jewish people through exhibition, education and cultural endeavours. Special attractions in the museum include the Feher Jewish Music Centre, the

Douglas E Goldman Jewish Genealogy Centre (where visitors can register their family tree to be preserved for future generations) and a Visual Documentation Centre, which is the largest photo-documentation centre of Jewish life in the world. The beautifully constructed and innovative methods of telling this experience are completely absorbing, and this place can take the best part of a day to get around. Visit their Web site (www.bh.org.il) for a preview.

The museum is open Sunday, Monday, Tuesday and Thursday from 10 am to 4 pm, Wednesday from 10 am to 6 pm, and Friday from 9 am to 1 pm, closed Saturday. Admission is 24NIS (students 18NIS). To get there take bus No 25 from HaMelekh George St, or Reines St near the corner of Frishman St, or take No 27 from the central bus station. Get off at the university, either Matatia Gate No 2 or Frenkel Gate No 7.

Eretz Y'Israel Museum The Eretz Y'Israel (Land of Israel) Museum actually consists of 11 linked, small museums built around an archaeological site, Tel Qasile. The museum complex (☎ 641 5244) is made up of, among others, a planetarium, a glass museum, a folklore pavilion, a reconstruction of a medieval bazaar, a ceramics museum and a couple of halls with temporary exhibitions. Although not all of it is exactly enthralling, it's all very well done and can easily occupy a few hours of your time. To get there take bus No 24, 27 or 86.

The museum is at 2 Chaim Levanon St and is open Sunday to Thursday from 9 am to 2 pm (Wednesday until 6 pm) and Saturday from 10 am to 2 pm. Admission is 25NIS, or 20NIS; the show at the planetarium at 3 pm on Wednesday is an extra 15NIS.

Art Galleries

The greatest concentration of galleries is along Gordon St, with a few spilling out down Ben Yehuda St. Opening hours vary greatly with many galleries only viewing for short periods each day; 10 am to 1 pm and 5 to 8 pm seem to be among the favoured opening times. See also the Jaffa section, later in this chapter.

Beaches

Possibly the major attraction in Tel Aviv is the lengthy stretch of fine white sand which fringes the alluringly blue Mediterranean Sea. When the sun is out (and it usually is) the beaches are an Israeli 'Copacabana' (Koshercabana?) a strutting ground for the local poseurs and a vast sandy court for pairs playing *matkot* (Israeli beach tennis), the incessant thok-thok-thok of which will haunt your every bathing hour.

If it's peace that you require then visit in the mornings when the only company will be groups of hardy old-timers, congregated to dip and exercise. On summer nights the beaches remain crowded as they serve as impromptu sites for concerts and discos.

Bear in mind that drownings are a tragically regular occurrence – a combination of the strong undertow and reckless swimmers

overestimating their capabilities. It's wise to take heed of the warning flags posted along the beaches: a black flag means that swimming is forbidden; red means that swimming is dangerous and you certainly shouldn't swim by yourself; white means that the area is safe.

Theft is a widespread problem so try not to take any valuables with you when you go to the beach.

The most crowded beaches are situated between the Hilton to the north and Opera Square to the south where Allenby St starts. If you want more privacy there's a **religious beach** north of the Hilton up towards the old port. On Sunday, Tuesday and Thursday only women are permitted to use the area and it is a good place for any woman, Jewish or not, to enjoy a swim or to sunbathe without the constant attention of an amorous Israeli male.

There's a beach hotline (☎ 604 2257) for further information.

Organised Tours

Egged Tours (☎ 527 1212, fax 527 1229) at 59 Ben Yehuda St do a half-day tour of Tel Aviv and Jaffa ending up at the Diaspora Museum. It goes every Sunday and Thursday from 10 am to 2 pm and costs US$26 per person.

Late Night Tel Aviv (☎ 525 6484, fax 528 7127 or 052-45 3753), specialises in after-hours tours of the 'happening' places in town. It is operated by Shira Skolnik and Maia Hoffman, originally from the USA, who moved here some years ago and have been busy ever since wining, dining and socialising. The resulting knowledge gained is put to use in their two hour tours which are 150NIS per person which includes a drink. Tours can also be custom-made for groups of a minimum of five people. Alternatively you can buy a 'tour kit' for US$13, which is basically a self-paced tour using a 42 page booklet.

Target Tours (☎ 517 5149) at 9 Ahad Ha'am St, has a good reputation in the gay community for helping with the travel needs of gays and lesbians.

TEL AVIV

Walking Tours Though not officially 'organised' in the normal sense, Tel Aviv's so-called Orange (Tapuz) Route walking trails are designed to take city walkers through the main sites in a leisurely two to four hours of walking. There are three walking routes in all which take in most of the city south of the Yarkon River and also Jaffa. There is also a driving route which takes in sights north of the Yarkon River. The walking trails are marked by orange-and-green signs, and start at 5 Shalom Aleikham St (between Ha-Yarkon and Ben Yehuda Sts). Orange Route maps can be obtained from the tourist information office (☎ 639 5660) in the central bus station.

Route 1 Takes in the First Town Hall, Bialik House, Reuven Rubin House, Shalom Tower, Independence Hall, the Haganah Museum, the Neve Tsedek neighbourhood and the Suzanne Dellal Centre and can be conveniently finished at the Dan Panorama hotel on the south promenade. Allow about 3½ hours to complete this tour.

Route 2 This tour first heads north from Shalom Aleikham St, then east, then south, then north-east, finally doubling back west to finish at the City Hall. Sights en route include the Habimah Theatre, the Tel Aviv Performing Arts Centre, the Mann Auditorium, the Tel Aviv Museum of Art, the Holocaust Monument and the Yitzhak Rabin Memorial on Rabin Square. Allow 2½ hours for this tour.

Route 3 While nominally commencing at Shalom Aleikham St, this walk can also be picked up in Jaffa itself since it mainly covers the relatively small area of the Jaffa Old Town. Other than the Old Town itself the only other advertised sight en route is the Etzel Museum in Charles Clore Park on the South Tel Aviv promenade.

Places to Stay

Virtually all of Tel Aviv's hostels and hotels are on or around Ben Yehuda and HaYarkon Sts, all just minutes from the beaches, popu-

lar eating and shopping places and night-spots. The flip side is that a lot of these places, especially in the lower price bracket, tend to be quite noisy, especially if you are in a room facing the street. If serenity is your bag then consider staying in the more sedate North Central area or in Jaffa (see later in this chapter).

Two buses leaving from the central bus station will get you to the general hostel/hotel area: No 4 goes along Allenby and Ben Yehuda Sts, and No 5 along Dizengoff St.

Places to Stay – Budget

Generally speaking, the majority of budget travellers in Tel Aviv fall into one of two categories. Most tend to stay for as short a time as possible, either as a stopover en route to or from a kibbutz or moshav or simply to have a quick look around before moving on to devote their time to other places. A significant number, though, become long-term 'residents', often finding a job to keep their heads above water. Some hostels are particularly popular with the latter; these tend to be the more laid-back places, where the housekeeping is of less importance, the bar is busy, and the noise level is somewhat high.

Backpacker hostels for the short-term visitors have taken a beating in recent years due to a downturn in tourism and quite a few have closed, so the pickings are not all that appetising and more often than not you will end up sharing your space with longer-term guests.

The charge per night for a dorm bed in a Tel Aviv hostel is generally 25 to 40NIS – exceptions are noted below. For slightly less, many places will also let you sleep on the roof. No curfew unless noted.

Central Tel Aviv One of the better options in this category, *Dizengoff Square Hostel* (☎ 522 5184, fax 522 5181, email info@dizengoffhostel.co.il, 11 Dizengoff Square) has a great location on bustling Dizengoff Square, close to plenty of cheap eating places. Favoured by long-termers, the place has a very friendly atmosphere. Dorms have six or 11 beds with showers and toilets shared between two or three rooms. There's a kitchen and a roof-terrace bar overlooking the square but noise from the busy nightlife may be a problem here. Dorms cost 42NIS/ 36NIS with/without air-con. The hostel also has private rooms at 90NIS per night. The entrance is right across from the Rav-Chen Cinema and the reception is open 24 hours.

A very popular traveller hostel is the excellent *No 1 Hostel* (☎ *523 7807, email sleeping@inter.net.il, 84 Ben Yehuda St)* on the 4th floor and about 100m south of the intersection with Gordon St. Well organised, the No 1 has an international telephone line and reception can cash travellers cheques and help with cheap flights. There's a kitchen and a lovely conservatory-like common room overlooking the city rooftops. The single-sex dorms have their own bathrooms and there are reductions for longer stays. Dorm beds are 35NIS (10% discount on production of a valid ISIC student card) and you can sleep on the roof for 29NIS. There are also two private rooms (140NIS). Reception is open 24 hours.

Sharing the same management, *Gordon Hostel* (☎ *522 9870, 2 Gordon St)*, on the seafront, offers dorm beds at 32NIS. There's a kitchen, a TV area, a rooftop bar and a 24 hour cafe-bar on the ground floor; the hostel is closed between 11 am and 2 pm. Facilities here are not as flash as the No 1 hostel and because it is slightly cheaper, it attracts a younger crowd.

Also in the centre is *Noah Hostel* (☎ *620 0044, 34 Ben Yehuda St)*. It's a reasonable sort of place, though a bit rough around the edges, and there is now a rather heavy longtermer atmosphere. Security is fairly good with controlled access to the dorms; however, at least one reader has complained of having money stolen from the hostel's safe, so be on the alert. The six to eight-bed dorms are pretty much par for the course at 30NIS. There are a few private rooms available ranging in price from 80 to 140NIS. There's also a pool table and a kitchen for guests' use.

Better still, at least by guestbook and travellers' accounts, is *Hayarkon 48 Hostel* (☎ *516 8989, fax 510 3113, 48 HaYarkon St)*. This converted former school opened in January 1999 and offers dormitory accommodation at 37NIS per person and fully self-contained private rooms for 189NIS. Guests rave on about the good showers, though you do also get a free breakfast plus a TV and pool room thrown in for good measure.

On Trumpeldor St, *Seaside Hostel* (☎ *620 0513, fax 525 6965)* has dorms available with/without air-con for 35NIS/ 30NIS. Each eight-bed room has its own shower and toilet. There is a kitchen of sorts and a cramped common room with bar, TV and fridge for guests' use. Private rooms go for between 100NIS and 120NIS. Be alerted, though, this hostel is populated with mainly roughneck long-termers and is not really suitable for bona fide travellers. *Caveat emptor* – may the buyer beware.

While some of the smaller hotels can be within a budget traveller's price range they don't tend to represent particularly good value. *Hotel Nes Ziona* (☎ *510 6084)* at 10 Nes Ziona St, one block back from the seafront, has single/double rooms for US$45/55, but don't expect much sleep there – we've had letters warning of loud drunken parties in the corridors and a management indifferent to guests' complaints.

Around the corner at 58 HaYarkon St, *Hotel Eilat* (☎/*fax 510 2453)* has a few air-con singles/doubles at US$45/60 but the catch is the hotel is directly above a 24 hour bar with a very popular jukebox, and many rooms don't have windows.

Allenby St & the Yemenite Quarter

Overall the choices here are poor as many closures have taken place here in recent times. One exception is the rustic *Home Hostel* (☎ *517 6736, 20 Alsheikh St)* which has reasonable dorms for 35NIS and a small private room for twice that price. There are cooking facilities, a small courtyard, cheap beer plus a free dinner on Friday evening and a free breakfast on Saturday morning.

Bus 22 from the airport will drop you on Allenby St nearby.

Many long-termers are resident at the ramshackle *Central Hostel* (☎ 560 6705, 4 HaRakevet St) which offers the cheapest beds in town (22NIS with every fourth night free). While the crowd here are friendly, the grubby and overcrowded mixed-sex dorms might not be to everyone's liking. Another drawback is that the Central is, well, actually not very central at all: it's east of the southern end of Allenby St, and Central Tel Aviv is a bus ride away.

At *Hotel HaGalil* (☎ 517 5036, 510 1782, 23 Beit Josef Ave), it's years since anybody dusted let alone renovated but that all adds to the antiquated charm of the place. Singles/doubles cost US$25/35; toilets and showers are shared.

North Central This area no longer offers much in the way of cheap pickings. About the only viable option is *Wandering Dog* (☎ 546 6333, 3 Yordei Hasira St) close to the port area. It opened in 1996 and attracts a mixed bag of longer-term residents and travellers. There is a pretty convivial rooftop lounge with cable TV, billiards, a sauna and great seaside views. Dorm beds cost 28NIS.

Way out of the centre, *HI Tel Aviv Youth Hostel* (☎ 544 1748, fax 544 1030, 36 B'nei Dan St), just west of HaYarkon Park, is mainly used by Israelis. It has no cooking facilities, although you can get standard HI food. Dorm beds in air-con rooms cost US$15 for members while singles/doubles are US$40/50 with breakfast (prices for nonmembers are a US$1.50 higher). Take bus No 5, 24 or 25 from the central bus station and get off on Yehuda HaMaccabi St, then walk north two blocks.

Places to Stay – Mid-Range

Unless otherwise stated, prices include breakfast and private bathrooms. Rates can vary dramatically according to the season; the prices given below are generally the rates you could expect to encounter in July and August.

Central Tel Aviv *The Gordon Inn Guest House* (☎ 523 8239, fax 523 7419, email sleeping@inter.net.il, 17 Gordon St) is a hybrid hostel-hotel, beautifully kept and good value with singles from US$37 to US$41 and doubles from US$47 to US$52.

The rest of the hotels at the lower end of the mid-range price are mostly well past their prime, like *Aviv Hotel* (☎ 510 2784, fax 510 2785, 88 HaYarkon St) with singles priced at US$40 and doubles from US$50, though this place has had good reports from readers. *Hotel Imperial* (☎ 517 7002, fax 517 8314, 66 HaYarkon St), flying the Israeli flag, has singles/doubles at US$58/84, but it's in need of some serious renovation. The shabby but pleasant *Moss Hotel* (☎/fax 517 1655, 6 Nes Ziona St) has singles/doubles at US$80/90.

Down where Allenby St meets the seafront there's a string of seedy hotels of the kind that characters in a *film noir* might hole up in. The least sleazy is *Hotel Bell* (☎ 517 7011, fax 517 4352, 12 Allenby St), which has singles from US$63 to US$67 and doubles from US$79 to US$91; a couple of doors along is *Miami Hotel* (☎ 510 3868) which has singles/doubles at US$50/60 and then *Tayelet Hotel* (☎ 510 5823) which has singles/doubles from US$35/45. We recommend you dig a little deeper into your pocket and go for *Ambassador* (☎ 517 7301, fax 517 6308, email ambasdor@netvision.net.il, 56 Herbert Samuel St), in the same block as the Tayelet and Miami but in a different class. It's well maintained and the rooms face on to the sea; singles are from US$75 to US$98 and doubles are from US$98 to US$115.

Also recommended is *Hotel Adiv* (☎ 522 9141, fax 522 9144, email iladiv01@ibm.net, 5 Mendele St) between Ben Yehuda and HaYarkon Sts. It has an excellent self-service restaurant which is worth visiting for breakfast even if you're not staying here. Singles range from US$64 to US$71 and doubles from US$89 to US$98.

The hotels belonging to the Atlas chain are all modern, three-star-style establishments with high standards of service. Central Tel

Aviv Atlas hotels can all be emailed on atlashot@netvision.net.il. *City Hotel (☎ 524 6253, fax 524 6250, 9 Mapu St)*, between Ben Yehuda and HaYarkon Sts; *Top Hotel (☎ 517 0941, fax 517 1322, 35 Ben Yehuda St)*; and *Center Hotel (☎ 629 6181, fax 629 6751, 2 Zamenhoff St)*, just off Dizengoff Square. In all three, single rooms cost somewhere between US$76 and US$111, and doubles from US$91 and US$145.

A couple of other good but more expensive mid-range options are *Astor Hotel (☎ 522 3141, 105 HaYarkon St)*, with singles from US$73 to US$79 and doubles from US$88 to US$101, and the newly renovated *Hotel Metropolitan (☎ 519 2727, fax 517 2626, email reserve@metrotlv.co.il, 11-15 Trumpeldor St)*, which has a terrace pool. Singles are US$102 to US$128, doubles US$122 to US$164.

Furnished Apartments Centrally located and offering tastefully furnished air-con apartments are *Kikar Dizengoff Apartments (☎ 620 0107, fax 620 0108, email neemanam@netvision.net.il, 4 Kikar Dizengoff)*. These apartments are ideal for both long and short-term stays and can't be beaten for price and quality. All rooms offer digital phones, cable TV, cooking facilities and are close to restaurants and shops. Singles start at $US50 and doubles range from US$64 to US$84. Check www.inisrael.com/kda for full details and current rates.

North Central Way up at the lonely end of town are two mid-range hotels facing each other. *Hotel Armon HaYarkon (☎ 605 5271, fax 605 8485, 268 HaYarkon St)* is small but smart-looking offering singles/doubles from US$69/81, while *Tal Hotel (☎ 544 2281, fax 546 8697, email atlashot @netvision.net.il, 287 HaYarkon St)*, is a member of the quality Atlas chain with singles at US$103, doubles at US$125.

Located above the Stagecoach Restaurant, *Shalom Hotel (☎ 524 3277, fax 523 5895, 216 HaYarkon St)* has a little more life about it. Singles/doubles cost from US$65 to US$85.

Places to Stay – Top End
Almost all of these places are on HaYarkon St with the beach just a quick shuffle away. Not so *Grand Beach Hotel (☎ 543 3333, fax 546 6589, 250 HaYarkon St)* which is set some way back from the sand on the wrong side of a busy road. It's way north of the Central Tel Aviv activity and it could prove quite a tiresome trudge home every evening. Singles are from US$110 to US$139 and doubles from US$134 to US$199.

Tel Aviv Hilton (☎ 520 2222, fax 522 4111, Gan Ha'Atzmaut) is also in the North Central area but it compensates by having the best beach access of any hotel and also benefits from its parkland setting. Then again, it is one of Tel Aviv's most expensive hotels with singles starting at US$270 and doubles at US$285.

The density of hotels starts to increase around Namir Square, which is unfortunate as this concrete complex is the most unpleasant public zone in all of Tel Aviv. To the north of the square is the *Carlton Hotel (☎ 520 1818, fax 527 1043, email request@ carlton.co.il, 10 Eliezer Peri St)* where singles cost from US$170 to US$249 and doubles from US$200 to US$314. South of the square on HaYarkon St are three virtually indistinguishable establishments: the *Radisson-Moriah Plaza (☎ 521 6666, fax 527 1065, email radisson-moriah-il@ibm.net, 155 HaYarkon St)* with singles from US$194 to US$230 and doubles from US$230 to US$303; the *Crown Plaza (☎ 520 1111, fax 520 1122, 145 HaYarkon St)* which has singles from US$298 to US$358, doubles from US$318 to US$378 (breakfast not included); and the *Renaissance (☎ 521 5555, fax 521 5588, reservation@ramada.co.il, 121 HaYarkon St)* with singles from US$160 to US$205, and doubles from US$170 to US$215 (breakfast not included). All three are right on the beach and relatively convenient for the Central Tel Aviv shopping areas.

With *Tel Aviv Sheraton (☎ 521 1111, fax 523 3322, shtelviv@netvision.net.il, 115 HaYarkon St)*, we move into the prime hotel location: good for the beaches, right in among the restaurants, shops and cafes, and close to the important bus routes. The Sheraton also enjoys a reputation as one of the best hotels in town – singles cost from US$267 to US$345, doubles from US$290 to US$368. A block south is **Dan Tel Aviv** (☎ 520 2525, fax 524 9755, email danhtls@danhotels .co.il, 99 HaYarkon St), the city's first luxury hotel, but since modernised and appended with an apartment wing; singles cost from US$163 to US$232 and doubles from US$313 to US$389.

In the same strip is the smaller **Yamit Park Plaza** (☎ 519 7111, fax 517 4719, 79 HaYarkon St) which has singles from US$147 to US$174, doubles from US$232 to US$277.

One more top-end establishment is **Dan Panorama** (☎ 519 0190, fax 517 1777, email danhtls@danhotels.co.il, 10 Kaufmann St) opposite Charles Clore Park. It is a decent enough hotel but its location on the coastal road to Jaffa makes it awkward to get to by bus (No 10) and just a bit too far from Central Tel Aviv to have to walk there on a regular basis. Singles cost from US$163 to US$232, doubles from US$186 to US$255.

Places to Eat

Fast or even medium-paced food is big business in Tel Aviv, with sandwich bars, *felafel* joints, pizza parlours and all the big-name hamburger retailers saturating the food scene. With the increasing exposure of Israeli travellers to Far East destinations, Asian street food is also slowly taking off and around Central Tel Aviv you will soon come across little hole-in-the-wall places offering stir-fried whatever you fancy. The only concession to Israeli tastes is that they often serve the stir-fried dish in baguettes! Look out for the flaming woks in the shop window and pop your head in to see what is on offer.

For fresh fruit, head for Carmel Market. For one-stop shopping there's a convenient Supersol supermarket at 79 Ben Yehuda St, between Gordon and Mapu Sts. It's open Sunday to Tuesday from 7 am to midnight,

Wednesday and Thursday for 24 hours, Friday from 7 am to 3 pm, closed Saturday.

Felafel, Shwarma, Humous & Fuul The heaviest concentrations of these Middle Eastern fast-food staples are on the southern stretches of Ben Yehuda and Dizengoff Sts and along Allenby St. On Frishman St, near the corner of Dizengoff St, is **Frishman Felafel** – a cheapie felafel joint with the usual range of felafel, *shwarma* and varied salads.

Felafel in Tel Aviv isn't always the best but one guaranteed good place is **Bezalel Market**, near Allenby St and the Yemenite Quarter. The 'felafel market', as it's also known, is no more than two stalls side by side, but each has a fantastic array of salads and for 11NIS you are free to stuff your own *pitta* bread with as much felafel and greenery as you can fit in.

While the title of 'Israel's best shwarma' is claimed by **Poondak Chem** in the Florentine district near Allenby St (see Restaurants – Budget) some of the places just north of Dizengoff Square are very good too.

Anyone who's visited Egypt and enjoyed the *fuul* there should visit **Chaim's** at 16 Lilienblum St, south-west of the Shalom Tower. This is a small hole-in-the-wall eatery that dishes out huge plates of the bean paste accompanied by *tahina*, humous and lemon, with salad, egg and pitta, all for 14NIS.

Israelis in north Tel Aviv head for **Humous Ashkara** (☎ 546 4547, 45 Yirmiyahu St) for what they consider the best humous and fuul in town. Their sign is in Hebrew only, so look out for the Coca-Cola sign and the tables on the street.

Cafes Tel Aviv's many cafes exist as centres of gossip and to provide ringside seating for the ongoing pavement carnival. Good or cheap food is not always a priority and the locals tend to fuel themselves on black coffee, croissants and cheesecake. **Espresso Mersand** – which incidentally also serves great cakes – on the corner of Ben Yehuda and Frishman Sts is typical of the city's cafes. However, the chain-smoking staff might offend the health-conscious. Come in the morning to observe its unique

CHRISTINE OSBORNE

ANTHONY PIDGEON

Tel Aviv (top) is a modern hub with a laid-back Mediterranean feel and the sophistication of a European city, while its historical port suburb of Jaffa (bottom) is a step back in time.

PAUL HELLANDER

CHRISTINE OSBORNE

CHRISTINE OSBORNE

The coastline of Tel Aviv is fringed by hotels and, in summer, the white beaches are swarming with sun-worshippers and water sports fans; there's even something for art lovers!

collection of regulars, comprising journalists, actors and elderly German Jews – known derisively as 'Yekkes' for their distinct pronunciation of 'J' as 'YE'.

Cafe Noir (*43 Ahad Ha'am*), four blocks south of Sheinkin St, is the current hot cafe and attracts a youngish clientele. Its interior decor of wood and tile is very conducive to romantic evenings.

Another cafe with a clientele of character is *Kassit Restaurant* (*117 Dizengoff St*) 100m north of Frishman St. This is a long-established bohemian hang-out whose past customers included Frank Sinatra and Harry Belafonte. These days, the equally long-established regulars are still a boisterous lot at times.

The fashionable hang-outs are to be found along Sheinkin St, which runs east off Allenby St. Try *Cafe Kazze* (*19 Sheinkin St*) a popular spot with a pleasant courtyard out the back, *Souss Etz* at No 20 or *Orne Ve'Ela* at No 33.

Cafe Nordau (*145 Ben Yehuda St*) on the corner of Arlosoroff St has been a trendy spot for a long time, but its hipness has been diminished somewhat lately. Still, the placemats are printed on recycled paper, the cafe serves as a collection point for used batteries, and dogs have their own menu. The food here is very good, ranging from light lunches such as soups and baked potatoes (actually, not so light) to full-blown meals. The place gets packed in the evenings so come early if you want to eat. It's the gay and lesbian community's most popular eating place, and they have a bar/club upstairs, open nightly from 9 pm.

There is another cafe strip in North Tel Aviv along Basel Street. *Cafe Basel* is the pick of the bunch here. It's relaxed and laid-back and easier to get to if you are staying in the northern end of town.

If you take your tea without frills then *Shakespeare Cafe* is a pleasant unpretentious air-con place with large picture windows looking on to the beach. It's part of the British Council on HaYarkon St, just north of Gordon St. You can catch up on the latest British newspapers while you sip your tea.

Vegetarian The unique vegan tofu-cuisine at *Taste of Life* (*60 Ben Yehuda St*), is well worth a try. Dishes include vegetable shwarma, vegetarian hot dogs, tamali, tofulafel, barbecue twist burgers, cheeses, ice cream, yoghurts and shakes. It's open Sunday to Thursday from 9 am to 11 pm, Friday from 9 am to 3 pm, and Saturday from sunset to midnight.

The menu at *Cafe Nordau* (see earlier in this section) is also heavily weighted towards vegetarians. It's open from noon daily. Great vegetarian sandwiches can be constructed at *Subway Sandwich Bar* on the northern side of Dizengoff Square. A scrumptious 30cm baguette stuffed with whatever you fancy will cost you around 15NIS. Subway is on the ground floor of the Dizengoff Square Hostel.

Cafe Kazze also does a good line in vegetarian dishes.

Restaurants – Budget If there's one place to break your budget-dictated felafel diet then this is it. Of all Israel's towns and cities, Tel Aviv offers the widest variety of cuisine, and while dining here isn't particularly cheap, you can get away with eating better for less than almost anywhere else in the country.

Central Tel Aviv Besides felafel, easily the cheapest eating in Tel Aviv can be found at the few remaining travellers' bars. *Buzz Stop* and *International Bar* (see Bars later in this chapter) have constantly changing menus, typically featuring English breakfasts, stir-fries and fish, chips and peas. In all cases the cook is a resident traveller (and you don't find many cordon bleu chefs hiding under a backpack) but if the quality is variable, the quantity gives little cause for complaint.

Also very basic but reasonable is *Chicken 'n' Chips* (*73 Ben Yehuda St*), on the corner of Mapu St, where a half chicken with fries (or rice) and salad is 32NIS. On Frishman St, near the corner of Dizengoff St, is *Chin Chin* – a cheapie Chinese restaurant with vegetable dishes at 20NIS and chicken/

pork/beef dishes at around 25NIS. Open noon to midnight, they also do takeaway.

At the eastern end of the Sheinkin St cafe strip at the junction with Ahad Ha'am St is **Slice Pizza** another hole in the wall fast-food outlet, but the generous pizza slices are scrumptious and attract a loyal following. Whole pizzas come in three sizes and prices: small at 35NIS, large at 46NIS and extra large at 53NIS.

Brazilian Sandwich Bar & Bakery at the lower end of Ben Yehuda St is a simple no-nonsense sandwich joint that does pretty reasonable quick snacks and sandwiches for around 15NIS.

Across the road, the cafe/restaurant **Acapulco** does fantastic mushroom *blintzes* (30NIS), after which you won't need to eat for another week.

In the same clutch of eateries is **Basta la Pasta** no more than a hole in the wall where delicious pasta dishes (around 12NIS) are cooked in front of you. Look for the sign 'Best Italian Pasta to Go'.

Just off Dizengoff Square is a quietly popular oriental Israeli restaurant, **Derby Bar Restaurant** (☎ 523 6128, 94 Dizengoff St), with a rich variety of meat and vegetable dishes and some delicious flavoured rice. A hearty meal here with beer should not set you back more than 40NIS.

North Central For those needing a good feed the best value is probably offered by **M.A.S.H.**, (275 Dizengoff St) the travellers' bar. Their hamburgers are top notch and their Guinness is a treat.

Hungarian Blintzes (☎ 545 0674, 35 Yirmiyahu St), east of Dizengoff St, specialise in, well, blintzes – spicy ones and sweet ones in all flavours and permutations. Sweet ones are cheaper with prices ranging from 24 to 34NIS and spicy ones cost 28 to 34NIS.

Allenby St and the Yemenite Quarter These older areas contain a number of inexpensive eating places, mainly family run workers' restaurants serving simple oriental fare such as humous, spicy meat soups and

meat and offal grilled on the fire. Walk along Peduyim St (it's the fifth on the right as you walk down HaCarmel St from Allenby St) for a choice of three or four places. One street back, **Big Mama** (22 Rabbi Akiva St) serves excellent Arab-style crispy pizzas for around 22 to 30NIS each. It's open from 8 pm to the early hours of the morning. Israelis vote Big Mama's thin crust pizza as the best in the country.

In the wholesaling Florentine district, south of Jaffa Rd, **Poondak Chem** (41 Levinsky St) – look for the 'Best Shwarma in Israel' sign – is a small Turkish-owned workers' restaurant that, besides shwarma, does good humous, *ishkambe* (sheep's stomach soup) and grilled meats and offal. It's open Sunday to Friday, lunch time only. There are several other excellent quick-stop eating places around this area. Next door to Poondak Chem is a busy **bakery** with trays of various breads, including sweet breads. Still on Levinsky St but closer to Ha'Aliyah St, is a corner **takeaway** that does great chicken rolls and chicken stir-fries.

On Nekhemia Beach at the end of Nekhemia St is **Banana Beach**, a collection of beach chairs and recliners set out facing the Mediterranean – a great spot to chill out after a hard night clubbing. Try their recommended *shakshuka,* a stewed Iraqi/Yemenite dish made with tomatoes, onions, garlic and with a poached egg on top.

Restaurants – Mid-Range Israelis dine late and most places only start to fill up around 9 or 10 pm; in fact up in North Central some restaurants don't even open much before that time. Unless otherwise stated reservations are not generally needed although sometimes you may have to wait a little while for a table.

Central Tel Aviv Avoid the restaurants on HaYarkon St. They are wildly popular with Israelis but what matters here is the flavour of the month not the flavour of the food, which is generally fairly bland and way overpriced. An exception is **Regatta Cafe**, overlooking the seafront esplanade from the

1st floor of the King David Tower (the apartment tower abutting the southern end of the Dan Tel Aviv hotel). Excellent seafood and pasta dishes are priced in the 25 to 30NIS range.

Mongolian Bar & Grill (☎ 517 4188, 62 HaYarkon St) is a fixed-price (79NIS) all you can eat Mongolian BBQ extravaganza with filling starters and meat dishes that you design and flavour yourself such as Cornish Hen, Mulard Breast and Sole Fish. Self-help cook cards help you design your dish to the optimum texture and flavour.

Looking very like a refugee from South Beach Miami, the puce-painted *The Chicago (☎ 517 7505, 63 HaYarkon St)* on the corner of Trumpeldor St, has deep-pan pizzas for 55NIS (regular) or 70NIS (large), chilli (25NIS) and lasagne (32NIS). There's draught beer and American sports on TV.

For a true celebration of kitsch, head for *Punchline (☎ 561 0785, 6 Ha'Arba'a St)* across from the Cinematheque (see under Cinemas later in this chapter for directions). The serving staff are a bunch of would-be Liza Minellis and Tom Joneses who throughout the evening break off from taking orders to hit the stage and indulge in some karaoke-style camping to the likes of *Cabaret* and *Big Spender*. While the stage is off-limits to the diners/audience, you're free to get up and conga and wave your spare ribs in the air. There's a minimum cover charge of 50NIS per person which, of course, there's no trouble in reaching with main dishes beginning at around 35NIS and beer at 15NIS. The food is superb (though limited to variations of meat in barbecue sauce) and served in extremely generous portions. Punchline opens at 10 pm and closes about 2 am; reservations are essential.

North Central Little Tel Aviv is close to becoming Little China with a few oriental restaurants clustered around the top end of Dizengoff St. An extremely good but pricey restaurant is *The Red Chinese (☎ 544 8405, 326 Dizengoff St)*, specialising in Sichuan province cuisine and a few Thai dishes. A cheaper alternative is the bustling *Yosi Pe-*

king (☎ 544 3687) on the corner of Dizengoff and Yirmiyahu Sts. They serve *glatt kosher* (super kosher) Chinese dishes in the 30 to 40NIS range. At the corner of Yirmiyahu and Yeshayahu St is *Jasmin Garden (☎ 604 7984, 54 Yirmiyahu St)* another popular Chinese eatery, despite its jaded exterior facade. If you ask for a 'Hong Kong menu' inside you will get to eat real Chinese food as opposed to Israeli-Chinese fare. Prices are mid-range.

Not far away and further west along Yirmiyahu St is another popular place, *Hippopotame (☎ 546 8907, 12 Yirmiyahu St)*, a Parisian-style bistro with fish and steaks as staples. It's homey and welcoming and has a good wine selection. Prices are 55 to 65NIS for fish dishes and 60 to 80NIS for meat dishes.

Yakimono (☎ 546 5164, 5 Yordei Hasira), over towards the derelict-looking port, is a Japanese restaurant-cum-sushi bar. It's a pretty decent kind of place with typically sparse Japanese decor and it pulls in the patrons. Prices are, not surprisingly, on the high side.

Allenby St & the Yemenite Quarter There are several upmarket versions here of the workers' restaurants already mentioned, serving the familiar meat, offal and salad specialities in more expensive surroundings. The best is the atmospheric *Restaurant Zion (☎ 510 7414, 28 Peduyim St)*, which besides such lovelies as ox testicles (40NIS) and veal brains (36NIS) has a variety of stuffed vegetable dishes at 12NIS.

In contrast to the intimate Levantine air of the Zion, the nearby *Maganda (☎ 517 9990, 26 Rabbi Meir St)*, is loud and lively with tightly packed tables. It's a good lunch time place. Expect to spend 35 to 45NIS per person without drinks.

Shaul's Inn (☎ 517 7619) is nearby and, despite the name, is not somewhere to stay the night but another similar yet more expensive variant of the earlier two restaurants.

All these places are closed Friday evening and Saturday lunchtime, but are otherwise open daily from noon until midnight.

TEL AVIV

Pasta fans should head for **Spaghettim** (*☎ 566 4467, 18 Yavne St*), one block east of Allenby St. It's spaghetti only but there's a choice of more than 50 sauces. It's open from noon to 1 am.

A popular and long-standing Chinese restaurant worth checking out is **Ying Yang** (*☎ 560 6833, 64 Rothschild Ave*). It was the first restaurant of its kind opened in Israel and is owned by the same chef who owns the award-winning Golden Apple French restaurant.

Tel Aviv's poshest bar-cum-restaurant is **Tel Aviv Brewhouse** (*☎ 516 8555, 11 Rothschild Ave*) down in the financial district. Here, well-heeled yuppies sup four kinds of designer ales – try the Masters, a strong, dark ale with 6% alcohol – in a cosy copper and wood ambience. Their food is predictable pub fare with sausages and sauerkraut being the most popular dish. Beers cost between 9NIS and 23NIS depending on what you order.

A few doors east is **Kashmir** (*☎ 517 5171*) another bar/restaurant ensemble specialising in sushi and sashimi. A combination of the former will cost you 60NIS, while a combination of both will set you back 105NIS. There is a mind-boggling array of whiskies, cognacs and vodkas that you can wash it all down with. It is only open in the evenings.

About five minutes walk south-west of Kashmir you will find **Suzana** (*☎ 517 7580, 9 Shabazi St*) opposite the Suzanne Dellal Centre in quiet and trendy Neve Tzedek. Enjoy a relaxing lunch or light salad dinner on a tree-shaded outdoor patio, or in the warm Mediterranean-style interior. Prices are reasonable.

Entertainment

Crowds of locals and visitors are out people-watching after dark, especially around Dizengoff Square and the seafront. The bars, cafes and restaurants fill up, and people also go down to visit Old Jaffa. For more organised activities, pick up the Friday edition of the *Jerusalem Post* with its 'What's On' supplement.

Bars Israelis don't drink very much and prefer cafes to bars, but check out Sheinkin and Basel Sts, Ha'Arba'a St near the Cinematheque, and the Florentine area down at the southern end of Allenby St. To compensate for the lack of serious beer venues, various non-Israelis have over the past few years opened a number of places aimed mainly at travellers and other nonlocal traffic. Most of the travellers' bars are on or around HaYarkon St in the Central Tel Aviv area. They don't spend much on the decor but the beer is cheap and they tend to stay open just as long as there are people drinking. Most of the bars have an early evening happy hour when they shave a couple of shekels off the price of a beer – as if anyone needed encouraging.

At the bottom end of HaYarkon St is **The Down South Pub**, underneath the Hotel Eilat. It has a good jukebox that the clientele constantly abuse by programing back-to-back Bob Marley and The Doors. This place gets pretty rowdy at times, so move on if things start looking lively.

Still on HaYarkon St, just north of the junction with Frishman St, **International Bar** is another really popular bar with a terrace out the back overlooking the seafront, a couple of pool tables and satellite TV for football fans. The barbed wire ringed view over the tatty car park is a bit off-putting, but the sea is no more than 150m beyond that.

Possibly Tel Aviv's best travellers' bar is **Buzz Stop**, a great 24-hour, seven-day a week joint, popular with dawn watchers. It's next to Planet Hollywood on the esplanade, in the lower half of the Yamit Park Plaza complex and is right in the middle of all the activity. Tel Aviv's oldest travellers' bar is **M.A.S.H** (*275 Dizengoff St*) which stands for More Alcohol Served Here, up at in the North Central area. It's a haunt of the city's long-stay community.

Joey's Bar (*42 Allenby St*), is an American bar where beers cost 15NIS, more expensive than most other bars. There's another nontraveller bar, **The Balcony**, on Nahalat Binyamin St, just south of Magen

What to do on Shabbat in Tel Aviv & Jaffa

As most shops and businesses rush to close early for Shabbat, many people take the opportunity to hang out at their favourite cafe before the sun goes down, making Friday night a busy one.

On Friday afternoon, say between 1 and 3 pm, head for Nahalat Binyamin St. The streets are packed with artists' stalls and musicians, the cafes are full and there is usually dancing. Walk also through neighbouring Carmel Market to witness the scenes as the traders slash prices and even give away bags of fruit and vegetables.

Another great happening is the Friday afternoon/evening party on the Western Beach, towards Jaffa. South American residents play music from home and dance on the sand. There's no charge for turning up, and you can buy food and drinks.

On Saturday, if the weather is fine, the beaches are packed solid and Israelis flock there en masse. On the other hand and despite the beaches and beautiful open countryside close by, large numbers of Israelis can be seen picnicking on the small grass area near the central railway station, surrounded by busy traffic.

Tel Avivians also flock down to Jaffa, where the eating and entertainment places are open and busier than at any other time.

While all the city buses grind to a halt, a sherut service runs the No 4 route up and down Ben Yehuda and Allenby Sts. Mercedes sheruts operate to Jerusalem and Haifa from HaHashmal St, east of the southern end of Allenby St. The other operational public transport is the United Services bus No 90, running from the Dan Panorama Hotel along Allenby, Ben Yehuda, Bograshov, Dizengoff, Reines and Arlosoroff Sts to Herzlia up the coast.

Plenty of cheap eating places stay open through Shabbat, including those on Dizengoff St, just north of the square, as well as a few along the seafront. All the travellers' bars continue serving uninterrupted. There are a number of small delicatessens and small convenience stores open too, so you will never go hungry.

David Circle. There's no indication of it at ground level but look up and you'll spot it: the entrance is down a little side alley and up the stairs. It's worth searching for.

Swing on Nahalat Binyamin, just north of Rothschild Ave is a trendy bar and poser's paradise. It's also great for lovers of cognac and Cuban cigars. Sit at a round wooden bar and be cool to your heart's content.

Lovers of real ale should head for the *Tel Aviv Brewhouse* (see Places to Eat for address details), around the corner from Swing. They brew and serve their own excellent ale on the premises. There are currently four ales on offer: *Blondelight* a lager kicking in at 3.7% alcohol; *Moonshine* a red-tinged lager with 4.7% alcohol; *Quantum* a tasty pilsener with 3.7% alcohol and finally *Masters*, a beefy dark ale packing 6% alcohol. Try all four with a 25NIS taster pack.

For live music visit *Logos* which has local blues, R&B and rock bands playing every night at about 10 pm. It's at 8 HaShomer St, a sidestreet running off Nahalat Binyamin St to HaCarmel St.

Tel Aviv is Israel's gay centre and has numerous gay bars and clubs. Situated above Logos is *He-She*, a gay bar, open Monday to Saturday from 8 pm. Another gay bar with the same opening hours is *ZAZ* (*105 HaHashmona'im St*). There's also *Abi's* (*40 Geula St*) near Allenby St.

There are gay and lesbian discos at *Playroom* (*58 Allenby St*), and also at *Zman Amiti* (☎ 683 7788, *22 Eilat Rd, Jaffa*) where

TEL AVIV

Dana International – Israel's Pride and Shame

When transsexual singer Dana International won the Eurovision song contest in 1998 with a catchy sugarpop hit called *Diva*, divisions between Israelis and Palestinians were briefly put on hold as orthodox Jews took on secular Jews over an issue that divided a nation as much as the politics of Islamic extremists Hamas.

Pop queen Dana International was formerly a male known as Yaran Cohen and gained fame in Israel as a female impersonator in Tel Aviv night clubs before her sex change operation in 1993. She was selected to represent Israel at the annual schmalzy music fest held in Birmingham, England. Her unprecedented win sparked spontaneous demonstrations of joy in Tel Aviv, Israel's secular capital, with people waving flags and dancing in the street.

Her win also drew flack from Israel's influential orthodox lobby with the ultraorthodox religious party Shas declaring that the win 'symbolised the sickness of secular Israel'. Both secular and religious Jews see Dana's victory as a battle in the constant cultural civil war they are fighting against each other.

Religious Jews are horrified that Dana International, who was born a man, represented Israel. Israelis are every bit as divided about religion and culture as they are about peace with the Palestinians, which is, at least, the subject of negotiations. There is no real dialogue between secular and religious Israelis, and Dana's victory is another sign that the gulf between them is growing wider. Despite continuing opposition, Israel won the right to host the 1999 Eurovision Song Contest in Jerusalem.

---

the Society for the Protection of Personal Rights (SPPR) organises extremely popular parties here every Thursday night, starting at midnight.

Nightclubs The action rarely gets underway before midnight and goes right on through until the morning. Expect queues at the more popular places and the kind of scrutiny from the style-police on the door that is normally reserved for departing passengers at Ben-Gurion airport. If you're accepted and admitted then cover charges range from 25 to 40NIS.

Judging by the line outside, the trendiest club in town is *Lemon* (☎ 681 3313, 17 HaNagarim St). The type of music varies nightly. *House on 26* (☎ 527 5576, 26 Allenby St) plays purely house, hip hop and dance and is popular with students.

The same kind of thing makes up the playlist at *Allenby 58* (☎ 517 6019), a spacious former cinema on Allenby St, just north of Magen David Circle. *Soweto Club* (☎ 516 0222, 61 HaYarkon St), as the name suggests, specialises in reggae and African sounds. There's also *The Coliseum* (☎ 527 1177) at Namir Square, originally a supermarket, and now a tacky tourist disco; however, it does have arguably the best sound, light and laser system in Israel.

Names (☎ 510 7722, 22 Ahad Ha'am St) may be one of the most beautiful clubs in Tel Aviv; it's located in an old house and is one of the best places to dance. *Camelot* (☎ 528 5222) is the place for jazz and blues lovers. It's at 16 Shalom Aleikham St (on the corner of Ben Yehuda St), and is open daily from 10 pm to 3 am.

Cinemas The centrally located cinemas in town are:

Dizengoff 1-3
    (☎ 620 0485) in the Dizengoff Centre
Gordon
    (☎ 524 4373) on the corner of Ben Yehuda and Gordon Sts
Hod 1-4
    (☎ 522 6226) underneath the Cameri Theatre on the corner of Dizengoff and Frishman Sts

Lev 1-4
(☎ 528 8288) also in the Dizengoff Centre
Rav-Chen
(☎ 528 2288) on Dizengoff Square
Rav-Or 1-5
(☎ 510 2674) in the Opera Tower
Tel Aviv
(☎ 528 1181) at 65 Pinsker St, again, close to Dizengoff Square

Anyone seriously interested in good cinema should drop by the *Cinematheque* (☎ 691 7181, 1 Ha'Arba'a St), part of a membership chain which shows a variety of classics, avante-garde, new wave, and offbeat movies. Tickets for nonmembers are also sold just before the performance. Actress Goldie Hawn donated enough to have one of the screens named in her honour – but thankfully the donation came free of the obligation to show any of her films. A monthly program is available in the foyer and there's a good cafe here too. To get there, follow Dizengoff St south to the junction with Ibn Gvirol St. Continue south on Ibn Gvirol, forking left onto Carlibach St and the Cinematheque will be visible to your left across a triangular piazza.

During the summer months, check to see if free films are being screened at night on the beach near Allenby St.

Theatre, Music & Dance Theatre is very well attended and by all accounts productions at the Cameri and Habima are often impressive. However, swayed by the intimacy of the venue, we recommend that you check the schedules and attend any performance of interest at the Suzanne Dellal Centre:

Cameri Theatre
(☎ 523 3335) 101 Dizengoff St, entrance on Frishman St. Plays in Hebrew with simultaneous translation into English on Tuesdays. Tickets are 65NIS and 80NIS, with earphone rental an extra 5NIS.
Habima Theatre
(☎ 526 6666) on Tarsat Blvd, opposite Habima Square. Home of Israel's leading theatre group, Habima. The performances on Thursdays have simultaneous English-language translation.

Mann Auditorium
(☎ 528 9163) Habima Square. Home of the Israeli Philharmonic Orchestra and venue for occasional stage shows.
Suzanne Dellal Centre for Dance & Theatre
(☎ 510 5656) 1 Yechieli St, Neve Tzedek. Beautiful complex, home to the Inbal and Bat Sheva dance companies as well as the Neve Tzedek Theatre.
Tel Aviv Performing Arts Centre
(☎ 692 7710) 28 Leonardo da Vinci St. Also known as the Golda Meir Centre, this new complex is home to the New Israeli Opera and venue for concerts and theatrical productions.
Tzavta Theatre
(☎ 695 0156) 30 Ibn Gvirol St

Getting There & Away

With Ben-Gurion airport close by, Tel Aviv-Jaffa is often the visitor's first stop. Just about in the centre of Israel's Mediterranean coast, the city is a popular choice as a base from which to visit other places in this small country.

The highway north of Tel Aviv (Route 2) leads to Haifa and the Galilee. The same highway south leads to Ashdod, Ashkelon, Gaza and the Negev. The busy highway to the east (Route 1) leads to Jerusalem.

Air Arkia flights depart from the Sde Dov airport, north of the Yarkon River. These connect directly with Eilat (US$80 one way, several flights daily) and Rosh Pina in the Upper Galilee, with further connections to Haifa and Jerusalem. There are no flights on Saturday. Its Central Tel Aviv offices (☎ 699 2222) are located at 11 Frishman St.

Other airline offices are:

Air Canada
(☎ 527 3781) 59 Ben Yehuda St
Air France
(☎ 516 1144) 1 Ben Yehuda St
Air Sinai
(☎ 510 2481) 1 Ben Yehuda St
Alitalia
(☎ 520 0000) 98 Dizengoff St
American Airlines
(☎ 510 4322) 1 Ben Yehuda St
British Airways
(☎ 510 1581) 1 Ben Yehuda St
Canadian Airlines International
(☎ 517 2163) 1 Ben Yehuda St

TEL AVIV

Cathay Pacific
(☎ 522 8444) 43 Ben Yehuda St
Delta Airlines
(☎ 620 1101) 29 Allenby St
El Al
(☎ 526 1222) 32 Ben Yehuda St
Lufthansa
(☎ 514 2350) 1 Ben Yehuda St
Qantas
(☎ 517 2163) 1 Ben Yehuda St
SAA
(☎ 510 2828) 1 Ben Yehuda St
Sabena
(☎ 517 4411) 74 HaYarkon St
SAS
(☎ 510 1177) 1 Ben Yehuda St
Swissair
(☎ 511 6666) 1 Ben Yehuda St
Tower Air
(☎ 517 9421) 78 HaYarkon St
TWA
(☎ 517 1212) 76 HaYarkon St
United Airlines
(☎ 527 9551) 41 Ben Yehuda St

For airport information call ☎ 971 0111; for recorded English-language flight information call ☎ 972 3344.

Bus Doubling as a multistorey shopping centre, Tel Aviv's central bus station is a mammoth complex in which, if unlucky, you could easily spend the first few days of your visit to Tel Aviv trying to find the way out. Intercity buses arrive at and depart from the 6th floor, where there's also an information point. Departure bays are well indicated with electronic boards that show information in both Hebrew and English. Suburban and interurban (Dan) buses leave from the 4th floor but these are not well signposted so you'll need to ask to find the correct bay. There are some Dan departures from the 1st floor also. Tickets can usually be bought from the driver as well as from the ticket booths.

Left luggage offices are on the 6th floor (☎ 638 4058) adjacent to the information point and on the 4th floor at the bottom of the ramp beside the post office. Security is tight and if you want to leave anything you have to provide passport details. Opening

hours are Sunday to Thursday from 7 am to 7 pm, Friday from 7 am to 3 pm and closed Saturday; the fee for each item you check-in is 10NIS per day.

Taxis and urban buses leave from the Levinsky St entrance on the 4th level.

The following mainline services leave from the station:

Beersheba – 23NIS, 80 minutes; departing every 10 to 20 minutes
Eilat – 37NIS, five hours; departing hourly between 6.30 am and 5 pm, plus an overnight service departing at 12.30 am
Haifa – 22NIS, 1½ hours; departing every 15 to 20 minutes
Jerusalem – 17NIS, one hour; departing every 10 to 15 minutes
Tiberias – 32.5NIS, 2½ hours; departing every hour

Unless otherwise stated buses run daily between about 5.30 am and 11 pm, with the last buses on Friday being around 3 pm and the first buses on Saturday leaving about 6 pm. For the West Bank go via Jerusalem. Call ☎ 537 5555 for intercity bus information.

There is also a second bus station in Tel Aviv, called the Arlosoroff terminal (see the Tel Aviv map), which is up by the train station in the north-eastern part of town. One or two services from Jerusalem and Haifa finish up here rather than at the central bus station. To get into town walk over to the bus stands in the station forecourt and catch a No 10, 12 or 18 bus which run to various city centre destinations.

Train Tel Aviv now has one main (central) train station and one suburban stop, Ha-Shalom, on the southern line to Rehovot. The central train station (☎ 693 7515 for information) serves Haifa (19.50NIS, 1¼ hours) and Nahariya (30NIS, two hours) up near the Lebanese border, both via Netanya, with trains leaving virtually every hour between 6 am and 8 pm. There are a further 12 trains a day to the dormitory suburb of Rehovot (10.50NIS, 30 minutes), two of which continue on to Ashdod (12.50NIS, one hour) to serve afternoon commuters.

The main train station is at the junction of Haifa Rd, Arlosoroff St and Petah Tikva Rd – take bus No 61 or 62 north up Dizengoff St. To get to HaShalom station, take bus No 51 (stand 51) from the central bus station and alight just before the Dizengoff interchange from where it's a five minute signposted walk to the train station.

Car Rental Most of the car rental places are on HaYarkon St near the Sheraton hotel.

Avis	☎ 527 1752
Budget	☎ 524 5233
Eldan	☎ 527 1166
Europcar	☎ 524 8181
Hertz	☎ 684 1011
Reliable	☎ 524 9794
Sa-Gal	☎ 510 6103
Splendid	☎ 522 1611
Thrifty	☎ 561 2050
Traffic	☎ 524 9187

Those in Ben-Gurion airport are:

Avis	☎ 977 3200
Budget	☎ 971 1504
Eldan	☎ 977 3400
Europcar	☎ 977 2895
Hertz	☎ 977 2444
Reliable	☎ 977 2511
Thrifty	☎ 977 3500

Sherut (Service Taxi) Sherut services operate from outside the central bus station (where bus Nos 4 and 5 alight). To Jerusalem, the cost is 45NIS and to Haifa, 32NIS. On Saturday they leave from Ha-Hashmal St, east of lower Allenby St and cost about an extra 20%.

Getting Around

To/From the Airport Bus No 222 provides an excellent service between the city centre and the airport, running at 45 minute intervals between 4 am and midnight (last bus Friday at 6.45 pm; first bus Saturday at noon). Timetables are posted at the stops.

Going out to the airport, the bus picks up passengers at: Dan Panorama Hotel; HaYarkon St south of Allenby St; north of

Shalom Aleikham St (opposite the Yamit Park Plaza); 104 HaYarkon St (opposite the Dan Tel Aviv); 144 HaYarkon St (opposite the Diplomat Hotel); 196 HaYarkon St (opposite the Hilton); 248 HaYarkon St (near the Grand Beach Hotel); Weizmann St (corner of Pinkas St); central train station; and HaTayasim Rd. The city-airport fare is 18NIS and the journey from Central Tel Aviv takes about an hour. (See also the Getting Around chapter.)

From the central bus station, bus No 475 leaves every 30 minutes for the airport also.

Bus For Dab city bus information call ☎ 639 4444. Buses generally run from 5.30 am to midnight. Currently, these are the major Tel Aviv bus routes:

Bus No 4
  Central bus station via Allenby St, Ben Yehuda and Dizengoff Sts to the Reading terminal, north of the Yarkon River.
Sherut No 4
  Same route as bus No 4 for the same price. Its advantage is that it's more comfortable, taking only as many passengers as there are seats, and it's quicker – once it's full it only stops to let people off. It also operates on Shabbat (when the price doubles), between the northern end of Ben Yehuda St to the interurban sheruts at the bottom of Allenby St.
Bus No 5
  Central bus station, along Allenby St, up Rothschild Ave, along Dizengoff St, Nordau Ave, Ibn Gvirol, Pinkas, Weizmann and Ha-Maccabi Sts and then back. Useful for the HI hostel, the Egyptian embassy, Habima Square and the Dizengoff St hostels.
Bus No 10
  Central train station via Arlosoroff St, Ben Yehuda St, Allenby St, Herbert Samuel Ave, Jaffa Rd and on to Bat Yam.
Bus No 18
  Central train station along Petah Tikva Rd and Shaul HaMelekh Blvd to Ibn Gvirol then Frishman, Dizengoff, Pinsker, Trumpeldor and Ben Yehuda Sts, Allenby St, Yerushalayim Ave and to Bat Yam.
Bus No 25
  Tel Aviv University via the Diaspora Museum, then HaMaccabi St, Ibn Gvirol St, Arlosoroff St, then Shlomo HaMelekh St, HaMelekh George St, Allenby St and Carmel Market.

TEL AVIV

Bus No 46
    Central bus station via Jaffa Rd to Jaffa.
Bus No 61
    Carmelit, along HaMelekh George, Dizengoff, Arlosoroff and Jabotinksy to Ramat Gan in east Tel Aviv.

Taxi All Tel Aviv taxis charge by the meter, but they are still an expensive way of getting around the city. They operate according to two tariffs: the lower tariff between 5.30 am and 9 pm and the 25% higher night tariff between 9 pm and 5 am. (For complaints about taxi service see the Getting Around chapter).

JAFFA   יפו يَافَا
☎ Area Code: 03

The Jaffa (Yafo, in Hebrew) of today exists largely as a quaint harbourside setting for an expensive seafood meal. Moneyed residents of Tel Aviv flock down here at weekends for serenity and great views across the bay. Serenity, however, has not always been Jaffa's lot and diners at this site in ages past might have had their shrimp cocktails interrupted by the sight of Jonah stepping ashore from the mouth of the whale or by the spectacle of Perseus circling the harbour on his winged horse Pegasus. Both of these legends are connected to Jaffa, a place that lays claim to the title of world's oldest working harbour.

Founded, according to the Old Testament, by Japheth, in the wake of the famed flood that shot his father Noah to fame, Jaffa came to prominence as a port during the time of Solomon. The King of the Israelites lost the town in 1468 BC to the Egyptians, whose soldiers made their surprise entry hidden in clay pots.

The tides of Islam swept over the port in the 8th century to be repelled briefly during the time of the Crusader conquests. From that time on, Jaffa remained in Muslim hands until the British General Allenby drove out the Turks in 1917. Jews had lived here since at least 1840 and by the end of the century, Jaffa had become a major gateway for boatloads of arriving immigrants. There were tensions between the new arrivals and the existing Arab community and, in 1921,

these boiled over into full-blown anti-Jewish riots. The riots were to recur every few years until the decisive fighting of 1948 which saw the defeat and subsequent flight of the majority of Jaffa's Arab population, leaving the ancient town in Jewish hands.

Since that time, Jaffa has been extensively renovated and developed as – that perennial Israeli favourite – an artists' quarter, with attendant galleries, craftshops and cafes. In financial terms, at least, it would seem that the plan has paid off. Making good use of the simple beauty of the Arab architecture, the heart of the old town has become an unashamed till-ringing tourist attraction. But away from the babble of guided tour groups and the coterie of candlelit couples dining down by the water's edge, 'Ye Olde Jaffa' remains empty at heart.

Every Wednesday a free guided walking tour of Old Jaffa is led by the Association for Tourism, Tel Aviv-Jaffa. Meet by the clocktower at 9 am; the tour ends at about noon.

The Clocktower & Flea Market
From Tel Aviv most people arrive at Jaffa via the Herbert Samuel Esplanade and are met by the Ottoman **clocktower**, built in 1906, on Yefet St. To the south-west of the clocktower is **Mahmudiya Mosque** (1812), which was built using columns filched from Caesarea and Ashkelon; unfortunately it's closed to non-Muslims. To the east of Yefet St is the **flea market**, which has a decent reputation for antiques and interesting oriental bits and pieces. It requires several visits if you want to shop seriously, as new items appear regularly. Bargaining is the order of the day, and the stallholders' traditional sales patter includes the one about making a quick first sale early on Sunday morning to bring good luck for the coming week. It's closed on Saturday.

Old Jaffa
To properly see Old Jaffa requires at least two visits: one made during the day and another at night. Only in clear daylight is it possible to appreciate the great view up the coast to Tel Aviv and the sun coaxing out

warmth in the dusty yellow buildings. However, it's at night that the place really comes to life and that the galleries, restaurants and cafes do most of their business.

Past the main entrance of the Mahmudiya Mosque and up the hill is the **Antiquities Museum of Tel Aviv-Jaffa** (☎ 682 5375) at 10 Mifraz Shlomo St. Originally a Turkish administrative and detention centre, the building is now home to a display of local archaeological discoveries. It's open Sunday to Thursday from 9 am to 1 pm and closed Friday and Saturday. Admission is 10NIS (students 7NIS).

The grassy knoll behind the museum, known as the **HaPisga Gardens**, has a small amphitheatre with a panorama of the Tel Aviv seafront as its backdrop. Excavations nearby have uncovered Egyptian, Israelite, Greek and Roman remains. The bizarre, white neo-Mayan sculpture on one of the hills purportedly depicts the fall of Jericho, Isaac's sacrifice and Jacob's dream.

A footbridge connects the gardens to **Kedumim Square** (Kikar Kedumim), the reconstructed centre of Old Jaffa, ringed by restaurants, clubs and galleries but dominated by the bulk of **St Peter's Monastery**. This cream-painted Franciscan church was built above a medieval citadel and in its later guise as a Christian hostelry it was visited by Napoleon. It's open to the public daily, October to February from 8 to 11.45 am and 3 to 5 pm; March to September from 8 to 11.45 am and 3 to 6 pm.

In a chamber underneath the square is the well-designed **visitors centre** (☎ 518 2680), where you can view partially excavated remains from the Hellenistic and Roman era and watch a six minute film on Jaffa. You can also pick up an informative free map down here. It's open daily from 9 am to 10 pm (2 pm on Friday).

Descending the steps beside the monastery will lead you to a tightly squeezed lane, at the southern end of which is **Simon the Tanner's House**. This is the traditional site of the house where the Apostle Peter stayed after restoring Tabitha to life (Acts 9:32).

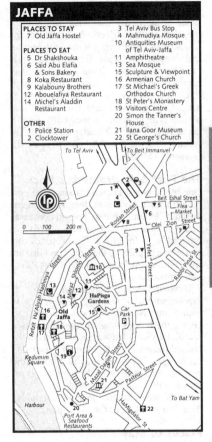

In the courtyard you can see a well, believed to have been used in Peter's day, and a stone coffin from the same period. When Muslims built a mosque on the site in 1730, they used the coffin as an ablutions font. Now a private house, the building is officially open daily from 8 am to 7 pm; just ring the bell and see if anyone answers. There is a small admission charge.

The main **artists' area** is stepped Mazal Dagim St and its branching stone alleyways named for the signs of the zodiac. Among the galleries at 4 Mazal Dagim is the **Ilana**

Goor Museum (☎ 683 7676, fax 683 6699), home of the first Jewish khan and built in the 18th century. It served as a hostel for Jewish pilgrims arriving at the Jaffa port on their way to Jerusalem. Today it is the private home of artist Ilana Goor who has turned her home into a tasteful display with three floors of modern eclectic pop and ethnic art, created by artists from Israel and abroad. The museum is open daily from 8 am to 10 pm, except Tuesday and Thursday when it closes at 2 pm. Admission is 19NIS (students 15NIS).

The Port & Andromeda's Rock

One of the oldest known harbours, the port of Jaffa (then known as Joppa) was mentioned by Hiram, King of Tyre, in conversation with Solomon (II Chronicles 2:16) and referred to in Jonah 1:3. For centuries this was where pilgrims to the Holy Land first arrived en route to Jerusalem and it was Palestine's main port.

Beyond the sea wall are a cluster of blackened rocks, the largest of which is named after Andromeda, who according to Greek mythology was chained here as a sacrificial victim but was snatched from the jaws of the great sea monster by Perseus on his winged horse. Reconstruction of the port and the dredging of the approaches resulted in the rock being damaged.

At the weekend and on Jewish holidays there is a small entry fee to the port.

Places to Stay

A pleasant Israeli couple have converted a beautiful old Turkish house into the lovely **Old Jaffa Hostel** (☎ 682 2370, fax 682 2316, email ojhostel@shani.net, 8 Olei Zion St). Up the twisting wooden staircase with its walls hung with sepia Jewish family portraits, there's a large bar/common room and airy dorms complete with armchairs and tables. A dorm bed costs 35NIS while private doubles are 100NIS. There's also the option of taking a mattress on the roof for only 25NIS. The hostel is in the flea market area, although the entrance is a little hard to find because it is actually from

A 12th century minaret in Jaffa

Ami'ad St. There's no sign at eye level – it's under your feet set in stone at the foot of an unmarked door, though you will see a sign if you look up. There can be noise problems from the street, so be prepared for a bit of a racket at times.

The other place to stay is the Christian hospice **Beit Immanuel** (☎ 682 1459, fax 682 9817, email beitimm@netvision.net.il, 8 Auerbach St). Built in 1884 by Baron Ustinov, Peter Ustinov's father, it was originally the Park Hotel, in which guise it entertained guests such as Kaiser Wilhelm II of Germany. Nicely renovated, and with a garden, it now comprises a pilgrims' hostel, study facilities and a worship centre for a Hebrew-speaking congregation. Dormitory beds are US$12 with breakfast, and private singles/doubles are US$40/65 (US$33/55 in the low season). The hospice is just outside Jaffa, south of Jaffa Rd. To get there take bus No 44 or 46 from the central bus station and get off at the Nechustan Lift factory (look for the sign) – Auerbach St can be located by the rocket-like spire of Immanuel Church.

Places to Eat

Almost reason alone to visit Jaffa, *Said Abu Elafia & Sons* (*7 Yefet St*) has become near legendary in Israel. This was Jaffa's first bakery, established in 1880, and four generations down the line the Abu Elafia family are busier than ever.

The main attraction is their version of pizza, prepared in the traditional Arab manner of cracking a couple of eggs on top of pitta, stirring in tomato, cheese and olives and baking it in the oven. Other items include 24 varieties of bread, such as pitta coated in sesame seeds or spices; ask for *za-'atar*, and *sambusa* – triangular shaped pastries with various fillings. Try *sambusa mayorav* which contains mushrooms, egg, potato and cheese and costs 10NIS.

The popularity of the place has led to a string of copycat bakeries along the street but the crowds still choose to swarm around the original. It's open 24 hours daily except Sunday.

Other cheap eating in Jaffa is limited. *Kalabouny Brothers* (*132 Yefet St*) serves humous, fuul, salad, chips, pitta and coffee, all for about 24NIS. Continue past Old Jaffa along Yefet St and the cafe is on the right just before the Hapoalim Bank on the corner (there is no English sign). *Dr Shak-shouka* (*☎ 682 2842, 3 Beit Eshel*) also serves typical Arab fare and is just around the corner from Abu Elafia.

For Israelis, the main culinary attraction in Jaffa is fish and both Mifraz Shlomo St and the port area have numerous outdoor restaurants – there is even a floating one – some of which also serve meat grilled on the fire. These restaurants are extremely popular with Israelis and tourists alike, but they are not surprisingly on the expensive side since you are paying as much for atmosphere as for your food. Try *Michel's Aladdin Restaurant* (*5 Mifraz Shlomo St*), if only for the views from its terrace. The restaurant is housed in an 800-year-old building that was originally a Turkish bath. Most of the dishes are priced in the 40 to 70NIS range but there are things like blintzes at 34NIS.

Diagonally opposite Michel's Aladdin you can't miss the fortress-like *Abouelafiya Restaurant* (*☎ 681 4335, fax 683 2144, 4-6 Mifraz Shlomo St*) owned by the same family of the bakery fame. Fish dishes are their speciality. Try *makloubeh*, a delicious combination of shrimps, pine and hazelnuts cooked in a special sauce (55NIS) or *tajeen*, groper steak and tahina, with pine and hazelnuts (66NIS). The rooftop dining affords spectacular views over to Tel Aviv at night.

At the lower end of Mifraz Shlomo St you will find *Koka Restaurant* (*☎ 681 0488, 30 Roslan St*) serving the same meat and fish as the restaurants with the view but at a more approachable cost.

Getting There & Away

From Central Tel Aviv it's a pleasant 2.5km stroll along the seafront to Old Jaffa. If you don't fancy walking then catch bus No 10 from Ben Yehuda St, bus No 18 from Dizengoff St, or bus No 18 or 25 from Allenby St.

In the reverse direction, you can catch bus No 10 from beside the clocktower to go to Ben Yehuda St.

BAT YAM   בת-ים

South of Jaffa, Bat Yam (Daughter of the Sea) is a modern seafront suburb. The beaches here are wide expanses of fine white sand that are much less crowded than those further north in Tel Aviv, but apart from that, there's little other reason to visit. Bat Yam has all the lack of charm of any concrete city-overspill zone. But people obviously do come, a fact borne out by the large number of new hotels along the seafront – none of which, incidentally, is particularly cheap. If you do want to soak up the sun or hit the surf on Bat Yam's beaches it makes much more sense budgetwise to stay in Central Tel Aviv or Jaffa and make the 20 minute bus ride down here.

There's a municipal tourist information office (*☎ 507 2777, fax 659 6666*) at 43 Ben-Gurion Ave, just north of the intersection with Rothschild Ave; it's open Sunday to Thursday from 8 am to 6.30 pm, Friday from 8 am to 1 pm, closed Saturday. In winter they close between 1.30 and 4 pm on Monday and Wednesday.

Getting There & Away
Bus Nos 10, 18, 25 and 26 provide a regular service to and from Central Tel Aviv.

B'NEI BRAK
בני-ברק

This orthodox Jewish community was established in 1924 by Warsaw Hasidim. B'nei Brak was mentioned in Joshua 19:45 as a city of the Dan tribe and during the Roman period it became a home to many famous sages of Israel and a centre of Hebrew study. Today the new city, with its numerous yeshivot, has once again become a centre for religious study. A sign of its status is the busy sherut service between here and Mea She'arim in Jerusalem.

Around Tel Aviv

All of the places mentioned in this section are easy day trips from Tel Aviv and can be visited by local bus or train. Telephone codes do change from town to town so note the local exchange code before calling any of the places listed here.

HERZLIA
הרצליה

Pop: 83,000 ☎ Area Code: 09

Named in memory of Theodor Herzl and established in 1924 as an agricultural centre, Herzlia was greatly affected by the rapid expansion of Tel Aviv. As the city grew, the fine northern beaches of Herzlia became more accessible and the small town become the address of choice for wealthy Israelis and diplomats.

The town has retained its air of affluence and Herzlia Pituah, the seafront area, is dominated by luxury hotels while the beaches (which charge admission) are the hang-out for the Israeli equivalent of the Beverly Hills 90210 set.

Orientation & Information
Basel St, Shalit Square and the seafront are the areas you should head for. The Sharon

Hotel, situated among various cafes, bars and restaurants, is the major landmark and the beach stretches out from it in both directions. To the north and just a short walk away is Sidna Ali Beach, which is free and is often less crowded than surrounding beaches. Sharon Beach is next to the Sharon Hotel, Dabush Beach is near the Daniel Hotel and Accadia Beach is to the south by the Accadia Hotel.

Coming in by bus, get off at the Sharon Hotel stop for the Sidna Ali or Sharon beaches. For the other beaches wait until the Accadia Hotel stop.

Sidna Ali Beach & the Caveman
In addition to the sand, cliffs and nearby Roman ruins, Sidna Ali Beach boasts a unique attraction – Nissim Kahalon, or the Caveman.

Formerly a plasterer, some 15 years ago Nissim decided to opt for an open-air lifestyle and decided on this spot to begin constructing himself a home in the cliff above the beach. He's been building and sculpting ever since, relying mainly on finds from the beach for his raw materials. The result is a bizarre piece of living sculpture that wouldn't look out of place in *Mad Max* or some other post-Apocalyptic movie.

Nissim makes a living from his cafe, which does good business despite the steep prices, and he's usually willing to show visitors around his home for a small fee.

The beach takes its name from **Sidna Ali Mosque**, built under the direction of Saladin in the late 12th century and currently undergoing renovation. **Apollonia**, a Roman port, is a few hundred metres to the north but the few remains are not really worth a special trip.

To get to Sidna Ali Beach, head north from the Sharon Hotel along Galei Thelet St and turn left along the dirt path just before the US Embassy residence. Then go right along the clifftop, past the army installation, continue down the slope and turn left down the road to the beach – it's just over 15 minutes walk. Nissim's cave is about 100m north of the entrance.

Places to Stay

Herzlia has no budget accommodation. *Eshel Inn (☎ 956 8208, fax 956 8797)*, across from Sharon Hotel, provides about the only cheap deal. Singles cost US$60, and doubles US$70.

Cymberg Hotel (☎ 957 2179, 29 Ha-Ma'apilim St) is an attractive villa with a very pleasant garden, lawn and veranda. It is peaceful but only has 11 rooms available. HaMa'apilim St, which runs parallel with Basel St, is two blocks north of Shalit Square.

Herzlia's premier hotel, *Daniel (☎ 952 8282, fax 952 8280)*, is a rather plush business centre hotel with singles from US$207 to US$297 and doubles from US$227 to US$317. The other equally expensive options are *Dan Accadia (☎ 959 7070, fax 959 7090, email danhtls@co.il)* with singles from US$198 to US$393 and doubles from US$221 to US$354, and the *Sharon Hotel (☎ 952 5777, fax 957 2448, email ha sharon@netvision.net.il)* with singles costing from US$100 to US$210 and doubles from US$96 to US$151.

Places to Eat

Nissim's *Caveman Cafe* down on Sidna Ali Beach does filled sandwiches and sometimes fish. Otherwise, highly recommended is *Mama's Traditional Homemade Food*, opposite the central bus station. The menu is whatever's in the pot and the cuisine ranges from Italian to Indian. Prices are very reasonable. It's open Sunday to Thursday from 9 am to 7 pm, Friday from 8 am to 3.30 pm, closed Saturday.

Getting There & Away

United Tours bus No 90 leaves Tel Aviv from the Dan Panorama Hotel and passes along Allenby St, then Ben Yehuda, Bograshov, Tchernikovsky, Dizengoff, Arlosoroff and Weizmann Sts. The bus runs throughout Shabbat, making Herzlia quite a popular Saturday outing. Alternatively, take bus No 501 or 502 from the central bus station. The journey takes less than 40 minutes and the fare is 6NIS.

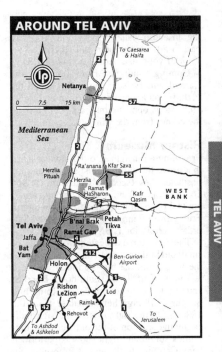

AROUND TEL AVIV

To Caesarea & Haifa

Netanya

0 7.5 15 km

Mediterranean Sea

Herzlia Pituah

Ra'anana Kfar Sava

Herzlia

Ramat HaSharon

Kafr Qasim

WEST BANK

Tel Aviv

B'nai Brak Petah Tikva

Jaffa

Ramat Gan

Bat Yam

Holon

Ben-Gurion Airport

Rishon LeZion

Lod

Ramla

Rehovot

To Jerusalem

To Ashdod & Ashkelon

RISHON LEZION

ראשון לציון

Pop: 169,500 ☎ Area Code: 03

Now a small town about 40km south of Tel Aviv, Rishon LeZion was the first Jewish settlement in Palestine. Meaning 'First in Zion', it was founded by Russian immigrants in 1882. After battling with agricultural problems and disease for five years, the settlers were given financial assistance by Baron Benjamin Rothschild – his first direct involvement with Zionism in Palestine. The vineyard and cellars that he helped establish are still among the town's major attractions.

Carmel Winery

To arrange a guided tour of the winery call ☎ 965 3662; alternatively, arrive early and a tour can probably be arranged for some time later that same day. As part of the tour you get a brief explanation of Carmel's history and the vinification process as well watching an audio-visual presentation. You take part in a tasting session and receive a souvenir of your visit. Admission is 13NIS.

Coming south-east from Tel Aviv, the Carmel winery is on Herzl St beyond the park. If you are arriving in town on bus No 19, it stops opposite the park, right around the corner from the winery.

History Museum

Providing an insight into the pioneer spirit that drove the early Zionist settlers and the obstacles they faced, this museum (☎ 964 1621) is open Sunday to Thursday from 9 am to 2 pm, (Monday also from 4 to 8 pm), Friday from 9 am to 1 pm; it's closed Saturday. Admission is 8NIS.

The museum is located in a series of small old buildings at 4 Ahad Ha'am St, but the walk from the bus station is a history lesson in itself. Head south down Herzl St and turn left onto pedestrianised Rothschild St (the buildings here all date from the 1880s). On the right, notice the sign indicating the location of the old well. The museum's sound and light show is performed here. Continue to the end of Rothschild St, where facing you is the **Great Synagogue**, built in 1885 and registered as a warehouse because the Turkish authorities wouldn't allow the Jews to build a place of worship – step inside, it's open during the day. The museum is on the corner, to the right.

Getting There & Away

Take bus No 19 from Tel Aviv. It leaves from Shalom Aleikham St, between Ha-Yarkon and Ben Yehuda Sts, and also from Allenby St. Alternatively, take bus No 200 or 201 from the central bus station.

Many visitors follow a visit to the winery with a visit to the Weizmann Institute in nearby Rehovot – a 10 minute ride from the bus station at Rishon LeZion.

REHOVOT   רחובות
Pop: 86,400 ☎ Area Code: 08
Situated about 60km from Tel Aviv, Rehovot is another Jewish town ideally lo-

cated for a day visit. Established in 1890 by Polish Jews, *rehovot* means 'expanses' and the name (taken from Genesis 26:22) was chosen to symbolise the community's aims of Zionist expansion throughout Palestine. Today this quiet town is best known for the Weizmann Institute of Science and its distinctive architecture.

Weizmann Institute of Science

This world-renowned centre was named after the first president of Israel, Chaim Weizmann, who was a leading research chemist as well as statesman. During WWI, Weizmann's scientific researches proved valuable to the Allied war effort and the goodwill generated may have been a factor in squeezing the Balfour Declaration out of the British in 1917. The institute in its present form was established in 1934, on moshav land, to provide facilities for research and study in the sciences. Students and staff continue the work today, conducting research into fields as wide-ranging as disease, agriculture, the environment and computer technology.

As you enter the institute campus, on your right is the Wix library building that houses the **visitors centre**. Here you can watch a multimedia presentation and receive assistance in selecting an appropriate route for a self-guided campus tour. A souvenir 'smart card' purchased at the centre will provide you with access to sites along the route, called the SciTrek Visitors' Trail.

Located along SciTrek are outdoor video monitors featuring short films about particular aspects of the institute's history or research. Other campus highlights include the Solar Tower Observation point, the History Pavilion, the Physics Pavilion and the **Clore Garden of Science**, an outdoor science museum and learning centre. The garden's hands-on exhibits are designed to demonstrate scientific phenomena in an accessible and exciting way.

Also on the institute's grounds next to the tombs of Dr Chaim Weizmann and his wife Vera is the stunning **Weizmann House**. Designed by the renowned German architect

Eric Mendelsohn, a refugee from Nazism, the house was built in 1937 in the daring international style. Parked outside is the Lincoln limousine presented to Weizmann by Henry Ford, one of only two ever made (the other was given to US President Truman).

For information on campus visits and opening hours call the visitors centre call ☎ 934 4500.

Getting There & Away

Bus Nos 200, 201 and 203 leave frequently from the Tel Aviv central bus station (10.50NIS, 40 minutes) or you can catch these buses at the Rishon LeZion bus station. You can also take a sherut from the Tel Aviv or Rishon LeZion bus stations or take a train from Tel Aviv's Merkaz and Ha-Shalom train stations.

RAMLA   רמלה الرملة
Pop: 60,000 ☎ Area Code: 03

The only town in Israel that was founded and originally developed by Arabs, Ramla was a stopover on the trade routes between Damascus, Baghdad and Egypt. Prior to the

arrival of the Crusaders in the 11th century, Ramla was Palestine's capital. It maintained its importance in the Middle Ages as the first stop for the Jerusalem-bound pilgrims who came ashore at Jaffa. Following the 1948 War the majority of the Arab population was forced to flee and they were replaced by Jewish immigrants from various countries.

Now, 20km south-east of Tel Aviv, bypassed by the major roads, of no interest to modern-day pilgrims and unknown to tourists, Ramla minds its own business with just one or two worn Islamic monuments standing as testaments to former glories. However, the mix of an old Arab quarter of crumbling stone buildings with lots of green parkland and eucalyptus tree-lined avenues makes for a very attractive small town, definitely worth a visit, especially on market day.

Orientation & Information

The bus from Tel Aviv terminates at the bus station off Herzl Ave, the town's main thoroughfare. All the sites of interest are within a kilometre or two of here; walk west along

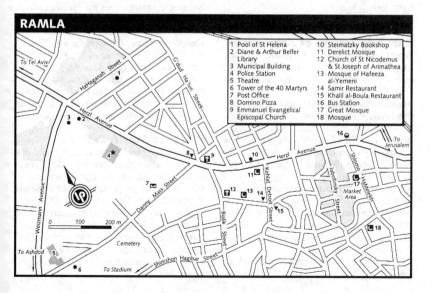

RAMLA

1 Pool of St Helena
2 Diane & Arthur Belfer Library
3 Municipal Building
4 Police Station
5 Theatre
6 Tower of the 40 Martyrs
7 Post Office
8 Domino Pizza
9 Emmanuel Evangelical Episcopal Church
10 Steimatzky Bookshop
11 Derelict Mosque
12 Church of St Nicodemus & St Joseph of Arimathea
13 Mosque of Hafeeza al-Yemeni
14 Samir Restaurant
15 Khalil al-Boula Restaurant
16 Bus Station
17 Great Mosque
18 Mosque

Herzl Ave and you'll spot the various minarets and towers.

There's no tourist information office but the Diane & Arthur Belfer library, near the corner of Weizmann and Herzl Aves, might have some local information or a town map. There's a Steimatzky bookshop on Herzl Ave, 300m west of the bus station.

The Great Mosque & Market

From the forecourt of the bus station the white minaret of Ramla's Great Mosque is easily visible south across Herzl Ave. Also known as the Omari Mosque, the building is very untypical of Islamic architecture and, in all likelihood, was probably originally a Crusader church. It's still used for Friday prayers but is open to visitors the rest of the week between 8 and 11 am.

The mosque stands on the fringes of Ramla's sprawling market, much of which is housed in the shells of Turkish-era buildings. Most of the week the stalls are limited to fruit, vegetables and foodstuffs, but on Wednesday morning the number of stalls doubles and the wares are expanded to include every conceivable kind of goods. Get there before noon.

Church & Hospice of St Nicodemus & St Joseph of Arimathea

According to Christian tradition, Ramla is the site of Arimathea, the hometown of Joseph who arranged the burial of Jesus with Nicodemus (John 19:38-39) hence the name of this church and hospice. Owned by the Franciscans, this church with its distinctive square bell tower was originally begun in the 16th century, although much of it was only completed as late as 1902. The painting above the altar is claimed to be a Titian *(The Deposition from the Cross)* but it's so covered by grime that it is impossible to make anything out. Napoleon stayed in the adjacent monastery during his unsuccessful campaign against the Turks. If you ask, one of the monks will usually show you the emperor's chambers.

The entrance to the church is off Bialik St, through the first gate on your left. Ring the bell and one of the monks living here will let you in. It's open Monday to Saturday from 9 to 11.30 am and closed Sunday. Admission is free but donations are accepted.

Tower of the 40 Martyrs

The tower is a 14th century minaret, built as an addition to the 8th century White Mosque (Jamaa al-Abiad), of which only traces remain. However, from those traces it's apparent that this was obviously a mosque of some size. This fact is best appreciated from the top of the tower; if you're there in the morning an attendant should be around to unlock the door and allow you up.

Stairs also descend down to the 9m-deep cisterns, which date back to the time of the mosque. Visitors are supposedly able to hire rowing boats to explore the spot-lit watery chambers but we saw no evidence of this; you could call ☎ 925 0319 and inquire. Opening times for the site are Sunday to Thursday from 8.30 am to 2 pm, Friday from 8 am to noon and Saturday from 8.30 am to 3.30 pm.

Pool of St Helena

Set in pleasant gardens off HaHaganah St, this 8th century reservoir was reputedly built for Haroun ar-Rashid of *The Thousand and One Nights* fame, although the name it goes by refers to the mother of the Roman Emperor Constantine. (In Arabic it's called the Pool of Al-Anazia and in Hebrew it's called Breichat Hakeshatot, The Pool of Arches.)

To reach the water, enter the small building next to the blue and white murals.

Places to Stay & Eat

There is nowhere to stay in Ramla and few places to eat. Other than the *felafel stalls* around the market, the best budget eatery we found was the popular *Khalil al-Boula Restaurant* on Kehlat Detroit St, which serves cheap oriental food in cafeteria-type surroundings. Across the narrow street, *Samir Restaurant* is much more pricey and formal. There's also a *Domino Pizza* franchise at the junction of Danny Mass St and Herzl Ave.

Getting There & Away

Buses to Tel Aviv (9NIS, 45 minutes) run every 20 minutes with slightly less frequent services to Jerusalem (18NIS, 75 minutes). While buses to Tel Aviv depart until around 10 pm, the last Jerusalem bus is at 7.50 pm. For information call ☎ 922 0222.

LOD   לוד

Pop: 55,500   ☎ Area Code: 03

Familiar to every visitor to Israel as the location of Ben-Gurion airport, what is much less well known is that Lod is the **burial site of St George**, the slayer of the dragon and patron saint of England.

George was a conscript in the Roman army who was executed in 303 AD for tearing up a copy of the emperor Diocletian's decree that forbade the practice of Christianity. He was buried in Lod (then Lydda) and a Byzantine church was built over his tomb. This church was subsequently dismantled by the Mamluk sultan Beybars (the stones were used to build a nearby bridge) and replaced with a mosque dedicated to Al-Khader, the 'Green One', a saintly Islamic folkloric figure who roughly equates to George. How this character came to be patron saint of England is unknown, although the fantastic legends of George that were doing the rounds in the Levant would have been carried back to Europe by the Crusaders.

The Greek Orthodox community built a new **Church of St George** beside the mosque in 1870. To get in, you usually need to persuade the caretaker to open it up; he lives in the Greek-style building across the cobbled lane.

A 2km walk north along the main street leads you to the oldest functioning bridge in Israel, the one built by Sultan Beybars with the stones taken from the Church of St George. Pass through the industrial site, look for the petrol station on your left and the signposted turn-off for Yagel and Zetan, then continue to follow the road as it turns right and crosses the Ayalon River. From here it is also possible to catch a bus to Tel Aviv.

ASHDOD   אשדוד

Pop: 138,000   ☎ Area Code: 08

Along with Gath, Gaza, Ekron and Ashkelon, Ashdod was one of the five great Philistine cities and an important cultural and religious centre. That was 3000 years ago; there is little great about the Ashdod of today. Established only as recently as 1957, modern Ashdod is a 'planned' city of uniform buildings, industrial sites and earnest attempts at gardening. It's also a major port with a deep-water harbour that has taken much work from Haifa and caused the closure of the port at Tel Aviv. Other industries based in Ashdod include cosmetics and textiles plants and a power plant which provides about half the country's supply of electricity.

For visitors to Ashdod, the prime historical attraction is a **Fatimid fortress** but, unfortunately, only a very small part of this early-Islamic structure remains and it's not particularly impressive. These ruins are on the outskirts of town; to get there take local bus No 5 and ask the driver to let you off at 'metzudat Ashdod yam'.

From the top of **Yaffa Ben-Ami Memorial Hill** you have a good view of Ashdod and its surroundings. According to Muslim tradition, these ruins mark the site of Jonah's tomb. He is believed to have settled in the area following his encounter with the whale.

If you happen to be in Ashdod on a Wednesday, you could take a look at the **flea market** on Lido Beach (the market lasts all day). The city's beaches are pleasant enough and, unlike those elsewhere, no one seems to mind if you camp here – there are showers and toilets.

For further information call in at the Bureau of Public Relations (☎ 864 0485/0090) in the municipality building next door to the bus station.

Getting There & Away

Tel Aviv is the nearest main centre, connected by frequent direct buses which often continue on to Ashkelon. You can also reach Ashdod from Beersheba and Jerusalem.

TEL AVIV

ASHKELON אשקלון
Pop: 88,900 ☎ Area Code: 07

Another of the great Philistine cities, Ashkelon is also believed to be the birthplace of Herod the Great. It gets a couple of good biblical mentions, most notably as a town which Samson visited and slew 30 of its men (Judges 14:19). Under the Romans, Byzantines and conquering early Muslims, the town remained as a thriving port and trade route stopover. The good times came to an abrupt end in 1270 when the Mamluk sultan Beybars completely destroyed Ashkelon.

In the early 19th century an aristocratic English adventuress, Lady Hester Stanhope, led excavations here, looking for gold and silver treasures rumoured to be buried in the area. Later diggings were carried out by the British Palestine Exploration Fund in the 1920s, but although a few foundations of buildings, statues and columns were uncovered, the ruins of ancient Ashkelon have yet to be found.

The town today has a large population of Jews from North Africa and, more recently, Russia. The local tourist board is marketing the place as the new resort capital of the country and the sandy beaches are popular with large numbers of Israelis. Aside from that, Ashkelon is really quite dull.

Orientation
Situated 56km south of Tel Aviv, Ashkelon is not a large town but its various neighbourhoods are quite spread out. Arriving by bus you will go through the old Arab town of Migdal before reaching the bus station on the southern edge of the new commercial centre, Afridar. South-west of the bus station, on the seafront, is Ashkelon National Park, the biggest draw for most visitors. You will need to use the local buses to get about.

Information
There's a tourist information office (☎ 673 2412, fax 671 0312) on Zefania Square in central Afridar, open Sunday and Tuesday from 8.30 am to 1.30 pm, and Monday, Wednesday and Thursday from 8.30 am to 12.30 pm, closed Friday and Saturday. The municipality of Ashkelon runs a Web page that may be of interest to potential visitors to the town. Check it out at www.ashkelon .gov.il.

The main post office and international telephones are at 18 Herzl St in Migdal. The office is open Sunday to Thursday from 8.30 am to 12.30 pm and 4 to 6 pm, Friday from 8.30 am to noon, closed Saturday. There are branches in Afridar and near the bus station in the civic centre.

Byzantine Church & Mosaic Floor
These 5th to 6th century Byzantine church ruins were uncovered in Ashkelon's newest neighbourhood, residential Shkunat Barnea, along with a mosaic floor of the same period. The church is within walking distance of central Afridar. You can also take local bus No 5 from either the bus station or Zefania Square. Ask to be let off at Yerushalayim St and walk half a block to Zui Segal St. Bus No 4 stops one block further south on the corner of Yerushalayim and Bar Kochba Sts.

Afridar
Largely residential and very suburban in appearance, Afridar is nevertheless Ashkelon's modern centre. The focus is **Zefania Square**, a small well-manicured green, fringed by some pleasant cafes and a few shops and banks. Across the road from the green, beside the tourist information office, is the **antiquities courtyard**, which contains two old Roman sarcophagi. It's open Sunday to Friday from 9 am to 2 pm, closed Saturday; admission is free.

To get to central Afridar from the bus station take bus No 4 or 5, or it's a 20 minute walk north along HaNassi Ave.

Migdal
During its formative years, the district of Migdal was inhabited by Arabs, brought here by the Turks to work on Lady Hester Stanhope's excavations. In the wake of the 1948 War, most of them were later forced to flee to the Gaza Strip. Their place has been taken by new Russian immigrants. Most

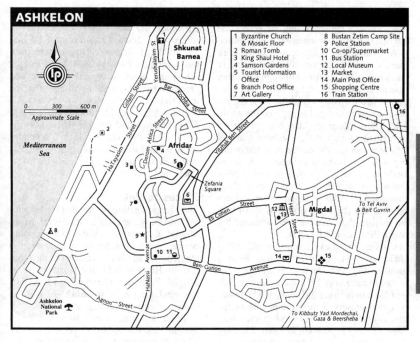

ASHKELON

1 Byzantine Church & Mosaic Floor	8 Bustan Zetim Camp Site
2 Roman Tomb	9 Police Station
3 King Shaul Hotel	10 Co-op/Supermarket
4 Samson Gardens	11 Bus Station
5 Tourist Information Office	12 Local Museum
6 Branch Post Office	13 Market
7 Art Gallery	14 Main Post Office
	15 Shopping Centre
	16 Train Station

TEL AVIV

shop front signs in Migdal are lettered in Cyrillic and at the cafe outside the old mosque vodka is now the preferred drink. Such is the influence of the Russians that we even heard African Jews hailing *dobry dyen* rather than the customary 'shalom'.

Centred on **Herzl St**, Migdal continues to serve as Ashkelon's main shopping quarter, with a fruit and vegetable market on Monday and Wednesday and a produce, clothing and jewellery market on Thursday. Most Israeli Jews, however, prefer to visit the large modern shopping centre on Ben-Gurion Ave rather than trawl Herzl's motley collection of bargain-basement and verge-of-bankruptcy stores.

At the northern end of Herzl St, at the junction with Eli Cohen St, is an attractive old caravanserai and mosque, now converted into shops, galleries and a small **local museum** (☎ 672 7002). Strange as it may seem,

the dust-blown, desolate square in front of the building is the place where Israel's declaration of independence was first made in 1948, an event commemorated in photographs inside the museum. It's open Sunday to Thursday from 9 am to 1 pm and 4 to 6 pm, Friday from 9 am to 1 pm and Saturday from 10 am to 1 pm. Admission is free.

Local bus No 4, 5 or 7 from either the bus station or central Afridar will take you to Migdal, or you could walk.

Ashkelon National Park

Mixing Crusader walls and surf-battered, sandy beaches, Ashkelon National Park (☎ 673 6444) attracts large numbers of Israelis, especially weekends and holidays.

The park covers the site of 4000-year-old Canaanite remains buried under the ruins of other successive cities. Scattered around, and unfortunately unlabelled, the archaeological detritus includes the ruins of two Crusader churches and one Byzantine church as well as an open-air auditorium.

A quadrangle in the centre of the park marked out by Roman columns probably dates to the 2nd century, although it is often associated with Herod the Great. The columns are only partly visible because the excavators were obliged to replace the earth. The original floor level has been preserved in a small section at the southern end and here you can see various parts of the building which have been collected. These include three major **pillar reliefs**: two of Nike the winged goddess of victory on a globe supported by Atlas, and one of the goddess Isis with the child god Horus. Made of Italian marble, they date back to sometime between 200 BC and 100 AD.

Outside the park, heading north along HaTayasim St, is an interesting Roman tomb with places for four bodies; it's believed to have been built for a wealthy Hellenistic family in the 3rd century AD. Inside is a well-preserved fresco depicting Greek mythological scenes. The tomb is open Sunday to Friday from 9 am to 1 pm, Saturday from 10 am to 2 pm. Admission is free; just unbolt the door and go in.

Places to Stay

Camping is the only really cheap way to stay in Ashkelon. *Bustan Zetim Camp Site* (☎ *673 6777*) is run by the national park (20NIS with your own tent) but you can probably pitch a tent elsewhere in the grounds or on the beach if you are discreet. Do not camp on the kibbutz's beach (south of the national park). It is unsafe for women to camp alone.

Renting a private room can be the cheapest deal outside of canvas-dwelling. Contact the tourist information office. Rooms vary in quality, and the prices are around 80 to 130NIS per person per night. Bargain hard and see the room and facilities before agreeing to anything.

Considering the popularity of the place with Israelis, there is surprisingly little choice when it comes to hotels. *Samson*

Gardens (☎ 673 4666, fax 673 9615, 38 HaTamar St) has single/double air-con rooms with attached bathroom for US$63/75, breakfast included. To get there from the bus station, take bus No 4, 5 or 7 and get off at the junction of HaNassi Ave and Derom Africa St; walk north and take the third right.

In the same neighbourhood, there's also *King Shaul Hotel (☎ 673 4124, fax 673 4129, 28 HaRakevet St)* which is a nondescript if comfortable establishment, popular with Jewish families and somewhat overpriced at US$70/85.

Places to Eat

The cheapest eating is provided by the felafel and shwarma stalls on Herzl St in Migdal. Otherwise visit the two shopping centres: one behind the bus station and the other, newer and larger, just east of the junction of Herzl St and Ben-Gurion Ave in Migdal. Both have plenty of fast food outlets, including a *McDonald's*, as well as some more upmarket restaurants.

There are also a few bars and cafes around Zefania Square in central Afridar which become quite lively in the evening and a clutch of cafes and restaurants on HaNassi Ave around the junction with Eli Cohen St.

For picnics, there's a co-op supermarket two blocks west of the bus station. It's open Sunday to Thursday from 8.30 am to 8.30 pm, Friday from 8 am to 2 pm. It's closed Saturday.

Getting There & Away

There are buses running every 20 minutes to Tel Aviv (17NIS, 1¼ hours) and hourly services to Jerusalem (23NIS) and Beersheba (17.50NIS). For bus information call ☎ 675 0221.

Getting Around

You have to rely on the town's bus network to get around. For the beach, take No 13 – but only in July and August. Nos 3 and 9 will take you to within walking distance of the national park. Bus Nos 4, 5 and 7 will take you to Zefania Square, No 5 continues to Shkunat Barnea, and all serve Migdal.

AROUND ASHKELON
Kibbutz Yad Mordechai
Established in 1943 this kibbutz is named after Mordechai Anilewicz, a resistance leader in the Warsaw Ghetto uprising. Over the hill to the left of the kibbutz entrance is another monument to ferocious resistance, in the form of a rather bizarre model of the battle which took place on this site during the 1948 War. The scene shows how the kibbutzniks, outnumbered 15 to one, withstood the assault of the Egyptian Army for five days, allowing precious time for Jewish forces to regroup in Tel Aviv.

There is also a **museum** (☎ 051-205 28) dedicated to Jewish resistance in the Warsaw Ghetto. It's open Sunday to Thursday from 8 am to 4 pm, Friday from 8 am to 2 pm, closed Saturday; admission is 7NIS (students 5NIS).

Bus No 19 runs between Ashkelon and Yad Mordechai but there are only two services a day, one at noon and one at 6 pm; the last return bus from the kibbutz is at 3.10 pm (12.40 pm on Friday).

Kiryat Gat & Beit Guvrin
A rapidly growing industrial town at the heart of the Lakhish region, Kiryat Gat lies about 22km east of Ashkelon. Established in 1954, it is named after the biblical town of Gat which is believed to have stood nearby at Tel Gat, the hill to the north-east. This was another major Philistine city and the birthplace of the stone-prone Goliath. There's nothing here today of interest but the town serves as a hub for visits to some excellent nearby archaeological sites.

Foremost of these are the **Beit Guvrin Caves**, some 4000 hollows and chambers that create a Swiss cheese landscape. Some of the caves are natural, the result of water eroding the soft limestone surface. Others, however, are thought to be the result of quarrying by the Phoenicians, builders of Ashkelon's port between the 7th and 4th centuries BC. During the Byzantine period

the caves were used by monks and hermits and some of the walls are still discernibly marked with crosses. St John the Baptist is said to have been one of the pious graffitists. Sylvester was here, too – Stallone and crew used the caves as a setting in one of the *Rambo* films.

To get to the caves you'll need to take a bus from Kiryat Gat to Kibbutz Beit Guvrin. Start walking back from the kibbutz along the road to Kiryat Gat and after about 300m you'll reach the turn-off for the site beside a large tree. The caves cover an extensive area south of here. After a very short distance the road forks and if you follow it to the right, about 2km along, you'll come to the circular road leading to **Tel Maresha**. Excavations here have uncovered remains from a 3rd century synagogue and various Greek and Crusader artefacts, all of which are now on display at Jerusalem's Rockefeller Museum. Some Byzantine mosaics also found here are now in the Israel Museum, Jerusalem. Among the finds that haven't been carted away are the ruins of the 12th century Crusader **Church of St Anna** (or Sandhanna).

The easiest caves to explore are those west of Tel Maresha – you can see tracks leading from the road. Check each interesting hole in the ground that you see. Some of the caves have elaborate staircases with banisters leading down below ground level. The rows of hundreds of small niches suggest that they were created for raising small domesticated doves used in the worship of Aphrodite by the Sidonian colony between the 3rd and 1st centuries BC.

Because the area covered by the caves is so large (some 1250 acres), during the summer National Parks Authority minibuses carry visitors from one section to another and trained guides are on hand to explain the significance of the different spots. Entry to the caves is currently 17NIS.

Places to Stay *Gal'on Guesthouse* (☎ 07-687 2410, fax 687 2677, email galon@ kibbutz.co.il) is run by Kibbutz Gal'on, on the fringes of the Beit Guvrin Caves. The modern air-con guest cottages here cost from US$101 to US$147 for a double.

Getting There & Away Getting to the site is difficult unless you have a car as public transport is limited. Bus No 11 runs twice a day from Kiryat Gat to the kibbutz, at 8 am and 5 pm, with return journeys at 8.25 am and 12.30 pm. Kiryat Gat is well served by buses from both Tel Aviv and Jerusalem and it should be possible to get an early enough bus from either city to connect with the 8 am service to Kibbutz Beit Guvrin. Alternatively, SPNI Tours do a one-day tour of Beit Guvrin from Jerusalem for US$59.

NETANYA   נתניה
Pop: 149,400   ☎ Area Code: 09
A perceived resemblance to the Riviera has made Netanya, 35km north of Tel Aviv, a big favourite with immigrant Jews from France. As a result the lively pedestrianised main street is lined with patisseries and the local Steimatzky carries prominent displays of *Le Monde* and *Paris-Match*. Away from the seafront and its generous sweeps of soft sandy beaches, Netanya is also a major industrial centre specialising in diamonds, citrus packing and beer making.

Named after Nathan Strauss, an American philanthropist, Netanya was established in 1929 as a citrus growing centre, soon developing as a holiday resort. In the early 1940s the British used it as a convalescent centre for the Allied armed forces. Now aimed at an older clientele, there are limited facilities for budget travellers, but those who choose to stay can enjoy a great climate, lovely surroundings and free entertainment almost every day during the summer.

Orientation
Though quite a large place, Netanya is easy to get to know. The main axis is east-west Herzl St, coming off the main Tel Aviv-Haifa highway and running straight through the centre of town to the seafront Ha'Atzmaut Square (Independence Square). The westernmost, pedestrianised end of Herzl St (the *midrahov*) is the happening part of

town, where most of the shops, cafes and restaurants are found. The bus station is about 1km east of here, at the junction of Herzl St and Binyamin/Weizmann Blvd, the town's main north-south axis.

Information
Tourist Office The local tourist information office (☎ 882 7286, fax 884 1348) is housed in a small kiosk-like building near the south-western corner of Ha'Atzmaut Square. The staff member encountered by Lonely Planet was not particularly friendly or helpful, but you can help yourself to the brochures, though many are only in Hebrew or French. It's open Sunday to Thursday from 8.00 am to 4 pm, and Friday from 9 am to noon, closed Saturday.

Money There are numerous banks along the seafront end of Herzl St. The Bank Hapoalim, where the midrahov hits Ha'Atzmaut Square, has an ATM that dispenses cash off a credit card as well as a foreign currency exchange ATM accessible 24 hours a day, as does Bank Leumi on the corner of Herzl and Dizengoff Sts.

Post & Communications The main post office is at 59 Herzl St but there are more convenient branches at 2 Herzl St and on Harazv Verner, just south of the midrahov. Opening times are Sunday, Monday, Tuesday and Thursday from 8 am to 12.30 pm and 3.30 to 6 pm, Wednesday from 8.30 am to 1.30 pm, Friday from 8 am to noon, closed Saturday.

For discount telephone calls go to Solan Telecom on the southern side of Ha'Atzmaut Square; it's open 24 hours daily.

Emergency For the police call ☎ 860 4444 or in emergencies call ☎ 100. For first-aid call the Magen David Adom ☎ 660 4444 or in medical emergencies call ☎ 101.

Things to See & Do
You can see diamonds being cut and polished as part of a free guided tour put on to attract potential buyers at the commercial

NETANYA

To The Seasons

Mediterranean Sea

PLACES TO STAY
1 Hotel Orly
2 King Solomon Hotel
3 Park Hotel
4 Hotel Ginot Yam
5 Hotel Maxim
8 Hof Hotel
11 King Koresh Hotel
16 Hotel Goldar
17 Atzmaut Hostel
19 Hotel Jeremy
20 Metropol Grande Hotel
21 Residence Hotel

22 Hotel Palace
23 Hotel Galei HaSharon
24 Hotel Orit

PLACES TO EAT
9 Burger King
10 Pundak HaYam Grill
12 Blondy's
25 Felafel Stalls

OTHER
6 Clifftop Amphitheatre
7 Tourist Information Office

13 Branch Post Office
14 Steimatzky Bookshop
15 Branch Post Office
18 Solan Telecom
26 Sherut Stand
27 Market
28 Bus Station
29 Police Station
30 Ohel Shem Auditorium
31 Main Post Office
32 Shopping Centre

TEL AVIV

0   250   500 m

National Diamond Centre showrooms (☎ 862 4770) at 90 Herzl St or inquire at the tourist information office about **citrus packing house** visits (January to March only). Most people, however, come to Netanya for its 11km stretch of **free beaches** – some of the best in the country. The eight lifeguard stations dotted along the beach are an indication of how strong the currents are. The **Kiryat Sanz Beach** in the north is for religious Jews; there are separate bathing times for men and women.

The municipality arranges beachfront concerts, fireworks displays and other events throughout the summer (check at the tourist information office for detasils). However, if you want to get into something more active, The Ranch (☎ 866 3525) and Cactus Ranch (☎ 865 1239) organise **horse riding** through the surf at a cost of about 75NIS per hour. Alternatively, you could launch yourself off Netanya's beachfront cliffs with **Dvir Paragliding** (☎ 899 0277, 052-546 077) at 17/4 Ussishkin St.

Places to Stay – Budget

Opened in 1995, *Atzmaut Hostel* (☎ *862 1315, fax 882 2562*) occupies a prime position on the southern side of Ha'Atzmaut Square. The rooms are air-con, clean and comfortable but a little on the expensive side at US$10 per person in an eight-bed dorm or US$30 for a private double. There are also lockers (US$3 per day) for use both by guests and nonguests who may wish to leave belongings while visiting the beach.

A similarly pleasant but pricey alternative is *Hotel Orit* (☎ *861 6818, 21 Chen St*), a guesthouse run by friendly Swedish Christians. Singles are 133NIS and doubles are 200NIS per person, breakfast included. It's often full with parties of Scandinavians so book ahead.

Places to Stay – Mid-Range

Netanya has over 30 listed hotels, most of which fall into the middle bracket. The majority of these places are grouped along the seafront on HaMelekh David and Ha-Maapilim Sts to the north of Ha'Atzmaut Square, and Gad Machnes St to the south.

On the northern side of the square itself, among the bustle, is *Hof Hotel* (☎ *862 4422*) with singles/doubles at US$65/75. The intriguingly South-East-Asian-styled *King Koresh Hotel* (☎ *861 3555, fax 861 3444, 6 Harav Kook St*), also benefits or suffers, depending on your disposition, from a lively setting just off the midrahov. Prices here are US$65 to US$90 a single and US$80 to US$120 a double.

North of Ha'Atzmaut Square, the hotels include the efficient *Hotel Maxim* (☎ *862 1062, fax 862 0190, 8 HaMelekh David St*) with singles/doubles at US$69/92 and, further along, *Park Hotel* (☎ *862 3344, fax 862 4029, email parkhotl@netvision.net.il, 7 HaMelekh David St*) with singles/doubles starting at US$65/80, and the cheaper *Hotel Ginot Yam* (☎ *834 1007, fax 861 5722, 9 HaMelekh David St*) with singles/doubles starting at US$60/70 but no seaviews.

Nearby, but with wonderful views over the Mediterranean, *King Solomon Hotel* (☎ *833 8444, fax 861 1397, 18 HaMaapilim*

St) has singles starting at US$58 and doubles at US$71, while next door, *Hotel Orly* (☎ *833 3091, fax 862 5453, 20 HaMaapalim St*) has doubles starting at US$75.

To the south of the square, the Euro-friendly *Hotel Jeremy* (☎*/fax 862 2651, email hojermy@netvision.net.il, 11 Gad Machnes St*) offers singles/doubles starting at US$52/63. Next along, *Metropol Grand Hotel* (☎ *862 4777, fax 861 1556, 17 Gad Maches St*) is somewhat higher class, with singles costing between US$58 and US$86, and doubles between US$69 and US$115.

Hotel Palace (☎ *862 0222, fax 862 0224, 33 Gad Machnes St*) is a small four-storey building and has singles/doubles from US$45/55 but has its view of the sea obstructed by the towering *Residence Hotel* (☎ *862 3777, fax 862 3711, 18 Gad Machnes St*) across the street, where singles are US$51 to US$108, doubles US$60 to US$133.

One block inland from Gad Machnes St, *Hotel Galei HaSharon* (☎ *834 1946, fax 833 8128, 42 Ussishkin St*) isn't a bad option with doubles around the US$35 to US$85 mark. Right on the corner of Ha'Atzmaut Square is *Hotel Goldar* (☎ *833 8188, fax 862 0680, 1 Issishkin St*), one of Netanya's better mid-range hotels, with singles kicking in at US$58 in low season and doubles at US$127 in high season.

Places to Stay – Top End

The Seasons (☎ *860 1555, fax 862 3022, email seasons@netmedia.co.il, Nice Blvd*) is a pretty decent hotel, but quite a distance from the centre. Singles start at US$94 and can reach a published US$328 in high season. Doubles start at US$131 in low season and reach a pricey US$424 in high season.

Places to Eat

The cheapest eating options are the *Egged self-service restaurant* at the bus station and the numerous *felafel stalls* that line nearby Sha'ar HaGay St.

Some of the cafes and restaurants on the midrahov have reasonably priced menus. *Blondy's* has various pasta dishes priced at under 20NIS, served in very generous portions and accompanied by complimentary garlic bread.

Pundak HaYam Grill (*1 Harav Kook St*), off the midrahov, specialises in oriental cuisine, with humous, tahina, grilled meats and offal; a full meal here will come to about 25 to 30NIS. For something more familiar, there's a ***Burger King*** on the northern side of Ha'Atzmaut Square where most of the items are under 10NIS. It's open daily from 11 am to midnight.

Entertainment

Netanya is proud of its reputation for providing visitors with a wide program of organised events, although most of it is geared towards older tourists – bingo, bridge, chess and lawn bowls, for example.

During the summer months in particular, the range of activities available is varied and the crowds of visitors obviously appreciate it. The Netanya Orchestra plays free concerts each Tuesday evening in Ha'Atzmaut Square and there is also free Israeli folk dancing in the square on Saturday evening. Also check out what's going on at the ***Ohel Shem Auditorium*** – the city's theatre and arts complex – over on David Raziel St.

Getting There & Away

Bus There are buses about every 15 minutes travelling to and from Tel Aviv (10NIS, 30 minutes) and services to Haifa (17NIS, one hour) and Jerusalem about every 30 minutes. To reach Caesarea, Meggido, Afula, Nazareth or Tiberias, take a bus from Netanya to Hadera and change there. For bus information call ☎ 860 6202.

Train The commuter-filled Haifa to Tel Aviv services stop at Netanya. The station is about 2.5km east of Ha'Atzmaut Square; follow Herzl St and cross over the main Tel Aviv-Haifa highway.

Rental Car Check out Herzl St down around Ha'Atzmaut Square for car rental places.

Hertz	☎ 09-882 8890
Reliable	☎ 09-862 9042
Sa-Gal	☎ 09-832 1390
Traffic	☎ 09-861 0454

Sherut (Service Taxi) Services operate from just north of Zion Square to Tel Aviv and Haifa.

TEL AVIV

Haifa & the North Coast

HAIFA

חיפה   حيفا

Pop: 262,600   ☎ Area Code: 04

It is often said that in Jerusalem they pray, in Tel Aviv they dance, in Haifa they work. There's more than an element of truth in all this. While Jerusalem is swathed in historical mystique and Tel Aviv buzzes with unbounded credit-card hedonism, Haifa, Israel's third-largest city, contents itself with being the cornerstone of the country's technological industry. For the visitor, this translates into attractions like tours of a giant harbourside grain silo.

Clinging to the wooded slopes of Mt Carmel, however, Haifa is not an unattractive place. The upper sections of the city include some breezy residential areas and promenades with superb panoramic views north along the coastline. Halfway down the mountain, the gardens of the golden-domed Baha'i Shrine of the Bab are one of the most beautiful places in Israel. In addition, there are quite a few destinations nearby that are worth a brief visit and, as the regional transport hub, Haifa makes a convenient base for some good day trips.

History

The city's name first appeared in 3rd century Talmudic literature and, although its origin remains obscure, it has been suggested that 'Haifa' is related to the Hebrew words *hof yafe*, which mean 'beautiful coast'. The Crusaders called the city Caife, Cayfe and sometimes Caiphas, which suggests alternatively that Haifa may have been named after Caiaphas, the high priest of Jerusalem at the time of Jesus, and a native of the coastal town.

Haifa was an important Arab town during the Mid-range Ages, but early in the 12th century it was destroyed in battles with the Crusaders. Nearby Akko superseded the town in importance, and at the time of the Ottoman conquest of Palestine, Haifa was an insignificant village.

HIGHLIGHTS

- **Baha'i Shrine of the Bab** – the spectacular building which dominates the cityscape of Haifa

- **Old Akko** – the timeless, workaday Arab town with its stunning subterranean Crusader city

- **Rosh HaNikra** – the beautiful sea caves reached by an almost vertical cable car, right next to the Lebanese border

- **Megiddo (Armageddon)** – the historic site with profound significance for doom-watchers

- **Dor** – a beautiful hidden resort with sandy beaches, safe swimming and scuba diving

- **Caesarea** – the impressive Herodian ruins accidentally discovered in 1951

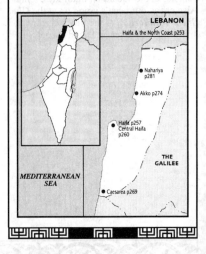

By the early 19th century, Haifa's Jewish community had begun to increase. With the growth of political Zionism the town expanded quite dramatically, although early in the 20th century the population was still only 10,000. What today is the port area was then marshland, and the slopes of Mt Carmel were home only to grazing sheep.

In 1898, Theodor Herzl, the founder of political Zionism, visited Haifa and visualised what lay ahead for the fledgling city: 'Huge liners rode at anchor ... a serpentine road led up to Mt Carmel', and 'at the top of the mountain there were thousands of white homes and the mountain itself was crowned with imposing villas'. His predictions have proved amazingly accurate.

Haifa's modern revival truly got under way with the construction of the Hejaz railway between Damascus and Medina in 1905, and the later development of lines to Akko and the south of the country. Land was reclaimed from the sea to create an area of offices and warehouses, and Haifa was rapidly became the country's shipping base, naval centre and oil terminal. Much of this development took place under the rule of the British Mandate – the British were the first to exploit Haifa's naturally sheltered position as a harbour, bucking the ancient trend of favouring Caesarea and Akko.

As the country's major new port, Haifa was the first sight of the 'Promised Land' for shiploads of arriving Jewish immigrants. Prior to the British withdrawal from Palestine, Haifa became a Jewish stronghold and it was the first major area to be secured by the newly declared State of Israel in 1948. The city earned a reputation for liberalism which, to a certain extent, it still maintains. The mostly secular Jewish community is under considerably less pressure to follow religious laws than elsewhere and it also enjoys a better than average relationship with the local Arab population, who are mainly Christian.

Orientation

Haifa is divided into three main tiers, with the poorest parts of town at the bottom of Mt Carmel and the most affluent suburbs at the top. Whether you arrive by bus, train or boat, the first place you will see is the port

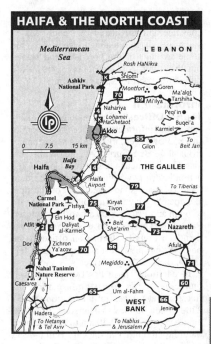

area, also known as Downtown. The two major port area roads are Ha'Atzmaut St and, one block inland, Jaffa Rd. At the north-western end of Jaffa Rd is the central bus station and central train station, and at its other end is Kikar Paris (Paris Square), the lower terminal of the city's subway line (the Carmelit).

About a half-kilometre hike uphill is the Hadar HaCarmel (Glory of the Carmel) area, or Hadar for short. Centred on Herzl St, Hadar is the city's commercial centre, with a heavy concentration of shops, office blocks, restaurants and cafes.

The Carmel district occupies the higher slopes of the city, where exclusive residences benefit from cool breezes and magnificent views. Carmel Central, focused on HaNassi Ave, is a small commercial district with a cluster of bars and eating places all charging fittingly high-altitude prices.

HAIFA & THE NORTH COAST

Many roads in Haifa run parallel to the coastline and are linked by steeply angled stairways. It is feasible to walk between some sections of the port area and Hadar, but the tiring slopes encourage you to use public transport to Carmel Central.

Information

Tourist Offices Haifa's main government-run tourist information office (☎ 853 5606, fax 853 5610, email haifa5@netvision.net.il) is at 48 Ben-Gurion Ave below the Persian Gardens near the German Colony. It's a nondescript building and a bit hard to identify; entry is via a steel door on the side. It's open Sunday to Thursday from 8.00 am to 6 pm and Friday 8.00 am to 1 pm, closed Saturday. There's also a second government-run tourist information office at the port (☎ 864 5692), usually open when ferries and cruise ships arrive.

In addition, Haifa has two less glossy, municipality-run tourist information offices: one at the central bus station (☎ 851 2208), open Sunday to Thursday from 9.30 am to 5 pm, Friday 9.30 am to 2 pm, closed Saturday; the other in the City Hall (☎ 835 6200) at 14 Hassan Shukri St, open Sunday to Friday from 8 am to 1 pm.

There's also a prerecorded, English line called 'What's On' ☎ 837 4253.

Money There are several banks on Ha'Atzmaut St in the port area and on and around HaNevi'im St in Hadar. All banks are closed on Saturday and Monday, and on Wednesday and Friday afternoons. If you are caught short of shekels out of banking hours, Haifa's port area is a popular haunt for black marketeers. While they offer a better rate than the banks, they take cash only and there's a definite risk of being ripped off.

The American Express office (☎ 864 2266, fax 864 2267) is situated in the port area at Meditrad Ltd, 2 Khayat Square (Kikar Khayat), but it won't cash travellers cheques, only sell them. The entrance is in the alleyway near the Steimatzky bookshop off Ha'Atzmaut St. The office is open Sunday to Thursday from 8.30 am to 5 pm, Friday 8.30 am to 1 pm and closed Saturday.

Post & Communications The main post office, poste restante and international telephones are at 19 HaPalyam Ave in the port area, 300m east of Kikar Paris. There's a more central branch office in Hadar on the corner of HaNevi'im and Shabtai Levi Sts, and there are also post offices at the central bus station, at 7 Wedgewood St in Carmel Central, at 27 Ben-Gurion Ave, and two more in Hadar. Post offices are usually open Sunday to Thursday from 8 am to 12.30 pm and 3.30 to 6 pm; Friday 8 am to 12.30 pm, closed Saturday and Wednesday afternoons.

Call ☎ 177 to reach an international operator, or ☎ 177 100 2727 to reach an AT&T operator, or ☎ 177 102 2727 to reach a SPRINT operator if you have call home arrangements with your phone company.

Travel Agencies ISSTA and ISIC (☎ 866 9139, 867 0222) are at 2 Balfour St in Hadar. They're open Sunday to Thursday from 9 am to 6 pm, Friday 8.30 am to 1 pm and closed Saturday.

Bookshops Steimatzky has bookshops in the central bus station arcade, at 82 Ha'Atzmaut St in the port area, on the lower floor of the HaNevi'im Tower shopping mall, at 16 Herzl St and at 126 HaNassi Ave in Carmel Central.

There are also several good, if a little pricey, secondhand bookshops in Hadar. Beverly's Books on the upper floor at 18 Herzl St and the Book Exchange (go through to the back) at 31 HeHalutz St. Both have a good selection of new and used English-language fiction. Around the corner from the Book Exchange, another store simply called Books (at 13 Shapira St) is less Anglocentric, with shelves of French and German titles. Books is open Sunday and Tuesday to Friday from 9.30 am to 1 pm, and Monday 9.30 am to 6 pm.

French readers also have their own bookshop in the Alcheh Librairie Française at 34 Nordau St.

Emergency The central police station is at 28 Jaffa Rd in the port area (emergency ☎ 100). First aid is available at the Haifa Medical Centre (☎ 830 5222) at 15 Horev St in Carmel Central or through the Magen David Adom (☎ 851 2233). In an emergency call ☎ 101.

Baha'i Shrine of the Bab & Carmel Central

Amid the beautifully manicured and dizzily sloped **Persian Gardens**, Haifa's most impressive attraction is the gold-domed **Shrine of the Bab**. This is one of the two main spiritual centres of the Baha'i faith, an independent religion which claims some four million followers worldwide. The faith set out by Baha'u'llah (see Bahje House in the Around Akko section) was heralded in the prophecies and teachings of Mirza Ali Mohammed, a Shi'ite Muslim, known as the Bab (Gateway). After he was executed in Persia in 1844 for heretical preaching, his remains were brought to Haifa. His shrine, which was completed in 1953, combines the style and proportions of European architecture with designs inspired by the Orient.

To get to the shrine take bus No 22 from the central bus station; No 23, 25 or 26 from HaNevi'im or Herzl Sts (in Hadar) also stop outside. The shrine is open daily from 9 am to noon. Admission is free but remove your shoes before entering and do not wear tops showing your arms and shoulders, or shorts. The gardens remain open until 5 pm.

Higher up the hill, behind the shrine, stands the **Universal House of Justice**, an impressive, classically styled pseudo-temple that also belongs to the Baha'i but is closed to the public.

Continuing up HaZiyonut Blvd, just 200m beyond the Baha'i Shrine of the Bab is the **Sculpture Garden** (Gan HaPesalim), a small park peopled with bronze sculptures by Ursula Malbin.

As a means perhaps of off-setting its blue-collar worker image, Haifa has always been keen to encourage artists to settle within the city. Mane Katz, an influential member of the group of Jewish Expressionists based in Paris earlier this century, was given free, quality accommodation in Carmel in return for the bequest of his works to the city. Perched precariously on the upper slopes of Carmel, the house where he spent the last years of his life is now the **Mane Katz Museum** (☎ 838 3482), containing some of his paintings and collected *objets d'art*. It's at 89 Ye'fe Nof St and is open Sunday to Thursday from 10 am to 1 pm and 4 to 6 pm, Saturday 10 am to 1 pm, closed Friday. Admission is free except when there is a visiting exhibition.

On the crest of Carmel, across from the upper Carmelit subway station is **Gan Ha'em** (Mother's Park), a cool swathe of greenery with an arcade of shops and cafes, and an amphitheatre which hosts summer evening concerts. The northern area of the park is given over to an extremely attractive small **zoo**, within the grounds of which is also the **M Stekelis Museum of Prehistory**, the **Biological Museum** and the **Natural History Museum**. The zoo and museums are open Sunday to Thursday from 8 am to 3 pm, Friday 8 am to 1 pm, and Saturday and holidays 10 am to 2 pm. Admission to the zoo is 13NIS (10NIS for students and children) and includes entry to the museums. Bus No 21, 28 or 37 will take you to the zoo.

Haifa Museum & Hadar

The Haifa Museum (☎ 852 3255, 26 Shabtai Levi St) is ostensibly three museums in one – ancient art, modern art, and music and ethnology – however, the combined displays would hardly fill a telephone kiosk and there's more bare wall here than in China. Of the scant items of interest are some floor mosaics from Roman Caesarea and Tel Shikmona, the original ancient site of Haifa. The museum is open Sunday, Monday, Wednesday and Thursday from 10 am to 4 pm, Tuesday 4 to 7 pm, Friday and holidays 10 am to 1 pm, and Saturday 10 am to 2 pm. Admission is 20NIS (students 15NIS), which also gets you entrance to the National Maritime Museum.

The work of contemporary Israeli artists are exhibited at the **Chagall Artists' House**

(☎ 852 2355) at 24 HaZiyonut Blvd on the corner of Herzlia St. The house is open Sunday to Thursday from 9 am to 1 pm and 4 to 7 pm, Saturday 10 am to 1 pm, closed Friday. Admission is free. Further along HaZiyonut Blvd, on the corner of HaGefen St, is the **Beit HaGefen Arab-Jewish Centre** (☎ 852 5252), which sponsors joint Arab-Jewish social activities, and could be worth a visit – check to see if there are any social events or lectures during your stay.

Travelling east, HaGefen St undergoes a change of name to Shabtai Levi and then to Herzl, at which point it becomes the main thoroughfare of Hadar, the city's original residential district, now a little worse for wear. Pedestrianised **Nordau St** has become a favoured haunt of the city's Russian immigrant community, so much so that it now bears an uncanny resemblance to Moscow's Arbat.

An exception to Hadar's shabbiness is the elegant 1920s concoction of European Orientalism that is the **National Museum of Science** (☎ 862 8111). Sometimes referred to as the Technodea, the museum specialises in interactive exhibits, of which it has more than 200, and it's a great place to visit with children. The museum is open Monday, Wednesday and Thursday (and Sunday in July/August only) from 9 am to 5 pm, Friday 9 am to 1 pm and Saturday 10 am to 2 pm. Admission is 22NIS (students 17NIS). Walk uphill on Balfour St from Herzl St and it's on the right, opposite No 15.

Wadi Nisnas & the Port Area

A maze of twisting streets between west Hadar and the port, Wadi Nisnas is Haifa's small central Arab quarter. The sandy block architecture, heavily laden donkey carts and smells of cumin and cardamom firmly place Haifa back in the Middle East. There is nothing specific to see – no mosques even, as the Arab community here is predominantly Christian – but it's a pleasant area to stroll in.

For mosques, head down to Kikar Paris and then 100m east to the dilapidated **Al-Kebir Mosque** (Great Mosque), which has a curiously un-Islamic minaret resembling

nothing so much as a provincial English town clocktower. A short distance away is the better maintained, typically Ottoman **Esteklayl Mosque** (Independence Mosque), still in use for worship.

Housed in the old Haifa East train station, the **Railway Museum** (☎ 856 4293) features a collection of stamps, photographs, tickets, timetables and rolling stock. Old timetables remind you that you could at one time travel from here by train south to Cairo or north to Beirut or Damascus. The museum is only open Sunday, Tuesday and Thursday from 9 am to noon; admission is 8NIS (students 6NIS). To get there follow HaPalyam Ave past the mosque — the museum is a few minutes walk further, on the left.

The port area, which is basically the streets which are immediately either side of Ha'Atzmaut St, is not particularly interesting, although the Kikar Paris end of Jaffa Rd with its market, bakeries and cafes is lively and worth some exploration.

The main landmark here is perhaps not quite what most people come to Israel to see, but the **Dagon grain silo** (☎ 866 4221) might be worth a visit. The distinctive fortress-like construction on Ha'Atzmaut St dominates the skyline of lower Haifa and is the country's tallest industrial building. There's a **museum** within the plant where you can take a free guided tour to learn something about the other oldest profession: the cultivation, handling, storing and distribution of grain. Tours are at 10.30 am Sunday to Friday, and the museum closes for the day once the tour is over. It's closed Saturday.

Maritime Museums

A kilometre west of the central bus station, at the junction of HaHaganah Ave and Allenby Rd, are a couple of museums as well as one of Israel's holiest sites.

Don't be put off by the unappealing name, the **Clandestine Immigration & Navy Museum** (☎ 853 6249) is actually quite fascinating. It deals with the successes and failures of the Zionists' illegal attempts to infiltrate into British-blockaded Palestine in the 1930s and 40s. The centrepiece of the

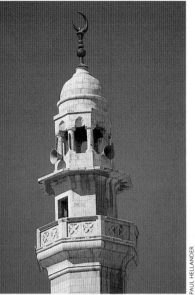

PAUL HELLANDER

TONY WHEELER

GADI FARFOUR

RUSSELL MOUNTFORD

The charming city of Akko features towering stone minarets (top left), the Sinan Pasha Mosque (top right) and Khan al-Umdan (bottom left), the grandest *caravanserai* in town. Haifa is home to the beautiful Baha'i Shrine of the Bab (bottom right).

Marble Corinthean column at Caesarea.

Megiddo has remains dating back to 4000 BC.

One of two large aqueducts along the coastline at the great archaeological site of Caesarea.

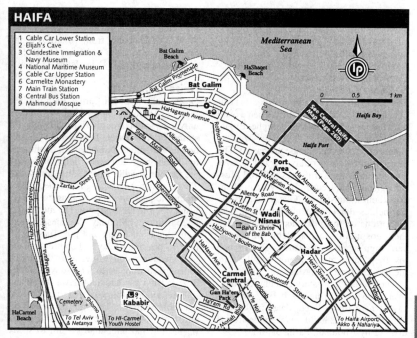

HAIFA

1 Cable Car Lower Station
2 Elijah's Cave
3 Clandestine Immigration & Navy Museum
4 National Maritime Museum
5 Cable Car Upper Station
6 Carmelite Monastery
7 Main Train Station
8 Central Bus Station
9 Mahmoud Mosque

Mediterranean Sea

Bat Galim Beach

HaShaqet Beach

Bat Galim Promenade

Bat Galim

HaHaganah Avenue

Rothschild Ave

Stella Maris Road

Allenby Road

Chernichovsky St

Haifa Bay

See Central Haifa Map (Pg 260)

Haifa Port

Port Area

Ha'Atzmaut Street

HaMeginim Ave

Allenby Road

Hacefen St

Khuri St

HaPalyam Avenue

Wadi Nisnas

HaZiyonut Boulevard

Baha'i Shrine of the Bab

Hadar

HaNassi Ave

Herzl Street

Zarfat Street

Humphrey Avenue

Hubert Avenue

HaHagana

HaMelekh

Shlomo

Cemetery

Kababir

Gan Ha'em Park

Carmel Central

HaYam Rd

Eliezer

Golomb Street

Arlosoroff Street

Ye'fe Nof St

Moriah Blvd

Bat Yehuda St

HaCarmel Beach

To Tel Aviv & Netanya

To Hl-Carmel Youth Hostel

To Haifa Airport, Akko & Nahariya

0   0.5   1 km

museum (quite literally – the building has been constructed around it) is a boat, the *Af-Al-Pi-Chen*, whose hold carried 434 refugees to Palestine in 1947. The museum is open Sunday to Thursday from 9 am to 4 pm, Friday 9 am to 1 pm and is closed Saturday. Admission is 5NIS.

Of less interest is the neighbouring **National Maritime Museum** (☎ 853 6622) at 198 Allenby Rd, which deals with the history of shipping in the Mediterranean area. The collection also contains some underwater archaeological finds. It's open Sunday, Monday, Wednesday and Thursday from 10 am to 4 pm, Tuesday 4 to 7 pm, Friday 10 am to 1 pm and Saturday 10 am to 2 pm. Admission is 8NIS (students 6NIS).

Elijah's Cave

Over the road from the National Maritime Museum, up a narrow string of steps, is a small garden and the hollow known as Elijah's Cave. This is where the prophet Elijah is believed to have hidden from King Ahab and Queen Jezebel after he slew the 450 priests of Ba'al (I Kings 17-19). There is also a Christian tradition that the Holy Family sheltered here on their return from Egypt, hence the alternative Christian name, Cave of the Madonna.

Although prior to 1948 the cave was a mosque dedicated to Khadar (the Green Prophet), Elijah in Muslim guise, these days the rock chamber is usually crammed full of praying Haredim. Outside, the garden is a favourite picnic spot for local Christian Arabs. The cave is open Sunday to Thursday from 8 am to 6 pm, Friday 8 am to 1 pm, with slightly shorter hours in winter. Admission is free.

To reach the cave and the museums you can walk the few blocks from the central bus station, or from town take bus No 5, 26, 43, 44, 45 or 47. The path running by Elijah's Cave leads, after a short, steep ascent, to the Carmelite Monastery.

Carmelite Monastery & Cable Cars

The Carmelites are a Catholic order that originated in the late 12th century when a band of Crusaders, inspired by the prophet Elijah, opted for a hermetic life on the western slopes of Mt Carmel (hence the name). The desired solitude was rarely granted as, over the centuries, the Carmelites suffered Muslim persecution, frequently having to abandon their monasteries. Occasionally, the Carmelites did have a hand in their own misfortune, as in 1799 when they extended their hospitality to Napoleon during his campaign against the Turks. The French lost their battle for the region and the Carmelites lost their monastery.

The present monastery and church, built over what the Carmelites believe to be a cave where Elijah lived, dates from 1836 after the previous buildings were destroyed in 1821 by Abdullah, Pasha of Akko.

It's worth visiting the church to view the beautiful painted ceiling which portrays Elijah and the famous chariot of fire, King David with his harp, the saints of the order, the prophets Isaiah, Ezekiel and David, and the Holy Family with the four evangelists below. A small adjoining **museum** contains ruins of former cloisters dating from Byzantine and Crusader times. The museum is open daily from 8.30 am to 1.30 pm and 3 to 6 pm. Admission is free.

The pyramid in the garden close by the church's entrance is the **tomb of French soldiers** commemorating those who died during Napoleon's campaign.

To get to the monastery take bus No 25 or 26 from Hadar, or No 31 from Carmel Central. There is also a cable car that runs up to the monastery from Bat Galim Promenade below, not far from the cave and museums. While the views from the cabins aren't as good as those from the observation point on Stella Maris Rd up at the top, on a hot day you'd certainly want to skip climbing to the monastery. The cable car operates Sunday to Thursday from 10 am to 8 pm, Friday 9 am to 2 pm and Saturday 10 to 9 pm; a single trip is 14NIS, return is 18NIS.

Haifa University

On the summit of Mt Carmel with the best views of Haifa and far beyond, the modern university campus is dominated by the 25 storey **Eshkol Tower**. Designed by the renowned architect Niemeyer, it features a top-floor observatory and, in the basement, the **Reuben & Edith Hecht Museum** (☎ 825 7773), which houses a good collection of archaeological artefacts relating to Jewish history before the Diaspora. The museum is open Sunday, Monday, Wednesday and Thursday from 10 am to 4 pm, Tuesday 10 am to 7 pm, and Friday and Saturday 10 am to 2 pm. Admission is free, as are the guided tours given Sunday to Thursday at noon, Tuesday at 5 pm, and Saturday at 11.30 am.

Free guided tours of the campus are available Sunday to Thursday between 8 am and 1 pm. On arrival, call ☎ 2093 or 2097 on the internal telephone system to speak with the Public Affairs Department or call ☎ 824 0097 in advance.

To get to the university take bus No 92 from the central bus station, or No 24, 36 or 37 from Herzl St, Hadar.

Beaches & Pools

Haifa's city beaches, awash with debris from a sea coated with port-residue scum, are not very pleasant. The closest to the centre are **HaShaqet Beach**, five minutes walk north of the central bus station or reached on bus No 41 from Hadar. Half a kilometre to the west, taking a detour around the waterfront naval base, is **Bat Galim Beach**. If you really fancy some sun-worshipping in Haifa, you should head for the much more attractive **HaCarmel Beach** on bus No 44 or 45 from Hadar. **Zamir** and **Dado** beaches south of HaCarmel are also quite clean.

The **Maccabi pool** (☎ 838 8341) on Bikurim St, Carmel is heated in winter and admission is around 30NIS (less for students). The pool is open daily, except Saturday, from about 6 am with a break of a couple of hours from 2 pm. It's almost 1km south of the zoo. From Gan Ha'em subway station, walk south down HaNassi Ave, which becomes Bikurim St. Some of the large hotels, such as the Dan Carmel, also open their pools to nonresidents, but the admission fees tend to be exorbitant.

Carmel National Park
Known to locals as Shveytsaria HaK'tana (Little Switzerland), Israel's largest national park covers the scenic southern slopes of Mt Carmel. It is renowned for its fertility; vineyards covered the area in ancient times and the name Carmel is derived from the Hebrew Kerem-El (Vineyard of God). For some pleasant walking or for a picnic, take bus No 92 from the central bus station, Herzl St in Hadar or Carmel Central and just get off when it gets green enough for you.

Organised Tours
The Haifa Tourism Development Association organises a free guided walking tour every Saturday at 10 am. Meet at the signposted observation point on the corner of Sha'ar HaLevenon and Ye'fe Nof Sts (close to the upper Carmelit subway station). The guide leads you down to the Haifa Museum (cover your own admission), taking in most of the sights en route – including the Baha'i Shrine of the Bab, so dress modestly. It's not exactly mind-blowing, but it's a convenient way to get your initial bearings in Haifa.

Egged Tours also buses people around the city on a half-day programme as well as running excursions out to the Druze villages and up to Akko. Its office is at the central bus station (☎ 854 9486).

Places to Stay – Budget
There are not many budget places to choose from and most travellers end up at the friendly *Bethel Hostel (☎ 852 1110, 40 HaGefen St)*. It's quiet, comfortable and clean, and the Christian emphasis of the management is relatively unobtrusive. There are no private rooms (separate male and female dorms; US$12 per night) or a kitchen. However, there's a lounge with tea and coffee-making

---

What to do on Shabbat in Haifa

Haifa municipality's liberal approach to Jewish religious law makes timing a visit here to coincide with Shabbat something of a good idea. Many of the sights stay open and some buses actually run throughout the day, though they have a late starting time of around 9.30 am.

In the city itself there are plenty of Saturday options, several of them free. The Baha'i Shrine of the Bab and Gardens, and the Haifa, Mane Katz, Science and National Maritime museums are all open for at least part of the day (see individual entries). The free Saturday morning guided walking tour takes in a number of these places.

Or take bus No 23 from HaNevi'im St in Hadar up to Carmel Central where Gan Ha'em, the zoo, the museums and the cafes and restaurants are all open. In good weather the beaches are packed – bus No 40 runs from Hadar.

The Arab market and grocers in Wadi Nisnas stay open, as do some of the felafel merchants, the bakeries and the cafes along HaNevi'im and HeHalutz Sts in Hadar.

There are also a couple of options for a Shabbat excursion from Haifa: to Akko, about 40 minutes away, and to the villages of Isfiya and Daliyat al-Karmel. Shabbat is the busiest day of the week for these two Druze villages, with crowds of Israelis coming along to see the locals, their market and nearby Mukhraqa's Carmelite Monastery of St Elijah. There are no buses to the villages on Shabbat, but the sheruts operate from Eliyahu St, between Paris Square and Ha'Atzmaut St in the port area.

CENTRAL HAIFA

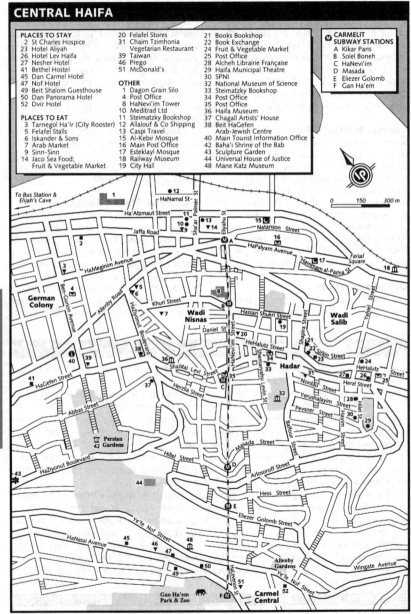

PLACES TO STAY
2 St Charles Hospice
23 Hotel Aliyah
26 Hotel Lev Haifa
27 Nesher Hotel
41 Bethel Hostel
45 Dan Carmel Hotel
47 Nof Hotel
49 Beit Shalom Guesthouse
50 Dan Panorama Hotel
52 Dvir Hotel

PLACES TO EAT
3 Tarnegol Ha'Ir (City Rooster)
5 Felafel Stalls
6 Iskander & Sons
7 Arab Market
9 Sinn-Sinn
14 Jaco Sea Food;
    Fruit & Vegetable Market

20 Felafel Stores
31 Chaim Tzimhonia
    Vegetarian Restaurant
39 Taiwan
46 Prego
51 McDonald's

OTHER
1 Dagon Grain Silo
4 Post Office
8 HaNevi'im Tower
10 Meditrad Ltd
11 Steimatzky Bookshop
12 Allalouf & Co Shipping
13 Caspi Travel
15 Al-Kebir Mosque
16 Main Post Office
17 Esteklayl Mosque
18 Railway Museum
19 City Hall

21 Books Bookshop
22 Book Exchange
24 Fruit & Vegetable Market
25 Post Office
28 Alcheh Librairie Française
29 Haifa Municipal Theatre
30 SPNI
32 National Museum of Science
33 Steimatzky Bookshop
34 Post Office
35 Post Office
36 Haifa Museum
37 Chagall Artists' House
38 Beit HaGefen
    Arab-Jewish Centre
40 Main Tourist Information Office
42 Baha'i Shrine of the Bab
43 Sculpture Garden
44 Universal House of Justice
48 Mane Katz Museum

Ⓜ **CARMELIT
SUBWAY STATIONS**
A Kikar Paris
B Solel Boneh
C HaNevi'im
D Masada
E Eliezer Golomb
F Gan Ha'em

facilities, a snack bar open for breakfast and, on Friday, a free evening meal. Everyone has to be out of the dorms by 9 am and the hostel stays closed until 5 pm (4 pm Friday), but newcomers arriving before then can leave their luggage in a safe room, and the lounge and garden remain open. The strict 11 pm curfew generally doesn't seem to be a problem as few travellers find much to keep them busy in Haifa in the evenings. To get to the hostel from the central bus station, take bus No 22, get off at the first stop on HaGefen St, then walk back past Ben-Gurion Ave and it's on your right; or it's a 15 minute walk up Rothschild Ave.

An often overlooked alternative is the peaceful *St Charles Hospice* (☎ 855 3705, fax 851 4919) at 105 Jaffa Rd in the port area, which is owned by the Latin Patriarchate and run by the Rosary Sisters. It is housed in a beautiful building with large rooms that are simple but comfortably furnished, has a lovely garden, and is kept spotlessly clean by the nuns. Singles/doubles are US$30/50, all including breakfast. The hospice closes at 10 pm.

A third option exists in *HI – Carmel Youth Hostel* (☎ 853 1944, fax 853 2516), but its location at the south-western approach to the city makes it too isolated. Other factors against it are the frequency of muggings in the area after dark, the absence of food shops or eating places nearby and its proximity to a cemetery. Bus No 43 goes right to the hostel from the central bus station about every hour and the slightly more frequent bus No 45 will drop you off on the main road about 20 minutes walk away.

Places to Stay – Mid-Range

Haifa's mid-range hotels are, with a few exceptions, all in the Hadar area and they're a pretty sleazy lot. The least objectionable is *Nesher Hotel* (☎ 862 0644) at 53 Herzl St, which has fairly clean air-con rooms with their own shower, though the toilet is shared. Singles/doubles cost 84/120NIS. Much less agreeable are *Hotel Lev Haifa* (☎ 867 3753, fax 867 3754, 61 Herzl St), beside the Haifa Towers Hotel, with rooms at 140NIS with

shared bathroom and 220NIS with private bathroom; and the Russian-run *Hotel Aliyah* (☎ 862 3918, 35 HeHalutz St), which has doubles at 90NIS. We really don't recommend either of these places and include them only as a last resort.

Up in Carmel Central prices lean towards the high end of mid-range but the quality is considerably better. *Beit Shalom Guesthouse* (☎ 837 7481, fax 837 2443, 110 HaNassi Ave) is a very comfortable German Protestant-run 'evangelical guesthouse', open to all (although, in summer at least, there's a minimum three night stay policy). The guesthouse has good hotel-style facilities, with rooms at US$50/70. You need to book ahead, as it's often full. Also check out *Vered HaCarmel* (☎ 838 9236, 1 Heinrich Heine Square), four blocks south of the Haifa Auditorium. It's in a quiet location and has a pretty garden terrace. Rooms are priced similarly to the Beit Shalom Guesthouse. To get there head along Moriah Blvd and turn right onto HaMayim St, which is a small street leading to the square.

Places to Stay – Top End

All of Haifa's upmarket hotels are in Carmel Central where the views and pleasant surroundings provide compensation for the distance from the city centre. *Dvir Hotel* (☎ 838 9131, fax 838 1068, 124 Ye'fe Nof St) is run by the Dan hotel group's training department, so the service is better than usual. The views are excellent and the surroundings clean and comfortable. Singles/doubles cost from US$62/107.

The twin towers of *Dan Panorama Hotel* (☎ 835 2222, fax 835 2235, email danhtls@ danhotels.co.il, 107 HaNassi Ave) dominate not just HaNassi Ave but the whole Carmel skyline. It has a busy international air about it and is linked to a multilevel shopping mall. Singles cost from US$184 to US$216, and doubles from US$207 to US$239. In stark contrast is the almost funereal *Dan Carmel Hotel* (☎ 830 6211, fax 838 7504, email danhtls@danhotels.co.il, 85-87 HaNassi Ave). Silence costs, and here rooms start at US$223/246.

An alternative to the Dan stranglehold and less of a budget-breaker is the comfortable *Nof Hotel (☎ 835 4311, fax 838 8810, 101 HaNassi Ave)*. Singles cost from US$121 to US$150; doubles from US$144 to US$190.

Places to Eat

Markets & Food Stores For the cheapest fruit and vegetables, shop at the great little market occupying a couple of alleyways between Ha'Atzmaut St and Jaffa Rd next to Kikar Paris. It operates Sunday to Friday. There are a couple of good bakeries here, too. In the Wadi Nisnas area, there is a small Arabic market on St John St, just south of Khuri St near the junction with HaZiyonut Blvd; it's open Monday to Saturday. In Hadar, the market is just north of the junction of HeHalutz and Yehiel Sts.

Felafel, Shwarma & Bakeries After the Baha'i Shrine and gardens, one of Haifa's major attractions must be its street food, which is cheap, delicious and easily available. Head for the HaNevi'im St end of HeHalutz St, where some of the country's best felafel and *shwarma* (lamb, turkey or chicken sliced from a veritcal spit) is sold, alongside bakeries selling sweet pastries, ring doughnuts, sticky buns and other delights.

The other good felafel area, convenient to the Bethel Hostel, is Allenby Rd, east of Ben-Gurion Ave. For the connoisseurs, *Avraham's (☎ 852 5029, 36 Allenby Rd)*, among the felafel stalls, proclaims itself the 'King of Felafel'.

Cafes There are several pleasant *konditereis* (pastry shops and cafes combined) around the Hadar area, many of them on Nordau St. The best coffee we found in town was served at a little *cafe/bar* on HaNevi'im St, across from the post office.

A self-service cafeteria on the 1st floor of *Dan Panorama Centre*, adjacent to the hotel of the same name, provides some of the cheapest eating in Carmel, with an odd selection ranging from burgers (priced from 10NIS) to Chinese stir-fry (20 to 25NIS).

Carmel Central has no shortage of fashionable cafes, but to avoid choking, finish your food before requesting the bill.

Restaurants The Egged self-service restaurant at the *central bus station* provides the usual value for money, and there are several fast-food outlets around the precinct too. Around Kikar Paris, near the market, there are a couple of cheap places that do soups, humous, grilled meats and offal. In the Wadi Nisnas area, *Iskander & Sons (170 HaZiyonut St)* has more of the same, with dishes around the 20 to 25NIS mark, and it's open on Saturday.

Tarnegol Ha'Ir (The City Rooster, ☎ 851 7413, 17 Ben-Gurion Ave) is an excellent chicken restaurant. The menu is in Hebrew, but most of the staff seem to speak English. Besides the variations on chicken (roast, schnitzel, kebab, shashlik, wings, livers etc) there are some interesting side dishes available from a self-service trolley. Prices for entrees are in the 25 to 30NIS range. The place is open 11.30 am to midnight and gets very busy in the evenings. The restaurant's sign is in Hebrew only, but just look for a frontage adorned with big red chickens.

In Hadar, head for 30 Herzl St and *Chaim Tzimhonia Vegetarian Restaurant – Dairy Farm Food* (only the last part of the name is written in English). Here you will find plain but tasty vegetarian dishes served in a fairly busy, though unexciting, atmosphere. You can eat for as little as 17NIS. The restaurant is open Sunday to Thursday from 9 am to 8 pm, Friday 9 am to 1 pm and is closed Saturday

Sinn-Sinn (☎ 867 6161, 28 Jaffa Rd) is a reasonable Chinese restaurant which does a special set meal of appetiser, soup, main dish and rice for 31NIS. It's open daily from noon to 10 pm.

Jaco Sea Food (☎ 862 6639, 12 HaDekalim St) is a famous seafood restaurant and a bit of a Haifa institution. The seedy neighbourhood belies the establishment's culinary excellence. Try the deep fried blue crabs or the sea bass at around 50NIS per serve. It's open Sunday to Thursday from noon to 11 pm and closes earlier on Friday and Saturday.

Another Chinese restaurant popular with locals is *Taiwan* (☎ 853 2082, 59 Ben-Gurion Ave), down from the Baha'i Shrine. It's in a wooden house with a lovely garden. The fare is standard Chinese-Thai, with a pretty decent fried rice in pepper sauce. Prices are around 40NIS per dish, though business lunches are usually better deals.

Up in Carmel Central is *Prego* (☎ 837 3455, 97 HaNassi Ave) having relocated from midtown Hadar. The fare is standard Italian done to a tee. Try the Prego salad – sauteed strips of chicken with fruit in a cream and apple sauce. Count on around 100NIS per person for a meal with wine.

1873 (☎ 853 2211, 102 Jaffa Rd) is Haifa's best restaurant, with a warm and welcoming atmosphere. Housed in an old building dating back to 1873 (hence the name) the fare is classic European. The seafood ravioli and the goose liver have been recommended by gastronomes in the know, though its rich and original desserts get a more than favourable mention too. It's open from Sunday to Thursday from noon to 3 pm and 7.30 pm to 11 pm, with the usual restricted hours on the Shabbat. A decent feed for two will set you back about 350NIS.

Entertainment

Haifa is not renowned for entertainment, but pick up a copy of the free leaflet *Events in the Haifa & Northern Region* from the tourist information office or call ☎ 837 4253 – you might find something going on which appeals to you.

Bars There are plenty of bars in the port area, especially around Sha'ar Palmer St, but this isn't a safe part of town and we don't recommend that you hang around here, especially in the evening.

Most of the city's nightlife goes on up in Carmel, and there's a string of late night/ early morning *terrace bars* along Ye'fe Nof St where moneyed young Haifans come out to preen and be seen. If you have the cash to cover 12NIS a beer, the best places are

those like *Café 29* at 29 Moriah Blvd or *Pundak Hadov* on the corner of Moriah Blvd and HaNassi St.

Other Entertainment There are several cinemas around town screening US and other imports (subtitled not dubbed). The most central cinemas are *Atzmon 1-5* (☎ 867 3003) on HaNevi'im St near the junction with Herzlia St and *Rav-Gat* (☎ 867 4311) in the HaNevi'im Tower. Up in Carmel Central, *Cinematheque* (☎ 838 3424) at 142 HaNassi Ave (part of the Haifa Auditorium) tends towards movie classics and art cinema. For details of what's showing check the *Jerusalem Post*.

Performances at *Haifa Municipal Theatre* (☎ 862 0670), across the park south of the junction of Herzl and Arlosoroff Sts, are unfortunately in Hebrew only. *Haifa Auditorium* (☎ 838 0013), at 142 HaNassi Ave up in Carmel Central, is where the Israel Philharmonic perform, when in town, and other classical concerts and opera are also staged here. *Al-Pasha* (☎ 867 1309), on Hammam al-Pasha St, just south of the main post office on HaPalyam Ave in the port area, regularly features Israeli folk singers and can be a lively spot – dancing on the tables and all that. In Carmel Central, *Rothschild Centre* (☎ 838 2749), next door to the Haifa Auditorium, has folk dancing some evenings.

The Haifa Social Group organises parties and cultural events at the *Gay & Lesbian Community Centre*, Top Floor, 1 Arlosoroff St, in the Hadar district, just off Herzl St.

Getting There & Away

For thousands of ferry and cruise ship passengers, Haifa is the first port of call on a visit to Israel. Most of the city's other visitors arrive from Tel Aviv or Jerusalem, although there are bus services to several other areas. Haifa is also the original home of the country's railway network.

Air Arkia, the Israeli domestic airline, flies in and out of the airport in the industrial zone east of Haifa. Flights connect directly with Eilat (US$94), with further connections to Tel Aviv and Jerusalem. The Arkia city office (☎ 864 3371) is at 80 Ha'Atzmaut St in the port area.

Bus The central bus station, on HaHaganah Ave in the Bat Galim neighbourhood of the port area, has intercity buses arriving and departing on the northern side, and local buses operating from the southern side.

Tel Aviv (22NIS, 1½ hours) is served by three buses: Nos 900 and 901 go direct to Tel Aviv's central bus station while bus No 980 runs to the Arlosoroff terminal in the north-east of the city. Departures on all three routes are around every 20 minutes. Bus No 940 departs for Jerusalem (34NIS, two hours) every hour, with extra services at peak times.

Heading north, bus Nos 271 and 272 (express) go to Nahariya (13.50NIS, 45 to 70 minutes) via Akko, bus Nos 251 and 252 (express) go to Akko (10NIS, 30 to 50 minutes) only. Akko and Nahariya buses also stop on Daniel St, Wadi Nisnas, after departing from the central bus station. Other regular services to include those to Nazareth, Tiberias and Safed.

At the bus station, the 'Department of Losses & Belongings Keepings' is opposite platform 10, and is open Sunday to Thursday from 8 am to 3 pm, Friday 8 am to 1 pm, closed Saturday. The left-luggage office is at the same place – it's open Sunday to Thursday from 8 am to 4.30 pm and Friday 8 am to noon.

For intercity bus information call ☎ 854 9555.

Car If you have hired a car, be prepared for long delays in getting through the bottleneck of Haifa's main roads, particularly along Jaffa Rd. At any time of the day there is a long, slow stream of traffic trying to squeeze into and through the city when entering from either side. If approaching Haifa along main Route 2 from Tel Aviv, consider entering the city via Routes 721 and 672 – turn right onto Route 721 at the Atlit Interchange and turn left onto Route 672 at Damun Junction after 12km. This will bring you into the city via Carmel and is a much more scenic and less congested approach road.

Rental Most of the car rental places are down in the port area on Ha'Atzmaut St or Jaffa Rd.

Avis	☎ 851 3050
Budget	☎ 852 0666
Eldan	☎ 852 0910
Hertz	☎ 852 3239
Reliable	☎ 842 2832
Sa-Gal	☎ 876 3901
Thrifty	☎ 872 5525
Traffic	☎ 862 1330

Sherut (Service Taxi) Amal sheruts (☎ 852 2828) to Tel Aviv leave from 157 Jaffa Rd, next to the central bus station and from HeHalutz St, up from HaNevi'im St, from 6 am to late at night each day. Kavei Ha-Galil (☎ 866 4442) to Akko and Nahariya depart from 16 HaNevi'im St in Hadar and from Kikar Plumer St by the Dagon grain silo in the port area. Fares are the same as by bus.

The trip to Isfiya and Daliyat al-Karmel will cost about 10NIS, and sheruts (☎ 866 4640) depart from the corner of Shemaryahu Levin and Herzl Sts and from Eliyahu St, north of Kikar Paris. There are frequent services except on Friday, when most shops and businesses in the Druze villages are closed.

The sherut to Nazareth also departs from Eliyahu St and costs around 19NIS. Departures are not as frequent as those to Tel Aviv, Akko and the Druze villages.

Train Haifa has three train stations: from west to east, Bat Galim (sometimes labelled on maps as central train station), Central (sometimes given as Kikar Plumer Station) and Mizrah (or East Haifa). Of the three, Bat Galim is the one to use. It's adjacent to the central bus station and reached through an underground passage next to bus platform 34. Timetables are given in English for the hourly trains south, via Netanya, to

Tel Aviv (19.50NIS) and north, via Akko, to Nahariya (11NIS).

For train information call ☎ 856 4564.

Ferry For trips to Athens, Crete and Cyprus, try Caspi Travel (☎ 867 4444, fax 866 1958) at 76 Ha'Atzamaut St, or Allalouf & Co Shipping Ltd (☎ 867 1743, fax 867 0530) at 40 HaNamal St. See the Getting There & Away chapter for full details.

Getting Around
Bus For city bus information call ☎ 854 9131. The main city bus destinations are:

Carmel Central
    No 22 from HaGefen St near the Bethel Hostel, No 24 from the central bus station and Herzl St, Hadar, and No 37, also from Herzl St
Hadar
    Nos 6, 19, 21, 24, 28 and 51 from the central bus station to Herzl St

Carmelit Subway The Carmelit provides an interesting, albeit limited, alternative to the bus service. Opened in 1959, the 1800m funicular subway has just one steeply angled line which serves six stops from Kikar Paris (named in honour of the French, who constructed the subway) in the port area, straight up through Hadar to Carmel Central. From top to bottom, or vice versa, the complete journey takes eight minutes. A single ticket is 4.30NIS or you can get a 10 ride multi-ticket for 38NIS – though if you're only staying in Haifa a couple of days you are unlikely to use the Carmelit so often. The Carmelit runs Sunday to Thursday from 6 am to 10 pm, Friday 6 am to 3 pm and Saturday from half an hour after sundown until 11 pm.

The six stations are: Kikar Paris (lower station, port area), Solel Boneh (bottom end of HaNevi'im St), HaNevi'im (junction with Herzl St, Hadar), Masada (Masada St), Eliezer Golomb (Eliezer Golomb St) and Gan Ha'em (upper station, Carmel Central).

DRUZE VILLAGES
The dusty Druze villages of Isfiya and Daliyat al-Karmel, on the slopes of Mt Carmel, are a popular attraction for both foreigners and Israelis, who come to shop at the high-street bazaar (though the mix of imported Indian clothing and trinkets on offer is unlikely to appeal to the well travelled). In reality, there isn't much to see here and a visit may disappoint you if you're expecting a taste of rustic, rural Israel. However, a visit does provide an opportunity to observe and possibly meet the Druze. Though many Druze men choose to wear western-style clothes, and look no different from Arabs or Oriental Jews, the male elders are instantly recognisable by their thick moustaches, distinctive robes and fez-style hats covered by a turban. Most of the women still wear the traditional long dark dress and white headscarf. For more information on the Druze, see Population & People in the Facts about the Country chapter.

Isfiya עוספייה يوسفيا
It is possible to stay in Isfiya, the nearer of the two Druze villages to Haifa. The *Stella Carmel Hospice* (☎ 04-839 1692), in an idyllic setting on the outskirts of the village, was originally built as an Arab hotel, and provides clean and comfortable accommodation in a quiet atmosphere. Dorm beds are 35NIS (with breakfast), 50NIS (half-board), and 70NIS (full board). Single rooms cost from 70 to 120NIS, doubles from 130 to 180NIS. The sherut from Haifa will drop you off on request.

Daliyat al-Karmel דלית אל-כרמל دالية الكرمل
Pop: 11,800 ☎ Area Code: 04
A few minutes drive from Isfiya, Daliyat al-Karmel is the larger of the two Druze villages and the last stop for buses and sheruts from Haifa. Most people visit for the **market**, a 100m stretch of bazaars along the main street cluttered with brightly coloured shawls and trousers, metalwork and factory-manufactured tabla drums, pottery and paintings. As much of this stuff is imported, prices tend to be unreasonably high.

Following the road due west from the sherut stop, about 800m along is a square little building, whitewashed with a crude red pimple of a dome. This is the **Mausoleum of Abu Ibrahim**, which serves as a local mosque. An inscription beside the door in Arabic warns would-be vandals 'Do not stain the walls with blood' – not a reference to Arab-Israeli tensions but to the Islamic practice of daubing bloody handprints everywhere after slaughtering sheep on feast days. Heads must be covered to enter, but you can glance in from the doorway.

A few minutes further on is **Beit Oliphant** (signposted as Beit Druze), which was the home of the Christian Zionists Sir Lawrence Oliphant and his wife between 1882 and 1887. The Oliphants were among the few non-Druze to have a close relationship with the sect, and did much to help the community. In the garden is a cave where they hid insurgents from the authorities. The house was recently renovated and is now a memorial to the many Druze members of the Israeli Defence Forces (IDF). The house faces a modern sports hall, outside which stands a **tank and artillery piece** with an 18m-long wall mural depicting the 1973 Arab-Israeli War and the signing of the Camp David peace treaty.

Mukhraqa About 4km south of Daliyat al-Karmel is one of the most renowned viewpoints in Israel, the **Carmelite Monastery of St Elijah**, built to commemorate Elijah's showdown with the 450 prophets of Ba'al (I Kings 17-19). Climb to the roof of the monastery to enjoy the great views across the patchwork of fields of the Jezreel Valley.

The monastery is open Monday to Saturday from 8 am to 1.30 pm and 2.30 to 5 pm, and Sunday 8 am to 1.30 pm. Admission is 4NIS. There is no public transport, so you have to walk/hitch from Daliyat al-Karmel. Bear left at the signposted junction or you'll end up miles away and be part of the view you are meant to be admiring.

Getting There & Away

The Druze villages are a half-day trip from Haifa. Bus No 192 runs from Haifa's central bus station, via Herzl St, Sunday to Friday, but only two or three times a day – all departures are in the afternoon. It's much better to take a sherut. These leave continually all day until about 5 pm, take about half as long as the bus and are no more expensive. See under Sherut in the Getting There & Away section in the Haifa chapter for details.

Returning to Haifa, the sheruts become less frequent after about 5 pm, and you run the risk of either a long wait for a stretch-Mercedes to fill up, or of being forced to pay more for a special taxi. The last bus back to Haifa leaves Daliyat al-Karmel at about 3.15 pm. Buses and sheruts pass through Isfiya en route between Haifa and Daliyat al-Karmel.

ATLIT
עתלית

The old Haifa-Hadera coastal road passes Atlit and its **Crusader castle ruins** about 16km south from Haifa. Known in Latin as Castrum Pergrinorum and in French as Château Pèlerin (Pilgrims' Castle), Atlit was built by the Crusaders around 1200 and, in 1291, was the last of their castles to fall to the Arabs. An earthquake in 1837 seriously damaged the structure, and the Turkish authorities moved much of the crumbling masonry to Akko and Jaffa to be used for reconstructing damaged buildings there. British-sponsored archaeologists excavated the site in 1930 and uncovered not only Crusader relics but others from the Persian, Hellenistic and Phoenician periods as well. Today, the castle is off-limits, as it is part of a naval installation.

EIN HOD
עין הוד
☎ Area Code: 04

Inland from Atlit, Ein Hod (Well of Beauty) is an artists' village founded in 1953 by painter Marcel Janco (who, when living in Paris and Zürich, was also one of the founders of the Dadaist movement). The site was designed and developed as a sort of artists' cooperative by painters, sculptors and potters who decided that this would be an ideal setting in which to live and work.

There are various working studios and Israelis come here to learn such skills as ceramics, weaving and drawing. The studios are mainly closed to casual visitors. Works by the colony residents are exhibited at the **Ein Hod Gallery**, open daily from 9.30 am to 5 pm (admission 4NIS); and at the **Janco-Dado Museum** (☎ 984 2350), which also exhibits collages, drawings and paintings by Marcel Janco himself. From the museum's top-floor porch you can appreciate the kind of view that inspired Janco to settle here. The museum is open Saturday to Thursday from 9.30 am to 5 pm and Friday 9.30 am to 4 pm. Admission is 5NIS (students 3NIS).

A blue gate beside the Artists' Cafe marks another museum-gallery, **Beit Gertrude**, dedicated to Gertrude Krause, a co-founding member of the colony. The museum contains more locally produced artwork and hosts occasional concerts, lectures and other cultural events. It's open between September and June on Saturday only, from 11 am to 2 pm. At other times you can inquire at the Ein Hod Gallery and if staff are not busy they will let you in. Admission is free.

Occasional Friday evening concerts are held at the restored **Roman Amphitheatre**, up the road from Beit Gertrude.

Getting There & Away

Bus Nos 202, 222 and 922 go past the Ein Hod junction on the Haifa-Hadera coastal road. Buses are fairly frequent and the trip takes about 20 minutes from Haifa. From the junction, walk up the hill for about 10 minutes, and the village is on the right.

DOR   דור
☎ Area Code: 06
Back on the coast, about 29km south of Haifa, Dor is a modern settlement mainly populated by Greek Jews. It is next to the site of an ancient town and near one of Israel's loveliest and most peaceful stretches of sand, **Tantura Beach**. Just out to sea here are four small, rocky islands which serve as **bird sanctuaries**.

This is actually one of Israel's 'forgotten' resorts. With the burgeoning popularity of Eilat, Dor has become all but forgotten by the mass Israeli travel industry, and for that reason it remains an absolutely delightful

spot to spend a few days or more. The beaches are clean, safe and ideal for children, sheltered as they are by the rocky islets offshore. A diving centre, The Aqua Dora Diving Club (☎ 639 0008, 052-796 695), offers introductory dives for US$40 and full-blown courses for around US$80. It also has equipment for hire.

Atop a small hill at the northern end of the beach are the ancient ruins of **Tel Dor**, a town that probably dates as far back as the 15th century BC. It was mentioned in an ancient Egyptian papyrus and was well known during the reign of King Solomon. You can just about distinguish the ancient harbour and the fortress by the shore. There are also Roman and Hellenistic remains, and the ruins of a 6th century Byzantine church.

The area is ideal for camping, and there are many appealing places to pitch a tent. There is a nearby campsite (40NIS per person) run by the *Dor Holiday Village* (☎ 639 9121, fax 639 2781) which also offers chalets and air-conditioned 'igloos'. There is also a *restaurant* and a small *grocery store* on hand.

For a bit of a splurge, the *Nahsholim Kibbutz Hotel* (☎ 639 9533, fax 639 7614, email nahsholim@kibbutz.co.il) at the northern end of the beach has singles from US$62 to US$104 and doubles from US$84 to US$160 depending on the season. It's right on the beach, has its own *restaurant* and offers various water-based activities to keep you occupied.

To get there, take any of the buses going along the Haifa-Hadera highway and ask the driver to drop you off at Dor.

ZICHRON YA'ACOV   זכרון יעקב
Pop: 8,800   ☎ Area Code: 06
Established in 1882 by Romanian Jews as one of the region's first modern Zionist settlements, these days Zichron Ya'acov (Jacob's Memorial) is more renowned for its role in Israel's wine industry. Visitors are welcome at the **Carmel Winery** (☎ 639 6709), which produces wines both for export and domestic consumption. There is, of course, a tasting room. The winery is open

Sunday to Thursday from 8.30 am to 3.30 pm, Friday 8.30 am to 1.30 pm and closed Saturday; admission is 12NIS, but you will need to call ahead to arrange a guided tour in English.

To get there, from the bus station walk north and turn left down Jabotinsky St, then turn right on HaNadiv St – the winery is signposted at the bottom of the hill.

Not too far away is the **Aaronsohn House Museum** (☎ 639 0120), named after a noted agronomist and botanist who lived in Zichron Ya'acov. He and his family were also leaders of the NILI, a network of agents who spied on the Turks during WWI, and so the museum not only houses his collection of Palestinian plants but also tells the story of NILI. The museum is open Sunday to Thursday from 9.30 am to 1 pm, Friday from 10 am to noon, closed Saturday. Admission is 10NIS. Following Jabotinsky St down from the bus station, a paved pathway leads up to the left – the museum is up here on the right.

In the early days, the town owed its survival to donations from the Baron de Rothschild, who funded the establishment of the vineyards. When the baron and his wife died, they were brought over from France aboard an Israeli warship and honoured with a state funeral before being interred in a family tomb on the outskirts of Zichron Ya'acov.

The **Rothschild family tomb** is surrounded by beautifully landscaped gardens and meadows with views across the Sharon Plain to the bordering mountains. The site is open to visitors Sunday to Thursday from 7 am to 4 pm, Friday to 2 pm and Saturday from 8 am to 4 pm. Admission is free. The tomb and gardens lie off to the left, just before the road approaches the town from the coastal road, in an area called Ramat Ha-Nadiv.

Getting There & Away
Zichron Ya'acov is about 5km south-east of Dor. From Haifa take bus No 202 or 222, from Netanya No 707 or 708, and from Tel Aviv No 872, 876 or 877.

CAESAREA קיסריה
☎ **Area Code: 06**
Caesarea is one of the country's premier archaeological sites and a fast growing coastal resort with development continuing at a pace with the excavations. The Israeli developers will have to go some way, however, to exceed the almost megalomaniacal achievements of the founder of Caesarea, Herod the Great.

History
This place was initially a small Phoenician settlement in the 3rd or 4th century BC. Herod inherited the site and set about building his city in 22 BC. Dedicating it to his patron, the Roman emperor Augustus Caesar, Herod apparently aimed to build the most grandiose city imaginable. For several years, hundreds of builders and divers worked around the clock to complete the project. To create the two lofty breakwaters which stretched for 540m on the southern side and 270m on the north, stones of 230 cubic metres were lowered into the open sea. Towers bearing colossal statues marked the entrance, and there was a massive oil-fuelled lighthouse. On land, the city enjoyed an advanced sewage system as well as a temple dedicated to Caesar, a palace, a theatre and an amphitheatre.

In the pursuit of his desire Herod became increasingly tyrannical and those who questioned, let alone disobeyed, his orders were often executed. Following Herod's death (sighs of relief all round, no doubt), Caesarea became the local Roman capital. Pontius Pilate resided here as prefect from 26 to 36 AD, and his name appears on an inscription found in the ruins of the theatre. The Bible also records (Acts 10) that a Roman centurion serving at the garrison here was the first Gentile to be converted to Christianity, baptised by Peter.

Following the First Revolt (66-70 AD), in which the Jews rose up against – and were crushed by – the Romans (and expelled from Jerusalem), thousands of captives were executed in Caesarea's amphitheatre. Some 65 years later, after the Romans put down the

Bar Kochba Revolt, the amphitheatre again became an arena of cruelty as 10 Jewish sages were tortured to entertain the masses.

The city was seized by the Arabs in 640 AD only to fall into disrepair. In 1101 the Crusaders took Caesarea from the Muslims and discovered in the city a hexagonal, green-glass bowl which they believed to be the Holy Grail, the vessel from which Jesus drank at the Last Supper. It is now kept at the Cathedral of St Lorenzo in Genoa. The Crusaders favoured Akko and Jaffa as their principal ports and therefore only a part of Herod's Caesarea was rehabilitated.

The city was to change hands between Arabs and Crusaders four times until King Louis IX of France captured it in 1251. That same year he added most of the fortifications visible today. They proved totally inadequate under the onslaught of the Mamluk sultan Beybars, who in 1261 broke through the Crusader defences and devastated the city.

The ruins remained deserted and over time were swallowed by shifting wind-blown sands. More than 600 years later, in 1878, groups of refugees from Bosnia (soon to become part of ill-fated Yugoslavia) were installed here by the Turks but driven out again during the 1948 War, making their tenancy relatively short-lived.

It was only with the establishment of Kibbutz Sdot Yam that ancient Caesarea began to re-emerge. Initial discoveries by the kibbutzniks while farming the land led to archaeological digs which continue today.

Orientation & Information

Caesarea's remains are spread along a 3km stretch of the Mediterranean coast, just west of the old Haifa-Hadera coastal road. Most visitors approach from the highway, first seeing the walled Crusader city with its citadel and harbour. Beyond the walls, is Caesarea's oldest structure, Strato's Tower, and 1km beyond that, littered across the beach are the skeletons of the Roman aqueducts.

A short walk south is the amphitheatre and following the road brings you to Kibbutz Sdot Yam. Maintained by the National Parks Authority (☎ 636 1010), everything at

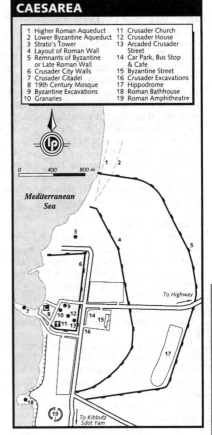

CAESAREA

1	Higher Roman Aqueduct	11	Crusader Church
2	Lower Byzantine Aqueduct	12	Crusader House
3	Strato's Tower	13	Arcaded Crusader
4	Layout of Roman Wall		Street
5	Remnants of Byzantine	14	Car Park, Bus Stop
	or Late Roman Wall		& Cafe
6	Crusader City Walls	15	Byzantine Street
7	Crusader Citadel	16	Crusader Excavations
8	19th Century Mosque	17	Hippodrome
9	Byzantine Excavations	18	Roman Bathhouse
10	Granaries	19	Roman Amphitheatre

Mediterranean Sea

0   400   800 m

To Highway

To Kibbutz Sdot Yam

Caesarea is well signposted and labelled. Entrance to the Roman amphitheatre and the Crusader city is on the same ticket that is sold at kiosks beside the entrance to both sites. Opening hours are Saturday to Thursday from 8 am to 6 pm, Friday to 5 pm, closed Saturday. Admission is 17NIS, free for Green Card holders.

Roman Amphitheatre

Just beyond the ticket kiosk is a replica of the Pontius Pilate inscription, mentioned earlier. The plaque is of enormous historical significance, as it's the only physical evidence that the man who the Bible says ordered the crucifixion of Jesus Christ actually existed. The original is on display at the Israel Museum in Jerusalem.

The original Herodian structure of the amphitheatre has been modified and added to over the centuries. The semicircular platform behind the stage is an addition dating back to the 3rd century, and the great wall with the two towers is part of a 6th century Byzantine fortress built over the ruins. A great deal more reconstruction has gone on in more recent times to transform the amphitheatre into a spectacular venue for concert performances.

Crusader City

Surrounded on three sides by walls and open only to the sea, the Crusader city is entered via the restored 12th century **East Gate**. Once inside you should follow the marked route to the left which takes you along the vaulted street to the remains of a Crusader-era **church**, built over the site of Caesar's temple and destroyed by the Arabs in 1291.

Down by the harbour and easily identifiable is the **mosque** constructed by the Turks for the Bosnian refugees in the late 19th century; beyond it, out on the jetty, the **Crusader Citadel** has been breached and occupied by souvenir stores and an expensive restaurant.

Jewish Quarter & Strato's Tower

Immediately to the north of the Crusader city wall is the Jewish Quarter, with the remains of its 3rd to 5th century synagogue. Also, foundations of houses dating from the Hellenistic period (4th to 2nd century BC) were found at the lowest level. The large wall in the sea below may have been part of the harbour.

Although it may seem logical to continue northwards up the beach to see the Roman aqueducts, it is easier to backtrack via the road past the Roman hippodrome and take the road to the left from there.

Byzantine Street

Among the trees to the east of the Crusader city's entrance, behind the cafe and car park, is an excavated Byzantine street with two large 2nd or 3rd century statues. Some steps lead down to the street where an inscription in the mosaic floor attributes it to Flavius Strategius, a 6th century mayor. The statues originally belonged to temples and were unearthed by the ploughs of local kibbutzniks. The white marble figure is unidentified but the red porphyry one is most probably the Emperor Hadrian holding an orb and sceptre.

Hippodrome & Aqueducts

About 1km east (inland) from the Crusader city, a rectangular ploughed field marks the site of Caesarea's hippodrome. Possibly built by Herod (Caesarea's horse races were apparently world-famous in the 4th century), the racetrack could accommodate 20,000 spectators. The best way to find it is to look for the modern arch by the roadside.

The easiest path to the Roman aqueducts is reached by heading eastwards (inland) from the hippodrome and then taking the next turn left. Although most of it has been buried by sand, the aqueduct nearest to the sea is about 17km long. Built by the Romans in the 2nd century, it carried water from mountain springs to Caesarea. The other, lower aqueduct dates from the 4th or 5th century and runs for about 5km before connecting to an artificial lake to the north.

Beaches

Swimming at the beach near the amphitheatre, or within the walls, costs an outrageous 17NIS. There's a free beach south of the amphitheatre, but take heed of any 'No Bathing' signs – they indicate waters dangerously polluted by the kibbutz's factory. Even in the safe area you should watch out for tar from the oil tankers.

Places to Stay

Accommodation in this area is expensive and while free camping is possible on the beach, theft is common.

Kibbutz Sdot Yam (☎ 636 2211) has comfortable air-con guest apartments with singles/doubles for US$56/82. The kibbutz entrance is immediately south of the Roman amphitheatre. Continue through the kibbutz to *Caesarea Sports Centre* (☎ 636 0879) which has dorm beds from 75 to 100NIS, depending on the time of year.

Dan Caesarea (☎ 626 9111, fax 626 9122, email danhtls@danhotels.co.il) offers five star luxury and service, with regular singles from a hefty US$115 to US$331, and doubles from US$138 to US$125. Facilities include a pool, tennis court, health club, sauna and Israel's only 18 hole golf course.

Getting There & Away

From Haifa, Tel Aviv or Netanya take any bus going along the coastal road to Hadera. You then have two choices. You can get off at Hadera bus station and hope for a reasonable connection with the No 76 bus which goes to Caesarea – the catch being this service only goes six times a day and, if unlucky, you risk a long wait. A taxi from Hadera will cost 40NIS or more. Alternatively, you can jump off the bus at the Caesarea intersection, but that leaves you with a 3.5km walk to the excavations. Neither choice is appealing.

AROUND CAESAREA

The very pleasant **Kibbutz Ma'agan** has a wildlife preserve and a small archaeological museum. The kibbutz *guesthouse* (☎ 06-675 3753, fax 675 3707) offers comfortable rooms with private bathroom for around US$25 per person, and breakfast is provided. Cheaper still is the nearby *SPNI Field Study Centre* (☎ 06-639 5166, fax 639 1618) at **Nahal Tanimin Nature Reserve**. This place is often full but if there is room, you will generally be able to stay for about US$40 per person. Either the kibbutz or the field study centre might prove a better place to stay than Caesarea. Your only problem is getting to and from the site, and hitching may be the only viable option.

BEIT SHE'ARIM   בית שערים

The archaeological site of Beit She'arim, about 19km south-east of Haifa, features a network of burial caves and some ruins from the 2nd century. Don't confuse this place with the extensive ruins of Beit She'an, near the Sea of Galilee. Beit She'arim is nowhere near as impressive and does not justify a major detour, but if you're in the area with time on your hands, it may be worth a visit.

During the 2nd century, Beit She'arim was the meeting place of the Sanhedrin, the Jewish supreme court, headed at the time by Rabbi Yehuda HaNassi, compiler of the Mishnah (Jewish holy law). When he died he was buried here. The Jews traditionally buried their dead on the Mount of Olives, where the Messiah was expected to appear, but after they were expelled from Jerusalem many followed the lead of Rabbi Yehuda HaNassi and chose Beit She'arim as a place of burial.

During the 4th century the town was destroyed by the Romans, presumably in the process of suppressing a Jewish uprising. During the following 600 years the many tombs suffered further destruction and looting, and the catacombs gradually became covered by earth and rock falls until they were eventually forgotten. It was not until 1936 that archaeologists first discovered Beit She'arim's remains, although extensive exploration only truly began after Israel's independence in 1948.

The site today is basically in two parts – the town's remains on the crest of the hill, and the tombs below.

Ancient Synagogue & Basilica

As you are coming down the hill from the Haifa-Nazareth road, the ruins of a 2nd century synagogue are off to the left. Destroyed by the Romans around 350 AD as punishment for unrest, it was probably one of the largest synagogues in the country. A hoard of some 1200 coins dating from the 4th century was found in the two storey building between the synagogue and the road.

About 100m further on are the ruins of a 4th century **olive press**. Olives were stacked between two uprights on the circular stone, and a heavy horizontal beam let into a notch in the wall acted as a lever to press out the oil which flowed from the circular groove into a plastered basin in the rock floor.

Further up the slope from the road are the ruins of a 2nd century basilica; a public meeting place divided by two rows of columns with a raised platform at the end opposite the doors, which opened onto a wide court.

Museum & Catacombs

Now called the Beit She'arim National Park, there are 31 catacombs here and a small museum in an ancient rock-cut reservoir. The catacombs are slightly spooky caves – cool chambers filled with now-empty stone coffins.

The national park is open Saturday to Thursday to 5 pm, Friday from 8 am to 4 pm. Admission is 13NIS (students 10NIS).

Getting There & Away

Take bus No 301 from Haifa to Kiryat Tivon, which is a 30 minute ride. Get off by the King Garden Chinese Restaurant and walk back up the hill to the side road on the left; follow the orange signs downhill.

MEGIDDO   מגידו

Otherwise known as Armageddon (from the Hebrew *Har Megiddo*, meaning Mount of Megiddo), this is the site synonymous with the last great battle on earth (Revelation 16:16). Megiddo is today a very popular attraction for doomsday watchers or just the plain curious.

Although nothing too apocalyptic has happened yet, Megiddo has been the scene of important and bloody battles throughout the ages. Details of the first blood to be spilt at the site come from hieroglyphics on the wall of Karnak Temple in Luxor which describe the battle that Thutmose III fought here in 1468 BC. Megiddo remained a prosperous Egyptian stronghold for at least 100 years, holding out against the Israelites (Judges 1:27) and probably only falling to David. Under his son, Solomon, Megiddo became one of the jewels of the kingdom,

known as the Chariot City – excavations have revealed traces of stables extensive enough to have held thousands of horses.

For a while Megiddo was a strategic stronghold on the Roman Empire's Via Maris trade route, but by the 4th century BC the town had inexplicably become uninhabited. However, its strategic importance remained, and among those armies which fought here were the British in WWI. On being awarded his peerage, General Allenby took the title Lord Allenby of Megiddo. More recently, Jewish and Arab forces fought here during the 1948 War.

Excavations have unearthed the remains of 20 distinct historical periods, from 4000 to 400 BC, but it takes some stretch of the imagination to see in the modern-day site any traces of former grandeur. Help is given through some excellent models in the visitors centre **museum** and by informative signs planted around the site sketching out the relevance of the earthen hummocks and depressions. The most tangible aspect of the excavations is the preserved 9th century BC water system. This consists of a shaft sunk 30m through solid rock down to a 70m tunnel. This hid the city's water source from invading forces, rather like Hezekiah's version in Jerusalem. There is no water to slosh through here, though. Save the tunnel until last as it leads you out of the site, depositing you on a side road some distance away from the visitors centre.

The site is open Saturday to Thursday from 8 am to 5 pm, Friday to 4 pm. Admission is 17NIS, or free to holders of a valid Green Card.

Getting There & Away

The archaeological site is 2km north of Megiddo Junction, which is the well signposted intersection of the Haifa-Jenin road and the Afula-Hadera highway. There are several Haifa-Afula buses passing by daily as well as half-hourly Tiberias to Tel Aviv services – ask the driver to let you off at Megiddo Junction and then walk or hitch a lift up the slight hill. Megiddo can also be reached from Nazareth via Afula.

AKKO (ACRE) עכו עכו

Pop: 45,300 ☎ Area Code: 04

Surpassing even Jerusalem, there is no city in Israel more timeless than Akko. Long considered a relative backwater, it has been passed over for development and investment. While every other place in Israel is busy packaging up its heritage for the tourist buck, Akko soldiers on oblivious, with families, not artists, in its houses; household goods, not souvenirs, in the *souq*; and the fish on the quayside in nets and buckets, not white wine sauce.

Akko is the Acre of the Crusaders, a town of solid stone buildings, surrounded by a muscular sea wall. As the capital and port of the Latinate Kingdom of Palestine, it received ships from Amalfi, Genoa, Pisa and Venice. St Francis of Assisi and Marco Polo were among the guests in the knights' dining halls.

History

Long before it was graced with the royalty of Europe, Akko could already boast a distinguished and colourful history. It received mention in Egyptian sacred texts of the 19th century BC and it's reputedly the place where Hercules, the Rambo of Greek mythology, took refuge to heal his wounds. Another theory on the origins of the town's name suggests that it is derived from the Ancient Greek word *ake*, meaning 'point' (headland).

Always an important port, Alexander the Great established a mint here in 333 BC, which operated for 600 years. After the Greek conqueror's death, Akko was taken by the Egyptian Ptolemites, who called it Ptolemais. In 200 BC they lost it to the Syrian Seleucids, who struggled to keep it until the Romans, led by Pompey, began two centuries of rule.

In 636, Akko fell to the Arabs, who enjoyed a fairly untroubled reign until the coming of the Crusaders. The arrival of the Christian armies heralded the most turbulent period in Akko's history. The Crusaders siezed the town and established it as their principal port and lifeline. They lost it to Saladin (Salah ad-Din) for a time but it was retaken during the Third Crusade by armies under the command of Richard the Lionheart and King Philip of Spain. The town expanded in size and grew in wealth from trade with Europe; however, disputes arose over the line of succession in the Latinate Kingdom and open war erupted between different Crusader factions. Venice and Genoa fought sea battles within sight of the town.

Every now and again the differences had to be settled long enough to repel an attack from the Muslims, but in 1291 the Mamluks appeared with an army that outnumbered the defenders 10-to-one. After a two month siege, during which most of Akko's inhabitants escaped to Cyprus, the town fell. It was pounded to rubble by the Mamluks and remained in ruins for the next 450 years.

The rebirth of Akko was undertaken by an unlikely midwife, an Albanian mercenary, Ahmed Pasha Al-Jazzar, known as 'the Butcher' (*jazzar* means 'butcher' in Arabic) – a nickname which had nothing to do with his skill with meat cutlets. Taking advantage of the weak and corrupt Ottoman administration, Al-Jazzar established a virtually independent fiefdom and bullied the port back into working order. Old Akko, as it exists today, was shaped by the decrees of Al-Jazzar. By 1799 the city had become important enough for Napoleon to attempt its capture, but he was repulsed by Al-Jazzar with some help from the English fleet.

Akko remained in Turkish hands until the British captured Palestine in 1917. They set up their headquarters in Haifa, and Akko's importance dwindled, although its citadel was maintained as the main prison in Palestine. During the 1930s, Akko became a hotbed of Arab hostility towards increased Jewish immigration and the notion of a Zionist state, but Jewish forces captured the town fairly easily in 1948.

Since then the Jews have more or less left Old Akko to the Arabs, preferring to develop their own new town east of Al-Jazzar's walls.

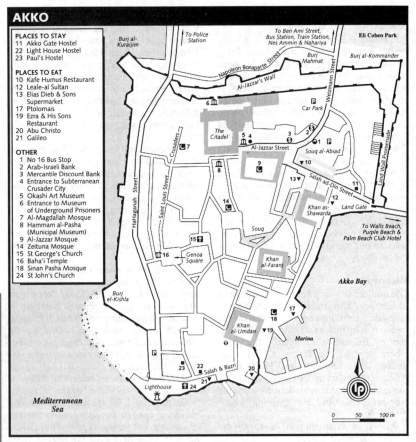

AKKO

PLACES TO STAY
11 Akko Gate Hostel
22 Light House Hostel
23 Paul's Hostel

PLACES TO EAT
10 Kafe Humus Restaurant
12 Leale-al Sultan
13 Elias Dieb & Sons
     Supermarket
17 Ptolomais
19 Ezra & His Sons
     Restaurant
20 Abu Christo
21 Galileo

OTHER
1 No 16 Bus Stop
2 Arab-Israeli Bank
3 Mercantile Discount Bank
4 Entrance to Subterranean
    Crusader City
5 Okashi Art Museum
6 Entrance to Museum
    of Underground Prisoners
7 Al-Magdallah Mosque
8 Hammam al-Pasha
    (Municipal Museum)
9 Al-Jazzar Mosque
14 Zeituna Mosque
15 St George's Church
16 Baha'i Temple
18 Sinan Pasha Mosque
24 St John's Church

Orientation

With all the places of interest firmly enclosed within the walls of Old Akko, you really only need to get to know a small, albeit confusing, area. From the bus station it's a short walk to Old Akko; turn left as you leave the station, walk one block to the traffic lights and turn right onto Ben Ami St. After walking through the pedestrianised shopping precinct (midrahov), turn left onto Weizmann St and you'll see the city walls ahead.

Once in the labyrinth of Old Akko, expect to get lost frequently but never for too long – the place is so small that a few minutes walking will always bring you to some recognisable landmark.

If you're driving a hire car, you can park just inside the main gate of Old Akko in one of two car parks located on either side of the road. Alternatively, you can park close to the lighthouse on the south-western corner of Old Akko. To get there, follow Napoleon Bonaparte St west until you get to HaHaganah St, then turn left and follow the road to the end.

Information

Tourist Office At the time of writing, Akko had no tourist information office. Instead, the ticket office at the subterranean Crusader city (☎ 991 1764) doubles as an information bureau. It sells a good map of Akko and surrounding areas for 5NIS. It's open Saturday to Thursday from 9 am to 6 pm and Friday from 8.30 am to 2.30 pm.

Money Within Old Akko there's a branch of the Mercantile Discount Bank on Al-Jazzar St, opposite the mosque, with an exchange bureau on the 1st floor. It's open Sunday, Tuesday and Thursday from 8.30 am to noon and 4 to 5.30 pm, Monday and Wednesday from 8.30 am to 1 pm and Friday from 8.30 am to noon. There's also a branch of the Arab-Israeli Bank around the corner on Weizmann St, and many banks outside the city walls on Ben Ami St. All keep more or less the same hours. Banks with ATMs can be found in the new city.

Post & Communications The main post office, poste restante and international phones are next door to the municipality building at 11 Ha'Atzmaut St in the new city, four blocks north of Ben Ami St. Opening hours are Monday, Tuesday and Thursday from 8 am to 12.30 pm and 4 to 6 pm, Wednesday and Friday from 8 am to 12.30 pm; it's closed weekends.

There's also a branch post office in Old Akko, in the entrance hall to the subterranean Crusader city. It's open in July and August on Sunday to Thursday from 8 am to 2 pm, Friday from 8 am to noon and closed Saturday; and September to June on Sunday, Tuesday and Thursday from 8 am to 12.30 pm and 3.30 to 6 pm, Monday and Wednesday from 8 am to 1 pm, closed Saturday.

Emergency The police station (☎ 991 0244, emergency ☎ 100) is at 16 HaHaganah St. First aid (☎ 991 2333, emergency ☎ 101) is available in the same building.

Danger & Annoyances The one drawback of Old Akko is that foreign women are frequently subject to an excess of unwanted attention and occasional sexual harassment. Women should definitely not walk around town on their own and both males and females should avoid wandering alone around the lighthouse area at night. Gangs of youths frequent the sea walls and have been known to physically harass tourists.

Walls & Gates

As you approach Old Akko on Weizmann St, you first come to the wall and moat built by Al-Jazzar in 1799 after Napoleon's retreat. Today they serve as a very physical division between the predominantly Arab Old Akko and the sprawl of the modern Jewish town to the north.

Heading west along Al-Jazzar's wall brings you to **Burj al-Kuraijim** (Vineyard Tower), also known as the British Fortress. From here, the 12th century sea wall (refaced in the 18th century by Al-Jazzar with stones scavenged from the Crusader castle at Atlit) runs due south before looping around to the harbour. In the shadow of the sea wall is HaHaganah St, which terminates in a car park beside the lighthouse at the southernmost tip of Old Akko.

Back at the point where Weizmann St breaches Al-Jazzar's wall, some stairs to the east ascends to the **Land Wall Promenade** and the **Burj al-Kommander**, the squat bastion that anchors the north-eastern corner of Old Akko. From the platform atop the tower there are good views across the bay to Haifa. The promenade terminates 200m south at the 12th century **Land Gate**, once the city's only land entrance – the only other way in was via the **Sea Gate** in the harbour, now occupied by the Abu Christo restaurant.

Al-Jazzar Mosque

Perhaps a little bit patchy up close, from a distance the large green dome and slender pencil minaret of the Al-Jazzar Mosque form a beautiful ensemble. The mosque was built in 1781 in typical Ottoman Turkish style with a little local improvisation in

Before entering the Al-Jazzar Mosque, worshippers stop at the ablutions fountain.

parts; the columns in the courtyard, for example, were looted from Roman Caesarea. Around by the base of the minaret, the small twin-domed building contains the sarcophagi of Al-Jazzar and his adopted son and successor, Suleyman.

The mosque stands on the site of a former Crusader cathedral, the cellars of which were put into use by the Turks as cisterns. Renovated some years ago, the vaulted waterfilled chambers are open to the public – bear over to the left as you enter the courtyard.

The mosque is open Saturday to Thursday from 8 am to 12.30 pm and 1.30 to 4 pm, and Friday from 8 to 11 am and 2 to 4 pm. Admission is 2NIS. Guides will often try to force themselves on you as you enter. If you don't want their brief tour, tell them immediately so as to avoid hassles when you leave. There are public toilets inside the complex.

Subterranean Crusader City

Across the street from the mosque is the entrance to the subterranean Crusader city, a haunting series of echoing vaulted halls beneath present-day Akko.

This excavated area was the quarter of the crusading Knights Hospitallers but, like the rest of Acre, it was laid to waste and buried under rubble when the Mamluks breached the walls in 1291. When the city came to be reconstructed some 450 years later it was simpler to start all over again and build on top of the ruins. The street level of the new Old Akko is some 8m above that of Crusader times.

The entrance to the underground city is from a 19th century Turkish hall, but as you descend into the first of the chambers the architecture skips down the ages to medieval Gothic. Beyond a courtyard dominated by the 30m-high citadel walls is an imposing Turkish gate leading through to the **knights' halls**. One of the ceilings here has a cement patch in the centre plugging a tunnel dug in 1947 by Jewish prisoners held in the British prison above. Not knowing what lay beneath in the dark halls, they returned to their cells to plot a more successful mass escape. Today the halls are occasionally used for concerts and the annual Akko Underground Theatre Festival is, aptly enough, staged here.

The signposted route then leads on to the **Grand Meneir**, the centre of the Crusader government, from where a narrow passage leads to the knights' dining hall or **crypt**. As a frequent visitor to Acre, it's highly likely that at some point Marco Polo would have dined in this room. From the crypt, there is a stairway leading to a long and claustrophobic underground passage, (purpose unknown) which surfaces in the rooms and courtyard of the Crusaders' Domus Infirmorum, or **hospital**. The Turks used the area as a post office, so it's also known as Al-Bosta.

Some of the chambers may be closed when you visit, as the digging and excavating process is ongoing. It's believed that there is still a great amount to be opened up, but archaeologists wield their trowels gingerly for fear of collapsing the buildings above. The subterranean Crusader city is open Saturday to Thursday from 8.30 am to 6.30 pm, Friday from 8.30 am to 2.30 pm.

Tickets are 15NIS (students 12NIS) and also cover admission to the Hammam al-Pasha, the entrance of which is directly opposite the exit of the Crusader hospital.

Hammam al-Pasha

You'll hear this place referred to as the Municipal Museum, but that's a little misleading, as the only exhibit is the building itself, the Hammam al-Pasha, the bathhouse of Al-Jazzar. Built in 1780, the baths were in use right up until the 1940s. They've been well preserved with original marble floors, tiled walls and domed ceilings inset with coloured glass. The place is definitely worth a walk through. If you're left with a yearning to actually experience a Pasha-style bath, you might consider a trip to Nablus (see The Gaza Strip & The West Bank chapter) where you'll find the country's only working Turkish baths.

The museum generally has the same operating hours as the subterranean Crusader city, and the same ticket is valid for both.

As you exit the bathhouse, following the alleyway south will bring you into the **souq** and another slice of unadulterated Orient.

Other Museums

Akko Citadel This was built by the Turks in the late 18th century on 13th century Crusader foundations. However, it's rich historical pedigree plays second fiddle to its role as home to the **Museum of Underground Prisoners** (☎ 991 8264), which is dedicated to the Jewish resistance during the British Mandate.

The citadel served for a while as a prison whose inmates included Baha'u'llah, founder of the Baha'i faith, in the late 19th century; and Ze'ev Jabotinsky, a leader of the Jewish underground, in the 1920s. Exhibits include memorials to nine Jewish resistance fighters who were executed here (the gallows room is open to the public) and a model illustrating the successful mass breakout of 1947 – that scene in the movie *Exodus* was filmed here.

The museum is open Sunday to Thursday from 9 am to 5 pm and admission is 5NIS

(students 2NIS). The entrance is from Ha-Haganah St, which is opposite the Burj al-Kuraijim.

Next door to the subterranean Crusader city entrance is the **Okashi Art Museum**, a gallery devoted to the works of Avshalom Okashi (1916-80), one of the most influential Israeli painters and a resident of Akko for the last half of his life. Despite being housed in a fine vaulted hall, the exhibition is unlikely to appeal to anyone who doesn't possess a keen interest in art. The museum is open Sunday to Thursday from 8.30 am to 5 pm, Friday from 8.30 am to 2 pm and Saturday from 9 am to 5 pm. Admission is 5NIS.

Khan al-Umdan & the Harbour

Old Akko has several large *khans* (an inn enclosing a courtyard, used by caravans for accommodation) which once served the camel caravans bringing in grain from the hinterland. The grandest is the **Khan al-Umdan**, down by the harbour. Its name means 'Inn of the Pillars', and it was built by Al-Jazzar in 1785. The pillars that give the khan its name were looted from Caesarea. It's a two storey structure and the ground floor would have housed the animals, while

Sculptured stone head found in Akko.

their merchant owners would have slept upstairs. The courtyard now serves as Akko's unofficial soccer stadium.

Atop the khan is an ugly Ottoman clocktower added in 1906. Just inside the northern entrance to the khan are the stairs up to the gallery level and roof. If you're lucky enough to find the gate at the foot of the stairs unlocked, go up and you should be able to ascend the tower for a great view of the harbour below.

The harbour is still very much in service and if you are around early.enough, you can watch the fishing boats come in and offload the day's catch.

Boat Rides

Throughout the day and until well after sundown, the *Akko Princess* departs regularly from the end of the breakwater and makes a 20 minute cruise around the walls. The boat leaves whenever a sufficient amount of passengers are aboard and the trip costs 13NIS per person.

Some 50m beyond Ezra & His Sons Restaurant another smaller boat is available for tours. It takes about eight people, and the sailing time and cost are negotiable. It's a favourite with wedding parties – look for the Arabic lettered sign depicting a bride and groom.

Beaches

The best bathing spot is **Purple Beach** (Hof Argaman), so named because of the royally favoured dye obtained from the snails that frequented the area in ancient times. With wonderful views of Old Akko on the horizon, the beach is popular with Israelis who happily pay the 10NIS admission.

To reach Purple Beach, either get off the bus from Haifa when you see the Palm Beach Club Hotel and the Argaman Motel, or walk east from Land Gate along Yonatan HaHoshmonai St – it's about a 10 minute walk.

Closer to the Land Gate is the unattractive Walls Beach (Hof HaHomot), popular with windsurfers. You can rent a board here for about 14NIS an hour. There is a changing room near the entrance to the beach.

Places to Stay – Budget

Akko has only three accommodation options in the old town. *Akko Gate Hostel* (☎ 991 0410, fax 981 5530) is a reasonable place and offers more creature comforts than Paul's Hostel. Owner Walied is affable and hospitable and also organises tours to the Golan. The hostel is next to the Land Gate on Salah ad-Din St. Dorm beds are 30NIS while private rooms are 90NIS.

Walied has also taken over the old HI – Youth Hostel and has renamed it *Light House Youth Hostel* (☎ 981 5530, fax 991 1982). This former mansion on the seafront near the lighthouse has been extensively renovated and now offers dorm beds (six to 10 per room) for 25NIS and single/double rooms for 70/100NIS. Breakfast is not included. There is a TV room, you can hire bikes for the day and you can be picked up at the bus station – just phone ahead.

The third option is *Paul's Hostel* (☎ 991 2857), a small family run concern in a converted Arab house near the harbour. The management keeps a low profile and the place has the laid-back feel of a communal house. There are two mixed dorms (beds are 25NIS) and a couple of private 'rooms' for 120NIS, which are essentially dorms with a double bed thrown in. The showers and toilets are clean but spartan and probably would not meet the demands of a full house. However, there's a well maintained kitchen with an ivy-hung courtyard that acts as a common room. All guests are issued with their own locker and a key to get in and out of the house, so there's no curfew. To find the place, go to the souvenir stall with the dark blue Kodak-emblazoned awning by the lighthouse and ask for Jerry, the manager. If you phone ahead, you can have somebody pick you up from the bus station.

Places to Stay – Top End

Outside Old Akko on Purple Beach is *Argaman Motel* (☎ 991 6691, fax 991 6690), a modern complex with free access to the sand and the great view of walled Akko. Singles/doubles start at US$50/70. However, at least one LP reader left here somewhat disgruntled with conditions, so do check your room before committing yourself. The adjacent *Palm Beach Club Hotel* (☎ 981 5815, fax 991 0434) has much better facilities, including a pool, sauna, tennis court and water sports. Singles cost from US$91 to US$116 and doubles from US$120 to US$155.

On the outskirts of Akko, *Nes Ammin* (☎ 982 2522, fax 982 6872) is a Christian-run guesthouse whose aim is to promote an understanding between Christians and Jews. Rooms start at US$50/75. It's off the Akko-Nahariya road about 5km north-east of town.

Places to Eat

There are a few cheap felafel and shwarma places near the junction of Salah ad-Din and Al-Jazzar Sts. One of the better ones is *Kafe Humus Restaurant* (☎ 991 8126) owned and run by Abu Yusuf. This recently expanded restaurant sports an easily spotted English language menu, and does pretty good kebabs, steaks and chicken dishes – all for around 25 to 30NIS.

The romance of a waterfront moonlit meal means that the restaurants around the lighthouse and the harbour are easily the most popular venues for sit-down dining. They're pretty good places if you just want to throw back a few beers, too. Most of these places are open daily from 11 am to about midnight. Fish is the obvious thing to order, but despite the quantities hauled in every morning it's still extremely expensive, clocking in at a minimum of 35NIS on most menus.

The best dishes are served at *Abu Christo* (☎ 991 0065) but then it's also one of the priciest places; expect to pay around 45NIS per person whatever you order. An alternative is *Galileo* (☎ 991 4620, 176/11 Ha-Migdalor St) built into the sea wall. While much of the menu is similarly priced to that at Abu Christo, there are some dishes around the 30 to 35NIS mark; the food is admittedly good and served in very generous portions. Neither restaurant capitalises on their great locations by creating a really cosy, waterside atmosphere, and the omnipresent plastic chairs and harsh lighting really do not do the establishments any justice, geared as they are to groups of packaged tourists.

Ezra & His Sons Restaurant and the nearby *Ptolomais* (☎ 991 6112) on the harbourfront both have a more laid-back and cosy ambience, but 'plastic fantastic' furniture still rules and the food, while reasonably priced (30 to 40NIS for meat dishes, more for fish) and filling, is generally unspectacular.

For an after-dinner smoke and a coffee, seek out *Leale-al Sultan* coffee shop near the Khan as-Shawarda. Here, mainly local youths sip cardamom coffee and suck on a *nargila* (water pipe) in this rather trendy new establishment.

If you've got the use of a kitchen, supplies can be bought at *Elias Dieb & Sons* (no English sign), a great little cave-like supermarket on Salah ad-Din St, opposite the Souq al-Abiad.

Getting There & Away

Bus Nos 252 and 272 connect Akko with Haifa (10NIS, 30 to 50 minutes), as do bus Nos 251 and 271, but these are the slower stopping services. There are departures around every 20 minutes. Bus Nos 270, 271 and 272 (express) run north to Nahariya (7NIS, 15 to 25 minutes). There are also buses about every 30 minutes to and from Safed. For bus information call ☎ 954 9555.

There is also a small train station just north of the bus station on David Remez St. There are 10 departures daily in either direction, with the earliest trains south to Haifa and Tel Aviv departing at 6 am and the last one at 6.50 pm. Nahariya, the last stop northwards, is only a 15 minute ride away. There is an automatic ticket machine on the platform. Purchase your ticket before boarding the train.

Getting Around

There's no need for transport within Old Akko, but rather than walk there you could catch a bus from platform 16, which will drop you off on Weizmann St beside Al-Jazzar's wall.

HAIFA & THE NORTH COAST

AROUND AKKO
Bahje House & the
Baha'i Gardens

This is the holiest site for the Baha'is. It is where Baha'u'llah, a follower of the Bab and the founder of the faith, lived after his release from prison in Akko and where he died in 1892. His tomb is in lovely gardens, similar in style to those in Haifa. You can visit the gardens daily, between 9 am and 5 pm. The shrine, known as Bahje House, contains a small museum and is open Friday to Sunday from 9 am to noon. Admission is free.

The gardens are about a kilometre north of the town centre on the main Akko-Nahariya road. Take bus No 271 and get off at the stop after the main gate to the gardens, which you should see off to the right 10 minutes out of the station. Unless you're a Baha'i, you'll have to use the entrance about 500m up the side road to the north of the main gate.

Turkish Aqueduct

On your right as you go north on the Nahariya road is a long Roman-style aqueduct. Built by Al-Jazzar in about 1780, it supplied Akko with water from the Galilee uplands.

Kibbutz Lohamei HaGhetaot

Just north of the aqueduct, this kibbutz was established in 1949 by former resistance fighters from the ghettoes of Germany, Poland and Lithuania. With models, documents and artefacts, their museum, **The House of the Ghetto Fighters** (Beit Lohamei Ha-Ghetaot, ☎ 06-692 0412), tells the story of the Jewish communities in those countries prior to the Holocaust and of the Jewish resistance movement.

The museum is open Sunday to Thursday from 9 am to 4 pm, Friday from 9 am to 1 pm, and Saturday from 10 am to 5 pm. Admission is free, although donations are requested. Ask the bus driver to let you off; it's a short distance from the main road.

Nahal Shagur
(Nahal Beit Hakerem)

Known by either name, this small river flows through an attractive valley. SPNI has marked out a pleasant and only slightly arduous 12km hike which follows the river bed, and it makes a good day trip from Akko. Note that the walk is not possible when the river is flowing.

The hardest part is negotiating a couple of steep drops which become waterfalls in season. With these in mind, it is inadvisable to go alone in case you twist an ankle or worse. Also, be sure to take plenty of water.

Take bus No 361, which leaves Akko for Gilon about every 30 minutes, and get off at the intersection for Gilon. It's marked by the Spanish-Jewish sign for Nahal Beit Hakerem. Take the steps by the sign down to the river bed and head right (west). For a short hike, take the path to the left to head back to Gilon when you reach the first steep drop. Otherwise, follow the river bed to the path which leads up to the road between Yasur and Alihud. Turn left to hitch back to Akko.

NAHARIYA   נהריה
Pop: 38,100 ☎ Area Code: 04

One of Israel's quietest seaside resorts, Nahariya seems to exist in a perpetual state of Shabbat. It livens up once a year when Jewish honeymooners flood in on the Lag B'Omer holiday in spring, the only day a Jew can marry during the six weeks between the Passover and Shavuot holidays.

Established in 1934 by German Jews escaping Nazism, Nahariya was western Galilee's first Jewish settlement. Following some unsuccessful attempts to establish itself as an agricultural settlement, the town switched to wooing the tourist trade. It enjoyed great popularity for a while until the increasing frequency of rocket and mortar attacks from neighbouring south Lebanon seriously began to detract from the quiet charm of the place. The explosive incursions were brought to a halt by Israel's 1982 invasion of Lebanon and since then the town has been struggling to regain its share of sun-worshippers.

The appeal of Nahariya lies solely in its beaches. There is nothing else. And while the town is close to the grottoes of Rosh Ha-Nikra, the beach and national park at Akhziv,

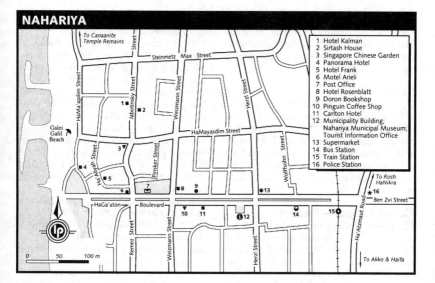

NAHARIYA

To Canaanite Temple Remains

Steinmetz Max Street

HaMa'apilim Street

Jabotinsky Street

Weizmann Street

Herzl Street

Galei Galil Beach

HaMayasdim Street

Pinsker Street

Wolffsohn Street

Ha'Aliyah Street

HaGa'aton Boulevard

Remez Street

Weizmann Street

Herzl Street

Ha'Atzmaut Road

To Rosh HaNikra

Ben Zvi Street

To Akko & Haifa

0   50   100 m

1 Hotel Kalman
2 Sirtash House
3 Singapore Chinese Garden
4 Panorama Hotel
5 Hotel Frank
6 Motel Arieli
7 Post Office
8 Hotel Rosenblatt
9 Doron Bookshop
10 Pinguin Coffee Shop
11 Carlton Hotel
12 Municipality Building;
   Nahariya Municipal Museum;
   Tourist Information Office
13 Supermarket
14 Bus Station
15 Train Station
16 Police Station

the Crusader castle at Montfort, and Peqi'in, it suffers badly from a lack of budget accommodation.

Orientation

A visit to Nahariya, almost the definitive one-street town, probably won't extend beyond HaGa'aton Blvd. At one end is the bus and train station, at the other the beach; and in between are the tourist information office, shops, banks, cafes and restaurants.

Information

Tourist Office The well provisioned and helpful municipal tourist information office (☎ 987 9800) is on the ground floor of the municipality building just west of the bus station on HaGa'aton Blvd. The office has a comprehensive accommodation list and plenty of information on places to visit in the surrounding region. It's open Sunday to Thursday from 8 am to 1 pm and 4 to 7 pm, Friday from 8 am to 1 pm only.

Post & Communications These services are at 40 HaGa'aton Blvd (☎ 992 0180),

three blocks west of the bus station on the opposite side of the street. Opening hours are Sunday, Monday, Wednesday and Thursday from 7.45 am to 12.30 pm and 3.30 to 6 pm, Tuesday from 7.45 am to 2 pm, Friday from 7.45 am to 1 pm, closed Saturday.

Emergency The police station (☎ 992 0344 or in emergencies call ☎ 100) is on Ben Zvi St, which runs north off HaGa'aton Blvd, east of the train station.

Things to See

The **Nahariya Municipal Museum** (☎ 987 9863) is home to a small and uninspiring collection of local archaeological finds, seashells and modern art. It occupies the top three floors of the municipality building. The museum is open Sunday and Wednesday from 10 am to noon and 4 to 6 pm; and Monday, Tuesday, Thursday and Friday from 8 am to noon. Admission is free.

Though most will find it not worth the 20 minute walk from the town centre, there are the 4000-year-old remains of a **Canaanite temple** south along the seafront. Of slightly more interest is a **mosaic floor**, all that remains of a 4th century Byzantine church on Bielefeld St – check with the tourist information office for directions and opening hours.

Beaches
The municipal **Galei Galil Beach** just north of HaGa'aton Blvd has shower and toilet facilities, and charges 15NIS admission. The entrance fee also includes use of the indoor heated swimming pool. It's open from 8 am to 6 pm daily. Otherwise, for free and less crowded beaches simply walk south from HaGa'aton Blvd.

Places to Stay – Budget
The closest Nahariya comes to budget accommodation is **Sirtash House** (☎ 992 2586, 22 Jabotinsky St), which offers clean doubles with air-con and private bathroom from 100 to 130NIS. **Hotel Kalman** (☎ 992 0355, fax 992 6539, 27 Jabotinsky St), while affiliated to HI, has no dorm beds. Private rooms, all with air-con and bathrooms, start at US$30/55 for singles/doubles. **Motel Arieli** (☎ 992 1076, 1 Jabotinsky St), near the corner of HaGa'aton Blvd, has attractive two-person bungalows for 180NIS.

During the summer months it is also possible to rent a room in a private home, and this may be a cheaper option. There are currently about 10 places offering *zimmer* (private room) style accommodation. Prices for these hover around 90NIS per person but can be higher during July and August, or lower depending on your bargaining skills. Look for the signs on Jabotinsky St in particular or ask for the list at the tourist information office.

See also the two or three accommodation options in Akhziv in the Around Nahariya section.

Places to Stay – Top End
In Nahariya, just because a building sports a 2m-high sign reading 'hotel', it does not necessarily mean that it has beds to let. The lack of business has meant that many former hotels are now forced to operate as retirement homes, but they keep the old signs up in the hope of better times.

Of the survivors, the modern **Panorama Hotel** (☎ 992 0555, fax 992 4647, 6 HaMa'apilim St), right across from the beach, has good seaviews, especially from the rooftop terrace. Singles/doubles are 200NIS. One block back, **Hotel Frank** (☎ 992 0278, fax 992 5535, 4 Ha'Aliyah St) is a little drab, but the rooms do have balconies with sea views and guests get to use the hotel's heated open-air pool. Rooms cost from US$75/98. The somewhat cheaper **Hotel Rosenblatt** (☎ 992 3469, fax 992 8121, 59 Weizmann St), has rooms for US$50/69.

Nahariya's plushest accommodation is found at **Carlton Hotel** (☎ 992 2211, fax 982 3771, 23 HaGa'aton Blvd) just west of the municipality building. Modern and attractive with some tasteful interior design and a pool, solarium and jacuzzi, this place is very popular and reservations are recommended. Singles are from US$93 to US$187 and doubles from US$124 to US$251, depending on the season.

Places to Eat
Nahariya suffers from a shortage of decent eating places and, although the cafes and restaurants on HaGa'aton Blvd seem to attract the crowds, the food and service are generally mediocre. An exception is the cheerful **Pinguin Coffee Shop** (☎ 992 8855, 31 HaGa'aton Blvd), which has a good menu of light meals such as pastas and salads costing from 25NIS.

Singapore Chinese Garden (☎ 992 4952, 17 Jabotinsky St), has pleasant decor, good service, excellent food and will charge you about 45 to 55NIS for a full meal, although you could eat for less.

For cheaper eating, shop at the **supermarket** on HaGa'aton Blvd, at the corner of Herzl St. The bus station has an **Egged self-service restaurant**.

Getting There & Away
Bus Nos 270, 271 and 272 (express) operate to Akko (5NIS, 15 to 25 minutes), with the 271 and 272 services running on to Haifa

(13.50NIS, 45 to 70 minutes). Departures are every 20 minutes until 10.30 pm. Change at Haifa for Tel Aviv, Jerusalem, Tiberias and other destinations.

There are 10 departures daily heading southwards from Nahariya's train station to Akko, Haifa, Netanya and Tel Aviv. The first train leaves at 5.53 am and the last one at 6.40 pm.

For a rental car, call:

Avis	☎ 951 1880
Budget	☎ 992 9252
Europcar	☎ 992 1614

AROUND NAHARIYA
Montfort

Montfort is not the most impressive of Israel's Crusader castles, but it is interesting and a visit here involves a pleasant hike. Originally built in 1226 by the French Courtenays, the castle's name was changed from Montfort (Strong Mountain) to Starkenburg (Strong Castle) when they sold it to the Teutonic knights, the Templars and the Hospitallers. They modified the castle, which became their central treasury, archives and Holy Land headquarters, although it had no real strategic value. In 1271 the Muslims, led by the Mamluk sultan Beybars, took the castle after a previous attempt (five years earlier) had failed. The Crusaders retreated to Akko and the castle was razed.

Little remains to be seen today. To the right of the entrance is the governor's residence, with the tower straight ahead. The two vaulted chambers to the right are the basement of the knights' hall; next to them is the chapel. The site is open from Saturday to Thursday from 8 am to 5 pm, and Friday from 8 am to 4 pm; admission costs 5NIS (students 3NIS).

Akhziv

The short stretch of coastline between Nahariya and Rosh HaNikra on the Lebanese border is known as Akhziv. Once one of the towns of the Asher tribe in ancient Israel, it was also a Phoenician port, and Bronze Age remains have been found here.

Akhziv Beach & National Park About 4km north of Nahariya, this national park has a pleasant beach – with changing rooms, sun-shades, showers and snack bar – and costs 11NIS to use.

Just a little further north is an area of well manicured parkland on the site of an 'abandoned' Arab village. You can see traces of a Phoenician port and use the beach. There are changing rooms and a snack bar at the beach but admission is 15NIS (students 10NIS). It's open April to September from Saturday to Thursday from 8 am to 5 pm and Friday to 4 pm; the rest of the year it closes an hour earlier.

Akhzivland In 1952, Eli Avivi settled in an old Arab house by the beach just north of the national park and declared his land to be an independent state, which he called Akhzivland. Since then he has established a museum housing his varied collection of artefacts found nearby. Some of them date from the Phoenician, Roman and Byzantine periods. The museum (☎ 04-823 250) is open daily, April to September from 8 am to 5 pm, and October to March from 8 am to 4 pm. Admission is 10NIS (students 7 NIS).

Avivi also runs a basic *hostel* with dorm beds at 30 to 40NIS. Guests here undoubtedly gain an unassailable advantage in the one-upmanship stakes by getting an Akhzivland stamp in their passports.

Campsite Just up the road from Akhzivland is a *campsite* (☎ 04-825 054) with small, basic two-berth or four-berth cabins for 55NIS per person. If you have your own tent you pay 20NIS per person. There's a supermarket, shower, toilet blocks and a pool.

Yad LeYad In 1946, 14 Haganah soldiers were killed trying to blow up the railway bridges on this stretch of the line in an effort to cut British communication links. A **monument** to them stands by the road.

SPNI The Galil Ma'aravi Field Study Centre (☎ 04-982 3762, fax 982 3015) is a useful stop for anyone interested in exploring this region. Drop by between 8 am and 4.30 pm. Bus Nos 22, 26 and 28 run up here (via Akhzivland) from Nahariya, and it's just a 10 minute ride. The study centre also has *accommodation*, though it's a little pricey at US$40 for a dorm bed.

Rosh HaNikra   ראש הניקרה   رأس الناقورة

Cheek by jowl with the closed Israel-Lebanon border and carved by the sea into the base of tall white cliffs, these caves were enlarged by the British for a railway and by the Israelis to improve access for visitors. They are at their most interesting in bad weather when the sea is wild. Access to the caves and the former railway tunnel is via a steep cable car with equally steep ticket prices, but the ride down is probably worth it.

The caves are explored via a meandering path that leads you to various points where the sea caves can be seen in all their glory – or tempestuousness, if the sea is seething. The path also leads you to the craggy exterior of the cliffs and exits a few hundred metres south of the entry point, leading you back past a guard post of wary-looking IDF soldiers. At the northern end the tunnel leads you into a small theatre, slap-bang on the Lebanese border where you can watch a 20 minute film on the history of this historic railway. In the other direction the tunnel leads out to where the 'Little Train' operates on weekends, taking visitors for a ride along the shoreline (15NIS).

Other than the caves there is a very pleasant and reasonably priced self-service restaurant, and the views from the restaurant back along the coast to Nahariya and Akko are splendid. You can also walk up to the border gate, which sports an optimistic, jazzy-looking yellow and blue sign proclaiming the Israeli-Lebanese border, though only United Nations (UNIFIL) vehicles are currently allowed across the border into the security zone currently occupied by the Israeli army. Photography is technically forbidden, but no one seems to mind as long as you don't point your camera directly at the watchtowers above.

The road up from Nahariya (10km to the south) halts at the observation point/tourist centre (☎ 04-985 7109), where there is car parking and from where you take the cable car. The two cars operate Sunday to Friday from 8.30 am to 4 pm. The 30NIS fare (students 26NIS) is a rip-off but there is no other way down to the caves.

Places to Stay The nearest hostel accommodation is in the hillside town of Shlomi, 6km inland. *HI – Shlomi Hostel (☎ 04-980 8975, fax 980 9163)* is in the hills of the Hanita Forest and is best approached by bus Nos 22 and 23 from Nahariya bus station. From there you may be able to hitch or even walk to Rosh HaNikra.

Getting There & Away Bus Nos 20 and 22 from Nahariya go direct to Rosh HaNikra (5NIS, 15 minutes) but there are only three services a day. Other more frequent services pass the Rosh HaNikra junction, but from there it's a 3km walk to the site.

Peqi'in   פקיעין   بقين

A predominantly Druze village, Peqi'in has also been home to a centuries old Jewish community which, according to tradition, has never been exiled from the Holy Land. In 1936 though, the political situation forced the residents to leave the area and only a small number returned after Israel became independent.

The village is believed to be where Rabbi Shimon Bar Yochai and his son, Eliezer, hid from the Romans in the 2nd century to escape a decree which made it illegal to study the Torah. The legend has it that they stayed in a cave here for 13 years, during which the rabbi compiled the Zohar, the most important book in Jewish mysticism. Outside the cave a freshwater spring and a carob tree miraculously appeared. The two are said to have fed on the fruit from the tree, drunk from the spring and embedded themselves in the sand up to their necks while they spent all their time studying the Torah.

The **cave of Bar Yochai** is now a holy site, and you can see the spring (trickling unattractively through a modern-day pipe into a pool), an ancient synagogue now housing a **museum**, the Jewish community's old cemetery, and an old flour mill and oil presses. The village is a maze of twisting streets and it is hard to find these visually disappointing sites. To save time, stop off at the Druze cafe next to the bus stop by the entrance to the village for a free map, directions and a friendly chat.

Peqi'in's other point of note is its speciality food, *pitta-eem-leben*. This is wafer-thin pitta bread served with a soft, sour white cheese which is mixed with olive oil and marjoram. Try this for about 6NIS at the *Jewish Community Restaurant*, on your left as you arrive from Nahariya. Despite its name, it is owned by Arabs; the old lady has been baking the pitta for over 30 years. Across the street by the bus stop, another *cafe* serves this pitta. It is owned by a friendly Druze man, and his sister does the baking. You can also order humous and very good coffee at both cafes.

Getting There & Away Bus No 44 runs about every hour from Nahariya (13NIS, 45 minutes). Get off at the old village, Peqi'in Atika, not the modern settlement of Peqi'in Hadasha, one stop before.

Beit Jan
Another friendly Druze community, this small village enjoys lovely views of the surrounding countryside and receives much fewer visitors than those villages near Haifa. Take bus No 44 from Nahariya, stay on after Peqi'in, then get off 3km later at the Beit Jan junction. From here the village is a 2.5km walk or hitch.

Getting There & Away From Nahariya take a bus to Goren and ask for the Akhziv National Park. From here you'll see Montfort castle in the distance, about a 1½ hour walk. Another, perhaps more interesting (albeit strenuous) way to get there is by taking the Ma'alot Tarshiha bus from Nahariya, getting off at Mi'ilya, and walking through this large Arab Christian village. After the turn-off for Hilah, a small Jewish village, the road deteriorates into a dirt path. Follow the signs and scale the cliff to reach the castle.

HAIFA & THE NORTH COAST

The Galilee

הגליל

Taken from the Hebrew word *galil* (district), the Galilee, with its rich combination of beautiful scenery and religious heritage, is probably the most popular area of the country, both with Israelis and foreign visitors. This is Israel's lushest region, with green valleys, verdant forests, lots of fertile farmland and, of course, the Sea of Galilee. Serious Bible territory, the Galilee is where Jesus did most of his preaching as well as some fish-multiplying and a spot of water-walking. It's also where Jewish scholars produced the rabbinical texts, the Talmud and the Kabbalah.

NAZARETH נצרת النّاصرة
Pop: 54,100 ☎ Area Code: 06

Believed to be the home of Mary and Joseph and the infant Jesus, Nazareth often fails to match the high expectations of pilgrims and tourists. The important churches are unfortunately overshadowed by the unattractive and rapidly expanding modern town. Still, as home to some of the most important Christian shrines, Nazareth remains the main centre of the Christian mission movement in the Holy Land and is always going to attract a large pilgrim crowd.

In preparation for an anticipated major influx of pilgrims for the new millennium, the Nazareth city council has embarked on a major renovation of the town centre, and particularly of the streets bordering the Basilica of the Annunciation. While this is a welcome move to dress up what was earlier a pretty grotty streetscape, Nazareth will still be hard-pressed to cope with the hordes of expected visitors in what are essentially narrow and congested streets.

All women visiting Nazareth should dress and behave in a manner that will not cause offence (see the Women Travellers section in the Facts for the Visitor chapter).

History
It's thought that Nazareth was home to a Christian community until the 3rd century,

HIGHLIGHTS

- **Sea of Galilee** – for relaxing by, sailing on, cycling around and dining next to

- **Monasteries, churches and tombs** – biblical sites in abundance

- **Nazareth** – lively, vibrant, crowded and a magnet for devout Christians

- **St Peter's fish** – a trout-like speciality found only in the Sea of Galilee and a must for fish lovers

- **Kibbutzim** – some of the best in the whole of Israel

- **Safed** – Israel's highest town and major centre for Jewish mysticism

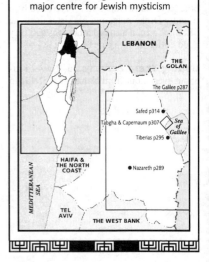

when interest in the town dwindled, only to be rekindled late in the 6th century. This was due to reports that the town had been the site of a number of miracles, and that a local synagogue had kept the book in which Jesus learnt to write, and the bench he sat on. It can't have done Nazareth's reputation any harm either that it was rumoured to have the region's most beautiful women, a result, it was said, of them all being related to the Holy Virgin Mary. Despite being predominantly Jewish at the time, the town experienced a boom in church construction.

The Crusaders, who'd made Nazareth their Galilean capital, dedicated a church here to the Annunciation, and another to the Angel Gabriel. After the Christian knights' defeat at the Horns of Hittin in 1187, pilgrims were still able to visit Nazareth owing to a series of truces, but by the 13th century the danger from Muslim attack was too great.

In the 17th century the Franciscans were able to buy back the ruins of the Church of the Annunciation and a Christian presence was re-established, albeit under difficult and often hostile conditions. In 1730 they built a new church which had been demolished in 1955 to be replaced by the modern basilica that you see today.

During the British Mandate, Nazareth was the administration's headquarters in the Galilee. When the British pulled out in 1948 Israeli forces siezed the town. Modern day Nazareth is one of the largest Arab towns in Israel (known to them as An-Nasra), with a population that's half Christian, half Muslim. Since the 1950s it has also grown to include Jewish Nasrat Illit, or Upper Nazareth, a new industrial town.

Orientation

The main places of interest are concentrated in the centre of the old Arab town. The main street is Paul VI St which runs from the junction with the Haifa-Afula highway to the south, up through the town centre and to Mary's Well, where it becomes Namsawi Rd. The other important street is the short Casa Nova St, which intersects with Paul VI St, and runs up to the market in front of the basilica. The tourist information office and the best accommodation and eating places are here.

Nazareth has no bus station, just bus stops on either side of St Paul VI St, located northeast of its intersection with Casa Nova St –

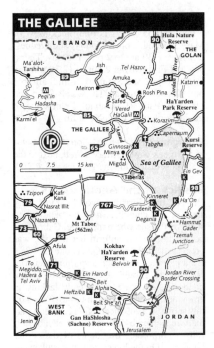

the Hamishbir department store is your landmark here.

Information

Tourist Office The local tourist informtion office (☎ 657 3003, fax 657 5279) is on Casa Nova St, just downhill from the basilica. It is open Monday to Friday from 8.30 am to 5 pm, and Saturday from 8.30 am to 2 pm, closed Sunday.

Money To change money, you should try the bureau at 81 Paul VI St. Alternatively, there are a couple of banks located within 100m of the intersection with Casa Nova St; opening hours are generally Monday and Tuesday from 8.30 am to 12.30 pm and 4 to 6.30 pm, Wednesday, Friday and Saturday from 8.30 am to 12.30 pm, Thursday from 8.30 am to 12.30 pm and 4 to 6 pm, closed Sunday.

Post & Communications The main post office (☎ 655 4019) is one block west of Mary's Well. It's open Monday and Wednesday from 8.30 am to 2 pm, Tuesday, Thursday and Friday from 8 am to 12.30 pm and 3.30 to 6 pm, and Saturday from 8 am to 1 pm, closed on Sunday. There's also a branch office on Paul VI St, about 400m south of the junction with Casa Nova St.

Emergency The police station (☎ 657 4444) is one block west of Mary's Well, next to the main post office. In emergencies call ☎ 100.

Basilica of the Annunciation

One of the Christian world's most holy shrines, this church is held by believers to stand on the site where the Angel Gabriel appeared to Mary to inform her that she was pregnant with the son of God (Luke 1:26-38). It's a pity then that such a spiritual scenario, fable or not, should be celebrated by such a ponderous structure, completely lacking in any grace. The fifth church to have stood on this spot, this 1969 incarnation is at least partially redeemed by its interior, which beautifully incorporates fragments of the earlier buildings. On the lower floor is a sunken enclosure focused on the apse of a 5th century Byzantine church, itself built around the **Grotto of the Annunciation**, the traditional site of Mary's house. Lining the north wall behind it are the remains of the apse of a 12th century Crusader church.

Stairs near the main entrance lead to the upper level which is used for regular services. The bare stone walls here are hung with a collection of murals depicting Mary and the infant Jesus, created and donated by Christian groups from around the world. Leave the upper level via the northern door to exit into a courtyard under which lie more excavations of ancient Nazareth.

No visitors are allowed inside the basilica during services; otherwise it is open from Monday to Saturday from 8.30 am to noon and 2 to 4 pm, and Sunday and holy days from 2 to 4 pm. Admission is free. Most of the other churches in Nazareth have the same visiting hours.

St Joseph's Church

Just north of the basilica and monastery is St Joseph's Church, built in 1914 and occupying the site considered to be that of **Joseph's carpentry shop**. This belief probably originated in the 17th century and today's church was built over the remains of an existing medieval church. Down in the crypt you can see an underground cave used for grain storage in pre-Byzantine times.

Sisters of Nazareth Convent

Up the side street across from the basilica (the side street with the Casa Nova Hospice on the corner), this convent operates a school for deaf and blind Arab children. It also provides accommodation for travellers in its hospice and hostel. The convent boasts one of the best examples of an ancient tomb sealed by a rolling stone. It lies under the present courtyard and can only be viewed by appointment.

Market

At the top of Casa Nova St is the Arab market (*souq*), occupying a maze of steep and narrow, winding streets. As in the lower part of the town, local authorities have taken steps to clean up the streets of the souq and make them a lot more presentable than they were previously.

The market operates on Monday, Tuesday, Thursday and Friday from 9 am to 5 pm, and Wednesday and Saturday from 9 am to 2 pm; it's closed on Sunday.

Greek Catholic Synagogue-Church

In a prominent position in the market, this church is beside the synagogue traditionally believed to be where Jesus regularly prayed and later taught (Luke 4:15-30).

Mensa Christi Church

Built in 1861, this small Franciscan church contains a large rock known in Latin as *Mensa Christi* (Table of Christ). Tradition has it that Jesus dined here with his disciples after the Resurrection. It is north of the Sisters of St Charles Borramaeus Convent,

Nazareth's modern Basilica of the Annunciation was built on the reputed site of Mary's home.

LEE FOSTER

The famous 'Mona Lisa of Galilee' is one of many beautiful Byzantine-era mosaic floors at Tzipori.

ISRAELI MINISTRY OF TOURISM

Church of the Mount of Beatitudes, Galilee

Basilica of the Transfiguration, Mt Tabor

The simple Church of the Primacy of St Peter in a tranquil setting by the Sea of Galilee.

LEE FOSTER

TONY WHEELER

PAUL HELLANDER

near the Maronite Church and Ecumenical Christian Child Care Centre.

St Gabriel's Church & Mary's Well

The story surrounding this Greek Orthodox church and the nearby well conflicts with the story associated with the basilica. According to Orthodox tradition, the Angel Gabriel appeared before Mary while she was fetching water, not while she was home in what is now the grotto in the basilica. The church was built in the late 17th century on the site of earlier churches and the crypt at the far end contains the source of the spring supplying the nearby well. Before entering the church take a look at the ancient graffiti carved around the doorway.

The church is about a 10 minute walk north of the Basilica of the Annunciation, one block north of where Paul VI St ends. It's open from 8 to 6 pm daily.

Mary's Well is also known as the Virgin's Fountain. In late 1998, renovations were still underway with stone paving being laid out in preparation for a handsome-looking plaza and shrine to replace what had previously been an unimpressive-looking faucet. The new plaza is just down from St Gabriel's Church on Paul VI St. Some believe that the Angel Gabriel appeared here and the water is said to have powers of healing.

Basilica & School of Jesus the Adolescent

Built in 1918 in a mock-Gothic style, this is probably the most beautiful of Nazareth's many churches. It belongs to the French Salesian Order and its attractive architecture, both inside and out, and the great views of the town below justify the steep hike to get up there. Unfortunately, there are no buses to the church.

Chapel of Fright

Luke 4:29-30 tells of the occasion when the people of Nazareth tried to throw Jesus off the top of a hill. In the southern part of the town, the Franciscan Chapel of Fright, or Notre Dame de l'Effroi, is built on the sup-

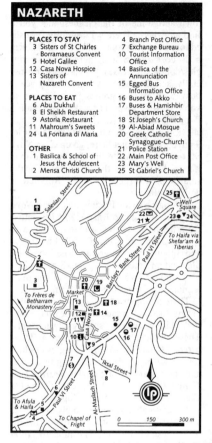

NAZARETH

PLACES TO STAY
3 Sisters of St Charles Borromaeus Convent
5 Hotel Galilee
12 Casa Nova Hospice
13 Sisters of Nazareth Convent

PLACES TO EAT
6 Abu Dukhul
8 El Sheikh Restaurant
9 Astoria Restaurant
11 Mahroum's Sweets
24 La Fontana di Maria

OTHER
1 Basilica & School of Jesus the Adolescent
2 Mensa Christi Church
4 Branch Post Office
7 Exchange Bureau
10 Tourist Information Office
14 Basilica of the Annunciation
15 Egged Bus Information Office
16 Buses to Akko
17 Buses & Hamishbir Department Store
18 St Joseph's Church
19 Al-Abiad Mosque
20 Greek Catholic Synagogue-Church
21 Police Station
22 Main Post Office
23 Mary's Well
25 St Gabriel's Church

posed site from where Mary witnessed this event. The nearby hill is known as the 'precipice', or the Leap of the Lord. Look for the signposted gate in the wall on Paul VI St, opposite the Hotel Galilee, south of the town centre. The church is behind the wall, beyond St Claire's Convent.

Places to Stay

With beautiful architecture and a delightful cloistered courtyard, the *Sisters of Nazareth Convent* (☎ 655 4304, fax 646 0741)

THE GALILEE

provides by far the best accommodation in town and some of the cleanest that you'll find anywhere. There's a tastefully furnished lounge-dining room and a kitchen. Dorm beds cost 28NIS and there are also singles/doubles for US$19/38. At Easter especially, and throughout summer, the place is busy with pilgrim groups from Europe so you'd be well advised to make a reservation if possible. Check-in time is after 4 pm, check-out time is 9 am, and there is a strict 9 pm curfew. To get there, go up Casa Nova St, turn left opposite the Basilica and then it's up the street on the right. Look for the small sign in French that reads, 'Religieuses de Nazareth'.

Belonging to the Franciscans, *Casa Nova Hospice* (☎ 645 6660, fax 657 9630), across from the basilica on Casa Nova St, is also very popular and is usually filled by Italian and Spanish pilgrim groups. The rooms are pleasant and the food is good. Singles/doubles are US$39/54; breakfast and one meal is included. Doors close at 11 pm.

There are other Christian institutions that provide accommodation, but they have limited facilities and may specify pilgrims only. These include *Frères de Betharram Monastery* (☎ 657 0046) with singles/doubles for US$40 per person, including breakfast, and the *Sisters of St Charles Borramaeus Convent* (☎ 655 4435), above the Carmelite Convent up on the western slopes.

Nazareth also has three hotels to provide a secular but not great alternative to the religious establishments. The modern *Hotel Galilee* (☎ 657 1311, fax 655 6627), on Paul VI St about five minutes walk south of the basilica, is the most central and probably the nicest of the three, with singles/doubles for US$65/90. *Nazareth Hotel* (☎ 657 7777, fax 657 8511) is out of the way, on the edge of town at the intersection of the Haifa-Afula highway, while further out still, towards Haifa, is *Grand New Hotel* (☎ 657 3020, fax 657 6281) on St Joseph St.

Places to Eat

The best places to eat in Nazareth are undoubtedly in the Christian hospices. Failing

that, the next best thing to do is to cook for yourself.

The market is the place to buy fresh vegetables and fruit, and there are grocery shops and bakeries along Paul VI St in both directions from Casa Nova St. Between the basilica and the bus station are some good felafel stalls, while a decent place for shwarma (18NIS), humous (15NIS) and a bottle of beer is *Astoria Restaurant* (☎ 657 7965) on the corner of Casa Nova and Paul VI Sts.

A little way further south on Paul VI, *Abu Dukhul* does excellent grilled meats seasoned with parsley, pine nuts and onions. Expect to pay 25 to 30NIS.

El Sheikh Restaurant (☎ 656 7664, Iksal St) is only open from 7 am to 2 pm but enjoys a good reputation among lovers of humous. Prices are ridiculously low, perhaps reflecting its unattractive location in a street full of car workshops.

For classier dining but with a heavier price tag, *La Fontana di Maria* (☎ 646 0435) just off Well Square is a large ornate restaurant in oriental style. It also has a car park – a necessity in cramped Nazareth. It is popular with pilgrim groups, so avoid it if you want a quiet meal. A meal for two will cost around 250NIS.

Mahroum's Sweets enjoys a reputation as the best place in town for baklava and other honey-soaked pastries. Several places have the same name, but the original is the one on Casa Nova St nearest to the basilica.

Getting There & Away

Bus Nazareth is a stopover for several buses that cross the Galilee. From just outside of the Hamishbir department store catch bus No 431 for Tiberias (15NIS, 45 minutes), departing every hour. For Haifa (16NIS, 45 minutes) and Afula (8NIS, 20 minutes) stand on the opposite side of the street. There are also several buses a day that run direct to Akko (take bus No 343 from the stop opposite the Egged information office; 18NIS) and Tel Aviv (bus Nos 823 and 824; 30NIS).

The Egged information office (☎ 656 9956) is on Paul VI St, across the road and

50m south of the Hamishbir department store, next to the Mazrawi Restaurant. This office is unmarked except for a small sign in Hebrew, and it's open Sunday to Thursday from 6 am to 7 pm, and Friday from 4 am to 3 pm, closed Saturday.

Sheruts (Service Taxis) Sheruts to Tiberias leave from in front of the Hamishbir department store. For Haifa and Tel Aviv sheruts, go to the street by the side of the Paz petrol station just south of the Hamishbir department store. You will also get sheruts looking for some extra passengers coming through Nazareth from Haifa, Tiberias and other places, so keep a lookout for them around the bus stands on Paul VI St.

AROUND NAZARETH
Kafr Kana
Historically known as Cana, this Arab town 7km north-east of Nazareth on the road to Tiberias is the purported site of Jesus' first miracle (John 2:1-11), when he changed water into wine at a wedding reception. A **Franciscan church** built in 1881 now stands on the site. It contains an old jar of the type that contained the water he turned into wine. Under the church floor you can see a fragment of a mosaic pavement that bears an ancient Jewish Aramaic inscription. Not to be outdone, Kafr Kana's **Greek church** contains some ancient stone vats that the Orthodox claim were the actual ones involved in the miracle.

This was also the home town of Jesus' disciple Nathanael (John 21:2) and the Franciscans administer a chapel built over the traditional site of his house.

Getting There & Away Arab buses depart about every 45 minutes from near Mary's Well in Nazareth bound for Kafr Kana. Alternatively, there is bus No 431 that operates between Tiberias and Nazareth which passes through the village – ask the driver to let you off there. The Greek church is the nearest to the main road, the Franciscan church and chapel are situated in the town centre.

Tzipori
This national park (☎ 656 8272) is a rapidly expanding archaeological site that is being assiduously developed as a prime tourist attraction. Given the amount of money being poured into it, it could well become one of the major attractions of the whole Galilee region.

Under the name Sepphoris, this place flourished as a major Roman city, subsequently occupied by Byzantines, Arabs and Crusaders.

Excavations in the late 1980s uncovered some fantastic **Byzantine mosaics**, now exhibited in a purpose-built mock-Roman villa. One of these, a portrait of a contemplative young woman nicknamed the 'Mona Lisa of the Galilee', is alone worth making the visit for. Other mosaics depict the Greek god of wine, Dionysus, and an Egyptian Nilometer. All are labelled with explanatory text in English.

Beside the villa, the ruins of a **Crusader-era fortress** house a resource centre that has a lively and informative video presentation, as well as several computer terminals with interactive programs, including one in which you create an on-screen mosaic. Visitors can also explore the ancient city's **water cisterns**. Hewn out of rock, they're 15m deep and 260m long and form part of a continuous system that brought water from a spring near Nazareth over 13km away.

The site is open daily from 8 am to 4 pm, and Friday from 8 am to 3 pm. Admission is 17NIS. It's 10km north of Nazareth on the Akko road. From Nazareth take the No 343 Akko bus (there's about one an hour until 4.45 pm) or the No 341 Tiberias to Haifa bus and ask to be let off at the Tzipori junction, from where it's about a 2.5km hike to the park. Alternatively, take bus No 16, which goes from Nazareth directly to the site once a day at 1.10 pm, and returns at 5.45 pm.

Mt Tabor
With glorious views across the Jezreel Valley's multicoloured patchwork of fields, Mt Tabor is the traditional site of the Transfiguration (Matthew 17:1-9, Mark 9:2-8 and

THE GALILEE

Luke 9:28-36). This was the occasion when Jesus was seen by some of the disciples to be talking with the prophets Moses and Elijah. Two large churches on the mountain summit, Franciscan and Greek, commemorate the event.

A Byzantine church probably already existed here when Benedictine monks were installed on the mount in 1099 by the Crusaders. They were massacred in a Turkish attack in 1113 that also saw their buildings destroyed. The monks later returned to build a new church and monastery which survived an attack by Saladin (Salah ad-Din) in 1183 but not the defeat of the Crusaders at the Horns of Hittin in 1187.

The Muslims then built their own fortress on the mount and, as it was on the believed site of the Transfiguration, this inspired the 5th Crusade. Although a Crusader siege in 1217 failed, the Muslims dismantled the fortress because they realised that it would continue to be a major provocation. Later in the 13th century a series of truces made it possible for Christians to return to the mount but in 1263 they were expelled by Sultan Beybars.

Basilica of the Transfiguration The entrance to the Franciscan complex is through the main gate of the Muslim's 13th century fortress, restored in 1897. Its defensive wall, including 12 towers, goes all the way around the summit. About 150m inside the gate to the right is a small chapel. Built on Byzantine foundations it commemorates the conversation between Jesus and his disciples after the Transfiguration (Mark 9:9-13). The cemetery to the north is medieval, the one to the south from the 1st century.

At the end of the drive is the basilica (built in 1924), definitely one of the Holy Land's most beautiful churches, both inside and out. A particular highlight is the lovely mosaic of the Nativity. On the right of the piazza, in front of the basilica, stands the Franciscan monastery and hospice, while on the left are remains of the Byzantine monastery.

No visitors are allowed inside the basilica during services; otherwise it's open Sun-

day to Friday from 8 am to noon and 2 to 5 pm, closed on Saturday. Admission is free.

Getting There & Away Mt Tabor is visited most easily by bus from Tiberias – all Tel Aviv buses stop at the turn-off for the mount. Coming from Nazareth (50 minutes), you need to change buses at Afula, where you can also connect with buses to most of the major destinations in Israel. However, Mt Tabor buses from Afula are infrequent, so check the schedule to avoid a long delay, especially for the return bus.

All buses drop you off at the bottom of the steep and winding road that leads to the summit; the climb takes about 30 minutes on foot. At the top the turning to the left leads to the Greek church; go straight ahead to reach the Franciscan basilica.

BEIT SHE'AN   בית שאן
Pop: 15,000 ☎ Area Code: 06

The attraction here is one of the country's most extensive archaeological sites (yes, another one), including its best-preserved Roman amphitheatre.

Located on a busy trade route, 5000 years of continuous occupation testify to the ancient importance of Beit She'an. Archaeologists believe that the first real town was established here circa 3000 BC and its name is mentioned in 19th century BC Egyptian texts as one of the strongholds from which the region was ruled by the Pharaohs. In the 13th century BC, the Israelite tribe of Manasseh inherited the area (Judges 1:27), losing it 200 years later to the Philistines, who hung the body of King Saul on the city walls (I Samuel 31).

The action didn't stop there – excavations have revealed no less than 18 cities superimposed on top of one another. Jewish sages were moved to write of one incarnation, 'If the Garden of Eden is in Israel, then its gate is at Beit She'an'. Unfortunately we missed that version and the late 20th century Beit She'an is an unattractive, drab little town that no discerning Adam or Eve is likely to want to linger in. Instead, from the bus station head west (left) and follow the road as far as the Bank Leumi, then turn right to go downhill through the park to the site of the ancient cities. It's a walk of about 800m.

Roman Amphitheatre & Byzantine Street

Not to be confused with the main site, these ruins are just a short walk from the bus station. The amphitheatre was used for gladiatorial contests and had 12 rows of seats for 6000 spectators. Only three rows can be seen today. The Byzantine street dates from the 5th century AD and connected this area with the main town. A Greek inscription notes that the drainage system dates from 522 AD.

Tel Beit She'an

Excavations and restoration work are ongoing but included among the structures so far revealed are a temple, a basilica, a nymphaeum and a wide colonnaded Roman street leading down to the great theatre, another 6000 seater. North of the herringbone-patterned street are the extensive Byzantine baths covering over half a hectare, with a paved courtyard and surrounding porticoes, paved with marble and mosaics. One of the

One of the busts recovered from the extensively excavated Tel Beit She'an site.

mosaics, dating from the 6th century, depicted Tyche, the goddess of prosperity and good fortune – the latter of which aided the thief who made off with it in 1989.

For a good overview of the site climb the hill on the northern side, beyond the baths. There's a free map of the excavations along with English-language information available at the ticket kiosk. Tel Beit She'an (☎ 658 7189) is open to visitors Saturday to Thursday from 8 am to 4 pm, and Friday from 8 am to 3 pm. Admission is 17NIS (students 12.80NIS).

Getting There & Away

Beit She'an is a stopover for the Tiberias to Jerusalem bus and there are also regular services between here and Afula, making it accessible from Nazareth.

AROUND BEIT SHE'AN
Beit Alpha Synagogue

In 1928, members of Kibbutz Beit Alpha (☎ 653 3650) uncovered the remains of a 6th century BC synagogue while digging an irrigation channel. Its mosaic floor is in good condition and is one of the country's best Jewish relics. The site is 8km northwest of Beit She'an.

The floor consists of three panels. The upper panel shows religious emblems, including *menorahs* (candelabras), the *lulav* (bundle of branches), *shofars* (ram's horn) and *etrog* (citrus fruit). A zodiac circle with the seasons symbolised in each corner makes up the central panel. Abraham's sacrifice is depicted in the lower panel. The site is open Saturday to Thursday from 8 am to 5 pm, and Friday from 8 am to 4 pm. Admission is 7NIS (students 5.25NIS).

Members of the Makoya, a Japanese Christian sect, study Hebrew on the kibbutz, and their lovely little Japanese garden can be seen up the hill from the synagogue, beyond the swimming pool.

To get there take bus No 412 or 415 from Afula or Beit She'an and get off at Kibbutz Heftziba (look for the orange signs), *not* Kibbutz Beit Alpha, which is 1km closer to Beit She'an.

Gan HaShlosha
(Sachne) Reserve

This is a pleasantly landscaped park (☎ 658 6219) with spacious lawns, trees and beautifully clear natural pools connected by gentle waterfalls. The water, with a year-round temperature of 28°C, comes from a spring *(sachne* is Arabic for warm). It's a very popular place for a swim or a picnic, but avoid Friday and Saturday when it becomes just a little bit too popular. There is a snack bar and cafe, too.

The park is open Saturday to Thursday from 8 am to 6 pm, and Friday from 8 am to 5 pm. Admission is 21NIS (students 14NIS). It's about 1km south-east of Beit Alpha and is reached by a signposted side road off Route 71; tell the bus driver where you want to get off.

The entrance fee to the park also covers admission to the **Nir David Museum of Regional & Mediterranean Archaeology** (☎ 658 6094), which houses a good collection of artefacts relating to the country's ancient history and that of neighbouring countries. It's open Sunday to Thursday from 8 am to 2 pm, Friday from 8 am to 1 pm, and Saturday from 10 am to 1 pm. The museum is a 10 minute walk up the road behind the park.

BELVOIR   כוכב הירדן

Belvoir is a ruined 12th century Crusader castle with great views over the Jezreel Valley, Jordan's Gilead Mountains and, on a clear day, even the Sea of Galilee. It is part of the **Kokhav HaYarden Reserve**, and one of those places that perhaps isn't worth making a great detour for; however, if you happen to be passing, it's definitely worth visiting.

The castle was built by the French Knights Hospitallers in 1168 and was held through two attacks by Saladin in 1182-83. However, after being under siege from July 1187 to January 1191, the defenders at Belvoir were forced to surrender. They were permitted to retreat to Tyre unharmed, in acknowledgment of their courage. Saladin also left the castle intact but it was systematically destroyed in the early 13th century by the

Sultan of Damascus who was afraid that the Crusaders would return. They did, in 1241, but they weren't around long enough to do any rebuilding.

The Belvoir ruins are still quite impressive, although it's the setting which is the main attraction. The castle (☎ 658 7000) is open Saturday to Thursday from 8 am to 5 pm, and Friday from 8 am to 4 pm. Admission is 8.50NIS (students 6.50NIS).

Getting There & Away

The reserve is 30km south of the Tzemah junction at the southern tip of the Sea of Galilee. Buses running between Tiberias and Beit She'an will drop you off at the signposted intersection of the road that leads up to the castle. From here it is a steep 6km walk or hitch. In the hot summer months it is best to make an early start. Make sure to cover your head and bring plenty of water.

TIBERIAS   טבריה
Pop: 36,700 ☎ Area Code: 06

As the only town on the shores of the Sea of Galilee, Tiberias is the obvious base from which to enjoy the beauty spots surrounding the lake.

With its mix of spas and tombs of venerated sages, Tiberias has grown as a popular holiday centre where observant Jews can combine treatment of the body with purification of the soul. The not-so-observant also flock here, to dine on fish and drink wine beside the lake, and enjoy the lively nightlife and water activities such as soaking in sulphur pools and hurtling down a waterslide.

In the summer months Tiberias is Sweat City – incredibly humid – but the rule regarding acceptable clothing when visiting the holy places still applies.

History

The town owes its origins to a series of hot springs that lured pleasure-seekers of Roman times and attracted the attention of Herod Antipas.

Herod Antipas was almost as egotistical as his father, Herod the Great, founder of Caesarea: the son's town included a grand

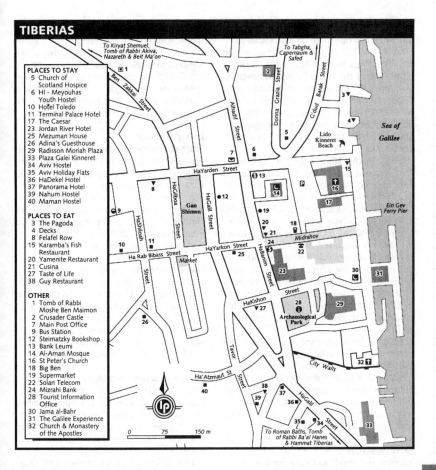

TIBERIAS

To Kiryat Shemuel,
Tomb of Rabbi Akiva,
Nazareth & Beit Ma'on

To Tabgha,
Capernaum &
Safed

Sea of
Galilee

Ein Gev
Ferry Pier

PLACES TO STAY
5 Church of
   Scotland Hospice
6 HI - Meyouhas
   Youth Hostel
10 Hotel Toledo
11 Terminal Palace Hotel
17 The Caesar
23 Jordan River Hotel
25 Mezuman House
26 Adina's Guesthouse
29 Radisson Moriah Plaza
33 Plaza Galei Kinneret
34 Aviv Hostel
35 Aviv Holiday Flats
36 HaDekel Hotel
37 Panorama Hotel
39 Nahum Hostel
40 Maman Hostel

PLACES TO EAT
3 The Pagoda
4 Decks
8 Felafel Row
15 Karamba's Fish
   Restaurant
20 Yamenite Restaurant
21 Cusina
27 Taste of Life
38 Guy Restaurant

OTHER
1 Tomb of Rabbi
  Moshe Ben Maimon
2 Crusader Castle
7 Main Post Office
9 Bus Station
12 Steimatzky Bookshop
13 Bank Leumi
14 Al-Amari Mosque
16 St Peter's Church
18 Big Ben
19 Supermarket
22 Solan Telecom
24 Mizrahi Bank
28 Tourist Information
   Office
30 Jama al-Bahr
31 The Galilee Experience
32 Church & Monastery
   of the Apostles

0   75   150 m

To Roman Baths, Tomb
of Rabbi Ba'al Hanes
& Hammat Tiberias

cardo, a stadium, a gold-roofed palace and a great synagogue.

The population was mixed, but following the Bar Kochba Revolt (132-35 AD) and the resulting exile of the Jews from Jerusalem, Tiberias became the centre of Jewish life in Israel. The work of the great sages was continued beside the shores of the Sea of Galilee and academies of rabbinical study were founded. A Tiberian system of punctuation and grammar was applied to the Torah, thus becoming the standard for all Hebrew, and the Mishnah was completed here around the year 200 AD – achievements which elevated Tiberias to the status of one of the country's four most holy Jewish cities. The population at this time is estimated to have been around 40,000, making the city larger than the Tiberias of today.

The Crusaders took Tiberias in 1099, built a fortress slightly to the north and generally shifted the focus of the town away from its original Roman-Byzantine centre. However, the new fortifications proved inadequate and failed to keep out Saladin when he turned up at the head of an army in 1187. The loss of Tiberias to the Muslims sparked the battle at the Horns of Hittin, which proved to be another inglorious defeat for the Crusaders, heralding the demise of the Latin kingdom. Tiberias also went into decline, after being seriously damaged by the many battles fought here and severely rattled by the occasional earthquake.

Early in the 16th century, the Ottoman Turks gained possession of the Holy Land and in 1562 Suleyman the Magnificent granted the rights to farm the taxes of Tiberias to a Jew, Don Joseph Nussi. Aided by his mother-in-law, Donna Grazia, he attempted with some degree of success to revive the town as a Jewish enclave. The next player was an Arab sheikh named Daher al-Omar who, in the 18th century, established an independent fiefdom in the Galilee, with Tiberias as its capital. He was assassinated in 1775. The town fared little better, with a great part of it demolished by an earthquake in 1837.

Many Jews of the First Aliyah (late 19th century) chose to settle in Tiberias and more followed with the expansion of the Zionist movement. By 1947 the population of Tiberias was again predominantly Jewish. The following year the Arabs and Jews went to war over the town. The defeated Arabs fled and Tiberias was left wholly Jewish.

Orientation

Tiberias is a small and easy place to get to know. Although the town is divided into three districts, all the places of interest, the hotels, hostels and restaurants are in and around the city centre, which is on the shores of the lake. The other two parts of town, Kiryat Shemuel, up the hill to the north, and Beit Ma'on, atop the hill, are both primarily residential districts.

Most visitors arrive at the bus station on the eastern end of HaYarden St. Between the station and the lake, intersecting with HaYarden and running parallel to the shore, are the two main streets of HaGalil and Ha-

Banim. On or around these two are the shops, banks, post office and tourist information office, as well as many of the town's hostels and hotels. Restaurants, cafes and the town's nightlife are centred on the *midrahov* (pedestrian mall), one block south of HaYarden, which connects HaBanim to the lake shore promenade and its string of eateries.

Information

Tourist Office The city tourist information office (☎ 672 5666) is in a small stone building in the HaKishon St Archaeological Park. It's reasonably well stocked with free literature though a lot of it is in Hebrew and has good maps of both Tiberias and the Galilee area for sale. The opening hours are Sunday to Thursday from 8 am to 5 pm, and Friday from 8 am to noon.

Money Bank Leumi, on the corner of HaBanim and HaYarden Sts, and Mizrahi Bank, on the corner of HaBanim St and the midrahov, have currency exchange ATMs, open 24 hours a day. The banking hours are Sunday, Tuesday and Thursday from 8.30 am to noon and 4 to 5.30 pm, and Monday, Wednesday and Friday from 8.30 am to 12.30 pm.

Post & Communications The main post office is on HaYarden St opposite the junction with HaBanim St. It's open Sunday, Monday, Tuesday and Thursday from 8 am to 12.30 pm and 3.30 to 6 pm, Wednesday from 8 am to 1.30 pm, and Friday from 8 am to noon.

For international telephones and faxes head for Solan Telecom (☎ 672 6470), on the midrahov, open from 8 am to midnight.

Emergencies For the police, phone ☎ 679 2444 or in an emergency dial ☎ 100.

There's a Magen David Adom first-aid station (☎ 679 0111) on the corner of HaBanim and HaKishon Sts, across from the Jordan River Hotel. In an emergency call ☎ 101.

Old Town Walls & Castle

Remnants of the black basalt wall built by Daher al-Omar in 1738 can be seen in various places in the old town, most notably stretching between HaBanim St and the Church of the Apostles. North of HaYarden St, off Donna Grazia St, is a lone grey stone bastion, sometimes called the Crusader Castle (it dates from the 18th century, and was probably built by Daher al-Omar's son, Chulabi) but more commonly known as **Rivka's Castle** after the woman who, along with her husband, restored the place. An artist, Rivka Ganun now uses the three storey tower as a studio and gallery for her work. Visitors are welcome to wander up and take a look around. Admission is 10NIS.

Al-Amari Mosque

As out of place as a pin-stripe suited gent at a teenage rave, the dignified little Al-Amari Mosque on HaBanim St looks threatened and lost, squeezed between some gaudy shops and a brusque concrete supermarket. Built by Daher al-Omar in the mid-18th century, the mosque is one of the very few buildings in Tiberias that predates 1948. It is generally held that its construction was partly paid for by the town's Jewish community, presumably grateful to the sheikh for being permitted to return. Needless to say, the mosque is no longer used for worship and is locked up pending the local council finding a use for it.

Jama al-Bahr & The Galilee Experience

Tiberias' other mosque, the waterfront Jama al-Bahr (1880), was built with a special entrance for those arriving by boat. It now stands forlornly abandoned, and no one appears to have any plans to utilise its potential.

Part of a modern waterfront development across from the museum, the Galilee Experience (☎ 672 3620, fax 672 3195) is a 37 minute summation of the history, geography and spiritual significance of the region presented in the form of a state-of-the-art slide show. With hourly screenings in English, and daily screenings in German and French, it's open Sunday to Thursday from 9 am to 10 pm, Friday from 9 am to 4 pm, and Saturday evening from 5 to 10 pm. Admission

is US$8 (students US$6). The marina complex also features an art gallery, a cafe, a souvenir shop and a bookshop.

St Peter's Church

This Franciscan church, commonly called Terra Sancta, was built in the 12th century by the Crusaders. The Muslims converted it into a mosque and you can make out an area of uneven stone on the southern wall filling in the hole where a *mihrab* (prayer niche indicating the direction of Mecca) was carved. Later, the Turks used the building as a caravanserai before it reverted to use as a church. In 1870 it was rebuilt, in 1903 enlarged and in 1944 restored. Its two main points of interest are the boat-shaped nave (St Peter was a fisherman) and the courtyard built by the Polish soldiers stationed here during WWII. It's open daily from 8 to 11.45 am and 2 to 5 pm. Admission is free. The church entrance is on the promenade next to the Galei Gil restaurant.

Church & Monastery of the Apostles

By the water's edge south of the Radisson Moriah Plaza Hotel, this Greek Orthodox complex is on the site of a Byzantine monastery that was destroyed by the Persians in the 7th century. Since then the complex has been rebuilt and destroyed numerous times; the buildings standing today date from the late 19th century but they've been restored as recently as 1975.

Three monks live here and they'll usually admit visitors who ring the bell. There are four chapels beyond the pleasant walled courtyard. One chapel is dedicated to St Peter, one to the disciples and one to Mary Magdalene; the one in the ancient round tower is dedicated to St Nicholas.

Roman Baths

Half a kilometre south of the Galei Kinneret Hotel, opposite Sironit Beach, are the partial excavations of some 4th century Roman baths. The archaeologists have uncovered fragments of mosaics that illustrate elephants, panthers, fish and geometric designs.

THE GALILEE

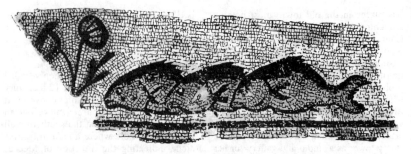

Byzantine fish and lotus mosaic found in Tiberias. The mosaics on church floors from this period rarely feature religious symbols as leaders didn't like the idea of the symbols being trodden on.

Non-claustrophobics can crawl through a hole near the palm tree into a tight, low-ceilinged underground chamber.

To find the site of the remains, cross the unsurfaced car park on the western side of the road and walk about 100m south to the roofed enclosure on the right.

Hammat Tiberias

The hot springs of Hammat Tiberias are now 2km south of the modern town, but during Roman times, they were the focus, if not *raison d'être*, of a community of 40,000 fervent bathers. The fame of Hammat Tiberias was such that in 110 AD the Emperor Trajan had a coin struck dedicated to the springs, with the image of Hygia, the goddess of health, shown sitting on a rock enjoying the water. The springs were also mentioned by Al-Idris, an Arab writer who lived during the Crusades, and recommended by the Jewish sage Rambam to his patients.

The near 2000-year-old traditions of Hammat Tiberias are maintained by the **Tiberias Hot Springs complex** (☎ 679 1967), which these days consists of two separate buildings. The older one across the road from the lake – the Health Springs Centre – is for people with serious skin problems. The more modern Relaxation Springs Centre, on the shore of the lake, is open to the general public and you don't need to suffer from any particular ailment to enjoy a good

soak or massage. There's a whole menu of available options and treatments but they tend to be a little expensive; as an example, a dip in the thermal pools costs 45NIS, a massage 90NIS, and a combined dip and massage 110NIS. The Relaxation Springs Centre is open Sunday, Monday and Wednesday from 8 am to 8 pm, Tuesday and Thursday from 8 am to 11 pm, Friday from 8 am to 6 pm and Saturday from 8.30 am to 8 pm.

The history of the site has been packaged up in the **Hammat Tiberias National Park** (☎ 672 5287), which comprises the Ernest Lehman Museum, housed in what was originally part of a Turkish bathhouse, the ruins of another, 6th century, bathhouse and the partially excavated remains of the 4th century Severus Synagogue. The highlight – which alone is worth the admission – is the synagogue's beautiful zodiac **mosaic floor**. Much has been made of the mosaic's curious mixing of Jewish and pagan symbols, but somehow this seems quite apt in Tiberias, a town that, historically, seems to have been able to reconcile the spiritual with the more earthly.

The national park is open Sunday to Thursday from 8 am to 5 pm, and Friday from 8 am to 4 pm. Admission is 7NIS. To get there you can either walk along the road on the lake shore south of the town centre (20 to 25 minutes), or you can try waiting for the infrequent bus No 2 or 5.

King Solomon & the Springs

An imaginative legend attributes the creation of the springs to King Solomon. The story has it that the king was approached by a group of sick men who begged him to find a cure for them. Solomon summoned a posse of demons and set them to work down below, heating the water in the earth's mineral rich crust and blasting it up to the surface. The wise old king also took the precaution of making the demons deaf, so that they would never hear of the news of his death and so never cease their labours.

The nauseatingly sulphurous smell of the spring waters certainly lends credence to the story. But in addition to the sulphur, the waters contain high amounts of muriatic and calcium salts which are believed to have excellent curative powers for such ailments as rheumatism, arthritis, gout, and nervous and gynaecological disorders.

Tomb of Rabbi Meir Ba'al Hanes

Up the hill from the Hammat Tiberias is one of Judaism's holiest sites, the tomb of Meir Ba'al Hanes, the 2nd century rabbi who helped to compile the Mishnah.

The tomb is marked by two synagogues: the one on the left with the white dome (Sephardic) and the other, with the blue dome (Ashkenazi). In the courtyard of the Sephardic synagogue is a pillar topped by a large bowl and four days before the Lag B'Omer holiday a bonfire is lit here on the Pesah Sheni (second Passover). Crowds of religious Jews visit throughout the year to pray and it is a tradition that God will answer the prayers of pilgrims who have personal problems.

The tomb is open Sunday to Thursday from 7 am to 8 pm, and Friday from 7 am to 3 pm.

Tomb of Rabbi Akiva

Above the old town, beyond Kiryat Shemuel and the police station, a white dome covers the cave-tomb of Rabbi Akiva. Born in 50 AD, he was one of the great Jewish scholars, and was killed by the Romans for his role in the Bar Kochba Revolt (132-35 AD). Take bus No 4 from Ben Zakkai St to get to the tomb.

Tomb of Rabbi Moshe Ben Maimon

This interesting complex of tombs is only a few minutes walk from the centre of town and is worth visiting simply so that you can observe at close hand some of the rituals of Jewish sacred life.

Better known by the names Rambam and Maimonides, Ben Maimon was born in Spain in 1135 and was one of the most highly regarded sages of the 12th century. An Aristotelian philosopher, astronomer and scientist, and physician to Saladin, he died in Cairo in 1204. Other well-known people buried here are Ben Zakkai, the Holy Land's most eminent sage at the time of the Roman destruction of Jerusalem; Rabbi Eliezer the Great, a prominent 2nd century scholar; Rav Ammi and Rav Assii, who lived in the 3rd century; and Rabbi Isaiah Horowitz, who died around 1630.

The tombs are busy all hours of the day with praying Hasidim; modest dress is essential. They are on Ben Zakkai St, 250m north of Gan Shimon (Shimon Park).

Beaches

Although the best things in life may be free, the best beaches on the lake are not. Most of the beaches immediately around Tiberias are owned by hotels, which do at least provide facilities such as changing rooms and showers. **Lido Kinneret** just north of Ha-Yarden St charges 15NIS admission (open daily from 8 am to 5 pm); further north, **Nelson Beach** is a little cheaper but its facilities are poorer. South of Tiberias is the fairly unpleasant and stony **Municipal (Ganim) Beach** (8NIS) or you can really go for it and splash out 45NIS for a day at the **Gai Beach Water Park** (☎ 679 0790) with giant water slides, including the wave-machine-rippled pools and the terrifying 70° angle of the kamikaze slide. The water park is 1km south of the town centre.

If you don't like the idea of paying for access to the lake, either head for the harbour wall to the south of the Radisson Moriah Plaza Hotel, or leave Tiberias altogether and walk, hitch or take a bus further south, beyond the hot springs, and stop when you see an appealing site.

Special Events
Check out the tourist information office for special events. For example, every Passover there's the Ein Gev Music Festival; there's also an annual summer Sea of Galilee Festival, which attracts a lot of attention.

Places to Stay
Tiberias offers some of Israel's better hostels, a lovely Christian hospice in the midprice range, and one of the country's best top-end hotels. Note that you can choose between staying in Tiberias itself and staying in more peaceful and scenic surroundings on the shores of the adjacent sea (see Places to Stay in the Around the Sea of Galilee section).

Places to Stay – Budget
The hostels are all within walking distance of the bus station, though the majority of the backpacker places are clustered around the southern end of town. Be aware that prices are subject to dramatic changes – up during Jewish holidays when Israelis flock here and down immediately afterwards when nervous proprietors outbid each other to attract the travellers.

Beds in Tiberias generally cost a little more than those in other parts of Israel; dorm beds (unless otherwise stated) are from 25 to 30NIS while private rooms start at 80NIS. This is about on a par with the rest of the country. However, add about 25% to hotel room prices during the summer high season and on Jewish holidays.

Easily spotted as you enter the town from the south is *HaDekel Hotel* (*☎/fax 672 5318, 1 HaGalil St)*, the latest addition to the hostel scene and a very good choice at

that. It offers a limited number of small four-bed dorms with comfortable beds (not bunks) air-con and fridge in each room for 25NIS a bed. Private rooms go for 120NIS and have cable TV. There is a large, pleasant courtyard with a bar and snack counter and guests can do their laundry for a small fee. There is also a safe for the deposit of travellers' valuables. You can get a decent breakfast here as well.

Nahum Hostel (☎ 672 1505, Tavor St)* is another backpackers' favourite. It's popular for its rooftop terrace and bar where you can watch the latest news or video clips on cable TV. It also has a kitchen. Dorm beds are 25NIS. Owner Yakov has some very attractive air-con double rooms at 90NIS with their own shower and toilet and even a kitchen area and, for groups of guests, small apartments at negotiable rates. The hostel also has bicycles for hire (30NIS per day).

A good alternative is *Maman Hostel (*☎ 679 2986, fax 672 6616, Ha'Atzmaut St)* two minutes away from the Nahum. It's well looked after, with large airy dorms and spotless showers, and there's a garden and terrace around the back with a small swimming pool. There is no curfew as guests are given keys. Dorm beds are 20NIS and private air-con rooms go for 80 to 120NIS.

Popular also is *Aviv Hostel (*☎ 672 0007, fax 672 3510, HaGalil St)*, close to the other hostels. The small dorms are a little claustrophobic but are at least air-conditioned; beds go for 25NIS. Doubles are available at 100 to 150NIS, the more expensive ones having air-con and a private bathroom. The place could do with a brush and scrub up, but does have a TV lounge, and soft drinks and beer in the fridge. There's also an outside terrace where you can sit and relax. The Aviv is the main place in town for bicycle rentals, charging 40NIS per day (or 30NIS for hostel guests). The management also runs full-day tours around the Upper Galilee and the Golan for 130NIS per person.

A bit more pricey but a good place to stay is *HI – Meyouhas Youth Hostel (*☎ 672 1775, fax 672 0372, 2 Jordan St)*, formerly the prestigious Hotel Tiberias (built 1862), now one of the country's most pleasant HI hostels. Accommodation is in two to four-bed dorms at US$13 per night for non-members, breakfast included. There are also single/double rooms at US$40/50. This place was destined for renovation in 1999 and should be up and running again by the time you read this: check to be sure though.

A three minute walk south of the bus station is *Adina's Guesthouse* (☎ 672 2507, 052-902 088, 15 HaShiloah St). Run by an orthodox Yemenite family, this is a guesthouse with separate kitchen and bathroom facilities for guests, and a terrace. You have a key so there's no curfew. Accommodation in private double air-con rooms with a bathtub costs 80/100NIS a single/double.

Mezuman House (☎ 672 3767) on Ha-Yarkon St is a B&B place frequented mainly by holidaying Israeli families – the family management don't speak much English but their young daughter does. The double air-con rooms are cosy and go for 150NIS, but showers and toilets are shared.

Places to Stay – Mid-Range

Just past the Meyouhas Youth Hostel, towards the lake, is the *Church of Scotland Hospice* (☎ 672 3769, fax 679 0145, email scottie@rannet.com). A lovely place, it has friendly staff, is comfortably furnished and has excellent facilities, including a garden and private beach. B&B is US$40 to US$45 per person in larger than average doubles, though there is a US$20 surcharge for one person. Rooms with sea views are US$5 extra. This place is often full, especially at weekends and on holidays, so book ahead if you can. It also provides dinner for US$12 and packed lunches for US$6.

Elsewhere, most hotel rooms seem overpriced when compared to some of the private rooms available in the better hostels. Close to the bus station is *Hotel Toledo* (☎ 672 1649, HaRab Bibass St), 50m west of the junction with HaShiloah St, which has air-con doubles with bathroom for 280NIS. *Panorama Hotel* (☎ 672 4811, fax 679 0146, 15 HaGalil St) is more basic, with singles/doubles for 210/270NIS – breakfast

and other meals are extra but are reasonably priced.

Opened in 1997, *Terminal Palace Hotel* (☎ 671 7176, fax 671 7175, 3 HaPrahim St) is as close to the bus station as you can get. It's a modern mid-range hotel with all expected comforts. Singles range from US$60 to $US67, doubles from US$72 to US$90. Enter the hotel via the shopping mall and take the lift to the 2nd floor.

The owners of the Aviv Hotel also run a very pleasant and airy block of apartments called *Aviv Holiday Flats* (☎ 671 2272, fax 671 2275) on Ahawa St. These are ideal for longer-term stays and offer cable TV and air-con. The rooms are quite large and airy, though a little under-furnished and the kitchenettes could be better provisioned for guests, but they are an ideal choice for visitors wanting location and independence. Apartments cost from US$50 to US$70 depending on the season.

There are also several mid-range hotels up in Kiryat Shemuel, a bit out of the way unless you have a car. Some of them do have great views across the lake, though. Recommended to Lonely Planet was *Kolton Inn* (☎ 679 1641, fax 672 0633, 2 Ohel Ya'acov St), which has a restaurant and nightclub and sea-facing rooms with balconies. Other alternatives you might try are *Eden Hotel* (☎ 679 0070, fax 672 2461, 4 Ohel Ya'acov St), and further up the street on the corner with Naiberg, *Astoria Hotel* (☎ 672 2351, fax 672 2352, email dany@kinneret.co.il, 13 Ohel Ya'acov St). *Beit Berger* (☎ 672 0850, fax 679 1514, 25 Neiberg St) is another one that has been recommended by readers. Located across from the Astoria, it's a private pension with air-con rooms all with bath and fridge.

Places to Stay – Top End

The long-established top hotel in Tiberias is *Plaza Galei Kinneret* (☎ 672 8888, fax 679 0260, email hhemda@irh.co.il), at the southern end of the town centre on the lake shore and run by the Howard Johnson chain. Mentioned in books by Leon Uris, James D McDonald and Taylor Caldwell, it has a charm and class badly lacking in its modern competitors. The facilities include an outdoor pool, gardens, water sports and a fine restaurant. Singles cost from US$223 to US$362, doubles from US$236 to US$452.

The other central top-end hotels, by comparison, are characterless though domineering in their bulk. There's little to choose between them. At *Radisson Moriah Plaza* (☎ 679 2233, fax 679 2320, email radisson-moriah-il@ibm.net) singles are priced from US$194 to US$218 in the low season and doubles from US$290 to US$327 in the high season. At *Jordan River Hotel* (☎ 671 4444, fax 672 3950, HaBanim St) singles are priced from US$115 to US$184 and doubles from US$150 to US$230; and at *The Caesar* (☎ 672 7272, fax 679 1013), entered off the midrahov down towards the promenade, singles go for US$209 to US$261, doubles from US$246 to US$308.

About 1km south of town on the road by the lake shore is *Gai Beach Hotel* (☎ 670 0700, fax 679 2776), right next to the water park, which guests can use free of charge; singles are priced from US$205 to US$293 and doubles from US$209 to US$309. Further south, right by the hot springs complex, is *Holiday Inn* (☎ 672 8555, 672 4443); singles are priced from US$158 to US$223 and doubles from US$173 to US$238.

Places to Eat – Budget

For picnicking supplies there's a small market with some fruit and vegetable stalls, just south of Gan Shimon, off HaYarkon St. It's open Sunday to Friday and closed on Saturday. There is also a very convenient supermarket right near the Al-Amari Mosque which is open Sunday to Thursday from 7 am to 6.45 pm, Friday from 7 am to 3.30 pm, and Saturday from 8 to 10 pm.

With a lengthy parade of felafel stands on HaYarden St, just west of the junction with HaGalil, Tiberias is a great place for fans of the deep-fried chickpea. These *Felafel Row* stalls are open until about 7 pm during the week, and until 2 pm on Friday; most stay closed on Saturday, although one or two sometimes open in the evening.

The cheapest sit-down dining is at the restaurants and cafes along HaBanim St, at the top end of the midrahov. *Cusina*, on the corner here, does inexpensive standards like kebab or schnitzel with salad and chips for 29NIS, while *Yamenite Restaurant* next door serves up *malawach*, large flaky-pastry pancakes, filled with either meat, mushrooms, egg or honey, for 16 to 18NIS each – one makes a substantial meal.

Vegetarians might head for the modern vegan eatery *Taste of Life* (☎ 671 2133, 4 HaKishon St) on a little pedestrian mall not far from the hostel colony. Takeaway BBQ twists and vegie shwarmas at 18NIS a pop are very popular choices, though you can have sit-down main dishes like a tofu medley for around 39NIS with all the trimmings. This is the sister shop to the Tel Aviv Taste of Life.

Places to Eat – Mid-Range

Most of the town's liveliest restaurants are to be found on the midrahov, along the promenade and on HaKishon St. The majority serve a very similar menu with little variation in price from one place to the next. The staple speciality is St Peter's fish and it's a popular choice among the town's diners. It tastes and looks a bit like trout in texture, though not as delicate. It is worth giving it a shot at least once during your stay here. The waterfront restaurants are easily the most attractive places to eat – grab a table at the water's edge and you can watch the fish, some up to almost 1m in length, flit and glide through the shallows and wonder why the hell, with such an abundance available, you have to pay 35 to 45NIS for the one on your plate. One of the better restaurants offering fish is *Karamba's Fish Restaurant* (☎ 672 4505), at the northern end of the promenade and it's open daily from about noon until the early hours. A pretty decent St Peter's fish dish will cost you around 40NIS.

Just north of the Lido promenade is a newly developed marina with a couple of popular, but fairly pricey restaurants catering to the better-heeled of the Tiberias set. Both are owned by local personality Eitan

What to do on Shabbat in Tiberias

The fact that no buses run on the Shabbat poses no problems as by far the best way of getting around the lake is by bicycle anyway. If the weather is fine then it may be too hot to do anything energetic and you may just want to cycle to a suitable site to lie in the sun or go swimming. Otherwise you can cycle up to Tabgha where the churches are all open and entry is free. Capernaum is open too, for a small fee. In the other direction you could visit Kibbutz Degania and Beit Gordon or carry on and cycle the whole way around the lake.

If you don't mind hitching and risking a long wait, go to Hammat Gader for the day. Make as early a start as possible to improve your chances of getting a ride. Remember that Saturday sees the place packed with Israelis.

On the food front, the popular eating and drinking places are open as usual on Friday evening for their busiest night of the week. However, stock up on food at the market and supermarket on Friday morning because on Saturday virtually everything is closed until after sundown.

'Mr Galilee' Gross, a former farmer turned restaurateur, and he has done spectacularly well out of both these enterprises. *The Pagoda* (☎ 672 5513) on G'dud Barak St is a flash kosher Chinese joint with just enough red and gold paint and bamboo to convince you that you are in the Far East.

Across from the Pagoda is *Decks* (☎ 672 1538) which is a large, cavernous marquee overlooking the water. It's popular with wedding parties, so it may not even be open to the public when you get there. Decks' speciality is its hickory charcoal grill and their entrecôte sword of mixed grilled meats at 78NIS sounds expensive, but it can feed up to three people. Try also the focaccia with onion cake – it is absolutely scrumptious. To get to the marina you have to walk along to G'dud Barak St for about 200m until you find the entrance on the right. Bookings are recommended at both places.

Away from the water and extremely popular with locals, the tiny *Guy Restaurant* (☎ 672 3036) often has queues of people waiting to get in. Strange, because the food is neither outstanding (a variety of averagely done grilled meat dishes) or particularly cheap (20 to 30NIS). However, the place does have a comfortable family atmosphere and excellent service, and the menu contains one or two interesting starters worth

trying, such as meatballs with nuts (15NIS) and spicy meat cigars (10NIS). It's open Sunday to Thursday from noon to midnight, Friday from noon to sunset, and Saturday from sunset to midnight. It's just west of the junction of HaBanim and HaGalil Sts, south of the city centre.

Entertainment

The cafes and bars on and around the midrahov are where the crowds form in the evening, bunching at *La Pirat* and *Big Ben*, both of which are loud and raucous through until well gone midnight. There are a couple of other popular places at the northern end of the promenade, too. All these bars, however, are geared to the Israeli tourist, which means 14NIS or more for a beer and awful music to boot. Budget travellers may prefer the rooftop bar at the *Nahum Hostel* which serves bottled beer at 8NIS and offers cable TV for travellers needing a fix on the news back home.

Live jazz is played on Thursday evening upstairs at *Taste of Life* (see Places to Eat – Budget) starting at 9 pm. This is a very popular activity so bookings are advised if you want to secure a table. There is an 'authentic' English pub of sorts called the *Red Lion* offering a variety of live and canned music and occasional events like 'Oriental Greek

THE GALILEE

Evenings' or 'Nisim Yemini Songs From All Times'. The Red Lion is in the Royal Plaza Tiberias hotel about 3km south of the town centre.

From October to May there is a free folk-loric dancing display daily at 9 pm at the Jordan River Hotel. For some strange reason this activity is not continued during the busy summer months.

Among the most infuriatingly popular evening activities are those offered by the many disco boats that ply the waters off the Lido and out into the lake each evening (20NIS per person). This mind-numbing entertainment is obviously popular with Israeli teens, and continues unabated for most of the evening. The worst of it is that the disco boats can make a peaceful waterside dinner almost an impossibility.

Getting There & Away

Bus There is a direct bus service to Tel Aviv (32.50NIS, 2½ hours) departing at least every hour until late evening, with the last bus on Friday leaving at 3 pm. Services to Jerusalem (39NIS, 2½ hours) are even more frequent.

There are also regular services to Haifa (22NIS, 1¼ hour), Nazareth (16.70NIS, 45 minutes) and Safed (16NIS, one hour), and Beit She'an (19NIS, 45 minutes).

Getting to the Upper Galilee and the Golan is not so easy. From the bus station you have to take a bus to the Rosh Pina junction (11.80NIS) and change there, which can involve a lot of waiting around.

The left-luggage office is just outside the bus station in shop No 1, a cafe that looks after bags for 6NIS a piece. It's open Sunday to Thursday from 7 am to 6 pm, and on Friday from 7 am to 3 pm, closed Saturday. For further bus information in Tiberias call ☎ 672 9222.

Car Rental All the car rental agencies are on HaBanim St.

Avis	☎ 06-672 2766
Budget	☎ 06-672 0864
Eldan	☎ 06-679 1822
Europcar	☎ 06-672 2777
Hertz	☎ 06-672 3939
Reliable	☎ 06-672 3464

Sheruts (Service Taxis) Outside the bus station and across the grass is where sheruts leave in the morning for Nazareth and occasionally Haifa. At other times you might find one looking for passengers to subsidise the journey back to some other destination but don't count on it. Sheruts also line up outside the Mizrahi Bank on HaBanim St.

Getting Around

In town you should be able to walk to most places, although if you stay up the hill in Kiryat Shemuel your legs will no doubt prefer you to use the bus.

Bicycle As long as you can deal with the heat, the ideal and most popular way of getting around Tiberias and the lake is by bicycle. The road by the lake shore is relatively hill-free and many of the sites are close together. You can rent bicycles from a few of the hostels including the Aviv (☎ 672 3510) and Nahum (☎ 672 1505). It isn't necessary to be a guest at these places. Expect to pay 30 or 40NIS for the day. Most cyclists do the lake circuit which can be done in four or five steady hours. Start early (around 7 am) to beat the heat and take plenty of water because there is little shade along the road.

Ferry Three times a day a ferry belonging to the Ein Gev kibbutz, on the opposite shore of the lake, departs Ein Gev for Tiberias and then shuttles back. Sailing times from Tiberias are 11.30 am and 1.30 and 4 pm, but check the schedule at the pier, which is just at the bottom of the midrahov. Alternatively you could call Kinneret Sailing Company (☎ 672 1831) for more details. A one-way crossing takes 45 minutes and costs 15NIS (25NIS return). Bicycles are carried for free.

Lido Kinneret Sailing Co (☎ 672 1538) also operates cruises up and down the lake departing the Lido Beach at 11.45 am daily. By special arrangement they also operate between Capernaum and Tiberias.

Sea of Galilee

Not just a natural beauty spot, the Sea of Galilee is Israel's major water supply. A freshwater lake which is fed by the Jordan River, the Sea of Galilee lies 212m below sea level and, in a good summer, the lake can be as warm as 33°C. Its length is 21km and its width, opposite Tiberias, is 9km, and it extends to 13km at its greatest. The average depth of 49m is changeable, depending on the region's unpredictable rainfall.

There are over 20 species of fish found in the lake and fishing has been an important industry since biblical times. The unique St Peter's fish is highly recommended in Israeli restaurants; however, it now mostly comes from fish farms rather than the Sea of Galilee.

Prehistoric tribes are known to have lived by the lake, in the Amud Caves south-west of Tabgha. The oldest human skull found in the country was discovered here in 1925. It was that of a man who lived in the Palaeolithic period, circa 100,000 BC. Bet Yerah, north of Kibbutz Degania, was an important Canaanite city 5000 years ago.

The Sea of Galilee has been known by several different names. The Old Testament calls it the Sea of Kinnereth (Numbers 34:11; Joshua 12:3, 13:27), which is linked to the Hebrew word *kinnor* (harp) – supposedly because the lake is shaped like a harp. The New Testament is where we get the term Sea of Galilee from (Matthew 4:18, 15:29; Mark 1:16, 7:31), although to Israelis it's still 'the Kinneret'.

Capernaum became the lake's most important site when Jesus made what was then a fishing village the centre of his ministry in the Galilee. With the destruction of Jerusalem and the Galilee's emergence as the new centre of Jewish life, schools of religious study were established on the shores of the lake and synagogues went up at Capernaum, Hammat Tiberias and Hammat Gader. The Byzantine period saw Christians flock here, and new churches were built in Heptapegon (Tabgha), Capernaum, Bet Yerah, and, on the eastern shore, Kursi and Susita.

AROUND THE SEA OF GALILEE

In about the 1st century BC there were nine large towns around the lake, each with a population of at least 15,000. Today, Tiberias is alone and virtually no trace exists of the other eight. However, there are numerous places of interest either on the shores of the Sea of Galilee or close by, many of them connected with the Bible. We recommend visits to Tabgha and Capernaum and also to Hammat Gader.

The best way to explore is to use Tiberias as a base and spend a day or two on a bicycle. It's 55km all the way around the Sea of Galilee, and if you're in shape it's possible to cycle the whole way around in a day, taking time out at one or two of the sites. But perhaps a better way of tackling it is to take the lake in two halves, each day finishing up at Kibbutz Ein Gev, opposite Tiberias, from where the regular ferry crosses back to town.

The descriptions below follow a route around the lake in a clockwise direction, starting from Tiberias.

Migdal

Six kilometres north of Tiberias, the road by the shore of the lake passes ancient Migdal, or Magdala, birthplace of Mary Magdalene. Its name is Hebrew for 'tower', and it was named after the defensive tower which dominated the important fishing village. A tiny, white-domed shrine marks the site.

Minya

Following the road by the lake, 1km north from Migdal, a side road leads eastwards to Minya. Here you'll find the ruins of a 7th century palace with the remnants of a mosaic

THE GALILEE

floor and, on the south-eastern side, a mosque with its tell-tale *mihrab* (prayer niche) oriented towards Mecca. This is the most ancient Muslim prayer place in Israel.

Beit Yigal Allon

Within the grounds of Kibbutz Ginossar, housed in a circular building at the water's edge, is the **Yigal Allon Centre** (☎ 672 1495, email betalon@netvision.net.il), a museum devoted to the theme 'man in the Galilee'. It contains exhibits on the region's archaeology, history and ethnography. The museum is open Sunday to Thursday from 8.30 am to 5 pm, Friday from 8 am to 1 pm, and Saturday from 9 am to 5 pm. Admission is 15NIS.

Since the late 1980s, however, the real interest at Yigal Allon has been in a murky tiled pool wherein, obscured by opaque waters, have lain the pickled remains of a 2000-year-old boat. Dubbed **'the Jesus boat'** by shrewd tour operators attuned to the pilgrimage buck, the vessel does date to roughly around the time of the Nazarene's ministry. It was discovered in 1986, uncovered by a severe drop in the lake's water level. The hard-packed mud of the lake bed had preserved the boat by denying oxygen to the otherwise wood-devouring bacteria. On 6 June 1995, after 9½ years soaking, the preservative solution was drained off and the skeletal boat is now fully visible beached inside the emptied pool. It's on view during museum hours and efforts are being made to build a suitable dedicated museum for the boat. If you can't get there yourself, view it virtually on the Internet at mahal .zrc.ac.il/ancient-boat.

To get here, noncyclists should take bus No 459, 841 or 963 from Tiberias bus station and get off at the orange signpost reading, 'Nof Ginnosar Guesthouse'. Walk 1km along the side road towards the lake and follow the signs to the museum.

Tabgha & the Mount of the Beatitudes

Generally considered to be the most appropriately beautiful and serene of the Christian holy places in the country, this site has managed to escape much of the commercialisation of modern Israel. Tradition locates three of the New Testament's most significant episodes here: the Sermon on the Mount, the Multiplication of the Loaves and Fishes, and Jesus' post-Resurrection appearance where he conferred the leadership of the church on Peter.

Tabgha is an Arab version of the Greek name Heptapegon (Seven Springs), and it is given to the small valley that lies south of the main road 12km north of Tiberias. A side road branches off to the right towards the lake and runs through the valley and past Capernaum to continue the circuit of the water, while the main road continues north towards Rosh Pina.

Church of the Multiplication of the Loaves & Fishes
This pleasant complex (which is also known as the Church of the Heptapegon) belongs to the German Benedictine Order and includes an adjacent monastery and pilgrims' hospice as well as the church. The current church building dates back only to 1936 and the monastery to 1956 but they're both constructed on the site of a 5th century Byzantine church whose well-preserved mosaic floor is probably the most beautiful in the country. The larger mosaic depicts a variety of flora and fauna, nearly all of which could have been found locally at the time the mosaic was laid. The mosaic immediately in front of the altar depicts two fish flanking a basket of loaves.

As the name implies, the churches were constructed on the site where it's traditionally believed that Jesus fed 5000 people with five loaves of bread and two fish (Mark 6:30-44).

The church is open Monday to Saturday from 8.30 am to 5 pm, and Sunday from 10 am to 5 pm. Admission is free.

Church of the Primacy of St Peter
This church occupies the site at which it's believed that Jesus appeared for the third time after his Resurrection (John 21). The current modest, black basalt structure was

built in 1933 by the Franciscans on the site of a 4th century church. At the base of the newer walls, at the end furthest away from the altar, you can clearly see the ancient wall on three sides. The flat rock in front of the altar is believed to be the table at which Jesus and his disciples ate; it was known to Byzantine pilgrims as Mensa Christi (Christ's Table).

Outside the church, by the water, are a few steps cut out of the rock. Some say that this was where Jesus stood when the disciples saw him, but they were possibly cut in the 2nd or 3rd century, when this area was quarried for limestone. Six double, or heart-shaped, column bases lie below the steps, although they are sometimes underwater if the lake level is high. These were probably taken from nearby buildings and intended to commemorate the 12 disciples. The church is open daily from 8 am to 6 pm. Admission is free.

Church of the Mount of Beatitudes

This marks the place where it's believed that Jesus gave the Sermon on the Mount (Matthew 5-7) and also where he chose his disciples (Luke 6:12). The present structure, built on the site of earlier churches, dates from 1937.

Owned by the Franciscans, whose nuns live in the adjacent hospice, the church's octagonal shape symbolises the eight beatitudes (Matthew 5:3-10). The seven virtues (justice, charity, prudence, faith, fortitude, hope and temperance) are also represented by symbols in the pavement around the altar. From the gallery you have some of the best views of the lake, particularly towards Tiberias to the south, and Capernaum, with the red domes of the Greek Orthodox monastery beyond, to the east. The church is open daily from 8 am to noon and 2.30 to 5 pm. Admission is free.

Springs

These powerful springs lie to the east of the Church of the Primacy and with a bit of searching you can locate a pleasant little waterfall for a refreshing shower on a hot sticky day.

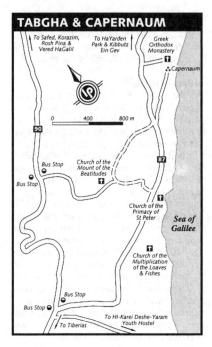

Getting There & Away Bus Nos 459, 841 and 963 leave from Tiberias bus station and go northwards, past Migdal and Minya. Just before the bus stop at the Tabgha turn-off, the road passes an electric power plant on the right as you climb a steep slope. Watch out for this so you have time to remind the driver that you want to get off at Tabgha. The Egged school of grand prix driving seems to teach its drivers to build up speed here to negotiate the approaching steep climb.

From this bus stop follow the side road as it bends to the left; the Church of the Multiplication is a few minutes walk further. Continuing along the road, above the lay-by is a rough path that leads up the slope to the Church of the Beatitudes. Alternatively, you can stay on the bus until the next stop; after the Tabgha turn-off the road veers away from the lake and zigzags up the hill, and the next stop is beside a turn-off marked by an

THE GALILEE

orange sign reading, 'Hospice of the Beatitudes'. Follow this side road to reach the church. From here you can walk down the slope to reach the Church of the Primacy.

Vered HaGalil

As the road to Rosh Pina continues northwards from the Mount of the Beatitudes, it steadily climbs to reach sea level just before the intersection with the road to Almagor. Here an orange signpost directs you to Vered HaGalil (Rose of the Galilee, ☎ *693 5785, fax 693 4964, email vered@veredhagalil .co.il*), a riding farm and stable that offers horse riding and guesthouse facilities (see Places to Stay later in this section). The US-style complex enjoys a good reputation and is beautifully situated in great riding country. You can go on half-day escorted trail rides for 310NIS; the stables also hires out horses for 89NIS an hour or 160NIS for two hours, and prices are negotiable for the whole day.

There is a pretty decent country restaurant here also, in case you are looking for a bite to eat on a hot Shabbat afternoon, when the restaurant will be open. See also www .veredhagalil.co.il for full details.

Korazim

Continue east along the road from Vered HaGalil and after 4km you come to the ruins of ancient Korazim. There was a Jewish town here in the 1st century and, along with Capernaum and Bethsaida, its people were condemned by Jesus for their lack of faith (Matthew 11:20-24). Although it probably benefited from the Galilee's influx of Jews following the exile from Jerusalem (135 AD), records show that the town was in ruins by the 4th century.

Some restoration has gone on and the remains give an idea of the layout of a small town of that time. The feature of the ruins is a black basalt synagogue of the 3rd to 4th century, similar in style to the limestone one at Capernaum. The site is open Sunday to Thursday from 8 am to 5 pm, and Friday from 8 am to 4 pm (but it closes one hour earlier in winter). Admission is 13NIS (students 9.80NIS).

Beyond Korazim to the east, the ground is covered with large basalt rocks. Many of these are dolmens – large blocks of broad and flat stone placed on other stones and used as burial chambers between 6000 and 4000 BC.

You can either backtrack from here to Tabgha or continue east along the minor road (No 8277) for a further couple of kilometres to a junction, the southern fork of which leads back to the road encircling the lake.

Capernaum

Capernaum is a Greek rendering of the Hebrew Kfar Nahum (Village of Nahum). Who Nahum was, nobody really knows. Capernaum, though, is well known as the home

The original Capernaum synagogue was built in about 100 AD.
The reconstructed building still includes these impressive Roman friezes.

base of Jesus when he started his ministry (Matthew 4:12-17, 9:1; Mark 2:1). There are several other references to the town in the New Testament, including Jesus teaching in the synagogue (Mark 1:21), getting rid of a man's evil spirit (Mark 1:23-26), the curing of Peter's step-mother (Mark 1:29-31), the leper (Luke 5:12-16), the centurion's servant (Luke 7:1-10), the paralytic (Mark 2:11-12; Luke 5:17-25), and walking on the water and discussing the bread of life (John 6:16-59).

Jesus is believed to have moved here from Nazareth because it was the home of his first converts (Peter and Andrew). There seems to have been a strong Christian presence here in the 2nd century, according to both rabbinical texts and archaeological discoveries, and we know that by the 4th century the town had expanded to cover the surrounding hills. However, after the Arab conquest sometime around 700 AD, the town was destroyed and never again inhabited.

Archaeological Museum In 1894, the Franciscans purchased the site and set about restoring the ancient synagogue and church, which are now the major attractions of a well-labelled museum.

Synagogue Not the synagogue frequented by Jesus. Although the specific date of construction is unknown, it's agreed by archaeologists that this particular house of worship was built at least a century after the Crucifixion took place. The reconstructed building consists of an annexe and a main prayer hall with an impressive Roman facade and a column with a Greek inscription. The entrance to the annexe, standing to the east of the hall, has a nicely carved lintel, with an eagle and palm tree design. Other carvings adorning various parts of the synagogue include the Star of David, a palm (once the symbol of Israel), a menorah, a wagon that may represent the ancient Holy Ark that carried the Torah, an urn, and a half-horse, half-fish figure.

St Peter's House The ruins of a church mark what is believed to have been St Peter's home where Jesus stayed. A mosaic

Ancient coin found at the site of St Peter's House, where it is believed Jesus stayed.

floor decorates the room believed to have been host to Christ. The beginnings of the church, built around the mosaic room, have been traced to the 4th century. It's open daily from 8.30 am to 4.15 pm; Admission is 2NIS. Modest dress is required – no shorts, bare shoulders etc. There are toilets and a snack bar outside.

Getting There & Away From the Church of the Mount of the Beatitudes you have a pleasant walk across the fields to Capernaum. Just follow the various tracks down the hill and aim for the red domes of the Greek Orthodox monastery. To reach the museum, you should walk down the signposted side road; it's at the end. From Tabgha just follow the road 3km to the east to reach the turn-off for the museum, and then keep going for the Greek Orthodox monastery which is easily spotted down to your right.

Greek Orthodox Monastery
Known also as the Church of the Twelve Apostles, with its peeling paint this place looks far better from a distance; up close there's nothing to see. Probably the only person you will meet is a friendly Greek caretaker who will be happy to spend some time with you.

THE GALILEE

Easily spotted because of its two red domes, the monastery is on the lake shore 2km east of the open-air museum.

Kursi

Seven kilometres north of Ein Gev, the Kursi archaeological site features the remains of the largest Byzantine monastery in the Holy Land. This is also the traditional site of the miracle of the swine (Luke 8:26-39; Matthew 8:23-34). When Jesus exorcised the body of a man the fleeing demons then possessed a herd of swine grazing nearby, which stampeded into the lake and were drowned.

Probably built in the 5th century, the walled monastery measured 145m by 123m, and has been partially reconstructed. At a nearby rock, assumed to be close to the spot of the pig possession episode, additional excavations include a chapel paved with three separate layers of mosaics, columns, a damaged inscription and a bench which overlooks the Sea of Galilee.

The Kursi site (☎ 673 1983) is open Saturday to Thursday from 8 am to 5 pm, and Friday from 8 am to 4 pm; from October to March closing times are one hour earlier. Admission is 8NIS (students 6NIS).

Kibbutz Ein Gev

Established in 1937 by German and Czech pioneers, Ein Gev was the first permanent Jewish settlement on the eastern shore of the Sea of Galilee. As a frontier post (and the kibbutz was stockaded like a fortress), security concerns ruled out agriculture as a means of existence so the kibbutz developed a fishing industry. One of Ein Gev's major attractions today is its restaurant, well supplied by the kibbutz fish farm. Reminiscent of a school dining hall and not particularly cheap, the attraction is hard to fathom. If you are going to eat there then the starters are the best value: very large helpings of cheese and mushroom flan or kosher prawns for 22NIS. Kids might enjoy leaning out of the windows to feed their leftovers to the giant catfish in the pool below. Ein Gev is also

well known for its 5000 seat **amphitheatre** which is the setting for some major music festivals.

The kibbutz runs the ferry service across the lake to Tiberias, with departures three times a day at 11.30 am and 1.30 and 4 pm – see Getting Around in the Tiberias section. To book tours around the kibbutz to see the vineyards, banana and date plantations and the fish farm, or for ferry details, call ☎ 675 8030 or fax 675 8888.

Kibbutz Ha'On

Its name meaning strength, this kibbutz was established in 1948. Next to the holiday village here is an **ostrich farm** (☎ 675 7555). It's open to visitors Sunday to Thursday from 9 am to 4 pm, and Friday from 9 am to 1 pm. Admission is 15NIS (students 10NIS) in the high season, and 12NIS (students 8NIS) in the low season.

Hammat Gader

One of the highlights for many visitors to the Galilee, and a regular attraction for locals, the Hammat Gader complex is an area of pleasant parkland dotted with some impressive Roman ruins, hot springs, amusements and crocodiles (in pens, you'll be relieved to know). Although the sulphur smell can be a bit pungent, the springs here provide a cheaper and more earthy alternative to the baths at Hammat Tiberias. The facilities also include a modern pool with massage jets, a waterfall, and an area with black mud which is reputed to be good for the skin. However, one reader ruined a 70-year old silver necklace while wearing it in the hot sulphur springs – so be warned.

The partially reconstructed **Roman ruins** are quite impressive and include various bathing areas, such as a smaller pool reserved for lepers and the hottest spring (51°C) which is called in Hebrew Ma'ayan HaGehinom (Hell's Pool) and in Arabic Ain Makleh (Frying Pool). There is also a ruined 5th or 6th century synagogue just west of the Roman baths and past the picnic area. From the top of the excavation site you have a fine view of the valley crossed by the bridge that used to carry the Haifa-Damascus railway.

The alligator park was started off with reptiles imported from Florida but they are now born and raised for export in the hothouse by the entrance to the pools.

Hammat Gader (☎ 675 1039, fax 675 2745) is open Monday to Thursday from 7 am to 9.30 pm, Friday from 7 am to 11.30 pm, and Saturday and Sunday from 7 am to 6.30 pm. Admission is 40NIS (students 35NIS), which gives access to all the amenities, although some health and beauty facilities are charged extra. The site is 8km south-east of the Sea of Galilee (21km from Tiberias) in the valley of the Yarmuk River, on the border with Jordan, so you'll see lots of barbed wire and sentry posts. Buses from Tiberias are not very frequent so you need to make an early start to get the most out of your admission fee. From the central station bus No 24 departs Sunday to Thursday at 8.45 and 10.30 am, and Friday at 8.30 and 9.30 am. Buses depart from Hammat Gader Sunday to Thursday at noon and 3 pm, and Friday at noon and 1 pm. No buses run on Saturday.

Tzemah

A roofless two storey building at the junction of Route 90 and the ring road beside the lake is the remains of a Turkish railway station; once a stop on the former Haifa-Damascus railway. There is a tourist information centre (☎ 675 2056) in the shopping centre, open daily from 8 am to 4 pm.

Kibbutz Degania

Also known by the Saddam-esque title of Em Hakevutsot, or 'Mother of all Cooperative Villages', Degania, established in 1909, was the world's first kibbutz. Located between the Jordan River and Beit She'an junction, there are in fact two kibbutzim here but the one of interest (minimal though it may be) is the original, Degania A (or Degania Alef).

The main entrance is 50m south of the road alongside the lake, down a well-signposted drive flanked by banana plantations.

Outside the gate is a Syrian tank, a souvenir from the 1948 War when the kibbutzniks, armed with molotov cocktails and rifles, defeated an enemy armoured column.

Within the grounds of the kibbutz is **Beit Gordon** (☎ 675 0040), an archaeological and natural history museum dedicated to the memory of the father of the kibbutz movement, AD Gordon. The museum is open Sunday to Thursday from 9.30 am to 4 pm, Friday from 8.30 am to noon, and Saturday from 9.30 am to noon. Admission is 10NIS (students 8NIS).

The entrance to the museum and a car park are on the road that runs beside the lake. On Saturday the entrance here is closed to cars (pedestrians and cyclists can still get through) and you should drive through the main entrance (marked by the tank).

Next to Beit Gordon is the **SPNI Kinnrot Field Study Centre** (☎ 675 2639), which has information on hikes in the region.

Beit Yerah & Kinneret Cemetery

Some 9km south of Tiberias, just south of the Afula junction, you come to a hill where, up on the left by the water, excavations have revealed the remains of a 3rd century Roman fort and the ruins of a 5th century Byzantine church and synagogue. However, all the finds from here have been distributed among museums and there's little left to see.

The nearby cemetery belongs to Kibbutz Kinneret and among those buried here are the Hebrew poets Rahel and Elisheva, and Berl Katsenelson, a leader of the Jewish labour movement.

Yardenit Baptism Site

Kibbutz Kinneret has built a flash-looking baptism site south of the bridge crossing the Jordan River where it leaves the Sea of Galilee. This is not the site where Jesus was baptised, which is at Al-Maghtes near Jericho – out of bounds to pilgrims because of its proximity to the Jordanian-West Bank border. The site boasts custom-built 'baptism pens' where white-garbed devotees line up to be dipped in the river.

The river here is quite beautiful, over-hung with trees and swarming with fish and is, not surprisingly, very popular all year round. For full information call ☎ 675 9486, fax 675 9648 or write to Yardenit Kvutsat, Kinneret, 15118.

Places to Stay

There is a variety of places to stay around the Sea of Galilee, most of them kibbutzim.

Places to Stay – Budget

Camping If you thought camping was an alternative to paying high prices, think again. Camp sites on the shores of the Sea of Galilee, mostly run by kibbutzim, are quite expensive. However, if you have your own tent then there are 20 or so spots around the lake where you can pitch for free. The SPNI Field Study Centre and the tourist information centre at Tzemah can give you details.

Ein Gev Holiday Village (☎ 675 2540, fax 675 1590) is about 1.5km south of the kibbutz entrance. It is set amid pleasant parkland and there is a rocky beach, boats and canoes for hire, crazy golf, a cafeteria and a restaurant. Prices go up considerably for the summer months and Jewish holidays. There are sites (approximately 60NIS per two people, 20NIS per extra person), little bungalows and caravans/trailers fitted out with showers, toilets and kitchens; the latter work out at around US$60 per person.

Kibbutz Ha'On Holiday Village (☎ 675 7555, fax 675 7557) is 5km further south on the lake shore. With your own tent you pay from 60NIS. A caravan/trailer with shower, toilet and kitchen costs from US$75 for two, rising steeply during weekends, the summer months and Jewish holidays.

Hostel In Tabgha itself is the modern and extremely elegant *HI – Karei Deshe-Yoram Youth Hostel (☎ 672 0601, fax 672 4818)*. This place is well worth considering if you want to spend some time in the immediate area. Set in attractive grounds with eucalyptus trees, a rocky beach and a few peacocks, its rooms are clean and air-conditioned, the management pleasant and the food good.

Dorm beds are US$16 for members, while nonmembers pay US$17.50. There's also a family sized room. Meals are available, or there's a kitchen for self-catering; no curfew is imposed.

Bus Nos 459, 841 and 963 from Tiberias stop on the main road nearby. Get off at the orange 'Karei Deshe' signpost just before the road heads up the hill past the power station. Walk straight down the side road, past the turning to the left, and the hostel is at the end after about a 1.5km walk.

Places to Stay – Mid-Range

Vered HaGalil Guest Farm (☎ 693 5785, fax 693 4964, email vered@veredhagalil .co.il) has lovely accommodation in Swiss-style chalets along with the horse riding facilities. Singles/doubles cost from 220 to 370NIS and 395 to 500NIS respectively, breakfast included. Prices go up by about 45% at weekends. It is usually possible to camp out on the lawn for free and use the shower and toilet facilities if you are going riding the next day. Get off the bus from Tiberias at the signposted Korazim junction.

Places to Stay – Top End

An attractive alternative to Tiberias for many visitors is to stay outside the town for at least some of their time in the region. The four-star-styled *Nof Ginnosar Guesthouse (☎ 679 2161, fax 679 2170, email ginosar@ netvision.net.il)*, run by Kibbutz Ginnosar, provides comfortable accommodation beside the lake. It offers gardens, a private beach and water-sports facilities in a very quiet and unhurried atmosphere. Singles cost from around US$95 to US$126 and doubles from US$121 to US$156. South of Tabgha, the kibbutz is off the main road from Tiberias, and clearly signposted.

SAFED   צפת
Pop: 23,000 ☎ Area Code: 06

Alternatively spelt Zefad, Tzfat or Tsfat, this is an attractive hilltop town with a rich heritage of Jewish mysticism and an industrious artists' colony. The town is also blessed with a beautiful high-altitude setting and a temperate climate. It's definitely worth a visit but because of the lack of good budget accommodation and evening entertainment most people make a day trip of it from Tiberias. Avoid Safed on the Shabbat when even the birds stay grounded.

History

Safed was founded sometime in the 2nd century BC as a *masu'of* (beacon) village – one of a chain of hilltop fire sites stretching to Jerusalem. The beacons were lit to mark the beginning of a new month or holy day. During the First Revolt (66-73 AD), Safed was fortified by Josephus, leader of the Jewish forces in the Galilee.

The Crusaders led by Fulke, King of Anjou, also chose to site a citadel here to control the highway to Damascus. Fulke's fortification, known as Saphet, was destroyed by Saladin, rebuilt by the Knights Templar and destroyed once again by the Sultan Beybars in 1266.

During the 15th and 16th centuries the Jewish community of Safad, or Safat, as it was now called, was enlarged by an influx of immigrants fleeing the Inquisition and persecution in Spain. Many of the new arrivals were Kabbalists, or mystical truth seekers. The name comes from the Hebraic root *kbl*, meaning 'to receive', and the movement originated in the region of Safed around the time of the First Revolt, before being carried abroad with the Diaspora. It flourished particularly among the Jews of the Iberian Peninsula and for a time Spain was a world centre of Jewish learning and culture. With the relocation of the Kabbalists that mantle passed to Safed.

In the latter part of the 18th century Safed welcomed a further influx of Jewish hasidim, this time from Russia. However, in 1837 an earthquake destroyed much of the town, killing up to 5000 people and levelling many of the 69 synagogues.

As throughout all of Palestine, increased Jewish immigration was intensifying Arab hostility to the newcomers. Violence between the two had been sporadic but with the growth of nationalistic aspirations on both

sides, clashes became increasingly frequent. During the 1920s and 30s there was rioting in Safed with loss of life on both sides, culminating in a pitched battle for the town in 1948. Though outnumbered, the Jews prevailed and the Arabs were forced to flee.

What had been the Arab quarter of town was filled with more, newly arrived Jewish immigrants, and today 25% of Safed's population is made up of recent arrivals from the former Soviet Union and Ethiopia. Many of the Arab properties, including the main mosque, have been turned into gallery space and studios and the resulting 'Artists' Quarter' has become one of Safed's major tourist attractions.

Orientation

The highest town in the country, Safed sits at 800m above sea level on a huddle of hilltops. It consists basically of three main areas, with the town centre on one hill, south Safed on another, and Mt Cana'an, a residential suburb, to the east.

Most, if not all, of your time will be spent in central Safed, which is small enough to cover on foot. Spread neatly over one perfectly rounded hill, the crown of central Safed is wooded Gan HaMetsuda, where the old Crusader citadel once stood. A little downhill, Jerusalem (Yerushalayim) St, Safed's main thoroughfare, completely encircles the park in an unbroken loop. The bus station is just off Jerusalem St on the eastern side of the hill, while the old town centre is 180° away, directly opposite on the western side – so, from the bus station head either north or south, you'll end up in the same place.

The old quarters which make up the heart of central Safed tumble down from Jerusalem St in a snakes and ladders compendium of ankle-straining stairways and slithering alleys. They are divided uncompromisingly in two by Ma'alot Olei HaGardom (see Ma'alot Olei HaGardom later in this section), a broad, stiff stairway running down from Jerusalem St; the area to the north of the stairway is known as the Synagogue Quarter, haunt of black-robed

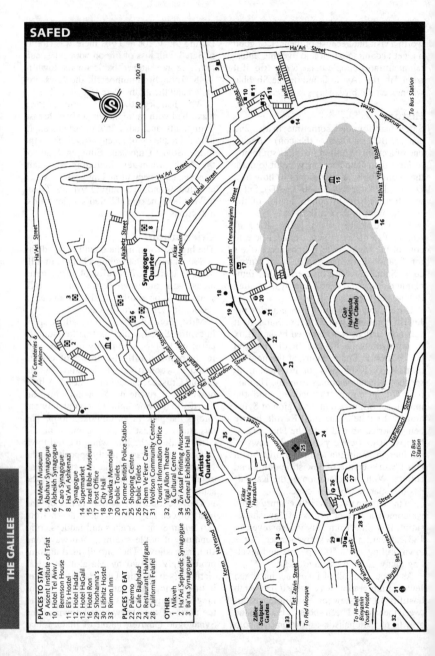

SAFED

PLACES TO STAY
9 Ascent Institute of Tsfat
10 Hotel Tel Aviv/
    Berenson House
11 Eli's Hostel
12 Hotel Hadar
13 Hotel HaGalil
16 Hotel Ron
29 Shoshanna's
30 Lifshitz Hostel
33 Rimon Inn

PLACES TO EAT
22 Palermo
23 Cafe Baghdad
24 Restaurant HaMifgash
28 California Felafel

OTHER
1 Mikveh
2 Ha'Ari Sephardic Synagogue
3 Ba'na Synagogue

4 HaMeiri Museum
5 Abuhav Synagogue
6 Alsheikh Synagogue
7 Caro Synagogue
8 Ha'Ari Ashkenazi
   Synagogue
14 Supermarket
15 Israel Bible Museum
17 Post Office
18 City Hall
19 Davidka Memorial
20 Public Toilets
21 Former British Police Station
25 Shopping Centre
26 Public Toilets
27 Shem Ve'Ever Cave
31 Wolfson Community Centre,
    Tourist Information Office
32 Yigal Allon Theatre
    & Cultural Centre
34 Zvi Assaf Printing Museum
35 General Exhibition Hall

THE GALILEE

Hasidic Jews, while south of the steps is Safed's famed Artists' Quarter.

Information

Tourist Office Safed's local tourist information office (☎ 692 0961) is not one of Israel's best. At the time of our last visit it was a very makeshift affair and any printed information it had was in Hebrew only. No maps either. It does, however, have a computerised information terminal which carries some historical site descriptions and a limited accommodatioh list. The office is in Wolfson Community Centre and is open Sunday to Thursday from 8 am to 4 pm, closed Friday and Saturday.

Money All the bank branches are on Jerusalem St west of the Citadel. Opening hours are generally Sunday, Tuesday and Thursday from 8.30 am to 12.30 pm and 4 to 6 pm, Monday, Wednesday and Friday from 8.30 am to noon; they're closed on Saturday. An exception is the First International Bank at 34 Jerusalem St, which is closed Sunday, Tuesday and Thursday afternoon, but open 4 to 7 pm on Monday and Wednesday.

Post & Communications Although the main post and telephone office is on Ha-Palmach St (look for the radar dish next door, visible from the corner of Aliyah Bet St) some way from the centre, there is a convenient branch office at 37 Jerusalem St. Both offices are open Sunday to Tuesday and Thursday from 8 am to 12.30 pm and 3.30 to 6 pm, Wednesday from 8 am to 1.30 pm, and Friday from 8 am to noon.

Emergencies For the police, call ☎ 693 0444 or in emergencies call ☎ 100. The Magen David Adom first-aid centre (☎ 692 0333) is next to the bus station. In medical emergencies call ☎ 911.

Gan HaMetsuda & the Bible Museum

Gan HaMetsuda is the pleasant breeze-cooled park and viewpoint at the summit of Mt Safed, the citadel of old. Though at one

time the largest in the Middle East, little evidence remains today of the Crusader-era fortress that once stood up here. Its outer walls once followed the line now marked by Jerusalem St but you can only see remains of one of the inner walls on Hativat Yiftah Rd, near the Israel Bible Museum (☎ 697 3472). Once the home of a Turkish pasha, the 120-year-old building is now home to the work of American-Jewish sculptor and artist, Phillip Ratner. He has established a museum of his sculpture, painting, lithography and tapestry, which depict scenes from the Bible. The collection is constantly being added to as Ratner works at his studio in the building for part of each year.

The museum is open Sunday to Thursday from 10 am to 4 pm, Friday from 10 am to 1 pm, and Saturday from 10 am to 2 pm (Sunday to Thursday from 10 am to 2 pm only from October to May); it's closed all through January. Admission is free, but donations are accepted.

Jerusalem & Ma'alot Olei HaGardom Streets

On Jerusalem St, a few metres south of City Hall, the **Davidka Memorial** incorporates an example of the primitive and unreliable Davidka mortar made by the Jews and used to great effect in 1948. Somewhat dangerous to use, it did little physical damage but the story goes that it made such a loud noise that it scared the living daylights out of the Arabs.

Across from the memorial is the former **British police station**, riddled with bullet holes – the result of Arab-Jewish skirmishing in May 1948. For many subsequent years the place served as an income tax office and obvious jokes are made about the 'real' reason for the bullets.

Just south of the police station, and over the road, is **Ma'alot Olei HaGardom St**, the wide stairway that leads down from Jerusalem St. It was built by the British after the riots of 1929 to divide the town and keep the Arab community (living mainly in what's now the Artists' Quarter) and Jewish community (inhabiting the Synagogue Quarter) apart. Tarpat St, which crosses Ma'alot Olei HaGardom St at its mid-point, is the main street where the rioting took place. Note the ruins of 16th century Jewish houses which were built using stones removed from the Crusader wall up the hill.

Look back from Ma'alot Olei HaGardom St, across Jerusalem St, and you'll notice on the roof of the building at the top the search-light remaining from a one-time British gun position.

Synagogue Quarter

The Synagogue Quarter, the town's old trad-itional Jewish neighbourhood, is centred on what's now known as Kikar HaMaginim (Defenders' Square) – or just HaKikar (The Square) – reached by descending the steps just north of City Hall. The name refers to the fact that the building that now houses the Tiferet Gallery was, during the 1948 War, the headquarters of the Haganah.

Within a few minutes walk of the square are all of Safed's major Kabbalist syna-gogues. They are usually open throughout the day to visitors, and admission is free al-though donations are requested. Suitable clothing must be worn – no shorts, no bare shoulders – and cardboard *yarmulkes* (skull caps; see the boxed text 'Jews & Kippas' opposite) are provided. Photography is per-mitted in the Synagogue Quarter except on Shabbat (sundown Friday to sundown Sat-urday). If you are a little short of time, then the two to visit are the Ha'Ari and Caro synagogues.

Ha'Ari Ashkenazi Synagogue Just down from the Kikar, on the right, this is one of two synagogues dedicated to 'the Ari', one of the major figures of Jewish mysticism. Ari (Lion) is an acronym of his name, Ad-oni (or Ashkenazi) Rabbi Yitzhak Luria.

Born in Jerusalem in 1534, Rabbi Yit-zhak moved to Cairo where he quickly mas-tered conventional Jewish teachings and began to study the Kabbalah. In 1569, after some 12 years of study, he brought his fam-ily to Safed so that he could study with the Ramak – Rabbi Moshe Cordeviero, the leading teacher of mysticism at the time. When he died, the Ari took over and taught the secrets of the Torah to a select group of students until his death in a sudden plague in 1572.

The Ha'Ari Ashkenazi Synagogue was built after his death on the site of the field (in those days it was outside the city) where the Kabbalists would gather to welcome Shabbat. The original building was destroy-ed in an 1852 earthquake.

The olive-wood ark was carved in the 19th century and represents over 10 years work. The *bimah* (central platform) bears a shrapnel hole in the side facing the door from an Arab attack during the 1948 siege. The synagogue was packed with worship-pers at the time but the congregation was bowed in prayer and the projectile flew over their heads – the hole is now stuffed with messages to God.

At the rear of the synagogue, in a small room, is a chair carved at about the same time as the ark. Called Kise Eliyahu (Eli-jah's Chair), it's used during the circumci-sion ceremony and legend has it that any Jewish couple who sits here will have a son within a year.

Caro Synagogue Rabbi Yosef Caro was another leading Kabbalist. He was born in Spain in 1488, and after the expulsion of the Jews in 1492, he moved to the Balkans, ar-riving in Safed in 1535. He later became the chief rabbi here, but he attained fame for his important written works which included the Shulchan Aruch, basically an extensive blueprint for living a Jewish life.

So influential are his teachings and their interpretations of the Jewish Law that mod-ern-day rabbis still refer to him for guidance with contemporary issues.

Destroyed in the 1837 earthquake and re-built around 1847, the synagogue stands above Rabbi Caro's yeshiva. The ark con-tains three ancient Torah scrolls: the one on the right is from Persia and is about 200 years old; the centre one, from Iraq, is about 300 years old; and the scroll on the left, from Spain, is over 500 years old.

Jews & Kippas

The most common sign that a male Jew is religiously observant is a *kippa* (skullcap), known in Yiddish and outside Israel as a *yarmulke* (pronounced YAH-muh-kuh). Contrary to what many people think, there is no religious requirement that men wear head covering – from the point of view of *Halacha* (Jewish law), the wearing of a kippa, cap, trilby, beret etc is merely a custom. There is no standard size for *kippot* and you will see various styles, colours and materials used.

You can very often tell the religious and political affiliation of a man by the kind of kippa he is wearing. Ultraorthodox men usually wear black velvet kippot under their black hats, which – like the *shtreimels* (fur hats) worn by some Hasidim on Shabbat and certain holidays – are often protected from the rain by plastic bags. Jews affiliated with the National Religious Party, the mainly right-wing party from which the Gush Emunim settler movement sprang, wear colourful, crocheted kippot with variegated designs around the edge. As a rule of thumb, the larger the kippa the more ideologically committed the wearer is. The newer models have an intricate design that goes all the way to the middle of the kippa.

If a man is wearing such a crocheted kippa (probably knitted by his wife or girlfriend), has *tzitziot* (tassels) flying from his hips and has an M16 slung over his shoulder, he's almost certainly a settler from the West Bank or the Gaza Strip. A huge crocheted kippa, often in white, is a sign that the wearer is either a Braslav Hassid or a Messianist of some sort, perhaps an extreme right-wing settler. (Don't confuse the large, white, messianic kippot with the patterned, all-white, crocheted skullcaps worn by Hajis – Muslims who have made the Haj to Mecca.) Orthodox men of moderate politics often wear knitted kippot of a single, unostentatious colour, often brown or tan. Tiny knitted kippot are sometimes worn by traditional (but not necessarily orthodox) Mizrahi men so that Jewish passers-by don't think that they're Arabs.

Since the assassination of Yitzhak Rabin, Conservative and Reform men (and, increasingly, women) have tried to find a kippa style that doesn't imply that the wearer is an opponent of the peace process, as the colourful crocheted models do. Some have adopted the Bucharian kippa, a large, round embroidered cap, while others have gone in for kippot crocheted with thick (rather than thin) yarn.

Alsheikh Synagogue Not always open, this synagogue is named after Rabbi Moses Alsheikh, another leading Kabbalist. Built in the 17th century, it's the only synagogue that survived the 1827 earthquake intact. The walls along this street are traditionally painted an attractive blue – a colour which represents royalty and heaven.

Abuhav Synagogue This synagogue is believed to have been built by followers of Rabbi Yitzhak Abuhav in the 1490s, using a plan based on the Kabbalah. The four central pillars represent the four elements which, according to Kabbalists, make up all

of the creation. The dome has 10 windows to represent the Commandments, pictures of the 12 tribes of Israel which represent Jewish unity, illustrations of the musical instruments used in the Temple, pomegranate trees (which traditionally have 613 seeds – the same number as the commandments in the Torah), and the Dome of the Rock, a reminder of the destruction of the Temple. The silver candelabrum hanging opposite the central ark is a memorial to the Holocaust victims.

Ba'na Synagogue Named after Rabbi Yossi Ba'na (the Builder) who is buried

THE GALILEE

here, this synagogue is also known as the Shrine of the White Saint – in Hebrew it's called HaTsadik HaLavan. This is based on a legend that tells of the time when an Arab governor of Safed ruled that the Jews had to use only white chickens for the Yom Kippur ceremony. The distressed Jews prayed at Rabbi Ba'na's tomb for a way out of the problem and the result was that all the black chickens turned pure white. Another version of the legend has it that the Jews were told to bring to the governor a certain number of white chickens, or face expulsion.

The synagogue is not normally open to visitors except in the afternoons when children's classes are held here.

Ha'Ari Sephardic Synagogue On the lower slopes of the Old City, just up from the cemeteries, this synagogue is built on the site where Ari prayed. The small room on the left in the back is said to be where he learned the mystical texts with the prophet Elijah.

In the 1948 War, the synagogue, which faced a then-Arab neighbourhood, was pressed into service as a military post and a machine gun was set up by the window above the ark.

HaMeiri Museum Just up the slope from the Ha'Ari Sephardic Synagogue, this complex comprises a museum, a research institute and a centre for educational tourism; call ☎ 697 1307 for details.

Established by Yehzkel HaMeiri, a fifth-generation Safedian, the stated aim of this museum is to impart an understanding of Safed's Jewish community during the last century and its struggle to survive. The presentation includes collections of documents, papers, ancient books, utensils from homes and workplaces, clothes, furniture and holy objects. There are also photographs, recordings and video tapes of both sites and older residents.

The museum is open Sunday to Thursday from 9 am to 2 pm, and Friday from 9 am to 1 pm, closed Saturday, and admission is 5NIS.

Cemeteries

Below the Synagogue Quarter on the lower western slopes of Mt Safed lie three adjoining cemeteries. The small building to the left of the path that leads down from the Ha'Ari Sephardic Synagogue is its gents' *mikveh* (ritual bath).

The oldest of the cemeteries contains the graves of many of the famous Kabbalists who believed that Safed's pure air would benefit the souls of those buried here and fly them immediately to the Garden of Eden.

The domed tomb was built by the Karaites of Damascus and is believed by them to contain the body of the biblical prophet, Hosea. Legend has it that also buried on this hill are Hannah and her seven sons, martyred by the Greeks on the eve of the Maccabaean Revolt. The feeling of fatigue experienced when you climb the hill is said to be due to walking over their graves.

The more recent cemeteries contain victims of the 1948 siege and, at the bottom of the slope, seven of the eight members of the Irgun and Lehi who were hanged by the British in Akko Citadel Prison. The eighth is buried at Rosh Pina, where he lived.

Artists' Quarter

The part of the old town south of the Ma'alot Olei HaGardom stairway used to be the Arab quarter but since the Arabs' defeat and subsequent withdrawal in 1948 the place has been developed by the Jews as an artists' colony.

The best place to start any walk is at the **General Exhibition Hall**, housed in a white-domed Ottoman-era mosque just a little to the south of Ma'alot Olei HaGardom St. The general exhibition features a representative selection of Safed's artists, a great many of whom, unfortunately, seem to belong to the 'Sunday afternoon' school of painting. Better work comes from the new wave of Russian immigrants who, at the time of our visit, had a separate exhibition that is well worth visiting in a neighbouring building. If you see anything of interest you can ask for directions to the particular artist's studio to see more. The galleries and studios around the quarter are mostly open to visitors with many artists happy to talk about their work and even happier to make a sale. The opening hours of the exhibition hall vary but it's usually open for at least a part of every day, Saturday included. Many of the individual artists' studios are also open on Saturday, which makes art appreciation one of the few possibilities for a Shabbat in Safed.

Much of the charm of the Artists' Quarter is still derived from its traditional Arab architecture and meandering streets. One of the few overt reminders of the area's Islamic heritage is the 13th century **Red Mosque**, built by Sultan Beybars after he drove the Crusaders out of Safed. The building is in quite a poor state but it has a typically splendid Mamluk entrance.

Zvi Assaf Printing Museum It was in Safed that the first printing press in the Holy Land was set up and the first Hebrew book printed (1578), and this is commemorated here. The museum (☎ 692 3022) on Tet Zayin St in the Artists' Quarter is open Sunday to Thursday from 10 am to noon and 4 to 6 pm, and Friday and Saturday from 10 am to noon. Admission is free.

Shem Ve'Ever Cave

Back on Jerusalem St, climb the stairs up to the bridge that carries HaPalmach St to reach this holy cave where Noah's son (Shem) and grandson (Ever) supposedly studied the Torah.

The entrance to the cave is generally locked, in which case there's nothing to see, but according to Muslim tradition it was here that a messenger told Jacob of the death of his son Joseph. The Arabs therefore call the cave the 'Place of Mourning', and they believe that the messenger lies buried here.

Organised Tours

Every Monday to Thursday at 9.45 am and Friday at 10 am, Aviva Minoff (☎ 692 0901) leads a walking tour of Safed. The price is 60NIS per person. The walk starts from the Rimon Inn, which is where you should inquire for further details.

Yisrael Shalem (☎ 697 1870), the author of a very good guidebook to the town, *Safed: Six Guided Tours in and Around the Mystical City* (available at all branches of Steimatzky for around 35NIS), is also available to conduct tours by arrangement, tailored to individual interests like archaeology, Judaism and mysticism.

Special Events

Each August, Safed hosts the Klezmer Festival. For three to five days, thousands of Israelis flock to the city to enjoy a busy line-up of Jewish soul music. Depending on your outlook, it's either a great time to be here, or a great time to be somewhere else. Accommodation is hard to find at this time; you could be better off visiting Safed from Tiberias or some other nearby location, but note that the heavy traffic makes getting in and out of Safed a lengthy ordeal during the festival.

Places to Stay – Budget

Shoshanna's (☎ 697 3939) is run by Shoshanna Briefer, a Romanian woman who rents out beds (25NIS) in a couple of centrally located but dingy apartments. Travellers' reports, however, have suggested that bed lice may be a problem here, so be aware. From the bus station climb the stairs up to Jerusalem St, turn left and follow the road to the bridge, climb the stairs up to the bridge and cross, heading south away from Gan HaMetsuda. Take the first alley to your right, running diagonally in the same general direction as HaPalmach St. The apartments are towards the end – one is on the right, with a grey door, about two-thirds of the way along and the other is at the end, on the left, behind a large green metal door.

Along the same alley and just before Shoshanna's apartments, is *Lifshitz Hostel* (☎ 052-472 360). The Lifshitz's are an orthodox family who offer accommodation from 35NIS per night. The rooms, off a central courtyard, have from two to four beds and are quite attractive in a spartan sort of way. Look for the makeshift handwritten sign on the gate.

THE GALILEE

A better option would have to be *Eli's Hostel* (☎ 050-514 956) under the same management as the Hotel Tel Aviv/Berenson House (see Places to Stay – Mid-Range & Top End). Dorm beds cost US$12 and singles/doubles go for US$20/40. However, this place is closed in winter, except on weekends.

Easily mistaken for a modern high school, *HI – Beit Binyamin Youth Hostel* (☎ 692 1086, fax 697 3514, 1 Lohamei HaGeta'ot St) in South Safed suffers badly from being a 20 to 25 minute walk up a steep gradient from the town centre. You can take bus No 6 or 7 from the central bus station. It also has a very off-putting institutional air about it. A dorm bed is US$16 and there are also single (US$35) and double (US$45) rooms available.

For Jewish travellers, another option is *Ascent Institute of Tsfat* (☎ 692 1364, fax 692 1942, email seminars@ascent.org.il, 2 Ha'Ari St). In a renovated former hotel, this complex has a lovely hostel (there's a fridge but no kitchen), and visitors are strongly encouraged to attend regular classes in Jewish mysticism. Arrangements are made for Shabbat meals with local families, hikes and city tours. Dorm beds are 50NIS, private single/double rooms for 150NIS, with a 20NIS rebate for those attending daily classes. Non-Jews are accommodated only if with a group of Jews. From the central bus station, turn right and take the first street on your right, which is Ha'Ari, and Ascent is on your left about 300m on.

Places to Stay – Mid-Range & Top End

All of the following hotels are reached by walking north from the central bus station along Jerusalem St. Taking the first left, the steep, curving Hativat Yiftah Rd brings you to *Hotel Ron* (☎ 697 2590) which, despite a very unattractive exterior, is comfortable enough inside. There's a private swimming pool with views of Mt Cana'an. Singles are priced from US$70 to US$90, doubles from US$90 to US$110. *Hotel Hadar* (☎ 692 0068) and *Hotel HaGalil* (☎ 692 1247),

both on Ridbaz St, one block west of Javitz, are converted apartments. Of the two, Hadar is easily the nicest, with a great rooftop terrace; singles/doubles are from US$22/49. The more basic HaGalil has beds in single or triple rooms at US$20.

At the bottom of Ridbaz St is *Hotel Tel Aviv/Berenson House* (☎ 697 2382, fax 697 2555), a clean, modern hotel with singles ranging in price from US$35 to US$50, doubles from US$70 to US$100.

The top hotel in town is *Rimon Inn* (☎ 692 0665, fax 692 0456), housed in a converted Ottoman-era post house in the Artists' Quarter. Singles cost from US$100 to US$120, doubles from US$115 to US$130 (prices are 20% higher in July and August, 20% lower in January and February).

Places to Eat

Safed is not the place to plan on breaking your diet of felafel and shwarma – away from street food your experiences of dining here may well be disappointing.

Most cafes and restaurants are on the pedestrianised part of Jerusalem St, although there are several good felafel places on the stretch between the bus station and HaPalmach. One of the best here is *California Felafel*, right beside the bridge. Another good snacking place is *Palermo*, which serves up reasonably priced pizza by the slice; it's on Jerusalem St right by the top of the Ma'alot Olei HaGardom stairway.

Cafe Baghdad (☎ 697 4065, 61 Jerusalem St) also near the Ma'alot Olei Ha-Gardom stairway is a dairy and vegetarian restaurant that, apart from reasonable dinners, does breakfasts, blintzes and sandwiches. The view from the streetside terrace is great too.

Further west along the same street is *Restaurant HaMifgash* (☎ 692 0510, 75 Jerusalem St), which although nothing flash, does purport to produce the best burgers in town.

There is a fruit and vegetable *market* on Wednesday morning next to the bus station and a *supermarket* at the eastern end of Jerusalem St near the Javitz St steps.

Entertainment

Originally built as a Turkish caravanserai, *Wolfson Community Centre* (☎ 697 1222), on HaPalmach St at the junction with Aliyah Bet St, is the venue for occasional chamber music concerts throughout the course of the year and a musical workshop in the summer. The *Yigal Allon Theatre & Cultural Centre* (☎ 697 1990), opposite the Wolfson, also doubles as a cinema and sometime art hall. Check the tourist information office for the schedules of any current local events.

Getting There & Away

There are services to Haifa (25NIS, two hours) every half an hour until 9 pm (5.45 pm on Friday) and to Tiberias hourly (16NIS, one hour) until 7 pm (4 pm on Friday). Three buses a day go to Tel Aviv (44NIS, otherwise change at Haifa) and one a day to Jerusalem (40NIS otherwise change at Rosh Pina).

For bus information call ☎ 692 1122.

AROUND SAFED
Meiron

This small orthodox Jewish settlement lies 9km north-west of Safed and though it contains the almost intact facade of a 2nd century synagogue, the village is best known as the site of the **tomb of Rabbi Shimon Bar Yochai**, 2nd century author of the *Zohar*, the Book of Wonders, the major work of Jewish mysticism. His son, Ele'azar, is also buried here. On the eve of Lag B'Omer, crowds of orthodox Jewish pilgrims take part in a traditional procession that starts in Safed's Synagogue Quarter and ends here at the tomb of Rabbi Shimon.

From the tomb a path leads down to the right to a **cave** where it's believed that Hillel the Elder, a famous Jewish scholar who lived in Jerusalem in the 1st century BC, is buried with his 30 disciples. The cave is often mentioned by medieval pilgrims.

Close by the tombs of Rabbi Shimon and his son and Hillel's cave lies a deep gorge. Beyond it, on top of the hill, is the **tomb of Rabbi Shammai** and the rock known as the **Throne of the Messiah**. According to tradition, when the Messiah comes he will sit on this rock and Elijah will blow a trumpet to announce the event.

Jish

This Arab village 4km north of Meiron is notable because most of its inhabitants are of the Maronite faith and originally came from Lebanon. This was an important town in ancient times, known as Gush HaLa'av (Abundance of Milk). Yohanan, a leader of the Jewish Revolt against the Romans in 66 AD, came from here, and the town was renowned for its olive oil.

On the outskirts of the village are the tombs of Shamai'a and Avtalion, two famous Jewish sages who taught in Jerusalem at the beginning of the 1st century. The remains of a 3rd or 4th century synagogue can be seen in a small valley 2km east of the village.

Bar'am

In this former Arab village are the oldest and perhaps most impressive remains of any ancient synagogue in the entire country. Dated back to the 2nd century, legend has it that Queen Esther is buried in the grounds here.

Bat Ya'ar

Beautifully located in the Birya forest, this activity centre (☎ 692 1788) offers visitors variety with a steak restaurant, trail riding, jeep tours, country walks, children's activities and rappelling. You need a car to get here; from Safed take the road north-east to Amuka.

THE GALILEE

The Upper Galilee & the Golan

הגליל העליון   הגולן

The Upper Galilee is an area of lush greenery watered by the runoff from the surrounding mountains. These streams come together in the Hula Valley to form the Jordan River, provider of most of Israel's fresh water. The chain of high peaks known as the Golan rises to form a barrier between the fertile Jordan Valley and the arid Syrian lands to the east. The Golan also acts as a political wedge between the two neighbouring countries, with Syria asserting that there will never be peace while the Israelis occupy the Heights.

Israel captured the Golan during the fighting in 1967, making further gains in 1973. The first Israeli settlers were kibbutzniks from the Hula Valley in the Upper Galilee who were determined to establish a presence on the Heights where Syrian gun emplacements had once been. The land in this area is extremely fertile and the new Jewish frontier settlements have flourished. The area is also growing as a scenic, off-track Israeli tourist destination.

However, under Rabin new settlements in the Golan were halted as the government declared its willingness to talk about returning the Heights to the Syrians in return for peace. This is far from a universally popular option among Israelis. The Golani settlers are against it because they would have to leave (and that would probably mean abandoning the Golan-produced wine which has made quite a name for itself). But more troubling to Israel's right wingers is that allowing the Syrians back onto the Heights puts the Arabs within easy striking distance of the valuable and vulnerable Galilee region. At the time of writing, Israeli prime minister Ehud Barak had indicated his willingness to discuss the idea of returning the Golan, and this issue continues to divide the electorate.

Recent years have seen giant strides made in developing the region as a leisure and tourist destination with guesthouses and

HIGHLIGHTS

- **Mt Hermon** – Israel's only skiing centre

- **Jordan River** – try white-water rafting; it's exhilarating and accessible to novices

- **Golan Heights** – great hiking, from commando treks to two-hour strolls

- **National parks and nature reserves** – get back to nature in the Golan

- **Wineries** – sip wines made from grapes grown in the unique black basalt soils of the Golan terrain

- **Sea of Galilee** – quiet, relaxing beaches on the eastern shores

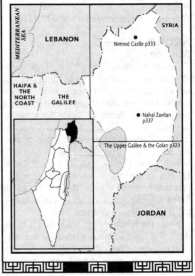

speciality restaurants in scenic locations, and soft-adventure activities like inner-tube floating, kayaking, horse and donkey riding, even ice skating; as well as the more

The Church of the Multiplication of the Loaves & Fishes at Tabgha (top) and the red-domed Greek Orthodox monastery (bottom) are two significant biblical sites on the shores of the Sea of Galilee.

ANDREW HUMPHREYS

TONY WHEELER

The synagogue at Capernaum – built of imported limestone – dates back to the 4th century AD.

Spectacular Roman amphitheatre, Beit She'an

Arch at Belvoir, a 12th century Crusader castle

THE UPPER GALILEE & THE GOLAN

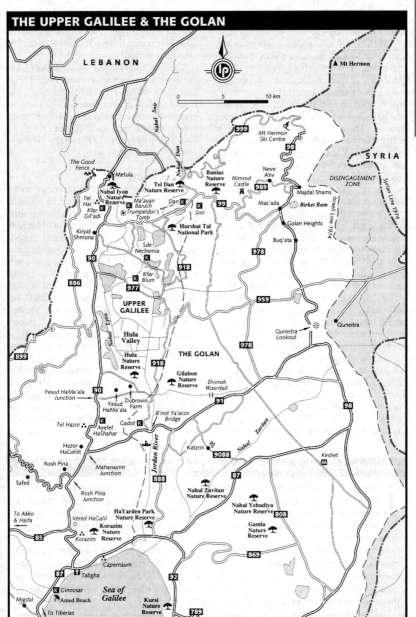

LEBANON

Mt Hermon

SYRIA

999

Mt Hermon Ski Centre

98

Neve Ativ

DISENGAGEMENT ZONE

The Good Fence

Metula

Nahal Iyon Nature Reserve

Tel Har Kfar Gil'adi

Ma'ayan Baruch

Trumpeldor's Tomb

Tel Dan Nature Reserve

Banias Nature Reserve

Nimrod Castle

989

Majdal Shams

Mas'ada

Birket Ram

Dan

Snir

99

Hurshat Tal National Park

Golan Heights

Buq'ata

Kiryat Shmona

Sde Nechemia

978

90

886

Kfar Blum

977

918

UPPER GALILEE

959

Hula Valley

Quneitra Lookout

Quneitra

Hula Nature Reserve

918

THE GOLAN

978

899

Nahal Iyon

Gilabon Nature Reserve

Dvorah Waterfall

91

Yesud HaMa'ala Junction

Yesud HaMa'ala

Dubrovin Farm

B'not Ya'acov Bridge

98

Tel Hazor

Ayelet HaShahar

Gadot

Katzrin

Nahal Zavitan

Keshet

Hazor HaGelilit

9088

Rosh Pina

Mahanayim Junction

Jordan River

888

87

Safed

Rosh Pina Junction

Vered HaGalil

HaYarden Park Nature Reserve

Nahal Zavitan Nature Reserve

Nahal Yehudiya Nature Reserve

808

To Akko & Haifa

Korazim Nature Reserve

Gamla Nature Reserve

85

Korazim

869

Capernaum

87

Tabgha

92

Ginnosar

Amud Beach

Migdal

Sea of Galilee

Kursi Nature Reserve

789

To Tiberias

Mahanayim

Disengagement Zone

Israeli Line 1974

Syrian Line 1974

Nahal Snir

Nahal Dan

Nahal Zavitan

obvious natural and historic attractions like hikes, archaeological sites and birdwatching. However, for the independent traveller, a relative lack of frequent public transport makes the Upper Galilee and the Golan considerably more difficult to explore than most other parts of Israel. How you travel will depend on how much time and money you have, and whether or not you have your own car. This is one part of Israel where it really can be an advantage to have your own vehicle. You can see a lot in one day by car, although two days, at least, are preferable; spend less than that and you risk missing out on some great hikes, waterfalls and bathing pools.

Those with limited time and money might decide to participate in one of the tours mentioned later in this chapter and visit the area for a day with a guide to point out the major places of interest. If you are following your own schedule, we recommend that you plan on spending a couple of days in the area, staying for one or possibly two nights. The only budget accommodation is at Tel Hai, near Kiryat Shmona, or Katzrin. For those with sufficient funds, there are some pleasant kibbutz guesthouses in other areas.

Anyone intending to spend more time in the region should consider picking up *Golan Pocket Guide* published by the Golan Tourist Association. This nifty little 144 page pocket book has top class information on hikes, sites, attractions and tours around the region. It can be bought at the Mahanayim junction tourist office (see the following Information entry) for 25NIS or order from the Golan Tourist Association (see Information).

The now rather dated *Guide to the Golan Heights* by Aviva Bar-Am and Yisrael Shalem badly suffers from a lack of maps, but has 20 to 30 well-described walks as well as plenty of background information on the indigenous flora and fauna. You can normally find it at any branch of Steimatzky for about 35NIS.

Information

There's a local tourism authority information office (☎ 06-693 5016, email saram@netvision.net.il) at the Mahanayim junction, 3km north of Rosh Pina. Staff will be able to help with current details of accommodation and local sites. The office is open daily from 10 am to 4.30 pm. It also has a privately maintained and potentially useful Web site (www.zimmer.co.il) with listings of accommodation – especially B&B accommodation. The site when last viewed catered mainly for Hebrew readers, but an English-language version is under development and should be up and running by the time you read this.

The Golan Tourist Association (☎ 06-696 2885, fax 696 3630, email tour@golan.org.il) in Katzrin promotes ecofriendly tourism for groups individuals around the region. You can also write to them at PO Box 175, 12900 Katzrin.

Warning – Unexploded Mines & Live Rockets

Parts of the Golan Heights are still littered with undetonated Syrian land mines. These areas have been sealed off with barbed-wire fences and warning signs – so stay away from them, and any fenced-off areas in general. Unfortunately, there have been people who have ignored these warnings – some lost limbs, others were killed. Don't make the same mistake.

Although notoriously inaccurate, Russian-made Katyusha rockets are occasionally lobbed into the Golan by Hezbollah guerillas operating somehow from within the Israel-Lebanon security zone. The town of Kiryat Shmona has been targeted by the guerillas on more than one occasion and, although you are highly unlikely to be hit by a stray rocket, travel to and around the area may be difficult if a spate of rocketing has started.

If you want up-to-date hiking and day-trip information, the best bet is to call in at one of the two SPNI Field Study Centres in the region:

Golan
(☎ 06-696 1352, fax 696 1947) in Katzrin
Hermon
(☎ 06-694 1091, fax 695 1480) south off Route 99, near Kibbutz Snir, midway between the Tel Dan and Banias nature reserves

Parks & Reserves

There are several nature reserves and numerous national parks in the region. All are open daily April to September from 8 am to 5 pm, and October to March from 8 am to 4 pm, closing one hour earlier on Friday and the day before holidays.

The nature reserves all charge around 17NIS to get in, but a 60NIS Green Card can be bought that covers admission to Banias, Gamla, Hula, Nahal Iyon and Tel Dan over a specified period.

For further information contact the National Parks Authority head office in Tel Aviv (☎ 03-576 6888, fax 751 1858), Twin Tower, 35 Jabotinsky St, Ramat Gan 52511.

Inner-Tube Floating, Rafting & Kayaking

Cataraft
(☎ 06-693 2992, fax 693 2017) kayaking and white-water rafting near Kibbutz Kfar HaNassi
Eretz HaKayakim
(☎ 06-694 8755, fax 694 8440) kayaking on the Jordan River at Kibbutz Kfar Blum
Huliot Jordan Rafting Park
(☎ 06-694 6010) at Kibbutz Sde Nechemia, south-east of Kiryat Shmona, off Route 90
Jordan River Rafting
(☎ 06-693 4622, fax 693 8977) at Kibbutz Gadot, next to the B'not Ya'acov bridge
Kibbutz Ma'ayan Baruch Adventure Park
(☎ 06-695 4624) inner-tube floating, rafting, kayaking and ice skating at Kibbutz Ma'ayan Baruch – look for the signposted exit off Route 99, north of Kiryat Shmona

Ice Skating

Canada Centre
(☎ 06-695 0370) see the Metula section later in this chapter
Kibbutz Ma'ayan Baruch Adventure Park
for contact details see under the Inner-Tube Floating, Rafting & Kayaking section

Horse & Donkey Riding

Baba Yona Ranch
(☎/fax 06-693 8773) 2km east of the Yesud HaMa'ala junction, 11km north of Rosh Pina
Bat Ya'ar
(☎ 06-692 1788) see Around Safed in the Galilee chapter
Kibbutz Ayelet HaShahar
(☎ 06-693 2611, fax 693 4777) horse riding 8km north of Rosh Pina
Vered HaGalil
(☎ 06-693 5785, fax 693 4964) a stud farm and riding stable – see Around the Sea of Galilee in the Galilee chapter

All Terrain Vehicle Rides

Baba Yona Ranch
for contact details see the Horse & Donkey Riding section
Jordan River Rafting
(☎ 06-693 4622, fax 693 8977) at Kibbutz Gadot, next to the B'not Ya'acov bridge

Skiing

Mt Hermon Ski Centre
(☎ 06-698 1337) see the Mt Hermon Ski Centre section later in this chapter

Organised Tours

From Akko, the Akko Gate Hostel (☎ 04-991 0410) runs a bus trip two or three times a week depending on the demand. The tour departs at 8.30 am and takes in Safed, Metula and the Good Fence, Banias and Majdal Shams, returning to Akko about 6 pm. The cost is 150NIS per person. From Tiberias, the Aviv Hostel (☎ 06-672 0007) organises something similar for 130NIS per person.

Egged Tours (☎ 06-672 9220) also operates from Tiberias, every Tuesday and Saturday (all year). The company takes an air-con bus on a circuit of Tabgha, Capernaum, Jordan Park, Mitzpe Gadot, Metula and the Good Fence, Banias and Bikat Ram. Some of the stops, however, are way too brief and the blatantly Zionistic commentary grates rather than enlightens. The cost per person is US$38.

Best of the lot, if you can afford it, is SPNI Tours' three day hike through the Galilee and the Golan. The action begins at Gamla Nature Reserve with vulture spotting, and continues with a hike down a basalt canyon. The next day takes in Nimrod Castle, the Banias Nature Reserve, a Druze village and, in summer, kayaking on the Jordan River. Day three is spent hiking through the western Galilee. Nights are spent in kibbutz accommodation (halfboard). The package costs US$298. See the SPNI section under Organised Tours in the Getting Around chapter for contact details.

There's also a company called TourGolan operating out of Katzrin which takes groups of no more than 12 on jeep safaris in the Golan area. Call ☎ 06-696 1511, 052-666 567 or fax 06-696 3493 for further details.

Getting Around

The bus services in this region are very infrequent so you need to check schedules in advance and plan carefully. The best idea is to sketch out your itinerary and then go to one of the SPNI field study centres (see under Information earlier in this chapter) for advice. Hitching is not recommended as attacks have occurred.

The Golan is one area of Israel where hiring a car might be a better alternative than testing your luck with the skeletal public transport system. A small car should cost no more than US$50 to US$60 per day (less if you shop around). Two or three people a car can work out as a pretty reasonable deal.

ROSH PINA ראש פינה
☎ Area Code: 06

The busy junction at Rosh Pina, just a few kilometres east of Safed, is the main point of entry to the region, with roads converging from Haifa, Akko and Safed from the west and Tiberias from the south. If you choose to travel by bus in the region, you will often have to change at this junction. Proceeding north from Rosh Pina, the road heads up to Metula on the Israel-Lebanon border via Kiryat Shmona, site of the Golan's major airport.

Rosh Pina Pioneer Settlement Site

This site (☎ 693 6603) is up on a hill, just to the west of the Rosh Pina junction. Rosh

Pina, established in 1882, was the first settlement in the Galilee. Although there is nothing much to see, the original houses have been renovated and it is an attractive spot for a meal or a drink at the local pub. The discovery of wild wheat in the area by leading Jewish botanist Aaron Aaronsohn in 1906 was an important development in the search for the origins of cultivated cereals.

Places to Stay

HI – Rosh Pina Youth Hostel (☎ 693 7086, fax 693 4312, HeHalutzim Rd) is housed in an attractive stone building in the centre of town. Dorm beds cost US$14 which includes breakfast.

If you don't fancy sleeping in dorms, *Mitzpe HaYamim Health Farm* (☎ 699 9666, fax 699 9555, email Sea_View@actom.co .il) is another more expensive option. Singles go for US$144 to US$155 and doubles from US$161 to US$173.

TEL HAZOR חצור

About 7km north of the Rosh Pina junction are the excavations of ancient Tel Hazor (or Khatsor). It is mentioned in ancient Assyrian and Egyptian records as early as the 19th century BC, and it was the most important town in northern Canaan when the Israelites conquered the area (Joshua 11:10-13 and 19:36) in the 13th century BC. In the late 10th century BC, King Solomon made it one of his chariot towns (I Kings 9:15). It was captured by the Assyrians during the 8th century BC (II Kings 15:29) and razed.

Across the road from Tel Hazor, by the entrance to Kibbutz Ayelet HaShahar, is the Hazor Museum (☎ 693 4855/7290). This houses an exhibit of two pre-Israelite temples, a scale model of ancient Hazor and a selection of artefacts. It's open Sunday to Thursday from 8 am to 4 pm, and Friday from 8 am to 1 pm; closed Saturday. Admission to the archaeological site is 13NIS, which includes entry to the Hazor Museum.

Places to Stay

The four star guesthouse at *Kibbutz Ayelet HaShahar* (☎ 693 2611, fax 693 4777, email *atlashot@netvision.net.il)* is one of the most pleasant guesthouses in the country. It is set in pleasant gardens with good facilities, including a swimming pool. There is a good restaurant, art gallery and free lectures on kibbutz life. Singles cost US$83 to US$95, and doubles US$102 to US$120.

Getting There & Away

Buses running between Tiberias or Safed and Kiryat Shmona go by the archaeological site and museum. Be sure to get off at Tel Hazor and not the town of Hazor HaGelilit, which is on the same road but 5km further south, near Rosh Pina.

HULA VALLEY & NATURE RESERVE עמק החולה ושמורת הטבע

This beautiful valley between the Lebanese border and the Golan mountains was once a huge malarial swamp dominated by Lake Hula, the northernmost and smallest of the three lakes fed by the Jordan River. In order to provide rich, well-watered land for intensive agricultural development, the Israelis implemented a massive engineering project here in the 1950s to drain the lake and the surrounding swamps. In addition, there was a plentiful supply of peat to be dug out of the former lake bed.

The Hula project, however, endangered a unique plant and wildlife habitat. Papyrus reed grows wild here – nowhere else in the world does it grow so far north – and the region's characteristic flowers are the white water lily and the yellow pond lily. These were threatened, along with great numbers of birds and animals, ranging from small waders to pelicans, sea eagles, otters, jungle cats, boar and many other creatures. The valley is a migratory station for birds, with many coming from as far as Scandinavia, Russia and India.

The fear that all of this might be lost spurred the formation of the Society for the Protection of Nature in Israel (SPNI) in 1953, which launched a successful campaign to retain an area of the swamp as a nature reserve. The result of its initial campaign is the Hula Nature Reserve (☎ 693 7069), which is

a unique wetlands wildlife sanctuary. There is a visitors centre which exhibits and explains much of the flora and fauna to be seen in the reserve, and also rents binoculars (10NIS) so you can go in search of the real thing in the wild.

The track around the reserve is about 1.5km long and although it only covers a relatively small part of the whole reserve, it takes in the best areas starting off with some spectacular views of the region. The track then takes you along a wooden swamp bridge which leads around to a raised observation tower from where you spot some indigenous wildlife.

The reserve is open to visitors Saturday to Thursday from 8 am to 4 pm, and Friday until 3 pm. There are free guided tours on Saturday, Sunday, Tuesday and Thursday between 9.30 am and 1.30 pm. Admission is 15NIS.

Buses running between Rosh Pina and Kiryat Shmona will drop you off at a signposted junction about 2.5km from the entrance to the reserve from where you have to walk or hitch.

Griffon vultures are common in the Hula Valley.

Dubrovin Farm

To the north-east of the Yesud HaMa'ala junction, this is a reconstructed turn-of-the-century Jewish settlers' farm (☎ 693 7371). In addition to the buildings and tools on display, there is a pottery workshop, an audiovisual presentation and a restaurant. It's open Sunday to Thursday from 9 am to 5 pm, and Friday from 9 am to 3 pm. In winter, closing times are an hour earlier. Admission is 8NIS, which is deducted from the cost of a main course in the restaurant.

Buses running between Rosh Pina and Kiryat Shmona will drop you off at the Yesud HaMa'ala junction on Route 90, from where the farm is about a 4km walk or hitch.

KIRYAT SHMONA   קרית שמונה

Pop: 19,900   ☎ Area Code: 06

The name is Hebrew for Town of the Eight, after the eight Jewish settlers killed at nearby Tel Hai in 1920. There have been more casualties since as the town's proximity to the Lebanese border has made it the object of first PLO and, more recently, Hezbollah rocket attacks. It was purportedly attacks on Kiryat Shmona that led to the Israeli shelling of Lebanon in 1996 which resulted in the massacre at the UN refugee camp at Qana.

Despite its frontier-post position, Kiryat Shmona is to all appearances a standard Israeli new town, with the familiar wide main boulevard, bus station and carefully laid-out residential districts. One of the very few reminders of its militarised nature is a children's playground built from three old army tanks which have been painted in bright colours.

This is the Upper Golan's big town and its administrative and transport centre, but other than for hopping off one bus and onto another, most visitors will find no reason to hang around.

Information

The post office, just south of the bus station on Tel Hai Rd, also has international telephone facilities. It's open Sunday to Thursday from 8 am to 1 pm and 4 to 6.30 pm, and Friday from 8 am to 12.30 pm. There's a Bank Hapoalim nearby.

In case of medical emergencies call ☎ 06-694 4334 or contact the Magen David Adom on ☎ 101.

Places to Stay

There's only *Hotel North* (☎ *694 4703, fax 694 1390, Tel Hai Rd*) across the street from the bus station. It is a three star establishment with a bar, lounge and pool. Singles/doubles are US$50/65.

North of the Hula Nature Reserve and 3km along a side road to the east of Route 90, *Kibbutz Kfar Blum* (☎ *694 3666, fax 694 8555)* has a three star-style guesthouse. There is a swimming pool, and opportunities for fishing, birdwatching and jogging. Singles cost US$75 to US$95 and doubles US$96 to US$136.

Places to Eat

The choice of places to eat is limited. There is an open-air *market* on Tel Hai Rd, north of the bus station, and a *supermarket* to the south, behind Bank Hapoalim. *Felafel* (deep-fried chickpeas) and *shwarma* (sandwich of meat sliced off a spit) are sold nearby, there is a *pastry and snack shop* near the Hotel North and a basic oriental-style *restaurant* near the petrol station to the south.

Getting There & Away

Kiryat Shmona is the major junction of the Upper Golan with connecting services to Tel Hai, Metula and the Israel-Lebanon border to the north, and Tel Dan, Banias, Nimrod Castle, Mt Hermon and Katzrin to the east. It's connected to the rest of Israel via bus Nos 541, 841 and 963 which run down to Tiberias via the Hula Valley and Rosh Pina.

Check bus routes and timetables carefully before setting off and stock up on food, especially for Shabbat. For Kiryat Shmona bus information call ☎ 694 0740.

TEL HAI   תל חי

Just north of Kiryat Shmona, off the Metula road, is Tel Hai. An incident here in 1920 led to the naming of the nearby town and the elevation of Josef Trumpeldor to the status of Zionist hero.

Born in Russia in 1880, Trumpeldor served in the czar's army where he lost an arm, and was decorated for gallantry. He later founded the HeHalutz Jewish pioneer movement. In 1912 he emigrated to Palestine and with his self-styled Zion Mule Corps fought with the British Commonwealth forces in the disastrous Gallipoli campaign. Returning to Palestine in 1917, he established Tel Hai (Hill of Life) as a shepherds' camp. Three years later it was attacked by Arabs, and eight of the settlers were killed, including Trumpeldor, whose reported last words were: 'It is good to die for our country'.

The death of those settlers has become a symbol of political Zionism, and Trumpeldor in particular is regarded as a model of courage and heroism. A statue of the Lion of Judah, with Trumpeldor's famous last words inscribed on it, stands in the **military cemetery** where the eight are buried. The 11th day of the month of Adar is Tel Hai Day and many young Israelis make a kind of pilgrimage up here to visit the graves.

The original settlement's watchtower and stockade have now been converted into a **museum** (☎ 695 1333, 694 1800) showing its history and purpose. An audiovisual show in English will usually be screened for a small group on request. The museum is open Sunday to Thursday from 8 am to 4 pm, Friday from 8 am to 1 pm and Saturday from 9 am to 2 pm. Admission is 13NIS (students 8NIS).

Places to Stay
HI – Tel Hai Youth Hostel (☎ 694 0043, fax 694 1743) is one of the IYHA's real treasures. It's a new HI establishment housed in a modern spacious building and run by veteran traveller Ofir who is particularly welcoming to backpackers and hikers. A dorm bed costs US$16.50 including breakfast, though a couple will pay only US$20. Advice is offered on hiking and trekking in the region, and there is a wood-panelled disco/

bar for aprés-hike activities. Kosher meals can be bought at reasonable prices.

Getting There & Away
Take bus No 20 or 23 from Kiryat Shmona (7NIS), or walk the 3km.

KIBBUTZ KFAR GIL'ADI   כפר גלעדי
About 1km north on the road to Metula from the Tel Hai turn-off, Kibbutz Kfar Gil'adi has a museum and a guesthouse.

Just inside the gates to the kibbutz is Beit HaShomer (House of the Guardian; ☎ 694 1565), an IDF museum that documents the history of the early Zionist settlers' regiments in the British Army during WWI. The museum is open Sunday to Thursday from 8 am to noon and 2 to 4 pm, and Friday and Saturday from 9 am to noon. Admission is 7NIS.

Kfar Gil'adi can also be reached via a track from the Tel Hai cemetery.

Places to Stay
Kfar Gil'adi Kibbutz Guesthouse (☎ 690 0000, fax 690 0069, email kfar_giladi@ kibbutz.co.il) offers singles for US$75 to US$98, and doubles for US$96 to US$136.

METULA
☎ Area Code: 06
Established in 1896 with a grant from the Rothschild family, this frontier town's name is Arabic for 'overlooking'. While the Jewish residents continue to farm, grow fruit and keep bees, it is their town's location that makes it important. Right on the border with Lebanon, Metula lives up to its name, overlooking barbed wire and concrete fortifications and Iyon Valley on the other side.

Israelis flock here to visit the **Canada Centre**, otherwise known as the Metula Sports Centre (☎ 695 0370) which, in addition to the country's largest ice-skating rink, has a heated swimming pool, water slides, squash courts, a gymnasium, firing range, saunas and a health centre. Admission is 35NIS (ouch!) or 27NIS for students, which includes skate hire and use of the pools. The place is open daily from 10 am to 10 pm.

Metula is a quiet peaceful place, perhaps worth a visit to say that you have 'seen' Lebanon at close quarters. It makes quite a good day trip if you combine it with a visit to the Good Fence and a hike back down to Kiryat Shmona through the Nahal Iyon Nature Reserve.

The Good Fence

On the Israel-Lebanon border near Metula, the Good Fence (HaGader HaTova) gives access to an Israeli medical clinic providing treatment (and referrals of serious cases to Israeli hospitals) for residents of southern Lebanon. Since 1976, over 300,000 Lebanese have crossed the border for medical attention courtesy of the Good Fence. Lebanese Christians and Druze are also permitted to visit relatives and to hold jobs in Israel; they commute each day from Lebanon through the checkpoint.

Although Metula has developed as a small-scale mountain resort, it's the Good Fence that is the major attraction here. The Good Fence is located to the west of town from where you can see into Lebanon. It's a kind of bizarre border crossing with Israeli tourist facilities cheek by jowl with razor wire separating the country from Lebanon. Security is surprisingly relaxed and photography is allowed as long as you don't point your camera at the military personnel. Across the border, you can see several Lebanese Christian villages. To the north-west is Beaufort Castle, once a stronghold of the Crusaders but more recently a PLO artillery position.

Nahal Iyon Nature Reserve

The reserve is focused on the deep gorge of the Iyon River (Nahal Iyon), east of the Kiryat Shmona-Metula road. About 2km before Metula, a turn-off leads to **Tanur Falls**, the largest and most attractive of the waterfalls. Some 18m high and surrounded by rocky walls, Tanur (Oven) is so-called because the density of mist that it creates when in full flow supposedly resembles billowing smoke. The falls are reduced to a trickle during summer, although the deep

pools below them are still good for a cool swim. The Iyon River continues to flow southwards to join the Jordan River. Further on, past the gate and down some stone steps, is a path leading to the Iyon waterfall. During the summer, it runs completely dry, bar a few stagnant pools.

Bus No 20 from Kiryat Shmona will drop you at the turn-off – from there it's a few minutes walk to the reserve. Follow the trail past Tanur Falls and you will see two smaller falls before ending up in Metula after about 45 minutes.

Places to Stay

Beit HaDekkel (☎ 695 0365, 8 HaGoren St) is a neat-looking villa surrounded by pleasant gardens with self-catering facilities and a TV in each room. Singles/doubles are 200/250NIS, breakfast included.

Other than this, there is no real budget accommodation in Metula – just three hotels with varying levels of facilities. The cheapest is *Hotel HaMavri* (☎ 694 0150) charging US$46/58; the most attractive is *Pension Arazim* (☎ 699 7143, fax 694 4666) with rooms from US$81/106; and *Sheleg HaLevanon Hotel* (☎ 699 7111, fax 694 4018) completes the trio by charging US$90/115 with no price hike during the high season.

Getting There & Away

About eight buses a day run from Metula to Kiryat Shmona where you can change for all other destinations.

HURSHAT TAL NATIONAL PARK

חורשת טל

Route 99 heads east from Kiryat Shmona, across the Iyon River and then the Snir River, one of the principal sources of the Jordan River, to reach Hurshat Tal National Park after about 5km.

A popular and, therefore, often crowded picnic spot, this forested area is famous for its ancient oaks. According to Muslim legend, 10 of Mohammed's messengers once rested here. With no trees to provide shade or hitching posts for their camels, they pounded sticks into the ground to fasten their mounts. Overnight the sticks grew into trees and in the morning the holy men awoke to find themselves in a beautiful forest. The oaks, some of them believed to be about 2000 years old, tower over the park with its lawns, pools and waterfalls. The Dan River has been diverted to create a series of pleasant but cold swimming pools.

The park (☎ 694 0400) is open daily from 8 am to 5 pm, closing an hour earlier on Friday, on the day before holidays and throughout winter. Admission is 10NIS.

Bus Nos 25, 26 and 36 from Kiryat Shmona will drop you off at this park.

Places to Stay

Hurshat Tal Camping Ground (☎ 694 2360) is 100m up the road, on the banks of the Dan River. Tent space costs 30NIS per person, and bungalows are available: three-bed for 160NIS, four-bed for 210NIS or five-bed for 230NIS.

Established by Turkish Jews in 1948, the guesthouse at nearby *Kibbutz HaGosherim (☎ 695 6231, fax 695 6234)* is of a three star standard and has a swimming pool. Singles cost US$75 to US$95 and doubles US$96 to US$136.

TEL DAN תל דן

When the land of Israel was divided after Joshua's conquest, the Dan tribe received territory in the coastal plain near Jaffa (Joshua 19:40-6). Unable to hold it against the chariots of the Philistines, they headed north to occupy a Canaan city-state which was called both Leshem (Joshua 19:47) and Laish (Judges 18:27), but which eventually became known as Dan. In the Old Testament, 'from Dan to Beersheba' is the standard expression defining the northern and southern limits of the Promised Land (I Samuel 3:20; II Samuel 3:10, 17:11, 24:2; Judges 20:1).

Tel Dan today is a densely forested nature reserve nourished by many small springs. There are some excavations but they're little distraction among the enchanting natural surroundings. It's open daily from 8 am to 4 pm; admission is 15NIS.

Buses from Kiryat Shmona will take you to the nearby Kibbutz Dan; continue up the main road and turn left at the orange sign to the reserve which is a 3km walk or hitch.

Beit Ussishkin Museum

Kibbutz Dan houses this museum (☎ 694 1704), which is near the Tel Dan Nature Reserve. Named after the director of the Jewish National Fund, it features audiovisuals, dioramas and other exhibits covering the flora and fauna, geology, topography and history of the region. It also has a birdwatching centre. The museum is open Sunday to Thursday from 8.30 am to 4.30 pm, Friday from 8.30 am to 3.30 pm and Saturday from 9.30 am to 4.30 pm. Admission is 13NIS.

Places to Stay

SPNI Hermon Field Study Centre (☎ 694 1091, fax 695 1480) has guest cottages set among oak tree-shaded lawns. The price per night is approximately US$40 per person but call in advance because this place is often booked up. The Field Study Centre is near Kibbutz Snir which is south of Route 99 about 2km east of the Tel Dan Nature Reserve (3km south-west of Banias).

BANIAS NATURE RESERVE בניאס

Spectacularly beautiful, the Banias Nature Reserve (☎ 695 1410) is probably the most popular spot in the whole Upper Galilee-Golan region. The heart of the reserve is a cave sanctuary, dedicated in ancient times to Pan, god of the countryside, flocks and herds (in Greek, *Paneas* is 'Pan's place', but the Arabs, who came later, have no 'p' in their alphabet). Before the arrival of the Arabs, Phillip, son of Herod, built his capital here and called it Caesarea Phillipi. According to the gospels, Jesus visited the city and it was here that he told the disciples that the church would be built on Peter, the rock (Matthew 16:13-20).

There is not really that much to see, although the Canaanites – and later the Greeks – built shrines and temples here. The niches in the cliff face next to the cave were cut during the Graeco-Roman period to receive statues and, although there have been no organised excavations, there are columns, capitals and blocks scattered around the site showing that this was an important 1st century city. To the north of the spring that flows from the rock face a room of an Herodian building can be seen; and above the cave to the north (left) is the Weli al-Khader (Tomb of St George), a Muslim saint, which is sacred to Muslims and Druze. Across the main road are some Crusader ruins.

Entry to the reserve costs 15NIS. It's open Saturday to Thursday from 8 am to 4 pm and from 8 am to 3 pm on Friday.

Banias Waterfall

About a kilometre from the park is this lovely waterfall, the largest in the region. Follow the path which starts near the stream in the park. Take the right fork just past the bakery, and you come to a pool built by the Syrian army. Past the pool you come to three paths – take either the middle or right path to the waterfall. Tempting as it looks, it is unfortunately forbidden to swim in the plunge pool. Regardless, it's a very popular site so try to come here early, and avoid visiting on Shabbat and Jewish holidays.

Places to Stay

See **SPNI Hermon Field Study Centre** under Places to Stay in the previous Tel Dan section. Private accommodation and B&B places come and go, so be sure to check out the Web site www.zimmer.co.il for some new and more obscure options in this region.

Getting There & Away

Bus No 55 travels from Kiryat Shmona via Banias to Mas'ada twice a day, with the last bus back to Kiryat Shmona leaving Banias around noon. An alternative, apart from hitching, is to walk the 5km west to Kibbutz Dan where bus Nos 25, 26 and 36 run more often and until early evening; check the schedules.

NIMROD CASTLE   קלעת נמרוד

Less than 2km east of Banias, this is the most impressive and best preserved of Israel's Crusader castles. Nimrod also enjoys some of the country's finest views from its prominent position, with the Hula Valley below and Mt Hermon to the north.

The castle was named after the biblical Nimrod (Genesis 10:8-10) to whom legend attributes its construction. In fact, Baldwin II had it built in 1129 by Reiner Brus to protect Banias from an attack from Damascus.

It took Reiner Brus three years to build the castle, which was not bad going judging by the size of the stones that had to be hauled up the steep slopes. However, in 1132 the castle was lost to the Damascenes, who later had it taken from them in 1137 by an Arab rival, Zengi, who wanted control of Damascus.

In 1140 the Crusaders and Arabs teamed up to win back the castle after a month-long siege, but their alliance ended in 1154 when Zengi's son, Nur ad-Din, won control of Damascus. He twice attempted to take Nimrod in 1157, but had to retreat both times when a Crusader relief force appeared on the horizon just in the nick of time. He succeeded at his next attempt in 1164, with the garrison surrendering before the Crusader army could return from Egypt.

During the 5th Crusade (1217-21) the castle was dismantled, but was later renovated by sultans of the Ayyubid dynasty during the early 13th century. There are 10 Arabic inscriptions which tell of this work, and in fact most of the remains seen today are from this period.

By 1260 the castle was under the control of the Mamluk sultan Beybars who constructed a citadel built from massive stones and decorated with inscriptions. From the 14th to the 16th century, the castle served as a jail for political prisoners. After that it was abandoned and used as a cow shed and sheepfold by local farmers.

In the Six Day War it was first used by the Syrians as an observation post and a mortar position, and then by the Israelis. Both parties seemed keen to avoid damaging the impressive remains.

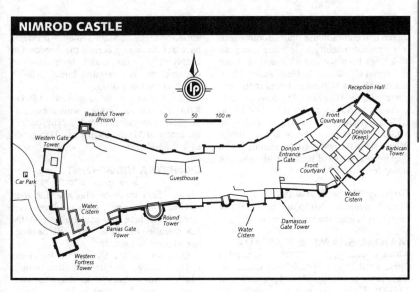

NIMROD CASTLE

0   50   100 m

Reception Hall

Beautiful Tower
(Prison)

Front
Courtyard

Donjon
(Keep)

Western Gate
Tower

Donjon
Entrance
Gate

Barbican
Tower

Front
Courtyard

P
Car Park

Guesthouse

Water
Cistern

Water
Cistern

Water
Cistern

Round
Tower

Damascus
Gate Tower

Banias Gate
Tower

Water
Cistern

Western
Fortress
Tower

The site (☎ 694 2360) is open Saturday to Thursday from 8 am to 5 pm, and Friday from 8 am to 4 pm. Admission is 15NIS (students 10NIS).

Getting There & Away

The most convenient way is to take a *sherut* (shared taxi) from Kiryat Shmona, costing about 17NIS. Alternatively, the bus running between Kiryat Shmona and Katzrin will drop you off nearby. You can also hike up the hill from Banias – give yourself about 1½ hours each way, cover your head and take plenty of water. A footpath starts from just above the spring.

MT HERMON SKI CENTRE

Mt Hermon is 2224m above sea level and Israel's highest peak. Only 7% of Hermon is in Israeli territory, the rest is in Syria and Lebanon. The scene of fierce fighting in the 1973 Yom Kippur War, most of Hermon is still heavily militarised and off-limits.

There are surprisingly decent, albeit limited, skiing facilities available here, based around **Neve Ativ** where there's a ski infor-

mation centre (☎ 698 1337). The season is usually from late December to early April and the slopes are pretty crowded on weekends. There are four runs from the upper station, the longest is about 2.5km and all designed for the average to fairly good skiers. Separate chair lifts take skiers and onlookers up from the base station. A shorter chair lift takes you up to a gentler run, with nursery slopes at the bottom of the hill.

Prices are as bad as you probably expect them to be. A round trip on the nonskiers' lift is about 50NIS. If you want to ski, the average daily cost of equipment hire, lift tickets and admission to the slopes is over 330NIS per person. Most Israelis hire their equipment, so you need to get here early to ensure that your boots fit.

The chair lifts operate between 8.30 am and 3.30 pm, depending on the conditions – call the Neve Ativ ski information centre to check.

Places to Stay

At *Howard Johnson Resort* (☎ 698 5888, fax 698 5666, email hhemda@irh.co.il) guests stay in members' homes. Meals are served in the guesthouse dining room which is a pleasant, country-style place complete with large fireplace and a great view down to Nimrod Castle and the Hula Valley. There is a disco/bar, a billiard and pool room, and horse riding is available. Singles cost US$101 to US$123, and doubles US$129 to US$152, rising on weekends and with mandatory half or full-board at busy times. All guests at the resort get free admission to the slopes and use of the chair lift, and free skiing lessons.

Getting There & Away

The infrequent bus No 55 runs to Neve Ativ from Kiryat Shmona and Katzrin.

MAJDAL SHAMS & MAS'ADA

מג'דל שאמס מסעדה مجدل شمس و مسعده

These are the two largest of four Druze villages in the region (combined population of 17,000). Unlike the communities on Mt Carmel, these Druze are fiercely anti-Israel and they have protested against the occupation and subsequent annexation of the area ever since Israel took the Golan Heights from Syria in 1967.

Not only have the Druze refused to accept Israeli citizenship, they actively support Syria and there have been several violent anti-Israeli demonstrations here over the years.

In addition to their political stance, these Druze are more traditional and, although they've had less contact with the western world, they are welcoming to visitors. The ramshackle villages are not especially attractive; however, the surrounding countryside is and the people themselves can make a visit extremely worthwhile. (For background on the Druze see Population & People in the Facts about the Country chapter.)

Majdal Shams (in Arabic, Tower of the Rising Sun), the Golan's largest town, is particularly close to the Syrian border – a UN building on the next hill across the valley and its adjacent white stone mark the furthest extent of Israeli territory.

The town was captured by the IDF in 1967 and many of Majdal Shams' residents have relatives just across the border. On Friday they go down and shout across to one another, as separated families do in Rafah in the Gaza Strip.

The only tourist site as such is the **Birket Ram**, a small round lake with a big rectangular restaurant nearby. It's 2km south of the centre of Majdal Shams and 1km north-east of Mas'ada.

QUNEITRA VIEWPOINT

תצפית אל-קוניטרה مرتفع لقنيطرة

About 15km south of Mas'ada, the road reaches a high mound with an observation point. From here you can look across the UN-patrolled border to Syria and the abandoned town of Quneitra.

Quneitra was the Syrians' major Golan town, mostly inhabited by Circassians, Muslim immigrants from the Caucasus. Captured and destroyed by the Israelis in 1967, it was subsequently returned under the cease-fire agreement but has since remained a ghost town. Damascus is a mere 30km north-east of here.

KATZRIN

קצרין

Pop: 5,600 ☎ Area Code: 06

Established in 1977, Katzrin is also known as Qazrin or Kazrin. The name is Hebrew for Forts, and is originally from the Latin *castra* (fortress). It's about 4km down a road that heads south off the Rosh Pina-Quneitra road. The new 'capital' of the Golan, Katzrin is as close to an ideal base for exploring the area as you can get, especially for those on a tight budget. Planned in the shape of a butterfly, with the wings as neighbourhoods and the body as the commercial district, it is far from fully grown, having a projected population of 10,000. Set among a bleak landscape, it is not a particularly attractive town, but its decent facilities certainly provide good living conditions by Israeli standards – further enhanced by various government grants and allowances for those who live and work here.

Orientation & Information

The town lies to the south of Route 91. The main street leads straight ahead past the shopping centre, which has a post office, bank, supermarket, eating places, cinema, museum and sports facilities. The post office is open Sunday, Tuesday and Thursday from 7.45 am to 12.30 pm and 3.30 to 6 pm; and Monday, Wednesday and Friday from 7.45 am to 2 pm. It's closed Saturday.

Bank Leumi is open Sunday, Tuesday and Thursday from 8.30 am to 12.30 pm and 4 to 6 pm, and Monday, Wednesday and Friday from 8.30 am to 12.30 pm; closed Saturday.

The swimming pool is open daily from 9 am to 5 pm, and admission is 15NIS.

There's also a TourGolan office located at 35 Ramot Gila'd St. See under Organised Tours earlier for more information.

In the event of a medical emergency you should call ☎ 696 1333 or the Magen David Adom on ☎ 101.

Things to See

Many of the artefacts at the **Golan Archaeological Museum** (☎ 696 1350) come from ancient Katzrin which was one of the original Jewish settlements in the Golan. The museum is open Sunday to Thursday from 8 am to 4 pm, Friday until 3 pm, and Saturday from 10 am to 4 pm, and admission is 15NIS (students 10NIS).

Not everything was hauled into the museum and there are still a few things left at the **ancient Katzrin Park**, like the remains of a 3rd century synagogue and two reconstructed houses. From the new town, return to the main road and head south (turn right). After about a 15 minute walk, you'll reach the park on the opposite side of the road. The museum ticket covers admission to the site, and the two share the same opening hours.

Less than a kilometre south of ancient Katzrin Park is the only petrol station in the Golan, which is beside a turn-off that leads to a new industrial area and the renowned **Golan winery**. Call ☎ 696 1841 for details of tours which cost 12NIS (students 10NIS) and include a short film, wine tasting of four different wines and a complimentary glass with the Yarden wine logo.

Places to Stay

SPNI's **Golan Field Study Centre** (☎ 696 1352, fax 696 1947, Daliyat St) has a modern, clean and comfortable guesthouse in which beds in air-con dorms are US$40 per person. It's often full, so phone ahead to make a reservation. To the south is a campsite with tent sites for 24NIS.

It is best to go straight to the main building of the field study centre regardless of where you want to stay. If no one is around (not unusual), leave a note and your stuff. The staff are friendly and helpful to travellers keen to explore the area. They will happily tell you about natural beauty spots to visit, such as waterfalls, springs and rivers. Most of these places require a few hours hiking, but nothing too strenuous.

Places to Eat

In the shopping centre there are a few cafes serving felafel, salads and grilled meats; some serve draught beer. Their main trade is provided by the IDF, with soldiers from nearby positions pouring in. Most of the staff are Druze from nearby villages. **Blue Berry Bar & Restaurant** is nothing flash, but it is fairly obvious and will see you through any hunger pangs you may have developed.

The town's **supermarket** is open Sunday to Thursday from 8 am to 6 pm, and Friday from 7 am to 3.30 pm, closed Saturday.

Getting There & Away

Bus Nos 55, 56 and 57 connect Katzrin with Rosh Pina (11NIS, 30 minutes), which is just a couple of kilometres east of Safed, and bus Nos 15, 16 and 19 all go to Tiberias (15NIS, 45 minutes).

Bus No 55 goes twice a day from Katzrin to Kiryat Shmona via Mas'ada.

AROUND KATZRIN
B'not Ya'acov Bridge

This bridge over the Jordan River is about 10km north-east of Katzrin, on Route 91 to Rosh Pina. The name means Daughters of

Jacob, and this is supposedly the spot where the said daughters crossed the river on their way to Canaan from Mesopotamia. It has also been the site of much conflict over the years as it marked the border between the Latin Kingdom of the Crusaders to the west, and the Muslims to the east and many battles were fought here during the 12th century. In 1799 Napoleon's forces were entrenched here to prevent Turkish reinforcements from reaching Akko which was under siege from the French. WWI saw the Turks in action here again, and in 1918 they were defeated in their campaign to liberate Syria. The bridge was used by Syria to invade Israel after it declared independence in 1948 and then, during the Six Day War, Israeli troops thundered across on their way to capturing the Golan Heights.

Little evidence remains of all this military coming and going except for the Crusader-era **Chastelet fortress**. The castle was built in 1179 to guard the routes into Palestine, but less than a year after its completion it was captured by Saladin and completely destroyed. The view from the overgrown ruins is more impressive than the stones themselves. To get there follow the dirt track which heads south off road No 91, about 1km west of the bridge.

Dvorah Waterfall

The road from Katzrin heading north-east (left) joins the B'not Ya'acov-Quneitra road. Turn right to head towards Quneitra and a side road on the left after 1km leads down to this attractive waterfall. Turn off after about 2km. The **Gilabon Nature Reserve** between the waterfall and Route 918 is another pleasant area of forest.

NAHAL YEHUDIYA NATURE RESERVE שמורת הטבע של נחל יהודיה

Stretching down to the Sea of Galilee from Katzrin, this lovely area boasts some of the country's most attractive hikes. The trails follow the route of the Nahal Zavitan (Zavitan River) and you see some pretty waterfalls. There are also amazing rock pools which feature interesting hexagonal formations, caused by the rapid cooling of molten rock and known as **Brekhat HaMeshushim**, the Hexagon Ponds.

To get here, either walk, hitch or drive 2km south from Katzrin until you see the orange sign for the reserve and head for the car park.

Nahal Zavitan

One of the highlights of this reserve is the following four to five hour hike. Possible year-round, it involves generally light walking and the opportunity for a refreshing swim.

Entering the car park, turn right to continue north on foot or by car along the blue-marked semi-paved road for 1.5km. Look for the lava flow and electricity pole to your left and park here. Bear to your left along the blue-marked dirt road heading west.

After about 1km there is a fork in the trail; take the black-marked trail to the right and head north for 1.5km. You should see a slope and the end point of a lava flow to your right. The trail heads down onto the western bank of Nahal Zavitan, then follows the stream. From here you can see the aqueduct built by local Arab villagers who left the area as a result of the fighting in 1967. After walking about half a kilometre downstream, you'll reach two of the large rock pools featuring unique hexagonal basalt formations. These were caused three million years ago when the lava cooled quickly and the basalt cracked into these interesting shapes.

Nahal Zavitan continues and runs into Nahal Meshushim where the Brekhat HaMeshushim features Israel's best examples of these amazing hexagons. Follow the trail across Nahal Zavitan to walk beside the aqueduct and after half a kilometre you'll come to another pool with hexagonal formations. From here, follow the red-marked trail to look out over the 25m **Zavitan Falls**. Head down to the right to reach Nahal Zavitan via the blue-marked trail which can be extremely slippery in winter. You can reach another pool under the waterfall by crossing the stream. Head back up the blue-marked

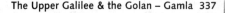

NAHAL ZAVITAN

To Katzrin

Nahal Zavitan

Old Semi-paved Road

Ya'ar Yehudiya Reserve

87

Yehudiya

Nahal Yehudiya

Yehudiya Forest

To Yehudiya Junction, Sea of Galilee & Tiberias

1 Zavitan River Bed
2 Hexagonal Basalt Formations
3 Aqueduct
4 Zavitan Falls & Swimming Hole
5 Hirbet Sheikh Hussein (Abandoned Arab Village)
6 Fork in Trail
7 Alternative Walk to Nahal Zavitan
8 Eucalyptus Grove
9 Car Park & Entrance
10 Nahal Yehudiya Walk

0   0.5   1 km

trail to reach the top and continue along the wadi to arrive at the Black Canyon.

Beautiful but dangerous, enough careless hikers have fallen to their deaths here to make unauthorised access illegal. Continue along the red-marked trail that bypasses the Black Canyon by taking you along the western bank of Nahal Zavitan.

Follow the blue-marked trail past a memorial site to reach a dirt road. Follow this to reach the abandoned Arab village of Hirbet

Sheikh Hussein and eventually to return to the starting point.

GAMLA   גמלה جملا

Gamla is the Masada of the Golan. A Jewish city on a high rock plateau, approachable only by a narrow ridge of highland, it is the site of a mass suicide in the face of an approaching enemy.

On 12 October in 67 AD, Gamla came under siege from the Romans. The numbers in the city were swollen by thousands of Jews who had fled north following an abortive revolt, pursued by three legions of the Roman army. The legionaries laid siege for months before attempting to storm the city across the ridge. Repelled once, they succeeded in taking the town on a second attempt, slaughtering 4000 Jews in the process. According to Flavius Josephus, a 1st century historian (known, incidentally, for his tendency to exaggerate), another 5000 committed suicide by leaping off the ridge's cliff-like face.

Josephus' account of the siege includes descriptions of the location and layout of the city, and it was from this information that the site was identified. However, some archaeologists believe that a site near Jamle on the Syrian side of the current Golan border is a more likely candidate. Authentic or not, the Israeli Gamla is an impressive place, particularly when viewed from the Golan with the Sea of Galilee below.

Although officially a nature reserve, the site is sometimes closed for military manoeuvres, so it's best to call ahead (☎ 676 2040, 050-205 362).

Getting There & Away

There are no buses to Gamla, which lies 15km south-east of Katzrin. The best advice we can give is that you could inquire at the SPNI's Golan Field Study Centre in Katzrin (see under Katzrin earlier in this chapter for details). It sometimes runs tours down to Gamla, and even if it has nothing going at the time of your visit, its staff will be able to suggest an alternative for you.

The Dead Sea

It's the ultimate Israeli cliché, the picture of the swimsuited bather lying in – almost on – the water, feet up and newspaper open, like a Sunday morning in bed. But unlike a camel ride at the pyramids or wrapping a *keffiyah* around your neck, this is one Middle Eastern cliché well worth indulging in. Floating in the Dead Sea is a sensation that cannot be duplicated anywhere else in the world.

With a shoreline of some 90km there is no one bathing spot but you are advised to take your dip somewhere with shower facilities – the Dead Sea has a slightly slimy quality. The nicest places are the well-kept sandy beach at Ein Bokek by the main hotel area, and at Hamme Zohar, a little further south. However, if you are short of time you may be better off using the beach at Ein Gedi which is closer to Jerusalem.

After the obligatory float, the next most popular thing to do is to visit Masada, a place which readers' letters consistently rate as Israel's number one attraction. Not as well known or as well frequented by travellers, Ein Gedi's nature reserves also deserve exploration. Visits to Qumran and Ein Feshka come lower on the scale of 'musts' for most people, although they are worth a look if your itinerary allows it.

For travellers that are short on time, perhaps the best way to enjoy the three most popular attractions is to take the early bus down from Jerusalem and visit Ein Gedi's Nature Reserve and beach, then head for Masada to spend the night. You can then beat the heat and reach the top of the fortress early the next morning and still have most of the day to move on elsewhere. Coming from Eilat or Beersheba, you reach Masada first. Spend the night here, explore it early, then head north to Ein Gedi's nature reserve before it closes in the early afternoon, and end the day with a float in the Dead Sea before heading up to Jerusalem. If you have an extra night to spare, stay over

HIGHLIGHTS

- **Masada** – symbol of Jewish resistance to Roman rule; best viewed after a pre-dawn hike up its snaking access path

- **The Dead Sea** – the lowest point on Earth; read a newspaper while floating on your back or soak in its health-promoting mud

- **Ein Gedi** – a welcome oasis in an otherwise arid landscape

- **Qumran** – the discovery site of the world-famous Dead Sea Scrolls

- **The Judean Desert** – unforgiving for beginners, unforgettable for those that respect it; challenging hiking and awe-inspiring desert tours

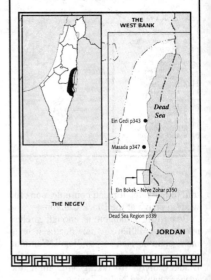

at Ein Gedi so you can get to the nature reserve early in the morning when it's cooler and less crowded, giving yourself more time to enjoy the beautiful surroundings of the region.

Be aware that bus services in the Dead Sea region are very infrequent and to avoid hanging around wilting under the sun, you need to plan your itinerary in advance. You also need to carry plenty of water as dehydration can be a very real problem. Deciding where to stay, or even whether to stay here at all, is another dilemma, particularly for shoestring travellers. The HI hostels at Ein Gedi and Masada are by far the cheapest places to stay but they are still more than double the price of private hostels in nearby Jerusalem. Rather than stay out here overnight, you could choose to 'do the Dead' in a series of day excursions from Jerusalem, but the cost of the return bus fares and the extra travelling time should be taken into account.

For travellers really short on time and with a felafel-only budget, the one-day Masada-Dead Sea-Ein Gedi trip offered by the hostels in Jerusalem can't be beaten; see Organised Tours later in this chapter.

Lastly, try to avoid the Dead Sea at weekends and holidays when it can be unpleasantly crowded.

History

Awareness of the Dead Sea's unique qualities goes back to at least the 4th century BC; luminaries such as Aristotle, Pliny and Galen all made mention of the sea's physical properties. The Nabataeans also knew a good thing when they saw it and collected the bitumen from the surface of the water and sold it to the Egyptians, who used it for embalming. Records show that this industry continued well into the Roman period.

Despite scientific interest and small-scale commercial activity, the sea was largely regarded as an unhealthy thing (common wisdom had it that no bird could fly over its waters) and shunned. This made the area a favoured retreat of religious ascetics and political fugitives – the future King David, King Herod, Jesus and John the Baptist all took refuge among its shoreline mountains and caves.

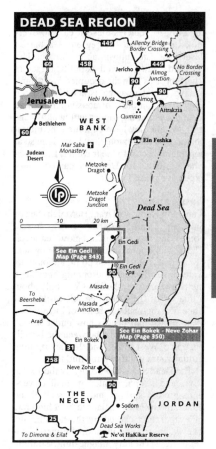

DEAD SEA REGION

THE DEAD SEA

Because of its 'Sea of the Devil' tag, the area remained desolate and untouched until it was finally explored by the US Navy in 1848. Still, it wasn't until the arrival of the British in Palestine that any real activity around the sea began. They set up two plants to tap the abundant mineral wealth and during the 1920s the Dead Sea provided half of Britain and the Commonwealth's potash needs. One of the plants was destroyed in the 1948 War but the other, at Sodom, is still working.

The luxuries of modern roads and air-conditioned vehicles make it easy to overlook the fact that the region is a barren desert with an inhospitable climate. The heat and aridity, as well as political factors – half the area is in the occupied West Bank – have meant that the Israelis have been slow to exploit the enormous potential here for moneyspinning tourist and health facilities. Where they have exploited the tourist potential of the region, they have done so at considerable cost to the traveller. Like elsewhere in Israel the Dead Sea can be a very expensive place to visit.

Geography

Known in Hebrew as Yam HaMelah (Sea of Salt), the Dead Sea is the world's lowest point lying at some 400m below sea level. The sea is approximately 65km long and 18km across at its widest point, although its water level fluctuates, dropping about one metre a year. After the 1948 War only about a quarter of the Dead Sea fell to the new State of Israel, but as a result of the Six Day War, almost half of it is now under Jewish control, with the border between the Israeli-occupied West Bank and Jordan running virtually straight down the middle.

The Dead Sea is fed mainly by the Jordan River, and is supplemented by smaller rivers, underground springs and floods. With no outlet, the inflow is balanced by a high rate of evaporation caused by the hot climate. The water arrives with normal mineral concentrations (mainly magnesium, sodium, calcium and potassium chlorides) but evaporation causes the levels of minerals to rise dramatically. The water's salt concentration is about 30% (compared to 4% for ordinary sea water) making it easy to sit up in and comfortably read this book. Contrary to the sea's 'dead' tag, 11 species of bacteria manage to survive – but no fish.

There are two very different sections to the Dead Sea. The northern basin is over three times the size of the southern one, and at some 400m is a lot deeper. The southern basin is only about 6m deep and has a higher salt level, resulting in iceberg-like crystal formations. The Lashon (Tongue) Peninsula, which juts out from the Jordanian eastern shore, now acts to separate the two sections.

At one time the lake was four or five times the size that it is today. Fluctuations in the water level were once due only to natural conditions, (mainly variations in rainfall) but the construction of Israel's National Water Carrier System, which draws on the Jordan River, has now disturbed the natural balance. Inspired by the Israelis, the Jordanians went on to build a similar project on the Yarmuk River, and together the two neighbours deprive the Dead Sea of over 600 million cubic metres of water per year. This has all but dried up the Dead Sea's southern basin and the sea has been shortened by over 25km in length.

Organised Tours

By far the cheapest way of sampling the Dead Sea region is to sign up for the 12 hour tour you'll see advertised in almost all the hostels in Jerusalem. The tour departs from Jaffa Gate in the Old City at 3 am, though in practice you don't usually leave until after 3.30 am. You are then bussed straight to Masada in time to climb the mountain and watch the sun rise over the desert. You get about an hour at the site before being shuttled to Ein Gedi for a float in the Dead Sea and a walk through the nature reserve. Then it's a brief photo stop at Qumran, the site of the Dead Sea Scrolls, followed by a quick visit to Jericho with a photo call at the Mount of Temptation. You arrive back in Jerusalem at about 3 pm. Despite the stopwatch schedule most travellers find that they see all they want; those who want to slow down can always drop out at Ein Gedi and make their own way back later using Egged buses.

The cost of the tour is 90NIS per person, excluding entry fees – still excellent value considering that the return fare to Masada on an Egged bus is around 63NIS. Bookings can be made at Jerusalem hostels such as Al-Arab, Cairo, Palm, New Swedish and Tabasco.

Dead Healthy?

Compared to regular sea water, the water of the Dead Sea contains 20 times as much bromine, 15 times as much magnesium and 10 times as much iodine – it is, in effect, 33% solid substance. Bromine, a component of many sedatives, relaxes the nerves, magnesium counteracts skin allergies and clears the bronchial passages while iodine has a beneficial effect on certain glandular functions – or so it's claimed, especially by local health spa owners and the various Dead Sea cosmetic companies.

The Dead Sea air is extremely dry, the temperatures are high all year-round, and rainfall averages only 5cm a year. Due to the low altitude (400m below sea level), there is 10% more oxygen in the Dead Sea air than at sea level, and the lack of urban development has kept it relatively free of pollution. All of this increases the body's metabolic rate which purportedly has a bracing effect. The misty haze of evaporating water over the Dead Sea contains large amounts of bromine and this supposedly also has a soothing effect.

Despite the high temperatures and around 300 cloudless days a year, the high atmospheric pressure filters the sun's burning ultraviolet rays which makes it harder to get sunburnt. Which isn't to say it's not possible; we met a few people with boiled lobster complexions who had wrongly presumed that their fair skins were safe without sunscreen.

Whether you are healthy or not, soaking in the water of the Dead Sea can also be extremely painful. Wade in with any exposed cuts or grazes and you will gain instant enlightenment as to the meaning behind the phrase to 'rub salt in one's wounds'. We guarantee that you are going to discover scratches and sores that you never knew you had. The magnesium chloride in the water gives it a revolting bitter taste and swallowing any can induce retching. Don't get the water in your eyes, either, as it will inflame them and sting – if this happens then rinse them immediately with fresh water.

Swimming in the buoyant water is a bit of a problem too since your legs tend to float towards the surface making normal swimming difficult; we have had reports of corpulent bathers turning turtle onto their fronts and being unable to turn around again to keep their faces out of the water. A number of drownings have occurred in this manner.

SPNI Tours operates a two-day program that is very similar to the above but with more time spent at Masada and Ein Gedi. The cost is US$185 per person, see Organised Tours in the Getting Around chapter for more details.

Metzoke Dragot (☎ 02-994 4222, fax 994 4333, email metzoke@netvision.net.il), also called the International Centre for Desert Tourism, is operated by Kibbutz Mitzpe Shalem and offers various tours and activities in the Judean Desert, with and without accommodation.

For those with limited time, Metzoke Dragot operates a full-day tour into the Judean Desert which picks up passengers in both Tel Aviv and Jerusalem. Heading south from Jerusalem towards the Dead Sea, you turn off the main road and head into the desert. Travelling in a custom-built Mercedes truck, you drive up and down mountains, along wadis and stop at some truly beautiful places. One of the many highlights is the view of Mar Saba Monastery (see Around Bethlehem in The Gaza Strip & the West Bank chapter). The trips depart every Tuesday and Saturday morning at 9 am and the cost per person is US$64.

Alternatively for longer-term visitors, the centre organises abseiling and rock climbing courses as well as hiking and mountain bike treks through the surrounding desert.

Getting There & Away

The entire west coast of the Dead Sea, about 90km in length, is served by a single main road (Route 90) which branches off the Jerusalem-Jericho highway in the north and follows the shoreline southwards to Sodom and Eilat, with intersections heading west to Beersheba via Arad or Dimona.

Although you can reach the Dead Sea by direct bus from Haifa, Tel Aviv, Beersheba, Arad, Dimona and Eilat, the most comprehensive service is from Jerusalem's central bus station. Buses to Eilat and Beersheba go by Qumran, Ein Feshka, Ein Gedi, Ein Bokek and Masada and there should be a bus this way departing at least every hour or so. In Jerusalem, the Old City tourist information office is a better place to go for the current Dead Sea bus schedules than the hectic central bus station.

Buses stop on request at all the major sites along the Dead Sea shoreline but it is important that you keep a sharp eye out for the place that you want. The Egged drivers speed along so fast that you can fly past Qumran or Ein Feshka, for example, without realising it. It takes about 1¾ hours to get from Jerusalem to Masada and the one-way fare is 35.50NIS. Intermediate fares and travel times are proportionately less. On Saturday, no buses operate until the late afternoon.

Attrakzia   אטרקציה

Offering much fun and frivolity at 400m below sea level, Attrakzia is a water-based amusement park on the shore of the Dead Sea. The park, of course, uses fresh water – a Dead Sea-water amusement park would be about as much fun as gargling with bleach. As well as numerous pools, water slides and wave machines, there is a good sandy beach on the sea with sunshades, public showers and toilets. The park (☎ 02-994 2391) is open daily from March to December from 9 am to 5 pm. Admission usually costs 24NIS, although those staying two hours or less pay only 10NIS. Attrakzia is located right at the northern end of the Dead Sea, just 12km south of the Almog junction. All of the Dead Sea buses from Jerusalem (25 minutes away) will stop here on request.

QUMRAN   קומרן قمران
☎ Area Code: 02

A modest and fairly uninspiring archaeological site, Qumran is principally famous as the place where the **Dead Sea Scrolls** were found, an event which has been described as the most important discovery in the history of the Jewish people. In early 1947, a Bedouin shepherd boy searching for a stray goat came upon the scrolls which were stored inside earthenware jars in a high cliffside cave. The scrolls are now on display at the Shrine of the Book, which is part of the Israel Museum in Jerusalem.

Subsequent excavations below the caves have revealed the place where the scrolls' authors lived. They are believed to have been Essenes, members of a breakaway Jewish sect who hid here to escape the liberalism and decadence they believed were corrupting their fellow Jews. The Essenes lived here from about 150 BC until 68 AD, working the land, tending their sheep and studying the Old Testament and other religious texts.

You can clearly make out the aqueduct, channels and cisterns that ensured the community's water supply. Elsewhere is a refectory, a council chamber, the scriptorium where the Dead Sea Scrolls were probably written, ritual baths, a pottery workshop with kilns and a cemetery.

The caves themselves are higher up although none of those in which the Dead Sea Scrolls were found are marked. If you interrogate the ticket office staff you might be given accurate directions. Give yourself about two hours for the return climb and take plenty of water.

The site (☎ 994 2235) is open from 8 am to 5 pm (4 pm on Friday). Admission is 13NIS (students 8NIS). There's a good map of the site on sale at the entrance for 10NIS, although the ruins are not extensive and they're clearly labelled in English. Don't miss the seven minute introductory video in the small building to the left of the ticket booth. It will give you a good potted history of the site as well as temporary relief from the heat outside. There is also a self-service cafeteria and an air-conditioned and extensive souvenir shop at the site.

Coming from Jerusalem, this is normally the first stop the bus makes after the road hits the Dead Sea shoreline (presuming no one gets off at Attrakzia). As soon as you spot the water remind the driver that you want to get off at Qumran – you're only minutes away. Coming from the south, Qumran is about 10km after Ein Feshka. From the bus stop the site is just a 200m walk up the signposted approach road.

EIN FESHKA   עין פשחה   عين فِيشكا
☎ Area Code: 02

Also known as Einot Tzukim (Spring of Cliffs), this nature reserve is unique in having freshwater pools adjacent to the highly saline Dead Sea. Difficult to imagine, and often made to sound more attractive than it actually looks, Ein Feshka is an area of salt-encrusted reeds and grass, with several small pools of spring water, leading down to the Dead Sea shore. Various animals can be found here, including ibex, hyrax and fish in the pools. The pools tend to become quite murky by the middle of the day and also when there are crowds of people here there's not much room.

The reserve (☎ 994 2355) is open daily from 8 am to 5 pm (closing at 4 pm from November to March); admission is 12NIS (students 13NIS). There is a cafeteria and snack bar.

EIN GEDI
Pop: 669   ☎ Area Code: 07

One of the country's most attractive oases, Ein Gedi (Spring of the Kid) is a lush area of freshwater springs, waterfalls, pools and tropical vegetation nestled in the arid desert landscape of the lowest place on earth. It's a haven for desert wildlife which hangs in there despite the terrifyingly raucous coach loads of kids that rampage through the reserves on an almost daily basis.

Still, the animals have had a while to get used to human intrusions – archaeologists reckon this area was first settled during the Chalcolithic Age (3000 BC) when tribes

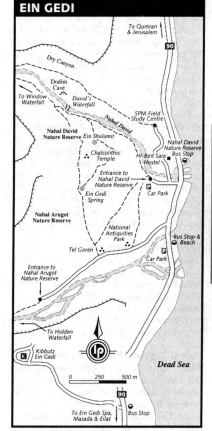

just out of the Stone Age worshipped the moon at a temple here. The encounter between David and Saul at Ein Gedi is described in 1 Samuel 24, and the place crops up again in Solomon's 'Song of Songs' (1:14). Human habitation continued at Ein Gedi until the Byzantine period when it stopped, resuming only in 1949 with the establishment of an Israeli military presence.

Apart from the odd machine gun-fitted jeep, today that military presence is low-key and instead Ein Gedi is now a decidedly

THE DEAD SEA

high-profile, coach party-guzzling tourist attraction. It includes the most (undeservedly) popular beach on the Dead Sea, the Ein Gedi Spa (probably the most popular place for experiencing the sea's health-giving qualities), a youth hostel, SPNI field study centre, restaurant, kibbutz guesthouse and petrol station.

Ein Gedi is spread over four kilometres and is served by four bus stops, so it's important to get off the bus at the right place to avoid a long, hot walk or wait. The nature reserves, youth hostel and field study centre are to the north, on the western side of the road. At the next stop, 1.5km further south, are the bathing beach, restaurant and petrol station. A kilometre further on is a stop for the kibbutz guesthouse, while another 1.5 to 2km to the south is the Ein Gedi Spa.

SPNI Field Study Centre

This complex (see Places to Stay & Eat later in this section) is the place to come for information on hiking in the region. There's also a small museum of local flora and fauna, a study centre and a hostel (groups only, however). It's just north of the HI hostel and is open daily from 8 am to 3 pm.

Nahal David Nature Reserve

This is the place most people associate with Ein Gedi – a pretty canyon in the desert near the Dead Sea, with lots of trees, plants, flowers, animals and cascading streams of water. Compared to some of the country's other great natural beauty spots, it may seem a little tame, as it's signposted and well trodden. However, if you can get here early in the morning when it opens (beating both the masses and the heat) it's like a little Garden of Eden.

The hikes in the Ein Gedi reserves are not particularly difficult or strenuous in themselves but you do need to bring along plenty of water to combat the heat. Bring swimwear (come wearing it, there's nowhere to change) and towels too for cooling off in the plunge pools.

The entrance to the reserve is beyond the car park at the end of the road leading from the bus stop. The road off to the right goes up to the HI hostel and the field study centre. Once inside, follow signs to **David's Waterfall**, the reserve's biggest attraction for most visitors, which is about a 15 minute walk. From here, follow the path around to head back towards the Dead Sea and pass another path leading up the slope. Climb up to reach the **Ein Shulamit** at the top of the cliff. Just beyond the place where water bubbles out of the ground, the path splits. To the right is a side path that leads to **Dodim Cave** (Lovers' Cave), just above the waterfall in a lovely setting. Give yourself about 40 minutes to make the side trip there and back. The steep main path to the left leads up to the fenced-in ruins of the **Chalcolithic temple** which, judging from artefacts discovered here, was most likely dedicated to the worship of the moon.

Continuing down the slope, signs point to the **Ein Gedi Spring**, reached after about 25 minutes. Find your way through the trees and reeds to join another path where there's a choice of going left to return to the main entrance, or going right to **Tel Goren**, the remains of the first Israelite settlement here. Beyond Tel Goren are the **ruins of an ancient synagogue** (see National Antiquities Park later in this section) with an interesting mosaic floor. Continue down to the road and either turn right to reach the Nahal Arugot Nature Reserve by the car park or turn left to reach the main road, a 15 minute walk. From here it's a 10 minute walk northwards along the main road to return to the bus stop and the turn-off to the main entrance.

Nahal David Nature Reserve (☎ 658 4285, fax 658 4517) is open daily from 8 am to 4 pm (you have to vacate the reserve by 5 pm) but you are not allowed to start the climb up to Ein Gedi Spring and Dodim Cave after 2.30 pm. In winter (December to February) closing times are an hour earlier. Admission is 15NIS. You can leave heavy bags at the entrance. Eating is not allowed in the reserve and you must keep to the paths.

Dry Canyon Hike This beautiful six hour hike takes you to less visited parts of the

Nahal David Nature Reserve. It involves straightforward walking over slightly rough ground, a few steep slopes and some scrambling over rocks here and there. Regular sports shoes are suitable footwear – sandals are not. It can be muddy underfoot in places, especially in winter, and you can also end up getting your feet wet wading through shallow water.

Flash floods are a danger in winter; it may not be raining at Ein Gedi but downpours in the hills further west can result in rushes of water through the canyons – make sure that you keep an ear out for the sound of rushing water and that you are ready to climb to higher ground.

The hike starts at the end of the road leading up past the field study centre. Follow the black-on-white painted trail markers past the reconstructed agricultural terraces. After 500m the trail reaches an intersection; go straight ahead, now following red painted markers. As you climb the small cliff, you can look down to the lush greenery between the David and Window waterfalls. The trail leads down to the dry canyon through a small gully. Take the left path down to Nahal David, with the springs a little further along. The canyon gets deeper and narrower and stakes have been provided to help you get past the waterfall.

The canyon ends at the picturesque **Window Waterfall**, which overlooks Nahal David. Come back to the stakes to climb the small ravine to the south. After 100m you come to a trail running parallel to the dry canyon. Turn left on this green marked trail, taking a right up the small hill. From the top you look down upon Ein Gedi and the Chalcolithic temple.

Follow the trail on your right down to the temple. About 250m to the right is the **Ein Gedi Spring**. You may well see hyraxes (dassies) here. From the spring, you can choose to either return to Nahal David via the upper part of the reserve and/or the **Shulamit Cave**, or continue down through Tel Goren and past the ancient synagogue.

To reach the upper part of Nahal David, take the wide path north from the spring,

passing underneath the ledge of the Chalcolithic temple. After 350m you intersect with the trail; continue straight down the southern bank and come to Nahal David Spring, with the Window Waterfall's overhang nearby. Take the path to the right across the stream until you reach a large boulder at the top of David's Waterfall. You can climb down the ladder to reach Shulamit Cave.

To return to Nahal David, follow the path to your left and head down through Ein Shulamit. The path eventually reaches David's Waterfall. Follow the path from here to reach the main entrance and car park.

To continue south, return to the Ein Gedi Spring and pass through a tunnel created by overhanging reeds. Note the ruins of a Crusader flour mill here. Follow the yellow marked trail, heading south-east, and crossing a dirt road. Take a right on the next dirt road you come to, and exit through the gate. To your left is a war memorial. The adjacent ruins are Tel Goren, dating from the late 7th century BC. Follow the dirt road till it intersects with a paved road. Turn left and pass by Tel Goren and the former field study centre and kibbutz buildings. At the next intersection, turn left, and go through the gate. After about 100m the road curves to the left. Head down to the right for another 100m and cross the fence to reach the ancient synagogue. Return to the paved road to make your way down to the main road, where you finish the hike about 3km south from where you started.

Nahal Arugot Nature Reserve

Signposted at the entrance as **Wadi Arugot** this is a larger area for walkers with more time and energy. It provides hikers with another lovely waterfall, **Hidden Waterfall**, involving a round-trip hike of about two hours. Another 30 minute hike beyond the Hidden Waterfall leads you to the **Upper Pools**. It is possible to make a loop by hiking up to the plateau on the northern side from the Hidden Waterfall and exiting the reserve via Nahal David. However, this is a difficult and long trek (five to six hours), you will need at least five litres of water per person and you must advise the reserve office before you leave. Food is not allowed in the reserve so eat well before you attempt any lengthy trekking.

The Nahal Arugot Nature Reserve closes one hour earlier than the Nahal David Nature Reserve. There is a separate entrance, open on the weekend and on holidays; admission is also 15NIS. Follow the signposted turn-off from the main road, about 2km south of the youth hostel, up to the car park for the start to the trail.

National Antiquities Park

This grandiloquent-sounding title describes an essentially small archaeological attraction featuring only one historic find: possibly the oldest synagogue discovered in Israel. Dating from the 3rd century AD the original synagogue was a trapezoid building paved with a black-and-white mosaic floor containing a moveable Torah Ark. The northern wall faced Jerusalem. The excavated remains that you see today date from the middle of the fifth century AD and are fairly well preserved, particularly the mosaic floor in the prayer hall.

The site is open from 8 am to 4 pm daily and entry costs 8NIS (students 6NIS).

Ein Gedi Beach

The popular but unpleasantly stony public beach (bring beach footwear) fulfils the bare requirements of Dead Sea floaters in that it has changing areas, large plastic shade umbrellas, toilets and showers. It also has a snack bar and a restaurant and is adjacent to a bus stop. What it lacks is the slightest hint of aesthetic appeal. Never mind, just keep your eyes shut while you float – although on second thoughts, better not; theft on the beach is rife.

Ein Gedi Spa

Further south, these therapeutic bathing facilities use hot sulphuric water from nearby mineral springs. There is a beach here and a decent vegetarian restaurant. Beach-goers are shuttled to and from the shore by a little train, now that the shoreline of the Dead Sea has receded so much in recent years. The complex belongs to the adjacent Hamme Mazor Kibbutz (☎ 659 4813) and guesthouse residents have free use of the facilities – nonresidents pay 52NIS, which includes mud and use of the private beach and sulphur pools.

Places to Stay & Eat

You can sleep for free by the beach, but watch your gear as theft is not uncommon. However, the beach is hard, stony and offers no shade.

HI – Beit Sara Hostel (☎ *658 4165, fax 658 4445)* charges US$16.50 for a bed in an eight bed dorm with air-con. A double room is US$40 (nonmembers pay a couple of dollars more). Breakfast is included and dinner is available. Check-in is from 3 to 7 pm and check-out is 9 am. The hostel is about 250m north-west of the Nahal David Nature Reserve bus stop.

SPNI Field Study Centre (☎ *658 4288, fax 658 4257)* has six-bed dorm rooms for visitors at US$40 per person (US$50 in the high season).

The only other accommodation option is the now expensive guesthouse at *Kibbutz Ein Gedi* (☎ *659 4222, fax 658 4328, email eb@kibbutz.co.il)* which is still, however, one of the most popular in the country. Surrounded by tree-filled gardens beside the Dead Sea, it has a swimming pool and a hot spa which are included in the price. Singles cost from US$122 to US$143 and doubles from US$174 to US$204, half board. Booking is recommended.

MASADA

☎ Area Code: 07

Shorthand for describing a kind of 'they'll never take us alive' attitude, the term 'Masada complex' is part of modern-day Israeli parlance. The story of the siege that took place here has been adopted as a symbol for the modern Jewish State. Israeli school children visit the site as part of their curriculum and some Israeli Defence Force (IDF) units hold their swearing-in ceremonies here, replete with the oath that 'Masada shall not fall again'.

A freestanding, sheer-sided plateau high above the Dead Sea, Masada (in Hebrew, *Metzuda*, meaning Stronghold) was fortified sometime between 103 and 76 BC before passing into the hands of Herod the Great in 43 BC. He saw the fortress as a potential refuge in the event of either a Jewish revolt or trouble from Cleopatra and Mark Anthony. Herod beefed up the defences with a casemate wall and towers, and added barracks, arsenals and storehouses. To make sure any enforced retreat would not be suffered in discomfort he added two luxurious palaces complete with swimming pools. After all that work, Herod died of natural causes in 4 BC without needing to use his desert hideaway. In 66 AD the Jews rose up against the Romans in what's known as the First Revolt. A group called the Zealots captured the lightly guarded Masada, which became a sanctuary for fleeing Jews. After four years the uprising was finally suppressed and the Romans then turned their attention to the mountain-top stronghold.

The sole account of what happened next comes from the chronicles of Flavius Josephus, a 1st century historian who was not a man to let the truth stand in the way of a good story. Josephus writes that under the command of Flavius Silva the Romans set up 15,000 men in eight camps around the base of the mountain and, using Jewish slave labour, began building an enormous earthen ramp up to the fortress walls. Inside the walls, the defenders of Masada numbered 967 men, women and children with enough food and water to last them for months. Once the ramp was complete, the Romans brought up their siege engines and prepared to breach the fortress. It's at this point that the Zealots, according to Josephus, began to set fire to their homes and all their possessions to prevent them falling into Roman hands. With that done, 10 men were chosen by lots and given the task of killing all of the others. Nine of the 10 were then executed by their companion before he finally despatched himself. When the Ro-

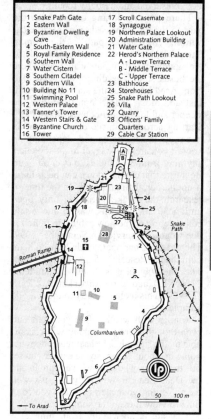

MASADA

1	Snake Path Gate	17	Scroll Casemate
2	Eastern Wall	18	Synagogue
3	Byzantine Dwelling Cave	19	Northern Palace Lookout
4	South-Eastern Wall	20	Administration Building
5	Royal Family Residence	21	Water Gate
6	Southern Wall	22	Herod's Northern Palace
7	Water Cistern		A - Lower Terrace
8	Southern Citadel		B - Middle Terrace
9	Southern Villa		C - Upper Terrace
10	Building No 11	23	Bathhouse
11	Swimming Pool	24	Storehouses
12	Western Palace	25	Snake Path Lookout
13	Tanner's Tower	26	Villa
14	Western Stairs & Gate	27	Quarry
15	Byzantine Church	28	Officers' Family Quarters
16	Tower	29	Cable Car Station

THE DEAD SEA

mans broke through they found alive just two women and five children who had survived by hiding. The mass suicide of Masada marked the end of the Jewish presence in Palestine.

Byzantine monks occupied the site during the 4th and 5th centuries after which Masada faded into legend. It was rediscovered in the early 19th century: in 1838 it was seen from Ein Gedi and correctly identified and in 1842 it was climbed. It wasn't, however, until 1963 that a major investigation was undertaken during which the site was excavated, preserved and partially rebuilt.

There are two hiking routes from the base to the top of Masada plus a cable car option. The easiest path is the **Roman Ramp** but this starts on the western side of the mountain, a 30 minute walk from where the buses stop. The direct approach road from Arad begins at the start of this path. Instead, most people opt to climb the steeper and longer switchback **Snake Path**. Starting across from the cable car station this route is hard going and, depending on how fit you are, the stagger to the top takes anything from 30 minutes to over an hour. Be aware that coming down can be as hard, if not harder, than going up. At the time of research the Snake Path was only open until 8.30 am, but this was to allow safe construction of the new cable car, which is due to go into service in September 1999. The old cable car operates daily from 8 am with the last descent at 5 pm (Friday 2 pm). The one-way fare is 38.80NIS (students 21.80NIS) and a return ticket is 47NIS (35NIS). This includes entry to the Masada complex.

Top up with water before you start out, even though there is drinking water available on the summit. The heat really does get going by about 10 am, so the earlier you set off, the better. The sunrise over Jordan and the Dead Sea can be lovely and it's well worth setting your alarm so that you're in time to view it from the summit.

The site is open daily from sunrise to about nightfall. Admission for walkers is 17NIS (students 12.80NIS). For further information call ☎ 658 4207, fax 658 4464.

Things to See

Depending on the level of your interest in archaeology, you could be up here for hours. A map is available at the lower terminal complex but it's perhaps not necessary as all the excavations are well labelled in English. The lines of black paint you'll see indicate which parts are the original remains and which parts are reconstructed. See Masada map on page 347:

1 **Snake Path Gate** The stone slab floor, wall benches, guardroom and white plaster wall made to resemble marble, are typical of Masada's gates.

2 **Eastern Wall** This section of the Herodian wall allows you to see how it was designed, with an outer and inner wall connected by partitions and the occasional tower. Herod's layout was, befitting a king, rather spacious, and the Zealots also built partitions to create more living quarters for themselves.

3 **Byzantine Dwelling Cave** Monks built this living space in an existing crater, believed to have been a quarry for plastering material.

4 **South-Eastern Wall** In this section of the wall, there's a tower with a little room built on to it. Inside, a small niche bears what might be a Roman inscription.

5 **Royal Family Residence** One of a few examples of the luxurious residential villas built for Herod. Designed around a courtyard, it had a wide roofed hall at the southern end, separated by two pillars. Frescoes cover the walls of the three rooms here. Again, the Zealots divided up the big rooms to accommodate their large numbers.

6 **Southern Wall** There's a lookout tower here, with what was probably a bakery added by the Zealots. The Zealots were strictly religious and built ritual baths for themselves. The bath here has a dressing room next to it (note the narrow niches for clothes). The southern gate led to cisterns and caves outside the wall.

7 **Water Cistern** This is an example of Herod's clever water supply system that was necessary to allow such a community to live in comfort in this barren location. There are another 12 cisterns up here, on the western slope.

8 **Southern Citadel** This defended Masada at its weakest spot.

9 **Southern Villa** An unfinished Herodian structure, the Zealots built more living quarters around it. One of the rooms has been restored to the state it was in when excavated, with pots left beside the kitchen hearth. A long hall with benches was built on to the north by the Zealots and may have been used as a study hall.

Wild ibex roam the Maktesh Ramon.

The Masada fortress overlooks the Rift Valley.

Tel Goren is the site of an ancient Israelite settlement near the springs of Ein Gedi.

Floating on the Dead Sea is a great experience – but don't get salt in your eyes!

Local women rummage for clothes at a Bedouin market in Beersheba.

The Negev

הנגב

The Negev Desert accounts for almost half of Israel's land area and although *negev* means 'dry land', it's far from being a simple expanse of sand. Starting by the Dead Sea where the Judean Desert ends, the northern Negev is a region of low sandstone hills, steppes and fertile plains furrowed with canyons and wadis. Moving south, the central Negev is drier and more mountainous – an area of bare rocky peaks, lofty plateaus, and more canyons and wadis. At its southern extreme are the grey-red Eilat Mountains and beyond is Egypt's Sinai Desert, of which, in geographic terms, the Negev is a natural extension.

The region's most outstanding features are the world's three largest craters. Of these, two are hard to get to without your own transport but the biggest, Maktesh Ramon, can easily be visited from the small dusty town of Mitzpe Ramon which huddles on the crater's edge.

Apart from the tourist magnet Eilat, squeezed tight between the Red Mountains and Red Sea, most of the Negev remains largely uninhabited, with only a handful of towns. However, the harsh environment is dotted with an increasing number of Jewish settlements, mainly kibbutzim and moshavim, and also Nahal military projects (military service combined with agricultural work in marginal areas).

David Ben-Gurion, Israel's first prime minister and so-called 'father of the Negev', was one of the first to publicly recognise the strategic importance and economic potential of the region. Under his leadership a development program of sorts was launched with the basic aim of transforming a wilderness into much needed farmland. Ben-Gurion's view was that 'if the state does not put an end to the desert, the desert may put an end to the state'. After much painstaking trial and error, some impressive results have been achieved and as you travel around the desert, occasionally

HIGHLIGHTS

- **The Maktesh Ramon** – a spectacular crater in the middle of the Negev Desert; great hiking opportunities

- **Eilat** – love it or leave it, Israelis and foreigners come here by the plane and bus load for its raucous, carnival atmosphere.

- **Camel trekking** – take your pick from a two or 15 day organised trip in the wilderness

- **Red Sea coral reefs** – great for snorkelling and scuba diving, or take a submarine if you don't want to get your feet wet

- **Hai-Bar Arava Biblical Wildlife Reserve** – view creatures featured in the Bible

- **Bedouins** – Israel's indigenous desert nomads live here along with their many camels

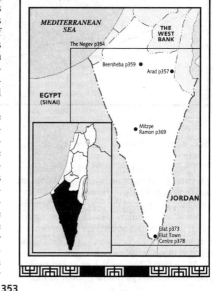

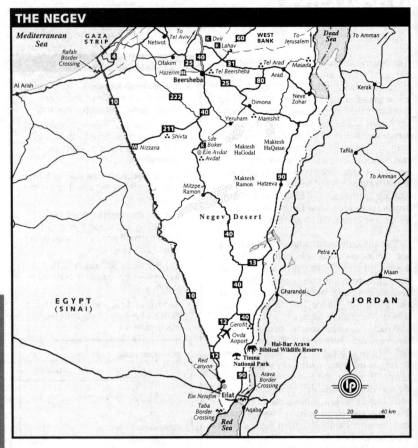

THE NEGEV

Mediterranean Sea
GAZA STRIP
To Tel Aviv
Netivot
Dvir
Lahav
WEST BANK
To Jerusalem
Dead Sea
To Amman
Rafah Border Crossing
Ofakim
Hazerim
Tel Arad
Masada
Al Arish
Tel Beersheba
Beersheba
Arad
Kerak
Dimona
Neve Zohar
Yeruham
Mamshit
Shivta
Nizzana
Sde Boker
Ein Avdat
Avdat
Maktesh HaGodal
Maktesh HaQatan
Tafila
To Amman
Mitzpe Ramon
Maktesh Ramon
Hatzeva
Negev Desert
Petra
Maan
EGYPT (SINAI)
Gharandal
JORDAN
Gerofit
Ovda Airport
Hai-Bar Arava Biblical Wildlife Reserve
Red Canyon
Timna National Park
Arava Border Crossing
Ein Netafim
Eilat
Taba Border Crossing
Aqaba
Red Sea
0   20   40 km

you will come across verdant agricultural oases.

The Negev is often overlooked by visitors or simply seen through a bus window en route to or from Eilat. However, just a short distance away from the main roads there are several spectacular natural beauty spots, such as Ein Avdat and Maktesh Ramon, and archaeological sites, such as Shivta and Avdat, that are well worth a visit.

Major roads in the Negev are limited to just two highways heading south to Eilat –

the one from the Dead Sea provides the most direct and also the fastest route, the other highway coming from Beersheba goes via Sde Boker, Ein Avdat and Mitzpe Ramon. Linking the Dead Sea and Beersheba there is a road via Arad and another via Dimona.

Hiking in the Negev

There are some excellent hikes in the Negev region taking in a surprisingly wide variety of landscapes. Particularly recommended are those around Sde Boker, Ein Avdat and Mitzpe Ramon (see individual entries in this chapter). There is also a locally produced book available called *Hikes Around Eilat* (50NIS) which details about 25 trails in and around the Red Mountains using the coastal resort as a base. You should be able to find a copy at one of the Steimatzky bookshops or at the Society for the Protection of Nature in Israel (SPNI) stores in Tel Aviv or Jerusalem.

There is a very good 1:50,000 map of the Eilat Mountain region produced by the Israeli Trails Committee of the SPNI which contains information on the flora and fauna of the region as well as individual trail maps for some of the more popular hikes. This map, No 20 in the very popular *Israel Hiking and Touring Maps* series and one of the few in English, is available for about 50NIS from any office of the SPNI. The current version was published in 1995 so check to see if a new one is out.

SPNI has field study centres at Sde Boker, Mitzpe Ramon and Eilat, and at Hatzeva, 50km south of the Dead Sea on road No 90 – these are the places to visit for detailed maps and information, and recommendations on routes and desert sights.

The Negev is a harsh desert, but due to its rapid development visitors can easily be lulled into a false sense of security and forget to follow the safety guidelines. It really is best to make an early start, avoid physical exertion in the middle of the day (say noon to 3 pm), cover your head and drink plenty of water.

Presumably due to the demands of IDF personnel (the Negev is highly militarised), bus services pass by most of the places of interest but they are very infrequent, so check the timetables to avoid too much waiting around.

Organised Tours

SPNI Tours offers a five day camel trek through the Eilat Mountains – meals around the campfire, sleeping out under the stars and all that. The departure dates are three times a month in summer and twice a

---

Bye Bye Bedouin

Critics point out that much of Israel's success in developing the Negev has been achieved at the expense of the estimated 70,000 Bedouin who still live in tents and breed camels and livestock here. Their encampments are all to the south and east of Beersheba, and you'll see the black oilcloth tents and animal compounds along the road to Eilat. However, only about 10% of the Bedouin remain nomadic; the rest of them have been forced into permanent, urban settlements.

Prior to 1948 the tribes roamed widely throughout the Negev but since the establishment of the State of Israel, traditional grazing lands have been lost to the kibbutzim and to the Israeli Defence Force (IDF) which has appropriated hundreds of sq km for bases, airstrips and ranges. Deprived of vital grazing areas for their flocks, the Bedouin have been left with little choice but to settle and attempt to adapt.

Meanwhile, the Israeli tourism industry long ago twigged to the appeal of the adjective 'Bedouin', and without a trace of irony operators offer accommodation in 'authentic Bedouin tents', and some up-market hotels welcome their guests with their 'traditional Bedouin hospitality'.

---

month in winter. The cost per person is US$320. SPNI Tours also does a four day hiking/driving tour which takes in Sde Boker, Maktesh Ramon, a camel ride in the mountains, snorkelling in Eilat and hiking around Timna National Park. The all-inclusive price per person is US$396. For contact details see the SPNI section under Flora & Fauna in the Facts about the Country chapter.

Out in the middle of the Negev at Shacharut some 20km south-east of Ovda airport, Camel Riders (☎ 07-637 3218, fax 637 1944) is an adventure tour operator that organises both group and individual tours.

Some of the SPNI trips also utilise the Shacharut setup, though you can just as easily contact it yourselves. It organises a variety of camel safaris and camping trips in the desert. Its prices range from as little as US$165 for a two day caravan along the 'Smugglers' Route' to a 15 day epic caravan 'Following the Footsteps of Past Cultures' for US$1520. In all cases, equipment and food are supplied.

Desert Shade (Zell Midbar; ☎ 658 6229, fax 658 6208) is one of the new wave of desert tour centres that are springing up in the Negev. It offers desert tours on camel (30NIS per hour) or in a 4WD (80NIS per person for two hours), rents mountain bikes (45NIS for a full day) and organises activities abseiling. While the camel tours are little more than a trot down the road and back, the 4WD tour is a real off the road trip, accompanied by some well-informed and interesting commentary.

ARAD   ערד
Pop: 21,600   ☎ Area Code: 07

On the road between Beersheba (48km) and the Dead Sea (28km), Arad is a new town even by Israeli standards. Established in 1961 after the discovery here of natural gas, Arad is one of the more attractive of Israel's pre-planned towns, with pedestrian and motor traffic separated as much as possible in residential quarters. Situated on a high plateau (620m above sea level), it has commanding views of the desert and, in the distance, the Dead Sea.

Renowned for its cool, dry and pollen-free air, Arad is promoted as an ideal health resort for those suffering from asthmatic and respiratory difficulties. The town itself doesn't offer too much to either see or do and so most travellers limit any time spent here to changing buses en route to or from the Dead Sea. However, it is an ideal place for making forays into the Judean and Negev deserts, and the visitors centre offers a wide variety of options.

Visitors to the Masada Sound and Light show will necessarily pass through Arad since the show venue is not connected by road to the main north-south highway linking the Dead Sea and Eilat.

Orientation & Information
Arad's tiny bus station on Yehuda St is easy enough to find. Across the street is the pedestrianised commercial centre (midrahov) with shops, eating places, banks, a cinema and the post office (open Sunday to Thursday from 7.45 am to 2 pm, and Friday from 7.45 am to noon; closed Saturday). Also on the midrahov is the town's tourist information office (☎ 995 4409, fax 995 5052), open Sunday to Tuesday from 8 am to 1 pm and 4 to 7 pm, Wednesday from 8 am to 4 pm and Friday from 8.30 am to noon. It's closed on Saturday.

If you choose to stay overnight the youth hostel is just a five minute walk to the east, as is one of the hotels.

Things to See & Do
New arrivals should head for the **Arad visitors centre** (☎ 995 4409, fax 995 5052) near the Arad Mall. The centre also includes exhibits on the archaeology of nearby Tel Arad, a simulated desert flood and a model of the Judean deserts complete with mini sound and light show. It is open Saturday to Thursday from 9 am to 5 pm and Friday from 9 am to 2.30 pm; admission is 14NIS.

In the industrial quarter to the south, the **Abir Riding School** (☎ 995 4147) offers horse-riding faciliies and there is a pleasant lookout at the far eastern end of Ben Yair and Moav Sts, near the Margoa Hotel.

Many people base themselves in Arad in order to visit the Dead Sea where accommodation and food prices are higher. Arad is also the jumping-off point for the spectacular Sound and Light show at Masada which is a 30 minute drive from the town. You can buy tickets for the show from the tourist information office. See the Masada section in the Dead Sea chapter for full details.

Places to Stay
HI – Blau Weiss Youth Hostel (☎ 995 7150, fax 995 5078, 34 Atad St) is on the corner of HaPalmach St. From the bus station walk

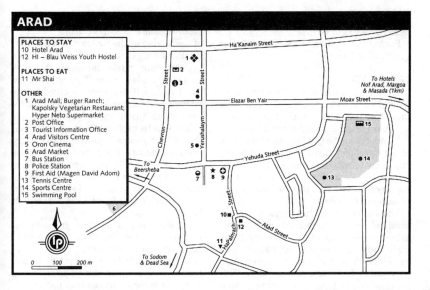

ARAD

PLACES TO STAY
10 Hotel Arad
12 HI – Blau Weiss Youth Hostel

PLACES TO EAT
11 Mr Shai

OTHER
1 Arad Mall; Burger Ranch;
   Kapolsky Vegetarian Restaurant;
   Hyper Neto Supermarket
2 Post Office
3 Tourist Information Office
4 Arad Visitors Centre
5 Oron Cinema
6 Arad Market
7 Bus Station
8 Police Station
9 First Aid (Magen David Adom)
13 Tennis Centre
14 Sports Centre
15 Swimming Pool

Ha'Kanaim Street
Elazar Ben Yair
To Hotels
Nof Arad, Margoa
& Masada (1km)
Moav Street
Chevron Street
Yerushalaym Street
Yehuda Street
To Beersheba
HaPalmach Street
Atad Street
To Sodom
& Dead Sea

0   100   200 m

east (past the police station) up Yehuda St,
and follow the signs to turn right on HaPalmach St. It's clean and quiet with kitchen facilities, and meals are available. Dorm beds
for HI card holders cost US$15. It's closed
from 9 am to 5 pm and there's no curfew.

The nearby *Hotel Arad* (☎ 995 7272, fax
995 4525, 6 HaPalmach St) is basic but
clean and comfortable – singles/doubles are
US$46/69. There are a couple of more ex-
pensive hotels 2km further east and each
has a swimming pool. At the three star *Nof
Arad* (☎ 995 7056, fax 995 4053, Moav St),
singles cost US$67 to US$76, and doubles
US$90 to US$110. The four star *Margoa*
(☎ 995 1222, fax 995 7778) has a clinic for
the climatic treatment of asthma. Singles/
doubles cost US$93 to US$133.

Places to Eat

The best choice of eating places is on the
midrahov. There's also one decent supermarket: *Hyperneto* in Arad Mall. There are
also a number of *felafel* (deep-fried chickpeas) and *shwarma* (sandwich of meat sliced
off a spit) places around the midrahov.

Burger Ranch has an outlet in Arad Mall
and is open Sunday to Thursday from 10 am
to 11 pm and on Saturday from noon to 11
pm – handy to note if you need a food fix
on the Shabbat. *Kapolsky* is one of a chain
of vegetarian restaurants.

Mr Shai (☎ 997 1956, 32 HaPalmach St)
is an unassuming little Chinese restaurant.
Recommended dishes include the goose in
lemon and the chicken in honey. Dinner for
two will come to around 250NIS with wine,
though its business lunches work out a lot
cheaper. It is open from noon to 3.30 pm
and 7 to 11 pm, closed Sunday.

Getting There & Away

With only a few buses connecting Beersheba to the Dead Sea, you will often have
to change at Arad. From here there are
fairly frequent buses to Masada (17NIS, 45
minutes), Ein Gedi (19NIS, one hour) and
Beersheba (15NIS, 45 minutes).

Remember that on Saturday morning a
special bus runs from Beersheba to Ein
Gedi via Arad and Masada. Egged provides
this service primarily for locals who would

be otherwise unable to benefit from the Dead Sea's health facilities.

For bus information call ☎ 995 7393. For a taxi call ☎ 997 3388.

TEL ARAD　　　　　　　תל ערד

Located some 10km west of modern Arad, this is the country's best example of an Early Bronze Age city and, as such, keen archaeologists may find Tel Arad worth a visit.

Mentioned in the Old Testament accounts of the Israelites' attempts to penetrate the Promised Land (Numbers 21:1-3, 33:40; Joshua 12:14), ancient Arad was then an important fortress guarding the southern approaches to the country.

The site covers several hectares, the excavations are clearly marked and an information leaflet is available. Opening hours are Saturday to Thursday from 8 am to 4 pm, and Friday from 8 am to 3 pm, closing one hour earlier in winter. Admission is 7NIS (students 4NIS). Buses going between Arad and Beersheba pass the orange signposted turn-off for Tel Arad – from here it's a 1.5km walk. Bus No 388 passes the Tel Arad turn-off.

BEERSHEBA　　　באר שבע بئر السبع
Pop: 156,400　☎ Area Code: 07

Unattractive and with little to see and do, Beersheba is unlikely to impress many visitors. It's the kind of town that gives most satisfaction when seen from the rear window of your departing bus.

Nevertheless, it's the 'capital' of the Negev and the region's transportation hub. Receiving mention in the Old Testament several times (Judges 20:1; I Samuel 3:20; II Samuel 3:10, 17:11, 24:2), Beersheba also has a rich history, though little of that is detectable today. The one surviving ancient monument, a well, attests to the town's association with the story of Abraham (Genesis 21:25-33) in which the name Beersheba (or Be'er Sheva) is given as meaning 'the well of the oath' after a covenant supposedly agreed in this place between the patriarch and Abimelek the Philistine.

In fact until the late 19th century, Beersheba remained little more than a collection of wells, used by the Bedouin to water their flocks. Changes came when the Turks began to develop this remote desert spot as an administrative centre. During WWI the small town fell to Allenby's allied forces after a spectacular and celebrated charge by units of the Australian Lighthorse.

The Israelis captured Beersheba in 1948, then still an Arab village of approximately 2000 inhabitants. Since then a continuous influx of Jewish immigrants (many Russian) have swollen the place to a drab, dusty urban sprawl of more than 140,000 people, making the city the fourth most populous in Israel.

For the visitor, probably the greatest point of interest is the weekly Bedouin market held every Thursday morning. The museum is also pleasant but a visit won't take much time and as accommodation is so pricey there's little reason to stay overnight.

Orientation

The town centre, where you will find most of the shops, eating places and accommodation, is in the not particularly old Old Town about 15 minutes walk west of the central bus station. It's laid out on a tight grid pattern, and centred on the pedestrianised Keren Kayemet Le-Y'Israel St.

The other place where you might find yourself spending a lot of time is the Kanyon (or Qanyon) shopping centre, near the central bus station and easily distinguishable by its great glass drum. The market is south of the shopping centre on the main Eilat Rd. The ancient site of Tel Beersheba is 5km outside town, to the east.

Information

Tourist Office The local tourist information office (☎ 623 6001/2) is on Nordau St, across from the entrance to the central bus station. You have to hard to find it as it's marked by just a small sign in the window – instead for Avis, and the tourist information office is next door. It's open Sunday to Thursday from 8 am to 4 pm.

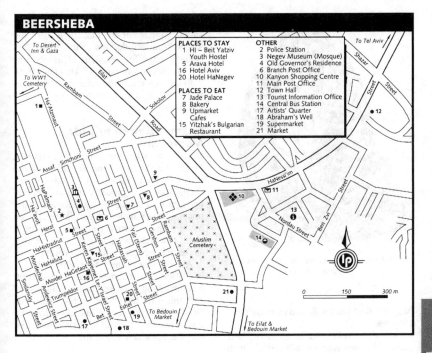

BEERSHEBA

PLACES TO STAY
1 HI – Beit Yatziv
   Youth Hostel
5 Arava Hotel
16 Hotel Aviv
20 Hotel HaNegev

PLACES TO EAT
7 Jade Palace
8 Bakery
9 Upmarket
   Cafes
15 Yitzhak's Bulgarian
   Restaurant

OTHER
2 Police Station
3 Negev Museum (Mosque)
4 Old Governor's Residence
6 Branch Post Office
10 Kanyon Shopping Centre
11 Main Post Office
12 Town Hall
13 Tourist Information Office
14 Central Bus Station
17 Artists' Quarter
18 Abraham's Well
19 Supermarket
21 Market

Money There are banks in the Kanyon centre, and a Bank Hapoalim on the corner of Ha'Atzmaut and HaHalutz Sts (Old Town) which is open Monday and Wednesday from 8.30 am to 1 pm, Tuesday and Thursday from 8.30 am to 12.30 pm and from 4 to 6 pm, and Friday from 8.30 am to noon.

Post & Communications The main post office is just north of the central bus station on the corner of HaNessi'im and Nordau Sts. It is open Sunday, Monday, Tuesday and Thursday from 8 am to 12.30 pm and 4 to 6 pm, Wednesday from 8 am to 1 pm, Friday from 8 am to 12.30 pm, closed Saturday. There is also a convenient branch in the Old Town, on the corner of HaHistradrut and Hadassah Sts.

Emergency The police station (☎ 642 6744 or in an emergency call ☎ 100) is on Herzl St at the northern end of Keren Kayemet Le-Y'Israel in the Old Town.

Bedouin Market

Thursday is the day for Beersheba's much talked-about Bedouin market. Traditionally this is when hundreds of the Negev's Bedouins come into town to buy and sell their livestock, food, carpets, clothes and jewellery to anyone who's willing to barter and buy, be they Israelis, tourists or each other.

It used to be truly authentic but now features things such as T-shirts and electronic goods. The southernmost part of the market is where you'll find the most interesting items such as Bedouin robes, rugs and ceramics. Only very early in the day can you really hope to see something that resembles a Bedouin scene – at about 6 am. It's south of the central bus station where you can see the arched rooftops across the main road.

Only 10% of Bedouins are now living a nomadic lifestyle.

Negev Museum & Governor's House

In one of the more attractive areas of Beersheba, this museum (☎ 628 2056) in the Old Town on Ha'Atzmaut St is housed in a Turkish-era mosque set in a green leafy park.

The exhibits include a history of the town itself as well as a series of archaeological artefacts from the whole Negev region. There is also a section on Bedouin culture, a collection of medieval maps of the Holy Land and a 6th century mosaic floor depicting animals in its geometric design.

The elegant building across from the museum is what used to be the governor's residence and was for a spell the city hall before becoming a small contemporary art gallery. It's open Sunday to Thursday from 10 am to 5 pm, Friday and Saturday 10 am to 1 pm; admission is 7NIS.

Abraham's Well

At the southern end of Keren Kayemet Le-Y'Israel St, where it meets Hebron Rd, is a very unimpressive reconstruction of what is claimed to be Abraham's Well. However, archaeologists believe that the well of the legend (see introduction to this section) is actually out at Tel Beersheba. This city centre site is open Sunday to Thursday from 8.30 am to 4 pm, and Friday from 8.30 am to 12.30 pm; it's closed Saturday. Admission is free.

Negev Palmach Brigade Memorial

North-east of the town on a hill, this is a bizarre and confusing modern tribute to the Jewish soldiers killed while taking Beersheba from the Egyptians in 1948. Hebrew inscriptions explain the significance of the images, which include a tent, a well, some battle maps, a narrow passage, a bunker, a bird, a watchtower, an aqueduct, and a snake that represents the evil enemy.

Also known as the Andarta Memorial, it is difficult to reach by public transport. Near the Arad road, you can get off bus No 388 and walk the 750m, or take local bus No 4 to the train station and cut across the tracks to reach the hill. Admission is free and there is a cafe at the site.

WWI Cemetery

Adjacent to the HI hostel, this is the largest British WWI cemetery in Israel. Most of those buried here were members of Australian and other Commonwealth regiments who were killed in action against the Turks.

Tel Beersheba

The site of the ancient town, this is some 5km east of modern Beersheba on the Jerusalem road. Here you can see remains of city walls and houses – it's a good idea to visit the Negev Museum first to have a better idea of what it's all about. Next to the ruins is a visitors centre (☎ 646 0103) with a cafeteria, a restaurant and a small museum featuring the Bedouin. The site is open daily from 9 am to 11 pm; admission is free. The Bedouin museum is open Sunday to Thursday from 10 am to 5 pm, and Friday and Saturday from 10 am to 1 pm; admission is 7NIS (students 4NIS).

Overeducated, Overwhelming & Over Here

Over 700,000 Jews from the former Soviet Union, seeking a better life and a surer future for their children, have made their way to Israel in the past decade, many of them settling in towns like Beersheba and Dimona This is a 10% population increase over and above natural growth.

The immigrants come with an extraordinarily high level of education, but not always in fields that are needed in Israel. The percentage of doctors in the country, already among the highest in the world, has grown, but what is a country without forests to do with forestry engineers and how many orchestras can six million people support? In the first years there was unemployment and under-employment, and headlines of brain surgeons sweeping the streets. Much of this has been resolved.

After initial euphoria (Israel is, after all, the country for the ingathering of the Jews), the immigration led to tensions and conflicting pressures for limited social welfare resources between veteran Israelis and the new arrivals. Some of these remain.

Shops with Russian signs in neighbourhoods where you hear nary a word of Hebrew are not uncommon; nor are special afternoon programs for children in Russian. And yet the Gesher Theater, which at first performed in Russian, is widely regarded as one of the leading companies in the world, while the teaching of music and art in Israel's schools has been literally saved from extinction.

Integrated but still apart. A separate culture? Maybe. The immigration was largely responsible for the dramatic growth in the Israeli economy and the rise in the standard of living. And their sons serve in the army, and get killed in Lebanon, and they have died in terrorist bus bombings over and above their percentage in the Israeli population. The bouillabaisse that is Israeli culture is a series of separate but integrated cultures, and this one has enriched the pot enormously.

Deborah Lipson

To reach Tel Beersheba, you should take the thrice-daily bus for nearby Tel as-Sab, a new Bedouin village that is part of the Israeli program of nomad settlement, and get off at the signs for the archaeological site.

Places to Stay

Beersheba has a limited selection of accommodation. *HI – Beit Yatziv Youth Hostel (☎ 627 7444, 627 5735, 79 Ha'Atzmaut St)* isn't quite the cheapest place in town but overpriced as it is, it still offers the best value for money. It's a clean, modern complex with a swimming pool, pleasant gardens and no curfew. Comfortable dorm beds, in a room for six with toilet and shower, are US$21. The adjoining guesthouse has singles/doubles for US$40/59. All prices include breakfast. Lunch and dinner at 45NIS are available if you want them.

The hostel is in the Old Town, a 20 minute walk from the central bus station. Cross the main Eilat Rd and head for the three large radio antennae visible above the buildings in front and slightly to your right. The road that runs in front of the antennae compound is Ha'Atzmaut; follow it past the mosque and the hostel is on the left-hand side, a further 400m on. Alternatively, take bus No 12 or 13 from the bus station.

It would really be pushing it to recommend any of the town's three central hotels since they are all mainly taken over by Russian migrants and other temporary residents. They are listed here purely as a last resort. The least unappealing of these places is *Hotel Aviv (☎ 627 8059, 48 Mordei Ha-Getaot St)* which is on the corner of Keren Kayemet Le-Y'Israel St. A little musty, it at least benefits from friendly management.

My Kibbutz Experience

The first kibbutz I worked on was in the hills of the Upper Galilee, overlooking the Hula Valley. The other volunteers and I would pick fruit in the morning wearing thick army jackets while in the afternoon we'd laze by the pool that had spectacular views across to the Golan Heights. Our daily roster was varied and sometimes we'd work in their glass factory making test tubes.

After a month, I headed south to a desert kibbutz near Beersheba where my fellow volunteers were two English skinheads as well as Canadians, French, Mexicans and Irish. We picked oranges, lemons and avocadoes and were each given a stint packing live chickens into wire mesh boxes at three in the morning. Occasionally we worked in the kitchen peeling potatoes or in the laundry ironing kibbutzniks' shirts. Friday nights were usually spent at the volunteers' club where we'd drink *arak* and dance; and, luckily for us, the kibbutzniks took us on trips to Masada, the Dead Sea and Ein Gedi.

Once we'd been around the kibbutz for a while, we were accepted as part of the community – one volunteer decided to stay forever, another developed cancer and the heartbroken kibbutzniks made sure he received the best possible treatment. As well as free accommodation and food, we were given some spending money. Five months later I left this kibbutz, suntanned and happy.

Julia Taylor

Singles will set you back 90NIS and doubles 120NIS. *Arava Hotel* (☎ *627 8792, 37 HaHistradrut St*) is extremely badly maintained. Singles are 80NIS and doubles 120NIS. *Hotel HaNegev* (☎ *627 7026, 26 Ha'Atzmaut St*) is scruffy and badly aged but at least it has a variety of prices (80 to 150NIS) to reflect the lack of amenities peculiar to each room.

Beersheba's top hotel is the four star *Desert Inn* (☎ *642 4922, fax 641 2772*) to the north of the Old Town in what is now a residential area, but was once the town's outskirts. It has a pool and a tennis court. Singles cost from US$65.50 and doubles from US$88.50, breakfast included.

Places to Eat

The best place to eat is *Kanyon shopping centre* which has the whole lower ground floor dedicated to felafel, shwarma and various fast-food franchises. The other place to go for inexpensive food is on and around Keren Kayemet Le-Y'Israel St, which is lined with cafes that serve all the standard versions of grilled meats and salads, along with ice-cream parlours and some fast-food outlets.

Beit Ha-Ful (☎ *623 4253, 15 HaHistradrut St*) is a popular fast *fuul* (fava bean paste) joint that does decent shwarma and felafel as well. You can stand up or sit down, inside or outside. A feed will set you back a mere 20NIS or so.

If you fancy a spot of Eastern European cuisine, try *Yitzhak's Bulgarian Restaurant* (☎ *623 8505, 112 Keren Kayemet Le-Y'Israel St*) which does kebabs, schnitzels, liver and so on for around 30NIS.

Jade Palace on the corner of HaHistradrut and Yair (Stern) Sts is a very good Chinese restaurant. You can expect to pay about 30 to 40NIS per person.

For coffee and cake check out some of the good-looking cafes at the eastern end of Herzl St, just further along from the Jade Palace.

Getting There & Away

Bus Bus Nos 370, 375 and 380 run every 15 minutes to Tel Aviv (21NIS, 80 minutes), headed for the central bus station and Arlosoroff terminal respectively. Bus Nos 470 and 446 head for Jerusalem (27.50NIS, 90 minutes), with one or the other departing every 30 minutes or so. For Eilat (35NIS, three hours), there's the hourly No 394 via Mitzpe Ramon (45NIS, 80 minutes) and a slow service which leaves four times a day.

There are also four buses daily for Ein Gedi, via Arad and Masada.

For information on intercity routes call ☎ 629 4311.

Car You can rent a car by calling:

Avis	☎ 627 1777
Dan-Rent-a-Car	☎ 623 5780
Europcar	☎ 623 1013
Reliable	☎ 057-237 123
Thrifty	☎ 628 2590
Traffic	☎ 627 3878

Sherut Moniot Ayal (☎ 623 3033) operate *sherut* (shared taxi) services to Tel Aviv, Jerusalem and Eilat for the same fares as the buses, but there's nothing running on Saturday and you have to wait until they fill up. They operate from a booth just outside the bus station.

Getting Around
You can easily walk from the central bus station to the Old Town and the market, otherwise the local buses leave from outside the central bus station's main entrance. Local bus No 13 departs every 20 minutes for the Beit Yatziv Youth Hostel.

AROUND BEERSHEBA
Museum of Bedouin Culture
With Israel's push to develop the Negev, the nomadic existence of the Bedouin and all its traditional trappings is fading fast. The aim of this museum is to preserve and present samples of the Bedouin's threatened culture and to represent their life as it is today. Most of the museum guides are Bedouins from the nearby area.

The idea for the museum came from Jews and Bedouins interested in preserving and promoting Bedouin culture and heritage. The collection, consisting of a variety of traditional items such as clothes, household utensils, tools and jewellery, was part of a private collection of the Jewish founders of the museum. Bedouins have also donated some items.

Other museum attractions include a 12 minute audiovisual program detailing the Bedouin existence in the Negev and Sinai, a demonstration of traditional home-making activities like bread-making and weaving, and a Bedouin tent of hospitality where visitors can sit with a local Bedouin, drink coffee and talk.

There is also an interesting archaeological section with a display of the cave culture dating from the Mishnaic and Talmudic eras. It features caves from the Chalcolithic, Israelite, Hellenistic, Roman and Byzantine periods.

The museum (☎ 991 8597, fax 991 9889) is part of the Joe Alon Regional & Folklore Centre, which is a combined museum, research institute and field school. It is open Sunday to Thursday from 9 am to 5 pm, and Friday 9 am to 2 pm; admission is 15NIS (students 13NIS). See its Web site: www.lahavnet.co.il/joalon.

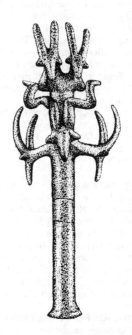

This antlered copper wand dates back to the Chalcolithic period (4500-3500 BC).

THE NEGEV

Getting There & Away The complex stands on the property of Kibbutz Lahav, which is near Kibbutz Dvir; both off a side road that intersects with the Beersheba-Kiryat Gat road. From Beersheba, bus No 369 to Tel Aviv passes the intersection quite often but from here it's an 8km hitch to the kibbutz. Bus No 42 runs directly to the kibbutz, but only once a day. Check with Egged for the current schedule.

Shivta (Subeita)

Some 58km south-west of Beersheba and out in the middle of nowhere, this is one of the Negev's most impressive archaeological sites. The ruins include Byzantine churches, houses and tiled streets.

The area was first settled in the 1st century by the Nabataeans, and by the 4th century Shivta had expanded to become an important Byzantine town on the caravan route between Egypt and Anatolia. In the 7th century the Arabs took the town but refrained from destroying any of the earlier Christian constructions. After a further two centuries, Shivta was abandoned due to the of water in the area. Being so isolated, its ruins escaped being pillaged which is why the buildings remain in such good condition.

The site is open Saturday to Thursday from 8 am to 5 pm, and Friday from 8 am to 4 pm. From October to March, the site closes one hour earlier. Admission is 10NIS (students 6NIS).

Getting There & Away You can take the infrequent bus No 44 from Beersheba to Nizzana, get off at the Horvot Shivta stop and walk the remaining 8.5km. With little traffic about, hitching can be a very time-consuming exercise. From the Nizzana road, the turn-off to Shivta has two lanes and is paved only for the first 2.5km. It then narrows considerably, passing a track to an army installation on the left after 1km.

Hazerim Air Force Museum

Anyone interested in aircraft or military history should make a trip to the Israeli Air Force (IAF) Museum at the Hazerim IAF base near Beersheba. As well as examples of almost every kind of aircraft in the history of the IAF, there are several planes on exhibit that were captured during the various Arab-Israeli conflicts, and various aerial weaponry and audiovisual displays, one screened inside an old airliner. Hazerim is an active training base and some of the aircraft you can examine on the ground may occasionally be seen zooming around above.

Inquire at Beersheba tourist information office about opening times.

Getting There & Away Hazerim (sometimes spelt Khatserim) is just 6km west of Beersheba. From the central bus station take bus No 31; the air base and museum are the last stop.

DIMONA   דימונה
Pop: 32,200   ☎ Area Code: 07

Established in 1955 and named after the biblical town of the tribe of Judah (Joshua 15:22), Dimona is one of the better known development towns. Its harsh desert location was the cause of considerable controversy as many thought that the climate would prove to be too fierce for people to live and work here. However, the initial brave collection of 36 North African families dumped here with tents and supplies has developed into a community now inhabiting a bleak collection of apartment blocks. Dimona's original settlers worked at the nearby chemical plants of the Dead Sea Works, but now the town also has glassmaking, ceramics and textiles as local industries, along with Israel's nuclear reactor. However, closure and cutbacks in the industrial base of the town have meant that up 20% of the potential workforce is unemployed, creating associated social problems within the town's community.

Unless you're involved in espionage, the sole attraction in Dimona is the controversial Black Hebrew community – see Population & People in the Facts about the Country chapter. This Community has grown from an initial 84 settlers who arrived in 1969-70, to a small village of 1300.

The Martyr Spy

In 1986 a technician at Israel's secret nuclear plant at Dimona in the Negev Desert blew the whistle on Israel's hitherto closely guarded nuclear program and earned himself a hefty jail stretch for his trouble. Mordechai Vanunu had been working at Dimona since 1976 and knew full well that Israel was making nuclear weapons. Concerned about Israel's brash invasion of Lebanon in 1982 and at what he perceived to be Israel's growing aggressiveness in foreign policy making, he smuggled out of Dimona a series of photographs and written documentation to show the world.

Acting through a bogus Colombian journalist 'Oscar Guerrero' he contacted London's *Sunday Times* and offered the story. Suspicious at first, the *Sunday Times* nevertheless pursued Vanunu's exposé and published it on 4 October 1986. What followed was a series of bungles that cost Vanunu his freedom and allowed the Israeli security service Mossad to capture him and imprison him with impunity.

A week before the publication of the exposé Vanunu disappeared with a woman he had befriended in London and headed for Rome where she took him to a flat. He was promptly pounced on by goons from Mossad, knocked out with an injection, bundled into a van to La Spezia and carried in the hold of a cargo ship to Israel.

He was subsequently tried in complete secrecy, charged with treason and espionage, and sentenced to 18 years in prison. Since then he has spent most of the time in complete isolation and in conditions that have been described by the European Parliament as cruel, inhuman and degrading. He has become something of a *cause célébre* for the peace movement and calls for his release are frequent.

Most Israelis are indifferent to his fate believing that he got what he deserved for betraying his country. In the meantime he has been nominated five times for the Nobel Peace Prize, none of which seems to have gone any way to mollifying the Israeli government's resolve to keep their martyr spy firmly behind bars.

They live a virtually self-contained lifestyle with their own school, and they make their own clothes (natural fibres only), jewellery and food (their religion prohibits meat, dairy products, fish, eggs, white sugar and white flour). They welcome visitors to discuss how they live, their aims and beliefs. Although the settlement is only 10 minutes walk from Dimona's bus station, the community prefers that you give advance notice of any visit; you can call ☎ 655 5400 or simply ask any of the staff in the Eternity Restaurant in Tel Aviv or Tiberias, or the Hebrews you meet selling jewellery.

Thirteen kilometres east of Dimona is the infamous **film factory** (known also as the 'chocolate' factory), a mysterious establishment reputedly at the centre of Israel's nuclear power industry. It was here that whistle-blower Mordechai Vanunu (see the boxed text 'The Martyr Spy' above) worked before revealing in 1986 to an incredulous public that the chocolate produced here contained more radon than proteins. Needless to say there are no visits allowed and you will almost certainly be pulled aside if you are caught lingering too long around the barbed wire fenced perimeter.

Places to Stay

There is a small **guesthouse** at the Hebrew Israelite Community which charges 80NIS per person, including breakfast and dinner. Alternatively, you can stay at **Drachim Youth Hostel** (☎ 655 6811, HaNassi St) (the bus will pass the hostel as it comes into town). Dorm beds are 44NIS, and for an extra fee guests can use a jacuzzi, sauna and heated pool. The owner is an ex-SPNI guide who can offer valuable advice to anyone touring the region.

Places to Eat
Vegans will love the *restaurant* of the Black Hebrew community where you can feast on imaginative dishes made from tofu. The community also runs a couple of restaurants in Tel Aviv and Tiberias serving similar dishes.

Getting There & Away
With frequent buses from Beersheba (40 minutes) Dimona is not difficult to reach. There are also occasional buses from Arad and Mitzpe Ramon.

AROUND DIMONA
Mamshit
Another Nabataean, Roman and Byzantine city, Mamshit is visually less impressive than Shivta, but it is particularly renowned for the engineering skills that were used in its construction.

The Nabataeans built their city here in the 1st century AD and it was later used by the Romans. About 6km south-east of Dimona, an abandoned British police station marks the site where the Romans built a series of dams to store rainwater to supply the town's inhabitants year-round. Razed by the Muslims in the 7th century, the site is dotted with explanatory signs and an information leaflet is available. The excavations include Nabataean remains, reservoirs, the dams, watchtowers, Roman military and Byzantine cemeteries, jewellery and coins, churches and mosaics.

The site is open April to September, Saturday to Thursday from 8 am to 5 pm and Friday from 8 am to 4 pm; October to March, Saturday to Thursday from 8 am to 4 pm and Friday from 8 am to 3 pm.

Getting There & Away Any of the buses heading to Eilat via Dimona will drop you at the signposted turn-off for the site.

SDE BOKER & EIN AVDAT
שדה בוקר

One of the best known of all kibbutzim, Sde Boker was established in 1952 by pioneers who planned to breed cattle in the desert; its name is Hebrew for Ranchers' Field. Although the initial aims have not been totally fulfilled the kibbutz is often seen to be a success, judged by its appearance as a lush oasis in the middle of the desert. Its main claim to fame, though, is that it was here that David Ben-Gurion chose to live when he retired as prime minister in 1953. Only 14 months later he returned to the political scene and went on to serve a second term as prime minister, returning to kibbutz life in 1963. He died here in 1973.

South of the kibbutz and overlooking the Wilderness of Zin nature preserve is the Sde Boker campus of the Ben-Gurion University, with the graves of Ben-Gurion and his wife, Paula, and the Ein Avdat spring nearby.

Ben-Gurion Home
Only slightly more regal than their fellow kibbutzniks' quarters, the small hut where David and Paula Ben-Gurion lived has been maintained as a museum. Kept essentially as it was when they were here, there is a collection of letters, photographs and books on display in the simply furnished rooms.

It's open Sunday to Thursday from 8.30 am to 3.30 pm, Friday from 8 am to noon and Saturday from 9 am to 1 pm. Admission is free. A cafe nearby serves meals and snacks, including fruit grown on the kibbutz.

Zoo
This small collection of animals is found near the Ben-Gurion home. From the museum and cafe, instead of turning right along the side road back to the main road, turn left past the tennis courts, turn right and the zoo is on your right. Feeding time is around 2 pm.

Ben-Gurion Graves
From the bus stop outside the entrance to the university campus, the graves of David and Paula Ben-Gurion are reached by turning

right then following the arrows to the left on the Hebrew signs. From here you have great views eastwards across the Wilderness of Zin, and southwards over to Ein Avdat.

Ein Avdat

Hidden from the main road and missed by most visitors, this is one of the highlights of the Negev. Ein Avdat is a freak of nature – a pool of icy water in the hot expanse of desert, fed by waters that flow through an intricate network of channels. Dominated by a steep, winding canyon, reaching it involves an easy hike through incredible scenery. The best way to reach Ein Avdat is by the Wilderness of Zin trail beginning near the Ben-Gurion University campus. At the very least, you should pause for a few minutes to admire the view from the observation point, clearly signposted and just off the main highway.

The area on top of the cliffs is where prehistoric tribes made their camps for over 100,000 years. They lived in huts made from branches and their flint tools can be seen protruding from the earth – especially on the northern rim of the canyon. Here and nearby, archaeologists have found evidence of dwellings from the Upper Palaeolithic and Mesolithic periods (35,000 to 15,000 BC).

Wilderness of Zin Nature Trail

Outside the main entrance to the Sde Boker campus of the Ben-Gurion University, an orange 'Ein Avdat' sign points the way. Follow the zigzagging road down into the Wilderness of Zin until it ends at the car park. Follow the path that leads off beyond, and about 40 minutes after leaving the campus you will see the large cave up on your right. Ibex and gazelles can often be seen along here, too. Simply follow the water and after another five minutes you will come to a spring. Despite the warning sign, many enjoy a refreshing dip. If tempted, be aware of the danger caused by the extreme difference in temperature between the hot sun and the cold water.

This is a dead end, so return the way you came and on your left out for steps cut into

the rock leading up the cliff (hidden behind a tree). Climb the steps to the paved ledge where there's a great view.

Carry on walking and after another few minutes you will reach the top of a waterfall, which in winter can be spectacular.

Some more steps have been cut into the rock to lead up the cliff to the right (not always easy to find – for the caves up above). There is a steep climb up steps cut into the cliff to reach the top of the canyon, or you can head back to the car park. The best views of all are from the steps, rather than at the very top, so be sure to take a good around before the end of the climb. An observation point has been provided a short distance away.

The whole hike usually takes two to three hours, allowing plenty of time for relaxing by the springs. The main road is a 10 to 15 minute walk along a side road from the observation point. You come out south of the university campus – unfortunately there is no bus stop here but you can usually hitch to either Mitzpe Ramon or Beersheba quite easily, or at least get a lift to Sde Boker or Avdat where you can catch a bus.

For those who just want to visit the observation point, out for the signpost, north of the Avdat archaeological site, south of Sde Boker (no bus stop, remember).

Entrance to Ein Avdat is free if you are on foot but there's a charge for drivers. The site is open Saturday to Thursday from 8 am to 5 pm, and Friday from 8 am to 4 pm, and closes an hour earlier in winter.

Sde Boker Field Study Centre

This field study centre (☎ 07-635 2902, fax 653 2721) on the campus of the Ben-Gurion University, is mainly responsible for nature conservation in the area. The staff are extremely knowledgeable and enthusiastic and, once you have shown an interest, will tell you all about the local wildlife and where and when to see it. Sights include griffin vultures having their breakfast of raw meat provided by the field school, ibex and other animals coming to drink at a spring, and sooty falcons nesting in the cliff side.

You should also inquire here about the various hikes in the desert where you can see a lot of this natural activity as well as some beautiful scenery.

Places to Stay
Although often filled by groups, the *hostel* at the Sde Boker Field Study Centre (see the previous page for details) is sometimes available for travellers – it's worth asking about if you want to spend some time in the area. Prices are around US$40 per person.

Alternative accommodation exists at *Beit Hamburg Guesthouse* (☎ 07-653 2902, fax 656 57212) or *Sde Boker Inn* (☎ 07-560 379), next to the Ben-Gurion home. None of these options, it should be warned, is cheap.

Getting There & Away
Bus No 60 running between Beersheba and Mitzpe Ramon is about the only way to get here by public transport. The bus makes three separate stops for Sde Boker: heading south from Beersheba it first stops beside the turn-off to the main entrance of the kibbutz, then at the turn-off for the Ben-Gurion Home and, finally, at the turn-off for the university campus, the Ben-Gurion graves and Ein Avdat. Warn the driver in advance where you want to get off.

AVDAT   עבדת
Not to be confused with Ein Avdat, this is a well-preserved Nabataean, Roman and Byzantine city perched on a hill that dominates the desert skyline. The place is now preserved as a national park, and its rich combination of impressive ruins and incredible vistas makes the steep climb well worth the effort. Parts of the film *Jesus Christ Superstar* were shot here.

Built by the Nabataeans in the 2nd century BC as a caravan stop on the road from Petra and Eilat to the Mediterranean coast, Avdat was taken by the Romans in 106 AD. Prosperous throughout the Byzantine period, the city was abandoned in 634 when it fell to the Muslims. The ruins include Nabataean burial caves, a pottery workshop and

a road, a Roman camp, and a Byzantine bath-house, wine press, house, church, monastery and castle.

The site (☎ 07-655 0954) is open Saturday to Thursday from 8 am to 5 pm and Friday from 8 am to 4 pm, closing an hour earlier in winter. Admission is 17NIS (students 10NIS).

Getting There & Away
On the Beersheba-Mitzpe Ramon road, Avdat lies 10km south of the Ben-Gurion home and 23km north of Mitzpe Ramon. The No 60 bus passes by in each direction about every hour.

MITZPE RAMON   מצפה רמון
Pop: 4,800   ☎ Area Code: 07
The word *mitzpe* is Hebrew for lookout and this small town, which began in 1956 as a camp for a 17 member road-building cooperative, is named after the nearby cliff that looks over the massive crater, the Maktesh Ramon.

Intended to be part of the desert development program, the town failed to take off as planned due to the lack of employment opportunities, and scores of apartments lie empty despite the many attempts at incentive schemes. In 1986 the government declared Mitzpe Ramon a tax-free zone in a vain bid to attract new businesses and residents. To hasten the process of revitalisation, the government resettled large numbers of Soviet immigrants in the town but that has only served to exacerbate the problems of unemployment. Other plans involve promoting the area's unique geological, ecological and archaeological sites and its clear, dry air as tourist attractions.

The town of Mitzpe Ramon is rendered insignificant by the impact of the Maktesh Ramon, the centre of attention for most visitors. Most people content themselves with just a couple of hours gazing across the canyon before moving on but there is also plenty of good hiking to be done around here. Mitzpe Ramon is also the best place to base yourself for visits to nearby Avdat, Ein Avdat and Sde Boker.

Orientation & Information

The town is centred on Ben-Gurion Blvd, a wide dual carriageway off the Beersheba-Eilat road. On Ben-Gurion Blvd is a small commercial concourse with a few shops, a cafe, a bank (open Sunday, Tuesday and Thursday from 8.30 am to noon and 4 to 6 pm, Monday and Wednesday and Friday from 8.30 am to 12.30 pm only) and cultural centre. The new youth hostel and the visitors centre are south of the commercial block, overlooking the Maktesh Ramon. All these places are within easy walking distance of each other.

The SPNI has the Har HaNegev Field Study Centre (☎ 658 8615, fax 658 8385) on the edge of the crater which is worth visiting for anybody planning any serious hiking. It's open Sunday to Thursday from 8 am to 5 pm and Friday from 8 am to 1 pm, closed Saturday. The study centre is about a 2km walk from the southern end of Ben-Gurion Blvd.

Visitors Centre & Bio-Ramon

Perched on the edge of the Maktesh Ramon, this attractive structure houses a museum which aims to explain everything you may want to know about the massive and intriguing crater. It does the job very well with a slide show and an exhibition of charts, illustrations, photographs, models and rock samples. The roof of the building serves as an excellent viewing platform.

Admission is 15NIS, and it's a worthwhile investment. The centre (☎ 658 8691) is open Saturday to Thursday from 9 am to 5 pm, Friday from 9 am to 4 pm.

The Bio-Ramon complex (☎ 658 8755) just down from the visitors centre has a collection of desert creatures, many that make you wonder just how secure the glass cases are. It's open Sunday to Thursday from 8 am to 3 pm, Friday from 8 am to 1 pm and Saturday from 9 am to 4 pm. Admission costs a few shekels; and a combined visitors centre/Bio-Ramon ticket costs 17NIS.

About 300m south of the visitors centre along the crater promenade is a breathtaking **lookout** which juts out over the edge of the

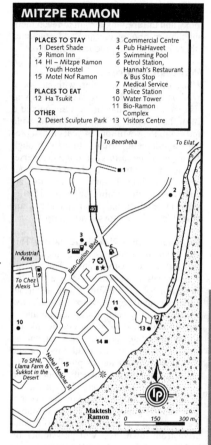

MITZPE RAMON

PLACES TO STAY
1 Desert Shade
9 Rimon Inn
14 HI – Mitzpe Ramon Youth Hostel
15 Motel Nof Ramon

PLACES TO EAT
12 Ha Tsukit

OTHER
2 Desert Sculpture Park

3 Commercial Centre
4 Pub HaHaveet
5 Swimming Pool
6 Petrol Station, Hannah's Restaurant & Bus Stop
7 Medical Service
8 Police Station
10 Water Tower
11 Bio-Ramon Complex
13 Visitors Centre

To Beersheba   To Eilat

Industrial Area

To Chez Alexis

To SPNI, Llama Farm & Sukkot in the Desert

Maktesh Ramon   0   150   300 m

THE NEGEV

crater. Don't look down from the platform if you're feint-hearted as there's nothing between your feet and the bottom of the crater. The views are indescribable, but better enjoyed early in the morning or late in the afternoon when the angled light casts fantastic shapes and shadows across the crater floor.

Desert Sculpture Park

North of the visitors centre is a rather stark and forlorn collection of stone sculptures assembled on the lip of the crater by Israeli artist Ezra Orion. You have to walk over rocky and unforgiving terrain to reach them but they're photogenic and add colour to otherwise hard to reproduce crater shots.

Maktesh Ramon

While difficult to describe without going overboard, the *maktesh* (crater) will remind visitors a little of the Grand Canyon and a lot of the moon. It is 300m deep, 8km wide and 40km long. Millions of years old, it presents a unique opportunity to walk through the stages of the earth's evolution in reverse.

A few nature trails have been marked out which lead through some of the most attractive and interesting sections. Hiking maps in English and other languages are available at the visitors centre shop.

Ein Sharonim – Nahal Gewanim This trail is recommended as one of the best by the staff at the visitors centre. The various rock formations seen along the way and the variety of colours are simply awe-inspiring. Taking about 4½ to 5½ hours, the walk covers occasionally steep rocky terrain and is usually walked in very hot conditions. Do not overestimate your stamina – take along plenty of water, wear a head covering and start as early in the day as possible.

To reach the trail, take the southbound bus from the petrol station in Mitzpe Ramon (to Eilat) and get off when you see the second orange signpost on the left-hand side of the road in the crater – about a 10 minute drive from town. You will pass mines on both sides of the road just before you get to the two signs. There is no bus stop, so tell the driver when you want to get off.

Follow the jeep track away from the road for about 30 minutes, then take the right fork after the electricity pylon on the left.

At the top of the steepish slope follow the green-on-white trail markers to your left. This narrow path takes you along the ridge, giving you excellent views across the crater to your left. There is a pleasant shaded spot for that necessary drink and rest after about 10 minutes – climb up to your right here. It should have taken you about an hour to reach this spot from the road. After a further five minutes, the path splits in two, but both the high and the low paths go the same way. Scramble up the rock face briefly to the top of the ridge for a commanding view in all directions. Here you can see all at once the variety of contrasting rock formations and colours with the maze of wadis and canyons winding through them. If you took the high path, climb down after about 20 minutes to join the low path to save an even steeper descent later. It's possible to take either of the three paths here as they all join up eventually to lead down to a wadi.

Follow the wadi to the right and around to the left. After 25 minutes it narrows considerably with large and small caves on both sides of the canyon. Another 15 minutes and you come to a Hebrew signpost. Follow the track just past it to the left, away from the wadi. The track forks after about five minutes; take the left track to the sign with the coloured trail markers. Go straight ahead following the blue-on-white trail markers.

After 20 minutes you should reach another signpost. Again, go straight and then follow the path to the left. Follow the wadi for 20 minutes and you will come to a couple of water holes. Follow the track to the left 10 minutes from here – there is a blue-on-white sign. After five minutes you will come to a jeep track going left to right with a signpost. Go to the left and after 25 minutes you will reach the electricity pylon that you passed at the start of the walk. Go to the right here and the road is 30 minutes away.

Scenic Pass This is part of the Trail of Israel, a series of hikes designed to run the length of the country. It is a leisurely and very scenic two hour hike that takes you down into the Maktesh Ramon to the Carpenter's Workshop and on to the main road. From the youth hostel, follow the path along the edge of the crater until you see the sign pointing down. Follow the green trail markings and you'll eventually come to the Carpenter's Workshop. Continue to reach the main road, where you can either hitch back to town, or flag down one of the infrequent buses.

Carpenter's Workshop Shortly after the road from Mitzpe Ramon zigzags down into the crater, an orange signpost points to this site of geological interest, 500m to the right.

This unique rock formation has been shaped by pressure and is said to resemble wood. The rock eventually breaks up into pieces, but among the rubble you can see unbroken parts.

Follow the jeep track from the road that ends with a car park. From here take the path up the hill to the left (past the refuse bins). This leads you around the hill to a wooden observation platform which gives you a close-up at the rocks in question. You can either take the Eilat bus or hitch from Mitzpe Ramon, or stop here on your way down on the Scenic Pass hike.

Other Craters The other two craters in the Negev are south of Dimona and are not accessible by public transport. **Maktesh Ha-Qatan** is the smallest. Roughly circular in shape, it looks more like it was caused by a large meteor than erosion. **Maktesh Ha-Gadol** is the easier of the two to reach. Both are worth a visit if you can get to them.

Alpaca & Llama Farm

These cameloids were flown here from Chile by an Israeli couple Ilan and Na'ama Dvir. Inspired by their love for South American wildlife and culture and for Israel, they worked hard to set up their farm. Starting with 188 creatures, they now have about 500. The animals are being raised for their wool, which is for sale. If your timing is right, you can see such activities as shearing, washing, spinning, weaving and, for the children, there is a llama ride. Llama tours in the desert are also planned. These charming, woolly quadrupeds wander around freely and will no doubt approach you fearlessly looking for handouts to nibble on.

Visitors are welcome. The farm (☎ 658 8047) is open Saturday to Thursday from 8.30 am to 6.30 pm (in winter from 8.30 am to 4 pm), and on Friday from 8.30 am to 4 pm. Admission is 14NIS. There is a small cafe selling snacks also.

To get here follow the signs from the southern end of Ben-Gurion Blvd; it's about a 3km walk.

Places to Stay

The modern *HI – Mitzpe Ramon Youth Hostel* (☎ 658 8443, fax 658 8074) is a great place to stay and the manager is pleasant. Beautifully located near the edge of the Maktesh Ramon, it's also just a short walk from the visitors centre. Dorm beds cost US$18 and singles/doubles are US$35/49, all with breakfast. There are no kitchen facilities for guests. Reception is open only from 3 pm onwards. *SPNI Field Study Centre* (see Orientation & Information earlier in this section) also has dorm accommodation for US$40 per person.

Chez Alexis (☎ 658 8258, 7 Ein Saharonim St) is an excellent choice for budget travellers. It's a villa that has been converted into a guesthouse and is on the western side of town. Beds are around US$12 per person and double rooms are US$30. You would be well-advised to phone ahead and make a reservation if you are heading this way.

Desert Shade (☎ 658 6229, fax 658 6208) (see Organised Tours earlier in this chapter) can put up guests in long wooden huts which are divided into two person cubicles. Showers and toilets are communal. The location is great, right on the edge of the Maktesh, and the food, served in a large Bedouin-style tent, is excellent. Call for prices. Desert Shade is located at the end of a dirt road east of the main road, a few hundred metres north of the petrol station.

The town also has two hotels, *Motel Nof Ramon* (☎ 658 8255, 7 Nahal Meishar St), which is just off the southern end of Ben-Gurion Blvd, opposite the school, with singles/doubles for US$20/35 (breakfast not included), and the swish new *Rimon Inn* (☎ 658 8822, fax 658 8151, 1 Ein Akev St) just up the hill from Ben-Gurion Blvd, which has air-con singles from US$92 to US$163 and doubles from US$115 to US$186 depending on what day of the week you stay. It's worth noting that the Rimon Inn has a swimming pool and sauna.

THE NEGEV

For something completely different, consider a stay at the unique and wonderful *Succah in the Desert* (☎ 658 6280, fax 658 6464), PO Box 272, 80600 Mitzpe Ramon. Located some 7km west of the town, this is a collection of seven *sukkot* (small dwellings) built of stones and palm leaves on the rocky slopes of a wadi amid some typically beautiful desert scenery. There is one larger sukkot that houses a kitchen, lounge and dining area, while the others provide accommodation that's tastefully furnished with rugs and other fabrics. Bathroom facilities are limited to using the desert that surrounds you; each sukkot is supplied with a trowel, an earthenware water jar, bedding, candles and solar-powered lighting. There is one shower, heated by solar energy. A night will cost you US$47 (US$58 on Friday nights) including two meals: breakfast and a hot vegetarian meal.

You can walk the 7km from Mitzpe Ramon, but if you call ahead, you will be met at the bus stop and driven here by 4WD. Reservations are a good idea.

Places to Eat

There is a *supermarket* in the commercial centre that's open Sunday to Thursday from 9 am to 1 pm and 4 to 7 pm, and Friday from 8.30 am to 1 pm. A few doors down is *Pub HaHaveet* which, open daily to around midnight, is the town's sole night spot. During the day it serves food as well as beer. There are two adjacent *cafes* serving fast food, kebabs and ice cream.

Next to the petrol station, *Hannah's Restaurant* serves surprisingly decent food and snacks. All Eilat-Beersheba buses take a 15 minute halt here and the custom they bring in seems to be the only thing that keeps the place going.

The restaurant next to the visitors centre, the self-service *HaTsukit* (meaning The Cliff – for obvious reasons), commands a wonderful view over the crater and the food isn't bad value either – around 28 to 32NIS a dish. It's open daily from 8 am to 5 pm. There's also a good *restaurant* at the Rimon Inn.

Getting There & Away

Mitzpe Ramon lies 23km south of Avdat and 136km north of Eilat, via the Gerofit junction. Bus No 392 stops here en route between Beersheba and Eilat (33NIS), via Dimona, but there are only about five buses a day, three of them before noon – check at the youth hostel or visitors centre for the current timetables. Catch bus No 932, in both directions, at the petrol station.

Bus No 60 shuttles between Beersheba (21NIS) and Mitzpe Ramon, via Sde Boker and Ein Avdat, with departures about every hour between 6 am and 9.30 pm. Again check the youth hostel and visitors centre for timetables. Catch it from Ben-Gurion Blvd, near the commercial centre.

EILAT אילת
Pop: 34,700 ☎ Area Code: 07

Eilat exists almost as an 'offshore', sybaritic mini city-state in which the major concerns are a good spot on the beach and an even tan.

From its beginnings as a small desert outpost wedged between Egypt and Jordan to prevent them snapping shut Israel's access to the Red Sea, Eilat has grown into a wannabe beachfront Las Vegas. Glitzy ziggurat-hotels surround a turquoise blue artificial lagoon, from which Walt Disney-style glass-bottomed boats set out on cruises around the bay. Evening entertainment is traditional Israeli folk dancing but it's choreographed Hollywood style.

However, for the independent traveller, it's a little being the wrong side of the movie set with all the scaffolding and unpainted plywood on view. Seen from anywhere but the lagoon-side hotels, the town is a mass of too hastily erected architecture that blights the beautiful natural surroundings. Neither is the town's sun, sand and sea image all it's cracked up to be; while there's plenty of the first named, decent beaches are limited to a cluttered strip in the hotel area and views across the bay tended to be blotted by great tankers docking at the port.

Despite Eilat's supposed free trade zone status, the only evidence of this the average visitor will encounter is the 60 agorot cut in the price of the *Jerusalem Post* and perhaps a few shekels off the purchase of CDs. In fact, the boom town image has attracted a large number of entrepreneurs and all too often you'll find yourself paying out and feeling hard done by. However, Eilat remains a popular stopover largely due to its proximity to border crossing points with Egypt and Jordan. Many travellers also find it a good place to hang around and try to find work, although there have been many stories about Eilat's unscrupulous employers not paying up. Hostel accommodation is also plentiful and relatively cheap, and there are one or two decent mid-priced options too.

Orientation

Eilat has three parts; the town centre, the hotel area and a trailing 5km coastal strip running down to the border with Egypt at Taba. Most readers of this book are going to be based in the town centre, the backbone of which is sloping HaTemarim Blvd. The bus station is off HaTemarim Blvd, with the main hostel area just to the north across Hativat HaNegev Ave. Downhill from the bus station is the main shopping area, with the modern Shalom and Red Canyon malls on one side of HaTemarim and the older commercial centre across the street.

At the base of the hill, HaTemarim ends in a T-junction with Ha'Arava Rd, which runs parallel to the runway of Eilat's town centre airport. Follow this road south and at the junction with Yotam Rd is the New Tourist Centre, a concrete collection of shops, bars and restaurants. Ha'Arava then becomes Mizrayim Rd as it continues along the shoreline and making a beeline for the border.

The airport runway serves as the no-man's land between the town centre and the hotel area. The hotels are dotted around a purpose-built lagoon and marina. Nearby are the most accessible beaches, known collectively as North Beach.

Information

Tourist Office Eilat's new tourist information centre (☎ 637 2111) is on the corner of

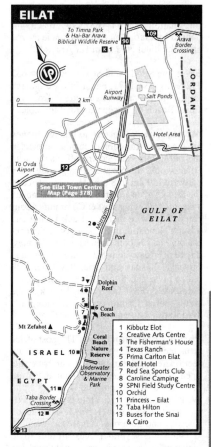

EILAT

To Timna Park
& Hai-Bar Arava
Biblical Wildlife Reserve
⊠ 1

To Timna Park 109
Arava Border Crossing

Airport Runway

Salt Ponds

JORDAN

Hotel Area

To Ovda Airport 12

See Eilat Town Centre Map (Page 378)

GULF OF EILAT

2 ● Mizrayim Road

Port

3 ▼ Dolphin Reef
4 ●

5 ●
6 Coral Beach
7 ●
8 ● ■

Mt Zefahot ▲ 9 ●

Coral Beach

ISRAEL 10 ■ Coral Nature Reserve

Underwater Observatory & Marine Park

EGYPT

11 ■

Taba Border Crossing

12 ■

13

1	Kibbutz Elot
2	Creative Arts Centre
3	The Fisherman's House
4	Texas Ranch
5	Prima Carlton Eilat
6	Reef Hotel
7	Red Sea Sports Club
8	Caroline Camping
9	SPNI Field Study Centre
10	Orchid
11	Princess – Eilat
12	Taba Hilton
13	Buses for the Sinai & Cairo

THE NEGEV

Yotam and Ha'Arava Rds, beside Burger King. Not only are there more maps and brochures here than you can fill a carrier bag with, the staff actually don't seem to mind answering inquiries about bus routes and opening times and places to go – all of the kind of queries that seem to irritate the hell out of the staff in Israel's other tourist information offices. They also have an excellent town plan. It's open Sunday to Thursday from 8 am to 9 pm, Friday from 8 am to 2 pm and Saturday from 10 am to 2 pm.

There's also a 24 hour Reservation and Information Centre (☎ 637 4741, 637 5944) housed in a kiosk on the promenade as you enter the hotel area from Ha'Arava Rd.

SPNI The SPNI Field Study Centre (☎ 637 1127, fax 637 1771, email info@eilat.spni .org.il) is just across the street from the Coral Beach on the coastal road to Taba.

Money The best places to change money are the no-commission exchange bureaus in the old commercial centre off HaTemarim Blvd which, the Sinai Exchange, are open daily from 9 am to 8 pm. The post office in the Red Canyon Centre also changes money – see the following Post & Communications entry. Otherwise there's a Bank Leumi and a Bank Hapoalim in the vicinity of the central bus station, both open Monday, Wednesday and Friday from 8.30 am to noon, and Sunday, Tuesday and Thursday from 8.30 am to noon and 5 to 6.30 pm; both closed Saturday. A First International Bank in the New Tourist Centre is open Monday and Wednesday afternoons from 4 to 7 pm.

Post & Communications The post office is in the Red Canyon Centre, in the back section reached through the car park; it's open Sunday, Monday and Thursday from 7.45 am to 12.30 pm and 4 to 6.30 pm, Wednesday from 7.45 am to 2 pm, and Friday from 7.45 am to 1 pm. It's closed on Tuesday and Saturday.

There are several places around town which offer cheaper international telephone rates than the post office, such as Starcom at the rear of the New Tourist Centre and Express International on the 1st floor of the Shalom Centre.

You can check your email at the only Internet centre in town at BJ's Books (see the following Bookshops entry for details). There are three terminals, a printer and scanner, and access time costs 7NIS for 15 minutes, 25NIS for an hour, or 100NIS will buy you 4½ hours of online time – good if you are in Eilat for a few days and are able to spread out your access times.

Bookshops Steimatzky has branches in the bus station and on the ground floor of the Shalom Centre. They are open Sunday to Thursday from 9 am to 7 pm, Friday from 9 am to 2 pm and are closed on Saturday.

In the New Tourist Centre, next to the Country Chicken restaurant, is BJ's Books (☎ 634 0905, email bjsbooks@eilatcity.co .il). Here you can buy, sell and swap used books. Recycle your Lonely Planet books here and pick up other titles for your next destination. There are also some computer terminals for email and Websurfing (see Post & Communications for costs).

Laundry The Gill laundromat, on the corner of Elot Ave and HaTemarim Blvd, is open Sunday to Thursday from 8 am to 1 pm and 4 to 7 pm, and Friday from 8 am to 1 pm. It's closed on Saturday.

Emergency The police station (☎ 636 2444, or in an emergency call ☎ 100) is on Avdat St, at the eastern end of Hativat Ha-Negev St. The police are very used to travellers reporting stolen bags and packs.

For medical aid call the Magen David Adom (☎ 637 2333) or in emergencies call ☎ 101.

Dolphin Reef
The management of this complex prefer not to have it labelled as a dolphinarium. An apparently sincere exercise in ecotourism, they purchased dolphins from Russian and Japanese fishing interests and brought them to the Red Sea with the aim of eventually releasing the mammals into the open water.

There are training demonstrations when visitors can see the dolphins. Admission costs 24NIS, which includes the use of the private beach facilities, documentary films and viewing the dolphin training sessions (10 am, noon and 2 and 4 pm). It's also possible to 'meet' the dolphins. For about 60NIS you can join the trainers to help feed the dolphins, for 124NIS you can swim with the dolphins, or if you're a certified diver you can dive with them for 176NIS. Snorkelling and scuba gear is available for hire. However, you may need to book long before your proposed visit, as it's a very popular activity.

To the south of the port, Dolphin Reef (☎ 637 5935, fax 637 3824, reef@netvision .net.il) is open daily from 9 am to 5 pm. Its bar stays open until the early morning. Visit its Web site (www.dolphin.co.il) too if you want a sneak preview.

Coral Beach Nature Reserve

The beach here is unpleasant, mostly stony and often overcrowded. Note also the constant procession of wet-suited groups flapping down to the water's edge – a clue to the reserve's main attraction and one of the few reasons to visit Eilat. It may be a bit tame compared to Sinai and the waters suffer from far too much two-legged traffic but if you've never snorkelled among coral before, it's definitely worth getting your hair wet for. There are a number of special trails to follow, marked out by buoys. The beach has showers and lockers (5NIS).

The reserve (☎ 637 6829) stretches from the Underwater Observatory to the Reef Hotel, and the entrance is opposite the SPNI Field Study Centre. It's open daily from 9 am to 5 pm; admission is 15NIS (children 8NIS). Snorkelling equipment is available for hire; masks for 7NIS, fins 8NIS and snorkels 6NIS, or 21NIS for a full set. All equipment hire requires a 70NIS refundable deposit.

Underwater Observatory & Marine Park

South of Coral Beach Nature Reserve is a rather pricey Disney underwater experience, consisting of the Marine Park and three additional attractions. Whether you visit all or some of them depends on the thickness of your wallet, whether you are claustrophobic, or whether you like looking at fish and coral from an underwater observatory.

Marine Park The 63NIS access fee will give you access to the general area, with souvenir shops, a restaurant and a marine museum. This is probably OK for parents who want to relax while their kids take in the fun bits.

Underwater Observatory For 76NIS you can visit the Marine Park and the Underwater Observatory with its 21 reinforced windows through which you can view the usually rich Red Sea marine life. The observatory is a glass-walled chamber 4.25m below the water's surface. In case the fish outside fail to put in an appearance there are plenty of captive specimens in the accompanying aquarium.

Oceanarium For 76NIS you can visit the Marine Park and the Oceanarium – a 150 seat simulator motion theatre and futuristic viewing hall. Billed as the only one of its kind in Israel (though the Time Elevator in Jerusalem gives participants a similar thrill), it most certainly is a unique experience and probably should not be missed if you want to experience a virtual ride under the sea.

Yellow Submarine For 255NIS you can visit the Marine Park and ride in the Yellow Submarine, which takes participants on a 60m underwater diving adventure. This purpose-built viewing craft takes 47 passengers on a 50 minute cruise across the seabed and along a sheer-sided coral cliff wall. If you have never been on a submarine before (and who has?) this is your chance.

If you are prepared to fork out just another 13NIS you can pay 268NIS per person and see the whole lot. For further information call (☎ 636 4200), or take a peak at its attractions at its Web site www.coralworld .com.

Texas Ranch

Across the street from the nature reserve, Texas Ranch (☎ 637 6663) is an unimpressive mock Wild West town inspired by the resemblance of the local terrain to that of American cowboy country. It was originally built as a movie set, and features a saloon bar and coffee house. Admission to the ranch is 15NIS (children 10NIS), which includes a beer or soft drink at the saloon. The complex also offers horse riding and half-day camel treks.

Airodium

Parcelled up in a balloon suit, thrill addicts are buffeted around in a vertical wind tunnel. Notices warn 'not for the weak-hearted' – in reference possibly to the charge of 120NIS for 10 minutes. Wind is up from 10 am to 6 pm, and the site is in the north-eastern corner of the hotel area. Call ☎ 633 2386 for full details.

Glass-Bottomed Boats

The *Stingray- Jules Verne Explorer* (☎ 637 7702, fax 633 4924) sets off from the North Beach marina four times a day for a two hour cruise in the tight little area hemmed in by the Egyptian and Jordanian borders. The underwater scenery is fairly spectacular and there's an accompanying English-language commentary. Cost per person is 55NIS (children 40NIS).

The boat is less snazzy but Israel Yam (reservations ☎ 637 5528) runs an almost identical operation from the jetty at the marina; cost per person is 35NIS.

International Birdwatching Centre

As the only land bridge between Africa, Europe and Asia, Eilat is the principle migration route for millions of birds. In particular, migrating birds of prey are an impressive attraction and over a million raptors of about 30 different species can be seen in season. In addition, some 400 species of songbirds, seabirds and waterfowl have been recorded passing through. The peak migration periods are in spring and autumn.

The International Birdwatching Centre (☎ 633 5339, fax 633 5319), PO Box 774, 88106 Eilat, coordinates all activities of research, surveys, tours and educational work in the area with the ultimate aim of promoting interest in the conservation of birds. The centre offers visitors a variety of activities, regardless of their depth of knowledge. Observation points and hiking trails have been established, mainly in the vicinity of the salt ponds to the east of town, and the centre can arrange half or full-day 4WD tours with a visit to a ringing station.

Other facilities include rental of field glasses, literature and background material, participation in migration surveys, lectures and nature films. The centre is just off HaTemarim Rd across from the central bus station, and is open Sunday to Thursday from 9 am to 1 pm and 5 to 7 pm, and Friday from 9 am to 1 pm only.

Beaches

Eilat's beaches are less than impressive. The most convenient is the North Beach strip fringing the hotel area, but the sands are incredibly crowded and cluttered with kiosks, stalls and other bits of beach paraphernalia. The best chance of avoiding the rush-hour commuter feeling is to head east towards the Jordanian border.

Although there is 5km of coastline stretching down to the Egyptian border, little of it is bikini territory. North of the Underwater Observatory, the shoreline looks like a building site of stones and gravel and muddy furrows. Further south, between the observatory and Coral Beach, part of the shoreline is cordoned off and posted with unexploded mine notices. The only other decent option seems to be HaDekel Beach, north of the port. Our advice would be to do as the Israelis do and head for Taba and Sinai.

In mitigation, however, the Eilat authorities are making every effort to tidy up the seafront and are busily constructing a pleasant promenade along the coastline down to the Taba border crossing. So if the beaches aren't all that crash hot you will still be able to enjoy a pleasant and eventually shaded walk along the Red Sea shoreline.

Scuba Diving

Despite the enthusiastic PR, Eilat's waters do not offer world-class diving – serious divers should head to the nearby Sinai Desert. However, most visitors find Eilat a great place to snorkel and to be introduced to the joys of black rubber suits and flippered feet.

The best place to check out the options is around Coral Beach where you'll find the

Red Sea Sports Club (☎ 637 6569, fax 637 0655, email manta1@netvision.net.il) and Aqua Sport (☎ 633 4404, fax 633 3771, email aquaspor@isdnet.net.il) on the other side of the street. Of the two companies, Aqua Sport is generally a little cheaper. Both charge about US$42 for an introductory dive. Designed for nondivers, this includes a training session and dive with an instructor and all equipment. A diving course leading to PADI or NAUI openwater certification lasts six days and costs around US$275 in a group class. See both company's Web sites: www.aquasport.com and www.redseasports.co.il.

Certified divers can consider Red Sea Sports Club's six day Manta Ray live-aboard from US$700 to US$770, including full-board and unlimited diving. Aqua Sport offers an Exclusive One Day Sinai Diving Cruise, diving an area that has not been touched by divers for the last 15 years for US$79, which includes lunch and two dives. There are also Diving Camping Safaris along the Sinai coast at US$255 for three days, or US$410 for five days. Prices include a guide, sleeping bag and mattress, transportation, full-board, tanks, weights and air refills.

Both operators have accommodation for divers who use their services, although we've received some serious security related complaints against the Red Sea Sports Club Hotel (☎ 637 3146, fax 637 4083), located across the road from Coral Beach. A little further north, Aqua Club Hostel is US$15 a night in a four bed dorm.

Snorkelling

Snuba (☎ 637 2722) is a guided underwater adventure for beginners who have no proficiency with tanks but would to see some of the underwater sights. Guides take snuba divers to the Caves reef, considered one of the best coral reefs in Eilat. Snuba is at South Beach and snorkel rental is around 30NIS per day.

Windsurfing & Water Sports

Both Aqua Sport at Coral Beach and the North Beach branch of Red Sea Sports Club rent windsurfers; expect to pay about 30 to 40NIS per hour. Red Sea also does water skiing (about 60NIS) and parasailing (about 100NIS), while Aqua Sport has underwater scooters for hire.

Desert Hikes

Although overshadowed by the activities on the beach and under water, there are some marvellous hiking possibilities in the Eilat region. The colourful mountains and valleys just outside the town have been enthusiastically explored by SPNI personnel, and marked nature trails enable visitors to see the most interesting of the beauty spots.

A company called Nature's Way (☎ 637 0057) leads ecology-minded half-day hikes into the Eilat Mountains and also takes parties to the National Reserve Authority's Predator Centre to witness feeding time. Other treks include Sunset on Mt Tsfahot, Red Canyon to Amram Pillars and Gishron Canyon. Drop by for details of the current program. It's based in the middle of town just off HaTemarim Blvd, next to the Birdwatching Centre.

When you go hiking in the desert be sure to abide by the safety guidelines: follow a marked path, take sufficient water, cover your head, beware of flash floods and avoid the Israel-Egypt border area and army installations – do not take photographs or hike at night near here.

Mt Zefahot Circular Trail This almost circular hike is within reach of nondrivers and is best enjoyed towards the end of the day. It involves about three hours of easy walking to give you a superb view of the Gulf of Aqaba and the four countries whose borders meet here: Israel, Egypt, Jordan and Saudi Arabia.

Take bus No 15 and get off by the Texas Ranch. Follow the sign pointing to Wadi Shlomo and walk upstream along the dirt road for about 2km, ignoring the numerous side paths, until you see the concrete buildings on your left. Now vacant, they were used to quarantine animals. Go left along Wadi Zefahot and follow the green trail

THE NEGEV

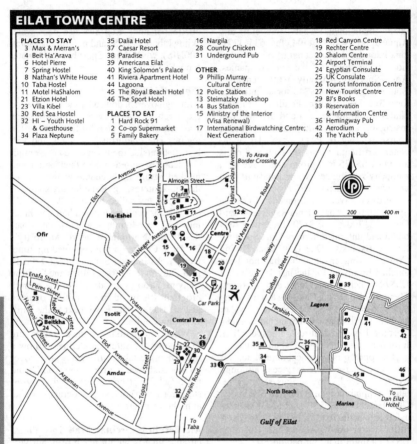

EILAT TOWN CENTRE

PLACES TO STAY
3   Max & Merran's
4   Beit Ha'Arava
6   Hotel Pierre
7   Spring Hostel
8   Nathan's White House
10 Taba Hostel
11 Motel HaShalom
21 Etzion Hotel
23 Villa Kibel
30 Red Sea Hostel
32 HI – Youth Hostel
    & Guesthouse
34 Plaza Neptune

35 Dalia Hotel
37 Caesar Resort
38 Paradise
39 Americana Eilat
40 King Solomon's Palace
41 Riviera Apartment Hotel
44 Lagoona
45 The Royal Beach Hotel
46 The Sport Hotel

PLACES TO EAT
1   Hard Rock 91
2   Co-op Supermarket
5   Family Bakery

16 Nargila
28 Country Chicken
31 Underground Pub

OTHER
9   Phillip Murray
    Cultural Centre
12 Police Station
13 Steimatzky Bookshop
14 Bus Station
15 Ministry of the Interior
    (Visa Renewal)
17 International Birdwatching Centre;
    Next Generation

18 Red Canyon Centre
19 Rechter Centre
20 Shalom Centre
22 Airport Terminal
24 Egyptian Consulate
25 UK Consulate
26 Tourist Information Centre
27 New Tourist Centre
29 BJ's Books
33 Reservation
    & Information Centre
36 Hemingway Pub
42 Aerodium
43 The Yacht Pub

markers. You pass by a dry waterfall on your right, and after 300m the path forks with a black marked trail veering off to the right. Keep going straight ahead on the green marked trail for another 200m. It then turns to the left and starts to climb quite steeply. Head up this path and keep climbing for about 15 minutes to reach the summit at about 278m.

From this vantage point, Sinai is visible to the south – for the Crusader castle on Coral Island – while across the gulf are the Jordanian port city of Aqaba and the Saudi border. To the north-east, the greenery of Kibbutz Elot and the reefs off Coral Beach can also be seen. Although the sunset can be beautiful from here, hikers are advised not to return after dark as the trail can be difficult to follow. The path continues down to bring you to the field school on the main road.

Places to Stay

Although Eilat is often referred to as a winter resort, its season actually lasts year-round. From November to March, the coolest months with an average daytime temperature of 24°C, the town is at its busiest and reaches an unbelievable peak of overcrowding at Passover. From April to October, with the average temperature zooming up to 36°C, the town is filled mainly with Israelis, particularly at Sukkot when once again it's sardine city. Stay away from Eilat during these two Jewish holidays. Not only is it hard to find a place to stay, but when you do, you will usually find that the price has doubled or trebled. Other Jewish holidays can present the same problems.

Places to Stay – Budget

Camping Camping is illegal on most of Eilat's beaches and it's a law that is enforced. Exceptions are the areas towards the Jordanian border and north of the port. Remember that there is a high theft rate on Eilat's beaches and if you sleep near the beach-front hotels you will also share your sleeping space with the rats who are attracted by the refuse areas.

Those who wish to pay for a rodent-free, amenity-served campsite should head for the Coral Beach area. *SPNI Field Study Centre* (☎ 637 1127, fax 637 1771, email info@eilat.spni.org.il) has a shaded campsite that is open year-round. Cost is 20NIS per person. *Caroline Camping* (☎ 637 5063) does not cater to campers as such but offers two-person bungalows for 100NIS. It has clean bathrooms and showers, and a basic cafeteria. Just a couple of hundred metres south, *Mt Zefahot Camping* (☎ 637 4411, fax 637 5206), next to the SPNI Field Study Centre, charges 20NIS for a pitching site, which gets you access to hot showers, toilets and an electricity supply if wanted.

All three of these sites might appeal to those who plan to spend a lot of time snorkelling or diving around Coral Beach. Local bus No 15 stops nearby.

Hostels Travellers are often greeted on arrival at the bus station by hostel and private room touts who have been known to fight over prospective guests. Be sure to see any

accommodation before deciding to stay there. Note that there is a considerable number of hostel accommodation options. Some are designed for travellers, others for longer-term residents and temporary workers, and a few cater to both. We recommend only those hostels that generally cater for bona fide travellers.

Top of the bill would have to be held by the excellent *Spring Hostel* (☎ 637 4660, fax 637 1543, 126 Ofarim St). This comparatively large place is a bit more expensive than other hostels, but is ideal for first-time travellers and couples. It is immaculately clean and each air-conditioned six to eight-bed dorm has its own modern toilet and shower. There's a kitchen, patio bar with a two hour 'happy hour' between 5 and 7 pm, a billiards table and the reception is open 24 hours. Breakfast is also available for a small charge. Beds are 30NIS, or 25NIS if you stay two nights or more.

Next in the comfort stakes is *Beit Ha'Arava* (☎ 637 4687, fax 637 1052, 106 Almogin St) near the police station and a three minute walk from the bus station. It is clean with comfortable air-con dorms (25NIS per bed) and a wonderful view from the patio. Private rooms cost 100 to 120NIS for two persons. Reception is open 24 hours, and there's a TV, bar, laundry facility and ample guest kitchen with a real gas cooker. There is no curfew.

A newie to the scene and away from the mid-town cluster of hostelries is *Red Sea Hostel* (☎ 637 2171, fax 637 4605, email hostel@hotmail.com) in the New Tourist Centre. It has clean, air-con dorm beds for 25NIS a night which, however, jump to a steep 70NIS during the peak summer season. Rooftop beds can be had for 15NIS year-round. Airy private rooms range from 100 to 180NIS.

There are several places favoured by Eilat's long-termer travellers which feel more boarding houses; many of the residents head out to work each morning (if they're enough to have any), drifting back later in the day to cook, watch TV in the lounge and find out what jobs are going.

Max & Merran's (☎ *637 1333, Agmonim St*) is one of those places and is very easy-going and friendly. The lounge has a TV and VCR, and there's free tea and coffee in the kitchen. Beds are squeezed in about 10 to a room for men and six to a room for the women, and the place could do with another bathroom to reduce the queues, but otherwise it's fine. It's 25NIS a night. The hostel is closed from 10 am to 1 pm for cleaning. There is also limited tent space for about six to eight tents (20NIS per person). Alcohol is not allowed.

Nathan's White House (☎ *637 6572*) is similar and has air-con dorms with fridges and attached bathrooms, and charges between 25NIS and 50NIS a night depending on the season. There is also a small bar and snooker table available for guests.

Finally, *Taba Hostel* (☎ *637 5982, 637 1435, Hativat HaNegev Ave*) is OK overall, though some of it's dorms (20 to 25NIS a bed) take up to 22 people. Girls' dorms are generally around the still-cramped nine-bed mark. There is an ample sitting and patio area, and breakfast can be had for 10NIS.

In its own category is *HI – Eilat Youth Hostel & Guesthouse* (☎ *637 0088, fax 637 5835, Mizrayim Rd*). The hostel is immaculate and beautiful, and there are good views out over the gulf from some of the balconies too. It's something of a bargain at the price, with dorm beds at US$16.50 to US$18.50, singles from US$36 to US$40.50 and doubles from US$52 to US$59 depending on the season. It's located just south of the New Tourist Centre.

Divers should consider *Aqua Club Hostel* (see Scuba Diving earlier in this section).

Places to Stay – Mid-Range

Eilat's hotels, unlike the hostels, are answerable to the Ministry of Tourism and so prices are more regulated. However, they still go up by over 30% for the winter and on Jewish holidays. Note, the single and double rooms at HI – Eilat Youth Hostel & Guesthouse (see Places to Stay – Budget) are equal in standard to much of the accommodation on offer in the mid-range price.

Next to the commercial centre at the bottom of HaTemarim Blvd is *Etzion Hotel* (☎ *637 0003, fax 637 0002*). It has a sauna, swimming pool and nightclub, with singles from US$60 to US$80 and doubles from US$80 to US$100.

New to the scene is the snazzy-looking *Hotel Pierre* (☎ *632 6601, fax 632 6602, 123 Ofarim Alley*). It's smallish but comfortable rooms are equipped, with fridge, phone, TV and air-con. Singles cost US$40 to US$50 and doubles from US$50 to US$60.

In the expensive hotel area by the lagoon, there are some more moderately priced beds available. Near the Galei Eilat Hotel, *Dalia Hotel* (☎ *633 4004, fax 633 4072*) has singles from US$53 to US$79 and doubles from US$68 to US$112. *Americana Eilat* (☎ *633 3777, fax 633 4174*) has a pool, nightclub and tennis, with singles from US$55 to US$75 and doubles from US$65 to US$99.

Out on Coral Beach is *Prima Carlton Eilat* (☎ *633 3555, fax 633 4088, email sales@prima.co.il*) part of the Prima Hotel chain. Its decent singles cost US$84 to US$120 and doubles US$108 to US$155.

Travellers who prefer independent apartment accommodation should look no further than *Villa Kibel* (☎ *050-345 366, fax 637 6911, email russell@eilat.ardom.co.il, 18 Peres St*). South African owner Russell Kibel has a range of apartments large and small to cater to all tastes and numbers of guests ranging from US$40 to US$150. Bookings are recommended and Russell will pick you up if given notice. To get to Peres St, head north up Yotam Rd, left at the junction with Elot Ave, right at Enafa St, left onto HaNesher and first right onto Peres St. No 18 is half-way up on the left. See Russell's Web site www.villakibel.com.il for more details.

The tourist office has a comprehensive list of all private rooms and apartments should you wish to do your own scouting or if Villa Kibel is full.

Places to Stay – Top End

Eilat's top-end hotels are generally of large and brash design, with swimming pools, nightclubs, and various sports and social activities. There are no less than 30 of these things clustered in a high-rise concrete-cube village centred around the North Beach lagoon and marina, with more going up all the time. There are also about a dozen large hotel complexes dotted along the coastal road down to Taba.

Eilat's top-end hotels are subject perhaps more than any others to wide seasonal variations in prices. Unless specified, the prices we quote are those for July/August, which is generally regarded as regular season.

Since being built in 1984, *King Solomon's Palace* (☎ *636 3444, fax 633 4189, email ksp@isrotel.co.il*) has remained Eilat's most popular populist hotel. Laden with poolside terraces, games rooms, health clubs and bars, it's a mini-resort in itself. Singles/doubles start at US$146/172 in the low season and reach US$269/316 in the high season.

Smaller and more sedate than the Solomon's Palace is its older but renovated *Lagoona* (☎ *636 6666, fax 636 6699, email lagoona@isrotel.co.il*), with singles/doubles starting at US$141/188. Slowing down the pace even more, *Riviera Apartment Hotel* (☎ *633 3944, fax 633 3939*) is a low-rise, poolside cluster of some 170 one and two-room flatlets with kitchenettes for self-contained holiday making; the prices are US$103 for a two person studio to US$164 for a four person chalet.

One possible drawback to the Riviera Apartment is that it's a distance away from the beach. This is not a problem with *The Royal Beach Hotel* (☎ *636 8888, fax 636 8811, email royal-beach@isrotel.co.il*), which practically has the sand drifting into the lobby. Rooms start at US$196/230.

There's also *The Sport Hotel* (☎ *637 9140, fax 633 2765*) which is similar to the Lagoona but has an Olympic array of facilities. All of the five previous hotels lie east of the marina, over the bridge. They are also all owned by the one company and together form a complex billed hideously as 'Israworld'.

West of the city's marina is *Dan Eilat* (☎ *636 2222, fax 636 2333, email danhtls@ danhotels.co.il*), which is a very sumptuous place but the ambience is all wrong; guests in thongs and shorts may feel a little uncomfortable and regret having left the tuxedo at home. As one tour operator put it, 'it's a five star hotel in a three star resort'. Rooms cost US$235/258 in the low season.

Similarly classy but a little more relaxed is the *Caesar Resort* (☎ *630 5555, fax 633 2624*). It has a good location and well-trained staff. Prices are in the US$133/184 range. The grand old *Plaza Neptune* (☎ *636 9369, fax 633 4389, email hhemda@irh.co .il*) was the previous holder of the 'classiest joint in town' title but these days the grand old place is full of senior citizens who can't afford the prices at the Dan. Here rooms go for US$207/259.

Another elegant hotel in town is *Princess – Eilat* (☎ *636 5555, fax 637 6333*). Unfortunately it may also be the biggest white elephant. The architecture (step in the lobby to see the screen glass back wall) and facilities can't be faulted, but the location down by the Taba border is just too far away from it all. For reclusive rock stars perhaps. Its rooms cost US$209/234 (low season).

A kilometre up the coast, *Orchid* (☎ *636 0360, fax 637 7279, email orchid@netvision .net.il*) is a hotel which is composed of a collection of oriental-style wooden bungalows. It's very attractive if a bit gimmicky but again, unless you're here specifically for the diving, it suffers greatly from being so isolated. Rooms start at US$202/253.

For visitors with children, one other place worth mentioning here is *Paradise* (☎ *637 8941*) which has a fantastic playroom that should keep kids engrossed for .hours. It's in the North Beach area, with rooms for US$105/139.

Places to Eat

The one saving grace of dining in Eilat is that the thermometer-busting heat means appetites tend to be smaller. If you can be satisfied with just a sandwich, there's a *Co-op supermarket* on Elot Ave, on the corner of HaTemarim Blvd, and another in the Shalom Centre.

Eilat's bakers win the prize for baking Is-rael's smallest *pitta*, and getting both felafel and salad into the same piece of bread is an acquired art. Most of the felafel and shwarma places are on HaTemarim near the bus station – there's a particularly good one next to the Birdwatching Centre. On the same boulevard, mainly between Hativat HaNegev Ave and Almogin St, are a couple of good bakeries; *Family Bakery*, where Ofarim meets HaTemarim, is worth noting as it stays open 24 hours, has a patio with seating and a jukebox. The sign is in Russian and Hebrew only. However, if you miss it there are also a couple of other decent bakeries on the same stretch of road.

For something a bit more substantial, but what are basically unimaginative permutations of chips, eggs, bacon, sausages and beans, *Underground Pub* (☎ 637 0239) in the New Tourist Centre serves up these staple traveller fillers for around 13NIS, or 20NIS for a chicken schnitzel with chips.

Nothing to do with its near-namesake, *Hard Rock 91* (☎ 637 2883, 179 Elot Ave) is a dim little cellar bar, but it does serve the best burgers and fries in town, and a few other dishes besides. Prices are around 15 to 20NIS. It's just west of HaTemarim.

The local branch of *Nargila* (☎ 637 6101) provides passable Yemenite food; try the *malawach*, which is a kind of large, flaky pastry pancake served with either meat, cheese, egg or something sweet. You'll find the Nargila next to the bus station.

None of the shopping malls has a truly recommendable eating place and you may find yourself having to resort to any of the fast-food chains that have made a presence in Eilat. However, *Country Chicken* (☎ 637 1312) in the Tourist Centre gets favourable comments in the local press where it is recommended for its chicken soup and its reasonable prices.

For a meal with a difference try Eilat's only Russian restaurant. *Favourite* (☎ 632 6319) (off map) is located in a quiet pedestrian mall called Beit Hamar centre, off Hatmarin St. Try the whole duck or any of the other menu items that you will not easily

find elsewhere. Prices average 32NIS for a main course, thought you can have caviar for 120NIS, or lobster for 180NIS should you be feeling in an expansive mood.

For fish, try *The Fisherman's House* (☎ 637 9830), across from Coral Beach, which offers a self-service meal of fish (there are seven kinds), various salads and baked potato – it's average quality food at best, but has the advantage that you can eat as much as you for little more than 30NIS.

Entertainment

Entertainment in Eilat is firmly bar-based. To find out what else is happening, either pick up the free *English in Eilat* newsletter from the tourist information office or email english@aquanet.co.il for details.

Cinematheque at the Phillip Murray Cultural Centre (☎ 633 2257) often screens something decent, and there is also a *cinema* in the Red Canyon Centre.

The *Creative Arts Centre* (☎ 637 0044) up behind the port is an occasional venue for music events, and also has studios for working artists and exhibitions of their painting, sculpture, jewellery and weaving.

Bars The most popular place with travellers for some time now is the *Underground Pub*, in the New Tourist Centre. Cheap beer and food fuel a loud and lively crowd, and for times when it's quieter there's a pile of current newspapers in a corner and a dartboard. It's open from around mid-morning until after midnight.

The atmosphere is downbeat at *Hard Rock 91*, though the place goes some way towards being redeemed by the friendly native New Yorker owner. It's at 179 Elot Ave, just west of HaTemarim and a short walk from the hostels.

Hemingway Pub is no more than a semi-circular room in a basement under a supermarket, but it pulls in a good crowd nightly. Tourists and expats make up the clientele for the first half of the evening and then the Israelis take over after midnight. Music is mixed but mainly pitched at the over 25s. The place can be a bit hard to find. It's sort of behind the Moriah Radisson hotel, near the Gulf Restaurant which is easy to spot.

Next Generation is run by the same management as Hemingways, but is only open three nights a week. This hot spot features 70s and 80s nights with free drinks for appropriately dressed patrons. The Next Generation is on Market Square behind the Leumi Bank, opposite the main entrance of the bus station.

Back at the marina on the Kings Wharf Prom-enade you'll find *The Yacht Pub*, part of the King Solomon's Palace Hotel complex on the marina, which features live music of varying quality. Its marble and wood tables and modern decor attract a thirsty crowd and it's a reasonably popular watering hole.

Getting There & Away

Air Arkia flights depart several times daily from the central airport for Tel Aviv and Jerusalem (both cost US$80), and less frequently for Haifa (US$94). The Arkia booking office (☎ 376 102) is in the Red Canyon centre, above the post office.

For information on flights with other airlines call Eilat airport (☎ 637 3553) or Ovda (☎ 635 9442).

Bus Bus No 394 leaves for Tel Aviv (58NIS, 5½ hours) every hour between 8 am and 5 pm, with an additional overnight service departing at 1 am. Last bus on a Friday is at 3 pm, the first on Saturday is at 1 pm. Bus No 444 departs for Jerusalem (58NIS, 4½ hours) at 7 and 10 am and 2 and 5 pm daily, except during Shabbat. On Friday there is no 5 pm bus, while on Saturday there's only one bus, leaving at 4 pm. There's also a Haifa (68NIS, 6½ hours) service, bus No 991, leaving Sunday and Thursday at 8.30 am and 2.30 and 11 pm, Monday to Wednesday at 8.30 am and 11.30 pm, and Friday at 8.30 am only. For these services it's advisable to book at least the day beforehand. If there are no Jerusalem or Tel Aviv buses available, go to Beersheba and change there.

If you want to stop off in the Negev en route, the No 392 Beersheba bus passes through Mitzpe Ramon and will also drop you at Avdat and Sde Boker. It departs Monday to Thursday at 7.45, 9.15 and 11 am and 3.45 pm, with additional 2 and 3 pm buses on Sunday. Note: the No 397 Beersheba bus does *not* go via Mitzpe Ramon.

All buses pass by the Timna National Park, Hai-Bar Biblical Wildlife Reserve and the Yotvata visitors centre.

For intercity bus information call ☎ 636 5111.

Bus to Egypt If you are heading to or from Sinai, local bus No 15 runs between Eilat's central bus station and Taba (4NIS). The service runs every 15 to 20 minutes between 7 am and 9.30 pm (last bus on Friday at 5 pm; first bus on Saturday at 9 am). You can also catch the less frequent bus No 16 which goes Arava-central bus station-Taba, but do check in which direction it's heading first.

See the Getting There & Away chapter for complete border crossing details.

Bus to Jordan Bus No 16 runs from Eilat's central bus station to the border at Arava, every 20 minutes on Monday to Thursday from 7 am to 4 pm.

See the Getting There & Away chapter for complete border crossing details.

Getting Around

Bus Local bus No 15 is the most used service, running daily between the bus station and Taba via the hotel area and Coral Beach. Distances within the town are not so great and most people prefer to walk. If you don't want to, bus Nos 1, 2 and 3 run between the town and the hotel area, with No 1A running between the town and Sun Bay Camping, towards the Israel-Jordan border. Bus Nos 392 and 395 run daily to Ovda airport, between 6.30 and 9 am and 1, 3 and 5 pm.

Car You can rent a car by calling:

Budget	☎ 371 063
Europcar	☎ 637 4014
Hertz	☎ 637 6682
Reliable	☎ 637 4126
Thrifty	☎ 637 3511

THE NEGEV

Taxi Eilat's taxis can be an inexpensive and comfortable way to get around, especially when there are two or more of you. Although distances are short, much of the town is on a hill and, worn out by the heat, you could well decide to take a smart Mercedes ride rather than walk. Fares are roughly 6NIS per kilometre; from the town centre to Taba is 28NIS.

Bicycle & Scooter The heat may prove to be too much of a deterrent, but you can hire a bicycle for 60NIS a day from Doobie Scooter (☎ 633 6557, 050-503 917) based in the Dalia Hotel. Alternatively beat the heat and let the wind whip your hair by slapping down 70NIS for four hours or 115NIS for 24 hour rental of a scooter from the same company.

AROUND EILAT

Unfortunately most of the places of natural beauty near Eilat can only be reached by private transport, and combined with the high temperatures and infrequent traffic, hitchhiking is impractical.

The area's incredible landscape is due to the Great Syrian-African Rift which terminates here with the Arava Valley. The result is a desert environment with glorious colours and a huge variety of flora and fauna. Of the Negev's 1200 recorded plant species, only 300 exist in this southern, more arid, area. These include palms, acacia, tamarisk, pistachio and the very rare horseradish tree. Animals found here include gazelles, wolves, foxes, ibex and Israel's largest bird, the almost extinct lappet-faced vulture.

There are also many archaeological sites in the area which show that ancient people managed not only to live here, but also dug copper mines in these harsh surroundings.

Places that should be seen if you have a car or decide to take a tour include **Ein Netafim**, a small spring at the foot of a 30m waterfall which attracts many animals who come to drink; the **Red Canyon**, one of the area's most beautiful sights, 600m long, one to 3m wide at its narrowest and some 10m at its deepest; and **Moon Valley**, which is

Egyptian territory but can be seen from the Red Canyon.

The following places are some of the attractions that can be reached by public transport.

Timna National Park

A popular excursion 25km north of Eilat, Timna Valley is the site of some stunning desert landscapes enlivened with multicoloured rock formations. King Solomon's Pillars are a series of sandstone ridges caused by gradual erosion on a 50m high cliff face. Erosion is also responsible for the aptly named rock formation, the Mushroom.

Among the other things to see are some ancient copper mines (mining is believed to have been going on here as early as 4000 BC) which now consist of sandstone arches and caves, underground shafts and galleries. About 3km away are some Egyptian and Midianite rock drawings. Other signs of ancient life include copper smelting camps and the ruins of the 14th century BC Temple of Hathor.

Information about walks is available at the booth (☎ 635 6215, fax 635 6217) at the park's entrance. A lot of kilometres are involved in walking around the park, so allow three to eight hours. It is open daily from 7.30 am to nightfall; admission is 18NIS.

Getting There & Away Any bus heading to/from Eilat passes the turn-off for Timna Valley. From the main road it's a 2.5km walk to the park's entrance. Make as early a start as possible to beat the heat and, as usual, take plenty of water and cover your head.

Hai-Bar Arava Biblical Wildlife Reserve

Hai-Bar is Hebrew for wild game and this wildlife reserve on 3200 hectares of salt flats was created to establish breeding groups of wild animals threatened with extinction.

Although the reserve was inspired by the desire to re-introduce animals mentioned in the Bible, other creatures are also found here.

Guided tours of the reserve are available by minivan (no private touring is allowed). Lasting about 1½ hours, these tours operate from 8.30 am to 1 pm every hour and cost 26NIS per person (children 15NIS), which includes admission to the Yotvata visitors centre (☎ 637 6018). In order to see more animals at feeding time, you are advised to take one of the earlier departures.

A prime source of information on the entire Eilat area, the **Yotvata visitors centre** features an audiovisual presentation that describes the region's natural attractions and an exhibition of maps, diagrams and photographs on the zoology, botany, geology, archaeology and history of the settlement here. It's open daily from 8 am to 3 pm. Admission to the visitors centre only is 8NIS.

A *cafeteria*, run by adjacent Kibbutz Yotvata, serves some of the local dairy produce. The wildlife reserve is around 40km north of Eilat and all buses to/from town pass by.

Taba

This is a controversial pocket of land that Israel and Egypt continued to argue about long after the 1979 signing of the Camp David accord. The matter was finally resolved some 10 years later when Taba was returned to the Egyptians. What they got was a pleasant public beach with freshwater showers, and the luxury Taba Hilton Hotel. You don't need an Egyptian visa to visit, just a passport.

To get to Taba take local bus No 15 from HaTemarim Blvd in the town centre to the last stop (5.10NIS). Private cars are permitted to enter Taba and Sinai from Israel, but taxis and rental cars are not.

THE NEGEV

The Gaza Strip & the West Bank

The Gaza Strip and the West Bank are two former Arab territories that were occupied by Israel during the Six Day War in 1967 and have remained in political limbo ever since, having neither been annexed outright (as were East Jerusalem and the Golan Heights) nor granted autonomy.

The West Bank is loosely defined by a pre-1967 border known as the 'green line'. It isn't marked by any signs, let alone a border post, and the majority of locals would be extremely hard pressed to point out exactly where Israel ends and the West Bank begins. The tiny Gaza Strip, on the other hand, is securely meshed around like a rabbit pen. The two areas are separated by a broad expanse of Israel.

Between them, these two parcels of land are home to approximately three million Palestinians; another estimated two million are widely dispersed throughout the region, with major concentrations in Jordan, Lebanon and Syria. The main objective of the Palestinians is to establish an independent state which is centred on the Gaza Strip and the West Bank. Their consistent efforts to achieve this goal have dominated Middle East politics for the past 50 years.

To date they have succeeded in securing a limited form of self-rule in the Gaza Strip as well as the West Bank towns of Bethlehem, Jenin, Jericho, Qalqilya, Nablus, Ramallah and Tulkarem. However, with the electoral victory in May 1996 of the Israeli right-wing leader Binyamin Netanyahu, all previous Palestinian gains are under threat of reversal. At the time of writing, following the general elections held in May 1999 which saw Ehud Barak take the helm as prime minister, a solution to the question of Palestine looked no nearer than it did in 1948, the year of the first major Arab-Israeli war.

HIGHLIGHTS

- **Bethlehem** – site of Jesus' birth and a lively Arab market town; focus of much Christian pilgrimage

- **Gaza** – chaotic, fast-paced, colourful and politically charged; life on the Palestinian side of the fence

- **Jericho** – the worlds' oldest continuously inhabited city, famous for its walls and its now booming casino

- **Ramallah** – a sophisticated and hip West Bank town near Jerusalem

- **Nablus** – the largest West Bank town, an hour from Jerusalem; busy, bustling and decidedly Palestinian

- **Hebron** – home to the contentious Tombs of the Patriarchs claimed by Jews and Muslims alike

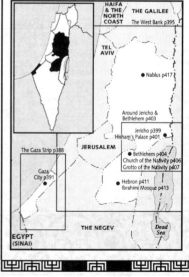

The Gaza Strip רצועת עזה

The Gaza Strip is a narrow stretch of land squeezed between the Mediterranean and the Negev Desert, severed from Sinai by the Egyptian-Israeli border and parcelled up in razor wire. It gained infamy in the late 1980s as the birthplace of the *Intifada* (the uprising against Israeli authorities in the Palestinian Territories and Jerusalem), but while the withdrawal of the Israeli Defence Force (IDF) has seen a cessation of the stone throwing and petrol bombing, the woes of the Gaza Strip are far from over.

Only 40km in length and as little as 6km wide in places, the Strip was filled to bursting by the arrival of some 200,000 Palestinian refugees in 1948, made homeless during the Arab-Israeli conflict. The resulting squalor and overcrowding have not been eased any by the Gazans' proclivity for procreation. The Strip has one of the world's highest birth rates, with a population that doubles each generation. To put this in perspective, a UN report made in 1952 stated that isolated from its natural hinterland, the Gaza Strip was too small and barren to support even its then-population of less than 300,000 – a number that had topped the million mark by 1997.

The Strip's Palestinian inhabitants are centred in three main towns, of which Gaza (often called Gaza City) is the largest, and in eight refugee camps. The Strip is also home to about 20 Jewish settlements and their 4000 occupants. The settlers arrived in the early 1970s and they control about a quarter of the land, mostly in the heavily guarded Gush Katif area to the south.

Except for the Jewish settlers, all of the Strip's residents, natives and refugees, are stateless. Under the auspices of the Palestinian National Authority, the Arabs in Gaza have had some limited control over their affairs but ultimately the IDF, which polices the borders, still calls the tune. Palestinians need to obtain a permit to go into Israel, and so reach Jerusalem or the West Bank; in the case that this is granted – and it's more often the case that it is not – the holder generally

WARNING

For the most part, the Gaza Strip and the West Bank are absolutely safe to visit. There are no problems with independent travellers just turning up in Bethlehem, Jericho, Nablus or Ramallah. Anyone intending to travel to Gaza or Hebron should make inquiries about the current situation before setting out (contact your embassy if necessary). Remember, this is a part of the world in which things can change dramatically from day to day.

Take Arab rather than Egged buses or, best of all, Arab service taxis. Note that cars with yellow Israeli registration plates, even rental cars, are not allowed into the Gaza Strip and have in the past been a stone-throwers' target in the West Bank.

This is a place in which to emphasise that you are a tourist. Speaking Hebrew or voicing pro-Israeli opinions is not a very smart idea.

must be back in Gaza by early evening that same day.

The Egyptian border at Rafah is also Israeli-controlled and permission to cross is rarely given to any except for those holding an air ticket to fly out of Cairo. Because of the difficulties involved in securing permission to travel, many young Palestinians born since 1967 have never left the Strip.

It used to be that journalists were fond of referring to Gaza as 'the Soweto of Israel', but the changes in South Africa may now have rendered that comparison inappropriate. For the Palestinians, recent years have seen matters worsen rather than improve.

Since 1967 the Strip has had an unofficial role as a source of cheap 'black' labour for the Israelis. At one time, up to 80,000 Palestinian workers were crossing the border each morning to be employed as agricultural, construction and light industrial labourers in Israel. Although these migrant workers have always earned a lot less than their non-Palestinian counterparts (an average US$25 a day), through sheer numbers

GAZA STRIP & WEST BANK

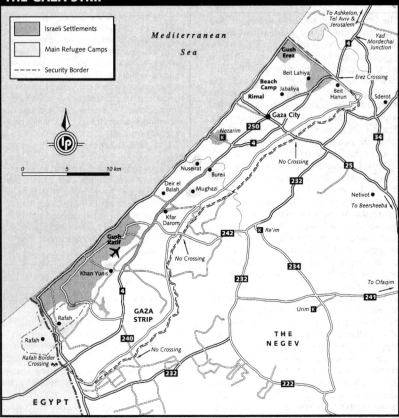

THE GAZA STRIP

- Israeli Settlements
- Main Refugee Camps
- ----- Security Border

Mediterranean Sea

To Ashkelon, Tel Aviv & Jerusalem

Yad Mordechai Junction

Gush Erez

Beit Lahiya

Erez Crossing

Beach Camp

Rimal

Jabaliya

Beit Hanun

Sderot

Gaza City

250

Nezarim

No Crossing

Nuseirat

Bureij

Deir el Balah

Mughazi

232

Netivot

To Beersheeba

Kfar Darom

Re'im

242

234

Gush Katif

No Crossing

232

To Ofaqim

Khan Yunis

Urim

241

GAZA STRIP

THE NEGEV

Rafah

240

Rafah

No Crossing

Rafah Border Crossing

232

222

EGYPT

0 5 10 km

34

25

their combined income has been the backbone of the Gazan economy, bringing in around two million dollars a day.

However in 1995, because of security worries, Israel set tough new restrictions on the availability of work passes, with the result that some days less than 10,000 workers are allowed to cross. The Palestinian coffers have suffered accordingly.

Investment within the Gaza Strip is minimal, kept at bay by the Israeli stranglehold on operation and exportation licences.

Until recently, the authorities would not permit any business to start up that might prove competitive to an Israeli company. As a result, the Strip hasn't developed even to the limited extent that the West Bank has, and the United Nations Relief & Works Agency (UNRWA) estimates put unemployment in Gaza at near 60%. Hopes are that with full Palestinian autonomy Israel will drop its virtual trade blockade and allow Gazan access to the West Bank and outside world.

So, with the situation as bleak as it currently is, why should the traveller visit Gaza City? True, there are no obvious tourist attractions such as ancient holy sites or beautiful landscapes, but there's a vibrancy in Gaza City rarely found in Israel. The place is teeming and chaotic and delivers an all-out sensory assault in the manner of a great Arab city like Cairo. On the streets you'll be greeted with a profusion of 'salaams', offered tea, choke on car fumes, trip in potholes and get your shoes filled with sand. It's not an easy place to be and it's not set up to deal with visitors, but life in Gaza tends to make a searing impact on all those who make the effort to investigate.

Entering & Leaving the Gaza Strip

The only entry/exit point at the time of writing was Erez, in the north of the Strip, though passengers to/from Egypt via the Rafah crossing could get to the crossing via a separate road corridor from Israeli territory. To get there from Jerusalem, essentially the only way nowadays is to take a special taxi from East Jerusalem with Al Zahra Taxi (☎ 628 2444) to the Erez crossing. The cost is 180NIS.

The other possible way to get to Erez is via the Israeli coastal town of Ashkelon, which is served by regular buses from Tel Aviv. From Ashkelon take a southbound bus, say for Beersheba, and ask to be let off at the Yad Mordechai junction. This is only about 5km from Erez and there are usually taxis at Yad Mordechai that will ferry you to the border.

Once at Erez, crossing into the Strip for non-Israeli or non-Arab passport holders is painless and takes minutes. However, make sure you don't join the usually long queue for Palestinian ID card holders. Head instead for the VIP control booth which is on the other side of the vehicle checkpoint. Flash your passport if challenged. The only headache is the swarm of taxi drivers just beyond the Palestinian checkpoint who literally fight over the right to drive you into Gaza City, only some 10km away. The fare

Refugee Camp Visits

As a result of land losses in the 1948 Arab-Israeli War, nearly 750,000 Palestinians became refugees. They fled what is now Israel and crossed into neighbouring Jordan, Lebanon and Syria or took shelter in the then Arab-held areas of the Gaza Strip and the West Bank. In 1950, when hopes for an early return of the refugees to their homes faded, the UN set up the United Nations Relief & Works Agency for Palestine Refugees (UNRWA).

As a result of the natural, but rapid, increases in population, there are now over three million Palestinian refugees registered with UNRWA. Around 600,000 are in the Gaza Strip, half of them housed in eight vast UNRWA-administered camps.

UNRWA's headquarters (signposted by a large blue UN flag) is in Gaza City, opposite the Islamic University on Al-Azhar St, just off Talatin St – follow the veiled girls. If contacted in advance, the public information department (☎ 07-286 7044) may, workload permitting, be able to arrange a visit to one of the refugee camps in the Strip. Try to avoid your visit coinciding with any Muslim holidays, including Ramadan, when almost everything grinds to a halt.

If UNRWA is otherwise occupied then it's possible to visit at least one of the camps on your own. Beach Camp is right on the fringes of Gaza City and a 15 minute walk north from where Omar al-Mukhtar St meets the seafront road. The camp is home to just over 63,000 refugees housed in rank upon rank of single storey huts.

Generally speaking the Palestinians are delighted to welcome visitors and appreciate any outside interest in their living conditions. However, visitors must dress modestly – covered upper arms and shoulders and absolutely no shorts for either men or women. UNRWA also advises visitors to avoid wearing any olive or military style clothing.

should be no more than 40NIS 'special', or 10NIS if you can get a service taxi with three other passengers.

Avoid crossing between 4.30 and 6 am, when the border is clogged by Palestinians heading out into Israel for a day's work, and likewise, from 3 to 4 pm when they are returning.

Scheduled flights have commenced to and from Gaza's Dahaniya airport (☎ 07-213 5696), which opened in November 1998. Flights to Egypt, Jordan, Morocco and Spain are currently operating, with more flights likely as the airport develops.

GAZA CITY   غزة
Pop: 292,567   ☎ Area Code: 07
Chiselled into the Temple of Amun at Karnak in Upper Egypt is a 3500-year-old inscription which states that the town of Gaza was 'flourishing'. Well, 3500 years is a long time and things have changed since then.

History
Gaza City was at one time one of the most strategically important towns in the Levant, a staging post on several well-trafficked trade routes linking central Asia and Persia with Arabia, Egypt and Africa. It was the last provisioning point before the caravans entered the Sinai Desert, and the town could also claim one of Palestine's best deep-water ports. Accordingly, its name in Arabic means 'the treasure' or 'prize'.

It was a prize often fought over. Alexander the Great laid siege to the town for two months in 332 BC before his forces prevailed. In a fit of pique at being defied for so long, the Greek had nearly 10,000 of the defenders executed. After Alexander, Gaza passed variously to the Romans, Crusaders, Mamluks and Ottoman Turks. Throughout the dynastic musical chairs Gaza continued to prosper; so much so that a French visitor in 1660 favourably compared the town with Paris. It's not recorded what another, more distinguished, French visitor thought of the place, but in 1779 Napoleon Bonaparte set up camp in Gaza as a prelude to his Egyptian campaign.

With Napoleon's departure and subsequent defeat in Egypt, Gaza passed back to the Turks until they were chased out in 1917 by British forces battling to conquer Palestine. With the withdrawal of the British, the Egyptian Army made the town its main military base and the area of land it held at the end of the 1948 Arab-Israeli conflict became the Gaza Strip of today. And that's when the problems really began.

The events of the last 50 years have buried Gaza's earlier history, in some cases quite literally. Uncontrolled building has seen Mamluk vaults and Ottoman courtyards disappear under makeshift breezeblock extensions, unavoidable as the city scrabbles to accommodate its penned-in and pent-up population. Half of these additions are falling down before they're completed, giving parts of the town the appearance of the aftermath of an earthquake.

However, since the establishment of limited self-rule in 1994, money has begun to be channelled into Gaza and businesses are experiencing a post-Intifada pick-up. Normal services are still some way from resuming but new, solid-looking apartment blocks are going up and the once neglected rubble-strewn square in the city centre has been transformed into a grassy park. Where just a couple of years ago there were only stone-throwing youths and IDF patrols roaming the streets after 9 pm, now in the evenings families are back strolling on the seafront and patronising the pastry shops along central Omar al-Mukhtar St.

Orientation & Information
Gaza is a fairly easy town to get to know, centred as it is on one long main street. This street, Omar al-Mukhtar St, climbs from Al-Shajaria Square, which marks the eastern extent of the city centre, to run downhill towards the seafront, some 3km away. Most of the city's shops, businesses and other facilities are either on Omar al-Mukhtar St or just off it.

The main activity is centred on Palestine Square (Midan Filisteen), which is about half a kilometre north-west of Al-Shajaria

Square on Omar al-Mukhtar St. The area surrounding Palestine Square is the oldest part of town and contains most of the city's sites of historical interest.

All Gaza's hotels and most of the restaurants are on the seafront at the end of Omar al-Mukhtar St. This coastal district is known as Rimal ('Sands'), and it's the posh bit, full of cool villas and Mediterranean apartment blocks, home to wealthy returned Palestinian migrants, expat aid workers and Yasser Arafat and family.

Money is best changed at the official moneychangers around Palestine Square, which is also where most of the town's banks are. There's an international telephone office, El-Baz (☎ 282 1910, fax 286 4120) near Gaza's only traffic lights on Omar al-Mukhtar St. The police station (☎ 100) is on the northern side of Al-Shajaria Square, while around the corner is the post office, which is open Saturday to Thursday from 8 am to 6 pm, but closed on Friday.

Great Mosque
Although mostly obscured by the surrounding buildings, the Jamaa al-Akbar (Great Mosque), or Mosque of Umar, is the town's most distinguished structure. It's a conversion of a Crusader-era church dedicated to John the Baptist, which itself is built on the site of a Hellenistic temple. Interestingly, the mosque contains a pillar from a 3rd century synagogue that bears a carving of a *menorah* (candelabra) with a Hebrew and Greek inscription. Nobody knows for sure where this was filched from.

Non-Muslims are usually allowed to enter the mosque between the daily prayers.

Mosque of Said Hashim
This mosque was built on the grave of the Prophet Mohammed's great-grandfather. Said Hashim was a merchant who travelled a great deal between the Arabian Peninsula and Damascus, and he died while passing through Gaza.

To reach the mosque, head north-east from Palestine Square to reach Al-Wahida St,

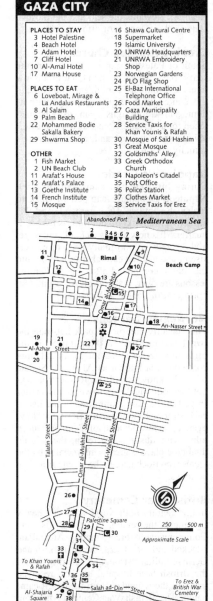

GAZA CITY

PLACES TO STAY
3 Hotel Palestine
4 Beach Hotel
5 Adam Hotel
7 Cliff Hotel
10 Al-Amal Hotel
17 Marna House

PLACES TO EAT
6 Loveboat, Mirage & La Andalus Restaurants
8 Al Salam
9 Palm Beach
22 Mohammed Bodie Sakalla Bakery
29 Shwarma Shop

OTHER
1 Fish Market
2 UN Beach Club
11 Arafat's House
12 Arafat's Palace
13 Goethe Institute
14 French Institute
15 Mosque
16 Shawa Cultural Centre
18 Supermarket
19 Islamic University
20 UNRWA Headquarters
21 UNRWA Embroidery Shop
23 Norwegian Gardens
24 PLO Flag Shop
25 El-Baz International Telephone Office
26 Food Market
27 Gaza Municipality Building
28 Service Taxis for Khan Younis & Rafah
30 Mosque of Said Hashim
31 Great Mosque
32 Goldsmiths' Alley
33 Greek Orthodox Church
34 Napoleon's Citadel
35 Post Office
36 Police Station
37 Clothes Market
38 Service Taxis for Erez

Abandoned Port   **Mediterranean Sea**

Rimal

Beach Camp

An-Nasser Street

Al-Azhar Street

Talatin Street

Omar al-Mukhtar Street

Al-Wahida Street

Palestine Square

0   250   500 m

Approximate Scale

To Khan Younis & Rafah

Salah ad-Din Street

To Erez & British War Cemetery

Al-Shajaria Square

GAZA STRIP & WEST BANK

which runs parallel to Omar al-Mukhtar St. Head left (towards the sea) and the mosque is down the second turn-off to the right.

Greek Orthodox Church
South of Palestine Square (away from the sea) is the town's Christian Quarter. Follow Omar al-Mukhtar St south and you come to this church on the right – although with its dome and Arabic signs it can easily be mistaken for a mosque. Someone may be available to show you around, although there's actually very little to see.

Napoleon's Citadel
During his Egyptian campaign in 1799, Napoleon Bonaparte camped in Gaza to replenish supplies. He commandeered this attractive Mamluk-era building as his headquarters. It's now a girls' school, and to get a close look you normally need to be persistent and ask the caretaker to let you into the school compound after 4 pm when the lessons are over. It stands on Al-Wahida St, north-east of the Great Mosque.

Norwegian Gardens
This recently completed park between the two lanes of Omar al-Mukhtar St is the pride of Gaza was previously an unkempt common area known as Al-Jundi (Square of the Unknown Soldier). Its creation was not without much controversy, as critics sniped that a park came low on the list of cash-strapped Palestinian priorities. However, as a rare swatch of greenery in an other-wise dusty ochre town, there is no doubt the place is greatly appreciated by the locals who flock here in the evenings and on holidays.

British War Cemetery
In this century both world wars saw heavy fighting in the region. In 1917 British and Commonwealth forces, mainly Australian, attacked and took Gaza, then a Turkish and German military stronghold. During WWII the British base hospital in Gaza received many of the wounded from the desert campaign. The British War Cemetery is about 3km from town on the Erez road, on the eastern side, across from the 7-Up factory.

Markets & Shops
The town's main food market is located just north-west of Palestine Square, under the corrugated iron roof. Much older is the short, vaulted **Goldsmiths' Alley**, which runs along the southern side of the Great Mosque. This is all that remains of what, during the Mamluk era, was a much larger covered market, similar to that in Jerusalem's Old Town. At the eastern end of the alley, a crowd of moneychangers stand around with fists full of dollars.

Just south of Al-Shajaria Square is a large clothes market, but if it's something a little more fancy you're after try the **UNRWA Embroidery Shop**, where all the profits go to the welfare of the refugees. The shop is between Omar al-Mukhtar and Talatin Sts, south of the Norwegian Gardens. It's open Saturday to Thursday from 6.30 to 11.45 am and 1.30 to 3.45 pm, closed Friday.

Souvenir hunters might also appreciate what's known locally as the '**PLO flag shop**'. As well as flags, this place has Palestinian stickers, badges and pennants, posters of Arafat or, for the enthusiast, 2m-high

The Palestinian *thob* (basic dress) often features densely patterned embroidery.

painted banners of the great fuzzy visage. This is also the place to buy one of the most bizarre pieces of political kitsch you're ever likely to come across: an inflatable Yasser Arafat. The shop is 100m from the junction of An-Nasser and Al-Wahida Sts.

Beaches

Although Gaza hopes to become a tourist resort (for West Bank Palestinians and Jordanians – hoteliers in Greece and Spain need not quake), little has been done so far to develop the seafront area. The beaches by the hotels are blighted by rubbish, the wreck of Gaza's abandoned, incomplete 'port', and two sewerage pipes that pump effluent directly into the sea. However, south-west of the fish market there are some appealing and relatively clean sandy stretches which are a big draw in summer for the locals. One major drawback for women though is that the Islamic laws of modesty prevail; suntanning opportunities are limited to hands, feet and the area from the neck up, and any swimming has to be done fully covered.

Places to Stay

Choices are limited and there's nothing really suitable for the traveller on a budget. The cheapest place in town to stay is *Al-Amal Hotel* (☎ 286 1832, fax 284 1317, Omar al-Mukhtar St) 300m east of the seafront. Though the plumbing is a little old, it's a well-run place, immaculately clean and not too badly priced at US$40/50 for singles/doubles.

For those with a fatter wallet, the other good option is *Marna House* (☎ 282 2624, fax 282 3322), a comfortable private villa, in a quiet residential street. With a large front garden, terrace and lounge, it's a faded reminder of pre-1948 Gaza. Singles/doubles are US$60/70, with breakfast. Marna House is two blocks north of Omar al-Mukhtar St, just west of An-Nasser St.

The rest of the hotels, all lined up along the seafront, are modern constructions that seem to have been surviving on the constant procession of foreign delegations, journalists, aid workers, election observers etc.

From the photos displayed at reception, Arafat favours *Hotel Palestine* (☎ 282 3355, fax 282 3356), where singles/doubles go for US$55/65. Otherwise, there seems little to choose between them; *Adam Hotel* (☎ 282 5580, fax 282 3521) has singles/doubles for US$40/50; and *Cliff Hotel* (☎ 286 1353, fax 282 0742) charges US$50/70 for singles/doubles. All three have restaurants and coffee shops.

The striking facade of the newer *Beach Hotel* (☎ 282 8800, fax 282 8604), with its white and glass exterior, cannot be missed. This is the best hotel on the seafront bunch and charges more – US$77/110 for singles/doubles – but it does have a very pleasant garden coffee shop, restaurant and rooms have air-con, mini-bar and TV.

For what it's worth, there's also a HI youth hostel in the Gaza Strip itself, though you're not going to meet many Palestinians there. *Hevel Katif 'Hadarom' Hostel* (☎ 684 7596, fax 684 7680) is just east of the Jewish settler enclave of Gush Katif overlooking the Mediterranean. You can get there on bus No 36 from Ashkelon or bus No 38 from Beersheba. A dorm bed will cost you around US$15.

Places to Eat

Cheap prices abound for fruit and vegetables in the markets. Felafel is easily found in the Palestine Square area and some of the best shwarma is here at a shop on the short street that connects the eastern end of the square to Al-Wahida St; a huge piece of *laffa* bread stuffed with meat and salad is only 10NIS.

Fish is a local speciality and restaurants on the seafront compete for the attention of the bigger spenders. *Al Salam*, *Loveboat*, *Mirage* and *La Andalus* restaurants, set above the beach between the hotels, are all fairly modern and well-run places and you can expect to pay 60 to 80NIS per person for meals at them.

Gaza also challenges Nablus' status as the best place for sweet pastries. Arguably the town's best bakery is *Mohammed Bodie Sakalla* (no English sign – look for the

GAZA STRIP & WEST BANK

white on green Arabic script) on Omar al-Mukhtar St next to the Norwegian Gardens. Fast food has arrived in Gaza too; there is a *Pizza Inn* in the middle of the Norwegian Gardens looking more than a tad similar to its mega-chain rival Pizza Hut.

Getting There & Away

For information about getting into Gaza from Israel, see Entering & Leaving the Gaza Strip earlier in this chapter.

Service taxis operate from two different places in Gaza: those just across from Al-Shajaria Square travel to the border at Erez (10NIS service or 40NIS 'special', 20 minutes), while those on Palestine Square will take you to places in the Strip.

Getting Around

Because Gaza City has a 3km-long main street, the unofficial local taxi setup is great. Instead of walking, stand by the roadside and, by pointing your index finger, hail a taxi. It seems like half of the cars in town act as pirate taxis and everyone uses them. Up and down Omar al-Mukhtar St the fare is 1NIS, no matter where you get in or out. If you want to go off the main road, to UNRWA headquarters for example, the fare jumps to 5NIS.

KHAN YOUNIS & RAFAH

خان يونس و رفح

Pop: 138,435 ☎ Area Code: 07

Aside from the refugee camps, the Strip's other main Palestinian settlements are Khan Younis and Rafah, both worth a visit on days when the colourful **Bedouin markets** set up shop. This means Wednesday and Thursday in Khan Younis and Saturday and Sunday in Rafah. Apart from the hectic trading there is very little to see, unfortunately, except more overcrowded slum conditions. You can get there by taking a service taxi from Palestine Square in Gaza City.

The situation is particularly sad in Rafah, which is a town divided by an international border. When Sinai was returned to Egypt under the Camp David Agreement of 1979,

part of the town and 5000 people went with it. As at Majdal Shams in the Golan region, this resulted in the separation of families. Israeli law prohibits Palestinians living outside the present-day borders to return to Gaza; similarly, those living in Gaza find it nearly impossible to acquire permission to get out. Unable to visit each other, Palestinian families have to resort to shouting to each other across the fenced-off wasteland. For details of the Israel-Egypt border crossing see the Land section in the Getting There & Away chapter.

The West Bank

הגדה המערבית (יו"ש)

The disputed nature of the territory has, to date, prevented the West Bank from developing as a major tourist venue, and the attendant violence of the Intifada years has discouraged many individual travellers from going ahead and exploring the area on their own. All of which is a great shame because the West Bank contains some of the region's most interesting places. Alongside the familiar biblical sites such as Bethlehem, the birth place of Jesus, and Jericho, of the horn-blasted walls, there is the striking monastery at Mar Saba, the beautiful scenery of Wadi Qelt and the medieval souqs of Nablus and Hebron.

Despite covering an area of less than 6000 sq km, the West Bank embraces a diverse range of geographical regions. Starting at the edge of the Jezreel Valley in the north, the Samarian Mountains are a range of green and brown peaks with a distinct red soil, with olive and fruit trees, tobacco and livestock as well as the occasional Arab village on the terraced slopes. Descending eastward towards the Dead Sea, the hills give way to the savage scenic splendour of the Judean Desert.

Moving down into the Jordan Valley you come to Jericho, a lush oasis with a steamy climate. Often overlooked is the fact that the shore of the Dead Sea, almost as far south as Ein Gedi, is also part of the West Bank. It includes Qumran, where the Dead

THE WEST BANK

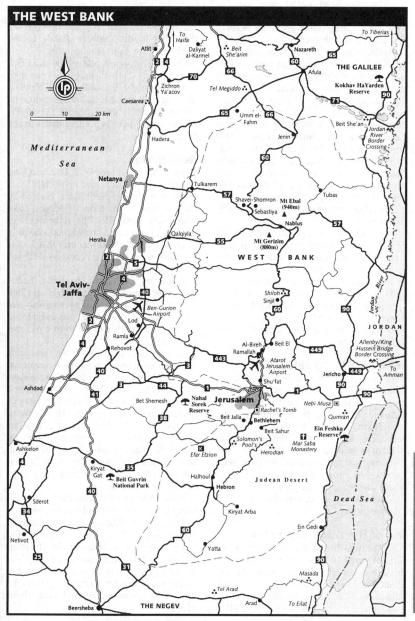

GAZA STRIP & WEST BANK

Sea Scrolls were found, and Ein Feshka, the freshwater spring (these areas are covered in the Dead Sea chapter).

To the west, the Judean Hills end where the Negev Desert begins, and you will find Bethlehem and Hebron, surrounded by hillsides of lush vineyards, orchards and olive trees set among the rocky brown terrain.

In the linguistic war, the Israelis officially designate the West Bank by the biblical names Judea and Samaria. As you travel around you will see fortified military installations, Jewish settlements, and periodic roadblocks and refugee camps that only begin to indicate the reality of the situation here. These aspects cannot be ignored, but do not allow them to deter you from visiting this area.

The Intifada has certainly done a great deal to dent the image of the West Bank as a tourist destination. Nonetheless, and despite the fact that many hotels closed down in the mid-90s, a cautious optimism prevails and new hotels and restaurants have sprung up in the major West Bank towns. There is no reason why you should not consider basing yourself here during your stay in the Territories.

JERUSALEM TO JERICHO

Between Jerusalem and Jericho there's a dramatic change in scenery and temperature as you experience the rapid descent from 820m above sea level to 395m below in less than 30km. You pass by Bethany (see the Jerusalem chapter) and the Inn of the Good Samaritan, with their New Testament connotations, and the road runs alongside Wadi Qelt, a nature reserve with a natural spring where you can bathe in a pool under a waterfall and hike along an aqueduct to a cliff-face monastery.

Inn of the Good Samaritan

After the tree-shaded slopes of Bethany, the Jericho road winds its way eastward through a suddenly barren landscape, enlivened occasionally only by a lone Bedouin camp. About 10km on, the road climbs a mountain called Ma'ale Adumim (Red

Ascent), so named because of the earth's reddish tint. In ancient Israel this marked the tribal border between Judah, to the south, and Binyamin, to the north.

On the right-hand side of the road is a 16th century Turkish building known to Christians as the Inn of the Good Samaritan. They believe that this is the traditional site of the inn in the parable, Luke 10:25-37; however, there is nothing much to see here.

Nebi Musa

Beyond the turn-off for Wadi Qelt, and 8km short of Jericho, a side road to the right leads to the monastery of Nebi Musa, revered by the Muslims as the tomb of Moses. Like many Holy Land sites, the authenticity of the claim is heavily disputed, but according to Deuteronomy 34, it was here that Moses was shown the Promised Land by God and here where he died.

A mosque was built on the spot at the behest of the Mamluk sultan Beybars in 1269. Accommodation for visiting pilgrims was added later and the complex was extended in the late 15th century to the form it remains in today.

At one time, each Easter the thousands of Muslims gathered for Friday prayers at Al-Aqsa Mosque would then make a day-long march to Nebi Musa, to be followed by five days of prayers, feasting and games before a return procession. This grew to become one of Palestine's most popular and colourful events; however, with the rise of Arab nationalism during the British Mandate the pilgrimage was carefully controlled by the British and eventually stopped by the Jordanians.

In the belief that this is the tomb of Moses, many Muslims choose to be buried here.

There are no fixed opening hours and admission is free. To get here, look out for the signpost on the main Jerusalem-Jericho road. It's about a 2km walk from the bus stop. Alternatively, you can take a taxi from the main square in Jericho; a round trip will take around an hour and should cost about 12NIS.

WADI QELT & ST GEORGE'S MONASTERY

ولدي كلت و دير لقسيس جورج

A wadi is a rocky watercourse, dry throughout the year except in the rainy season; not a definition to inspire perhaps, but Wadi Qelt is beautiful. In this case the wadi is sunk deep in a steep canyon, the limestone walls of which burst with clumps of trees and foliage. Added spectacle is lent by St George's Monastery, perched halfway up a cliff face, looking as though it has been carved out of the solid rock wall of the wadi.

There are two ways of visiting the wadi and monastery; a short walk of an hour or a long, strenuous hike which takes half a day. The starting point for both is the Wadi Qelt turn-off on the Jerusalem-Jericho road (ask the bus driver to drop you off here) and the finishing point is Jericho, from where you can continue sightseeing in the town or easily find transport back to Jerusalem.

Wadi Qelt Hike

Taking about four hours, this hike involves straightforward walking over slightly rough ground with some scrambling over rocks here and there. Regular sports shoes are suitable footwear, sandals are not. You may well have to get your feet wet wading through shallow water and, in winter, it's often muddy underfoot in places. There's also the danger in winter of flash floods, when a sudden downpour of rain can lead to torrential rushes of water; keep an eye on the weather and be ready to climb to higher ground.

In warmer weather take plenty of water and cover your head. Also remember to take suitable clothes for the visit to the monastery. Although the monks will usually provide some unflattering rags to cover your legs and arms, it's more respectful to provide your own clothing.

The Hike At the turn-off on the Jerusalem-Jericho road, follow the sign to the monastery. After you've been walking for five minutes, you'll see the road fork at another sign for the monastery, this one pointing to the right; this is the direct route that avoids

the wadi, so take the fork to the left. A further 100m on, turn right onto the dirt track that winds down to the valley, with a marvellous view before you. After 25 minutes of walking you arrive at the spring, Ein Qelt, and the nature reserve. The aqueduct here carries spring water from Ein Fuwwar, a few kilometres west of here, to Jericho. It was restored by the British, but note the ruins of the Herodian aqueduct.

Further along the wadi, on the left-hand side, there are some picturesque bathing possibilities; climb up the opposite bank and turn right, though, for the monastery and Jericho. Following the path beside the aqueduct you'll see occasional red-on-white painted trail markers showing the way. Judging by the infrequency of the markers, paint was obviously in short supply.

After following the aqueduct for about 40 minutes the trail leads down to the wadi; a descent that can be tricky if there is a lot of water. After another 45 minutes you'll pass under the ruined arches where the Herodian aqueduct crossed the canyon. Follow the wadi a little further and around the next bend you will see the monastery.

Moving on, stay on the same side of the wadi as the monastery, with the trail climbing high above the bed. Look out for the first sight of the Jordan Valley after about 25 minutes as you pass **caves** once used by hermits, and the ruins of other monasteries. The trail later splits; you can either follow the wadi or climb up the other side.

If you choose the latter route, you'll find yourself by a largely abandoned refugee camp. Head for the road that passes the mosque (look for the minaret) and follow it through the melon and banana fields to the main road by the restaurant and military camp.

If you choose the alternative route and follow the wadi to the main road you'll pass the Tulul Abu al-Alaiq excavations. On both sides of the wadi and very easy to miss, these are the remains of Hasmonean, Herodian and Roman winter palaces and villas.

At the main road, which is Jerusalem Rd, turn left to enter Jericho.

St George's Monastery

The more direct route to the monastery is the right fork on the turn-off from the Jerusalem-Jericho road, as directed by the orange signposts. Look out for the metal cross marking the monastery's location. Steps lead down into the canyon and the road continues and eventually passes the above-mentioned refugee camp and mosque, intersecting with Jerusalem Rd by the restaurant and military camp.

The monastery, named after St George of Koziba, was first built in the late 5th century, an elaboration of a small oratory built by hermits in the early 4th century. Wadi Qelt's numerous cave-dwelling hermits would attend the Divine Liturgy on Saturday and Sunday. The monastery was to all intents abandoned after the Persians swept through the valley and massacred the 14 monks. The Crusaders made some attempts at restoration in 1179 but a pilgrim travelling in 1483 wrote that he only saw ruins here. More significant reconstruction was begun by the Greek Orthodox Church in 1878 and completed in 1901.

The traditions attached to this monastery include a visit by St Elijah en route to Sinai, and St Joachim, whose wife Anne was infertile, weeping here when an angel announced to him the news of the Virgin Mary's conception.

The oldest part of the building is the 6th century mosaic floor of the Church of St George and John. The skulls of the martyred monks are kept here and a niche contains the tomb of St George. The larger church was added by the Crusaders during their 12th century renovations. It was dedicated to the Blessed Virgin, and it features a striking black, white and red double-headed Byzantine eagle. Most of the paintings and icons seen today date from the latest reconstruction; however, the doors at the centre of the iconostasis date from the Crusaders.

The monastery is open to visitors Monday to Saturday from 8 am to 5 pm but the hours can be flexible. There's a small admission charge.

Getting There & Away

Take the Jericho bus from East Jerusalem, or a service taxi, or any Egged bus that is heading for the Dead Sea from Jerusalem's central bus station. Tell the driver that you want to go to Wadi Qelt and/or the monastery and keep an eye out for the orange signpost after about 25 minutes.

JERICHO יריחו حيفا

Pop: 13,911 ☎ Area Code: 02

Reputedly the world's oldest town (not an uncommon claim in this part of the world), Jericho is best known for the biblical account of Joshua and the tumbling walls.

For visitors in winter, Jericho's warm climate is a pleasant alternative to the cold and rain of Jerusalem. The town's ancient ruins are surpassed by the shabby beauty of their surroundings as year-round the area is a lush oasis of colour, with fruit and flowers abundant among the greenery – quite a contrast to the desert valley setting which, at 250m below sea level, makes it (indisputably) the world's lowest town.

History

The Old Testament Book of Joshua tells how Jericho was the first town captured by the Israelites when, after years in the wilderness, they laid siege and brought down the city walls with the blare of their priests' trumpets.

Prior to the arrival of the Israelites in around 1200 BC, the climate and perennial spring of Ein as-Sultan had attracted prehistoric nomads to the area. They settled at an adjacent site, known today as Tel as-Sultan, or ancient Jericho. Archaeologists have now uncovered remains of the town built around 7000 BC and believe the site was abandoned as a result of the Babylonian exile around 586 BC.

During the reign of Alexander the Great (336 to 323 BC), Jericho became the private estate of the ruling sovereign, and later on, Mark Anthony made a gift of the oasis to Cleopatra. The sultry Queen of Egypt, in turn, leased Jericho out to Herod, to whom the town passed on her death. Herod fixed

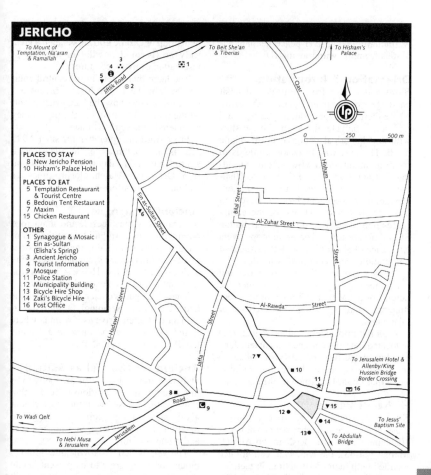

JERICHO

To Mount of Temptation, Na'aran & Ramallah

Jiftlik Road

To Beit She'an & Tiberias

To Hisham's Palace

Qasr

Hisham

Street

0   250   500 m

Ein as-Sultan Street

Bilal Street

Al-Zuhar Street

Al-Haddawi Street

Jaffa Street

Al-Rawda Street

Road

Jerusalem

To Wadi Qelt

To Nebi Musa & Jerusalem

To Jerusalem Hotel & Allenby/King Hussein Bridge Border Crossing

To Jesus' Baptism Site

To Abdullah Bridge

PLACES TO STAY
8 New Jericho Pension
10 Hisham's Palace Hotel

PLACES TO EAT
5 Temptation Restaurant & Tourist Centre
6 Bedouin Tent Restaurant
7 Maxim
15 Chicken Restaurant

OTHER
1 Synagogue & Mosaic
2 Ein as-Sultan (Elisha's Spring)
3 Ancient Jericho
4 Tourist Information
9 Mosque
11 Police Station
12 Municipality Building
13 Bicycle Hire Shop
14 Zaki's Bicycle Hire
16 Post Office

the place up, running in new aqueducts to supply his winter palace at Tulul Abu al-Alaiq. Prosperity followed, as evidenced by the Byzantine-era monasteries such as St George's and the 8th century Hisham's Palace which, even from the little that remains, was obviously a building of great opulence.

The decline of Jericho began in the 12th century when persistent Bedouin raids transformed what was a thriving town into a desolate village. Under the British Mandate, Jericho's natural resources were again used effectively with the development of fruit production, a lucrative source of income which fell to Jordan following the 1948 War. The town subsequently had to absorb great floods of Arab refugees from the new State of Israel. Refugee camps, among the largest on the West Bank, were hastily built to house them. During the Six Day War most of the refugees crossed the Jordan River to escape Jewish occupation. A couple of those camps near the site of Tel as-Sultan are now used as training centres for the new Palestinian police force, which is gradually taking over peace-keeping activities from the withdrawing IDF.

Orientation & Information

Buses and sheruts from Jerusalem deposit passengers on the main square of the town, where there are shops, eating places, a taxi rank and a bicycle hire shop. All the stuff with any historical pedigree is off to the north. The best way to tackle things is to move in an anti-clockwise direction, heading first north up Qasr Hisham St to Hisham's Palace, then west to the ancient synagogue and ancient Jericho. Here you can refresh yourself at one of the eating places before heading down Ein as-Sultan St to return to town. The basic loop covers a distance of about 6km, with the Mount of Temptation about 2km further north.

You need to be both an early starter and a fast mover if you plan on adding the heights of the Mount of Temptation to your itinerary – unless, that is, you have a car or take a taxi.

A tourist information cabin (☎ 922 935) is located near the entrance to ancient Jericho but at the time of our visit it had no maps and was, in fact, fairly short on anything that might be termed informative.

Hisham's Palace

Known in Arabic as Khirbet al-Mafjar, these impressive ruins are better known as Hisham's Palace after Hisham ibn Abd al-Malik (724-43), the Umayyad caliph once credited with their construction. In fact, it's now thought more likely that his nephew and successor, Al-Walid ibn Yazid, was the man responsible.

The remains of the palace are of special interest to historians as this is one of the earliest examples of Islamic architecture. At that time (7th century), Islam had yet to develop its own architectural vocabulary. Consequently, Hisham's Palace is a composite of borrowed styles with strong Persian and Byzantine influences. These probably reflect the origins of the builders. In particular there is one beautiful Byzantine-style mosaic floor depicting a lion pouncing on one of a group of gazelle grazing beneath a great leafy tree (Islam supposedly forbade the representation of living creatures).

The large monument in the central court was built by the archaeologists. Meant as a window, it shows how the Umayyads adapted the motifs they found in the places they conquered; this star is Roman.

From April to September, the site (☎ 922 522) is open Saturday to Thursday from 8 am to 5 pm, and Friday from 8 am to 4 pm; from October to March, closing times are an hour earlier. Admission is 8NIS.

Ancient Synagogue

An orange signpost beside the main road points to the modern building at the end of the gravel track. Inside is the mosaic floor of a 5th or 6th century synagogue, depicting a menorah with the Hebrew inscription 'Shalom al Israel' ('Peace Upon Israel').

The synagogue is open daily, although the hours are erratic. Seemingly absent, the attendant will often arrive as if from nowhere to unlock the door and think of a suitable fee. Pay no more than 8NIS.

Ancient Jericho (Tel as-Sultan)

Only true archaeology buffs are likely to be impressed by the excavations at Tel Jericho; even visitors blessed with the most visionary imagination are going to struggle to make anything of the signposted trenches and mounds of dirt.

The *tel*, which is a volcanic looking mound of earth, grew to its present height through a succession of towns being built one on top of another. The mud-brick wall at the tel's summit is not, as once believed, one of those brought down by Joshua's trumpets; it has now been dated back to 10 centuries before the arrival of the Israelites.

The site is open Saturday to Thursday from 8 am to 5 pm, and Friday from 8 am to 4 pm. Admission is 8NIS.

Ein as-Sultan

Across the street from ancient Jericho is Ein as-Sultan, or Sultan's Spring, also known as

CHRISTINE OSBORNE

There are good views of Jericho from the Mount & Monastery of Temptation.

TONY WHEELER

The 5th century St George's Monastery clings to a rock face high above the Wadi Qelt valley.

Church of the Nativity, Bethlehem

Fresco in the Church of the Nativity, Bethlehem

The fortress-like Ibrahimi Mosque (Cave of Machpelah) dominates the West Bank city of Hebron.

St Catherine's Monastery (top right) is inland at the foot of Mt Sinai, while the coast offers beautiful beaches, colourful coral reefs and marine life, and some of the best diving in the world.

The magnificent sandstone mountains of Wadi Arab surround the lost city of Petra.

One of Petra's 'High Places', the rock-hewn monastery (Al-Deir) is definitely worth the uphill hike.

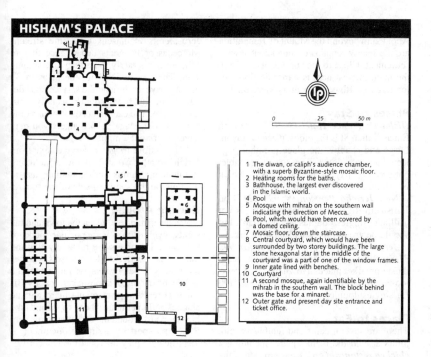

HISHAM'S PALACE

0   25   50 m

1 The diwan, or caliph's audience chamber, with a superb Byzantine-style mosaic floor.
2 Heating rooms for the baths.
3 Bathhouse, the largest ever discovered in the Islamic world.
4 Pool
5 Mosque with mihrab on the southern wall indicating the direction of Mecca.
6 Pool, which would have been covered by a domed ceiling.
7 Mosaic floor, down the staircase.
8 Central courtyard, which would have been surrounded by two storey buildings. The large stone hexagonal star in the middle of the courtyard was a part of one of the window frames.
9 Inner gate lined with benches.
10 Courtyard
11 A second mosque, again identifiable by the mihrab in the southern wall. The block behind was the base for a minaret.
12 Outer gate and present day site entrance and ticket office.

Elisha's Spring. Although this is the spring traditionally associated with II Kings 2:19-22, which tells of Elisha purifying the water with salt, there is now little to see apart from a shabby building and a UN sign barring admission.

Mount & Monastery of Temptation

This mountain is traditionally associated with the attempts of the Devil to goad Jesus into converting stones to bread to satisfy his hunger after 40 days and nights of fasting (Matthew 4:1-11). From this legend comes the Crusaders' name of Mont Quarantana (Mount of Forty), which the Arabs modified to Qarantal.

The cliff-clinging Greek Orthodox monastery here is similar in style to St George's in Wadi Qelt, although not quite as spectacular. It dates from the 12th century, which

makes it not quite as old either. The monastery is built around the cave where Jesus and the Devil met.

The mount is deceptively further north of ancient Jericho than it looks, so give yourself plenty of time if walking or cycling. The summit is officially out of bounds but if you ask nicely (a shekel or three sometimes does the trick) the attendant may let you through the back door of the monastery. It's worthwhile to hike the extra 20 minutes to the top for the knockout view of Jericho and the Jordan Valley, with the Dead Sea to the south and the Mount of Olives to the west.

During the summer months the monastery is open to visitors Monday to Saturday from 8 am to 5 pm (in winter from 7 am to 2 pm and 3 to 4 pm); it's closed on Sunday. Note that the cave-church is normally closed after 11 am.

Na'aran

About 2km beyond the Mount of Temptation are the scanty remains of an ancient Jewish settlement. Close to the springs of Ein Duq, the main interest here is a mosaic floor belonging to a 4th or 5th century synagogue.

Places to Stay

Hisham's Palace Hotel (☎ 992 2156) on Ein as-Sultan St is the oldest place to stay in. Large and shabby, the place is rather neglected and run-down. Prices are negotiable, but count on paying around 135NIS, which is still more than the room is worth.

New Jericho Pension (☎ 992 2215) on Jerusalem Rd is slightly better, but it's not brilliant. Singles/doubles are negotiable but should be around the 130/160NIS mark.

Jerusalem Hotel (☎ 992 1329, fax 992 3109), 2.5km east of the main square, is the most upmarket place in town to stay. Smart-looking bright new rooms go for US$65/90 for singles/doubles.

Places to Eat

There are several cafes and felafel/shashlik joints around the main square, including a *chicken restaurant* on the eastern side of the square, just up from Zaki's Bicycle Hire, that does a half roast chicken plus bread and salad for 14NIS and felafel for 4NIS.

The garden restaurants on Ein as-Sultan St seem to attract an enthusiastic crowd – they can be worth a splurge to enjoy Palestinian meat specialities and salads. Look out for *Bedouin Tent* with its bizarre water wheel. On the same street but closer to town, *Maxim* (☎ 992 2410) offers fairly good value, with a barbecued mixed grill and choice of salads for 32NIS.

On the upper floor of the modern tourist centre near the site of ancient Jericho is the easily resistible *Temptation Restaurant*, a large self-service diner with an 'eat all you want' salad bar (20NIS) or cold meat and salad platter for 28NIS.

Getting There & Away

There are, at present, no bus services to Jericho; instead, you could use the service taxis (sheruts). Operating from the rank opposite Jerusalem's Damascus Gate, the stretch-Mercedes or Peugeots depart once they're full, but that's rarely more than a 10 minute wait. The fare is 5NIS for the pleasant 30 minute drive. In Jericho the service taxis depart from the town square, usually until about 7 pm. You can find taxis after this time but with a shortage of passengers you may have to fork out a higher fare.

It's possible to get a service taxi from Jericho to other West Bank towns including Bethlehem, Nablus and Ramallah; ask at the rank on the southern side of the square.

Getting Around

Given the distance between the town and the sights, cycling is a very popular mode of transport. The roads are relatively flat and traffic-free, so decide for yourself whether the heat is easier to bear on foot or on the saddle of a rented boneshaker. Zaki's Bicycle Hire is on the town square and he charges 3NIS per hour. There's a second bike hire shop just around the corner on Jerusalem Rd. A passport or a similar document of identification may be asked for as security.

AROUND JERICHO
Jesus' Baptism Site

You'll see old-style milestones pointing the way to the traditional site of Jesus' baptism on the Jordan River. With a picturesque 19th century Greek Orthodox monastery nearby, it is unfortunately in a military zone normally out of bounds to visitors. Two exceptions are in January, when the Greek Orthodox celebrate Epiphany, and the third Thursday in October, when the Roman Catholic Church is permitted to celebrate Jesus' baptism. Contact the Christian Information Centre (☎ 02-27 2692, fax 628 6417) in Jerusalem for details – see Tourist Offices in the Jerusalem chapter for directions on where to find it.

The Dead Sea

The Palestinians have yet to capitalise on the tourism potential of their share of the Dead Sea coastline. Apart from special taxis,

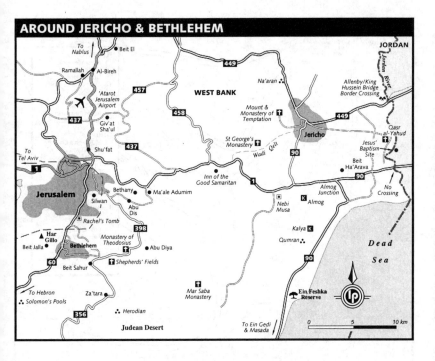

AROUND JERICHO & BETHLEHEM

To Nablus
Beit El
JORDAN
Ramallah Al-Bireh
449
Na'aran
Allenby/King Hussein Bridge Border Crossing
'Atarot Jerusalem Airport
457
WEST BANK
Mount & Monastery of Temptation
458
437
Giv'at Sha'ul
St George's Monastery
Jericho
449
Qasr al-Yahud
To Tel Aviv
437
Shu'fat
Wadi Qelt
90
Jesus' Baptism Site
1
Inn of the Good Samaritan
Beit Ha'Arava
90
Jerusalem
Bethany
Ma'ale Adumim
1
Almog Junction
No Crossing
Silwan
Abu Dis
Nebi Musa
Almog
Rachel's Tomb
398
Kalya
Har Gillo
Monastery of Theodosius
Qumran
Dead Sea
Beit Jalla
Bethlehem
Abu Diya
60
Beit Sahur
Shepherds' Fields
90
Ein Feshka Reserve
To Hebron
Za'tara
Mar Saba Monastery
Solomon's Pools
356
Herodian
0   5   10 km
Judean Desert
To Ein Gedi & Masada

there's no direct public transport running between Qumran, Ein Feshka and Jericho. You can change at the Almog junction, where the turn-off to Jericho intersects with the main road from Jerusalem. The Dead Sea is dealt with in a chapter of its own.

Allenby/King Hussein Bridge

This is the most trafficked crossing between Israel and Jordan. For details see the Land section in the Getting There & Away chapter.

BETHLEHEM   בית לחם بيت لحم
Pop: 21,437 ☎ Area Code: 02
Modern-day Bethlehem may be a cynic's delight, with a Manger Square, Manger St, two Shepherds' Fields, Shepherds' St, Star St and an unheavenly host of 'Christmases', but for most travellers with even the remotest Christian background, a trip to the Holy Land without visiting the site of the

Nativity is unthinkable, even if only to please a pious relative back home.

Happily, the Church of the Nativity, constructed over the accepted birthplace of Jesus, is a suitably august and venerable building which, unlike Jerusalem's Holy Sepulchre or Nazareth's Basilica, manages to avoid the 'holy site as sideshow' feel.

Bethlehem was actually well known long before the arrival of Jesus. Rachel the Matriarch died here (Genesis 35:19) and Ruth and Boaz romanced here (Ruth 1-4) which, down the line, resulted in David, local shepherd and future king of Israel.

Despite being the birthplace of Christ, for almost two centuries after his death, Bethlehem was a centre of paganism. It wasn't until 31 May in the year 339 that the town's first church was dedicated by Queen Helena on the site of the present-day Church of the Nativity.

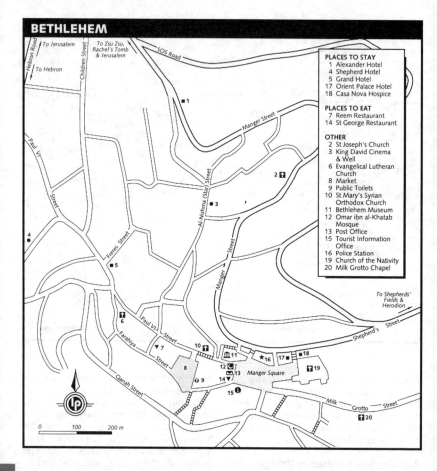

BETHLEHEM

To Jerusalem — Hebron Road

*To Zsu Zsu,
Rachel's Tomb
& Jerusalem*

SOS Road

Children Street

To Hebron

Manger Street

Paul VI Street

Al-Nizhma (Star) Street

Manger Street

Freres Street

Paul VI Street

Farahiya Street

Qanah Street

Shepherd's Street

*To Shepherds'
Fields &
Herodion*

Manger Square

Milk Grotto Street

0   100   200 m

PLACES TO STAY
1 Alexander Hotel
4 Shepherd Hotel
5 Grand Hotel
17 Orient Palace Hotel
18 Casa Nova Hospice

PLACES TO EAT
7 Reem Restaurant
14 St George Restaurant

OTHER
2 St Joseph's Church
3 King David Cinema
& Well
6 Evangelical Lutheran
Church
8 Market
9 Public Toilets
10 St Mary's Syrian
Orthodox Church
11 Bethlehem Museum
12 Omar ibn al-Khatab
Mosque
13 Post Office
15 Tourist Information
Office
16 Police Station
19 Church of the Nativity
20 Milk Grotto Chapel

In keeping with the history of the Holy Land, Bethlehem changed hands many times with a roll call that includes the Romans, Byzantines, Crusaders, Mamluks, Turks, British, Jordanians and Israelis. The most recent handover was in December 1995, when the Palestinians took the reins and at the traditional Christmas Eve gathering in Manger Square, Jesus had to share the billing with Yasser Arafat.

Bethlehem itself is very attractive: the area around central Manger Square has been spruced up especially for the Millennium celebrations, and the area around the souq is definetly worth exploring. It's also possible to take some excellent excursions to places situated just outside the town. The Mar Saba Monastery, for example, is in a stunning desert location, while the Herodian – the intriguing palace complex of Herod the Great – sits atop a volcano-like peak with outstanding views of the surrounding landscape. Other good day trips include Ruth's Field and Shepherd's Field.

Orientation

Manger Square, with the Church of the Nativity on its southern side, is the centre of town. At the time of research renovations to the square (a joint Palestinian-Swedish project) were not complete, but they should be finished by the time this book goes to print. Around the square are the tourist information office, police station, post office and various shops, hotels and eating places. Milk Grotto St heads off to the south-east, down past the Milk Grotto Chapel, while Paul VI St, which heads uphill to the northwest, has the museum, outdoor market and more shops and hotels.

Manger St, which comes off the northern side of the square, is the main, winding route through the new town. It eventually intersects with the Jerusalem-Hebron highway opposite the Jewish shrine of Rachel's Tomb.

Information

The Palestinian-run local tourist information office (☎ 274 1581) is on the western side of Manger Square. It's open Saturday to Thursday from 9 am to noon and 2.30 to 4 pm, closed Friday. During Ramadan the hours are Saturday to Thursday from 9 am to 2.30 pm and closed on Friday.

Next door to the tourist information office is the post office, open Monday to Saturday from 8 am to 5 pm, and closed on Sunday. During Ramadan the hours are Monday to Thursday and Saturday from 9 am to 3 pm, closed Friday and Sunday.

The town's banks are also on the square and there are moneychangers on Paul VI St.

Church of the Nativity

Built like a citadel over the cave where it's believed that Jesus was born, this is one of the world's oldest working churches. The original 4th century church commissioned by Emperor Constantine was altered considerably around 530 AD by Emperor Justinian, whose aim was to create a shrine that would overshadow all others, including those of Jerusalem. Apart from the roof and the floor, which have both been replaced

Battle of Bethlehem

While the Greek Orthodox, the Armenians and the Roman Catholics are united in a shared set of central beliefs, the equitable shared possession of the Church of the Nativity has proved completely beyond them. Territorial claims are zealously guarded and something as seemingly insignificant as the moving of a rug by a few centimetres has in the past resulted in blood being spilt. To this day the Greek Orthodox-controlled Grotto of the Nativity is still blocked off by a thick steel door employed to keep out the Catholics.

In recent years, the most talked about dispute has been between the Greek Orthodox and the Armenians. The Armenians object to the Orthodox priests perching on a particular 'Armenian' beam while sweeping above the entrance to the grotto. Matters have tended to come to a head on 29 December, the 'Annual General Cleaning Day'. In 1984 there were violent clashes as Greek and Armenian clergy fought running battles with staves and chains that had been hidden beneath their robes. Amid accusations and counter accusations of bully boys being hired for the day to take part in the violence, the Jewish authorities frantically tried to find a diplomatic solution.

In the end the Greek Orthodox were required to do their sweeping without stepping on the Armenian's beam. The result was far from well received by the Greek Patriarch, who penned a stiff letter of protest to the Israeli authorities.

several times, the basic structure of Justinian's church survives until today.

On 6 June 1099, the Crusaders captured the church, a major prize. They crowned their kings here and between 1165 and 1169 embarked on a major restoration program, renewing the interior decoration and replacing the roof. Under Saladin (Salah ad-Din) the church was respectfully preserved,

CHURCH OF THE NATIVITY

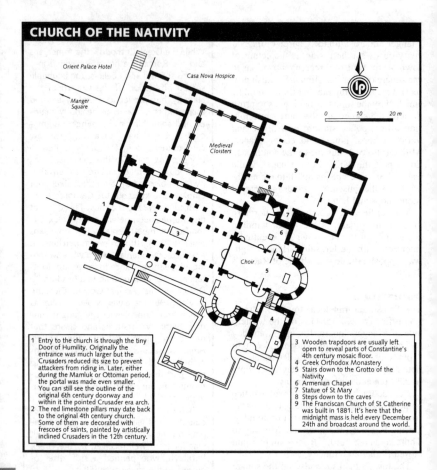

Orient Palace Hotel

Casa Nova Hospice

Manger Square

Medieval Cloisters

0   10   20 m

Choir

1 Entry to the church is through the tiny Door of Humility. Originally the entrance was much larger but the Crusaders reduced its size to prevent attackers from riding in. Later, either during the Mamluk or Ottoman period, the portal was made even smaller. You can still see the outline of the original 6th century doorway and within it the pointed Crusader era arch.
2 The red limestone pillars may date back to the original 4th century church. Some of them are decorated with frescoes of saints, painted by artistically inclined Crusaders in the 12th century.

3 Wooden trapdoors are usually left open to reveal parts of Constantine's 4th century mosaic floor.
4 Greek Orthodox Monastery
5 Stairs down to the Grotto of the Nativity
6 Armenian Chapel
7 Statue of St Mary
8 Steps down to the caves
9 The Franciscan Church of St Catherine was built in 1881. It's here that the midnight mass is held every December 24th and broadcast around the world.

but with his defeat by the Mamluks in the 13th century began a long period of abuse and neglect. Infrequent repairs and systematic looting, along with an earthquake in 1834 and a fire in 1869 that destroyed the cave's furnishings, all took their toll.

During winter, the church is open to visitors daily from 8 am to 5 pm (7 am to 6 pm in summer), and admission is free. The adjoining Church of St Catherine and the underground caves are closed daily from noon to 2 pm. You must wear suitably modest attire before entering the churches (no shorts or short sleeves) and be on the constant lookout for the rip-off artists standing by the church entrance who provide you with *kufeyyas* (chequered scarves) to cover your offending flesh and then seek to extort 30NIS or more from you for the 'rental' when you exit.

Milk Grotto Chapel

Tradition has it that on their way to Egypt the Holy Family took shelter at this Fran-

GROTTO OF THE NATIVITY

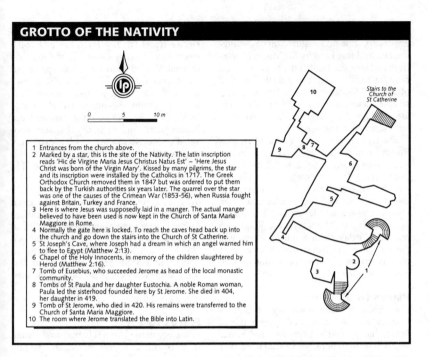

1 Entrances from the church above.
2 Marked by a star, this is the site of the Nativity. The latin inscription reads 'Hic de Virgine Maria Jesus Christus Natus Est' – 'Here Jesus Christ was born of the Virgin Mary'. Kissed by many pilgrims, the star and its inscription were installed by the Catholics in 1717. The Greek Orthodox Church removed them in 1847 but was ordered to put them back by the Turkish authorities six years later. The quarrel over the star was one of the causes of the Crimean War (1853-56), when Russia fought against Britain, Turkey and France.
3 Here is where Jesus was supposedly laid in a manger. The actual manger believed to have been used is now kept in the Church of Santa Maria Maggiore in Rome.
4 Normally the gate here is locked. To reach the caves head back up into the church and go down the stairs into the Church of St Catherine.
5 St Joseph's Cave, where Joseph had a dream in which an angel warned him to flee to Egypt (Matthew 2:13).
6 Chapel of the Holy Innocents, in memory of the children slaughtered by Herod (Matthew 2:16).
7 Tomb of Eusebius, who succeeded Jerome as head of the local monastic community.
8 Tombs of St Paula and her daughter Eustochia. A noble Roman woman, Paula led the sisterhood founded here by St Jerome. She died in 404, her daughter in 419.
9 Tomb of St Jerome, who died in 420. His remains were transferred to the Church of Santa Maria Maggiore.
10 The room where Jerome translated the Bible into Latin.

ciscan chapel. While Mary was breast-feeding her baby, so the story goes, some of the milk dripped to the floor, causing the rock out of which the cavern is built to turn chalky white. Women come here to pray in the belief that the white stone helps their lactation, and packets of the powdered stone are sold to pilgrims. The chapel – with a suitably kitsch entrance – is a few minutes walk from the square along Milk Grotto St. It's open daily from 8 to 11.45 am and 2 to 4.30 pm. Admission is free; for attention, ring the bell in the courtyard.

Bethlehem Museum

On Paul VI St, just up from Manger Square and on the northern side, this small museum has exhibits of traditional Palestinian crafts and costumes. It's open Monday to Saturday from 10 am to noon and 2.30 to 5.30 pm; it's closed Sunday. Admission is 5NIS.

King David Cinema & King David's Well

On Star St, about half a kilometre north of Manger Square, the King David Cinema presents a film, *Jesus*, which is a virtual word-for-word dramatisation of Luke's gospel. Poorly acted and directed, the film isn't as wonderful an experience as the Christian organisation responsible for it would have you believe.

Even more of a nonevent are the three restored water cisterns in the car park outside the cinema. They are associated with II Samuel 23:13-17, which relates the tale of the thirsty David offering the water to God as a sacrifice.

Rachel's Tomb

One of Judaism's most sacred shrines, also revered by Muslims and Christians, this is the tomb of the matriarch Rachel, wife of

Jacob and mother of Benjamin (Genesis 35:19-20). Located inside a plain, white-washed building built by Sir Moses Monte-fiore in 1860, the tomb attracts people who pray for fertility and a safe birth. You will often find Sephardic Jewish women here weeping and praying – although the sexes are segregated by a screen and have their own separate entrances.

The tomb is at the intersection of Hebron Rd and Manger St, which is a 30 minute walk from Manger Square. All buses between Jerusalem, Bethlehem and Hebron pass by. Alternatively, it's easy enough to flag down a service taxi to take you down into town or north to Jerusalem. The tomb's open Sunday to Thursday from 8 am to 5 pm, and Friday from 8 am to 1 pm, and closed Saturday. Admission is free; men must cover their heads, and cardboard kippas are provided.

Places to Stay

The choice of accommodation in Bethlehem is somewhat limited (some things never change) and at Christmas and Easter you will need to book well ahead to be sure of somewhere to stay. Most people prefer to stay in Jerusalem, with its wider choice and, often, lower prices.

Part of the Church of the Nativity complex is the recently renovated Franciscan *Casa Nova Hospice* (☎ 274 3981, fax 274 3540). This lovely place is the nicest looking in town but you will often have to deal with the holy bureaucracy of the staff to get in. Great facilities and good food make it worth the effort. It costs US$20 for B&B, US$25 for half-board, US$30 for full-board. There's also a 5% service charge. Curfew is at 11 pm. You can also get a decent meal at the hospice restaurant, which is open to the public, for US$8 per person.

Just down from the Church of the Nativity, the *Orient Palace Hotel* (☎ 277 7766, fax 274 1562), built by the Greek Orthodox, has been well renovated in time for 2000 and charges US$80/100 for singles/doubles.

You may have to resort to the hotels among the narrow streets to the north-west

of Manger Square, off Paul VI St. The large *Grand Hotel* (☎ 274 1603, fax 274 1604, email bandaks@p-ol.com), at the junction of Paul VI and Freres Sts, has sparse but clean singles/doubles for US$45/70 including breakfast. The hotel also sports a Mexican restaurant. *Shepherd Hotel* (☎ 274 0656, fax 274 4488), on Jamal abd en-Nasser St, off Paul VI St, has also been renovated to four star rating and has extremely comfortable singles/doubles for US$50/90 (breakfast extra). You need to book well in advance for Christmas and Easter.

Alexander Hotel (☎ 277 0780, fax 277 0782) is a great hotel with an enthusiastic owner called Joseph. It's tastefully furnished rooms have a great view over the valley at the back of the hotel; singles cost between US$40 and US$55 and doubles between US$50 and US$85. Smart-looking four-person apartments were being built at the time of inspection and will go for US$105 – a pretty good deal.

Places to Eat

While accommodation is hard to find, eating in Bethlehem, which means in Hebrew 'House of Bread' *(Beit Lechem)* and in Arabic 'House of Meat' *(Beit Lahem)*, should not be a problem. There are no outstanding restaurants but there are plenty of felafel and mixed grill merchants competing around Manger Square. *Reem Restaurant*, down the side street past the bakery on Paul VI St, is inexpensive with humous and other salads for about 14NIS

One of the better meat restaurants anywhere is *Zsu Zsu*, next to the Nissan Store on Manger St, just down from Rachel's Tomb. Named after the extrovert proprietor, it serves up some of the tastiest shashlik and kebabs you're likely to find in this area. Expect to spend 30 to 40NIS per person.

On the newly renovated Manger Square the smart-looking *St George Restaurant* (☎ 274 1833) is essentially a big tourist trap set up for large groups. Still, as an individual you can probably sneak into a corner and dine on a presentable main dish for around 35NIS.

Getting There & Away

Arab bus No 22 runs frequently from East Jerusalem and stops outside Jaffa Gate en route. It's about a 40 minute ride. Service taxis (costing 3NIS) from outside Damascus Gate are more convenient; they tend to depart more frequently and make the journey in half the bus time. The last bus leaves Bethlehem at about 6 pm; service taxis can be found after this time but you may have to pay more to cover the lack of passengers.

Jerusalem and Bethlehem are close together, and walking between the two is a popular option. At Christmas there's an official procession, but the two to 2½ hour, up and downhill-all-the-way hike will be shared with often heavy traffic. Follow Hebron Rd out past the Jerusalem railway station and eventually you will emerge into the countryside. Once past the Greek Orthodox Elias Monastery, you'll see Bethlehem ahead of you.

AROUND BETHLEHEM
Beit Jalla, Gillo & Cremisan

Past Rachel's Tomb in the direction of Hebron, a road heads west up the hill to the pleasant Christian Arab village of Beit Jalla. The road continues to the summit of Har Gillo, believed to be biblical Gillo, the home of King David's counsellor, Anhithophel. With great views of Jerusalem this is a popular picnic site. Back down the slope, a side road leads to the attractive Salesian monastery of Cremisan (☎ 274 2605), renowned for its wine and olive oil.

Getting There & Away Arab bus No 21 runs from Jerusalem to Beit Jalla. From here it is a steep walk to either the summit or the monastery.

Ruth's Field & Shepherds' Fields

The village of Beit Sahur is 1km east of Bethlehem. Nearby is Ruth's Field, traditionally associated with the events of the Old Testament Book of Ruth. In Hebrew, Beit Sahur means 'Village of the Watching'.

Not to be outdone, the Roman Catholics and the Greek Orthodox each have their own Shepherds' Field associated with the shepherds mentioned in Luke 2:8-18. The Roman Catholic site features a Franciscan chapel built in 1954, designed to resemble a shepherd's tent. There are ruins of a Byzantine monastery nearby, destroyed by the Persians in 614.

The Greek Orthodox site features a 5th century church built over a cave with a mosaic floor. Often closed, there is an admission fee of 8NIS when the caretaker is there to let you in.

Getting There & Away Arab bus No 47 leaves from Manger St by the police station for Beit Sahur. The respective fields are about a 20 minute walk further east from the village, beyond the fork in the road. Take the right fork for the Greek Orthodox field, left for the Roman Catholic.

Alternatively, you can walk the 4km from Bethlehem.

Mar Saba Monastery

Splendid architecture and a superb location combine to make this Greek Orthodox monastery one of the most impressive buildings in the Holy Land. Unfortunately, it's strictly closed to women but it is worth a visit if only to view the exterior.

The monastery is on the steep bank of the Kidron River in the proverbial middle of nowhere, which in this case is the Judean Desert. Unless you have your own car, you will have to walk the 8km from where the bus stops in the village of Abu Diya.

Just before the last stop there is another monastery. Overlooking Abu Diya, the large **Monastery of Theodosius**, or Deir Dosi, is built over a cave where the three wise men supposedly rested on their way home from Bethlehem. This monastery was founded by St Theodosius and accommodated 400 monks by the time he died in 529. The monastery was restored in 1893. There is little to see anyway; some 7th century mosaics and skulls of monks massacred by Persians are stored underground.

Mar Saba Monastery was founded in 482 by St Sabas (439-532). He had been living in a cave (look for the cross and letters A and C on the opposite side of the wadi), but with an increasing number of disciples he needed more room. The Persians massacred the occupants in 614 but the monastery managed to continue, with its 'golden age' occurring in the 8th and 9th centuries. However, until as recently as the 19th century the monks were still subjected to hostility, occasionally resulting in murderous attacks. After an earthquake in 1834 caused considerable damage the buildings were almost completely reconstructed, hence their impressive appearance today.

The body of St Sabas is displayed in the main church. It had been removed by the Crusaders but was returned by Pope Paul VI in 1965. More skulls of monks massacred by the Persians can also be seen. The adjacent **Tower of St Simeon** (1612) is sometimes open to women and a path runs past here down into the wadi, which is rather smelly (courtesy of the Jerusalemites who use the river as a sewer). You should make a point of crossing over to the other side for the superb view of the monastery. It is mainly this that makes the hot hike worthwhile. There were some 5000 men living over here in the caves before the monastery was built.

To enter the monastery, pull the bell chain by the blue door. To enter, you must be suitably dressed (and of acceptable sex) – with the heat it's best to bring long pants to slip over shorts on arrival. There are no set opening hours and the monks will normally let you in. However, on Sunday and at meal times your rings may be ignored. Saturday is quite busy with an influx of other visitors, so a morning visit during the week is best.

Getting There & Away Take Arab bus No 60 from Bethlehem bus station to Abu Diya, the last stop, or get off by the Monastery of Theodosius. The last bus back to Bethlehem leaves Abu Diya at about 4 pm. From here follow the road east. After 1km it forks; take the left branch. You will be hassled by children demanding baksheesh until you leave the outskirts of the village. The 6km walk takes 1½ to two hours

each way. Bring plenty of water – you can get a refill from the monastery for the return. Hitching is possible, although there is little traffic, and you will be especially grateful of a ride for the steep climb back from the monastery.

Herodian
Built by Herod the Great between 24 and 15 BC, the Herodian palace complex occupies the top of a hill reshaped as part of the construction program. About 100m above the surrounding area and looking rather like a volcano, it offers more great views and the remains of the citadel.

A lavish and luxurious place in its day, a stairway of white marble led up to the ring of round towers enclosing apartments, baths and a garden. It is not certain whether Herod was buried here as he had instructed. During the First Revolt (66-70 AD), the Jewish rebels attacked the Herodian and sheltered here. During the Second Revolt (132-35), they used it as an administrative centre. In the 5th century, Byzantine monks established a monastery among the ruins.

It's open Saturday to Thursday from 7.30 am to 6 pm, and Friday from 7.30 am to 5 pm; admission is 11NIS (students 7NIS).

Getting There & Away The Bethlehem tourist information office often seems to indicate that you can only reach the Herodian by taxi. Although infrequent, there are buses that can drop you near the site. Ask a few locals and use the most popular answer to determine which bus and when. We have used bus Nos 52 and 47 from Manger St to Beit Sahur and changed there. Egged bus No 66 also stops nearby.

Another alternative is simply to walk and hitch. The Herodian stands about 8km south of Beit Sahur – take the right fork past the Greek Orthodox Shepherds' Field.

BETHLEHEM TO HEBRON
Solomon's Pools
Eight kilometres south of Beit Jalla, a turnoff to the east leads to these large reservoirs and a Turkish fort. The trees and

shrubs help to make this a popular picnic site and there is a cafe here.

Legend associates the pools with Solomon (Ecclesiastes 2:6); others date them to Herod. The aqueducts supplied Jerusalem with water right up to the early years of the State of Israel. The fort (circa 1540) was built to defend the water supply.

Getting There & Away From Manger St, Bethlehem, take Arab minibus No 1 to Dashit, the nearby Arab village. You could also take Arab bus No 23 or one of the Egged buses which operate between Jerusalem and Hebron.

Kfar Etzion
Continuing south to Hebron, after 7km a side road to the right leads to Kfar Etzion, a religious kibbutz. First established by religious Zionists in 1943, it was destroyed by the Arabs in the 1948 War and most of the settlers were killed. In 1967 the settlement was re-established, with some of the new settlers being the children of those killed almost 20 years before.

There is a museum here highlighting the history of Jewish settlement in the Etzion region, which is the Judean hills between Jerusalem and Hebron.

Frequent Egged buses from Jerusalem go to the kibbutz.

Halhoul
Just outside Hebron, the main road passes through the small Arab village of Halhoul. The Tombs of Nathan and Gad (I Chronicles 29:29) are here.

HEBRON   חברון   لخليل
Pop: 119,230 ☎ Area Code: 02
At the time of writing, Hebron was continuing to be the place of greatest unrest within the disputed territories. A visitor to the majority of other West Bank towns is rarely made aware of the simmering hostilities underlying daily life, but here the proliferation of guns and concrete barricades, and the wary manner in which Palestinians and Jewish settlers passing on the street watch

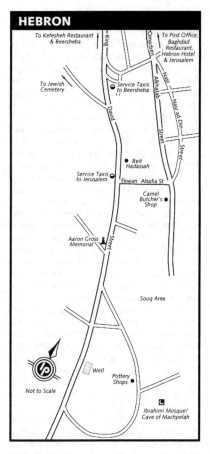

each other, are highly visible and unnerving reminders of the explosive nature of Hebron.

The dispute has its origins in Abraham (or in Arabic, Ibrahim), who made a covenant with God (Genesis 17) and also purchased the Cave of Machpelah from Ephron the Hittite (Genesis 23) as a burial place for his wife Sarah. When Abraham died, his sons Ishmael and Isaac buried him beside his wife. Later, Isaac and his wife Rebecca and Jacob and his wife Leah were all also entombed in the cave (Genesis 49:29-32, 50:7-9, 12-14).

The site became sacred to Jews and, following the 7th century sweep of Islamicism, to Muslims also. A mosque (today's Ibrahimi Mosque) was built over the cave but the Arabs and Jews coexisted and worshipped in relative peace. This state of affairs began to deteriorate in the late 19th century with the advent of political Zionism. Hebron's Jewish population began to become swollen with the arrival of immigrants from Eastern Europe and the Arabs reacted with fierce rioting. A large number of Jews were killed and the survivors were forced to flee the city for Jerusalem.

On the heels of Israeli successes in the Six Day War, the more extreme factions were keen to re-establish a Jewish presence in wholly Arab Hebron. Such an inflammatory idea alarmed the majority of moderate Israelis and the government was moved to put a ban on the establishment of Jewish settlements in Hebron. This did nothing to dampen the ardour of the extremists and, in 1972, with reluctant official agreement, they established Kiryat Arba, a large settlement right on the edge of Hebron, just 1km from the Cave of Machpelah. Since then, the settlers have advanced into the centre of the town itself, taking possession of a street in what used to be the old Jewish quarter.

Blatantly provocative, the 400 strong Hebron settler community has gone on record saying that it's their desire to see the Arabs driven out of Hebron. As protection from the overwhelming majority of Palestinians among whom they live, the settlers are guarded by some 2500 Israeli soldiers and police with numerous roadblocks, checkpoints and concrete barricades. The town centre has effectively been choked; the vegetable market has been closed and many shops have gone out of business, their customers have been scared away by their fear of gun-toting soldiers and settlers.

The situation shows no signs of an easy solution. Despite the apparent progress of the peace process, the streets of Hebron

have been the stage for a series of particularly unpleasant confrontations, resulting in a number of deaths. While the Ibrahimi Mosque and old market quarter are well worth seeing, call your embassy for details on the current situation. Go, but be careful.

Orientation & Information

The main areas of interest are within easy walking distance of each other and of the bus stops and taxi ranks. The bus or service taxi will drop you off on King David St on the northern edge of the market. Heading down through the market, directly south, brings you to the Ibrahimi Mosque.

Bearing in mind the political climate and the religious traditions of Hebron, visitors should act and dress sensibly. It is important that while wandering around the Old Town you look as touristy (ie non-Jewish) as you possibly can.

The Ibrahimi Mosque (Cave of Machpelah)

To Jews the site of the Cave of Machpelah is second only to Jerusalem's Western Wall, while to Muslims, of all the Holy Land shrines, only the Dome of the Rock is more venerated.

The cave was purchased by Abraham when, according to tradition, he learnt through divine inspiration that Adam and Eve were buried here. In time he, his wife, his sons and their wives (except Ruth) joined them. Around 20 BC, Herod the Great sealed off the cave and built above it the *haram* (enclosure), with a great hall known as the Hall of Isaac. The huge chiselled Herodian stones are still there as part of the wall on the exterior staircase leading up to the Muslim entrance.

In the late 6th century a Byzantine church was built, enclosing Herod's Hall of Isaac, and the Jews were permitted to build an adjacent synagogue. With the 7th century Arab conquest, the Christians were driven out and their church became a mosque but the Jews and their synagogue were allowed to stay. The Crusaders turned the tables for a while but the Mamluks settled matters for

IBRAHIMI MOSQUE (CAVE OF MACHPELAH)

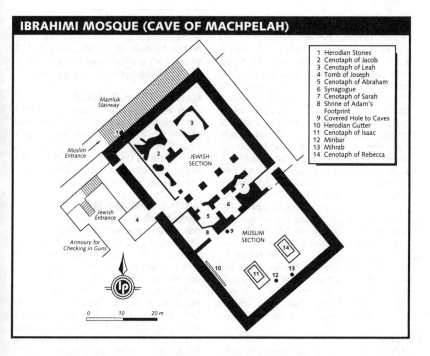

1 Herodian Stones
2 Cenotaph of Jacob
3 Cenotaph of Leah
4 Tomb of Joseph
5 Cenotaph of Abraham
6 Synagogue
7 Cenotaph of Sarah
8 Shrine of Adam's Footprint
9 Covered Hole to Caves
10 Herodian Gutter
11 Cenotaph of Isaac
12 Minbar
13 Mihrab
14 Cenotaph of Rebecca

Mamluk Stairway

Muslim Entrance

JEWISH SECTION

Jewish Entrance

Armoury for Checking in Guns

MUSLIM SECTION

0   10   20 m

good, driving the Christian knights out of town and building a new mosque on the site.

The Mamluks added the cenotaphs of Joseph, Jacob and Leah (those of Abraham and Sarah date to the 9th century), none of which represent the true location of the tombs, which are somewhere in the caves beneath. The walls of the former Hall of Isaac, now the main prayer hall of the mosque, are decorated in typical Mamluk fashion, inset with various coloured marble. Beside the *mihrab* (prayer niche) is a sumptuously carved and lapis-inlaid *minbar* (pulpit), donated by Saladin in 1191. The small room off the north-western corner includes a small shrine where, legend has it, Adam prayed so much that his foot left a mark in the stone.

The Arabs forbade Jews entry to the tombs and former synagogue, now encased within the mosque, a situation which was only changed when the Israelis took Hebron in the 1967 War. Under the terms of the surrender agreement the administration of the shrine remained under Muslim control but with equal Jewish access permitted. As fair-minded as this arrangement may seem, it ultimately led to bloody tragedy when on 25 February 1994 Baruch Goldstein, a Jewish settler, stepped through the green doors of the mosque and opened fire on the Muslims as they knelt with their backs to him in prayer; 29 were killed.

Since then the mosque has been segregated into separate Muslim and Jewish sections, each with its own entrance. Security is tight and visitors will be brusquely frisked and questioned before being allowed entry. The site is open to visitors Sunday to Thursday from 8 am to 4 pm; it's closed on Friday and Saturday.

Jewish Community of Hebron

In 1979 Miriam Levinger, mother of 11 and one of the original Jewish settlers, led a group of women and children from Kiryat Arba into the city and illegally occupied the rundown Beit Hadassah, Hebron's old Hadassah Hospital in the ruined Jewish quarter. They refused to leave, and their eight-month 'sit-in' succeeded in securing official permission for Jews to live in Beit Hadassah, a decision that eventually led to Jewish settlement in Hebron proper being allowed. These events were surrounded by much controversy and tragic violence, highlighted by the murder of six yeshiva students by Arabs in 1980 and revenge attacks by Jewish terrorists, whose subsequent capture and imprisonment did nothing to calm either side.

The Beit Hadassah complex of apartments and offices is on King David St, blocked off on either end by heavily armed security posts. Although there is a small museum of the Jewish Community of Hebron, it's not a good idea to visit if you are then going to be walking around town.

Souq

Hebron's souq is a compendium of marvellous Crusader and Mamluk facades, vaulted ceilings, tiny shops and narrow alleyways. Despite the tensions in the city, it's still fairly lively first thing in a morning. Among the most unusual/revolting things to see/avoid is the butcher's shop selling camel meat. The 'ship of the desert' can be seen moored to a meat hook, with that expression of nonchalance still on its face, hanging upside down while its intestines and feet are arranged on the shop floor.

Places to Stay & Eat

Should you decide to make a night of it in Hebron, your only accommodation option is *Hebron Hotel* (*☎/fax 992 6760*) on Al-Malik Feisal St near the town hall. It's modern and very pleasant and singles/doubles go for US$50/60.

There are the usual felafel and shwarma stands around the market and Bab al-Zawiya, but for something a little more sub-stantial try *Baghdad Restaurant* on Al-Malik Feisal St open most of the day, or *Kefesheh Restaurant* on Wadi al-Tufeah St which does a wide range of meat dishes. The soups are reputedly very good too.

Getting There & Away

There are no longer any direct buses to Hebron from Jerusalem so you will have to use one of the frequent service taxis (5NIS) from Damascus Gate. Heading back you can still take a taxi, or opt for a bus to Ramallah or Bethlehem and look for onward connections from those towns.

AROUND HEBRON
Kiryat Arba
Pop: 5,000 ☎ Area Code: 09

The name of this controversial Jewish settlement just north of the Hebron city centre means 'Town of the Four', referring to the four couples who are believed to be buried in Hebron: Adam and Eve, Abraham and Sarah, Isaac and Rebecca, and Jacob and Leah. There is little for the visitor to see here except the contrast between the crowded city and the settlement's modern apartment blocks, wide streets and gardens behind a barbed-wire perimeter.

Nearby, an unfinished mosque symbolises the tensions in and around Hebron. Beautifully designed, its construction was halted by the Israelis who believed that the main reason for a new mosque in an area with few Muslims would be to encourage Arabs to move closer to Kiryat Arba, thus creating a new round of potentially violent confrontations with Jewish settlers. However, if avoiding possible friction is the aim, the Israelis seem to have developed something of a blind spot in regard to Kiryat Arba's creation of a shrine to Baruch Goldstein, perpetrator of the Ibrahimi Mosque massacre and popular settler hero.

Oak of Abraham

An oak tree 2km west of Hebron marks the legendary site where Abraham pitched his tent (Genesis 18:1). Pilgrims through the ages have removed pieces from the tree for good luck charms, and in an ill-conceived attempt to thwart this habit the trunk is wrapped with rusted steel braces and wire, and studded with nails. The irony is that scientific tests have proved that the tree is in reality no more than 600 years old.

The Russian Orthodox Church owns the site and its monastery is nearby.

JERUSALEM TO RAMALLAH

Heading north out of Jerusalem, the highway crests Mt Scopus before descending to the village of Shu'fat. Across to the west, with the mountains in the distance, you can see Samuel's Tomb just above the modern suburban developments. In the Middle Ages, Jews came here for solemn religious celebrations and it's the vantage point from where the Crusaders had their first glimpse of Jerusalem – they named the spot Mt Joy.

Shu'fat is also the site of biblical Gilbeah, Saul's capital. It was for most of this century a cool summer retreat for wealthy Arabs; King Hussein of Jordan started to build a villa here, but its construction was interrupted by the Six Day War – the building is now used by the IDF.

Al-Bireh

After passing Jerusalem airport and Tel Nashe (biblical Mizpeh), you drive under the 'Welcome to Al-Bireh' archway just north of Ramallah, and 14km north of Jerusalem. Although there is little to see in this relatively affluent Arab suburb, one point of interest is the headquarters of the Inash al-Usra Society.

Inash al-Usra Society Established in 1965, this organisation was set up with the aim of improving the lot of Palestinian women by setting up vocational training centres, sponsoring students and initiating numerous other beneficial schemes. A spin-off of the society's work that may interest travellers is their promotion of Palestinian culture. The Folklore & Research Centre was initiated in 1972 with the aim of preserving, studying and developing Palestinian folklore and it produces journals and

books, stages folkloric festivals and has put together a museum open to the public.

For further information and to arrange a visit to the society's headquarters and museum, contact the Inash al-Usra Society (☎ 952 876/544), Al-Bireh, PO Box 3549, West Bank. The most convenient way of getting there is to take a special taxi from Ramallah (about 12NIS).

RAMALLAH رام الله
Pop: 18,300 ☎ Area Code: 02

Arabic for 'Heights of the Lord', Ramallah and its environs are among the more affluent areas of the West Bank region. Before the Israeli occupation the area was a summer resort popular with wealthy Jordanians wanting to escape the heat of Amman.

Although there are no real sights in Ramallah, it's a pleasant place to walk around and, for those who are put off by the political tensions in Hebron or Nablus, it's a safe experience of a Palestinian West Bank town. Don't be surprised to find yourself approached by locals full of questions about where you're from and what you're doing in their town – they don't see many 'tourists'. Ramallah now has plenty of places to stay and eat, and you may well find it an ideal place to base yourself in while you are visiting the West Bank.

Next to the bus station is the small market, with the Abu Nasser Mosque nearby; non-Muslims are not allowed to enter.

Places to Stay

New hotels are being built and the existing ones run the gamut from adequate to excellent. *Al-Wihdeh Hotel (☎ 295 6452, fax 298 0412, 26 Al-Nadah St)* has been refurbished and is now a bright and fresh-looking place to stay. This hotel has a friendly and relaxed atmosphere and no curfew. Prices for breezy well-equipped single/double rooms are 80/100NIS, and breakfast is 10NIS extra. A selection of food and drinks (including alcoholic drinks) are available in the communal lounge.

The Miami Pension (☎ 295 6808, fax 295 5874, Jaffa St) has decent rooms with bathroom, TV and phone. The room rates are 130/170NIS for singles/doubles including breakfast. The Italian restaurant attached to the hotel gets good reviews. *Al-Hajal Hotel* (☎ 298 7858, fax 295 6217, Lutheran St) is not the friendliest place but has singles/doubles for 150/190NIS including breakfast. All rooms have a bathroom, TV and phone and there is a communal lounge area and kitchen.

Nearby, *Plaza Hotel* (☎ 995 6020, Jaffa St) has similarly decent single/double rooms for 60/120NIS and there are attractive outdoor and indoor restaurants serving a variety of western and Arabic food in a beautiful flower filled environment.

Ramallah Hotel (☎ 295 2559, fax 295 5029) is sufficient distance from town to justify a taxi ride. Well-appointed rooms with cable TV, phone and bar fridge are US$55 to US$70 for singles and US$65 to US$85 for doubles (breakfast included); the honeymoon suite is US$150. The hotel also runs a travel agency that can assist you with your touring plans.

Grand Park Hotel & Resort (☎ 298 6194, fax 295 6950) is even further out. It's plusher and, naturally, more expensive, charging US$125/155 for singles/doubles.

Places to Eat

Ramallah has seen something of a restaurant boom since the darker days of the Intifada, with more than 20 eating places for the visitor to choose from. Among those that you might want to check out are *Muntaza* (☎ 295 6835, Jaffa St), an outdoor park-restaurant catering mainly to family groups and serving snacks and popular western and Arabic meals. *Palnet@K5M* (☎ 295 6813, email K5M@palnet.com, Rokab St) is Palestine's first Internet Cafe and is also a restaurant serving up cheap pizzas, pastas and burgers. It is near the Catholic church.

Maroush (☎ 050-587 943, Manara St) is a trendy European-style restaurant with a European-Arab mixed cuisine and an outdoor section for summer evenings. Prices are mid-range.

Bardounis (☎ 295 1410, Jaffa St) is a somewhat more expensive joint specialising in *mezze* dishes and buffets, while *Flamingo's* (☎ 298 5813, 69 Al-Ahlyah St) is a trendy bar/restaurant with decor featuring neon flamingos and flamingo tiles. The menu serves a mixture of Mexican, American and Arabic food. Try the chicken fajitas, the nachos and the buffalo wings.

Angelo's (☎ 295 6408, Rokab St) is a long-standing Ramallah favourite, specialising in pizzas and other Italian dishes and favoured by Ramallah's international community. It also does vegetarian lasagne and vegetarian soups.

Getting There & Away

Arab bus No 18 runs from the Nablus Rd bus station in East Jerusalem and takes about 40 minutes. The service taxis from opposite Damascus Gate take only 10 minutes. The last bus leaves Ramallah for Jerusalem at about 6 pm, while service taxis operate until about 9 pm.

RAMALLAH TO NABLUS

On the road heading to Nablus, you will pass by **Beit El**. This is the biblical Bethel (House of God), the site of Jacob's dream about a ladder (Genesis 28:10-17), as well as the home of Deborah (Judges 4:4-6). There is a hill called Jacob's Ladder but it's unremarkable and completely indistinguishable from any of the other hills in the vicinity.

Continuing north, you come to the Arab village of **Sinjil**. The name comes from the original Crusader settlement here, called St Giles. After 5km you come to the sparse ruins of ancient **Shiloh** (Seilun). It was here that the Tabernacle and the Holy Ark rested before the conquest of Jerusalem (Joshua 18:1-9, I Samuel 1:3, I Samuel 4, Jeremiah 7:12, Psalm 78:60).

NABLUS   شכם نابلس
Pop: 100,396   ☎ Area Code: 09
Beautifully situated between the scenic mountains of Gerizim and Ebal, Nablus is the largest of the West Bank towns. It's the

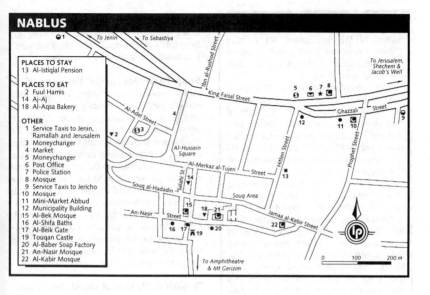

NABLUS

PLACES TO STAY
13 Al-Istiqlal Pension

PLACES TO EAT
2 Fuul Hamis
14 Aj-Aj
18 Al-Aqsa Bakery

OTHER
1 Service Taxis to Jenin,
  Ramallah and Jerusalem
3 Moneychanger
4 Market
5 Moneychanger
6 Post Office
7 Police Station
8 Mosque
9 Service Taxis to Jericho
10 Mosque
11 Mini-Market Abbud
12 Municipality Building
15 Al-Bek Mosque
16 Al-Shifa Baths
17 Al-Beik Gate
19 Touqan Castle
20 Al-Baber Soap Factory
21 An-Nasir Mosque
22 Al-Kabir Mosque

modern-day incarnation of another of the world's oldest towns, Shechem, which was first settled around 4500-3100 BC by Chalcolithic people. It was in Shechem that Abraham received the promise of the Land of Israel (Genesis 12:6-7), that Jacob purchased a field (Genesis 33:18-19), Joshua gathered his people to renew their covenant (Joshua 8:30-35, 24:1-29), and Joseph was buried (Joshua 24:32). The traditional site of ancient Shechem lies to the east of the Arab town of Nablus, and it derives its name from Flavia Neapolis, the Roman colony built here in 72 AD (note that the State of Israel persists in referring to modern-day Nablus by its biblical name of Shechem).

Nablus has become one of the main Palestinian centres of industry and commerce, with numerous soap factories, goldsmiths and a busy souq selling the produce of local farmers. It is a typical bustling Arab town, quite attractive with its breeze-block houses tumbling down the mountain sides and an enchanting old quarter. Situated only an hour away from Jerusalem, it's well worth a day visit.

Orientation & Information

The centre of Nablus is Palestine/Al-Hussein Square, home to a small market and the terminal for many buses and service taxis. Just south of the square is the Old Town, which stretches to the east along An-Nasir St. Beyond the Old Town rise the slopes of Mt Gerizim, considered a holy site to the Samaritans, while Mt Ebal stands to the north.

On the eastern outskirts of Nablus, about 3km from the town centre, is the site of ancient Shechem (Tel Balata), with Jacob's Well and Joseph's Tomb.

Being predominantly Muslim, the markets, shops and businesses are closed on Friday afternoon. Saturday is a particularly busy day, with crowds of Arabs who live in Israel coming to shop.

The Old Town

One of the grandest buildings in the Old Town is the Turkish mansion known as **Touqan Castle**. It's privately owned, but you're welcome to look at the architecture and garden. While this building hasn't been

Mt Gerizim

Sacred to the Samaritans, Mt Gerizim (881m above sea level) offers a superb panoramic view of Nablus and the surrounding countryside.

The Samaritans spend the 40 days of their Passover up here, living in the houses just below the summit. The highlight of their celebrations is a bloody sacrifice, carried out in strict conformity with the ritual prescribed by Moses (Exodus 12): they kill a sheep, pour water over it and strip off the fleece. The sheep's forefeet are then cut off and given to the priests. After being cleaned and salted, the sheep is put on a spit and roasted. After prayers, the sheep is eaten by the Samaritans, who must be fully clothed and wearing shoes. The meat bones must not be broken, and everything that is edible has to be eaten quickly. When they have finished eating they gather up the bones, hooves, horns and spits – in fact everything that came in contact with the sacrificial altar – and solemnly burn it all. This deeply religious event now attracts a crowd of bemused tourists. You can see where the ceremony takes place, just to the south of the road.

Further north is where the Samaritans believe Abraham sacrificed Isaac, disputing the Jewish tradition that it took place on Mt Moriah (the Temple Mount) in Jerusalem.

No buses go up the mountain, so you have to either walk (about two hours) or take a taxi (about 40NIS).

brilliantly maintained, you can still appreciate something of its former glory. From An-Nasir St walk south through Al-Beik Gate; the entrance is up the slope on your left.

There are about 30 minarets punctuating the Nablus skyline. **Al-Kabir Mosque**, with its beautiful arch, is at the corner of An-Nasir and Jamaa al-Kebir Sts and is the largest. One tradition has it that this is the site where Joseph's brothers showed their

father, Jacob, the blood-stained coat of many colours to convince him that his favourite son was dead. Non-Muslims aren't permitted inside the city's mosques.

Soap Factories Nablus, the centre of the Arab soap-making industry, has more than 40 factories and it's usually possible to visit one to see how soap is made. Although some modern technology is now used, the production process is still traditional. One of the more interesting factories is also the most convenient; Al-Bader (Full Moon) Soap at 20 An-Nasir St has been here for over 250 years and exports to other Arab countries via Amman. The soap's basic ingredients are caustic soda and olive oil. Local olive oil was once used, but its quality was so good it proved too expensive; it's more economical to buy Italian. By the way, the soap is particularly good for dandruff.

Turkish Bath West of the Al-Bek Mosque on An-Nasir St is Al-Shifa (☎ 838 1176), the oldest working Turkish bath in the country. Built around 1480 at the start of the Ottoman era, it was one of six in Nablus but all the others have been demolished or converted – in one case into a soap factory. Al-Shifa has been lovingly restored and, as well as the hot rooms, and there's a central hall with cushion-strewn platforms to recline on as you sip black coffee or mint tea and puff on a nargila.

It's open daily from about 8 am to 10 pm; it's men only except for Wednesday between 8 am and 5 pm, when it's women only. It costs 10NIS to use the baths, while a massage is 10NIS extra.

Amphitheatre

On the slopes, tucked away behind the markets and houses, is an excavated Roman amphitheatre. At the time of writing, there were no explanatory signs.

Samaritan Quarter

Nablus is home to the Samaritans (see Population & People in Facts about the Country chapter). The community lives in a small western section of the town and their synagogue houses what they claim to be the world's oldest Torah scroll, dated to the 13th year of the Israelites' settlement in Canaan.

Shechem

To reach **Tel Balata**, the site of biblical Shechem, take the main road 3km east from the town centre and follow the signposts. It's possible to walk or take a taxi. The bus will drop you nearby.

The remains, dating back to between 1650 and 1550 BC, are not particularly impressive to non-archaeologists, but walk a little further east to the **Greek Orthodox convent of Jacob's Well**. A Byzantine church was first built here in 380 but it stood for only 150 years before it was destroyed. The Crusaders erected a replacement church and it's the bones of this structure, heavily restored by first the Russian Orthodox and then the Greek Orthodox Church, which stand today. In the crypt is the deep well at which it's believed Jesus met the Samaritan woman (John 4) on the land purchased by Jacob (Genesis 33:18-20).

The church is open Monday to Saturday from 8 am to noon and 2 to 5 pm; it's closed Sunday. Admission is free.

Just north of Jacob's Well is the traditional site of **Joseph's Tomb**. The rather simple white-domed building, similar in style to Rachel's Tomb in Bethlehem, is believed to be where Joseph's remains were carried from Egypt (Joshua 24:32). Holy to Jews and Muslims, the tomb is presided over by the IDF. It's open daily from 6 am to 6 pm; admission is free.

Places to Stay

There are currently only a couple of hotels plying their trade in Nablus. At the bottom of the scale is **Al-Istiqlal Pension** (☎ 238 3618, 11 Hitteen St), which offers men-only dorm accommodation.

Al-Qasr Hotel (☎ 238 5444, 238 5944, email alqasr@netvision.net.il, Omar Ibn al-Khatib St) has singles/doubles for US$70/ 95 irrespective of the season. It's a newish business-oriented place with comfortable rooms, as the price suggests. It also boasts a fine restaurant. It's some 3km out of town.

Places to Eat

Along with soap, the Nablus speciality is sweets including all the various pastries, *halvah* and Turkish delight, but in particular *kunafeh* (cheese topped with wheat flakes and soaked in honey). The best bakery for this rich delicacy is **Al-Aqsa**, next to the An-Nasir Mosque and across from the soap factory on An-Nasir St in the Old Town.

In the heart of the Old Town souq, on Salahi St across from the carpenter's workshop, is a plain-looking restaurant called *Aj-Aj* which means 'Busy- Busy' (no English sign). It serves great humous, *laban* – a delicious cheese salad dip – and omelettes. For the best *fuul* in Nablus, head for **Fuul Hamis** (*39 Palestine St)*. It's on the right as you walk from the square (no English sign).

Mini-Market Abbud on Ghazzali St, a few hundred metres east of the municipality building, specialises in US and British 'luxury imports', ranging from confectionery and cigarettes to cosmetics and toiletries; it also stocks cold beer (do not drink it on the streets – alcohol is forbidden under Islamic law).

Getting There & Away

Arab buses run to Nablus from East Jerusalem (Nablus Rd station) via Ramallah. The journey takes two to 2½ hours, which makes the sherut option (11NIS, 1¼ hours) very appealing. Sheruts also operate to and from Jenin and Afula in the north, and to Jericho.

AROUND NABLUS
Sebastiya

This quiet little Arab village stands about 15km north-west of Nablus up on the scenic slopes of the Samarian hills. Just above it on the summit of the peak lie the impressive **ruins of Samaria**, the capital of the ancient Israelite kingdom.

Omri, King of Israel, established the city here in 876 BC (I Kings 16:24). It was greatly improved by his son Ahab, who built various great buildings and fortifications.

In 724-722 BC the Assyrians invaded and destroyed the Israelite Kingdom. Samaria's citi-zens were deported and it became a provincial capital under the Persians. Razed in 108 BC and restored in 57 BC, it came in 30 BC to Herod, who renamed it Sebaste (Greek for Augustus) and initiated a new construction program. It eventually declined with the development of Nablus. The Israelite, Hellenistic and Roman ruins include an amphitheatre, temple, palace, towers, columns and a hippodrome.

From April to September, the site (☎ 242 235) is open Saturday to Thursday from 8 am to 5 pm, and Friday from 8 am to 4 pm. From October to March, it's open Saturday to Thursday from 8 am to 4 pm, and Friday from 8 am to 3 pm. Admission is 10NIS (students 6NIS).

Inside the village is a 12th century Crusader church that was converted into a mosque by Saladin. Built on the site of a ruined 5th century church, it contains two tomb chambers. The prophets Elisha and Obadiah are believed to be buried here, along with the head of John the Baptist – the prophet Yahya to the Muslims. The Nabi Yahya Mosque is on the eastern side of the square.

Getting There & Away There are no buses that run directly to Sebastiya. Instead, take a service taxi from near Palestine/Al-Hussein Square (4NIS). Alternatively, you can also take the Arab bus from Nablus to Jenin or Egged buses from Netanya to Shavei-Shomron, and get off at the turn-off for the village. From here it's a steep 2km climb.

Excursions from Israel

Were the politics of the Middle East less convoluted, Israel would be an ideal base for a variety of excursions out of the country. In practice, visitors to Israel may only visit two of the country's neighbours – Jordan and Egypt. Distance and available attractions conspire to make Egypt's Sinai Desert and Jordan's spectacular rock city Petra the most obvious destinations.

Both can easily be visited on do-it-yourself day excursions, but it is advisable to allow at least two or three days to do both regions any justice. Jerusalem and Tel Aviv are just too far away to reach the regions easily, so excursions described in the following chapter are most conveniently made from Eilat.

Border crossing formalities between Israel and these two neighbours are now very relaxed. Visas for Jordan can be obtained at the border, and visas are not required for most of the Egyptian Sinai coastal strip. Visas are, however, required for trips further south or inland.

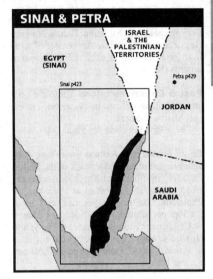

SINAI & PETRA

Sinai

The arid and mountainous Sinai peninsula belongs to Egypt. Between 1967 and 1982 it was occupied by Israeli forces but they were obliged to withdraw under the terms of the Camp David Agreement. The area is sparsely populated, mainly by Bedouins, although the Egyptian tourist industry is pouring millions into southern Sinai hoping to emulate the successes (and excesses) of Eilat.

Divers in-the-know rate the Sinai coast as having some of the most spectacular diving in the world. What's more it isn't even necessary to don expensive scuba gear to appreciate the marine life, a face mask and snorkel will do. And the beaches are superb. Most travellers head straight for the old part of Dahab, but there are plenty of other quieter places with better facilities.

Ecologists fear that the number of divers and snorkellers visiting this area will bring permanent damage to the coral and marine life. Try to enjoy it without touching or taking away anything and remember, don't feed the fish.

For more detailed coverage of the Sinai region and beyond, pick up Lonely Planet's *Egypt*.

Information

Visas If you are entering Sinai from Israel and only intend to visit the eastern coastal resorts from Taba down to Sharm el-Sheikh, no Egyptian visa is required – you will just need a 14 day pass which is issued at the border. However, if you want to visit Ras Mohammed National Park you will need to get an Egyptian visa (you can get one of these in Eilat). For more information see Visas & Documents in the Facts for the Visitor chapter.

Money Change money in Taba at the Hilton Hotel, at the small exchange booth in the customs and passport control building or at one of the moneychangers down by the bus stand. You should have no trouble off-loading shekels in Nuweiba, Dahab, Na'ama Bay or Sharm el-Sheikh. At the time of writing, one shekel equals 1.05 Egyptian pounds (E£).

Post & Communications There are post and telephone offices in Nuweiba, Dahab and Sharm el-Sheik.

The telephone code for Sinai is 062.

Email & Internet Access There's a cyber-cafe/bar just off the boardwalk at the Hilton Fayrouz in Sharm el-Sheikh; it charges E£15 per hour. In Dahab at the Snapper Photo Shop on the bay, you can send email for 50pt per minute, with a minimum charge of E£3. Email can also be sent at the White Hawk Souvenir Shop, opposite the entrance to Auski Camp. They charge E£7.50 per quarter hour or E£25 per hour.

Getting Around

East Delta Bus Co runs several buses from Taba. The 10 am bus goes down the coast to Nuweiba (E£10), then inland to St Catherine's Monastery (E£25) and on to Cairo (E£60). For Sharm el-Sheikh (E£35) there are buses at 9 am and 3 pm, stopping at Nuweiba (E£10) and Dahab (E£15). To Nuweiba only there's another bus at 2 pm. There's also an additional Cairo bus (E£65) departing at 2 pm.

The other way of travelling around Sinai is by service taxi. A taxi (taking up to seven people) to Nuweiba costs E£30 per person or E£40 to Sharm el-Sheikh. To Cairo you're looking at E£50 to E£60 per person. You may also find a minibus which will take you to Dahab for about E£15 per person.

TABA

A few hundred metres of beach and a solitary luxury hotel are the core of Taba, the busy border crossing 4km south of Eilat. Once through immigration, the small tourist village and bus station is about 1km beyond the 11 storey *Taba Hilton* (singles/doubles at US$160/208). There is a small post and telephone office in the tourist village, along with a bakery and an EgyptAir office (often closed). *Panorama Restaurant*, opposite the bus station, seems to have been abandoned by all and sundry, probably because of its overinflated prices. Slightly cheaper but pretty unwelcoming is the *cafeteria* at the bus station.

TABA TO NUWEIBA

South of Taba are some large, expensive 'tourist villages', in various stages of completion. However, there are still plenty of secluded beaches, best reached by service taxi.

Closest to Taba is **The Fjord**, a small protected bay which serves as a popular sun-bathing spot for Israelis. Up on the rise to the north is the small, clean *Salima Cafeteria* (☎ 530 130/1) with six basic rooms where you can stay for E£40/60; meals cost E£10/ 20/25 for breakfast/lunch/dinner. Book ahead if you want to stay overnight as it's very popular with Israelis.

Next down are *Club Aqua Sun* and *Sally Land Holiday Village*, both close to some good beaches and reefs. *Basata* (☎ 500 481 or Cairo ☎ 02-350 1829) is a simple, clean, ecologically minded travellers' settlement with a common kitchen hut, a bakery and a camping ground with 18 bamboo huts going for E£25 per person. If you want to snooze on the beach you'll pay E£15 per person. Again, it's highly advisable to book ahead as it gets very crowded on Egyptian and Israeli holidays.

Another 7km on is *Barracuda Village* which has a series of waterfront stone huts, and 3km further is the quite isolated *Bawaki* where you can virtually walk straight from your beachfront hut and dive into some great snorkelling sites.

NUWEIBA

Nuweiba is certainly not the most attractive of Sinai beach resorts; the area has become something of a major port, with a continual flow of people and vehicle traffic on and off the ferry between Nuweiba and Aqaba, Jordan. However, the mountain scenery is beautiful and the coral reefs, for which Nuweiba is renowned, are spectacular. There are many diving centres, although they're more expensive than those at Dahab or Na'ama Bay, and it's possible to go camel trekking in the mountains (for details, inquire at the Helnan Nuweiba Hotel, ☎ 500 401).

Nuweiba is divided into three parts: to the north is Tarabin, a once tranquil beachside oasis which is rapidly turning into a party and pick-up place; 2km south is 'Nuweiba City', while a further 8km south is the port with a large bus station, banks, a couple of fairly awful hotels and the new Hilton.

Camel & Jeep Treks

Nuweiba is probably the best place in Sinai to arrange camel and jeep trips into the dramatic mountains that line the coast here. The best trip is a one-day outing to Coloured Canyon, but there are some beautiful wadis and oases that can be visited on two or three-day trips – or longer if you prefer. Almost every camp and supermarket in Tarabin offers these trips, but take care that whoever you pick is a local Bedouin – there have been some nasty tales of travellers lost without water in the desert because their so-called guides didn't know where they were going. Travellers have recommended the guide Usama at *White Palace Camp* in Tarabin for day trips to Coloured Canyon. For longer excursions, ask around Tarabin for a local Bedouin called Aynaz.

Places to Stay

At Tarabin you can get a mattress in a bamboo or concrete hut at one of the camps for as little as E£5, and there are a couple of hotels. Most of these camps have cafes selling food and drinks and the differences between the camps are minimal. If forced to choose we'd plump for *Betra Camp* with 35 bungalows with fans and shared bathrooms at E£10 per person or *Soft Beach*, a 30 hut camp run by Sudanese that charges E£10 for one, or E£15 for two, staying in small huts.

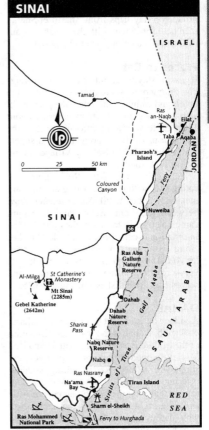

SINAI

ISRAEL

Tamad

Ras
an-Naqb

Eilat

Taba

Aqaba

JORDAN

Pharaoh's
Island

0   25   50 km

Coloured
Canyon

Nuweiba

SINAI

66

Ras Abu
Galluh
Nature
Reserve

Al-Milga

St Catherine's
Monastery

Mt Sinai
(2285m)

Gebel Katherine
(2642m)

Dahab

Dahab
Nature
Reserve

Sharira
Pass

Nabq Nature
Reserve

Nabq

Gulf of Aqaba

ARABIA

SAUDI

Ras Nasrany

Na'ama
Bay

Tiran Island

Straits of Tiran

RED

SEA

Sharm el-Sheikh

Ras Mohammed
National Park

Ferry to Hurghada

City Beach Village, halfway between Nuweiba City and Tarabin, is not a bad option if you just want to sit all day on a tranquil beach. You can pitch a tent for E£5, camp out in one of their reed huts for E£10 per person or go for a clean, comfortable single/double for E£45/55, breakfast included.

In Nuweiba City, *Habiba Camp* (☎/fax 500 770) has 10 huts at E£15/25, as well as dorm tents where you can sleep for E£10. The huts are fairly large and the camp has a beachfront restaurant where Bedouin bread is made. The only disadvantage is that groups on day trips from Sharm el-Sheikh stop here for lunch. Still, the beach is beautiful and it's a calm place to hang out.

Places to Eat

If you're staying at either the port or Tarabin, dining options are limited mainly to the hotels and camps, although at the port you'll also find a gang of cheap eateries about 150m off to your left (with your back to the port entrance). In Tarabin there's a supermarket in front of Elsebaey Village selling lots of junk food.

Across the street, *Blue Bus* is a popular eating spot with pizzas starting at E£12 and meals for about E£20. *Supermarket Aiwa* between the Palm Beach and El-Salam camps also sells food supplies and has an international-card phone outside. Further along on the seafront is the small but popular *Aid Abu Goma* fish restaurant. It gets very crowded during Israeli holidays and serves fresh fish dishes starting at E£25.

DAHAB

A village beach resort 85km north of Sharm el-Sheikh, Dahab is the wannabe Ko Samui of the Middle East – banana fritters and Bob Marley, stoned travellers in tie-dyes and shops with names like 'Laughing Buddha' offering tarot card readings. Accommodation virtually on the beach can cost as little as E£5 a night and many's the backpacker who pitches up here for a night or two and ends up saying on for weeks, if not months.

Despite the town's somewhat unfair reputation as a drug-infested hippie hang-out, there is more to it. A short walk away are tranquil beachside hotels and restaurants without the hippie hype. And while Dahab is not immune to the construction that plagues much of Sinai's coastline, it's still a place where individual travellers are the rule rather than the exception, making it an antidote to the big groups and plastic resorts of Sharm el-Sheikh and Hurghada.

There are two parts to Dahab – in the new part, referred to by the locals rather euphemistically as Dahab City, are some of the more expensive hotels, the bus station, post and phone offices and a bank. Along the beach to the north is the old part – Assalah was originally a Bedouin village but now has more low-budget travellers and Egyptian entrepreneurs than Bedouins in residence.

Activities

After loafing around, diving is the most popular activity in Dahab. The town's various dive clubs all offer a full range of diving possibilities, however, you should choose your club carefully as some places have lousy reputations when it comes to safety standards.

Many snorkellers head for Eel Garden, just north of the village. You can hire snorkelling gear from places along the restaurant strip for about E£20 a day, as well as pedalos (E£20 an hour) and kayaks (E£10 an hour). There's a windsurfing school at the Novotel Holiday Village – the bay there is excellent for windsurfing. Windsurfing sailboards can also be rented at the northern end of Dahab Bay.

There is no 'beach' to speak of in Assalah itself, instead, the rocky coastline leads straight out onto the reef. For the golden sands after which Dahab (Arabic for 'gold') was named, you must go down to the lagoon area where the resorts are clustered.

Many local Bedouins organise camel trips to the interior of Sinai. In the morning, the camel drivers and their camels congregate along the waterfront in the village. Register with the police before beginning the trek, and don't pay the camel driver until you return to the village. Prices for a one day trip start at E£70, including food. As the drivers seem to have agreed among themselves on this price, bargaining will probably get you nowhere.

Places to Stay

Most, if not all, low-budget travellers head for Assalah. There's a plethora of so-called camps, which are basically compounds with spartan stone, cement or reed huts, usually with two or three mattresses tossed on the floor, and communal bathroom facilities.

The camps south of Nesima Resort tend to be the best as they are sheltered from the wind, have more space and some even have attractive waterfront areas shaded by groves of palms. Many of the camps have started to introduce proper rooms with private bathrooms. These are considerably more expensive than the huts, although prices are negotiable.

There are some things to keep in mind when hunting for a good place. Remember that concrete huts with iron roofs are hotter than those made of reeds, but the latter may be less secure – ask for a padlock. Check that there's electricity and running water (some places have hot water) as well as decent mattresses, fly screens and fans.

A few of the better places include *Auski Camp*, next to Starcosa Hotel, a popular camp that charges E£10 for an ordinary room, E£15 with fans; *Bishbishi Garden Camp*, which is probably the cleanest camp in Dahab, charges from E£12 for a mattress on the floor to E£30/40 for rooms with fans and private bathroom; and *Star of Dahab* which charges E£15/20 for single/double occupancy in one of the small, apricot-toned rooms or a beehive-shaped reed huts (which have candles only) near the water.

Heading south from Assalah, *Starcosa Hotel* (☎/fax 640 388) is a comfortable place with rooms with fans, private bathroom and hot water for E£37/60, not including breakfast. The nearby *Sphinx House* (☎ 640 032) charges E£30/40 for a reasonable room with fan, fly screens and communal bath or E£100/120 with private bathroom and aircon; all include breakfast.

About 100m south of here on the other side of the road is the Swiss-run *Christina Residence Hotel* (☎ 640 390, fax 640 406). Very clean doubles with fans and private bathrooms cost US$15 to US$22, triples US$22 to US$30. Breakfast is about E£3 to E£10 extra.

Places to Eat
There is a string of places to eat along the waterfront in Assalah. They serve breakfast, lunch and dinner and most seem to have

Drugs & Dahab

Nothing anyone can say or write will stop people from buying and using marijuana in Dahab. It's freely available and widely used. If you are going to indulge, at least try to be discreet. Although there is not a huge police presence here, remember that the authorities take a dim view of drug use, especially as the business has escalated to harder drugs like heroin. You'll certainly gain no exemption from police attention just because you're a tourist – westerners have been arrested in Dahab for possession and jailed. Penalties for drug offences are high in Egypt: dealing and smuggling attract sentences of 25 years or death by hanging. Executions for such offences have been taking place since 1989.

identical menus hanging out the front. A meal will generally cost between E£6 and E£15.

Few travellers seem to stay at *Dolphin Camp* but the food here is good, the servings generous and it's one of the few camps where you can drink beer with your meal.

The sweet pancakes with fruit and ice cream, offered at most restaurants, are great. *Al-Salam* seems especially good for these.

Tota, a ship-shaped place in the heart of Assalah, has the best Italian cuisine on the strip. Next door, *Italy Pizzeria* does arguably better pizzas.

SHARK BAY
Also known as Beit al-Irsh, this low-key resort camp can be found about 5km before you reach Na'ama Bay (about 2km down a track off the main road).

At *Shark's Bay Camp* (☎ 600 947, fax 600 943) you can stay in clean and comfortable huts on the beach for E£50/65 or huts with fans higher up on the hillside for E£60/75. The camp has clean toilets and showers with hot water. There is also a mini-market and a Bedouin-style restaurant with meals starting at E£21.

SHARM EL-SHEIKH & NA'AMA BAY

The southern coast of the Gulf of Aqaba, between Tiran Island in the straits and Ras Mohammed at the tip of Sinai, features some of the world's most brilliant and amazing underwater scenery. The crystal-clear water, the rare and lovely reefs and the incredible variety of exotic fish darting in and out of the colourful coral have made this a snorkelling and scuba-diving paradise, attracting people from all over the globe.

Na'ama Bay is a seaside resort that has grown from virtually nothing since the early 1980s, while Sharm el-Sheikh (or Sharm) initially developed by the Israelis during their occupation of the peninsula (1967-82), is a relatively long-standing settlement. Although the two are 6km apart, they are rapidly joining together into one long development strip. Almost all the construction is of four and five star-resorts and the place is geared to package tourists flying in direct from Europe.

Information

All the main banks have branches in both towns. Banque Misr handles MasterCard and Bank of Alexandria handles Visa card. Egyptian American Bank (EAB) (in the shopping bazaar off the mall at Na'ama Bay) handles American Express. Thomas Cook has an office on the main road in Na'ama Bay.

The post office is on the hill in Sharm el-Sheikh. The nearby telephone office is open 24 hours.

Diving & Snorkelling

Na'ama Bay itself has reefs, but far better are the stunning Near and Middle gardens and the even more incredible Far Garden reefs. **Near Garden** is near the point at the northern end of the bay just below the Sofitel Hotel, and **Far Garden** is another hour's trek along the coast. You can try walking to the reefs but because large hotels have now been built on the shore, you may find access blocked and have to take a boat organised by one of the diving centres. No matter how you get there, remember to take plenty of water and sunscreen with you.

Another excellent spot for snorkelling is Ras um Sid near the lighthouse at Sharm el-Sheikh. The small beach here is now parcelled up between a number of resorts and gets quite crowded, but the area near the lighthouse is open to the public and is free, although there's no beach as such.

There are several wrecks including the prized *Thistlegorm*. Any of the dive clubs and schools can give you a full rundown on the possibilities. Among the better and more established of the dive clubs and schools are the Aquamarine Diving Centre (☎ 600 276); Aquanaute (☎ 600 187); Camel Dive Club (☎ 600 700); Red Sea Diving Club (☎ 600 342); and Red Sea Diving College (☎ 600 313). Just outside Sharm el-Sheikh there's a modern decompression chamber.

Most of the dive clubs rent out cameras for you to snap some underwater memories.

Places to Stay

Sharm el-Sheikh The cheapest place to stay in an area geared to tourists with comparatively fat wallets is the *Youth Hostel* (☎ 660 317), which is up on the hill. A bed in a fairly standard eight bed dorm costs E£18.60 (E£19.60 for nonmembers) with breakfast. It's open from 6.30 to 9 am and 2 to 10 pm, and they don't seem overly fussed about membership cards.

Safety Land (☎ 660 359, fax 660 458) was undergoing extensive renovation at the time of writing. The management claims that singles/doubles in their newly renovated bungalows will cost E£37/54; air-con rooms will be E£70/90/120 not including breakfast. They have a bit of beach to themselves, although this used to be Sharm's main marina and the water is none too clean.

Clifftop Hotel (☎ 660 251), part of the Helnan group of hotels, has reasonable singles/doubles/triples with TV, air-con, fridge, phone and bathroom for US$50/65/78 including breakfast. You also get the use of the beach at the Marina Sharm Hotel.

Sunset Hotel (☎/fax 661 673/4) is a brand new three star hotel and one of the better deals in town with singles/doubles for E£100/120 including breakfast. As with most of the other hotels along here, you get to use the beach at Ras um Sid.

Na'ama Bay *Pigeon House* (☎ 600 996, fax 600 965) on the northern edge of town is only a budget option because everything else around here is so expensive. It has three types of rooms. On the bottom rung are the basic huts with fans which go for E£38/56/76. Then there are small rooms, which though clean and comfortable are way overpriced at E£65/85/105. Both these options involve shared communal facilities. Superior rooms with air-con and private bathroom go for E£120/170/205. It is often fully booked, so reserve ahead.

Sanafir (☎ 600 197, fax 600 196) is one of the best mid-range places. You'll be looking at US$64/78/99 for a 'superior' air-con single/double/triple in the low season and US$82/98/126 in the high season; including breakfast but not tax. With a pool and the addition of new rooms, it's no longer the intimate place that it used to be, but the older rooms, with whitewashed walls, domed ceilings, and beds raised two or three steps above the floor are the nicest in town.

Not as nice to look at but slightly cheaper is *Kahramana Hotel* (☎ 601 071, fax 601 076), which sits one block back from the beach and has singles/doubles for US$50/60 including breakfast.

Back on the other side of the road at the northern end of Na'ama Bay, is *Oasis Hotel* (☎ 602 624). Rooms with air-con and shared bathroom go for US$32/39, including breakfast but not tax; rooms with private bathroom go for US$37/44. There are also basic huts available for E£40/60.

Places to Eat

Sharm el-Sheikh There are a couple of small restaurants/cafes in the shopping bazaar behind the bus station. *Sinai Star* serves excellent fish meals for about E£12. *Brilliant Restaurant* offers a range of trad-itional Egyptian food at reasonable prices – a plate of chicken with salad should cost about E£15, they also have sweets.

Safsafa in the old Sharm 'mall' is one of the best places in this area. It's a small, eight table, family run affair. Local residents say the fish here is the freshest in Sharm and the clientele is a mixture of families and divers. Whole fish is priced at E£45 per kilo, and a plate of calamari and rice, with *tahina* and *baba ghanoug*, will cost you E£18. There is no beer.

If you're into dining under the stars while the waves wash gently up onto the beach, try *Safety Land*. There's no formal restaurant here, but meals (fish or calamari for E£25) and snacks (omelettes and salad) can be arranged, and you can dine within metres of the water. Beers are a reasonable E£7.50.

Self-caterers will find quite a well-stocked supermarket in the bazaar, as well as a wholesale beer shop – talking the manager into selling a bottle or two (rather than the customary crate) is not too difficult.

Na'ama Bay *Tam Tam Oriental Cafe* is one of the cheapest restaurants in Na'ama Bay and is deservedly popular. Jutting out onto the beach, it's a laid-back place where you can delve into a range of Egyptian fare including mezzes for E£3.75 a bowl, a roast pigeon for E£17 and kushari for E£7.50. *Chef Jurgen's Restaurant* over at Pigeon House is also deservedly popular. Pasta dishes start at E£10.50 and there's a good selection of vegetarian food, plus fruit and pancakes for desert. Beers are E£9.50.

Another popular choice is *Danadeer Restaurant* (☎ 600 321), just on the corner along from the Sanafir. There's a selection of seafood and Egyptian dishes on offer and you can get a fish meal for about E£35.

The usual fast food outlets are also represented here: McDonald's, KFC and Pizza Hut are all on or close to the street that runs in front of the Sanafir. There's even a newly opened *Hard Rock Cafe* (☎ 602 665), which is very popular with the young middle-class Cairenes who flock to Sharm on weekends and national holidays.

RAS MOHAMMED NATIONAL PARK

Declared a national marine park in 1988, the headland of Ras Mohammed is about 30km from Sharm el-Sheikh. Camping permits (E£5 per person per night) are available from the visitors centre inside the park, but camping is allowed only in designated areas. Vehicles are permitted to enter (E£15 per person), but access is restricted to certain regions and, for conservation reasons, it's forbidden to drive off the official tracks. Take your passport with you, and remember that it is not possible to go to Ras Mohammed with only a Sinai permit in your passport.

Petra

If you are only going to see one place in Jordan make it majestic Petra, the ruined capital of the Nabataeans (Arabs who dominated the Trans-Jordan area in pre-Roman times). Like Jerash, this lost city was forgotten by the outside world for 1000 years. It was rediscovered in 1812 and excavations commenced in 1929, but the central city was not uncovered until after 1958.

This spectacular city was built in the 3rd century BC by the Nabataeans who carved palaces, temples, tombs, storerooms and stables from the rocky cliffs. From here they commanded the trade route from Damascus to Arabia, and through here the great spice, silk and slave caravans passed. In a short time the Nabataeans made great advances – they mastered iron production, hydraulic engineering, copper refining, stone carving and sculpture, all probably because of their great success in commerce. Archaeologists believe that it was several earthquakes, including a massive one in 555 AD which forced the inhabitants to abandon the city.

The most famous of Petra's ruins is the **Khazneh** (Treasury), the first main monument you come to after the trek through the incredibly narrow 1.2km long defile known as the **Siq**. The carved facade of the Khazneh is the finest of all of Petra's monu-

ments, familiar to viewers of *Indiana Jones & the Last Crusade*.

The other monument that shouldn't be missed is the **monastery** (Al-Deir), reached by a long, rock-cut staircase on the far side of the site. On the way up look out for the **Lion Tomb** – the eroded lions astride the entrance are difficult to see at first. The monastery has a similar facade to the Khazneh, but is far bigger and the views from there are stunning (especially out to Mt Haroun).

Other interesting sites are the 8000 seat **amphitheatre**, the **Qasr al-Bint** (one of the very few free-standing buildings), the **colonnaded street**, the **Temple of the Winged Lions**, the ruins of a **Byzantine church** with possibly the world's oldest Byzantine mosaic, and the facade known as the **Royal Tombs**. Walk to the Royal Tombs (known as the 'Urn', 'Corinthian', 'Silk' and 'Palace') to examine their eroded facades and colourful interiors.

Orientation

The ruins of Petra are isolated from Wadi Musa by the Siq, the main entry point. The centre of Wadi Musa, a sprawling town which clings to the sides of a 4km long valley, is defined by a roundabout – all of the main services are found near here and this is the place to catch buses to Aqaba and Wadi Rum. It is 2km downhill (along aptly named Tourist Street) from the circle to the star-studded hotels which guard the entrance to Petra. (Note that prices increase as the altitude drops.)

Information

One of the big talking points in Jordan's cheap digs is the high entry price to Petra – JD20/25/30 for a one/two/three day pass (which must be used on consecutive days). The visitors centre near the entrance gate provides some information and has periodic displays. At Jeff's Bookshop (just outside) you can purchase the excellent *Map of Petra* (JD5) which depicts the relief of the site. *Petra – a guide to the capital of the Nabataeans* by Rami Khouri, or his simply titled *Petra* are good aids. Also useful are

PETRA

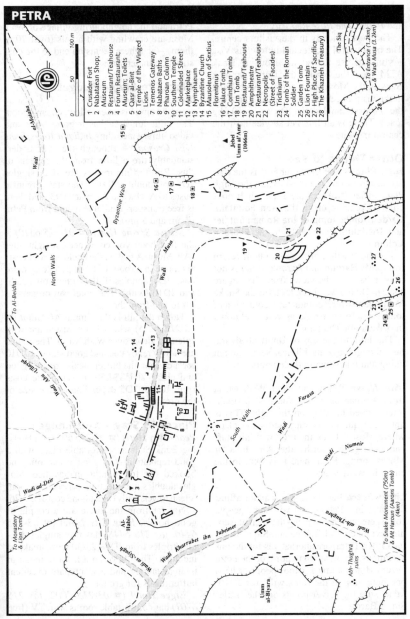

1 Crusader Fort
2 Nabataean Shop;
Museum
3 Restaurant/Teahouse
4 Forum Restaurant;
Museum; Toilets
5 Qasr al-Bint
6 Temple of the Winged
Lions
7 Temenos Gateway
8 Nabataen Baths
9 Pharoan Column
10 Southern Temple
11 Colonnaded Street
12 Marketplace
13 Nymphaeum
14 Byzantine Church
15 Mausoleum of Sextius
Florentinus
16 Palace Tomb
17 Corinthian Tomb
18 Urn Tomb
19 Restaurant/Teahouse
20 Amphitheatre
21 Restaurant/Teahouse
22 Necropolis
(Street of Facades)
23 Triclinium
24 Tomb of the Roman
Soldier
25 Garden Tomb
26 Lion Fountain
27 High Place of Sacrifice
28 The Khazneh (Treasury)

the free pamphlets *Petra: Panoramic Guide* and *Petra: The Rose Red City*

The post office is in the visitors centre. The only useful credit card in town is Visa – you can use this at the Housing Bank ATM near the circle, the Cairo-Amman Bank in the Mövenpick and the Arab Bank in the visitors centre. You can do laundry at the Twaissi Inn Hotel (JD6 for a 10.5kg load). There is an Internet service near the central mosque.

Other Things to See

High Places The **Crusader Fort** is the easiest climb (a few minutes), while the **High Place of Sacrifice** near the Siq is a half-hour climb. Continue on to the **Lion Fountain**, **Garden Tomb**, **Tomb of the Roman Soldier** and **Triclinium**, then down to the **Pharoan Column**.

For those with time, the five hour return trip to **Mt Haroun** and **Aaron's Tomb** is not to be missed as the views from the top are superb. On the way back look for the **Snake Monument** which dominates a collection of tombs, it's to your right as you head down into Wadi ath-Thughra.

The hike to the top of **Umm al-Biyara**, once thought to be the biblical Sela, is tough going and takes two to three hours.

'Ain Musa When you enter Wadi Musa from Amman or Aqaba you pass a small, three-domed building on the right. This is not a mosque but is supposedly the place where Moses struck the rock with his staff and water gushed forth – the 'Ain Musa' or Moses spring. From here it is 2km to the circle in Wadi Musa.

Little Petra For those who cannot afford the entry into Petra – and yes, some people come here and cannot pay – the ancient Neolithic village of Al-Beidha and Siq al-Barid (aka Little Petra) are alternatives for the impecunious. These are 8km north of the Petra Forum Hotel; a taxi for four people with a one hour stop at the ruins will cost JD10. Make sure the driver points out the 'little' Siq al-Barid.

Places to Stay

Petra and the neighbouring village of Wadi Musa are crawling with hotels (over 70 of them) – and there seems no end to the construction under way.

Places to Stay – Budget

Twaissi Inn Hotel (☎ 03-215 6423) just up from the circle is an excellent, cheap option. The common area has a good book and video library including *Indiana Jones & the Last Crusade* – although the staff understandably tire a little from the repeats of this. Rooftop mattresses are JD2, singles JD5 and doubles JD10. The staff organise buses to Aqaba and Amman (JD3) and there is free transport available to and from Petra (7 am and 5 pm).

Mussa Spring Hotel (☎ 03-215 6310) is the first hotel you come across, right after 'Ain Musa. A bed on the enclosed roof costs JD2, one in a room of three people or more costs JD4, doubles JD10 (without own bath) and JD16 (with). The hotel can organise a lift to and from the site.

Down the hill is the similar *Al-Anbat* (☎ 03-215 6275) which has a restaurant with splendid views over Wadi Musa. The rooms are newly renovated and good value at JD10 for a double; the buffet meals are also good and cheap at US$4.50. A camp site costs from JD3 to JD5 depending on the size of the group.

Places to Stay – Mid-Range

Peace Way Hotel (☎ 03-215 6963) on Housing Bank St is a comfortable place with a good reputation – so good it can often be booked out for months in advance. Singles/doubles with heating, private bathroom (clean towels daily) and phone cost JD22/26.

Not far from the circle are a couple of good hotels. *Rose City Hotel* (☎ 03-215 6440, fax 215 6448) has tidy singles/doubles/triples from JD18/23/30 with breakfast included. They have an à la carte menu in their restaurant and also prepare excellent buffet meals for groups.

Elgee Hotel (☎ 03-215 7002, fax 215 6701) has comfortable rooms with TV (free movies), phone and shower for JD15/24 including breakfast. It is popular with locals and the bar is a good place to meet Bedouin.

Similar to the previous two is **Moon Valley Hotel** (☎ 03-215 6824, fax 215 7131) on Tourist St. **Petra Hotel & Rest House** (☎ 03-215 6014, fax 215 6868), close to the entrance of Petra, has good rooms that are not unreasonably priced at JD31/58 in the older part, JD41/70 in the new wing. Part of it includes an old Nabataean tomb.

Places to Stay – Top End
Petra Forum Hotel (☎ 03-215 6266, fax 215 6977) is a more expensive option close to the Petra entrance. You get great views over the Siq from its poolside bar. Singles/doubles are from JD80/90 plus tax.

King's Way Inn (☎ 03-215 6799, fax 215 6796, Web site www.kingsway-petra.com) is a big, friendly four star place offering aircon rooms with satellite TV from JD90 plus tax. There is also a swimming pool and restaurant.

Mövenpick Hotel (☎ 03-215 7111, fax 215 7112) is the new five star darling of the prebooked European set and has every creature comfort they would expect from a top-end hotel in their own countries. It also has two excellent restaurants – **Al-Saraya** and **Al-Iwan** – and the best bar in Wadi Musa.

Places to Eat
For the cheapest eats, investigate the little restaurants clustered in the centre of town – which incidentally is where you can buy your own foodstuffs in shops frequented mainly by locals.

Wadi Petra Restaurant, right on the roundabout in town, is a curious little place where you can eat a few dishes beyond the usual fare. The chicken and mixed vegetable stew is good value at JD1.80.

Cleopatra (☎ 215 7099) offers chicken and Middle Eastern dishes, **Treasury** also serves chicken meals for about JD2.50, and **Abbysalama Flowers** gets the thumbs up from locals for its kebabs and chicken.

There is a collection of eateries on Tourist St near the new Mövenpick Hotel. The best value is **El Tafily** which specialises in Jordanian dishes. As you head downhill you pass the Pizza Hut which is the same as its American counterpart, **Papazzi** which does a poor imitation of Pizza Hut (a small pizza is JD4), and the classy but expensive **Red Cave Restaurant**.

If you want an ice cream then the shop at the Mövenpick is the place (900 fils for a scoop or try a big vase of fruit cocktail for JD2.50).

Most of the hotels have restaurants attached to them, those at Petra Rest House, Petra Forum Hotel and Mövenpick are particularly expensive.

Entertainment
Bar hopping is not really possible in Wadi Musa. Beer is expensive wherever you buy it in town – a big bottle of Amstel is JD3.50. Popular with locals is the cosy sports bar at **Petra Palace**.

Elgee Hotel has a liquor store as well as the upstairs **Bedwin Bar** with its distinctive puffer fish light; foreigners will be gawked at here for a little while. About the only other place to buy takeaway beer is at the Mövenpick, and surprisingly, it is cheaper than the Elgee. Mövenpick also has a superb bar – in the style of a lavishly decorated grand dining room – but the drinks are very pricey. Looks like it is a couple of takeaway beers and **Indiana Jones & The Last Crusade** at Twaissi Inn Hotel.

Getting There & Away
From Israel via the Arava border crossing, the easiest way is to get a taxi into Aqaba (JD5) and then a taxi from Aqaba to Petra which will cost around JD40 per taxi. However, the cheapest way is to take a local bus (JD3) from Aqaba to Petra. They leave the bus station at 8.30 and 10 am, noon, 2 and 3.30 pm. The bus trip takes about 2 hours.

From Amman, there's one JETT bus daily (3 hours) which you can catch one way for a hefty JD5.50, or take the day tour for JD32, which includes lunch and entry to the site – only for those with strictly limited time. It leaves for Amman at about 3 pm.

When it's time to leave Petra, there are a few minibuses departing for Aqaba (2 hours) between 6.30 am and 3.30 pm, for Amman between 5.30 am and noon; and one to the resthouse at Wadi Rum (1½ hours) at 6 am; all are JD3.

The most frequent connection is the minibus to Ma'an (500 fils, 1 hour), which is supposed to leave hourly. From Ma'an you can get another minibus or service taxi to Amman or Aqaba, or just get off on the highway and hitch. The rich can hire a car – readers have recommended Pioneer Rent a Car (☎ 03-215 7188) in Silk Road St where you can hire a car without/with air-con for JD30/35 per day.

Language

Israel's national language is Hebrew. It is the most spoken language, followed by Arabic. English is also widely spoken and you'll almost always be able to find someone who understands it. Most of the important road and street signs are in all three languages. With Jews arriving in Israel from around the world, many other languages are commonly understood too – French, German and Yiddish are the main ones, but also Spanish and Russian.

HEBREW

Written from right to left, Hebrew has a basic 22-character alphabet – but from there it starts to get very complicated. Like English, not all these characters have fixed phonetic values and their sound can vary from word to word. You just have to know that, for instance, *Yair* is pronounced 'Ya-ear' and doesn't rhyme with 'hare' or 'fire'.

Other letters change their sound value by the addition of diacritical marks but these diacritical marks are quite often left out. Like Arabic, the shape of certain characters will vary according to where they fall within a word (initial, medial or final position). There is also a second 'handwritten', more decorative form of the alphabet, often used in advertising and on store-front signs, in which many of the characters are dissimilar to their 'standard' forms.

It's worth noting that transliteration from Hebrew script into English is at best an approximate science. The presence of sounds not found in English, and the fact that the script is 'defective' (most vowels are not written) combine to make it nearly impossible to settle on one consistent method of transliteration. A wide variety of spellings is therefore possible for words when they appear in roman script, and that goes for place names and people's names as well. We take comfort in the knowledge that the Israelis themselves are no better at this inexact science than we are: one street in Haifa is labelled 'Hayim' at one end and

'Chaim' at the other, both transliterations of the same Hebrew name.

Basics

Hello.	*sha-LOM*
Goodbye.	*sha-LOM*
Good morning.	*BO-ker tov*
Good evening.	*erev tov*
Goodnight.	*lie-la tov*
See you later.	*le-HIT-rah-OTT*
Thank you.	*to-DAH*
Please.	*be-va-ka-SHA*
You're welcome.	*al low da-VAAR*
Yes.	*ken*
No.	*loh*
Excuse me.	*slee-KHA*
Wait.	*REG-gah*
What?	*mah?*
When?	*mah-tye?*
Where is ...?	*AYE-fo ...?*
right (correct)	*na-CHON*
money	*KES-sef*
bank	*bank*

I don't speak Hebrew.	*AH-NEELo m'dah-BEHR ee-VREET*
Do you speak English?	*ah-TAH m'dah-BEHR ang-LEET?*

Time & Days

What is the time?	*MA ha-sha-AH?*
seven o'clock	*ha-sha-AHSHEV-vah*
minute	*da-KAH*
hour	*sha-AH*
day	*yom*
week	*sha-voo-ah*
month	*KHO-desh*
year	*sha-NAH*

Monday	*shey-NEE*
Tuesday	*shlee-SHEE*
Wednesday	*reh-vee-EE*
Thursday	*cha-mee SHEE*
Friday	*shee-SHEE*
Saturday	*sha-BAT*
Sunday	*ree-SHON*

Getting Around

Which bus goes to ...?	AYE-zeh auto-boos no-SE-ah le ...?
Stop here.	ah-TSOR kahn
airport	sde t'oo-FAH
bus	auto-boos
near	ka-ROV
railway	rah-KEH-vet
station	ta-cha-na

Food & Accommodation

food	OKHEL
water	my-im
restaurant	MISS-ah-DAH
breakfast	ah-roo-CHAT BO-ker
lunch	ah-roo-KHAT-tsa-ha-RYE-im
dinner	ah-roo-KHAT erev
menu	taf-REET
egg	bay-TSA
vegetables	YEH-rah-KOHT
bread	LEKH-hem
butter	khem-AH
cheese	g'VEE-nah
milk	kha-LAV
ice cream	glee-DAH
fruit	pay-ROT
wine	yain
bill	KHESH-bon
hotel	ma-LON
room	khe-der
toilet	she-ru-TEEM

Around Town

How much is it?	KA-mah zeh ule?
post office	dough-ar
letter	mich-tav
stamps	boolim
envelopes	ma-ata-FOT
postcard	gloo-yah
telegram	miv-rack
airmail	dough-ar ah-veer
pharmacy	bait mer-kah-KHAT
shop	kha-NOOT
expensive	ya-KAR
cheap	zol

Numbers

1	eh-HAD
2	SHTA-yim
3	sha-LOSH
4	AR-bah
5	cha-MAYSH
6	shaysh
7	SHEV-vah
8	sh-MO-neh
9	TAY-shah
10	ESS-er
11	eh-HAD-ess-RAY
12	shtaym-ess-RAY
20	ess-REEM
21	ess-REEM v'ah-KHAD
30	shlo-SHEEM
31	shlo-SHEEM v'ah-KHAD
50	cha-MEESHLEEM
100	MAY-ah
200	mah-tah-YEEM
300	shlosh may-OAT
500	cha-MAYSH may-OAT
1000	alef
3000	shlosh-ET alef-EEM
5000	cha-maysh-ET alef-EEM

ARABIC

Any attempts, however unsuccessful, to speak Arabic will endear you to the Arabs of the region. Learning the characters for the Arab numerals is useful, as much of your shopping will be done in Arab markets.

Useful Words

Hello.	a-halan/mahr-haba
Goodbye.	salaam aleicham/ ma-ah-salameh
Good morning.	sabah-al-kheir
Good evening.	masa'al-kheir
Please.	min fadlach
Thank you.	shoo-khran
You're welcome.	afwan
I don't understand.	mish faahim
Do you speak English?	tech-kee Ingleesi?
How much is this?	ah-desh hadah?
Yes.	ay-wah
No.	la

Pardon?	*sa-mech-nee?*
Where?	*feen?*
right	*yemine*
left	*she-mal*
straight	*doo-ree*

Time & Days

Sunday	*el-ahad*
Monday	*itnein*
Tuesday	*talaata*
Wednesday	*el-arbi'a*
Thursday	*khamis*
Friday	*jumu'a*
Saturday	*sabit*

What is the time?	*gaddesh saa'ah?*
minute	*da'iah*
hour	*saa'ah*
day	*yawm*
week	*jum'a/usbuu'*
month	*shahr*
year	*saneh*

Getting Around

Which bus goes to ...?	*ayya baas yaruh 'ala ...?*
Is it far?	*ba'id?*
Stop here.	*wa'if huna*

railway station	*mahattat train*
airport	*mataar*
bus stop	*mawif al-baas*

Around Town

post office	*al-bostah*
letter	*maktuub*
stamps	*tabi'*
envelope	*mughallaf*
airmail	*al-barid al-hawwi*
pharmacy	*farmashiyyeh*

shop	*dukkaan*
expensive	*ghaali*
cheap	*rakhis*

Food & Accommodation

food	*akil*
water	*may*
restaurant	*mat'am*
breakfast	*futuur*
lunch	*ghada*
dinner	*'asha*
menu	*menu*
tea	*schai*
coffee	*kah-wah*

hotel	*oteyl*
room	*odah*
toilet	*beyt al-may*

Numbers

Arabic numerals are read from left to right, unlike the language, which is read from right to left.

0	٠	*sifr*
1	١	*wa-hid*
2	٢	*tinen*
3	٣	*talatay*
4	٤	*arbaha*
5	٥	*khamseh*
6	٦	*sitteh*
7	٧	*sabah*
8	٨	*tamanyeh*
9	٩	*taisah*
10	١٠	*ahsharah*
100	١٠٠	*miyyah*
500	٥٠٠	*khamsmiyyah*
1000	١٠٠٠	*alf*
5000	٥٠٠٠	*khamasta alaf*

Glossary

HEBREW

agam – lake

agora (s), **agorot** (pl) – smallest unit of the shekel; 1 shekel = 100 agorot

atar – site

be'er – well

beit/beth – house

beit knesset – synagogue

beth midrash – Jewish house of study

bimah – central platform in a synagogue

derekh – street or road

dunam – 1000 sq m (from Turkish)

ein – spring

Eretz Yisra'el – the Land of Israel

Eretz Yisra'el HaShlema – the Greater Land of Israel, used by Israel's right wing to refer to their claim that Israel's territory must include the Gaza Strip, the West Bank and the Golan Heights

gan – garden or park

gush – literally 'bloc'; appears in such names as Gush Emunim (Bloc of Believers), the West Bank settler movement; and Gush Etzion (Etzion Bloc), a group of Jewish settlements south of Bethlehem, Gush Dan (the Greater Tel Aviv area)

HaGanah – literally 'defence'; the Jewish underground army during the British Mandate; the forerunner of the modern-day Israeli Defence Force (IDF)

Halacha – Jewish law

Halachic – in accordance with Jewish law

har – mountain

Haredi (s), **Haredim** (pl) – an ultraorthodox Jew, either a *Hasid* or a member of one of the groups that oppose *Hasidism*, known as 'mitnagdim'

Hasid (s), **Hasidim** (pl) – member of an ultraorthodox (*Haredi*) movement with mystical tendencies that was founded in Poland in the 18th century by the Ba'al Shem Tov

hefetz hashud – literally 'suspicious object'; an object (eg a sack or backpack whose owner is nowhere to be found) that may be a bomb; passers-by are kept at a distance until the police sappers finish their work

hof – beach

hursha – grove

hurva – ruin

IDF – Israeli Defence Force, the national army

iriya – city hall or municipality

kaddish – prayer recited in memory of the deceased at the funeral, daily for 11 months following the funeral, and annually on the 'Jahrzeit' (anniversary of the death)

kanyon – shopping mall

kashrut – religious dietary laws, ie the rules of keeping *kosher*

kibbutz (s), **kibbutzim** (pl) – a communal settlement run cooperatively by its members; kibbutzim, once based solely on farming, are now involved in a wide range of industries

kibbutznik – member of a *kibbutz*

kikar – square, roundabout

kippa – skullcap worn by observant Jewish men (and among reform and conservative Jews, sometimes by women); known in Yiddish as a *yarmulke*

knesiya – church

Knesset – Israeli Parliament

kosher – food prepared according to Jewish dietary law (*kashrut*)

ma'agar – reservoir

ma'ayan – spring

malon – hotel

mapal – waterfall

matzeva – pillar, monument, gravestone

me'ara – cave

menorah – a seven-branched candelabra that adorned the ancient Temple in Jerusalem and has been a Jewish symbol ever since; it is now the official symbol of the State of Israel

metzuda – fortress, castle

midrahov – pedestrian mall

migdal – tower

mikveh – Jewish ritual bath

mitzpeh – lookout; a hilltop Jewish settlement, especially in the Galilee

mitzvah – religious obligation, commandment

Mizrahi (s), **Mizrahim** (pl) – a Jew from one of the Oriental Jewish communities, eg from one of the Islamic countries such as Morocco, Yemen or Iraq; this term is often used interchangeably with Sefaradi, though technically only the descendents of Jews expelled from Spain are Sefaradim

MK – member of the Knesset

moshav (s), **moshavim** (pl) – cooperative settlement, with a mix of private and collective housing and economic activity

moshavnik – a member of a moshav

nahal – river

naveh/neveh – oasis

oleh (s), **olim** (pl) – new immigrant

parochet – the curtain that covers the Holy Ark in synagogues (except in certain *Mizrahi* Jewish communities)

rakhava(t) – square

rehov – street

sabra – literally 'prickly pear'; native-born Israeli,

settler – a term for Israelis who have created new communities on territory captured from Jordan, Egypt and Syria during the 1967 war. The Hebrew word for settler is 'mitnachel'

sha'ar – gate

Shabbat – the Jewish Sabbath observed from sundown on Friday evening to an hour after sundown on Saturday

sharav – Hebrew word for *khamseen*; a hot dry wind or generally a very hot day

shdera(t)/shderot – boulevard, avenue

shekel – Israel monetary unit

shikun – housing estate, generally built in the 1950s to house new immigrants

Shin Bet/Shabak – Israel's feared internal security service

shmura/shmurat teva – nature reserve

shtetl – small, traditional Eastern European Jewish village

shvil – trail

tallit – prayer shawl

tayelet – promenade

tefillin – phylacteries, ie the two cube-shaped leather boxes containing exerpts from the Torah that are worn on the forehead and left arm by observant Jewish men during weekday morning prayers

tel – a hill; in archaeology, a mound built up during centuries of urban rebuilding

Torah – the Five Books of Moses, the Pentateuch, ie the first five books of the Old Testament

tzabar – the Hebrew word for *sabra*

Tzahal – Hebrew for Israeli Defence Force (IDF)

tzitzit – white tassles worn by orthodox Jewish men, attached to the four corners of a square undergarment

WZO – World Zionist Organisation

ya'ar – forest

yad – memorial

yarmulke – see *kippa*

yeshiva (s), **yeshivot** (pl) – Jewish religious seminary

zimmer – literally 'room' in German; B&B

ARABIC

abu – father (of), often used as part of a name

ain/ein – water spring or source

al – the definite article, 'the'

al-Naqba – literally the 'Catastrophe'; this is what the Palestinians call the Israeli War of Independence

bab – door, gate

bir – well

burj – fortress or tower

dunam – 1000 sq m (from Turkish)

fellah (s), **fellahin** (pl) – peasant, farmer

haj – annual Muslim pilgrimage to Mecca
Hamas – (Harakat al-Muqaama al-Is-lamiya) militant Islamic organisation which aims to create an Islamic state in the pre-1948 territory of Palestine
hamma – hot spring
hammam – public baths
haram – literally 'forbidden'; holy sanctuary
Hezbollah – literally 'Party of God'; Iranian-backed Shiite guerrilla group active in southern Lebanon
Hijra – Mohammed's flight from Mecca to Medina in 622 AD

Intifada – literally 'shaking off'; the Palestinian uprising against Israeli authorities in the West Bank, Gaza and East Jerusalem that began at the end of 1987
Islam – literally 'voluntary surrender to the will of God (Allah)'; the religion of the vast majority of the Palestinians

jabal – hill, mountain
jami' – mosque

kfar – village
khamseen – literally 'fifty' in Arabic; a hot, dry, dusty desert wind that blows from the south-east
khan – also called a caravanserai, a travellers' inn usually constructed on main trade routes, with accommodation on the 1st floor and stables and storage on the ground floor around a central courtyard
khatib – low, railed wooden platform where the reader sits to recite from the Quran
khirbet – ruins (of)
Koran – see *Quran*
kufeyyas – the black-and-white chequered Palestinian headscarf

madrasa – school, especially one associated with a mosque
majdal – tower

masjid – mosque
midan – public square
mihrab – prayer niche in a mosque, indicating the direction of Mecca
minaret – the tower of a mosque; from which the call to prayer is traditionally sung from here
minbar – pulpit used for mosque sermons
muezzin – the man who sings the call to prayer, traditionally from atop a minaret
mufti – a jurist who interprets Islamic law

nabi – prophet

PA – Palestinian Authority
PFLP – Popular Front for the Liberation of Palestine
PLO – Palestine Liberation Organisation
PNC – Palestinian National Council, ruling body of the PLO

qibla – the direction of Mecca, towards which Muslims pray; see *mihrab*
qubba – dome, cupola
Quran – the sacred book of the Muslims

ribat – pilgrim hostel

sabil – public drinking fountain
saray – palace
shabab – literally 'youths'; young Palestinian stone throwers and agitators, the backbone of the *Intifada*
Shariya – Muslim law
sheikh – learned or old man
souq – market
sufi – Muslim mystic

tariq – road
turba – tomb or graveyard

UNRWA – United Nations Reliefs & Works Agency for Palestine Refugees

wadi – dried up river bed
wali – Muslim saint or holy man

zawiya – Muslim religious dwelling
zuqaq – alleyway

LONELY PLANET

FREE Lonely Planet Newsletters

We love hearing from you and think you'd like to hear from us.

Planet Talk

Our FREE quarterly printed newsletter is full of tips from travellers and anecdotes from Lonely Planet guidebook authors. Every issue is packed with up-to-date travel news and advice, and includes:

- a postcard from Lonely Planet co-founder Tony Wheeler
- a swag of mail from travellers
- a look at life on the road through the eyes of a Lonely Planet author
- topical health advice
- prizes for the best travel yarn
- news about forthcoming Lonely Planet events
- a complete list of Lonely Planet books and other titles

To join our mailing list, residents of the UK, Europe and Africa can email us at go@lonelyplanet.co.uk; residents of North and South America can email us at info@lonelyplanet.com; the rest of the world can email us at talk2us@lonelyplanet.com.au, or contact any Lonely Planet office.

Comet

Our FREE monthly email newsletter brings you all the latest travel news, features, interviews, competitions, destination ideas, travellers' tips & tales, Q&As, raging debates and related links. Find out what's new on the Lonely Planet Web site and which books are about to hit the shelves.

Subscribe from your desktop: www.lonelyplanet.com/comet

LONELY PLANET

Mail Order

Lonely Planet products are distributed worldwide. They are also available by mail order from Lonely Planet, so if you have difficulty finding a title please write to us. North and South American residents should write to 150 Linden St, Oakland, CA 94607, USA; European and African residents should write to 10a Spring Place, London NW5 3BH, UK; and residents of other countries to PO Box 617, Hawthorn, Victoria 3122, Australia.

ISLANDS OF THE INDIAN OCEAN Madagascar & Comoros • Maldives • Mauritius, Réunion & Seychelles

MIDDLE EAST & CENTRAL ASIA Arab Gulf States • Central Asia • Central Asia phrasebook • Iran • Israel & the Palestinian Territories • Israel & the Palestinian Territories travel atlas • Istanbul • Jerusalem • Jordan & Syria • Jordan, Syria & Lebanon travel atlas • Lebanon • Middle East on a shoestring • Turkey • Turkish phrasebook • Turkey travel atlas • Yemen
Travel Literature: The Gates of Damascus • Kingdom of the Film Stars: Journey into Jordan

NORTH AMERICA Alaska • Backpacking in Alaska • Baja California • California & Nevada • Canada • Chicago • Florida • Hawaii • Honolulu • Los Angeles • Louisiana • Miami • New England USA • New Orleans • New York City • New York, New Jersey & Pennsylvania • Pacific Northwest USA • Rocky Mountain States • San Francisco • Seattle • Southwest USA • USA • USA phrasebook • Vancouver • Washington, DC & the Capital Region
Travel Literature: Drive Thru America

NORTH-EAST ASIA Beijing • Cantonese phrasebook • China • Hong Kong • Hong Kong, Macau & Guangzhou • Japan • Japanese phrasebook • Japanese audio pack • Korea • Korean phrasebook • Kyoto • Mandarin phrasebook • Mongolia • Mongolian phrasebook • North-East Asia on a shoestring • Seoul • South-West China • Taiwan • Tibet • Tibetan phrasebook • Tokyo
Travel Literature: Lost Japan

SOUTH AMERICA Argentina, Uruguay & Paraguay • Bolivia • Brazil • Brazilian phrasebook • Buenos Aires • Chile & Easter Island • Chile & Easter Island travel atlas • Colombia • Ecuador & the Galapagos Islands • Latin American Spanish phrasebook • Peru • Quechua phrasebook • Rio de Janeiro • South America on a shoestring • Trekking in the Patagonian Andes • Venezuela
Travel Literature: Full Circle: A South American Journey

SOUTH-EAST ASIA Bali & Lombok • Bangkok • Burmese phrasebook • Cambodia • Hill Tribes phrasebook • Ho Chi Minh City • Indonesia • Indonesia's Eastern Islands • Indonesian phrasebook • Indonesian audio pack • Jakarta • Java • Laos • Lao phrasebook • Laos travel atlas • Malay phrasebook • Malaysia, Singapore & Brunei • Myanmar (Burma) • Philippines • Pilipino (Tagalog) phrasebook • Singapore • South-East Asia on a shoestring • South-East Asia phrasebook • Thailand • Thailand's Islands & Beaches • Thailand travel atlas • Thai phrasebook • Thai audio pack • Vietnam • Vietnamese phrasebook • Vietnam travel atlas

ALSO AVAILABLE: Antarctica • Brief Encounters: Stories of Love, Sex & Travel • Chasing Rickshaws • Not the Only Planet: Travel Stories from Science Fiction • Travel with Children • Traveller's Tales

LONELY PLANET

Guides by Region

Lonely Planet is known worldwide for publishing practical, reliable and no-nonsense travel information in our guides and on our Web site. The Lonely Planet list covers just about every accessible part of the world. Currently there are nine series: travel guides, shoe-string guides, walking guides, city guides, phrasebooks, audio packs, travel atlases, diving and snorkeling guides and travel literature.

AFRICA Africa – the South • Africa on a shoestring • Arabic (Egyptian) phrasebook • Arabic (Moroccan) phrasebook • Cairo • Cape Town • Central Africa • East Africa • Egypt • Egypt travel atlas • Ethiopian (Amharic) phrasebook • The Gambia & Senegal • Kenya • Kenya travel atlas • Malawi, Mozambique & Zambia • Morocco • North Africa • South Africa, Lesotho & Swaziland • South Africa, Lesotho & Swazi-land travel atlas • Swahili phrasebook • Tanzania, Zanzibar & Pemba • Trekking in East Africa • Tunisia • West Africa • Zimbabwe, Botswana & Namibia • Zimbabwe, Botswana & Namibia travel atlas
Travel Literature: The Rainbird: A Central African Journey • Songs to an African Sunset: A Zimbabwean Story • Mali Blues: Traveling to an African Beat

AUSTRALIA & THE PACIFIC Australia • Australian phrasebook • Bushwalking in Australia • Bush-walking in Papua New Guinea • Fiji • Fijian phrasebook • Islands of Australia's Great Barrier Reef • Melbourne • Micronesia • New Caledonia • New South Wales & the ACT • New Zealand • Northern Ter-ritory • Outback Australia • Papua New Guinea • Papua New Guinea (Pidgin) phrasebook • Queensland • Rarotonga & the Cook Islands • Samoa • Solomon Islands • South Australia • Sydney • Tahiti & French Polynesia • Tasmania • Tonga • Tramping in New Zealand • Vanuatu • Victoria • Western Australia
Travel Literature: Islands in the Clouds • Sean & David's Long Drive

CENTRAL AMERICA & THE CARIBBEAN Bahamas and Turks & Caicos • Barcelona • Bermuda • Central America on a shoestring • Costa Rica • Cuba • Dominican Republic & Haiti • Eastern Caribbean • Guatemala, Belize & Yucatán: La Ruta Maya • Jamaica • Mexico • Mexico City • Panama
Travel Literature: Green Dreams: Travels in Central America

EUROPE Amsterdam • Andalucía • Austria • Baltic States phrasebook • Barcelona • Berlin • Britain • British phrasebook • Canary Islands • Central Europe • Central Europe phrasebook • Corsica • Croatia • Czech & Slovak Republics • Denmark • Dublin • Eastern Europe • Eastern Europe phrase-book • Edinburgh • Estonia, Latvia & Lithuania • Europe • Finland • France • French phrasebook • Germany • German phrasebook • Greece • Greek phrasebook • Hungary • Iceland, Greenland & the Faroe Islands • Ireland • Italian phrasebook • Italy • Lisbon • London • Mediterranean Europe • Mediterranean Europe phrasebook • Norway • Paris • Poland • Portugal • Portugal travel atlas • Prague • Provence & the Côte d'Azur • Romania & Moldova • Rome • Russia, Ukraine & Belarus • Russian phrasebook • Scandinavian & Baltic Europe • Scandinavian Europe phrasebook • Scotland • Slovenia • Spain • Spanish phrasebook • St Petersburg • Switzerland • Trekking in Spain • Ukrainian phrasebook • Vienna • Walking in Britain • Walking in Italy • Walking in Ireland • Walking in Switzer-land • Western Europe • Western Europe phrasebook
Travel Literature: The Olive Grove: Travels in Greece

INDIAN SUBCONTINENT Bangladesh • Bengali phrasebook • Bhutan • Delhi • Goa • Hindi/Urdu phrasebook • India • India & Bangladesh travel atlas • Indian Himalaya • Karakoram Highway • Nepal • Nepali phrasebook • Pakistan • Rajasthan • South India • Sri Lanka • Sri Lanka phrasebook • Trekking in the Indian Himalaya • Trekking in the Karakoram & Hindukush • Trekking in the Nepal Himalaya
Travel Literature: In Rajasthan • Shopping for Buddhas

Index

Text

Bold indicates maps.

Boxed Text

MAP LEGEND

BOUNDARIES

▪–▪▪–▪▪–▪	International
▪▪▪–▪▪▪▪	State
– – – –	Disputed

HYDROGRAPHY

	Coastline
	River, Creek
	Lake
	Intermittent Lake
	Salt Lake
	Canal
⊚ ⇢	Spring, Rapids
⊣⊢	Waterfalls
	Swamp

ROUTES & TRANSPORT

	Freeway
	Highway
	Major Road
	Minor Road
======	Unsealed Road
	City Freeway
	City Highway
	City Road
	City Street, Lane
	Pedestrian Mall
⇥=====	Tunnel
⊢⊢⊢●⊢	Train Route & Station
●Ⓜ●	Metro & Station
⊬⊢⊬⊢⊬	Cable Car or Chairlift
– – – –	Walking Track
·········	Walking Tour
– – – –	Ferry Route

AREA FEATURES

	Building
✿	Park, Gardens
+ + + +	Christian Cemetery
× × × ×	Non-Christian Cemetery
	Market
	Beach, Desert
	Urban Area

MAP SYMBOLS

⊙ CAPITAL	National Capital	☕	Café	☂	National Park
◉ CAPITAL	State Capital	🏛	Castle or Fort	)(	Pass
● CITY	City	⌢	Cave	★	Police Station
● Town	Town	⊞ ✝	Church	✉	Post Office
● Village	Village	⌒⌒	Cliff or Escarpment	❖	Shopping Centre
○	Point of Interest	❂	Embassy	▬	Swimming Pool
■	Place to Stay	✛	Hospital	▣	Synagogue
▼	Place to Eat	Ⓚ	Kibbutz	☎	Telephone
☕	Pub or Bar	✳	Lookout	🏛	Temple, Classical
✈	Airport	Ⓜ	Moshav	▣	Tomb
⌒⌒	Ancient or City Wall	Ⓒ	Mosque	❶	Tourist Information
∴	Archaeological Site	▲	Mountain or Hill	●	Transport
❸	Bank	🏛	Museum	🐾	Zoo

Note: not all symbols displayed above appear in this book

LONELY PLANET OFFICES

Australia
PO Box 617, Hawthorn 3122, Victoria
tel: (03) 9819 1877 fax: (03) 9819 6459
e-mail: talk2us@lonelyplanet.com.au

USA
150 Linden St, Oakland, CA 94607
tel: (510) 893 8555 TOLL FREE: 800 275-8555
fax: (510) 893 8572
e-mail: info@lonelyplanet.com

UK
10a Spring Place, London, NW5 3BH
tel: (0171) 428 4800 fax: (0170) 428 4828
e-mail: go@lonelyplanet.co.uk

France
1 rue du Dahomey, 75011 Paris
tel: 01 55 25 33 00 fax: 01 55 25 33 01
e-mail: bip@lonelyplanet.fr

World Wide Web: www.lonelyplanet.com *or* AOL keyword: lp
Lonely Planet Images: lpi@lonelyplanet.com.au